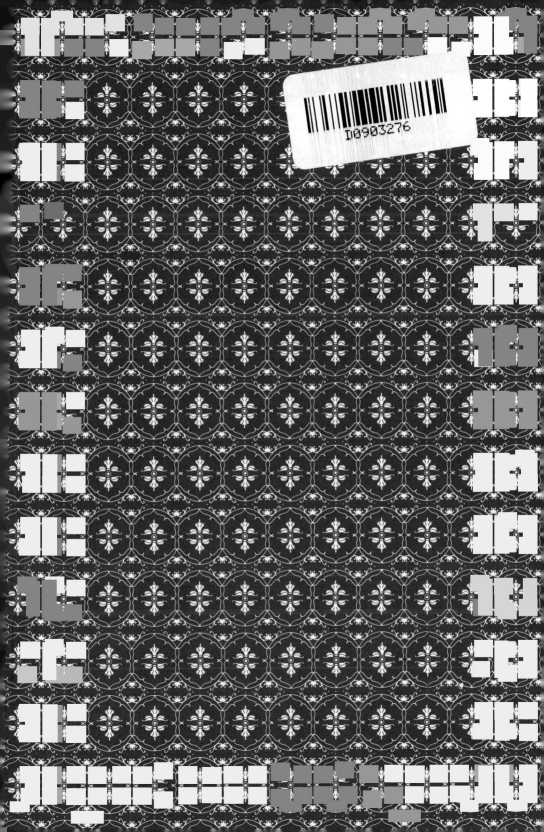

The
Divine Comedy

DANTE ALICHIERI

Dante Alighieri

The
Divine
Comedy

Translated by John Ciardi

With the Engravings of Gustave Doré

THE FRANKLIN LIBRARY
Franklin Center, Pennsylvania

Contents

Inferno   1

Purgatorio   187

Paradiso   373

Notes   553

Inferno

Canto 1

*Midway in his allotted threescore years
and ten, Dante comes to himself with a start and
realizes that he has strayed from the True Way
into the Dark Wood of Error, or Worldliness. As
soon as he has realized his loss, Dante lifts his
eyes and sees the first light of the sun, the symbol
of divine illumination, lighting the shoulders of a
little hill, the Mount of Joy. It is the Easter season,
the time of resurrection, and the sun is in its equinoctial rebirth. This juxtaposition of joyous symbols fills Dante with hope, and he sets out at once
to climb directly up the Mount of Joy. Immediately his way is blocked by the Three Beasts of
Worldliness—the Leopard of Malice and Fraud,
the Lion of Violence and Ambition, and the She-
Wolf of Incontinence—who drive him back despairing into the darkness of error. But just as all
seems lost, the shade of Virgil, Dante's symbol of
human reason, appears and explains that he has
been sent to lead Dante from error. There can,
however, be no direct ascent past the beasts: the
man who would escape them must go a longer
and harder way. First he must descend through
Hell, the recognition of sin; then he must ascend
through Purgatory, the renunciation of sin; and
only then may he reach the pinnacle of joy
and come to the light of God. Virgil offers to
guide Dante, but only as far as human reason
can go. Another guide—Beatrice, the symbol of
divine love—must take over for the final ascent,
because human reason is self-limited. Dante
submits himself joyously to Virgil's
guidance and they move off.*

The Divine Comedy

MIDWAY in our life's journey, I went astray
   from the straight road and woke to find myself
   alone in a dark wood. How shall I say
what wood that was! I never saw so drear,
   so rank, so arduous a wilderness!
   Its very memory gives a shape to fear.
Death could scarce be more bitter than that place!
   But since it came to good, I will recount
   all that I found revealed there by God's grace.
How I came to it I cannot rightly say,
   so drugged and loose with sleep had I become
   when I first wandered there from the True Way.
But at the far end of that valley of evil
   whose maze had sapped my very heart with fear!
   I found myself before a little hill   15
and lifted up my eyes. Its shoulders glowed
   already with the sweet rays of that planet
   whose virtue leads men straight on every road,
and the shining strengthened me against the fright
   whose agony had wracked the lake of my heart
   through all the terrors of that piteous night.
Just as a swimmer, who with his last breath
   flounders ashore from perilous seas, might turn
   to memorize the wide water of his death—
so did I turn, my soul still fugitive
   from death's surviving image, to stare down
   that pass that none had ever left alive.
And there I lay to rest from my heart's race
   till calm and breath returned to me. Then rose
   and pushed up that dead slope at such a pace   30
each footfall rose above the last. And lo!
   almost at the beginning of the rise
   I faced a spotted Leopard, all tremor and flow
and gaudy pelt. And it would not pass, but stood
   so blocking my every turn that time and again
   I was on the verge of turning back to the wood.
This fell at the first widening of the dawn
   as the sun was climbing Aries with those stars
   that rode with him to light the new creation.

Midway in our life's journey, I went astray
    from the straight road and woke to find myself
    alone in a dark wood.

Thus the holy hour and the sweet season
   of commemoration did much to arm my fear
   of that bright murderous beast with their good omen.
Yet not so much but what I shook with dread
   at sight of a great Lion that broke upon me
   raging with hunger, its enormous head   45
held high as if to strike a mortal terror
   into the very air. And down his track,
   a She-Wolf drove upon me, a starved horror
ravening and wasted beyond all belief.
   She seemed a rack for avarice, gaunt and craving.
   Oh, many the souls she has brought to endless grief!
She brought such heaviness upon my spirit
   at sight of her savagery and desperation,
   I died from every hope of that high summit.
And like a miser—eager in acquisition
   but desperate in self-reproach when Fortune's wheel
   turns to the hour of his loss—all tears and attrition
I wavered back; and still the beast pursued,
   forcing herself against me bit by bit
   till I slid back into the sunless wood.   60
And as I fell to my soul's ruin, a presence
   gathered before me on the discolored air,
   the figure of one who seemed hoarse from long silence.
At sight of him in that friendless waste I cried:
   "Have pity on me, whatever thing you are,
   whether shade or living man." And it replied:
"Not man, though man I once was, and my blood
   was Lombard, both my parents Mantuan.
   I was born, though late, *sub Julio,* and bred
in Rome under Augustus in the noon
   of the false and lying gods. I was a poet
   and sang of old Anchises' noble son
who came to Rome after the burning of Troy.
   But you—why do *you* return to these distresses
   instead of climbing that shining Mount of Joy   75
which is the seat and first cause of man's bliss?"
   "And are you then that Virgil and that fountain
   of purest speech?" My voice grew tremulous:

"Glory and light of poets! now may that zeal
    and love's apprenticeship that I poured out
    on your heroic verses serve me well!
For you are my true master and first author,
    the sole maker from whom I drew the breath
    of that sweet style whose measures have brought me honor.
See there, immortal sage, the beast I flee.
    For my soul's salvation, I beg you, guard me from her,
    for she has struck a mortal tremor through me."
And he replied, seeing my soul in tears:
    "He must go by another way who would escape
    this wilderness, for that mad beast that fleers   90
before you there, suffers no man to pass.
    She tracks down all, kills all, and knows no glut,
    but, feeding, she grows hungrier than she was.
She mates with any beast and will mate with more
    before the Greyhound comes to hunt her down.
    He will not feed on lands nor loot, but honor
and love and wisdom will make straight his way.
    He will rise between Feltro and Feltro, and in him
    shall be the resurrection and new day
of that sad Italy for which Nisus died,
    and Turnus, and Euryalus, and the maid Camilla.
    He shall hunt her through every nation of sick pride
till she is driven back forever to Hell
    whence Envy first released her on the world.
    Therefore, for your own good, I think it well   105
you follow me and I will be your guide
    and lead you forth through an eternal place.
    There you shall see the ancient spirits tried
in endless pain and hear their lamentation
    as each bemoans the second death of souls.
    Next you shall see upon a burning mountain
souls in fire and yet content in fire,
    knowing that whensoever it may be
    they yet will mount into the blessed choir.
To which, if it is still your wish to climb,
    a worthier spirit shall be sent to guide you.
    With her shall I leave you, for the King of Time,

who reigns on high, forbids me to come there
   since, living, I rebelled against His law.
   He rules the waters and the land and air   120
and there holds court, His city and His throne.
   Oh, blessed are they He chooses!" And I to him:
  "Poet, by that God to you unknown,
lead me this way. Beyond this present ill
   and worse to dread, lead me to Peter's Gate
   and be my guide through the sad halls of Hell."
And he then: "Follow." And he moved ahead
in silence, and I followed where he led.

Canto 2

*It is evening of the first day (Friday).
Dante is following Virgil and finds himself tired
and despairing. How can he be worthy of such a
vision as Virgil has described? He hesitates and
seems about to abandon his first purpose. To comfort him, Virgil explains how Beatrice descended
to him in Limbo and told him of her concern for
Dante. It is she, the symbol of divine love, who
sends Virgil to lead Dante from error. She has
come into Hell itself on this errand, for Dante
cannot come to divine love unaided; reason must
lead him. Moreover, Beatrice has been sent with
the prayers of the Virgin Mary, the symbol of compassion, and of St. Lucia, the symbol of divine
light. Rachel, symbol of the contemplative life,
also figures in the heavenly scene which Virgil
recounts. Virgil explains all this and reproaches
Dante: how can he hesitate longer when such
heavenly powers are concerned for him, and Virgil himself has promised to lead him safely?
Dante understands that such forces cannot fail
him, and his spirits rise in
joyous anticipation.*

The light was departing. The brown air drew down
   all the earth's creatures, calling them to rest
   from their day-roving, as I, one man alone,
prepared myself to face the double war
   of the journey and the pity, which memory
   shall here set down, nor hesitate, nor err.
O Muses! O High Genius! Be my aid!
   O Memory, recorder of the vision,
   here shall your true nobility be displayed!

Thus I began: "Poet, you who must guide me,
  before you trust me to that arduous passage,
  look to me and look through me—can I be worthy?
You sang how the father of Sylvius, while still
  in corruptible flesh won to that other world,
  crossing with mortal sense the immortal sill.   15
But if the Adversary of All Evil,
  weighing his consequence and who and what
  should issue from him, treated him so well—
that cannot seem unfitting to thinking men,
  since he was chosen father of Mother Rome
  and of her Empire by God's will and token.
Both, to speak strictly, were founded and foreknown
  as the established Seat of Holiness
  for the successors of Great Peter's throne.
In that quest, which your verses celebrate,
  he learned those mysteries from which arose
  his victory and Rome's apostolate.
There later came the chosen vessel, Paul,
  bearing the confirmation of that Faith
  which is the one true door to life eternal.   30
But I—how should I dare? By whose permission?
  I am not Aeneas. *I* am not Paul.
  Who could believe me worthy of the vision?
How, then, may I presume to this high quest
  and not fear my own brashness? You are wise
  and will grasp what my poor words can but suggest."
As one who unwills what he wills, will stay
  strong purposes with feeble second thoughts
  until he spells all his first zeal away—
so I hung back and balked on that dim coast
  till thinking had worn out my enterprise,
  so stout at starting and so early lost.
"I understand from your words and the look in your eyes,"
  that shadow of magnificence answered me,
  "your soul is sunken in that cowardice   45
that bears down many men, turning their course
  and resolution by imagined perils,
  as his own shadow turns the frightened horse.

To free you of this dread I will tell you all
  of why I came to you and what I heard
  when first I pitied you. I was a soul
among the souls of Limbo, when a Lady
  so blessed and so beautiful, I prayed her
  to order and command my will, called to me.
Her eyes were kindled from the lamps of Heaven.
  Her voice reached through me, tender, sweet, and low.
  An angel's voice, a music of its own:
'O gracious Mantuan whose melodies
  live in earth's memory and shall live on
  till the last motion ceases in the skies,   60
my dearest friend, and Fortune's foe, has strayed
  onto a friendless shore and stands beset
  by such distresses that he turns afraid
from the True Way, and news of him in Heaven
  rumors my dread he is already lost.
  I come, afraid that I am too late risen.
Fly to him and with your high counsel, pity,
  and with whatever need be for his good
  and soul's salvation, help him, and solace me.
It is I, Beatrice, who send you to him.
  I come from the blessed height for which I yearn.
  Love called me here. When amid Seraphim
I stand again before my Lord, your praises
  shall sound in Heaven.' She paused, and I began:
  'O Lady of that only grace that raises   75
feeble mankind within its mortal cycle
  above all other works God's will has placed
  within the heaven of the smallest circle;
so welcome is your command that to my sense,
  were it already fulfilled, it would yet seem tardy.
  I understand and am all obedience.
But tell me how you dare to venture thus
  so far from the wide heaven of your joy
  to which your thoughts yearn back from this abyss.'
'Since what you ask,' she answered me, 'probes near
  the root of all, I will say briefly only
  how I have come through Hell's pit without fear.

11

"It is I, Beatrice, who send you to him.
   I come from the blessed height for which I yearn.
   Love called me here."

Know then, O waiting and compassionate soul,
  that is to fear which has the power to harm,
  and nothing else is fearful even in Hell.   90
I am so made by God's all-seeing mercy
  your anguish does not touch me, and the flame
  of this great burning has no power upon me.
There is a Lady in Heaven so concerned
  for him I send you to, that for her sake
  the strict decree is broken. She has turned
and called Lucia to her wish and mercy
  saying: "Thy faithful one is sorely pressed;
  in his distresses I commend him to thee."
Lucia, that soul of light and foe of all
  cruelty, rose and came to me at once
  where I was sitting with the ancient Rachel,
saying to me: "Beatrice, true praise of God,
  why dost thou not help him who loved thee so
  that for thy sake he left the vulgar crowd?   105
Dost thou not hear his cries? Canst thou not see
  the death he wrestles with beside that river
  no ocean can surpass for rage and fury?"
No soul of earth was ever as rapt to seek
  its good or flee its injury as I was—
  when I had heard my sweet Lucia speak—
to descend from Heaven and my blessed seat
  to you, laying my trust in that high speech
  that honors you and all who honor it.'
She spoke and turned away to hide a tear
  that, shining, urged me faster. So I came
  and freed you from the beast that drove you there,
blocking the near way to the Heavenly Height.
  And now what ails you? Why do you lag? Why
  this heartsick hesitation and pale fright   120
when three such blessed Ladies lean from Heaven
  in their concern for you and my own pledge
  of the great good that waits you has been given?"
As flowerlets drooped and puckered in the night
  turn up to the returning sun and spread
  their petals wide on his new warmth and light—

just so my wilted spirits rose again,
    and such a heat of zeal surged through my veins
    that I was born anew. Thus I began:
"Blesséd be that Lady of infinite pity,
    and blesséd be thy taxed and courteous spirit
    that came so promptly on the word she gave thee.
Thy words have moved my heart to its first purpose.
    My Guide! My Lord! My Master! Now lead on;
    one will shall serve the two of us in this."   135
He turned when I had spoken, and at his back
I entered on that hard and perilous track.

14

Canto 3

*The Poets pass the Gate of Hell and are
immediately assailed by cries of anguish. Dante
sees the first of the souls in torment, the Opportunists, those who in life were neither for good nor
evil but only for themselves; mixed with them are
those outcasts who took no sides in the Rebellion
of the Angels. The Opportunists are neither in
Hell nor out of it; eternally unclassified, they race
to and fro after an aimlessly wavering banner,
urged on by swarms of wasps and hornets. The
law of Dante's Hell is the law of symbolic retribution; as they sinned so are they punished. They
took no sides, therefore they are given no place;
they sought the ever-shifting illusion of their own
advantage, so they pursue eternally an elusive,
ever-shifting banner. Dante recognizes several,
among them Pope Celestine V, but without delaying to speak to any of these souls the Poets move
on to Acheron, the first of the rivers of Hell. Here
the newly-arrived souls of the damned gather
and wait for Charon to ferry them over to punishment. Charon recognizes Dante as a living man
and angrily refuses him passage. Virgil forces
Charon to serve them, but Dante swoons with
terror and does not reawaken until he
is on the other side.*

I AM THE WAY INTO THE CITY OF WOE.
I AM THE WAY TO A FORSAKEN PEOPLE.
I AM THE WAY INTO ETERNAL SORROW.

SACRED JUSTICE MOVED MY ARCHITECT.
I WAS RAISED HERE BY DIVINE OMNIPOTENCE,
PRIMORDIAL LOVE AND ULTIMATE INTELLECT.

ONLY THOSE ELEMENTS TIME CANNOT WEAR
WERE MADE BEFORE ME, AND BEYOND TIME I STAND.
ABANDON ALL HOPE YE WHO ENTER HERE.

These mysteries I read cut into stone
 above a gate. And turning I said: "Master,
 what is the meaning of this harsh inscription?"
And he then as initiate to novice:
 "Here must you put by all division of spirit
 and gather your soul against all cowardice.   15
This is the place I told you to expect.
 Here you shall pass among the fallen people,
 souls who have lost the good of intellect."
So saying, he put forth his hand to me,
 and with a gentle and encouraging smile
 he led me through the gate of mystery.
Here sighs and cries and wails coiled and recoiled
 on the starless air, spilling my soul to tears.
 A confusion of tongues and monstrous accents toiled
in pain and anger. Voices hoarse and shrill
 and sounds of blows, all intermingled, raised
 tumult and pandemonium that still
whirls on the air forever dirty with it,
 as if a whirlwind sucked at sand. And I,
 holding my head in horror, cried: "Sweet spirit,   30
what souls are these who run through this black haze?"
 And he to me: "These are the nearly soulless
 whose lives concluded neither blame nor praise.
They are mixed here with that despicable corps
 of angels who were neither for God nor Satan,
 but only for themselves. The High Creator
scourged them from Heaven for its perfect beauty,
 and Hell will not receive them since the wicked
 might feel some glory over them." And I:
"Master, what gnaws at them so hideously
 their lamentation stuns the very air?"
 "They have no hope of death," he answered me,

"and in their blind and unattaining state
    their miserable lives have sunk so low
    that they must envy every other fate.   45
No word of them survives their living season.
    Mercy and Justice deny them even a name.
    Let us not speak of them; look, and pass on."
I saw a banner there upon the mist.
    Circling and circling, it seemed to scorn all pause.
    So it ran on, and still behind it pressed
a never-ending rout of souls in pain.
    I had not thought death had undone so many
    as passed before me in that mournful train.
And some I knew among them; last of all
    I recognized the shadow of that soul
    who, in his cowardice, made the Great Denial.
At once I understood for certain; these
    were of that retrograde and faithless crew
    hateful to God and to His enemies.   60
These wretches never born and never dead
    ran naked in a swarm of wasps and hornets
    that goaded them the more the more they fled,
and made their faces stream with bloody gouts
    of pus and tears that dribbled to their feet
    to be swallowed there by loathsome worms and maggots.
Then looking onward I made out a throng
    assembled on the beach of a wide river,
    whereupon I turned to him: "Master, I long
to know what souls these are and what strange usage
    makes them as eager to cross as they seem to be
    in this infected light." At which the Sage:
"All this shall be made known to you when we stand
    on the joyless beach of Acheron." And I
    cast down my eyes, sensing a reprimand   75
in what he said, and so walked at his side
    in silence and ashamed until we came
    through the dead cavern to that sunless tide.
There, steering toward us in an ancient ferry
    came an old man with a white bush of hair,
    bellowing: "Woe to you depraved souls! Bury

17

here and forever all hope of Paradise!
    I come to lead you to the other shore,
    into eternal dark, into fire and ice.
And you who are living yet, I say begone
    from these who are dead." But when he saw me stand
    against his violence he began again:
"By other windings and by other steerage
    shall you cross to that other shore. Not here! Not here!
    A lighter craft than mine must give you passage."   90
And my Guide to him: "Charon, bite back your spleen;
    this has been willed where what is willed must be,
    and is not yours to ask what it may mean."
The steersman of that marsh of ruined souls,
    who wore a wheel of flame around each eye,
    stifled the rage that shook his woolly jowls.
But those unmanned and naked spirits there
    turned pale with fear and their teeth began to chatter
    at sound of his crude bellow. In despair
they blasphemed God, their parents, their time on earth,
    the race of Adam, and the day and the hour
    and the place and the seed and the womb that gave them birth.
But all together they drew to that grim shore
    where all must come who lose the fear of God.
    Weeping and cursing they come for evermore,   105
and demon Charon with eyes like burning coals
    herds them in, and with a whistling oar
    flails on the stragglers to his wake of souls.
As leaves in autumn loosen and stream down
    until the branch stands bare above its tatters
    spread on the rustling ground, so one by one
the evil seed of Adam in its Fall
    cast themselves, at his signal, from the shore
    and streamed away like birds who hear their call.
So they are gone over that shadowy water,
    and always before they reach the other shore
    a new noise stirs on this, and new throngs gather.
"My son," the courteous Master said to me,
    "all who die in the shadow of God's wrath
    converge to this from every clime and country.   120

"I come to lead you to the other shore,
into eternal dark, into fire and ice."

And all pass over eagerly, for here
   Divine Justice transforms and spurs them so
   their dread turns wish; they yearn for what they fear.
No soul in grace comes ever to this crossing;
   therefore if Charon rages at your presence
   you will understand the reason for his cursing."
When he had spoken, all the twilight country
   shook so violently the terror of it
   bathes me with sweat even in memory;
the tear-soaked ground gave out a sigh of wind
   that spewed itself in flame on a red sky,
   and all my shattered senses left me. Blind,
like one whom sleep comes over in a swoon,
I stumbled into darkness and went down.

Canto 4

Dante wakes to find himself across Acheron. The Poets are now on the brink of Hell itself, which Dante conceives as a great funnel-shaped cave lying below the northern hemisphere with its bottom point at the earth's center. Around this great circular depression runs a series of ledges, each of which Dante calls a circle. Each circle is assigned to the punishment of one category of sin. As soon as Dante's strength returns, the Poets begin to cross the first circle. Here they find the Virtuous Pagans. They were born without the light of Christ's revelation, and, therefore, they cannot come into the light of God; but they are not tormented. Their only pain is that they have no hope. Ahead of them Dante sights a great dome of light, and a voice trumpets through the darkness welcoming Virgil back, for this is his eternal place in Hell. Immediately the great poets of all time appear—Homer, Horace, Ovid, and Lucan. They greet Virgil, and they make Dante a sixth in their company. With them Dante enters the Citadel of Human Reason and sees before his eyes the master souls of pagan antiquity gathered on a green, and illuminated by the radiance of human reason. This is the highest state man can achieve without God; the glory of it dazzles Dante, but he knows also that it is nothing compared to the glory of God.

A monstrous clap of thunder broke apart
    the swoon that stuffed my head; like one awakened
    by violent hands, I leaped up with a start.
And having risen, rested and renewed,
    I studied out the landmarks of the gloom
    to find my bearings there as best I could.

And I found I stood on the very brink of the valley
    called the Dolorous Abyss, the desolate chasm
    where rolls the thunder of Hell's eternal cry,
so depthless-deep and nebulous and dim
    that stare as I might into its frightful pit
    it gave me back no feature and no bottom.
Death-pale, the Poet spoke: "Now let us go
    into the blind world waiting here below us.
    I will lead the way and you shall follow."   15
And I, sick with alarm at his new pallor,
    cried out: "How can I go this way when you
    who are my strength in doubt turn pale with terror?"
And he: "The pain of these below us here
    drains the color from my face for pity
    and leaves this pallor you mistake for fear.
Now let us go, for a long road awaits us."
    So he entered and so he led me in
    to the first circle and ledge of the abyss.
No tortured wailing rose to greet us here
    but sounds of sighing rose from every side,
    sending a tremor through the timeless air,
a grief breathed out of untormented sadness,
    the passive state of those who dwelled apart,
    men, women, children—a dim and endless congress.   30
And the Master said to me: "You do not question
    what souls these are that suffer here before you?
    I wish you to know before you travel on
that these were sinless. And still their merits fail,
    for they lacked Baptism's grace, which is the door
    of the true faith *you* were born to. Their birth fell
before the age of the Christian mysteries,
    and so they did not worship God's Trinity
    in fullest duty. I am one of these.
For such defects are we lost, though spared the fire
    and suffering Hell in one affliction only:
    that without hope we live on in desire."
I thought how many worthy souls there were
    suspended in that Limbo, and a weight
    closed on my heart for what the noblest suffer.   45

"Instruct me, Master and most noble sir,"
    I prayed him then, "better to understand
    the perfect creed that conquers every error.
  Has any, by his own or another's merit,
    gone ever from this place to blessedness?"
  He sensed my inner question and answered it:
"I was still new to this estate of tears
    when a Mighty One descended here among us,
    crowned with the sign of His victorious years.
  He took from us the shade of our first parent,
    of Abel, his pure son, of ancient Noah,
    of Moses, the bringer of law, the obedient.
  Father Abraham, David the King,
    Israel with his father and his children,
    Rachel, the holy vessel of His blessing,   60
and many more He chose for elevation
    among the elect. And before these, you must know,
    no human soul had ever won salvation."
  We had not paused as he spoke, but held our road
    and passed meanwhile beyond a press of souls
    crowded about like trees in a thick wood.
  And we had not traveled far from where I woke
    when I made out a radiance before us
    that struck away a hemisphere of dark.
  We were still some distance back in the long night,
    yet near enough that I half-saw, half-sensed,
    what quality of souls lived in that light.
"O ornament of wisdom and of art,
    what souls are these whose merit lights their way
    even in Hell. What joy sets them apart?"   75
  And he to me: "The signature of honor
    they left on earth is recognized in Heaven
    and wins them ease in Hell out of God's favor."
  And as he spoke a voice rang on the air:
    "Honor the Prince of Poets! The soul and glory
    that went from us returns. He is here! He is here!"
  The cry ceased and the echo passed from hearing;
    I saw four mighty presences come toward us
    with neither joy nor sorrow in their bearing.

23

"Note well," my Master said as they came on,
  "that soul that leads the rest with sword in hand
  as if he were their captain and champion.
It is Homer, singing master of the earth.
  Next after him is Horace, the satirist,
  Ovid is third, and Lucan is the fourth.   90
Since all of these have part in the high name
  the voice proclaimed, calling me Prince of Poets,
  the honor that they do me honors them."
So I saw gathered at the edge of light
  the masters of that highest school whose song
  outsoars all others like an eagle's flight.
And after they had talked together awhile,
  they turned and welcomed me most graciously,
  at which I saw my approving Master smile.
And they honored me far beyond courtesy,
  for they included me in their own number,
  making me sixth in that high company.
So we moved toward the light, and as we passed
  we spoke of things as well omitted here
  as it was sweet to touch on there. At last   105
we reached the base of a great Citadel
  circled by seven towering battlements
  and by a sweet brook flowing round them all.
This we passed over as if it were firm ground.
  Through seven gates I entered with those sages
  and came to a green meadow blooming round.
There with a solemn and majestic poise
  stood many people gathered in the light,
  speaking infrequently and with muted voice.
Past that enameled green we six withdrew
  into a luminous and open height
  from which each soul among them stood in view.
And there directly before me on the green
  the master souls of time were shown to me.
  I glory in the glory I have seen!   120
Electra stood in a great company
  among whom I saw Hector and Aeneas
  and Caesar in armor with his falcon's eye.

24

So I saw gathered at the edge of light
  the masters of that highest school whose song
  outsoars all others like an eagle's flight.

I saw Camilla and the Queen Amazon
   across the field. I saw the Latian King
   seated there with his daughter by his throne.
And the good Brutus who overthrew the Tarquin;
   Lucrezia, Julia, Marcia, and Cornelia;
   and, by himself apart, the Saladin.
And raising my eyes a little I saw on high
   Aristotle, the master of those who know,
   ringed by the great souls of philosophy.
All wait upon him for their honor and his.
   I saw Socrates and Plato at his side
   before all others there. Democritus   135
who ascribes the world to chance, Diogenes,
   and with him there Thales, Anaxagoras,
   Zeno, Heraclitus, Empedocles.
And I saw the wise collector and analyst—
   Dioscorides, I mean. I saw Orpheus there,
   Tully, Linus, Seneca the moralist,
Euclid the geometer, and Ptolemy,
   Hippocrates, Galen, Avicenna,
   and Averroës of the Great Commentary.
I cannot count so much nobility;
   my longer theme pursues me so that often
   the word falls short of the reality.
The company of six is reduced by four.
   My Master leads me by another road
   out of that serenity to the roar   150
and trembling air of Hell. I pass from light
into the kingdom of eternal night.

Canto 5

*The Poets leave Limbo and enter the sec-
ond circle. Here begin the torments of Hell proper,
and here, blocking the way, sits Minos, the dread
and semi-bestial judge of the damned who assigns to each soul its eternal torment. He orders
the Poets back; but Virgil silences him as he earlier silenced Charon, and the Poets move on. They
find themselves on a dark ledge swept by a great
whirlwind, which spins within it the souls of the
Carnal, those who betrayed reason to their appetites. Their sin was to abandon themselves to the
tempest of their passions; so they are swept forever
in the tempest of Hell, forever denied the light of
reason and of God. Virgil identifies many among
them. Semiramis is there, and Dido, Cleopatra,
Helen, Achilles, Paris, and Tristan. Dante sees
Paolo and Francesca swept together, and in the
name of love he calls to them to tell their sad
story. They pause from their eternal flight to
come to him, and Francesca tells their history
while Paolo weeps at her side. Dante is so stricken
by compassion at their tragic tale
that he swoons again.*

So we went down to the second ledge alone,
   a smaller circle of so much greater pain
   the voice of the damned rose in a bestial moan.
There Minos sits, grinning, grotesque, and hale.
   He examines each lost soul as it arrives
   and delivers his verdict with his coiling tail.
That is to say, when the ill-fated soul
   appears before him it confesses all,
   and that grim sorter of the dark and foul

decides which place in Hell shall be its end,
    then wraps his twitching tail about himself
    one coil for each degree it must descend.
The soul descends and others take its place;
    each crowds in its turn to judgment, each confesses,
    each hears its doom and falls away through space.   15
"O you who come into this camp of woe,"
    cried Minos when he saw me turn away
    without awaiting his judgment, "watch where you go
once you have entered here and to whom you turn!
    Do not be misled by that wide and easy passage!"
    And my Guide to him: "That is not your concern;
it is his fate to enter every door.
    This has been willed where what is willed must be
    and is not yours to question. Say no more."
Now the choir of anguish, like a wound,
    strikes through the tortured air. Now I have come
    to Hell's full lamentation, sound beyond sound.
I came to a place stripped bare of every light
    and roaring on the naked dark like seas
    wracked by a war of winds. Their hellish flight   30
of storm and counterstorm through time foregone,
    sweeps the souls of the damned before its charge.
    Whirling and battering it drives them on,
and when they pass the ruined gap of Hell
    through which we had come, their shrieks begin anew.
    There they blaspheme the power of God eternal.
And this, I learned, was the never ending flight
    of those who sinned in the flesh, the carnal and lusty
    who betrayed reason to their appetite.
As the wings of wintering starlings bear them on
    in their great wheeling flights—just so, the blast
    wherries these evil souls through time foregone.
Here, there, up, down, they whirl and, whirling, strain
    with never a hope of hope to comfort them,
    not of release, but even of less pain.   45
As cranes go over sounding their harsh cry,
    leaving the long streak of their flight in air,
    so come these spirits, wailing as they fly.

And watching their shadows lashed by wind, I cried:
    "Master, what souls are these the very air
    lashes with its black whips from side to side?"
"The first of these whose history you would know,"
    he answered me, "was empress of many tongues.
    Mad sensuality corrupted her so
that to hide the guilt of her debauchery
    she licensed all depravity alike,
    and lust and law were one in her decree.
She is Semiramis of whom the tale is told
    how she married Ninus and succeeded him
    to the throne of that wide land the Sultans hold.   60
The other is Dido; faithless to the ashes
    of Sichaeus, she killed herself for love.
    The next whom the eternal tempest lashes
is sense-drugged Cleopatra. See Helen there,
    from whom such ill arose. And great Achilles,
    who fought at last with love in the house of prayer.
And Paris. And Tristan." As they whirled above
    he pointed out more than a thousand shades
    of those torn from the mortal life by love.
I stood there while my Teacher one by one
    named the great knights and ladies of dim time;
    and I was swept by pity and confusion.
At last I spoke: "Poet, I should be glad
    to speak a word with those two swept together
    so lightly on the wind and still so sad."   75
And he to me: "Watch them. When next they pass,
    call to them in the name of love that drives
    and damns them here. In that name they will pause."
Thus, as soon as the wind in its wild course
    brought them around, I called: "O wearied souls!
    if none forbid it, pause and speak to us."
As mating doves that love calls to their nest
    glide through the air with motionless raised wings,
    borne by the sweet desire that fills each breast—
just so, those spirits turned on the torn sky
    from the band where Dido whirls across the air;
    such was the power of pity in my cry.

"O living creature, gracious, kind, and good,
  going this pilgrimage through the sick night,
  visiting us who stained the earth with blood,   90
were the King of Time our friend, we would pray His peace
  on you who have pitied us. As long as the wind
  will let us pause, ask of us what you please.
The town where I was born lies by the shore
  where the Po descends into its ocean rest
  with its attendant streams in one long murmur.
Love, which in gentlest hearts will soonest bloom,
  seized my lover with passion for that sweet body
  from which I was torn unshriven to my doom.
Love, which permits no loved one not to love,
  took me so strongly with delight in him
  that we are one in Hell, as we were above.
Love led us to one death. In the depths of Hell
  Caïna waits for him who took our lives."
  This was the piteous tale they stopped to tell.   105
And when I had heard those world-offended lovers,
  I bowed my head. At last the Poet spoke:
  "What painful thoughts are these your lowered brow covers?"
When at length I answered, I began: "Alas!
  What sweetest thoughts, what green and young desire
  led these two lovers to this sorry pass."
Then turning to those spirits once again,
  I said: "Francesca, what you suffer here
  melts me to tears of pity and of pain.
But tell me, in the time of your sweet sighs
  by what appearances found Love the way
  to lure you to his perilous paradise?"
And she: "The double grief of a lost bliss
  is to recall its happy hour in pain.
  Your Guide and Teacher knows the truth of this.   120
But if there is indeed a soul in Hell
  to ask of the beginning of our love
  out of his pity, I will weep and tell.
On a day for dalliance we read the rhyme
  of Launcelot, how love had mastered him.
  We were alone with innocence and dim time.

30

I was swept
by such a swoon as death is, and I fell
as a corpse might fall, to the dead floor of Hell.

Pause after pause that high old story drew
   our eyes together while we blushed and paled;
   but it was one soft passage overthrew
our caution and our hearts. For when we read
   how her fond smile was kissed by such a lover,
   he who is one with me alive and dead
breathed on my lips the tremor of his kiss.
   That book, and he who wrote it, was a pander.
   That day we read no further." As she said this,   135
the other spirit, who stood by her, wept
   so piteously, I felt my senses reel
   and faint away with anguish. I was swept
by such a swoon as death is, and I fell,
as a corpse might fall, to the dead floor of Hell.

Canto 6

Dante recovers from his swoon and finds himself in the third circle. A great storm of putrefaction falls incessantly, a mixture of stinking snow and freezing rain, which forms into a vile slush underfoot. Everything about this circle suggests a gigantic garbage dump. The souls of the damned lie in the icy paste, swollen and obscene, and Cerberus, the ravenous three-headed dog of Hell, stands guard over them, ripping and tearing them with his claws and teeth. These are the Gluttons. In life they made no higher use of the gifts of God than to wallow in food and drink, producers of nothing but garbage and offal. Here they lie through all eternity, themselves like garbage, half-buried in fetid slush, while Cerberus slavers over them as they in life slavered over their food. As the Poets pass, one of the speakers sits up and addresses Dante. He is Ciacco, the Hog, a citizen of Dante's own Florence. He recognizes Dante, who asks eagerly for news of what will happen there. With the foreknowledge of the damned, Ciacco then utters the first of the political prophecies that become a recurring theme of the Inferno. The Poets then move on toward the next circle, at the edge of which they encounter the monster Plutus.

My senses had reeled from me out of pity
    for the sorrow of those kinsmen and lost lovers.
    Now they return, and waking gradually,
I see new torments and new souls in pain
    about me everywhere. Wherever I turn
    away from grief I turn to grief again.

I am in the third circle of the torments.
    Here to all time with neither pause nor change
    the frozen rain of Hell descends in torrents.
Huge hailstones, dirty water, and black snow
    pour from the dismal air to putrefy
    the putrid slush that waits for them below.
Here monstrous Cerberus, the ravening beast,
    howls through his triple throats like a mad dog
    over the spirits sunk in that foul paste.   15
His eyes are red, his beard is greased with phlegm,
    his belly is swollen, and his hands are claws
    to rip the wretches and flay and mangle them.
And they, too, howl like dogs in the freezing storm,
    turning and turning from it as if they thought
    one naked side could keep the other warm.
When Cerberus discovered us in that swill
    his dragon-jaws yawed wide, his lips drew back
    in a grin of fangs. No limb of him was still.
My Guide bent down and seized in either fist
    a clod of the stinking dirt that festered there
    and flung them down the gullet of the beast.
As a hungry cur will set the echoes raving
    and then fall still when he is thrown a bone,
    all of his clamor being in his craving,   30
so the three ugly heads of Cerberus,
    whose yowling at those wretches deafened them,
    choked on their putrid sops and stopped their fuss.
We made our way across the sodden mess
    of souls the rain beat down, and when our steps
    fell on a body, they sank through emptiness.
All those illusions of being seemed to lie
    drowned in the slush; until one wraith among them
    sat up abruptly and called as I passed by:
"O you who are led this journey through the shade
    of Hell's abyss, do you recall this face?
    You had been made before I was unmade."
And I: "Perhaps the pain you suffer here
    distorts your image from my recollection.
    I do not know you as you now appear."   45

And he to me: "Your own city, so rife
　with hatred that the bitter cup flows over
　was mine too in that other, clearer life.
Your citizens nicknamed me Ciacco, the Hog;
　gluttony was my offense, and for it
　I lie here rotting like a swollen log.
Nor am I lost in this alone; all these
　you see about you in this painful death
　have wallowed in the same indecencies."
I answered him: "Ciacco, your agony
　weighs on my heart and calls my soul to tears;
　but tell me, if you can, what is to be
for the citizens of that divided state,
　and whether there are honest men among them,
　and for what reasons we are torn by hate."　　　　　60
And he then: "After many words given and taken
　it shall come to blood; White shall rise over Black
　and rout the dark lords' force, battered and shaken.
Then it shall come to pass within three suns
　that the fallen shall arise, and by the power
　of one now gripped by many hesitations
Black shall ride on White for many years,
　loading it down with burdens and oppressions
　and humbling of proud names and helpless tears.
Two are honest, but none will heed them. There,
　pride, avarice, and envy are the tongues
　men know and heed, a Babel of despair."
Here he broke off his mournful prophecy.
　And I to him: "Still let me urge you on
　to speak a little further and instruct me:　　　　　75
Farinata and Tegghiaio, men of good blood,
　Jacopo Rusticucci, Arrigo, Mosca,
　and the others who set their hearts on doing good—
where are they now whose high deeds might begem
　the crown of kings? I long to know their fate.
　Does Heaven soothe or Hell envenom them?"
And he: "They lie below in a blacker lair.
　A heavier guilt draws them to greater pain.
　If you descend so far you may see them there.

35

But when you move again among the living,
   oh, speak my name to the memory of men!
   Having answered all, I say no more." And giving
his head a shake, he looked up at my face
   cross-eyed, then bowed his head and fell away
   among the other blind souls of that place.   90
And my Guide to me: "He will not wake again
   until the angel trumpet sounds the day
   on which the host shall come to judge all men.
Then shall each soul before the seat of Mercy
   return to its sad grave and flesh and form
   to hear the edict of Eternity."
So we picked our slow way among the shades
   and the filthy rain, speaking of life to come.
   "Master," I said, "when the great clarion fades
into the voice of thundering Omniscience,
   what of these agonies? Will they be the same,
   or more, or less, after the final sentence?"
And he to me: "Look to your science again
   where it is written: the more a thing is perfect
   the more it feels of pleasure and of pain.   105
As for these souls, though they can never soar
   to true perfection, still in the new time
   they will be nearer it than they were before."
And so we walked the rim of the great ledge
   speaking of pain and joy, and of much more
   that I will not repeat, and reached the edge
where the descent begins. There, suddenly,
we came on Plutus, the great enemy.

Canto 7

Plutus menaces the Poets, but Virgil silences him. The Poets then enter the fourth circle and find what seems to be a war in progress. The sinners are divided into two raging mobs, each soul among them straining madly at a great boulderlike weight. The two mobs meet, clashing their weights against one another, after which they separate, pushing the great weights apart, and begin over again. One mob is made up of the Hoarders, the other of the Wasters. In life they lacked all moderation in regulating their expenses; they destroyed the light of God within themselves by thinking of nothing but money. Thus in death, their souls are encumbered by dead weights (mundanity), and one excess serves to punish the other. Their souls, moreover, have become so dimmed and awry in their fruitless rages that there is no hope of recognizing any among them. The Poets pass on while Virgil explains the function of Dame Fortune in the divine scheme. As he finishes (it is past midnight now of Good Friday) they reach the inner edge of the ledge and come to a black spring which bubbles murkily over the rocks to form the Marsh of Styx, which is the fifth circle and last station of the Upper Hell. Across the marsh they see countless souls attacking one another in the foul slime. These are the Wrathful and the symbolism of their punishment is obvious. Virgil also points out to Dante certain bubbles rising from the slime and informs him that below that mud lie entombed the souls of the Sullen. In life they refused to welcome the sweet light of the divine illumination, and in death they are buried forever below the stinking waters of the Styx, gargling the words of an endless chant in a grotesque parody of singing a hymn.

"Papa Satán, Papa Satán, aleppy,"
    Plutus clucked and stuttered in his rage;
    and my all-knowing Guide, to comfort me:
"Do not be startled, for no power of his,
    however he may lord it over the damned,
    may hinder your descent through this abyss."
And turning to that carnival of bloat
    cried: "Peace, you wolf of Hell. Choke back your bile
    and let its venom blister your own throat.
Our passage through this pit is willed on high
    by that same Throne that loosed the angel wrath
    of Michael on ambition and mutiny."
As puffed out sails fall when the mast gives way
    and flutter to a self-convulsing heap—
    so collapsed Plutus into that dead clay.   15
Thus we descended the dark scarp of Hell
    to which all the evil of the universe
    comes home at last, into the fourth great circle
and ledge of the abyss. O Holy Justice,
    who could relate the agonies I saw!
    What guilt is man that he can come to this?
Just as the surge Charybdis hurls to sea
    crashes and breaks upon its countersurge,
    so these shades dance and crash eternally.
Here, too, I saw a nation of lost souls,
    far more than were above; they strained their chests
    against enormous weights and with mad howls
rolled them at one another. Then in haste
    they rolled them back, one party shouting out:
    "Why do you hoard?" and the other: "Why do you waste?"   30
So back around that ring they puff and blow,
    each faction to its course, until they reach
    opposite sides, and screaming as they go
the madmen turn and start their weights again
    to crash against the maniacs. And I,
    watching, felt my heart contract with pain.
"Master," I said, "what people can these be?
    And all those tonsured ones there on our left—
    is it possible they *all* were of the clergy?"

Inferno

And he: "In the first life beneath the sun
   they were so skewed and squint-eyed in their minds
   their misering or extravagance mocked all reason.
The voice of each clamors its own excess
   when lust meets lust at the two points of the circle
   where opposite guilts meet in their wretchedness.   45
These tonsured wraiths of greed were priests indeed,
   and popes and cardinals, for it is in these
   the weed of avarice sows its rankest seed."
And I to him: "Master, among this crew
   surely I should be able to make out
   the fallen image of some soul I knew."
And he to me: "This is a lost ambition.
   In their sordid lives they labored to be blind,
   and now their souls have dimmed past recognition.
All their eternity is to butt and bray:
   one crew will stand tight-fisted, the other stripped
   of its very hair at the bar of Judgment Day.
Hoarding and squandering wasted all their light
   and brought them screaming to this brawl of wraiths.
   You need no words of mine to grasp their plight.   60
Now may you see the fleeting vanity
   of the goods of Fortune for which men tear down
   all that they are, to build a mockery.
Not all the gold that is or ever was
   under the sky could buy for one of these
   exhausted souls the fraction of a pause."
"Master," I said, "tell me—now that you touch
   on this Dame Fortune—what *is* she, that she holds
   the good things of the world within her clutch?"
And he to me: "O credulous mankind,
   is there one error that has wooed and lost you?
   Now listen, and strike error from your mind:
That King whose perfect wisdom transcends all,
   made the heavens and posted angels on them
   to guide the eternal light that it might fall   75
from every sphere to every sphere the same.
   He made earth's splendors by a like decree
   and posted as their minister this high dame,

39

the Lady of Permutations. All earth's gear
    she changes from nation to nation, from house to house,
    in changeless change through every turning year.
No mortal power may stay her spinning wheel.
    The nations rise and fall by her decree.
    None may foresee where she will set her heel;
she passes, and things pass. Man's mortal reason
    cannot encompass her. She rules her sphere
    as the other gods rule theirs. Season by season
her changes change her changes endlessly,
    and those whose turn has come press on her so,
    she must be swift by hard necessity.   90
And this is she so railed at and reviled
    that even her debtors in the joys of time
    blaspheme her name. Their oaths are bitter and wild,
but she in her beatitude does not hear.
    Among the primal beings of God's joy
    she breathes her blessedness and wheels her sphere.
But the stars that marked our starting fall away.
    We must go deeper into greater pain,
    for it is not permitted that we stay."
And crossing over to the chasm's edge
    we came to a spring that boiled and overflowed
    through a great crevice worn into the ledge.
By that foul water, black from its very source,
    we found a nightmare path among the rocks
    and followed the dark stream along its course.   105
Beyond its rocky race and wild descent
    the river floods and forms a marsh called Styx,
    a dreary swampland, vaporous and malignant.
And I, intent on all our passage touched,
    made out a swarm of spirits in that bog
    savage with anger, naked, slime-besmutched.
They thumped at one another in that slime
    with hands and feet, and they butted, and they bit
    as if each would tear the other limb from limb.
And my kind Sage: "My son, behold the souls
    of those who lived in wrath. And do you see
    the broken surfaces of those water holes

on every hand, boiling as if in pain?
    There are souls beneath that water. Fixed in slime
    they speak their piece, end it, and start again: 120
'Sullen were we in the air made sweet by the sun;
    in the glory of his shining our hearts poured
    a bitter smoke. Sullen were we begun;
sullen we lie forever in this ditch.'
    This litany they gargle in their throats
    as if they sang, but lacked the words and pitch."
Then circling on along that filthy wallow,
    we picked our way between the bank and fen,
    keeping our eyes on those foul souls that swallow
the slime of Hell. And so at last we came
to foot of a great tower that has no name.

Canto 8

The Poets stand at the edge of the swamp, and a mysterious signal flames from the great tower. It is answered from the darkness of the other side, and almost immediately the Poets see Phlegyas, the boatman of Styx, racing toward them across the water, fast as a flying arrow. He comes avidly, thinking to find new souls for torment, and he howls with rage when he discovers the Poets. Once again, however, Virgil conquers wrath with a word, and Phlegyas reluctantly gives them passage. As they are crossing, a muddy soul rises before them. It is Filippo Argenti, one of the Wrathful. Dante recognizes him despite the filth with which he is covered, and he berates him soundly, even wishing to see him tormented further. Virgil approves Dante's disdain and, as if in answer to Dante's wrath, Argenti is suddenly set upon by all the other sinners present, who fall upon him and rip him to pieces. The boat meanwhile has sped on, and before Argenti's screams have died away, Dante sees the flaming red towers of Dis, the capital of Hell. The great walls of the iron city block the way to Lower Hell. Properly speaking, all the rest of Hell lies within the city walls, which separate Upper from Lower Hell. Phlegyas deposits them at a great iron gate which they find to be guarded by the Rebellious Angels. These creatures of ultimate evil, rebels against God Himself, refuse to let the Poets pass. Even Virgil is powerless against them, for human reason by itself cannot cope with the essence of evil. Only divine aid can bring hope. Virgil accordingly sends up a prayer for assistance and waits anxiously for a Heavenly Messenger to appear.

Returning to my theme, I say we came
   to the foot of a great tower; but long before
   we reached it through the marsh, two horns of flame
flared from the summit, one from either side,
   and then, far off, so far we scarce could see it
   across the mist, another flame replied.
I turned to that sea of all intelligence
   saying: "What is this signal and countersignal?
   Who is it speaks with fire across this distance?"
And he then: "Look across the filthy slew;
   you may already see the one they summon,
   if the swamp vapors do not hide him from you."
No twanging bowspring ever shot an arrow
   that bored the air it rode dead to the mark
   more swiftly than the flying skiff whose prow   15
shot toward us over the polluted channel
   with a single steersman at the helm who called:
   "So, do I have you at last, you whelp of Hell?"
"Phlegyas, Phlegyas," said my Lord and Guide,
   "this time you waste your breath; you have us only
   for the time it takes to cross to the other side."
Phlegyas, the madman, blew his rage among
   those muddy marshes like a cheat deceived
   or like a fool at some imagined wrong.
My Guide, whom all the fiend's noise could not nettle,
   boarded the skiff, motioning me to follow;
   and not till I stepped aboard did it seem to settle
into the water. At once we left the shore,
   that ancient hull riding more heavily
   than it had ridden in all of time before.   30
And as we ran on that dead swamp, the slime
   rose before me, and from it a voice cried:
   "Who are you that come here before your time?"
And I replied: "If I come, I do not remain.
   But you, who are *you*, so fallen and so foul?"
   And he: "I am one who weeps." And I then:
"May you weep and wail to all eternity,
   for I know you, hell-dog, filthy as you are."
   Then he stretched both hands to the boat, but warily

The Master shoved him back, crying, "Down! Down! with the other dogs!"

the Master shoved him back, crying, "Down! Down
   with the other dogs!" Then he embraced me saying:
   "Indignant spirit, I kiss you as you frown.
Blessed be she who bore you. In world and time
   this one was haughtier yet. Not one unbending
   graces his memory. Here is his shadow in slime.   45
How many living now, chancellors of wrath,
   shall come to lie here yet in this pigmire,
   leaving a curse to be their aftermath!"
And I: "Master, it would suit my whim
   to see the wretch scrubbed down into the swill
   before we leave this stinking sink and him."
And he to me: "Before the other side
   shows through the mist, you shall have all you ask.
   This is a wish that should be gratified."
And shortly after, I saw the loathsome spirit
   so mangled by a swarm of muddy wraiths
   that to this day I praise and thank God for it.
"After Filippo Argenti!" all cried together.
   The mad-dog Florentine wheeled at their cry
   and bit himself for rage. I saw them gather.   60
And there we left him. And I say no more.
   But such a wailing beat upon my ears,
   I strained my eyes ahead to the far shore.
"My son," the Master said, "the city called Dis
   lies just ahead, the heavy citizens,
   the swarming crowds of Hell's metropolis."
And I then: "Master, I already see
   the glow of its red mosques, as if they came
   hot from the forge to smolder in this valley."
And my all-knowing Guide: "They are eternal
   flues to eternal fire that rages in them
   and makes them glow across this lower Hell."
And as he spoke we entered the vast moat
   of the sepulcher. Its wall seemed made of iron
   and towered above us in our little boat.   75
We circled through what seemed an endless distance
   before the boatman ran his prow ashore
   crying: "Out! Out! Get out! This is the entrance."

Above the gates more than a thousand shades
   of spirits purged from Heaven for its glory
   cried angrily: "Who is it that invades
Death's Kingdom in his life?" My Lord and Guide
   advanced a step before me with a sign
   that he wished to speak to some of them aside.
They quieted somewhat, and one called: "Come,
   but come alone. And tell that other one,
   who thought to walk so blithely through Death's Kingdom,
he may go back along the same fool's way
   he came by. Let him try his living luck.
   You who are dead can come only to stay."   90
Reader, judge for yourself, how each black word
   fell on my ears to sink into my heart;
   I lost hope of returning to the world.
"O my beloved Master, my Guide in peril,
   who time and time again have seen me safely
   along this way, and turned the power of evil,
stand by me now," I cried, "in my heart's fright.
   And if the dead forbid our journey to them,
   let us go back together toward the light."
My Guide then, in the greatness of his spirit:
   "Take heart. Nothing can take our passage from us
   when such a power has given warrant for it.
Wait here and feed your soul while I am gone
   on comfort and good hope; I will not leave you
   to wander in this underworld alone."   105
So the sweet Guide and Father leaves me here,
   and I stay on in doubt with yes and no
   dividing all my heart to hope and fear.
I could not hear my Lord's words, but the pack
   that gathered round him suddenly broke away
   howling and jostling and went pouring back,
slamming the towering gate hard in his face.
   That great soul stood alone outside the wall.
   Then he came back; his pain showed in his pace.
His eyes were fixed upon the ground, his brow
   had sagged from its assurance. He sighed aloud:
   "Who has forbidden me the halls of sorrow?"

And to me he said: "You need not be cast down
  by my vexation, for whatever plot
  these fiends may lay against us, we will go on.   120
This insolence of theirs is nothing new;
  they showed it once at a less secret gate
  that still stands open for all that they could do—
the same gate where you read the dead inscription;
  and through it at this moment a Great One comes.
  Already he has passed it and moves down
ledge by dark ledge. He is one who needs no guide,
and at his touch all gates must spring aside."

Canto 9

At the Gate of Dis the Poets wait in dread. Virgil tries to hide his anxiety from Dante, but both realize that without divine aid they will surely be lost. To add to their terrors the three infernal Furies, symbol of eternal remorse, appear on a nearby tower, from which they threaten the Poets and call for Medusa to come and change Dante to stone. Virgil at once commands Dante to turn and shut his eyes. To make doubly sure, Virgil himself places his hands over Dante's eyes, for there is an evil upon which man must not look if he is to be saved. But at the moment of greatest anxiety a storm shakes the dirty air of Hell and the sinners in the marsh begin to scatter like frightened frogs. The Heavenly Messenger is approaching. He appears walking majestically through Hell, looking neither to right nor to left. With a touch he throws open the Gate of Dis while his words scatter the Rebellious Angels. Then he returns as he came. The Poets now enter the gate unopposed and find themselves in the sixth circle. Here they find a countryside like a vast cemetery. Tombs of every size stretch out before them, each with its lid lying beside it, and each wrapped in flames. Cries of anguish sound endlessly from the entombed dead. This is the torment of the Heretics of every cult. By Heretic, Dante means specifically those who did violence to God by denying immortality. Since they taught that the soul dies with the body, so their punishment is an eternal grave in the fiery morgue of God's wrath.

My face had paled to a mask of cowardice
    when I saw my Guide turn back. The sight of it
    the sooner brought the color back to his.

He stood apart like one who strains to hear
    what he cannot see, for the eye could not reach far
    across the vapors of that midnight air.
"Yet surely we were meant to pass these tombs,"
    he said aloud. "If not . . . so much was promised . . .
    Oh, how time hangs and drags till our aid comes!"
I saw too well how the words with which he ended
    covered his start, and even perhaps I drew
    a worse conclusion from that than he intended.
"Tell me, Master, does anyone ever come
    from the first ledge, whose only punishment
    is hope cut off, into this dreary bottom?"   15
I put this question to him, still in fear
    of what his broken speech might mean; and he:
    "Rarely do any of us enter here.
Once before, it is true, I crossed through Hell
    conjured by cruel Erichtho who recalled
    the spirits to their bodies. Her dark spell
forced me, newly stripped of my mortal part,
    to enter through this gate and summon out
    a spirit from Judaïca. Take heart,
that is the last depth and the darkest lair
    and the farthest from Heaven which encircles all,
    and at that time I came back even from there.
The marsh from which the stinking gases bubble
    lies all about this capital of sorrow
    whose gates we may not pass now without trouble."   30
All this and more he expounded; but the rest
    was lost on me, for suddenly my attention
    was drawn to the turret with the fiery crest
where all at once three hellish and inhuman
    Furies sprang to view, bloodstained and wild.
    Their limbs and gestures hinted they were women.
Belts of greenest hydras wound and wound
    about their waists, and snakes and horned serpents
    grew from their heads like matted hair and bound
their horrid brows. My Master, who well knew
    the handmaids of the Queen of Woe, cried: "Look!
    the terrible Erinyes of Hecate's crew.

That is Megaera to the left of the tower.
   Alecto is the one who raves on the right.
   Tisiphone stands between." And he said no more.   45
With their palms they beat their brows, with their nails they clawed
   their bleeding breasts. And such mad wails broke from them
   that I drew close to the Poet, overawed.
And all together screamed, looking down at me:
   "Call Medusa that we may change him to stone!
   Too lightly we let Theseus go free."
"Turn your back and keep your eyes shut tight;
   for should the Gorgon come and you look at her,
   never again would you return to the light."
This was my Guide's command. And he turned me about
   himself and would not trust my hands alone,
   but, with his placed on mine, held my eyes shut.
Men of sound intellect and probity,
   weigh with good understanding what lies hidden
   behind the veil of my strange allegory!   60
Suddenly there broke on the dirty swell
   of the dark marsh a squall of terrible sound
   that sent a tremor through both shores of Hell;
a sound as if two continents of air,
   one frigid and one scorching, clashed head on
   in a war of winds that stripped the forests bare,
ripped off whole boughs and blew them helter-skelter
   along the range of dust it raised before it
   making the beasts and shepherds run for shelter.
The Master freed my eyes. "Now turn," he said,
   "and fix your nerve of vision on the foam
   there where the smoke is thickest and most acrid."
As frogs before the snake that hunts them down
   churn up their pond in flight, until the last
   squats on the bottom as if turned to stone—   75
so I saw more than a thousand ruined souls
   scatter away from one who crossed dry-shod
   the Stygian marsh into Hell's burning bowels.
With his left hand he fanned away the dreary
   vapors of that sink as he approached;
   and only of that annoyance did he seem weary.

"That is Megaera to the left of the tower.
Alecto is the one who raves on the right.
Tisiphone stands between."

Clearly he was a messenger from God's Throne,
    and I turned to my Guide; but he made me a sign
    that I should keep my silence and bow down.
Ah, what scorn breathed from that angel-presence!
    He reached the gate of Dis and with a wand
    he waved it open, for there was no resistance.
"Outcasts of Heaven, you twice-loathsome crew,"
    he cried upon that terrible sill of Hell,
    "how does this insolence still live in you?   90
Why do you set yourselves against that Throne
    whose will none can deny, and which, times past,
    has added to your pain for each rebellion?
Why do you butt against Fate's ordinance?
    Your Cerberus, if you recall, still wears
    his throat and chin peeled for such arrogance."
Then he turned back through the same filthy tide
    by which he had come. He did not speak to us,
    but went his way like one preoccupied
by other presences than those before him.
    And we moved toward the city, fearing nothing
    after his holy words. Straight through the dim
and open gate we entered unopposed.
    And I, eager to learn what new estate
    of Hell those burning fortress walls enclosed,   105
began to look about the very moment
    we were inside, and I saw on every hand
    a countryside of sorrow and new torment.
As at Arles where the Rhone sinks into stagnant marshes,
    as at Pola by the Quarnaro Gulf, whose waters
    close Italy and wash her farthest reaches,
the uneven tombs cover the even plain—
    such fields I saw here, spread in all directions,
    except that here the tombs were chests of pain;
for, in a ring around each tomb, great fires
    raised every wall to a red heat. No smith
    works hotter iron in his forge. The biers
stood with their lids upraised, and from their pits
    an anguished moaning rose on the dead air
    from the desolation of tormented spirits.   120

Inferno

And I: "Master, what shades are these who lie
  buried in these chests and fill the air
  with such a painful and unending cry?"
"These are the arch-heretics of all cults,
  with all their followers," he replied. "Far more
  than you would think lie stuffed into these vaults.
Like lies with like in every heresy,
  and the monuments are fired, some more, some less;
  to each depravity its own degree."
He turned then, and I followed through that night
between the wall and the torments, bearing right.

Canto 10

As the Poets pass on, one of the damned
hears Dante speaking, recognizes him as a Tuscan, and calls to him from one of the fiery
tombs. A moment later he appears. He is Farinata
degli Uberti, a great war chief of the Tuscan
Ghibellines. The majesty and power of his bearing seem to diminish Hell itself. He asks Dante's
lineage and recognizes him as an enemy. They
begin to talk politics, but are interrupted by another shade, who rises from the same tomb. This
is Cavalcante dei Cavalcanti, father of Guido
Cavalcanti, a contemporary poet. If it is genius
that leads Dante on his great journey, the shade
asks, why is Guido not with him? Can Dante presume to a greater genius than Guido's? Dante replies that he comes this way only with the aid of
powers Guido has not sought. His reply is a clas-
sic example of many-leveled symbolism as well
as an overt criticism of a rival poet. The senior
Cavalcanti mistakenly infers from Dante's reply
that Guido is dead, and swoons back into the
flames. Farinata, who has not deigned to notice
his fellow sinner, continues from the exact point
at which he had been interrupted. It is as if he
refuses to recognize the flames in which he is
shrouded. He proceeds to prophesy Dante's banishment from Florence, defends his part in Florentine politics, and then, in answer to Dante's
question, explains how it is that the damned can
foresee the future but have no knowledge of the
present. He then names others who share his
tomb, and Dante takes his leave with considerable respect for his great enemy, pausing only long
enough to leave word for Cavalcanti
that Guido is still alive.

Inferno

We go by a secret path along the rim
 of the dark city, between the wall and the torments.
 My Master leads me and I follow him.
"Supreme Virtue, who through this impious land
 wheel me at will down these dark gyres," I said,
 "speak to me, for I wish to understand.
Tell me, Master, is it permitted to see
 the souls within these tombs? The lids are raised,
 and no one stands on guard." And he to me:
"All shall be sealed forever on the day
 these souls return here from Jehoshaphat
 with the bodies they have given once to clay.
In this dark corner of the morgue of wrath
 lie Epicurus and his followers,
 who make the soul share in the body's death.   15
And here you shall be granted presently
 not only your spoken wish, but that other as well,
 which you had thought perhaps to hide from me."
And I: "Except to speak my thoughts in few
 and modest words, as I learned from your example,
 dear Guide, I do not hide my heart from you."
"O Tuscan, who go living through this place
 speaking so decorously, may it please you pause
 a moment on your way, for by the grace
of that high speech in which I hear your birth,
 I know you for a son of that noble city
 which perhaps I vexed too much in my time on earth."
These words broke without warning from inside
 one of the burning arks. Caught by surprise,
 I turned in fear and drew close to my Guide.   30
And he: "Turn around. What are you doing? Look there.
 It is Farinata rising from the flames.
 From the waist up his shade will be made clear."
My eyes were fixed on him already. Erect,
 he rose above the flame, great chest, great brow;
 he seemed to hold all Hell in disrespect.
My Guide's prompt hands urged me among the dim
 and smoking sepulchers to that great figure,
 and he said to me: "Mind how you speak to him."

And when I stood alone at the foot of the tomb,
   the great soul stared almost contemptuously,
   before he asked: "Of what line do you come?"
Because I wished to obey, I did not hide
   anything from him; whereupon, as he listened,
   he raised his brows a little, then replied: 45
"Bitter enemies were they to me,
   to my fathers, and to my party, so that twice
   I sent them scattering from high Italy."
"If they were scattered, still from every part
   they formed again and returned both times," I answered,
   "but yours have not yet wholly learned that art."
At this another shade rose gradually,
   visible to the chin. It had raised itself,
   I think, upon its knees, and it looked around me
as if it expected to find through that black air
   that blew about me, another traveler.
   And weeping when it found no other there,
turned back. "And if," it cried, "you travel through
   this dungeon of the blind by power of genius,
   where is my son? why is he not with you?"   60
And I to him: "Not by myself am I borne
   this terrible way. I am led by him who waits there
   and whom perhaps your Guido held in scorn."
For by his words and the manner of his torment
   I knew his name already and could, therefore,
   answer both what he asked and what he meant.
Instantly he rose to his full height:
   "He *held!* What is it you say? Is he dead, then?
   Do his eyes no longer fill with that sweet light?"
And when he saw that I delayed a bit
   in answering his question, he fell backwards
   into the flame and rose no more from it.
But that majestic spirit at whose call
   I had first paused there, did not change expression,
   nor so much as turn his face to watch him fall.   75
"And if," going on from his last words, he said,
   "men of my line have yet to learn that art,
   that burns me deeper than this flaming bed.

But the face of her who reigns in Hell shall not
  be fifty times rekindled in its course
  before you learn what griefs attend that art.
And as you hope to find the world again,
  tell me: Why is that populace so savage
  in the edicts they pronounce against my strain?"
And I to him: "The havoc and the carnage
  that dyed the Arbia red at Montaperti
  have caused these angry cries in our assemblage."
He sighed and shook his head. "I was not alone
  in that affair," he said, "nor certainly
  would I have joined the rest without good reason.   90
But I *was* alone at that time when every other
  consented to the death of Florence; I
  alone with open face defended her."
"Ah, so may your soul sometime have rest,"
  I begged him, "solve the riddle that pursues me
  through this dark place and leaves my mind perplexed.
You seem to see in advance all time's intent,
  if I have heard and understood correctly;
  but you seem to lack all knowledge of the present."
"We see asquint, like those whose twisted sight
  can make out only the far off," he said,
  "for the King of All still grants us that much light.
When things draw near, or happen, we perceive
  nothing of them. Except what others bring us
  we have no news of those who are alive.   105
So may you understand that all we know
  will be dead forever from that day and hour
  when the Portal of the Future is swung to."
Then, as if stricken by regret, I said:
  "Now, therefore, will you tell that fallen one
  who asked about his son, that he is not dead
and that, if I did not reply more quickly,
  it was because my mind was occupied
  with this confusion you have solved for me."
And now my Guide was calling me. In haste,
  therefore, I begged that mighty shade to name
  the others who lay with him in that chest.

And he: "More than a thousand cram this tomb.
  The second Frederick is here, and the Cardinal
  of the Ubaldini. Of the rest let us be dumb."   120
And he disappeared without more said, and I
  turned back and made my way to the ancient Poet,
  pondering the words of the dark prophecy.
He moved along, and then, when we had started,
  he turned and said to me, "What troubles you?
  Why do you look so vacant and downhearted?"
And I told him. And he replied: "Well may you bear
  those words in mind." Then, pausing, raised a finger:
  "Now pay attention to what I tell you here;
when finally you stand before the ray
  of that sweet Lady whose bright eye sees all,
  from her you will learn the turnings of your way."
So saying, he bore left, turning his back
  on the flaming walls, and we passed deeper yet
  into the city of pain, along a track   135
that plunged down like a scar into a sink
which sickened us already with its stink.

Canto 11

*The Poets reach the inner edge of the
sixth circle and find a great jumble of rocks that
had once been a cliff, but which has fallen into
rubble as the result of the great earthquake that
shook Hell when Christ died. Below them lies the
seventh circle, and so fetid is the air that arises
from it that the Poets cower for shelter behind a
great tomb until they can grow accustomed to the
stench. Dante finds an inscription on the lid of the
tomb labeling it as the place in Hell of Pope
Anastasius. Virgil takes advantage of the delay to
outline in detail the division of Lower Hell, a theological discourse based on the* Ethics *and the*
Physics *of Aristotle with subsequent medieval
interpretations. Virgil explains also why it is that
the Incontinent are not punished within the walls
of Dis, and rather ingeniously sets forth the reasons why usury is an act of violence against
Art, which is the child of Nature and hence the
grandchild of God. (By Art, Dante means the
arts and crafts by which man draws from nature, i.e., industry.) As he concludes, he rises
and urges Dante on. By means known only to
Virgil, he is aware of the motion of the stars and
from them he sees that it is nearly
sunrise of Holy Saturday.*

We came to the edge of an enormous sink
   rimmed by a circle of great broken boulders.
   Here we found ghastlier gangs. And here the stink
thrown up by the abyss so overpowered us
   that we drew back, cowering behind the wall
   of one of the great tombs; and standing thus,

I saw an inscription in the stone, and read:
  "I guard Anastasius, once Pope,
    he whom Photinus led from the straight road."

I saw an inscription in the stone, and read:
  "I guard Anastasius, once Pope,
    he whom Photinus led from the straight road."
"Before we travel on to that blind pit
  we must delay until our sense grows used
    to its foul breath, and then we will not mind it,"
my Master said. And I then: "Let us find
  some compensation for the time of waiting."
    And he: "You shall see I have just that in mind.   15
My son," he began, "there are below this wall
  three smaller circles, each in its degree
    like those you are about to leave, and all
are crammed with God's accurst. Accordingly,
  that you may understand their sins at sight,
    I will explain how each is prisoned, and why.
Malice is the sin most hated by God.
  And the aim of malice is to injure others
    whether by fraud or violence. But since fraud
is the vice of which man alone is capable,
  God loathes it most. Therefore, the fraudulent
    are placed below, and their torment is more painful.
The first below are the violent. But as violence
  sins in three persons, so is that circle formed
    of three descending rounds of crueler torments.   30
Against God, self, and neighbor is violence shown.
  Against their persons and their goods, I say,
    as you shall hear set forth with open reason.
Murder and mayhem are the violation
  of the person of one's neighbor; and of his goods—
    harassment, plunder, arson, and extortion.
Therefore, homicides, and those who strike
  in malice—destroyers and plunderers—all lie
    in that first round, and like suffers with like.
A man may lay violent hands upon his own
  person and substance; so in that second round
    eternally in vain repentance moan
the suicides and all who gamble away
  and waste the good and substance of their lives
    and weep in that sweet time when they should be gay.   45

Violence may be offered the Deity
   in the heart that blasphemes and refuses Him
   and scorns the gifts of Nature, her beauty and bounty.
Therefore, the smallest round brands with its mark
   both Sodom and Cahors, and all who rail
   at God and His commands in their hearts' dark.
Fraud, which is a canker to every conscience,
   may be practiced by a man on those who trust him,
   and on those who have reposed no confidence.
The latter mode seems only to deny
   the bond of love which all men have from Nature;
   therefore within the second circle lie
simoniacs, sycophants, and hypocrites,
   falsifiers, thieves, and sorcerers,
   grafters, pimps, and all such filthy cheats.   60
The former mode of fraud not only denies
   the bond of Nature, but the special trust
   added by bonds of friendship or blood ties.
Hence, at the center point of all creation,
   in the smallest circle, on which Dis is founded,
   the traitors lie in endless expiation."
"Master," I said, "the clarity of your mind
   impresses all you touch; I see quite clearly
   the orders of this dark pit of the blind.
But tell me: those who lie in the swamp's bowels,
   those the wind blows about, those the rain beats,
   and those who meet and clash with such mad howls—
why are *they* not punished in the rust-red city
   if God's wrath be upon them? and if it is not,
   why must they grieve through all eternity?"   75
And he: "Why does your understanding stray
   so far from its own habit? or can it be
   your thoughts are turned along some other way?
Have you forgotten that your *Ethics* states
   the three main dispositions of the soul
   that lead to those offenses Heaven hates—
incontinence, malice, and bestiality?
   and how incontinence offends God least
   and earns least blame from Justice and Charity?

Now if you weigh this doctrine and recall
   exactly who they are whose punishment
   lies in that upper Hell outside the wall,
you will understand at once why they are confined
   apart from these fierce wraiths, and why less anger
   beats down on them from the Eternal Mind."   90
"O sun which clears all mists from troubled sight,
   such joy attends your rising that I feel
   as grateful to the dark as to the light.
Go back a little further," I said, "to where
   you spoke of usury as an offense
   against God's goodness. How is that made clear?"
"Philosophy makes plain by many reasons,"
   he answered me, "to those who heed her teachings,
   how all of Nature—her laws, her fruits, her seasons—
springs from the Ultimate Intellect and Its art;
   and if you read your *Physics* with due care,
   you will note, not many pages from the start,
that Art strives after her by imitation,
   as the disciple imitates the master;
   Art, as it were, is the grandchild of creation.   105
By this, recalling the Old Testament
   near the beginning of Genesis, you will see
   that in the will of Providence man was meant
to labor and to prosper. But usurers,
   by seeking their increase in other ways,
   scorn Nature in herself and her followers.
But come, for it is my wish now to go on;
   the wheel turns and the Wain lies over Caurus,
   the Fish are quivering low on the horizon,
and there beyond us runs the road we go
down the dark scarp into the depths below."

Canto 12

The Poets begin the descent of the fallen rock wall, having first to evade the Minotaur, who menaces them. Virgil tricks him, and the Poets hurry by. Below them they see the river of blood, which marks the first round of the seventh circle as detailed in the previous canto. Here are punished the Violent Against Their Neighbors, great war-makers, cruel tyrants, highwaymen— all who shed the blood of their fellowmen. As they wallowed in blood during their lives, so they are immersed in the boiling blood forever, each according to the degree of his guilt, while fierce Centaurs patrol the banks, ready to shoot with their arrows any sinner who raises himself out of the boiling blood beyond the limits permitted him. Alexander the Great is here, up to his lashes in the blood, and with him Attila, the Scourge of God. They are immersed in the deepest part of the river, which grows shallower as it circles to the other side of the ledge, then deepens again. The Poets are challenged by the Centaurs, but Virgil wins a safe-conduct from Chiron, their chief, who assigns Nessus to guide them and to bear them across the shallows of the boiling blood. Nessus carries them across at the point where it is only ankle deep and immediately leaves them and returns to his patrol.

The scene that opened from the edge of the pit
   was mountainous, and such a desolation
   that every eye would shun the sight of it;
a ruin like the Slides of Mark near Trent
   on the bank of the Adige, the result of an earthquake
   or of some massive fault in the escarpment—

for, from the point of the peak where the mountain split
  to the plain below, the rock is so badly shattered
  a man at the top might make a rough stair of it.
Such was the passage down the steep, and there
  at the very top, at the edge of the broken cleft,
  lay spread the Infamy of Crete, the heir
of bestiality and the lecherous queen
  who hid in a wooden cow. And when he saw us,
  he gnawed his own flesh in a fit of spleen.   15
And my Master mocked: "How you do pump your breath!
  Do you think, perhaps, it is the Duke of Athens,
  who in the world above served up your death?
Off with you, monster; this one does not come
  instructed by your sister, but of himself
  to observe your punishment in the lost kingdom."
As a bull that breaks its chains just when the knife
  has struck its deathblow cannot stand nor run
  but leaps from side to side with its last life—
so danced the Minotaur, and my shrewd Guide
  cried out: "Run now! While he is blind with rage!
  Into the pass, quick, and get over the side!"
So we went down across the shale and slate
  of that ruined rock, which often slid and shifted
  under me at the touch of living weight.   30
I moved on, deep in thought; and my Guide to me:
  "You are wondering perhaps about this ruin
  which is guarded by that beast upon whose fury
I played just now. I should tell you that when last
  I came this dark way to the depths of Hell,
  this rock had not yet felt the ruinous blast.
But certainly, if I am not mistaken,
  it was just before the coming of Him who took
  the souls from Limbo, that all Hell was shaken
so that I thought the universe felt love
  and all its elements moved toward harmony,
  whereby the world of matter, as some believe,
has often plunged to chaos. It was then,
  that here and elsewhere in the pits of Hell,
  the ancient rock was stricken and broke open.   45

At the very top, at the edge of the broken cleft,
lay spread the Infamy of Crete.

But turn your eyes to the valley; there we shall find
   the river of boiling blood in which are steeped
   all who struck down their fellow men." O blind!
O ignorant, self-seeking cupidity,
   which spurs us so in the short mortal life
   and steeps us so through all eternity!
I saw an arching fosse that was the bed
   of a winding river circling through the plain
   exactly as my Guide and Lord had said.
A file of Centaurs galloped in the space
   between the bank and the cliff, well armed with arrows,
   riding as once on earth they rode to the chase
And seeing us descend, that straggling band
   halted, and three of them moved out toward us,
   their long bows and the shafts already in hand. 60
And one of them cried out while still below:
   "To what pain are you sent down that dark coast?
   Answer from where you stand, or I draw the bow!"
"Chiron is standing there hard by your side;
   our answer will be to him. This wrath of yours
   was always your own worst fate," my Guide replied.
And to me he said: "That is Nessus, who died in the wood
   for insulting Dejanira. At his death
   he plotted his revenge in his own blood.
This one in the middle staring at his chest
   is the mighty Chiron, he who nursed Achilles;
   the other is Pholus, fiercer than all the rest.
They run by that stream in thousands, snapping their bows
   at any wraith who dares to raise himself
   out of the blood more than his guilt allows." 75
We drew near those swift beasts. In a thoughtful pause
   Chiron drew an arrow, and with its notch
   he pushed his great beard back along his jaws.
And when he had thus uncovered the huge pouches
   of his lips, he said to his fellows: "Have you noticed
   how the one who walks behind moves what he touches?
That is not how the dead go." My good Guide,
   already standing by the monstrous breast
   in which the two mixed natures joined, replied:

"It is true he lives; in his necessity
    I alone must lead him through this valley.
    Fate brings him here, not curiosity.
From singing *Alleluia* the sublime
    spirit who sends me came. He is no bandit.
    Nor am I one who ever stooped to crime.   90
But in the name of the Power by which I go
    this sunken way across the floor of Hell,
    assign us one of your troop whom we may follow,
that he may guide us to the ford and there
    carry across on his back the one I lead,
    for he is not a spirit to move through air."
Chiron turned his head on his right breast
    and said to Nessus: "Go with them, and guide them,
    and turn back any others that would contest
their passage." So we moved beside our guide
    along the bank of the scalding purple river
    in which the shrieking wraiths were boiled and dyed.
Some stood up to their lashes in that torrent,
    and as we passed them the huge Centaur said:
    "These were the kings of bloodshed and despoilment.   105
Here they pay for their ferocity.
    Here is Alexander; and Dionysius,
    who brought long years of grief to Sicily.
That brow you see with the hair as black as night
    is Azzolino; and that beside him, the blond,
    is Opizzo da Esti, who had his mortal light
blown out by his own stepson." I turned then
    to speak to the Poet, but he raised a hand:
    "Let him be the teacher now, and I will listen."
Further on, the Centaur stopped beside
    a group of spirits steeped as far as the throat
    in the race of boiling blood, and there our guide
pointed out a sinner who stood alone:
    "That one before God's altar pierced a heart
    still honored on the Thames." And he passed on.   120
We came in sight of some who were allowed
    to raise the head and all the chest from the river,
    and I recognized many there. Thus, as we followed

along the stream of blood, its level fell
    until it cooked no more than the feet of the damned.
    And here we crossed the ford to deeper Hell.
"Just as you see the boiling stream grow shallow
    along this side," the Centaur said to us
    when we stood on the other bank, "I would have you know
that on the other, the bottom sinks anew
    more and more, until it comes again
    full circle to the place where the tyrants stew.
It is there that Holy Justice spends Its wrath
    on Sextus and Pyrrhus through eternity,
    and on Attila, who was a scourge on earth;   135
and everlastingly milks out the tears
    of Rinier da Corneto and Rinier Pazzo,
    those two assassins who for many years
stalked the highways, bloody and abhorred."
And with that he started back across the ford.

Canto 13

Nessus carries the Poets across the river of boiling blood and leaves them in the second round of the seventh circle, the Wood of the Suicides. Here are punished those who destroyed their own lives and those who destroyed their substance. The souls of the Suicides are encased in thorny trees whose leaves are eaten by odious Harpies, the overseers of these damned. When the Harpies feed upon them, damaging their leaves and limbs, the wounds bleed. Only as long as the blood flows are the souls of the trees able to speak. Thus, they who destroyed their own bodies are denied a human form; and just as the supreme expression of their lives was self-destruction, so they are permitted to speak only through that which tears and destroys them. Only through their own blood do they find voice. And to add one more dimension to the symbolism, it is the Harpies—defilers of all they touch—who give them their eternally recurring wounds. The Poets pause before one tree and speak with the soul of Pier delle Vigne. In the same wood they see Jacomo da Sant' Andrea and Lano da Siena, two famous Squanderers and Destroyers of Goods pursued by a pack of savage hounds. The hounds overtake Sant' Andrea, tear him to pieces, and carry off his limbs in their teeth, a self-evident symbolic retribution for the violence with which these sinners destroyed their substance in the world. After this scene of horror, Dante speaks to an unknown Florentine suicide whose soul is in the bush that the hounds tore when they leaped upon Sant' Andrea.

Inferno

Nessus had not yet reached the other shore
  when we moved on into a pathless wood
  that twisted upward from Hell's broken floor.
Its foliage was not verdant, but nearly black.
  The unhealthy branches, gnarled and warped and tangled,
  bore poison thorns instead of fruit. The track
of those wild beasts that shun the open spaces
  men till between Cecina and Corneto
  runs through no rougher nor more tangled places.
Here nest the odious Harpies of whom my Master
  wrote how they drove Aeneas and his companions
  from the Strophades with prophecies of disaster.
Their wings are wide, their feet clawed, their huge bellies
  covered with feathers, their necks and faces human.
  They croak eternally in the unnatural trees.   15
"Before going on, I would have you understand,"
  my Guide began, "we are in the second round
  and shall be till we reach the burning sand.
Therefore look carefully and you will see
  things in this wood, which, if I told them to you
  would shake the confidence you have placed in me."
I heard cries of lamentation rise and spill
  on every hand, but saw no souls in pain
  in all that waste; and, puzzled, I stood still.
I think perhaps he thought that I was thinking
  those cries rose from among the twisted roots
  through which the spirits of the damned were slinking
to hide from us. Therefore my Master said:
  "If you break off a twig, what you will learn
  will drive what you are thinking from your head."   30
Puzzled, I raised my hand a bit and slowly
  broke off a branchlet from an enormous thorn;
  and the great trunk of it cried: "Why do you break me?"
And after blood had darkened all the bowl
  of the wound, it cried again: "Why do you tear me?
  Is there no pity left in any soul?
Men we were, and now we are changed to sticks;
  well might your hand have been more merciful
  were we no more than souls of lice and ticks."

71

Here nest the odious Harpies of whom my Master
wrote how they drove Aeneas and his companions
from the Strophades with prophecies of disaster.

As a green branch with one end all aflame
  will hiss and sputter sap out of the other
  as the air escapes—so from that trunk there came
words and blood together, gout by gout.
  Startled, I dropped the branch that I was holding
  and stood transfixed by fear, half turned about   45
to my Master, who replied: "O wounded soul,
  could he have believed before what he has seen
  in my verses only, you would yet be whole,
for his hand would never have been raised against you.
  But knowing this truth could never be believed
  till it was seen, I urged him on to do
what grieves me now; and I beg to know your name,
  that to make you some amends in the sweet world
  when he returns, he may refresh your fame."
And the trunk: "So sweet those words to me that I
  cannot be still, and may it not annoy you
  if I seem somewhat lengthy in reply.
I am he who held both keys to Frederick's heart,
  locking, unlocking with so deft a touch
  that scarce another soul had any part   60
in his most secret thoughts. Through every strife
  I was so faithful to my glorious office
  that for it I gave up both sleep and life.
That harlot, Envy, who on Caesar's face
  keeps fixed forever her adulterous stare,
  the common plague and vice of court and palace,
inflamed all minds against me. These inflamed
  so inflamed him that all my happy honors
  were changed to mourning. Then, unjustly blamed,
my soul, in scorn, and thinking to be free
  of scorn in death, made me at last, though just,
  unjust to myself. By the new roots of this tree
I swear to you that never in word or spirit
  did I break faith to my lord and emperor
  who was so worthy of honor in his merit.   75
If either of you return to the world, speak for me,
  to vindicate in the memory of men
  one who lies prostrate from the blows of Envy."

The Poet stood. Then turned. "Since he is silent,"
    he said to me, "do not you waste this hour,
    if you wish to ask about his life or torment."
And I replied: "Question him for my part,
    on whatever you think I would do well to hear;
    I could not, such compassion chokes my heart."
The Poet began again: "That this man may
    with all his heart do for you what your words
    entreat him to, imprisoned spirit, I pray,
tell us how the soul is bound and bent
    into these knots and whether any ever
    frees itself from such imprisonment."   90
At that the trunk blew powerfully, and then
    the wind became a voice that spoke these words:
  "Briefly is the answer given. When
out of the flesh from which it tore itself,
    the violent spirit comes to punishment,
    Minos assigns it to the seventh shelf.
It falls into the wood, and landing there,
    wherever Fortune flings it, it strikes root,
    and there it sprouts, lusty as any tare,
shoots up a sapling, and becomes a tree.
    The Harpies, feeding on its leaves then, give it
    pain and pain's outlet simultaneously.
Like the rest, we shall go for our husks on Judgment Day,
    but not that we may wear them, for it is not just
    that a man be given what he throws away.   105
Here shall we drag them and in this mournful glade
    our bodies will dangle to the end of time,
    each on the thorns of its tormented shade."
We waited by the trunk, but it said no more;
    and waiting, we were startled by a noise
    that grew through all the wood. Just such a roar
and trembling as one feels when the boar and chase
    approach his stand, the beasts and branches crashing
    and clashing in the heat of the fierce race.
And there on the left, running so violently
    they broke off every twig in the dark wood,
    two torn and naked wraiths went plunging by me.

The leader cried, "Come now, O Death! Come now!"
  And the other, seeing that he was outrun
  cried out: "Your legs were not so ready, Lano,   120
in the jousts at the Toppo." And suddenly in his rush,
  perhaps because his breath was failing him,
  he hid himself inside a thorny bush
and cowered among its leaves. Then at his back,
  the wood leaped with black bitches, swift as greyhounds
  escaping from their leash, and all the pack
sprang on him; with their fangs they opened him
  and tore him savagely, and then withdrew,
  carrying his body with them, limb by limb.
Then, taking me by the hand across the wood,
  my Master led me toward the bush. Lamenting,
  all its fractures blew out words and blood:
"O Jacomo da Sant' Andrea!" it said,
  "what have you gained in making me your screen?
  What part had I in the foul life you led?"   135
And when my Master had drawn up to it
  he said: "Who were you, who through all your wounds
  blow out your blood with your lament, sad spirit?"
And he to us: "You who have come to see
  how the outrageous mangling of these hounds
  has torn my boughs and stripped my leaves from me,
oh, heap them round my ruin! I was born
  in the city that tore down Mars and raised the Baptist.
  On that account the god of war has sworn
her sorrow shall not end. And were it not
  that something of his image still survives
  on the bridge across the Arno, some have thought
those citizens who of their love and pain
  afterwards rebuilt it from the ashes
  left by Attila, would have worked in vain.   150
I am one who has no tale to tell;
  I made myself a gibbet of my own lintel."

Canto 14

Dante, in pity, restores the torn leaves to
the soul of his countryman, and the Poets move
on to the next round, a great plain of burning sand
upon which there descends an eternal slow rain of
fire. Here, scorched by fire from above and below,
are three classes of sinners suffering differing de-
grees of exposure to the fire. The Blasphemers (the
Violent Against God) are stretched supine upon
the sand; the Sodomites (the Violent Against Na-
ture) run in endless circles; and the Usurers (the
Violent Against Art) huddle on the sands. The
Poets find Capaneus stretched out on the sands,
the chief sinner of that place. He is still blas-
pheming God. They continue along the edge of the
Wood of the Suicides and come to a blood-red rill
which flows boiling from the wood and crosses
the burning plain. Virgil explains the miraculous
power of its waters and discourses on the Old
Man of Crete and the origin of all the rivers of
Hell. The symbolism of the burning plain is obvi-
ously centered in sterility (the desert image) and
wrath (the fire image). Blasphemy, sodomy, and
usury are all unnatural and sterile actions: thus
the unbearing desert is the eternity of these sin-
ners; and thus the rain, which in nature should be
fertile and cool, descends as fire. Capaneus, more-
over, is subjected not only to the wrath of Nature
(the sands below) and the wrath of God (the fire
from above), but is tortured most by his own
inner violence, the root of blasphemy.

Love of that land that was our common source
   moved me to tears; I gathered up the leaves
   and gave them back. He was already hoarse.

Inferno

We came to the edge of the forest where one goes
  from the second round to the third, and there we saw
  what fearful arts the hand of Justice knows.
To make these new things wholly clear, I say
  we came to a plain whose soil repels all roots.
  The wood of misery rings it the same way
the wood itself is ringed by the red fosse.
  We paused at its edge; the ground was burning sand,
  just such a waste as Cato marched across.
O endless wrath of God! how utterly
  thou shouldst become a terror to all men
  who read the frightful truths revealed to me!   15
Enormous herds of naked souls I saw,
  lamenting till their eyes were burned of tears;
  they seemed condemned by an unequal law,
for some were stretched supine upon the ground,
  some squatted with their arms about themselves,
  and others without pause roamed round and round.
Most numerous were those that roamed the plain.
  Far fewer were the souls stretched on the sand,
  but moved to louder cries by greater pain.
And over all that sand on which they lay
  or crouched or roamed, great flakes of flame fell slowly
  as snow falls in the Alps on a windless day.
Like those Alexander met in the hot regions
  of India, flames raining from the sky
  to fall still unextinguished on his legions;   30
whereat he formed his ranks and at their head
  set the example, trampling the hot ground
  for fear the tongues of fire might join and spread—
just so in Hell descended the long rain
  upon the damned, kindling the sand like tinder
  under a flint and steel, doubling the pain.
In a never-ending fit upon those sands,
  the arms of the damned twitched all about their bodies,
  now here, now there, brushing away the brands.
"Poet," I said, "master of every dread
  we have encountered, other than those fiends
  who sallied from the last gate of the dead—

who is that wraith who lies along the rim
and sets his face against the fire in scorn,
so that the rain seems not to mellow him?"   45
And he himself, hearing what I had said
to my Guide and Lord concerning him, replied:
"What I was living, the same am I now, dead.
Though Jupiter wear out his sooty smith
from whom on my last day he snatched in anger
the jagged thunderbolt he pierced me with;
though he wear out the others one by one
who labor at the forge at Mongibello
crying again 'Help! Help! Help me, good Vulcan!'
as he did at Phlegra; and hurl down endlessly
with all the power of Heaven in his arm,
small satisfaction would he win from me."
At this my Guide spoke with such vehemence
as I had not heard from him in all of Hell:
"O Capaneus, by your insolence   60
you are made to suffer as much fire inside
as falls upon you. Only your own rage
could be fit torment for your sullen pride."
Then he turned to me more gently. "That," he said,
"was one of the Seven who laid siege to Thebes.
Living, he scorned God, and among the dead
he scorns Him yet. He thinks he may detest
God's power too easily, but as I told him,
his slobber is a fit badge for his breast.
Now follow me; and mind for your own good
you do not step upon the burning sand,
but keep well back along the edge of the wood."
We walked in silence then till we reached a rill
that gushes from the wood; it ran so red
the memory sends a shudder through me still.   75
As from the Bulicame springs the stream
the sinful women keep to their own use;
so down the sand the rill flowed out in steam.
The bed and both its banks were petrified,
as were its margins; thus I knew at once
our passage through the sand lay by its side.

"Among all other wonders I have shown you
   since we came through the gate denied to none,
   nothing your eyes have seen is equal to
the marvel of the rill by which we stand,
   for it stifles all the flames above its course
   as it flows out across the burning sand."
So spoke my Guide across the flickering light,
   and I begged him to bestow on me the food
   for which he had given me the appetite.   90
"In the middle of the sea, and gone to waste,
   there lies a country known as Crete," he said,
   "under whose king the ancient world was chaste.
Once Rhea chose it as the secret crypt
   and cradle of her son; and better to hide him,
   her Corybantes raised a din when he wept.
An ancient giant stands in the mountain's core.
   He keeps his shoulder turned toward Damietta,
   and looks toward Rome as if it were his mirror.
His head is made of gold; of silverwork
   his breast and both his arms; of polished brass
   the rest of his great torso to the fork.
He is of chosen iron from there down,
   except that his right foot is terra-cotta;
   it is this foot he rests more weight upon.   105
Every part except the gold is split
   by a great fissure from which endless tears
   drip down and hollow out the mountain's pit.
Their course sinks to this pit from stone to stone,
   becoming Acheron, Phlegethon, and Styx.
   Then by this narrow sluice they hurtle down
to the end of all descent and disappear
   into Cocytus. You shall see what sink that is
   with your own eyes. I pass it in silence here."
And I to him: "But if these waters flow
   from the world above, why is this rill met only
   along this shelf?" And he to me: "You know
the place is round, and though you have come deep
   into the valley through the many circles,
   always bearing left along the steep,   120

you have not traveled any circle through
   its total round; hence when new things appear
   from time to time, that hardly should surprise you."
And I: "Where shall we find Phlegethon's course?
   And Lethe's? One you omit, and of the other
   you only say the tear-flood is its source."
"In all you ask of me you please me truly,"
   he answered, "but the red and boiling water
   should answer the first question you put to me,
and you shall stand by Lethe, but far hence—
   there, where the spirits go to wash themselves
   when their guilt has been removed by penitence."
And then he said: "Now it is time to quit
   this edge of shade; follow close after me
   along the rill, and do not stray from it;   135
for the unburning margins form a lane,
and by them we may cross the burning plain."

Canto 15

*Protected by the marvelous powers of
the boiling rill, the Poets walk along its banks
across the burning plain. The Wood of the Suicides is behind them; the great cliff at whose foot
lies the eighth circle is before them. They pass one
of the roving bands of Sodomites. One of the sinners stops Dante, and with great difficulty the
Poet recognizes him under his baked features as
Ser Brunetto Latino. This is a reunion with a
dearly-loved man and writer, one who had considerably influenced Dante's own development,
and Dante addresses him with great and sorrow-
ful affection, paying him the highest tribute
offered to any sinner in the Inferno. Brunetto
prophesies Dante's sufferings at the hands of
the Florentines, gives an account of the souls
that move with him through the fire, and finally,
under divine compulsion, races
off across the plain.*

We go by one of the stone margins now
   and the steam of the rivulet makes a shade above it,
   guarding the stream and banks from the flaming snow.
As the Flemings in the lowland between Bruges
   and Wissant, under constant threat of the sea,
   erect their great dikes to hold back the deluge;
as the Paduans along the shores of the Brent
   build levees to protect their towns and castles
   lest Chiarentana drown in the spring torrent—
to the same plan, though not so wide nor high,
   did the engineer, whoever he may have been,
   design the margin we were crossing by.

Already we were so far from the wood
  that, even had I turned to look at it,
  I could not have made it out from where I stood,   15
when a company of shades came into sight
  walking beside the bank. They stared at us
  as men at evening by the new moon's light
stare at one another when they pass by
  on a dark road, pointing their eyebrows toward us
  as an old tailor squints at his needle's eye.
Stared at so closely by that ghostly crew,
  I was recognized by one who seized the hem
  of my skirt and said: "Wonder of wonders! You?"
And I, when he stretched out his arm to me,
  searched his baked features closely, till at last
  I traced his image from my memory
in spite of the burnt crust, and bending near
  to put my face closer to his, at last
  I answered: "Ser Brunetto, are *you* here?"   30
"O my son! may it not displease you," he cried,
  "if Brunetto Latino leave his company
  and turn and walk a little by your side."
And I to him: "With all my soul I ask it.
  Or let us sit together, if it please him
  who is my Guide and leads me through this pit."
"My son!" he said, "whoever of this train
  pauses a moment, must lie a hundred years
  forbidden to brush off the burning rain.
Therefore, go on; I will walk at your hem,
  and then rejoin my company, which goes
  mourning eternal loss in eternal flame."
I did not dare descend to his own level
  but kept my head inclined, as one who walks
  in reverence meditating good and evil.   45
"What brings you here before your own last day?
  What fortune or what destiny?" he began.
  "And who is he that leads you this dark way?"
"Up there in the happy life I went astray
  in a valley," I replied, "before I had reached
  the fullness of my years. Only yesterday

at dawn I turned from it. This spirit showed
  himself to me as I was turning back
  and guides me home again along this road."
And he: "Follow your star, for if in all
  of the sweet life I saw one truth shine clearly,
  you cannot miss your glorious arrival.
And had I lived to do what I meant to do,
  I would have cheered and seconded your work,
  observing heaven so well disposed toward you.   60
But that ungrateful and malignant stock
  that came down from Fiesole of old
  and still smacks of the mountain and the rock
for your good works will be your enemy.
  And there is cause; the sweet fig is not meant
  to bear its fruit beside the bitter sorb tree.
Even the old adage calls them blind,
  an envious, proud, and avaricious people;
  see that you root their customs from your mind.
It is written in your stars, and will come to pass,
  that your honors shall make both sides hunger for you:
  but the goat shall never reach to crop that grass.
Let the beasts of Fiesole devour their get
  like sows, but never let them touch the plant,
  if among their rankness any springs up yet,   75
in which is born again the holy seed
  of the Romans who remained among their rabble
  when Florence made a new nest for their greed."
"Ah, had I all my wish," I answered then,
  "you would not yet be banished from the world
  in which you were a radiance among men;
for that sweet image, gentle and paternal,
  you were to me in the world when hour by hour
  you taught me how man makes himself eternal,
lives in my mind and now strikes to my heart;
  and while I live, the gratitude I owe it
  will speak to men out of my life and art.
What you have told me of my course, I write
  by another text I save to show a Lady
  who will judge these matters, if I reach her height.   90

This much I would have you know; so long, I say,
  as nothing in my conscience troubles me
  I am prepared for Fortune, come what may.
Twice already in the eternal shade
  I have heard this prophecy; but let Fortune turn
  her wheel as she please, and the countryman his spade."
My guiding spirit paused at my last word
  and, turning right about, stood eye to eye
  to say to me: "Well heeded is well heard."
But I did not reply to him, going on
  with Ser Brunetto to ask him who was with him
  in the hot sands, the best born and best known.
And he to me: "Of some who share this walk
  it is good to know; of the rest let us say nothing,
  for the time would be too short for so much talk.   105
In brief, we all were clerks and men of worth,
  great men of letters, scholars of renown;
  all by the one same crime defiled on earth.
Priscian moves there along the wearisome
  sad way, and Francesco d'Accorso, and also there,
  if you had any longing for such scum,
you might have seen that one the Servant of Servants
  sent from the Arno to the Bacchiglione
  where he left his unnatural organ wrapped in cerements.
I would say more, but there across the sand
  a new smoke rises and new people come,
  and I must run to be with my own band.
Remember my *Treasure*, in which I still live on;
  I ask no more." He turned then, and he seemed,
  across that plain, like one of those who run   120
for the green cloth at Verona; and of those,
more like the one who wins, than those who lose.

Canto 16

The Poets arrive within hearing of the waterfall that plunges over the great cliff into the eighth circle. The sound is still a distant throbbing when three wraiths, recognizing Dante's Florentine dress, detach themselves from their band and come running toward him. They are Jacopo Rusticucci, Guido Guerra, and Tegghiaio Aldobrandi, all of them Florentines whose policies and personalities Dante admired. Rusticucci and Tegghiaio have already been mentioned in a highly complimentary way in Dante's talk with Ciacco in Canto 6. The sinners ask for news of Florence, and Dante replies with a passionate lament for her present degradation. The three wraiths return to their band, and the Poets continue to the top of the falls. Here, at Virgil's command, Dante removes a cord from about his waist, and Virgil drops it over the edge of the abyss. As if in answer to a signal, a great distorted shape comes swimming up through the dirty air of the pit.

We could already hear the rumbling drive
   of the waterfall in its plunge to the next circle,
   a murmur like the throbbing of a hive,
when three shades turned together on the plain,
   breaking toward us from a company
   that went its way to torture in that rain.
They cried with one voice as they ran toward me:
   "Wait, oh, wait, for by your dress you seem
   a voyager from our own tainted country."
Ah! what wounds I saw, some new, some old,
   branded upon their bodies! Even now
   the pain of it in memory turns me cold.

My Teacher heard their cries, and turning-to,
    stood face to face. "Do as they ask," he said,
    "for these are souls to whom respect is due;   15
and were it not for the darting flames that hem
    our narrow passage in, I should have said
    it were more fitting you ran after them."
We paused, and they began their ancient wail
    over again, and when they stood below us
    they formed themselves into a moving wheel.
As naked and anointed champions do
    in feeling out their grasp and their advantage
    before they close in for the thrust or blow—
so circling, each one stared up at my height,
    and as their feet moved left around the circle,
    their necks kept turning backward to the right.
"If the misery of this place, and our unkempt
    and scorched appearance," one of them began,
    "bring us and what we pray into contempt,   30
still may our earthly fame move you to tell
    who and what you are, who so securely
    set your live feet to the dead dusts of Hell.
This peeled and naked soul who runs before me
    around this wheel was higher than you think
    there in the world, in honor and degree.
Guido Guerra was the name he bore,
    the good Gualdrada's grandson. In his life
    he won great fame in counsel and in war.
The other who behind me treads this sand
    was Tegghiaio Aldobrandi, whose good counsels
    the world would have done well to understand.
And I who share their torment, in my life
    was Jacopo Rusticucci; above all
    I owe my sorrows to a savage wife."   45
I would have thrown myself to the plain below
    had I been sheltered from the falling fire;
    and I think my Teacher would have let me go.
But seeing I should be burned and cooked, my fear
    overcame the first impulse of my heart
    to leap down and embrace them then and there.

"Not contempt," I said, "but the compassion
 that seizes on my soul and memory
 at the thought of you tormented in this fashion—
it was grief that choked my speech when through the scorching
 air of this pit my Lord announced to me
 that such men as you are might be approaching.
I am of your own land, and I have always
 heard with affection and rehearsed with honor
 your name and the good deeds of your happier days.   60
Led by my Guide and his truth, I leave the gall
 and go for the sweet apples of delight.
 But first I must descend to the center of all."
"So may your soul and body long continue
 together on the way you go," he answered,
 "and the honor of your days shine after you—
tell me if courtesy and valor raise
 their banners in our city as of old,
 or has the glory faded from its days?
For Borsiere, who is newly come among us
 and yonder goes with our companions in pain,
 taunts us with such reports, and his words have stung us."
"O Florence! your sudden wealth and your upstart
 rabble, dissolute and overweening,
 already set you weeping in your heart!"   75
I cried with face upraised, and on the sand
 those three sad spirits looked at one another
 like men who hear the truth and understand.
"If this be your manner of speaking, and if you can
 satisfy others with such ease and grace,"
 they said as one, "we hail a happy man.
Therefore, if you win through this gloomy pass
 and climb again to see the heaven of stars;
 when it rejoices you to say 'I was,'
speak of us to the living." They parted then,
 breaking their turning wheel, and as they vanished
 over the plain their legs seemed wings. "Amen"
could not have been pronounced between their start
 and their disappearance over the rim of sand.
 And then it pleased my Master to depart.   90

A little way beyond we felt the quiver
    and roar of the cascade, so close that speech
    would have been drowned in thunder. As that river—
the first one on the left of the Apennines
    to have a path of its own from Monte Veso
    to the Adriatic Sea, which, as it twines
is called the Acquacheta from its source
    until it nears Forlì, and then is known
    as the Montone in its further course—
resounds from the mountain in a single leap,
    there above San Benedetto dell'Alpe
    where a thousand falls might fit into the steep;
so down from a sheer bank, in one enormous
    plunge, the tainted water roared so loud
    a little longer there would have deafened us.   105
I had a cord bound round me like a belt
    which I had once thought I might put to use
    to snare the Leopard with the gaudy pelt.
When at my Guide's command I had unbound
    its loops from about my habit, I gathered it
    and held it out to him all coiled and wound.
He bent far back to his right, and throwing it
    out from the edge, sent it in a long arc
    into the bottomless darkness of the pit.
"Now surely some unusual event,"
    I said to myself, "must follow this new signal
    upon which my good Guide is so intent."
Ah, how cautiously a man should breathe
    near those who see not only what we do,
    but have the sense which reads the mind beneath!   120
He said to me: "You will soon see arise
    what I await, and what you wonder at;
    soon you will see the thing before your eyes."
To the truth which will seem falsehood every man
    who would not be called a liar while speaking fact
    should learn to seal his lips as best he can.
But here I cannot be still. Reader, I swear
    by the lines of my Comedy—so may it live—
    that I saw swimming up through that foul air

Inferno

a shape to astonish the most doughty soul,
    a shape like one returning through the sea
    from working loose an anchor run afoul
of something on the bottom; so it rose,
its arms spread upward and its feet drawn close.

Canto 17

*The monstrous shape lands on the brink
and Virgil salutes it ironically. It is Geryon, the
monster of fraud. Virgil announces that they must
fly down from the cliff on the back of this monster, and while Virgil negotiates for their passage,
Dante is sent to examine the Usurers. These sinners sit in a crouch along the edge of the burning
plain that approaches the cliff. Each of them has a
leather purse around his neck, and each purse is
blazoned with a coat of arms. Their eyes, gushing
with tears, are forever fixed on these purses.
Dante recognizes none of these sinners, but their
coats of arms are unmistakably those of well-
known Florentine families. Having understood
who they are and the reason for their present condition, Dante cuts short his excursion and returns
to find Virgil mounted on the back of Geryon.
Dante joins his Master and they fly down from
the great cliff. Their flight carries them from the
Hell of the Violent and the Bestial, the Sins of the
Lion, into the Hell of the Fraudulent and
Malicious, the Sins of the Leopard.*

"Now see the sharp-tailed beast that mounts the brink.
 He passes mountains, breaks through walls and weapons.
 Behold the beast that makes the whole world stink."
These were the words my Master spoke to me,
 then signaled the weird beast to come to ground
 close to the sheer end of our rocky levee.
The filthy prototype of Fraud drew near
 and settled his head and breast upon the edge
 of the dark cliff, but let his tail hang clear.

The filthy prototype of Fraud drew near
    and settled his head and breast upon the edge
    of the dark cliff, but let his tail hang clear.

His face was innocent of every guile,
  benign and just in feature and expression;
  and under it his body was half reptile.
His two great paws were hairy to the armpits;
  all his back and breast and both his flanks
  were figured with bright knots and subtle circlets;   15
never was such a tapestry of bloom
  woven on earth by Tartar or by Turk,
  nor by Arachne at her flowering loom.
As a ferry sometimes lies along the strand,
  part beached and part afloat; and as the beaver,
  up yonder in the guzzling Germans' land,
squats halfway up the bank when a fight is on—
  just so lay that most ravenous of beasts
  on the rim which bounds the burning sand with stone.
His tail twitched in the void beyond that lip,
  thrashing, and twisting up the envenomed fork
  which, like a scorpion's stinger, armed the tip.
My Guide said: "It is time now we drew near
  that monster." And descending on the right
  we moved ten paces outward to be clear   30
of sand and flames. And when we were beside him,
  I saw upon the sand a bit beyond us
  some people crouching close beside the brim.
The Master paused. "That you may take with you
  the full experience of this round," he said,
  "go now and see the last state of that crew.
But let your talk be brief, and I will stay
  and reason with this beast till you return,
  that his strong back may serve us on our way."
So further yet along the outer edge
  of the seventh circle I moved on alone
  and came to the sad people of the ledge.
Their eyes burst with their grief; their smoking hands
  jerked about their bodies, warding off
  now the flames and now the burning sands.   45
Dogs in summer bit by fleas and gadflies,
  jerking their snouts about, twitching their paws,
  now here, now there, behave no otherwise.

92

Inferno

I examined several faces there among
   that sooty throng, and I saw none I knew;
   but I observed that from each neck there hung
an enormous purse, each marked with its own beast
   and its own colors like a coat of arms.
   On these their streaming eyes appeared to feast.
Looking about, I saw one purse display
   azure on or, a kind of lion; another,
   on a blood-red field, a goose whiter than whey.
And one that bore a huge and swollen sow
   azure on field argent said to me:
   "What are you doing in this pit of sorrow?   60
Leave us alone! And since you have not yet died,
   I'll have you know my neighbor Vitaliano
   has a place reserved for him here at my side.
A Paduan among Florentines, I sit here
   while hour by hour they nearly deafen me
   shouting: 'Send us the sovereign cavalier
with the purse of the three goats!'" He half arose,
   twisted his mouth, and darted out his tongue
   for all the world like an ox licking its nose.
And I, afraid that any longer stay
   would anger him who had warned me to be brief,
   left those exhausted souls without delay.
Returned, I found my Guide already mounted
   upon the rump of that monstrosity.
   He said to me: "Now must you be undaunted;   75
this beast must be our stairway to the pit;
   mount it in front, and I will ride between
   you and the tail, lest you be poisoned by it."
Like one so close to the quartanary chill
   that his nails are already pale and his flesh trembles
   at the very sight of shade or a cool rill—
so did I tremble at each frightful word.
   But his scolding filled me with that shame that makes
   the servant brave in the presence of his lord.
I mounted the great shoulders of that freak
   and tried to say: "Now help me to hold on!"
   But my voice clicked in my throat and I could not speak.

93

But no sooner had I settled where he placed me
   than he, my stay, my comfort, and my courage
   in other perils, gathered and embraced me.   90
Then he called out: "Now, Geryon, we are ready;
   bear well in mind that his is living weight
   and make your circles wide and your flight steady."
As a small ship slides from a beaching or its pier,
   backward, backward—so that monster slipped
   back from the rim. And when he had drawn clear
he swung about, and stretching out his tail
   he worked it like an eel, and with his paws
   he gathered in the air, while I turned pale.
I think there was no greater fear the day
   Phaeton let loose the reins and burned the sky
   along the great scar of the Milky Way,
nor when Icarus, too close to the sun's track,
   felt the wax melt, unfeathering his loins
   and heard his father cry: "Turn back! Turn back!"—   105
than I felt when I found myself in air,
   afloat in space with nothing visible
   but the enormous beast that bore me there.
Slowly, slowly, he swims on through space,
   wheels and descends, but I can sense it only
   by the way the wind blows upward past my face.
Already on the right I heard the swell
   and thunder of the whirlpool. Looking down
   I leaned my head out and stared into Hell.
I trembled again at the prospect of dismounting
   and cowered in on myself, for I saw fires
   on every hand, and I heard a long lamenting.
And then I saw—till then I had but felt it—
   the course of our down spiral to the horrors
   that rose to us from all sides of the pit.   120
As a flight-worn falcon sinks down wearily
   though neither bird nor lure has signaled it,
   the falconer crying out: "What! spent already!"—
then turns and in a hundred spinning gyres
   sulks from her master's call, sullen and proud—
   so to that bottom lit by endless fires

Inferno

the monster Geryon circled and fell,
    setting us down at the foot of the precipice
    of ragged rock on the eighth shelf of Hell.
And once freed of our weight, he shot from there
into the dark like an arrow into air.

Canto 18

Dismounted from Geryon, the Poets find
themselves in the eighth circle, called Malebolge,
the Evil Ditches. This is the upper half of the Hell
of the Fraudulent and Malicious. Malebolge is a
great circle of stone that slopes like an amphithe-
ater. The slopes are divided into ten concentric
ditches; and within these ditches, each with his
own kind, are punished those guilty of simple
fraud. A series of stone dikes runs like spokes
from the edge of the great cliff face to the center of
the place, and these serve as bridges. The Poets
bear left toward the first ditch, and Dante ob-
serves below him and to his right the sinners of
the first bolgia, the Panderers and Seducers.
These make two files, one along either bank of the
ditch, and are driven at an endless fast walk
by horned demons who hurry them along with
great lashes. In life these sinners goaded others
on to serve their own foul purposes; so in Hell
are they driven in their turn. The horned de-
mons who drive them symbolize the sinners'
own vicious natures, embodiments of their own
guilty consciences. Dante may or may not
have intended the horns of the demons to symbo-
lize cuckoldry and adultery. The Poets see Vene-
dico Caccianemico and Jason in the first pit,
and pass on to the second, where they find the
souls of the Flatterers sunk in excrement, the true
equivalent of their false flatteries on earth.
They observe Alessio Interminelli
and Thaïs, and then pass on.

There is in Hell a vast and sloping ground
    called Malebolge, a lost place of stone
    as black as the great cliff that seals it round.

Inferno

Precisely in the center of that space
    there yawns a well extremely wide and deep.
    I shall discuss it in its proper place.
The border that remains between the well pit
    and the great cliff forms an enormous circle,
    and ten descending troughs are cut in it,
offering a general prospect like the ground
    that lies around one of those ancient castles
    whose walls are girded many times around
by concentric moats. And just as, from the portal,
    the castle's bridges run from moat to moat
    to the last bank; so from the great rock wall   15
across the embankments and the ditches, high
    and narrow cliffs run to the central well,
    which cuts and gathers them like radii.
Here, shaken from the back of Geryon,
    we found ourselves. My Guide kept to the left,
    and I walked after him. So we moved on.
Below, on my right, and filling the first ditch
    along both banks, new souls in pain appeared,
    new torments, and new devils black as pitch.
All of these sinners were naked; on our side
    of the middle they walked toward us; on the other,
    in our direction, but with swifter stride.
Just so the Romans, because of the great throng
    in the year of the Jubilee, divide the bridge
    in order that the crowds may pass along,   30
so that all face the Castle as they go
    on one side toward St. Peter's, while on the other,
    all move along facing toward Mount Giordano.
And everywhere along that hideous track
    I saw horned demons with enormous lashes
    move through those souls, scourging them on the back.
Ah, how the stragglers of that long rout stirred
    their legs quick-march at the first crack of the lash!
    Certainly no one waited a second, or third!
As we went on, one face in that procession
    caught my eye, and I said: "That sinner there;
    it is certainly not the first time I've seen that one."

I stopped, therefore, to study him, and my Guide
  out of his kindness waited and even allowed me
  to walk back a few steps at the sinner's side.   45
And that flayed spirit, seeing me turn around,
  thought to hide his face, but I called to him:
  "You there, that walk along with your eyes on the ground,
if those are not false features, then I know you
  as Venedico Caccianemico of Bologna.
  What brings you here among this pretty crew?"
And he replied: "I speak unwillingly,
  but something in your living voice, in which
  I hear the world again, stirs and compels me.
It was I who brought the fair Ghisola 'round
  to serve the will and lust of the Marquis,
  however sordid that old tale may sound.
There are many more from Bologna who weep away
  eternity in this ditch; we fill it so
  there are not as many tongues that are taught to say   60
'sipa' in all the land that lies between
  the Reno and the Saveno, as you must know
  from the many tales of our avarice and spleen."
And as he spoke, one of those lashes fell
  across his back, and a demon cried: "Move on,
  you pimp, there are no women here to sell."
Turning away then, I rejoined my Guide.
  We came in a few steps to a raised ridge
  that made a passage to the other side.
This we climbed easily, and, turning right
  along the jagged crest, we left behind
  the eternal circling of those souls in flight.
And when we reached the part at which the stone
  was tunneled for the passage of the scourged,
  my Guide said: "Stop a minute and look down   75
on these other misbegotten wraiths of sin.
  You have not seen their faces, for they moved
  in the same direction we were headed in."
So from that bridge we looked down on the throng
  that hurried toward us on the other side.
  Here, too, the whiplash hurried them along.

Inferno

And the good Master, studying that train,
   said: "Look there, at that great soul that approaches
   and seems to shed no tears for all his pain—
what kingliness moves with him even in Hell!
   It is Jason, who by courage and good advice
   made off with the Colchian Ram. Later it fell
that he passed Lemnos, where the women of wrath,
   enraged by Venus' curse that drove their lovers
   out of their arms, put all their males to death.   90
There with his honeyed tongue and his dishonest
   lover's wiles, he gulled Hypsipyle,
   who, in the slaughter, had gulled all the rest.
And there he left her, pregnant and forsaken.
   Such guilt condemns him to such punishment;
   and also for Medea is vengeance taken.
All seducers march here to the whip.
   And let us say no more about this valley
   and those it closes in its stony grip."
We had already come to where the walk
   crosses the second bank, from which it lifts
   another arch, spanning from rock to rock.
Here we heard people whine in the next chasm,
   and knock and thump themselves with open palms,
   and blubber through their snouts as if in a spasm.   105
Steaming from that pit, a vapor rose
   over the banks, crusting them with a slime
   that sickened my eyes and hammered at my nose.
That chasm sinks so deep we could not sight
   its bottom anywhere until we climbed
   along the rock arch to its greatest height.
Once there, I peered down; and I saw long lines
   of people in a river of excrement
   that seemed the overflow of the world's latrines.
I saw among the felons of that pit
   one wraith who might or might not have been tonsured—
   one could not tell, he was so smeared with shit.
He bellowed: "You there, why do you stare at me
   more than at all the others in this stew?"
   And I to him: "Because if memory   120

99

He bellowed: "You there, why do you stare at me
more than at all the others in this stew?"

serves me, I knew you when your hair was dry.
   You are Alessio Interminelli da Lucca.
   That's why I pick you from this filthy fry."
And he then, beating himself on his clown's head:
  "Down to this have the flatteries I sold
   the living sunk me here among the dead."
And my Guide prompted then: "Lean forward a bit
   and look beyond him, there—do you see that one
   scratching herself with dungy nails, the strumpet
who fidgets to her feet, then to a crouch?
   It is the whore Thaïs who told her lover
   when he sent to ask her, 'Do you thank me much?'
'Much? Nay, past all believing!' And with this
let us turn from the sight of this abyss."

Canto 19

Dante comes upon the Simoniacs, the sell-
ers of ecclesiastic favors and offices, and his heart
overflows with the wrath he feels against those
who corrupt the things of God. This bolgia is lined
with round tubelike holes, and the sinners are
placed in them upside down with the soles of
their feet ablaze. The heat of the blaze is propor-
tioned to their guilt. The holes in which these sin-
ners are placed are debased equivalents of the
baptismal fonts common in the cities of northern
Italy and the sinners' confinement in them is
temporary: as new sinners arrive, the souls drop
through the bottoms of their holes and disappear
eternally into the crevices of the rock. As always,
the punishment is a symbolic retribution. Just as
the Simoniacs made a mock of Holy Office, so are
they turned upside down in a mockery of the bap-
tismal font. Just as they made a mockery of the
holy water of Baptism, so is their hellish baptism
by fire, after which they are wholly immersed in
the crevices below. The oily fire that licks at their
soles may also suggest a travesty on the oil used
in Extreme Unction, the last rites for the dying.
Virgil carries Dante down an almost sheer ledge
and lets him speak to one who is the chief
sinner of that place, Pope Nicholas III. Dante
delivers another stirring denunciation of those
who have corrupted Church Office, and Virgil
carries him back up the steep ledge
toward the fourth bolgia.

O Simon Magus! O you wretched crew
   who follow him, pandering for silver and gold
   the things of God which should be wedded to

love and righteousness! O thieves for hire,
    now must the trump of judgment sound your doom
    here in the third fosse of the rim of fire!
We had already made our way across
    to the next grave and to that part of the bridge
    which hangs above the midpoint of the fosse.
O Sovereign Wisdom, how Thine art doth shine
    in Heaven, on earth, and in the evil world!
    How justly doth Thy power judge and assign!
I saw along the walls and on the ground
    long rows of holes cut in the livid stone;
    all were cut to a size, and all were round.   15
They seemed to be exactly the same size
    as those in the font of my beautiful San Giovanni,
    built to protect the priests who come to baptize,
one of which, not so long since, I broke open
    to rescue a boy who was wedged and drowning in it—
    be this enough to undeceive all men.
From every mouth a sinner's legs stuck out
    as far as the calf. The soles were all ablaze,
    and the joints of the legs quivered and writhed about.
Withes and tethers would have snapped in their throes.
    As oiled things blaze upon the surface only,
    so did they burn from the heels to the points of their toes.
"Master," I said, "who is that one in the fire
    who writhes and quivers more than all the others?
    From him the ruddy flames seem to leap higher."   30
And he to me: "If you wish me to carry you down
    along that lower bank, you may learn from him
    who he is and the evil he has done."
And I: "What you will, I will. You are my Lord,
    and know I depart in nothing from your wish,
    and you know my mind beyond my spoken word."
We moved to the fourth ridge, and turning left
    my Guide descended by a jagged path
    into the strait and perforated cleft.
Thus the good Master bore me down the dim
    and rocky slope, and did not put me down
    till we reached the one whose legs did penance for him.

"Whoever you are, sad spirit," I began,
  "who lie here with your head below your heels
  and planted like a stake—speak if you can."   45
I stood like a friar who gives the Sacrament
  to a hired assassin, who, fixed in the hole,
  recalls him and delays his death a moment.
"Are you there already, Boniface? Are you there
  already?" he cried. "By several years the writ
  has lied. And all that gold and all that care—
are you already sated with the treasure
  for which you dared to turn on the Sweet Lady
  and trick and pluck and bleed her at your pleasure?"
I stood like one caught in some raillery,
  not understanding what is said to him,
  lost for an answer to such mockery.
Then Virgil said: "Say to him, 'I am not he,
  I am not who you think.'" And I replied
  as my good Master had instructed me.   60
The sinner's feet jerked madly; then again
  his voice rose, this time choked with sighs and tears,
  and said at last: "What do you want of me then?
If to know who I am drives you so fearfully
  that you descend the bank to ask it, know
  that the Great Mantle was once hung upon me;
and in truth I was a son of the She-Bear,
  so sly and eager to push my whelps ahead,
  that I pursed wealth above and myself here.
Beneath my head are dragged all who have gone
  before me in buying and selling Holy Office;
  there they cower in fissures of the stone.
I, too, shall be plunged down when that great cheat
  for whom I took you comes here in his turn.
  Longer already have I baked my feet   75
and been planted upside down than he shall be
  before the west sends down a lawless Shepherd
  of uglier deeds to cover him and me.
He will be a new Jason of the Maccabees;
  and just as that king bent to his high priests' will,
  so shall the French king do as this one please."

Maybe—I cannot say—I grew too brash
   at this point, for when he had finished speaking
   I said: "Indeed! Now tell me how much cash
our Lord required of Peter in guarantee
   before he put the keys into his keeping?
   Surely he asked nothing but 'Follow me!'
Nor did Peter, nor the others, ask silver or gold
   of Matthias when they chose him for the place
   the despicable and damned Apostle sold.   90
Therefore stay as you are; this hole well fits you—
   and keep a good guard on the ill-won wealth
   that once made you so bold toward Charles of Anjou.
And were it not that I am still constrained
   by the reverence I owe to the Great Keys
   you held in life, I should not have refrained
from using other words and sharper still;
   for this avarice of yours grieves all the world,
   tramples the virtuous, and exalts the evil.
Of such as you was the Evangelist's vision
   when he saw She Who Sits Upon the Waters
   locked with the kings of earth in fornication.
She was born with seven heads, and ten enormous
   and shining horns strengthened and made her glad
   as long as love and virtue pleased her spouse.   105
Gold and silver are the gods you adore!
   In what are you different from the idolator,
   save that he worships one, and you a score?
Ah, Constantine, what evil marked the hour—
   not of your conversion, but of the fee
   the first rich Father took from you in dower!"
And as I sang him this tune, he began to twitch
   and kick both feet out wildly, as if in rage
   or gnawed by conscience—little matter which.
And I think, indeed, it pleased my Guide; his look
   was all approval as he stood beside me
   intent upon each word of truth I spoke.
He approached, and with both arms he lifted me,
   and when he had gathered me against his breast,
   remounted the rocky path out of the valley,   120

nor did he tire of holding me clasped to him,
    until we reached the topmost point of the arch
    which crosses from the fourth to the fifth rim
of the pits of woe. Arrived upon the bridge,
    he tenderly set down the heavy burden
    he had been pleased to carry up that ledge
which would have been hard climbing for a goat.
Here I looked down on still another moat.

Canto 20

*Dante stands in the middle of the bridge
over the fourth bolgia and looks down at the souls
of the Fortune Tellers and Diviners. Here are the
souls of all those who attempted by forbidden
arts to look into the future. Among these damned
are Amphiareus, Tiresias, Aruns, Manto, Eurypylus, Michael Scott, Guido Bonatti, and Asdente.
Characteristically, the sin of these wretches is reversed upon them; their punishment is to have
their heads turned backwards on their bodies
and to be compelled to walk backwards through
all eternity, their eyes blinded with tears. Thus,
those who sought to penetrate the future cannot even see in front of themselves; they attempted to move themselves forward in time, so
must they go backwards through all eternity;
and as the arts of sorcery are a distortion of
God's law, so are their bodies distorted in Hell.
No more need be said of them. Dante names
them and passes on to fill the canto with a lengthy
account of the founding of Virgil's native
city of Mantua.*

Now must I sing new griefs, and my verses strain
   to form the matter of the twentieth canto
   of canticle one, the canticle of pain.
My vantage point permitted a clear view
   of the depths of the pit below, a desolation
   bathed with the tears of its tormented crew,
who moved about the circle of the pit
   at about the pace of a litany procession.
   Silent and weeping, they wound round and round it.

And when I looked down from their faces, I saw
   that each of them was hideously distorted
   between the top of the chest and the lines of the jaw;
for the face was reversed on the neck, and they came on
   backwards, staring backwards at their loins,
   for to look before them was forbidden. Someone,   15
sometime, in the grip of a palsy may have been
   distorted so, but never to my knowledge;
   nor do I believe the like was ever seen.
Reader, so may God grant you to understand
   my poem and profit from it, ask yourself
   how I could check my tears, when near at hand
I saw the image of our humanity
   distorted so that the tears that burst from their eyes
   ran down the cleft of their buttocks. Certainly
I wept. I leaned against the jagged face
   of a rock and wept so that my Guide said: "Still?
   Still like the other fools? There is no place
for pity here. Who is more arrogant
   within his soul, who is more impious
   than one who dares to sorrow at God's judgment?   30
Lift up your eyes, lift up your eyes and see
   him the earth swallowed before all the Thebans,
   at which they cried out: 'Whither do you flee,
Amphiareus? Why do you leave the field?'
   And he fell headlong through the gaping earth
   to the feet of Minos, where all sin must yield.
Observe how he has made a breast of his back.
   In life he wished to see too far before him,
   and now he must crab backwards round this track.
And see Tiresias, who by his arts
   succeeded in changing himself from man to woman,
   transforming all his limbs and all his parts;
later he had to strike the two twined serpents
   once again with his conjurer's wand before
   he could resume his manly lineaments.   45
And there is Aruns, his back to that one's belly,
   the same who in the mountains of the Luni
   tilled by the people of Carrara's valley,

made a white marble cave his den, and there
   with unobstructed view observed the sea
   and the turning constellations year by year.
And she whose unbound hair flows back to hide
   her breasts—which you cannot see—and who also wears
   all of her hairy parts on that other side
was Manto, who searched countries far and near,
   then settled where I was born. In that connection
   there is a story I would have you hear.
Tiresias was her sire. After his death,
   Thebes, the city of Bacchus, became enslaved,
   and for many years she roamed about the earth.   60
High in sweet Italy, under the Alps that shut
   the Tyrolean gate of Germany, there lies
   a lake known as Benacus roundabout.
Through endless falls, more than a thousand and one,
   Mount Apennine from Garda to Val Cammonica
   is freshened by the waters that flow down
into that lake. At its center is a place
   where the Bishops of Brescia, Trentine, and Verona
   might all give benediction with equal grace.
Peschiera, the beautiful fortress, strong in war
   against the Brescians and the Bergamese,
   sits at the lowest point along that shore.
There, the waters Benacus cannot hold
   within its bosom, spill and form a river
   that winds away through pastures green and gold.   75
But once the water gathers its full flow,
   it is called Mincius rather than Benacus
   from there to Governo, where it joins the Po.
Still near its source, it strikes a plain, and there
   it slows and spreads, forming an ancient marsh
   which in the summer heat pollutes the air.
The terrible virgin, passing there by chance,
   saw dry land at the center of the mire,
   untilled, devoid of all inhabitants.
There, shunning all communion with mankind,
   she settled with the ministers of her arts,
   and there she lived, and there she left behind

her vacant corpse. Later the scattered men
   who lived nearby assembled on that spot
   since it was well defended by the fen.   90
Over those whited bones they raised the city,
   and for her who had chosen the place before all others
   they named it—with no further augury—
Mantua. Far more people lived there once,
   before sheer madness prompted Casalodi
   to let Pinamonte play him for a dunce.
Therefore, I charge you, should you ever hear
   other accounts of this, to let no falsehood
   confuse the truth which I have just made clear."
And I to him: "Master, within my soul
   your word is certainty, and any other
   would seem like the dead lumps of burned out coal.
But tell me of those people moving down
   to join the rest. Are any worth my noting?
   For my mind keeps coming back to that alone."   105
And he: "That one whose beard spreads like a fleece
   over his swarthy shoulders, was an augur
   in the days when so few males remained in Greece
that even the cradles were all but empty of sons.
   He chose the time for cutting the cable at Aulis,
   and Calchas joined him in those divinations.
He is Eurypylus. I sing him somewhere
   in my High Tragedy; you will know the place
   who know the whole of it. The other there,
the one beside him with the skinny shanks
   was Michael Scott, who mastered every trick
   of magic fraud, a prince of mountebanks.
See Guido Bonatti there; and see Asdente,
   who now would be wishing he had stuck to his last,
   but repents too late, though he repents aplenty.   120
And see on every hand the wretched hags
   who left their spinning and sewing for soothsaying
   and casting of spells with herbs and dolls and rags.
But come. Cain with his bush of thorns appears
   already on the wave below Seville,
   above the boundary of the hemispheres;

and the moon was full already yesternight,
   as you must well remember from the wood,
   for it certainly did not harm you when its light
shone down upon your way before the dawn."
And as he spoke to me, we traveled on.

Canto 21

The Poets move on, talking as they go, and arrive at the fifth bolgia. Here the Grafters are sunk in boiling pitch and guarded by demons, who tear them to pieces with claws and grappling hooks if they catch them above the surface of the pitch. The sticky pitch is symbolic of the sticky fingers of the Grafters. It serves also to hide them from sight, as their sinful dealings on earth were hidden from men's eyes. The demons, too, suggest symbolic possibilities, for they are armed with grappling hooks and are forever ready to rend and tear all they can get their hands on. The Poets watch a demon arrive with a grafting Senator of Lucca and fling him into the pitch where the demons set upon him. To protect Dante from their wrath, Virgil hides him behind some jagged rocks and goes ahead alone to negotiate with the demons. They set upon him like a pack of mastiffs, but Virgil secures a safe-conduct from their leader, Malacoda. Thereupon Virgil calls Dante from hiding, and they are about to set off when they discover that the bridge across the sixth bolgia lies shattered. Malacoda tells them there is another further on and sends a squad of demons to escort them. Their adventures with the demons continue through the next canto. These two cantos may conveniently be remembered as the Gargoyle Cantos. If the total Commedia *is built like a cathedral (as so many critics have suggested), it is here that Dante attaches his grotesqueries. At no other point in the* Commedia *does Dante give such free rein to his coarsest style.*

Inferno

Thus talking of things which my Comedy does not care
   to sing, we passed from one arch to the next
   until we stood upon its summit. There
we checked our steps to study the next fosse
   and the next vain lamentations of Malebolge;
   awesomely dark and desolate it was.
As in the Venetian arsenal, the winter through
   there boils the sticky pitch to caulk the seams
   of the sea-battered bottoms when no crew
can put to sea—instead of which, one starts
   to build its ship anew, one plugs the planks
   which have been sprung in many foreign parts;
some hammer at a mast, some at a rib;
   some make new oars, some braid and coil new lines;
   one patches up the mainsail, one the jib—   15
so, but by art divine and not by fire,
   a viscid pitch boiled in the fosse below
   and coated all the bank with gluey mire.
I saw the pitch; but I saw nothing in it
   except the enormous bubbles of its boiling,
   which swelled and sank, like breathing, through all the pit.
And as I stood and stared into that sink,
   my Master cried, "Take care!" and drew me back
   from my exposed position on the brink.
I turned like one who cannot wait to see
   the thing he dreads, and who, in sudden fright,
   runs while he looks, his curiosity
competing with his terror—and at my back
   I saw a figure that came running toward us
   across the ridge, a demon huge and black.   30
Ah, what a face he had, all hate and wildness!
   Galloping so, with his great wings outspread
   he seemed the embodiment of all bitterness.
Across each high-hunched shoulder he had thrown
   one haunch of a sinner, whom he held in place
   with a great talon round each ankle bone.
"Blacktalons of our bridge," he began to roar,
   "I bring you one of Santa Zita's Elders!
   Scrub him down while I go back for more;

I planted a harvest of them in that city;
 everyone there is a grafter except Bonturo.
 There yes is no and no is yes for a fee."
Down the sinner plunged, and at once the demon
 spun from the cliff; no mastiff ever sprang
 more eager from the leash to chase a felon.   45
Down plunged the sinner and sank to reappear
 with his backside arched and his face and both his feet
 glued to the pitch, almost as if in prayer.
But the demons under the bridge, who guard that place
 and the sinners who are thrown to them, bawled out:
 "You're out of bounds here for the Sacred Face;
this is no dip in the Serchio; take your look
 and then get down in the pitch. And stay below
 unless you want a taste of a grappling hook."
Then they raked him with more than a hundred hooks
 bellowing: "Here you dance below the covers.
 Graft all you can there; no one checks your books."
They dipped him down into that pitch exactly
 as a chef makes scullery boys dip meat in a boiler,
 holding it with their hooks from floating free.   60
And the Master said: "*You* had best not be seen
 by these fiends till I am ready. Crouch down here.
 One of these rocks will serve you as a screen.
And whatever violence you see done to me,
 you have no cause to fear. I know these matters;
 I have been through this once and come back safely."
With that, he walked on past the end of the bridge;
 and it wanted all his courage to look calm
 from the moment he arrived on the sixth ridge.
With that same storm and fury that arouses
 all the house when the hounds leap at a tramp
 who suddenly falls to pleading where he pauses—
so rushed those fiends from below, and all the pack
 pointed their gleaming pitchforks at my Guide.
 But he stood fast and cried to them: "Stand back!   75
Before those hooks and grapples make too free,
 send up one of your crew to hear me out,
 then ask yourselves if you still care to rip me."

114

All cried as one: "Let Malacoda go."
  So the pack stood and one of them came forward,
    saying: "What good does he think *this* will do?"
"Do you think, Malacoda," my good Master said,
  "you would see me here, having arrived this far
    already, safe from you and every dread,
without divine will and propitious fate?
  Let me pass on, for it is willed in Heaven
    that I must show another this dread state."
The demon stood there on the flinty brim,
  so taken aback he let his pitchfork drop;
    then said to the others: "Take care not to harm him!"   90
"O you, crouched like a cat," my Guide called to me,
  "among the jagged rock piles of the bridge,
    come down to me, for now you may come safely."
Hearing him, I hurried down the ledge;
  and the demons all pressed forward when I appeared,
    so that I feared they might not keep their pledge.
So once I saw the Pisan infantry
  march out under truce from the fortress at Caprona,
    staring in fright at the ranks of the enemy.
I pressed the whole of my body against my Guide,
  and not for an instant did I take my eyes
    from those black fiends who scowled on every side.
They swung their forks saying to one another:
  "Shall I give him a touch in the rump?" and answering:
    "Sure, give him a taste to pay him for his bother."   105
But the demon who was talking to my Guide
  turned round and cried to him: "At ease there, Snatcher!"
    And then to us: "There's no road on this side;
the arch lies all in pieces in the pit.
  If you *must* go on, follow along this ridge;
    there's another cliff to cross by just beyond it.
In just five hours it will be, since the bridge fell,
  a thousand two hundred sixty-six years and a day;
    that was the time the big quake shook all Hell.
I'll send a squad of my boys along that way
  to see if anyone's airing himself below;
    you can go with them; there will be no foul play.

Front and center here, Grizzly and Hellken,"
   he began to order them. "You too, Deaddog.
   Curlybeard, take charge of a squad of ten. 120
Take Grafter and Dragontooth along with you.
   Pigtusk, Catclaw, Cramper, and Crazyred.
   Keep a sharp lookout on the boiling glue
as you move along, and see that these gentlemen
   are not molested until they reach the crag
   where they can find a way across the den."
"In the name of Heaven, Master," I cried, "what sort
   of guides are these? Let us go on alone
   if you know the way. Who can trust such an escort!
If you are as wary as you used to be
   you surely see them grind their teeth at us
   and knot their beetle brows so threateningly."
And he: "I do not like this fear in you.
   Let them gnash and knot as they please; they menace only
   the sticky wretches simmering in that stew." 135
They turned along the left bank in a line;
   but before they started, all of them together
   had stuck their pointed tongues out as a sign
to their captain that they wished permission to pass,
and he had made a trumpet of his ass.

Canto 22

The Poets set off with their escort of demons. Dante sees the Grafters lying in the pitch like frogs in water with only their muzzles out. They disappear as soon as they sight the demons, and only a ripple on the surface betrays their presence. One of the Grafters, an unidentified Navarrese, ducks too late and is seized by the demons who are about to claw him, but Curly-beard holds them back while Virgil questions him. The wretch speaks of his fellow sinners, Friar Gomita and Michel Zanche, while the un-controllable demons rake him from time to time with their hooks. The Navarrese offers to lure some of his fellow sufferers into the hands of the demons, and when his plan is accepted he plunges into the pitch and escapes. Hellken and Grizzly fly after him, but too late. They start a brawl in midair and fall into the pitch themselves. Curlybeard immediately organizes a rescue party, and the Poets, fearing the bad temper of the frustrated demons, take advantage of the confusion to slip away.

I have seen horsemen breaking camp. I have seen
   the beginning of the assault, the march and muster,
   and at times the retreat and riot. I have been
where chargers trampled your land, O Aretines!
   I have seen columns of foragers, shocks of tourney,
   and running of tilts. I have seen the endless lines
march to bells, drums, trumpets, from far and near.
   I have seen them march on signals from a castle.
   I have seen them march with native and foreign gear.

But never yet have I seen horse or foot,
  nor ship in range of land nor sight of star,
  take its direction from so low a toot.
We went with the ten fiends—ah, savage crew!—
  but, "In church with saints; with stewpots in the tavern,"
  as the old proverb wisely bids us do.   15
All my attention was fixed upon the pitch
  to observe the people who were boiling in it
  and the customs and the punishments of that ditch.
As dolphins surface and begin to flip
  their arched backs from the sea, warning the sailors
  to fall-to and begin to secure ship—
so now and then, some soul, to ease his pain,
  showed us a glimpse of his back above the pitch
  and quick as lightning disappeared again.
And as, at the edge of a ditch, frogs squat about
  hiding their feet and bodies in the water,
  leaving only their muzzles sticking out—
so stood the sinners in that dismal ditch;
  but as Curlybeard approached, only a ripple
  showed where they had ducked back into the pitch.   30
I saw—the dread of it haunts me to this day—
  one linger a bit too long, as it sometimes happens
  one frog remains when another spurts away;
and Catclaw, who was nearest, ran a hook
  through the sinner's pitchy hair and hauled him in.
  He looked like an otter dripping from the brook.
I knew the names of all the fiends by then;
  I had made a note of them at the first muster,
  and, marching, had listened and checked them over again.
"Hey, Crazyred," the crew of demons cried
  all together, "give him a taste of your claws.
  Dig him open a little. Off with his hide."
And I then: "Master, can you find out, please,
  the name and history of that luckless one
  who has fallen into the hands of his enemies?"   45
My Guide approached that wraith from the hot tar
  and asked him whence he came. The wretch replied:
  "I was born and raised in the Kingdom of Navarre.

My mother placed me in service to a knight,
  for she had borne me to a squanderer
  who killed himself when he ran through his birthright.
Then I became a domestic in the service
  of good King Thibault. There I began to graft,
  and I account for it in this hot crevice."
And Pigtusk, who at the ends of his lower lip
  shot forth two teeth more terrible than a boar's,
  made the wretch feel how one of them could rip.
The mouse had come among bad cats, but here
  Curlybeard locked arms around him crying:
  "While I've got hold of him the rest stand clear!"   60
And turning his face to my Guide: "If you want to ask him
  anything else," he added, "ask away
  before the others tear him limb from limb."
And my Guide to the sinner: "I should like to know
  if among the other souls beneath the pitch
  are any Italians?" And the wretch: "Just now
I left a shade who came from parts nearby.
  Would I were still in the pitch with him, for then
  these hooks would not be giving me cause to cry."
And suddenly Grafter bellowed in great heat:
  "We've stood enough!" And he hooked the sinner's arm
  and, raking it, ripped off a chunk of meat.
Then Dragontooth wanted to play, too, reaching down
  for a catch at the sinner's legs; but Curlybeard
  wheeled round and round with a terrifying frown,   75
and when the fiends had somewhat given ground
  and calmed a little, my Guide, without delay,
  asked the wretch, who was staring at his wound:
"Who was the sinner from whom you say you made
  your evil-starred departure to come ashore
  among these fiends?" And the wretch: "It was the shade
of Friar Gomita of Gallura, the crooked stem
  of every fraud; when his master's enemies
  were in his hands, he won high praise from them.
He took their money without case or docket
  and let them go. He was in all his dealings
  no petty bursar, but a kingly pocket.

119

With him, his endless crony in the fosse,
  is Don Michel Zanche of Logodoro;
    they babble about Sardinia without pause.   90
But look! See that fiend grinning at your side!
  There is much more that I should like to tell you,
    but, oh, I think he means to grate my hide!"
But their grim sergeant wheeled, sensing foul play,
  and turning on Cramper, who seemed set to strike,
    ordered: "Clear off, you buzzard. Clear off, I say!"
"If either of you would like to see and hear
  Tuscans or Lombards," the pale sinner said,
    "I can lure them out of hiding if you'll stand clear
and let me sit here at the edge of the ditch;
  and get all these Blacktalons out of sight,
    for while they're here, no one will leave the pitch.
In exchange for myself, I can fish you up as pretty
  a mess of souls as you like. I have only to whistle
    the way we do when one of us gets free."   105
Deaddog raised his snout as he listened to him,
  then, shaking his head, said: "Listen to the grafter
    spinning his tricks so he can jump from the brim!"
And the sticky wretch, who was all treachery:
  "Oh, I am more than tricky when there's a chance
    to see my friends in greater misery."
Hellken, against the will of all the crew,
  could hold no longer. "If you jump," he said
    to the scheming wretch, "I won't come after you
at a gallop, but like a hawk after a mouse.
  We'll clear the edge and hide behind the bank;
    let's see if you're trickster enough for all of us."
Reader, here is new game! The fiends withdrew
  from the bank's edge, and Deaddog, who at first
    was most against it, led the savage crew.   120
The Navarrese chose his moment carefully
  and, planting both his feet against the ground,
    he leaped, and in an instant he was free.
The fiends were stung with shame, and of the lot
  Hellken most, who had been the cause of it.
    He leaped out madly bellowing: "You're caught!"

Grizzly turned his talons against Hellken,
locked with him claw to claw above the ditch.

but little good it did him; terror pressed
   harder than wings; the sinner dove from sight
   and the fiend in full flight had to raise his breast.
A duck, when the falcon dives, will disappear
   exactly so, all in a flash, while he
   returns defeated and weary up the air.
Grizzly, in a rage at the sinner's flight,
   flew after Hellken, hoping the wraith would escape,
   so he might find an excuse to start a fight.   135
And as soon as the grafter sank below the pitch,
   Grizzly turned his talons against Hellken,
   locked with him claw to claw above the ditch.
But Hellken was sparrow hawk enough for two
   and clawed him well; and ripping one another,
   they plunged together into the hot stew.
The heat broke up the brawl immediately,
   but their wings were smeared with pitch and they
   could not rise. Curlybeard, upset as his company,
commanded four to fly to the other coast
   at once with all their grapples. At top speed
   the fiends divided, each one to his post.
Some on the near edge, some along the far,
   they stretched their hooks out to the clotted pair
   who were already cooked deep through the scar   150
of their first burn. And turning to one side
we slipped off, leaving them thus occupied.

Canto 23

*The Poets are pursued by the fiends and
escape them by sliding down the sloping bank of
the next pit. They are now in the sixth bolgia.
Here the Hypocrites, weighted down by great
leaden robes, walk eternally round and round a
narrow track. The robes are brilliantly gilded on
the outside and are shaped like a monk's habit,
for the Hypocrite's outward appearance shines
brightly and passes for holiness, but under that
show lies the terrible weight of his deceit which
the soul must bear through all eternity. The Poets
talk to two Jovial Friars and come upon Caiaphas, the chief sinner of that place. Caiaphas
was the High Priest of the Jews who counseled
the Pharisees to crucify Jesus in the name of public expedience. He is punished by being crucified to the floor of Hell by three great stakes,
and in such a position that every passing sinner
must walk upon him. Thus he must suffer upon
his own body the weight of all the world's hypo-
crisy, as Christ suffered upon his body the pain of
all the world's sins. The Jovial Friars tell Virgil how he may climb from the pit, and Virgil
discovers that Malacoda lied about the
bridges over the sixth bolgia.*

Silent, apart, and unattended we went
   as Minor Friars go when they walk abroad,
   one following the other. The incident
recalled the fable of the Mouse and the Frog
   that Aesop tells. For compared attentively
   point by point, "pig" is no closer to "hog"
than the one case to the other. And as one thought
   springs from another, so the comparison
   gave birth to a new concern, at which I caught

my breath in fear. This thought ran through my mind:
"These fiends, through us, have been made ridiculous
and have suffered insult and injury of a kind

to make them smart. Unless we take good care—
now rage is added to their natural spleen—
they will hunt us down as greyhounds hunt the hare." 15

Already I felt my scalp grow tight with fear.
I was staring back in terror as I said:
"Master, unless we find concealment here

and soon, I dread the rage of the fiends; already
they are yelping on our trail; I imagine them
so vividly I can hear them now." And he:

'Were I a pane of leaded glass, I could not
summon your outward look more instantly
into myself, than I do your inner thought.

Your fears were mixed already with my own
with the same suggestion and the same dark look,
so that of both I form one resolution.

The right bank may be sloping; in that case
we may find some way down to the next pit
and so escape from the imagined chase." 30

He had not finished answering me thus
when, not far off, their giant wings outspread,
I saw the fiends come charging after us.

Seizing me instantly in his arms, my Guide—
like a mother wakened by a midnight noise
to find a wall of flame at her bedside,

who takes her child and runs and, more concerned
for him than for herself, does not pause even
to throw a wrap about her—raised me, turned,

and down the rugged bank from the high summit
flung himself down supine onto the slope
which walls the upper side of the next pit.

Water that turns the great wheel of a land mill
never ran faster through the end of a sluice
at the point nearest the paddles as down that hill 45

my Guide and Master bore me on his breast,
as if I were not a companion, but a son.
And the soles of his feet had hardly come to rest

124

on the bed of the depth below, when on the height
    we had just left, the fiends beat their great wings.
    But now they gave my Guide no cause for fright;
for the Providence that gave them the fifth pit
    to govern as the ministers of Its will,
    takes from their souls the power of leaving it.
About us now in the depth of the pit we found
    a painted people, weary and defeated.
    Slowly, in pain, they paced it round and round.
All wore great cloaks cut to as ample a size
    as those worn by the Benedictines of Cluny.
    The enormous hoods were drawn over their eyes.   60
The outside is all dazzle, golden and fair;
    the inside, lead, so heavy that Frederick's capes,
    compared to these, would seem as light as air.
O weary mantle for eternity!
    We turned to the left again along their course,
    listening to their moans of misery,
but they moved so slowly down that barren strip,
    tired by their burden, that our company
    was changed at every movement of the hip.
And walking thus, I said: "As we go on,
    may it please you to look about among these people
    for any whose name or history may be known."
And one who understood Tuscan cried to us there
    as we hurried past: "I pray you check your speed,
    you who run so fast through the sick air;   75
it may be I am one who will fit your case."
    And at his words my Master turned and said:
    "Wait now, then go with him at his own pace."
I waited there and saw along that track
    two souls who seemed in haste to be with me;
    but the narrow way and their burden held them back.
When they had reached me down that narrow way,
    they stared at me in silence and amazement,
    then turned to one another. I heard one say:
"This one seems, by the motion of his throat,
    to be alive; and if they are dead, how is it
    they are allowed to shed the leaden coat?"

And then to me "O Tuscan, come so far
  to the college of the sorry hypocrites,
  do not disdain to tell us who you are."
And I: "I was born and raised a Florentine
  on the green and lovely banks of Arno's waters,
  I go with the body that was always mine.
But who are *you*, who sighing as you go
  distill in floods of tears that drown your cheeks?
  What punishment is this that glitters so?"
"These burnished robes are of thick lead," said one,
  "and are hung on us like counterweights, so heavy
  that we, their weary fulcrums, creak and groan.
Jovial Friars and Bolognese were we.
  We were chosen jointly by your Florentines
  to keep the peace, an office usually
held by a single man; near the Gardingo
  one still may see the sort of peace we kept.
  I was called Catalano, he, Loderingo."
I began: "O Friars, your evil—" and then I saw
  a figure crucified upon the ground
  by three great stakes, and I fell still in awe.
When he saw me there, he began to puff great sighs
  into his beard, convulsing all his body;
  and Friar Catalano, following my eyes,
said to me: "That one nailed across the road
  counseled the Pharisees that it was fitting
  one man be tortured for the public good.
Naked, he lies fixed there, as you see,
  in the path of all who pass; there he must feel
  the weight of all through all eternity.
His father-in-law and the others of the Council,
  which was a seed of wrath to all the Jews,
  are similarly staked for the same evil."
Then I saw Virgil marvel for a while
  over that soul so ignominiously
  stretched on the cross in Hell's eternal exile.
Then, turning, he asked the friar: "If your law permit,
  can you tell us if somewhere along the right
  there is some gap in the stone wall of the pit

90

105

120

126

through which we two may climb to the next brink
   without the need of summoning the Black Angels
   and forcing them to raise us from this sink?"
He: "Nearer than you hope, there is a bridge
   that runs from the great circle of the scarp
   and crosses every ditch from ridge to ridge,
except that in this it is broken; but with care
   you can mount the ruins which lie along the slope
   and make a heap on the bottom." My Guide stood there   135
motionless for a while with a dark look.
   At last he said: "He lied about this business,
   who spears the sinners yonder with his hook."
And the friar: "Once at Bologna I heard the wise
   discussing the Devil's sins; among them I heard
   that he is a liar and the father of lies."
When the sinner had finished speaking, I saw the face
   of my sweet Master darken a bit with anger;
   he set off at a great stride from that place,
and I turned from that weighted hypocrite
to follow in the prints of his dear feet.

Canto 24

The Poets climb the right bank labori-
ously, cross the bridge of the seventh bolgia, and
descend the far bank to observe the Thieves. They
find the pit full of monstrous reptiles who curl
themselves about the sinners like living coils of
rope, binding each sinner's hands behind his back
and knotting themselves through the loins. Other
reptiles dart about the place, and the Poets see
one of them fly through the air and pierce the jug-
ular vein of one sinner who immediately bursts
into flames until only ashes remain. From the
ashes the sinner reforms painfully. These are
Dante's first observations of the Thieves and will
be carried further in the next canto, but the first
allegorical retribution is immediately apparent.
Thievery is reptilian in its secrecy; therefore it is
punished by reptiles. The hands of the thieves are
the agents of their crimes; therefore they are
bound forever. And as the thief destroys his fel-
lowmen by making their substance disappear, so
is he painfully destroyed and made to disappear,
not once but over and over again. The sinner who
has risen from his own ashes reluctantly identi-
fies himself as Vanni Fucci. He tells his story, and
to revenge himself for having been forced to re-
veal his identity he utters a dark
prophecy against Dante.

In the turning season of the youthful year,
    when the sun is warming his rays beneath Aquarius
    and the days and nights already begin to near
their perfect balance, the hoarfrost copies then
    the image of his white sister on the ground,
    but the first sun wipes away the work of his pen.

The peasants who lack fodder then arise
    and look about and see the fields all white
    and hear their lambs bleat; then they smite their thighs,
go back into the house, walk here and there,
    pacing, fretting, wondering what to do,
    then come outdoors again, and there, despair
falls from them when they see how the earth's face
    has changed in so little time, and they take their staffs
    and drive their lambs to feed—so in that place   15
when I saw my Guide and Master's eyebrows lower,
    my spirits fell and I was sorely vexed;
    and as quickly came the plaster to the sore;
for when he had reached the ruined bridge, he stood
    and turned on me that sweet and open look
    with which he had greeted me in the dark wood.
When he had paused and studied carefully
    the heap of stones, he seemed to reach some plan,
    for he turned and opened his arms and lifted me.
Like one who works and calculates ahead
    and is always ready for what happens next—
    so, raising me above that dismal bed
to the top of one great slab of the fallen slate,
    he chose another saying: "Climb here, but first
    test it to see if it will hold your weight."   30
It was no climb for a lead-hung hypocrite;
    for scarcely we—he light and I assisted—
    could crawl handhold by handhold from the pit;
and were it not that the bank along this side
    was lower than the one down which we had slid,
    I at least—I will not speak for my Guide—
would have turned back. But as all of the vast rim
    of Malebolge leans toward the lowest well,
    so each succeeding valley and each brim
is lower than the last. We climbed the face
    and arrived by great exertion to the point
    where the last rock had fallen from its place.
My lungs were pumping as if they could not stop;
    I thought I could not go on, and I sat exhausted
    the instant I had clambered to the top.   45

"Up on your feet! This is no time to tire!"
    my Master cried. "The man who lies asleep
    will never waken fame, and his desire
and all his life drift past him like a dream,
    and the traces of his memory fade from time
    like smoke in air or ripples on a stream.
Now, therefore, rise. Control your breath, and call
    upon the strength of soul that wins all battles
    unless it sink in the gross body's fall.
There is a longer ladder yet to climb;
    this much is not enough. If you understand me,
    show that you mean to profit from your time."
I rose and made my breath appear more steady
    than it really was, and I replied: "Lead on
    as it pleases you to go; I am strong and ready."   60
We picked our way up the cliff, a painful climb,
    for it was narrower, steeper, and more jagged
    than any we had crossed up to that time.
I moved along, talking to hide my faintness,
    when a voice that seemed unable to form words
    rose from the depths of the next chasm's darkness.
I do not know what it said, though by then the Sage
    had led me to the top of the next arch;
    but the speaker seemed in a tremendous rage.
I was bending over the brim, but living eyes
    could not plumb to the bottom of that dark;
    therefore I said: "Master, let me advise
that we cross over and climb down the wall;
    for just as I hear the voice without understanding,
    so I look down and make out nothing at all."   75
"I make no other answer than the act,"
    the Master said. "The only fit reply
    to a fit request is silence and the fact."
So we moved down the bridge to the stone pier
    that shores the end of the arch on the eighth bank,
    and there I saw the chasm's depths made clear;
and there great coils of serpents met my sight,
    so hideous a mass that even now
    the memory makes my blood run cold with fright.

Let Libya boast no longer, for though its sands
  breed chelidrids, jaculi, and phareans,
  cenchriads, and two-headed amphisbands,
it never bred such a variety
  of vipers, no, not with all Ethiopia
  and all the lands that lie by the Red Sea.   90
Amid that swarm, naked and without hope,
  people ran terrified, not even dreaming
  of a hole to hide in or of heliotrope.
Their hands were bound behind by coils of serpents,
  which thrust their heads and tails between the loins
  and bunched in front, a mass of knotted torments.
One of the damned came racing round a boulder,
  and, as he passed us, a great snake shot up
  and bit him where the neck joins with the shoulder.
No mortal pen—however fast it flash
  over the page—could write down o or i
  as quickly as he flamed and fell in ash;
and when he was dissolved into a heap
  upon the ground, the dust rose of itself
  and immediately resumed its former shape.   105
Precisely so, philosophers declare,
  the Phoenix dies and then is born again
  when it approaches its five hundredth year.
It lives on tears of balsam and of incense;
  in all its life it eats no herb or grain,
  and nard and precious myrrh sweeten its cerements.
And as a person fallen in a fit,
  possessed by a demon or some other seizure
  that fetters him without his knowing it,
struggles up to his feet and blinks his eyes
  (still stupefied by the great agony
  he has just passed) and, looking round him, sighs—
such was the sinner when at last he rose.
  O power of God! How dreadful is Thy will,
  which in its vengeance rains such fearful blows.   120
Then my Guide asked him who he was. And he
  answered reluctantly: "Not long ago
  I rained into this gullet from Tuscany.

I am Vanni Fucci, the beast. A mule among men,
  I chose the bestial life above the human.
  Savage Pistoia was my fitting den."
And I to my Guide: "Detain him a bit longer
  and ask what crime it was that sent him here;
  I knew him as a man of blood and anger."
The sinner, hearing me, seemed discomforted,
  but he turned and fixed his eyes upon my face
  with a look of dismal shame; at length he said:
"That you have found me out among the strife
  and misery of this place grieves my heart more
  than did the day that cut me from my life.
But I am forced to answer truthfully;
  I am put down so low because it was I
  who stole the treasure from the Sacristy,
for which others once were blamed. But that you may
  find less to gloat about if you escape here,
  prick up your ears and listen to what I say.
First Pistoia is emptied of the Black,
  then Florence changes her party and her laws.
  From Valdimagra the god of war brings back
a fiery vapor wrapped in turbid air;
  then in a storm of battle at Piceno
  the vapor breaks apart the mist, and there
every White shall feel his wounds anew.
And I have told you this that it may grieve you."

135

Canto 25

*Vanni Fucci's rage mounts to the point
where he hurls an ultimate obscenity at God, and
the serpents immediately swarm over him, driving him off in great pain. The Centaur, Cacus, his
back covered with serpents and a fire-eating
dragon, also gives chase to punish the wretch.
Dante then meets five noble Thieves of Florence
and sees the further retribution visited upon
the sinners. Some of the Thieves appear first in
human form, others as reptiles. All but one of
them suffer a painful transformation before
Dante's eyes. Agnello appears in human form
and is merged with Cianfa, who appears as a
six-legged lizard. Buoso appears as a man and
changes form with Francesco, who first appears
as a tiny reptile. Only Puccio Sciancato remains
unchanged, though we are made to understand
that his turn will come. Endless and painful
transformation is the final state of the Thieves. In
life they took the substance of others, transforming it into their own. So in Hell their very bodies are constantly being taken from them, and
they are left to steal back a human form from
some other sinner. Thus they waver constantly
between man and reptile, and no sinner
knows what to call his own.*

When he had finished, the thief—to his disgrace—
    raised his hands with both fists making figs,
    and cried: "Here, God! I throw them in your face!"
Thereat the snakes became my friends, for one
    coiled itself about the wretch's neck
    as if it were saying: "You shall not go on!"

and another tied his arms behind him again,
   knotting its head and tail between his loins
   so tight he could not move a finger in pain.
Pistoia! Pistoia! why have you not decreed
   to turn yourself to ashes and end your days,
   rather than spread the evil of your seed!
In all of Hell's corrupt and sunken halls
   I found no shade so arrogant toward God,
   not even him who fell from the Theban walls!   15
Without another word, he fled; and there
   I saw a furious Centaur race up, roaring:
   "Where is the insolent blasphemer? Where?"
I do not think as many serpents swarm
   in all the Maremma as he bore on his back
   from the haunch to the first sign of our human form.
Upon his shoulders, just behind his head
   a snorting dragon, whose hot breath set fire
   to all it touched, lay with its wings outspread.
My Guide said: "That is Cacus. Time and again
   in the shadow of Mount Aventine he made
   a lake of blood upon the Roman plain.
He does not go with his kin by the blood-red fosse
   because of the cunning fraud with which he stole
   the cattle of Hercules. And thus it was   30
his thieving stopped, for Hercules found his den
   and gave him perhaps a hundred blows with his club,
   and of them he did not feel the first ten."
Meanwhile, the Centaur passed along his way,
   and three wraiths came. Neither my Guide nor I
   knew they were there until we heard them say:
"You there, who are you?" There our talk fell still,
   and we turned to stare at them. I did not know them,
   but by chance it happened, as it often will,
one named another. "Where is Cianfa?" he cried.
   "Why has he fallen back?" I placed a finger
   across my lips as a signal to my Guide.
Reader, should you doubt what next I tell,
   it will be no wonder, for though I saw it happen,
   I can scarce believe it possible, even in Hell.   45

Inferno

For suddenly, as I watched, I saw a lizard
   come darting forward on six great taloned feet
   and fasten itself to a sinner from crotch to gizzard.
Its middle feet sank in the sweat and grime
   of the wretch's paunch, its forefeet clamped his arms,
   its teeth bit through both cheeks. At the same time
its hind feet fastened on the sinner's thighs;
   its tail thrust through his legs and closed its coil
   over his loins. I saw it with my own eyes!
No ivy ever grew about a tree
   as tightly as that monster wove itself
   limb by limb about the sinner's body;
they fused like hot wax, and their colors ran
   together until neither wretch nor monster
   appeared what he had been when he began;   60
just so, before the running edge of the heat
   on a burning page, a brown discoloration
   changes to black as the white dies from the sheet.
The other two cried out as they looked on:
   "Alas! Alas! Agnello, how you change!
   Already you are neither two nor one!"
The two heads had already blurred and blended;
   now two new semblances appeared and faded,
   one face where neither face began nor ended.
From the four upper limbs of man and beast
   two arms were made, then members never seen
   grew from the thighs and legs, belly and breast.
Their former likenesses mottled and sank
   to something that was both of them and neither;
   and so transformed, it slowly left our bank.   75
As lizards at high noon of a hot day
   dart out from hedge to hedge, from shade to shade,
   and flash like lightning when they cross the way—
so toward the bowels of the other two,
   shot a small monster, livid, furious,
   and black as a peppercorn. Its lunge bit through
that part of one of them from which man receives
   his earliest nourishment; then it fell back
   and layed sprawled out in front of the two thieves.

135

Its victim stared at it but did not speak;
   indeed, he stood there like a post and yawned
   as if lack of sleep, or a fever, had left him weak.
The reptile stared at him, he at the reptile;
   from the wound of one and from the other's mouth
   two smokes poured out and mingled, dark and vile.   90
Now let Lucan be still with his history
   of poor Sabellus and Nassidius
   and wait to hear what next appeared to me.
Of Cadmus and Arethusa be Ovid silent.
   I have no need to envy him those verses
   where he makes one a fountain and one a serpent;
for he never transformed two beings face to face
   in such a way that both their natures yielded
   their elements each to each, as in this case.
Responding sympathetically to each other,
   the reptile cleft his tail into a fork,
   and the wounded sinner drew his feet together.
The sinner's legs and thighs began to join;
   they grew together so, that soon no trace
   of juncture could be seen from toe to loin.   105
Point by point the reptile's cloven tail
   grew to the form of what the sinner lost;
   one skin began to soften, one to scale.
The armpits swallowed the arms, and the short shank
   of the reptile's forefeet simultaneously
   lengthened by as much as the man's arms shrank.
Its hind feet twisted round themselves and grew
   the member man conceals; meanwhile the wretch
   from his one member generated two.
The smoke swelled up about them all the while;
   it tanned one skin and bleached the other; it stripped
   the hair from the man and grew it on the reptile.
While one fell to his belly, the other rose
   without once shifting the locked evil eyes
   below which they changed snouts as they changed pose.   120
The face of the standing one drew up and in
   toward the temples, and from the excess matter
   that gathered there, ears grew from the smooth skin;

while of the matter left below the eyes
  the excess became a nose, at the same time
  forming the lips to an appropriate size.
Here the face of the prostrate felon slips,
  sharpens into a snout, and withdraws its ears
  as a snail pulls in its horns. Between its lips
the tongue, once formed for speech, thrusts out a fork;
  the forked tongue of the other heals and draws
  into his mouth. The smoke has done its work.
The soul that had become a beast went flitting
  and hissing over the stones, and after it
  the other walked along talking and spitting.   135
Then turning his new shoulders, said to the one
  that still remained: "It is Buoso's turn to go
  crawling along this road as I have done."
Thus did the ballast of the seventh hold
  shift and reshift; and may the strangeness of it
  excuse my pen if the tale is strangely told.
And though all this confused me, they did not flee
  so cunningly but what I was aware
  that it was Puccio Sciancato alone of the three
that first appeared, who kept his old form still.
The other was he for whom you weep, Gaville.

Canto 26

Dante turns from the Thieves toward the
Evil Counselors of the next bolgia, and between
the two he addresses a passionate lament to Flor-
ence prophesying the griefs that will befall her
from these two sins. At the purported time of the
vision, it will be recalled, Dante was a chief mag-
istrate of Florence and was forced into exile by
men he had reason to consider both thieves and
evil counselors. He seems prompted, in fact, to
say much more on this score, but he restrains
himself when he comes in sight of the sinners of
the next bolgia, for they are a moral symbolism,
all men of gift who abused their genius, perverting
it to wiles and stratagems. Seeing them in Hell he
knows his must be another road; his way shall
not be by deception. So the Poets move on and
Dante observes the eighth bolgia in detail. Here
the Evil Counselors move about endlessly, hid-
den from view inside great flames. Their sin was
to abuse the gifts of the Almighty, to steal His vir-
tues for low purposes. And as they stole from God
in their lives and worked by hidden ways, so are
they stolen from sight and hidden in the great
flames which are their own guilty consciences.
And as, in most instances at least, they sinned by
glibness of tongue, so are the flames made into a
fiery travesty of tongues. Among the others, the
Poets see a great doubleheaded flame, and dis-
cover that Ulysses and Diomede are punished
together within it. Virgil addresses the flame,
and through its wavering tongue Ulysses nar-
rates an unforgettable tale of his
last voyage and death.

Inferno

Joy to you, Florence, that your banners swell,
    beating their proud wings over land and sea,
    and that your name expands through all of Hell!
Among the thieves I found five who had been
    your citizens, to my shame; nor yet shall you
    mount to great honor peopling such a den!
But if the truth is dreamed of toward the morning,
    you soon shall feel what Prato and the others
    wish for you. And were that day of mourning
already come it would not be too soon.
    So may it come, since it must! for it will weigh
    more heavily on me as I pass my noon.
We left that place. My Guide climbed stone by stone
    the natural stair by which we had descended
    and drew me after him. So we passed on,   15
and, going our lonely way through that dead land
    among the crags and crevices of the cliff,
    the foot could make no way without the hand.
I mourned among those rocks, and I mourn again
    when memory returns to what I saw;
    and more than usually I curb the strain
of my genius, lest it stray from virtue's course;
    so if some star, or a better thing, grant me merit,
    may I not find the gift cause for remorse.
As many fireflies as the peasant sees
    when he rests on a hill and looks into the valley
    (where he tills or gathers grapes or prunes his trees)
in that sweet season when the face of him
    who lights the world rides north, and at the hour
    when the fly yields to the gnat and the air grows dim—   30
such myriad flames I saw shine through
    the gloom of the eighth abyss when I arrived
    at the rim from which its bed comes into view.
As he the bears avenged so fearfully
    beheld Elijah's chariot depart—
    the horses rise toward Heaven—but could not see
more than the flame, a cloudlet in the sky,
    once it had risen—so within the fosse
    only those flames, forever passing by

were visible, ahead, to right, to left;
    for though each steals a sinner's soul from view
    not one among them leaves a trace of the theft.
I stood on the bridge and leaned out from the edge
    so far that, but for a jut of rock I held to,
    I should have been sent hurtling from the ledge   45
without being pushed. And seeing me so intent,
    my Guide said: "There are souls within those flames;
    each sinner swathes himself in his own torment."
"Master," I said, "your words make me more sure,
    but I had seen already that it was so
    and meant to ask what spirit must endure
the pains of that great flame which splits away
    in two great horns, as if it rose from the pyre
    where Eteocles and Polynices lay?"
He answered me: "Forever round this path
    Ulysses and Diomede move in such dress,
    united in pain as once they were in wrath;
there they lament the ambush of the Horse
    which was the door through which the noble seed
    of the Romans issued from its holy source;   60
there they mourn that for Achilles slain
    sweet Deidamia weeps even in death;
    there they recall the Palladium in their pain."
"Master," I cried, "I pray you and repray
    till my prayer becomes a thousand—if these souls
    can still speak from the fire, oh, let me stay
until the flame draws near! Do not deny me!
    You see how fervently I long for it!"
    And he to me: "Since what you ask is worthy,
it shall be. But be still and let me speak;
    for I know your mind already, and they perhaps
    might scorn your manner of speaking, since they were Greek."
And when the flame had come where time and place
    seemed fitting to my Guide, I heard him say
    these words to it: "O you two souls who pace   75
together in one flame!—if my days above
    won favor in your eyes, if I have earned
    however much or little of your love

in writing my High Verses, do not pass by,
   but let one of you be pleased to tell where he,
   having disappeared from the known world, went to die."
As if it fought the wind, the greater prong
   of the ancient flame began to quiver and hum,
   then moving its tip as if it were the tongue
that spoke, gave out a voice above the roar.
   "When I left Circe," it said, "who more than a year
   detained me near Gaeta long before
Aeneas came and gave the place that name,
   not fondness for my son, nor reverence
   for my aged father, nor Penelope's claim   90
to the joys of love, could drive out of my mind
   the lust to experience the far-flung world
   and the failings and felicities of mankind.
I put out on the high and open sea
   with a single ship and only those few souls
   who stayed true when the rest deserted me.
As far as Morocco and as far as Spain
   I saw both shores; and I saw Sardinia
   and the other islands of the open main.
I and my men were stiff and slow with age
   when we sailed at last into the narrow pass
   where, warning all men back from further voyage,
Hercules' Pillars rose upon our sight.
   Already I had left Ceuta on the left;
   Seville now sank behind me on the right.   105
'Shipmates,' I said, 'who through a hundred thousand
   perils have reached the West, do not deny
   to the brief remaining watch our senses stand
experience of the world beyond the sun.
   Greeks! You were not born to live like brutes,
   but to press on toward manhood and recognition!'
With this brief exhortation I made my crew
   so eager for the voyage I could hardly
   have held them back from it when I was through;
and turning our stern toward morning, our bow toward night,
   we bore southwest out of the world of man;
   we made wings of our oars for our fool's flight.

That night we raised the other pole ahead
  with all its stars, and ours had so declined
   it did not rise out of its ocean bed.   120
Five times since we had dipped our bending oars
  beyond the world, the light beneath the moon
   had waxed and waned, when dead upon our course
we sighted, dark in space, a peak so tall
  I doubted any man had seen the like.
  Our cheers were hardly sounded, when a squall
broke hard upon our bow from the new land;
  three times it sucked the ship and the sea about
   as it pleased Another to order and command.
At the fourth, the poop rose and the bow went down
till the sea closed over us and the light was gone."

Canto 27

*The double flame departs at a word from
Virgil and behind it appears another which contains the soul of Count Guido da Montefeltro, a
lord of Romagna. He had overheard Virgil speaking Italian, and the entire flame in which his soul
is wrapped quivers with his eagerness to hear recent news of his war-torn country. (As Farinata
has already explained, the spirits of the damned
have prophetic powers, but lose all track of events
as they approach.) Dante replies with a stately
and tragic summary of how things stand in the
cities of Romagna. When he has finished, he asks
Guido for his story, and Guido recounts his life
and how Boniface VIII persuaded him to sin.*

When it had finished speaking, the great flame
   stood tall and shook no more. Now, as it left us
   with the sweet Poet's license, another came
along that track and our attention turned
   to the new flame; a strange and muffled roar
   rose from the single tip to which it burned.
As the Sicilian bull—that brazen spit
   which bellowed first (and properly enough)
   with the lament of him whose file had tuned it—
was made to bellow by its victim's cries
   in such a way, that though it was of brass,
   it seemed itself to howl and agonize:
so lacking any way through or around
   the fire that sealed them in, the mournful words
   were changed into its language. When they found
their way up to the tip, imparting to it
   the same vibration given them in their passage
   over the tongue of the concealed sad spirit,

15

we heard it say: "O you at whom I aim
  my voice and who were speaking Lombard, saying:
  'Go now, I ask no more,' just as I came—
though I may come a bit late to my turn,
  may it not annoy you to pause and speak awhile;
  you see it does not annoy me—and I burn.
If you have fallen only recently
  to this blind world from that sweet Italy
  where I acquired my guilt, I pray you, tell me
is there peace or war in Romagna? for on earth
  I, too, was of those hills between Urbino
  and the fold from which the Tiber springs to birth."   30
I was still staring at it from the dim
  edge of the pit when my Guide nudged me, saying:
  "This one is Italian; *you* speak to him."
My answer was framed already; without pause
  I spoke these words to it: "O hidden soul,
  your sad Romagna is not and never was
without war in her tyrants' raging blood;
  but none flared openly when I left just now.
  Ravenna's fortunes stand as they have stood
these many years; Polenta's eagles brood
  over her walls, and their pinions cover Cervia.
  The city that so valiantly withstood
the French and raised a mountain of their dead
  feels the Green Claws again. Still in Verrucchio
  the Aged Mastiff and his Pup, who shed   45
Montagna's blood, raven in their old ranges.
  The cities of Lamone and Santerno
  are led by the white den's Lion, he who changes
his politics with the compass. And as the city
  the Savio washes lies between plain and mountain,
  so it lives between freedom and tyranny.
Now, I beg you, let us know your name;
  do not be harder than one has been to you;
  so, too, you will preserve your earthly fame."
And when the flame had roared awhile beneath
  the ledge on which we stood, it swayed its tip
  to and fro and then gave forth this breath:

144

"If I believed that my reply were made
    to one who could ever climb to the world again,
    this flame would shake no more. But since no shade   60
ever returned—if what I am told is true—
    from this blind world into the living light,
    without fear of dishonor I answer you.
I was a man of arms, then took the rope
    of the Franciscans, hoping to make amends;
    and surely I should have won to all my hope
but for the Great Priest—may he rot in Hell!—
    who brought me back to all my earlier sins;
    and how and why it happened I wish to tell
in my own words. While I was still encased
    in the pulp and bone my mother bore, my deeds
    were not of the lion but of the fox. I raced
through tangled ways; all wiles were mine from birth;
    and I won to such advantage with my arts
    that rumor of me reached the ends of the earth.   75
But when I saw before me all the signs
    of the time of life that cautions every man
    to lower his sail and gather in his lines,
that which had pleased me once, troubled my spirit,
    and penitent and confessed, I became a monk.
    Alas! What joy I might have had of it!
It was then the Prince of the New Pharisees drew
    his sword and marched upon the Lateran—
    and not against the Saracen or the Jew,
for every man that stood against his hand
    was a Christian soul; not one had warred on Acre,
    nor been a trader in the Sultan's land.
It was he abused his sacred vows and mine;
    his office and the cord I wore, which once
    made those it girded leaner. As Constantine   90
sent for Silvestro to cure his leprosy,
    seeking him out among Soracte's cells—
    so this one from his great throne sent for me
to cure the fever of pride that burned his blood.
    He demanded my advice, and I kept silent
    for his words seemed drunken to me. So it stood

145

until he said: 'Your soul need fear no wound;
   I absolve your guilt beforehand; and now teach me
   how to smash Penestrino to the ground.
The gates of Heaven, as you know, are mine
   to open and shut, for I hold the two Great Keys
   so easily let go by Celestine.'
His weighty arguments led me to fear
   silence was worse than sin. Therefore, I said:
   'Holy Father, since you clean me here   105
of the guilt into which I fall, let it be done;
   long promise and short observance is the road
   that leads to the sure triumph of your throne.'
Later, when I was dead, St. Francis came
   to claim my soul, but one of the Black Angels
   said: 'Leave him. Do not wrong me. This one's name
went into my book the moment he resolved
   to give false counsel. Since then he has been mine;
   for who does not repent cannot be absolved;
nor can we admit the possibility
   of repenting a thing at the same time it is willed,
   for the two acts are contradictory.'
Miserable me! with what contrition
   I shuddered when he lifted me, saying: 'Perhaps
   you hadn't heard that I was a logician.'   120
He carried me to Minos; eight times round
   his scabby back the monster coiled his tail,
   then biting it in rage he pawed the ground
and cried: 'This one is for the thievish fire!'
   And, as you see, I am lost accordingly,
   grieving in heart as I go in this attire.''
His story told, the flame began to toss
   and writhe its horn. And so it left, and we
   crossed over to the arch of the next fosse,
where from the iron treasury of the Lord
the fee of wrath is paid the sowers of discord.

Canto 28

*The Poets come to the edge of the ninth
bolgia and look down at a parade of hideously
mutilated souls. These are the Sowers of Discord,
and just as their sin was to rend asunder what
God had meant to be united, so are they hacked
and torn through all eternity by a great demon
with a bloody sword. After each mutilation the
souls are compelled to drag their broken bodies
around the pit and to return to the demon, for in
the course of the circuit their wounds knit in time
to be inflicted anew. Thus is the law of retribution observed, each sinner suffering according to
his degree. Among them Dante distinguishes
three classes with varying degrees of guilt within
each class. First come the Sowers of Religious
Discord. Mahomet is chief among them, and appears first, cleft from crotch to chin, with his internal organs dangling between his legs. His
son-in-law, Ali, drags on ahead of him, cleft from
topknot to chin. These reciprocal wounds symbolize Dante's judgment that these two sum up
the total schism between Christianity and Islam.
The revolting details of Mahomet's condition
clearly imply Dante's opinion of that doctrine.
Mahomet issues an ironic warning to another
schismatic, Fra Dolcino. Next come the Sowers of
Political Discord, among them Pier da Medicina,
the Tribune Curio, and Mosca dei Lamberti, each
mutilated according to the nature of his sin. Last
of all is Bertrand de Born, a Sower of Discord Between Kinsmen. He separated father from son,
and for that offense carries his head separated
from his body, holding it with one hand by the
hair and swinging it as if it were a lantern to light
his dark and endless way. The image of Bertrand
raising his head at arm's length in order that it
might speak more clearly to the Poets on the ridge
is one of the most memorable in the Inferno. For
some reason that cannot be ascertained, Dante*

makes these sinners quite eager to be remem-
bered in the world, despite the fact that many
who lie above them in Hell were
unwilling to be recognized.

Who could describe, even in words set free
   of metric and rhyme and a thousand times retold,
   the blood and wounds that now were shown to me!
At grief so deep the tongue must wag in vain;
   the language of our sense and memory
   lacks the vocabulary of such pain.
If one could gather all those who have stood
   through all of time on Puglia's fateful soil
   and wept for the red running of their blood
in the war of the Trojans; and in that long war
   which left so vast a spoil of golden rings,
   as we find written in Livy, who does not err;
along with those whose bodies felt the wet
   and gaping wounds of Robert Guiscard's lances;
   with all the rest whose bones are gathered yet   15
at Ceperano where every last Pugliese
   turned traitor; and with those from Tagliacozzo
   where Alardo won without weapons—if all these
were gathered, and one showed his limbs run through,
   another his lopped off, that could not equal
   the mutilations of the ninth pit's crew.
A wine tun when a stave or cant bar starts
   does not split open as wide as one I saw
   split from his chin to the mouth with which man farts.
Between his legs all of his red guts hung
   with the heart, the lungs, the liver, the gall bladder,
   and the shriveled sac that passes shit to the bung.
I stood and stared at him from the stone shelf;
   he noticed me and opening his own breast
   with both hands cried: "See how I rip myself!   30

"See how I rip myself!
See how Mahomet's mangled and split open!
Ahead of me walks Ali in his tears."

See how Mahomet's mangled and split open!
  Ahead of me walks Ali in his tears,
    his head cleft from the topknot to the chin.
And all the other souls that bleed and mourn
  along this ditch were sowers of scandal and schism;
    as they tore others apart, so are they torn.
Behind us, warden of our mangled horde,
  the devil who butchers us and sends us marching
    waits to renew our wounds with his long sword
when we have made the circuit of the pit;
  for by the time we stand again before him
    all the wounds he gave us last have knit.
But who are you that gawk down from that sill—
  probably to put off your own descent
    to the pit you are sentenced to for your own evil?"   45
"Death has not come for him, guilt does not drive
  his soul to torment," my sweet Guide replied.
    "That he may experience all while yet alive
I, who am dead, must lead him through the drear
  and darkened halls of Hell, from round to round;
    and this is true as my own standing here."
More than a hundred wraiths who were marching under
  the sill on which we stood paused at his words
    and stared at me, forgetting pain in wonder.
"And if you do indeed return to see
  the sun again, and soon, tell Fra Dolcino
    unless he longs to come and march with me
he would do well to check his groceries
  before the winter drives him from the hills
    and gives the victory to the Novarese."   60
Mahomet, one foot raised, had paused to say
  these words to me. When he had finished speaking,
    he stretched it out and down and moved away.
Another—he had his throat slit and his nose
  slashed off as far as the eyebrows and a wound
    where one of his ears had been—standing with those
who stared at me in wonder from the pit,
  opened the grinning wound of his red gullet
    as if it were a mouth, and said through it:

"O soul unforfeited to misery
  and whom—unless I take you for another—
  I have seen above in our sweet Italy,
if ever again you see the gentle plain
  that slopes down from Vercelli to Marcabò,
  remember Pier da Medicina in pain   75
and announce this warning to the noblest two
  of Fano, Messers Guido and Angiolello—
  that unless our foresight sees what is not true,
they shall be thrown from their ships into the sea
  and drown in the raging tides near La Cattolica
  to satisfy a tyrant's treachery.
Neptune never saw so gross a crime
  in all the seas from Cyprus to Majorca,
  not even in pirate raids, nor the Argive time.
The one-eyed traitor, lord of the demesne
  whose hill and streams one who walks here beside me
  will wish eternally he had never seen,
will call them to a parley, but behind
  sweet invitations he will work it so
  they need not pray against Focara's wind."   90
And I to him: "If you would have me bear
  your name to time, show me the one who found
  the sight of that land so harsh and let me hear
his story and his name." He touched the cheek
  of one nearby, forcing the jaws apart,
  and said: "This is the one; he cannot speak.
This outcast settled Caesar's doubts that day
  beside the Rubicon by telling him,
  'A man prepared is a man hurt by delay.' "
Ah, how wretched Curio seemed to me
  with a bloody stump in his throat in place of the tongue
  which once had dared to speak so recklessly!
And one among them with both arms hacked through
  cried out, raising his stumps on the foul air
  while the blood bedaubed his face: "Remember, too,   105
Mosca dei Lamberti, alas, who said,
  'A thing done has an end!' and with those words
  planted the fields of war with Tuscan dead."

"And brought about the death of all your clan!"
    I said, and he, stung by new pain on pain,
    ran off; and in his grief he seemed a madman.
I stayed to watch those broken instruments,
    and I saw a thing so strange I should not dare
    to mention it without more evidence
but that my own clear conscience strengthens me,
    that good companion that upholds a man
    within the armor of his purity.
I saw it there; I seem to see it still—
    a body without a head, that moved along
    like all the others in that spew and spill.   120
It held the severed head by its own hair,
    swinging it like a lantern in its hand,
    and the head looked at us and wept in its despair.
It made itself a lamp of its own head,
    and they were two in one and one in two;
    how this can be, He knows who so commanded.
And when it stood directly under us
    it raised the head at arm's length toward our bridge
    the better to be heard, and swaying thus
it cried: "O living soul in this abyss,
    see what a sentence has been passed upon me,
    and search all Hell for one to equal this!
When you return to the world, remember me.
    I am Bertrand de Born, and it was I
    who set the young king on to mutiny,   135
son against father, father against son
    as Achitophel set Absalom and David;
    and since I parted those who should be one
in duty and in love, I bear my brain
    divided from its source within this trunk;
    and walk here where my evil turns to pain,
an eye for an eye to all eternity;
    thus is the law of Hell observed in me."

Canto 29

*Dante lingers on the edge of the ninth
bolgia expecting to see one of his kinsmen, Geri
del Bello, among the Sowers of Discord. Virgil,
however, hurries him on, since time is short, and
as they cross the bridge over the tenth bolgia, Virgil explains that he had a glimpse of Geri among
the crowd near the bridge and that he had been
making threatening gestures at Dante. The Poets
now look into the last bolgia of the eighth circle
and see the Falsifiers. They are punished by afflictions of every sense: by darkness, stench, thirst,
filth, loathsome diseases, and a shrieking din.
Some of them, moreover, run ravening through
the pit, tearing others to pieces. Just as in life they
corrupted society by their falsifications, so in
death these sinners are subjected to a sum of
corruptions. In one sense they figure forth what
society would be if all falsifiers succeeded—
a place where the senses are an affliction (since
falsification deceives the senses) rather than
a guide, where even the body has no honesty,
and where some lie prostrate while others run
ravening to prey upon them. Not all of these details are made clear until the next canto, for Dante
distinguishes four classes of Falsifiers, and in the
present canto we meet only the first class, the Alchemists, the Falsifiers of Things. Of this class
are Griffolino d'Arezzo and Capocchio,
with both of whom Dante speaks.*

The sight of that parade of broken dead
   had left my eyes so sotted with their tears
   I longed to stay and weep, but Virgil said:

"What are you waiting for? Why do you stare
   as if you could not tear your eyes away
   from the mutilated shadows passing there?
 You did not act so in the other pits.
   Consider—if you mean perhaps to count them—
   this valley and its train of dismal spirits
 winds twenty-two miles round. The moon already
   is under our feet, the time we have is short,
   and there is much that you have yet to see."
"Had you known what I was seeking," I replied,
   "you might perhaps have given me permission
   to stay on longer." As I spoke, my Guide   15
 had started off already, and I in turn
   had moved along behind him, thus, I answered
   as we moved along the cliff: "Within that cavern
 upon whose brim I stood so long to stare,
   I think a spirit of my own blood mourns
   the guilt that sinners find so costly there."
And the Master then: "Hereafter let your mind
   turn its attention to more worthy matters
   and leave him to his fate among the blind;
 for by the bridge and among that shapeless crew
   I saw him point to you with threatening gestures,
   and I heard him called Geri del Bello. You
 were occupied at the time with that headless one,
   who in his life was master of Altaforte,
   and did not look that way; so he moved on."   30
"O my sweet Guide," I answered, "his death came
   by violence and is not yet avenged
   by those who share his blood, and, thus, his shame.
 For this he surely hates his kin, and, therefore,
   as I suppose, he would not speak to me;
   and in that he makes me pity him the more."
We spoke of this until we reached the edge
   from which, had there been light, we could have seen
   the floor of the next pit. Out from that ledge
Malebolge's final cloister lay outspread,
   and all of its lay brethren might have been
   in sight but for the murk; and from those dead

Inferno

such shrieks and strangled agonies shrilled through me
  like shafts, but barbed with pity, that my hands
  flew to my ears. If all the misery   45
that crams the hospitals of pestilence
  in Maremma, Valdichiano, and Sardinia,
  in the summer months when death sits like a presence
on the marsh air, were dumped into one trench—
  that might suggest their pain. And through the screams,
  putrid flesh spread up its sickening stench.
Still bearing left we passed from the long sill
  to the last bridge of Malebolge. There
  the reeking bottom was more visible.
There, High Justice, sacred ministress
  of the First Father, reigns eternally
  over the falsifiers in their distress.
I doubt it could have been such pain to bear
  the sight of the Acginian people dying
  that time when such malignance rode the air   60
that every beast down to the smallest worm
  shriveled and died (it was after that great plague
  that the Ancient People, as the poets affirm,
were reborn from the ants) as it was to see
  the spirits lying heaped on one another
  in the dank bottom of that fetid valley.
One lay gasping on another's shoulder,
  one on another's belly, and some were crawling
  on hands and knees among the broken boulders.
Silent, slow, step by step, we moved ahead
  looking at and listening to those souls
  too weak to raise themselves from their stone bed.
I saw two there like two pans that are put
  one against the other to hold their warmth.
  They were covered with great scabs from head to foot. 75
No stable boy in a hurry to go home,
  or for whom his master waits impatiently,
  ever scrubbed harder with his currycomb
than those two spirits of the stinking ditch
  scrubbed at themselves with their own bloody claws
  to ease the furious burning of the itch.

One lay gasping on another's shoulder,
   one on another's belly, and some were crawling
   on hands and knees among the broken boulders.

And as they scrubbed and clawed themselves, their nails
   drew down the scabs the way a knife scrapes bream
   or some other fish with even larger scales.
"O you," my Guide called out to one, "you there
   who rip your scabby mail as if your fingers
   were claws and pincers, tell us if this lair
counts any Italians among those who lurk
   in its dark depths; so may your busy nails
   eternally suffice you for your work."   90
"We both are Italian whose unending loss
   you see before you," he replied in tears.
   "But who are you who come to question us?"
"I am a shade," my Guide and Master said,
   "who leads this living man from pit to pit
   to show him Hell as I have been commanded."
The sinners broke apart as he replied
   and turned convulsively to look at me,
   as others did who overheard my Guide.
My Master, then, ever concerned for me,
   turned and said: "Ask them whatever you wish."
   And I said to those two wraiths of misery:
"So may the memory of your names and actions
   not die forever from the minds of men
   in that first world, but live for many suns,   105
tell me who you are and of what city;
   do not be shamed by your nauseous punishment
   into concealing your identity."
"I was a man of Arezzo," one replied,
   "and Albert of Siena had me burned;
   but I am not here for the deed for which I died.
It is true that jokingly I said to him once:
   'I know how to raise myself and fly through air';
   and he—with all the eagerness of a dunce—
wanted to learn. Because I could not make
   a Daedalus of him—for no other reason—
   he had his father burn me at the stake.
But Minos, the infallible, had me hurled
   here to the final bolgia of the ten
   for the alchemy I practiced in the world."   120

And I to the Poet: "Was there ever a race
  more vain than the Sienese? Even the French,
  compared to them, seem full of modest grace."
And the other leper answered mockingly:
  "Excepting Stricca, who by careful planning
  managed to live and spend so moderately;
and Niccolò, who in his time above
  was first of all the shoots in that rank garden
  to discover the costly uses of the clove;
and excepting the brilliant company of talents
  in which Caccia squandered his vineyards and his woods,
  and Abbagliato displayed his intelligence.
But if you wish to know who joins your cry
  against the Sienese, study my face
  with care and let it make its own reply.   135
So you will see I am the suffering shadow
  of Capocchio, who, by practicing alchemy,
  falsified the metals, and you must know,
unless my mortal recollection strays,
how good an ape I was of Nature's ways."

Canto 30

As Capocchio finishes speaking, two ravenous uncleaned spirits come racing through
the pit. One of them, sinking his tusks into Capocchio's neck, drags him away like prey. Capocchio's companion, Griffolino, identifies the two
as Gianni Schicchi and Myrrha, who run ravening
through the pit through all eternity, snatching at
other souls and rending them. These are the Evil
Impersonators, the Falsifiers of Persons. In life
they seized upon the appearance of others, and in
death they must run with never a pause, seizing
upon the infernal apparition of these souls, while
they in turn are preyed upon by their own furies.
Next the Poets encounter Master Adam, a sinner
of the third class, a Falsifier of Money, a Counter-
feiter. Like the Alchemists, he is punished by a
loathsome disease, and he cannot move from
where he lies; but his disease is compounded by
other afflictions, including an eternity of unbearable thirst. Master Adam identifies two spirits
lying beside him as Potiphar's wife and Sinon
the Greek, sinners of the fourth class, the False
Witnesses, the Falsifiers of Words. Sinon, angered
by Master Adam's identification of him, strikes
him across the belly with the one arm he is
able to move. Master Adam replies in kind, and
Dante, fascinated by their continuing exchange
of abuse, stands staring at them until Virgil turns
on him in anger, for "The wish to hear such baseness is degrading." Dante burns with shame, and
Virgil forgives him because of
his genuine repentance.

At the time when Juno took her furious
    revenge for Semele, striking in rage
    again and again at the Theban royal house,
King Athamas, by her contrivance, grew
    so mad that, seeing his wife out for an airing
    with his two sons, he cried to his retinue:
"Out with the nets there! Nets across the pass!
    for I will take this lioness and her cubs!"
    and spread his talons, mad and merciless,
and seizing his son Learchus, whirled him round
    and brained him on a rock; at which the mother
    leaped into the sea with her other son and drowned.
And when the Wheel of Fortune spun about
    to humble the all-daring Trojan's pride
    so that both king and kingdom were wiped out,   15
Hecuba—mourning, wretched, and a slave,
    having seen Polyxena sacrificed,
    and Polydorus dead without a grave—
lost and alone, beside an alien sea,
    began to bark and growl like a dog
    in the mad seizure of her misery.
But never in Thebes nor Troy were Furies seen
    to strike at man or beast in such mad rage
    as two I saw, pale, naked, and unclean,
who suddenly came running toward us then,
    snapping their teeth as they ran, like hungry swine
    let out to feed after a night in the pen.
One of them sank his tusks so savagely
    into Capocchio's neck, that when he dragged him,
    the ditch's rocky bottom tore his belly.   30
And the Aretine, left trembling by me, said:
    "That incubus, in life, was Gianni Schicchi;
    here he runs rabid, mangling the other dead."
"So!" I answered, "and so may the other one
    not sink its teeth in you, be pleased to tell us
    what shade it is before it races on."
And he: "That ancient shade in time above
    was Myrrha, vicious daughter of Cinyras,
    who loved her father with more than rightful love.

"That ancient shade in time above
was Myrrha, vicious daughter of Cinyras,
who loved her father with more than rightful love."

She falsified another's form and came
   disguised to sin with him just as that other
   who runs with her, in order that he might claim
the fabulous lead-mare, lay under disguise
   on Buoso Donati's deathbed and dictated
   a spurious testament to the notaries." 45
And when the rabid pair had passed from sight,
   I turned to observe the other misbegotten
   spirits that lay about to left and right.
And there I saw another husk of sin,
   who, had his legs been trimmed away at the groin,
   would have looked for all the world like a mandolin.
The dropsy's heavy humors, which so bunch
   and spread the limbs, had disproportioned him
   till his face seemed much too small for his swollen paunch.
He strained his lips apart and thrust them forward
   the way a sick man, feverish with thirst,
   curls one lip toward the chin and the other upward.
"O you exempt from every punishment
   of this grim world—I know not why—" he cried,
   "look well upon the misery and debasement 60
of him who was Master Adam. In my first
   life's time, I had enough to please me; here,
   I lack a drop of water for my thirst.
The rivulets that run from the green flanks
   of Casentino to the Arno's flood,
   spreading their cool sweet moisture through their banks,
run constantly before me, and their plash
   and ripple in imagination dries me
   more than the disease that eats my flesh.
Inflexible Justice that has forked and spread
   my soul like hay, to search it the more closely,
   finds in the country where my guilt was bred
this increase of my grief; for there I learned,
   there in Romena, to stamp the Baptist's image
   on alloyed gold—till I was bound and burned. 75
But could I see the soul of Guido here,
   or of Alessandro, or of their filthy brother,
   I would not trade that sight for all the clear

cool flow of Branda's fountain. One of the three—
    if those wild wraiths who run here are not lying—
    is here already. But small good it does me
when my legs are useless! Were I light enough
    to move as much as an inch in a hundred years,
    long before this I would have started off
to cull him from the freaks that fill this fosse,
    although it winds on for eleven miles
    and is no less than half a mile across.
Because of them I lie here in this pigpen;
    it was they persuaded me to stamp the florins
    with three carats of alloy." And I then: 90
"Who are those wretched two sprawled alongside
    your right-hand borders, and who seem to smoke
    as a washed hand smokes in winter?" He replied:
"They were here when I first rained into this gully,
    and have not changed position since, nor may they,
    as I believe, to all eternity.
One is the liar who charged young Joseph wrongly;
    the other, Sinon, the false Greek from Troy.
    A burning fever makes them reek so strongly."
And one of the false pair, perhaps offended
    by the manner of Master Adam's presentation,
    punched him in the rigid and distended
belly—it thundered like a drum—and he
    retorted with an arm blow to the face
    that seemed delivered no whit less politely,   105
saying to him: "Although I cannot stir
    my swollen legs, I still have a free arm
    to use at times when nothing else will answer."
And the other wretch said: "It was not so free
    on your last walk to the stake, free as it was
    when you were coining." And he of the dropsy:
"That's true enough, but there was less truth in you
    when they questioned you at Troy." And Sinon then:
    "For every word I uttered that was not true
you uttered enough false coins to fill a bushel;
    I am put down here for a single crime,
    but you for more than any fiend in Hell."

"Think of the Horse," replied the swollen shade,
 "and may it torture you, perjurer, to recall
  that all the world knows the foul part you played."   120
"And to you the torture of the thirst that fries
 and cracks your tongue," said the Greek, "and of the water
  that swells your gut like a hedge before your eyes."
And the coiner: "So is your own mouth clogged
 with the filth that stuffs and sickens it as always;
  if I am parched while my paunch is waterlogged,
you have the fever and your cankered brain;
 and were you asked to lap Narcissus' mirror
  you would not wait to be invited again."
I was still standing, fixed upon those two
 when the Master said to me: "Now keep on looking
  a little longer and I quarrel with you."
When I heard my Master raise his voice to me,
 I wheeled about with such a start of shame
  that I grow pale yet at the memory.   135
As one trapped in a nightmare that has caught
 his sleeping mind, wishes within the dream
  that it were all a dream, as if it were not—
such I became; my voice could not win through
 my shame to ask his pardon; while my shame
  already won more pardon than I knew.
"Less shame," my Guide said, ever just and kind,
 "would wash away a greater fault than yours.
  Therefore, put back all sorrow from your mind;
and never forget that I am always by you
 should it occur again, as we walk on,
  that we find ourselves where others of this crew
fall to such petty wrangling and upbraiding.
The wish to hear such baseness is degrading."

Canto 31

Dante's spirits rise again as the Poets approach the central pit, a great well, at the bottom of which lies Cocytus, the ninth and final circle of Hell. Through the darkness Dante sees what appears to be a city of great towers, but as he draws near he discovers that the great shapes he has seen are the Giants and Titans who stand perpetual guard inside the well-pit with the upper halves of their bodies rising above the rim. Among the Giants, Virgil identifies Nimrod, builder of the Tower of Babel; Ephialtes and Briareus, who warred against the gods; and Tityos and Typhon, who insulted Jupiter. Also here, but for no specific offense, is Antaeus, and his presence makes it clear that the Giants are placed here less for their particular sins than for their general natures. These are the sons of earth, embodiments of elemental forces unbalanced by love, desire without restraint and without acknowledgment of moral and theological law. They are symbols of the earth-trace that every devout man must clear from his soul, the unchecked passions of the beast. Raised from the earth, they make the very gods tremble. Now they are returned to the darkness of their origins, guardians of earth's last depth. At Virgil's persuasion, Antaeus takes the Poets in his huge palm and lowers them gently to the final floor of Hell.

One and the same tongue had first wounded me
so that the blood came rushing to my cheeks,
and then supplied the soothing remedy.

Just so, as I have heard, the magic steel
  of the lance that was Achilles' and his father's
  could wound at a touch, and, at another, heal.
We turned our backs on the valley and climbed from it
  to the top of the stony bank that walls it round,
  crossing in silence to the central pit.
Here it was less than night and less than day;
  my eyes could make out little through the gloom,
  but I heard the shrill note of a trumpet bray
louder than any thunder. As if by force,
  it drew my eyes; I stared into the gloom
  along the path of the sound back to its source.   15
After the bloody rout when Charlemagne
  had lost the band of Holy Knights, Roland
  blew no more terribly for all his pain.
And as I stared through that obscurity,
  I saw what seemed a cluster of great towers,
  whereat I cried: "Master, what is this city?"
And he: "You are still too far back in the dark
  to make out clearly what you think you see;
  it is natural that you should miss the mark.
You will see clearly when you reach that place
  how much your eyes mislead you at a distance;
  I urge you, therefore, to increase your pace."
Then taking my hand in his, my Master said:
  "The better to prepare you for strange truth,
  let me explain those shapes you see ahead;   30
they are not towers but giants. They stand in the well
  from the navel down; and stationed round its bank
  they mount guard on the final pit of Hell."
Just as a man in a fog that starts to clear
  begins little by little to piece together
  the shapes the vapor crowded from the air—
so, when those shapes grew clearer as I drew
  across the darkness to the central brink,
  error fled from me, and my terror grew.
For just as at Montereggione the great towers
  crown the encircling wall—so the grim giants
  whom Jove still threatens when the thunder roars

raised from the rim of stone about that well
    the upper halves of their bodies, which loomed up
    like turrets through the murky air of Hell.   45
I had drawn close enough to one already
    to make out the great arms along his sides,
    the face, the shoulders, the breast, and most of the belly.
Nature, when she destroyed the last exemplars
    on which she formed those beasts, surely did well
    to take such executioners from Mars.
And if she has not repented the creation
    of whales and elephants, the thinking man
    will see in that her justice and discretion;
for where the instrument of intelligence
    is added to brute power and evil will,
    mankind is powerless in its own defense.
His face, it seemed to me, was quite as high
    and wide as the bronze pine cone in St. Peter's
    with the rest of him proportioned accordingly;   60
so that the bank, which made an apron for him
    from the waist down, still left so much exposed
    that three Frieslanders standing on the rim,
one on another, could not have reached his hair;
    for to that point at which men's capes are buckled,
    thirty good hand-spans of brute bulk rose clear.
"Rafel mahee amek zabi almit,"
    began a bellowed chant from the brute mouth
    for which no sweeter psalmody was fit.
And my Guide in his direction: "Babbling fool,
    stick to your horn and vent yourself with it
    when rage or passion stir your stupid soul.
Feel there around your neck, you muddlehead,
    and find the cord; and there's the horn itself,
    there on your overgrown chest." To me he said: 75
"His very babbling testifies the wrong
    he did on earth; he is Nimrod, through whose evil
    mankind no longer speaks a common tongue.
Waste no words on him; it would be foolish.
    To him all speech is meaningless; as his own,
    which no one understands, is simply gibberish."

"His very babbling testifies the wrong
he did on earth; he is Nimrod, through whose evil
mankind no longer speaks a common tongue."

Inferno

We moved on, bearing left along the pit,
   and a crossbow-shot away we found the next one,
   an even huger and more savage spirit.
What master could have bound so gross a beast
   I cannot say, but he had his right arm pinned
   behind his back, and the left across his breast
by an enormous chain that wound about him
   from the neck down, completing five great turns
   before it spiraled down below the rim.   90
"This piece of arrogance," said my Guide to me,
   "dared try his strength against the power of Jove;
   for which he is rewarded as you see.
He is Ephialtes, who made the great endeavor
   with the other giants who alarmed the gods;
   the arms he raised then, now are bound forever."
"Were it possible, I should like to take with me,"
   I said to him, "the memory of seeing
   the immeasurable Briareus." And he:
"Nearer to hand, you may observe Antaeus,
   who is able to speak to us and is not bound.
   It is he will set us down in Cocytus,
the bottom of all guilt. The other hulk
   stands far beyond our road. He, too, is bound
   and looks like this one, but with a fiercer sulk."   105
No earthquake in the fury of its shock
   ever seized a tower more violently,
   than Ephialtes, hearing, began to rock.
Then I dreaded death as never before;
   and I think I could have died for very fear
   had I not seen what manacles he wore.
We left the monster, and not far from him
   we reached Antaeus, who to his shoulders alone
   soared up a good five ells above the rim.
"O soul who once in Zama's fateful vale—
   where Scipio became the heir of glory
   when Hannibal and all his troops turned tail—
took more than a thousand lions for your prey,
   and in whose memory many still believe
   the sons of earth would yet have won the day   120

169

had you joined with them against High Olympus,
  do not disdain to do us a small service,
  but set us down where the cold grips Cocytus.
Would you have us go to Tityos or Typhon?—
  this man can give you what is longed for here;
  therefore do not refuse him, but bend down.
For he can still make new your memory:
  he lives, and awaits long life, unless grace call him
  before his time to his felicity."
Thus my Master to that tower of pride;
  and the giant without delay reached out the hands
  which Hercules had felt and raised my Guide.
Virgil, when he felt himself so grasped,
  called to me: "Come, and I will hold you safe."
  And he took me in his arms and held me clasped.   135
The way the Carisenda seems to one
  who looks up from the leaning side when clouds
  are going over it from that direction,
making the whole tower seem to topple—so
  Antaeus seemed to me in the fraught moment
  when I stood clinging, watching from below
as he bent down; while I with heart and soul
  wished we had gone some other way, but gently
  he set us down inside the final hole
whose ice holds Judas and Lucifer in its grip.
Then straightened like a mast above a ship.

Canto 32

At the bottom of the well Dante finds himself on a huge frozen lake. This is Cocytus, the ninth circle, the fourth and last great water of Hell, and here, fixed in the ice, each according to his guilt, are punished sinners guilty of treachery against those to whom they were bound by special ties. The ice is divided into four concentric rings marked only by the different positions of the damned within the ice. This is Dante's symbolic equivalent of the final guilt. The treacheries of these souls were denials of love, which is God, and of all human warmth. Only the remorseless dead center of the ice will serve to express their natures. As they denied God's love, so are they furthest removed from the light and warmth of His sun. As they denied all human ties, so are they bound only by the unyielding ice. The first round is Caïna, named for Cain. Here lie those guilty of Treachery Against Blood Ties. They have their necks and heads out of the ice and are permitted to bow their heads—a double boon since it allows them some protection from the freezing gale and, further, allows their tears to fall without freezing their eyes shut. Here Dante sees Alessandro and Napoleone degli Alberti, and he speaks to Camicion, who identifies other sinners of his round. The second round is Antenora, named for Antenor, the Trojan who was believed to have betrayed his city to the Greeks. Here lie those guilty of Treachery to Country. They, too, have their heads above the ice, but they cannot bend their necks, which are gripped by the ice. Here Dante accidentally kicks the head of Bocca degli Abbati and then treats him with a savagery he has shown to no other soul in Hell. Bocca names some of his fellow traitors, and the Poets pass on to discover two heads frozen together in one hole. One of them is gnawing the nape of the other's neck.

The Divine Comedy

If I had rhymes as harsh and horrible
   as the hard fact of that final dismal hole
   which bears the weight of all the steeps of Hell,
I might more fully press the sap and substance
   from my conception; but since I must do
   without them, I begin with some reluctance.
For it is no easy undertaking, I say,
   to describe the bottom of the universe;
   nor is it for tongues that only babble child's play.
But may those Ladies of the Heavenly Spring
   who helped Amphion wall Thebes, assist my verse,
   that the word may be the mirror of the thing.
O most miscreant rabble, you who keep
   the stations of that place whose name is pain,
   better had you been born as goats or sheep!   15
We stood now in the dark pit of the well,
   far down the slope below the Giant's feet,
   and while I still stared up at the great wall,
I heard a voice cry: "Watch which way you turn;
   take care you do not trample on the heads
   of the forworn and miserable brethren."
Whereat I turned and saw beneath my feet
   and stretching out ahead, a lake so frozen
   it seemed to be made of glass. So thick a sheet
never yet hid the Danube's winter course,
   nor, far away beneath the frigid sky,
   locked the Don up in its frozen source;
for were Tanbernick and the enormous peak
   of Pietrapana to crash down on it,
   not even the edges would so much as creak.   30
The way frogs sit to croak, their muzzles leaning
   out of the water, at the time and season
   when the peasant woman dreams of her day's gleaning—
just so the livid dead are sealed in place
   up to the part at which they blushed for shame,
   and they beat their teeth like storks. Each holds his face
bowed toward the ice, each of them testifies
   to the cold with his chattering mouth, to his heart's grief
   with tears that flood forever from his eyes.

When I had stared about me, I looked down
  and at my feet I saw two clamped together
  so tightly that the hair of their heads had grown
together. "Who are you," I said, "who lie
  so tightly breast to breast?" They strained their necks,
  and when they had raised their heads as if to reply,   45
the tears their eyes had managed to contain
  up to that time gushed out, and the cold froze them
  between the lids, sealing them shut again
tighter than any clamp grips wood to wood,
  and mad with pain, they fell to butting heads
  like billy goats in a sudden savage mood.
And a wraith who lay to one side and below,
  and who had lost both ears to frostbite, said,
  his head still bowed: "Why do you watch us so?
If you wish to know who they are who share one doom,
  they owned the Bisenzio's valley with their father,
  whose name was Albert. They sprang from one womb,
and you may search through all Caïna's crew
  without discovering in all this waste
  a squab more fit for the aspic than these two;   60
not him whose breast and shadow a single blow
  of the great lance of King Arthur pierced with light;
  nor yet Focaccia; nor this one fastened so
into the ice that his head is all I see,
  and whom, if you are Tuscan, you know well—
  his name on the earth was Sassol Mascheroni.
And I—to tell you all and so be through—
  was Camicion de' Pazzi. I wait for Carlin
  beside whose guilt my sins will shine like virtue."
And leaving him, I saw a thousand faces
  discolored so by cold, I shudder yet
  and always will when I think of those frozen places.
As we approached the center of all weight,
  where I went shivering in eternal shade,
  whether it was my will, or chance, or fate,   75
I cannot say, but as I trailed my Guide
  among those heads, my foot struck violently
  against the face of one. Weeping, it cried:

"Why do you kick me? If you were not sent
  to wreak a further vengeance for Montaperti,
  why do you add this to my other torment?"
"Master," I said, "grant me a moment's pause
  to rid myself of a doubt concerning this one;
  then you may hurry me at your own pace."
The Master stopped at once, and through the volley
  of foul abuse the wretch poured out, I said:
  "Who are you who curse others so?" And he:
"And who are *you* who go through the dead larder
  of Antenora kicking the cheeks of others
  so hard, that were you alive, you could not kick harder?"   90
"*I am* alive," I said, "and if you seek fame,
  it may be precious to you above all else
  that my notes on this descent include your name."
"Exactly the opposite is my wish and hope,"
  he answered. "Let me be; for it's little you know
  of how to flatter on this icy slope."
I grabbed the hair of his dog's ruff and I said:
  "Either you tell me truly who you are,
  or you won't have a hair left on your head."
And he: "Not though you snatch me bald. I swear
  I will not tell my name nor show my face.
  Not though you rip until my brain lies bare."
I had a good grip on his hair; already
  I had yanked out more than one fistful of it,
  while the wretch yelped, but kept his face turned from me;   105
when another said: "Bocca, what is it ails you?
  What the Hell's wrong? Isn't it bad enough
  to hear you bang your jaws? Must you bark too?"
"Now filthy traitor, say no more!" I cried,
  "for to your shame, be sure I shall bear back
  a true report of you." The wretch replied:
"Say anything you please but go away.
  And if you *do* get back, don't overlook
  that pretty one who had so much to say
just now. Here he laments the Frenchman's price.
  'I saw Buoso da Duera,' you can report,
  'where the bad salad is kept crisp on ice.'

And if you're asked who else was wintering here,
    Beccheria, whose throat was slit by Florence,
    is there beside you. Gianni de' Soldanier   120
is further down, I think, with Ganelon,
    and Tebaldello, who opened the gates of Faenza
    and let Bologna steal in with the dawn.''
Leaving him then, I saw two souls together
    in a single hole, and so pinched in by the ice
    that one head made a helmet for the other.
As a famished man chews crusts—so the one sinner
    sunk his teeth into the other's nape
    at the base of the skull, gnawing his loathsome dinner.
Tydeus in his final raging hour
    gnawed Menalippus' head with no more fury
    than this one gnawed at skull and dripping gore.
"You there," I said, "who show so odiously
    your hatred for that other, tell me why
    on this condition; that if in what you tell me   135
you seem to have a reasonable complaint
    against him you devour with such foul relish,
    I, knowing who you are, and his soul's taint,
may speak your cause to living memory,
God willing the power of speech be left to me.''

Canto 33

*In reply to Dante's exhortation, the sin-
ner who is gnawing his companion's head looks
up, wipes his bloody mouth on his victim's hair,
and tells his harrowing story. He is Count Ugolino and the wretch he gnaws is Archbishop Ruggieri. Both are in Antenora for treason. In life
they had once plotted together. Then Ruggieri
betrayed his fellow-plotter and caused his death
by starvation, and that of Ugolino's four sons. In
the most pathetic and dramatic passage of the
Inferno, Ugolino details how their prison was
sealed and how his sons dropped dead before him
one by one, weeping for food. His terrible tale
serves only to renew his grief and hatred, and he
has hardly finished it before he begins to gnaw
Ruggieri again with renewed fury. In the immuta-
ble law of Hell, the killer-by-starvation becomes
the food of his victim. The Poets leave Ugolino
and enter Ptolomea, so named for the Ptolomaeus
of Maccabees, who murdered his father-in-law at
a banquet. Here are punished those who were
Treacherous Against the Ties of Hospitality. They
lie with only half their faces above the ice and
their tears freeze in their eye sockets, sealing
them with little crystal visors. Thus even the
comfort of tears is denied them. Here Dante finds
Friar Alberigo and Branca d'Oria, and discovers
the terrible power of Ptolomea: so great is its sin
that the souls of the guilty fall to its torments
before they die, leaving their bodies still
on earth, inhabited by demons.*

The sinner raised his mouth from his grim repast
and wiped it on the hair of the bloody head
whose nape he had all but eaten away. At last

he began to speak: "You ask me to renew
  a grief so desperate that the very thought
  of speaking of it tears my heart in two.
But if my words may be a seed that bears
  the fruit of infamy for him I gnaw,
  I shall weep, but tell my story through my tears.
Who you may be, and by what powers you reach
  into this underworld, I cannot guess,
  but you seem to me a Florentine by your speech.
I was Count Ugolino, I must explain;
  this reverend grace is the Archbishop Ruggieri;
  now I will tell you why I gnaw his brain.   15
That I, who trusted him, had to undergo
  imprisonment and death through his treachery,
  you will know already. What you cannot know—
that is, the lingering inhumanity
  of the death I suffered—you shall hear in full;
  then judge for yourself if he has injured me.
A narrow window in that coop of stone
  now called the Tower of Hunger for my sake
  (within which others yet must pace alone)
had shown me several waning moons already
  between its bars, when I slept the evil sleep
  in which the veil of the future parted for me.
This beast appeared as master of a hunt
  chasing the wolf and his whelps across the mountain
  that hides Lucca from Pisa. Out in front   30
of the starved and shrewd and avid pack he had placed
  Gualandi and Sismondi and Lanfranchi
  to point his prey. The father and sons had raced
a brief course only when they failed of breath
  and seemed to weaken; then I thought I saw
  their flanks ripped open by the hounds' fierce teeth.
Before the dawn, the dream still in my head,
  I woke and heard my sons, who were there with me,
  cry from their troubled sleep, asking for bread.
You are cruelty itself if you can keep
  your tears back at the thought of what foreboding
  stirred in my heart; and if you do not weep,

at what are you used to weeping?—The hour when food
   used to be brought, drew near. They were now awake,
   and each was anxious from his dream's dark mood.   45
And from the base of that horrible tower I heard
   the sound of hammers nailing up the gates;
   I stared at my sons' faces without a word.
I did not weep: I had turned stone inside.
   They wept. 'What ails you, Father, you look so strange,'
   my little Anselm, youngest of them, cried.
But I did not speak a word nor shed a tear;
   not all that day nor all that endless night,
   until I saw another sun appear.
When a tiny ray leaked into that dark prison
   and I saw staring back from their four faces
   the terror and the wasting of my own,
I bit my hands in helpless grief. And they,
   thinking I chewed myself for hunger, rose
   suddenly together. I heard them say: 60
'Father, it would give us much less pain
   if you ate us; it was you who put upon us
   this sorry flesh; now strip it off again.'
I calmed myself to spare them. Ah! hard earth,
   why did you not yawn open? All that day
   and the next we sat in silence. On the fourth,
Gaddo, the eldest, fell before me and cried,
   stretched at my feet upon that prison floor:
   'Father, why don't you help me?' There he died.
And just as you see me, I saw them fall
   one by one on the fifth day and the sixth.
   Then, already blind, I began to crawl
from body to body shaking them frantically.
   Two days I called their names, and they were dead.
   Then fasting overcame my grief and me."   75
His eyes narrowed to slits when he was done,
   and he seized the skull again between his teeth
   grinding it as a mastiff grinds a bone.
Ah, Pisa! foulest blemish on the land
   where "*si*" sounds sweet and clear, since those nearby you
   are slow to blast the ground on which you stand,

may Caprara and Gorgona drift from place
 and dam the flooding Arno at its mouth
 until it drowns the last of your foul race!
For if to Ugolino falls the censure
 for having betrayed your castles, you for your part
 should not have put his sons to such a torture;
you modern Thebes! those tender lives you split—
 Brigata, Uguccione, and the others
 I mentioned earlier—were too young for guilt!   90
We passed on further, where the frozen mine
 entombs another crew in greater pain;
 these wraiths are not bent over, but lie supine.
Their very weeping closes up their eyes;
 and the grief that finds no outlet for its tears
 turns inward to increase their agonies;
for the first tears that they shed knot instantly
 in their eye sockets, and as they freeze they form
 a crystal visor above the cavity.
And despite the fact that standing in that place
 I had become as numb as any callus,
 and all sensation had faded from my face,
somehow I felt a wind begin to blow,
 whereat I said: "Master, what stirs this wind?
 Is not all heat extinguished here below?"   105
And the Master said to me: "Soon you will be
 where your own eyes will see the source and cause
 and give you their own answer to the mystery."
And one of those locked in that icy mall
 cried out to us as we passed: "O souls so cruel
 that you are sent to the last post of all,
relieve me for a little from the pain
 of this hard veil; let my heart weep awhile
 before the weeping freeze my eyes again."
And I to him: "If you would have my service,
 tell me your name; then if I do not help you
 may I descend to the last rim of the ice."
"I am Friar Alberigo," he answered therefore,
 "the same who called for the fruits from the bad garden.
 Here I am given dates for figs full store."   120

"What! Are you dead already?" I said to him.
 And he then: "How my body stands in the world
 I do not know. So privileged is this rim
of Ptolomea, that often souls fall to it
 before dark Atropos has cut their thread.
 And that you may more willingly free my spirit
of this glaze of frozen tears that shrouds my face,
 I will tell you this: when a soul betrays as I did,
 it falls from flesh, and a demon takes its place,
ruling the body till its time is spent.
 The ruined soul rains down into this cistern.
 So, I believe, there is still evident
in the world above, all that is fair and mortal
 of this black shade who winters here behind me.
 If you have only recently crossed the portal   135
from that sweet world, you surely must have known
 his body; Branca d'Oria is its name,
 and many years have passed since he rained down."
"I think you are trying to take me in," I said,
 "Ser Branca d'Oria is a living man;
 he eats, he drinks, he fills his clothes and his bed."
"Michel Zanche had not yet reached the ditch
 of the Black Talons," the frozen wraith replied,
 "there where the sinners thicken in hot pitch,
when this one left his body to a devil,
 as did his nephew and second in treachery,
 and plumbed like lead through space to this dead level.
But now reach out your hand, and let me cry."
 And I did not keep the promise I had made,
 for to be rude to him was courtesy.   150
Ah, men of Genoa! souls of little worth,
 corrupted from all custom of righteousness,
 why have you not been driven from the earth?
For there beside the blackest soul of all
 Romagna's evil plain, lies one of yours
 bathing his filthy soul in the eternal
glacier of Cocytus for his foul crime,
while he seems yet alive in world and time!

Canto 34

"On march the banners of the King," Virgil begins as the Poets face the last depth. He is quoting a medieval hymn, and to it he adds the distortion and perversion of all that lies about him: "On march the banners of the King—of Hell." And there before them, in an infernal parody of Godhead, they see Satan in the distance, his great wings beating like a windmill. It is their beating that is the source of the icy wind of Cocytus, the exhalation of all evil. All about him in the ice are strewn the sinners of the last round, Judecca, named for Judas Iscariot. These are the Treacherous to Their Masters. They lie completely sealed in the ice, twisted and distorted into every conceivable posture. It is impossible to speak to them, and the Poets move on to observe Satan. He is fixed into the ice at the center to which flow all the rivers of guilt; and as he beats his great wings as if to escape, their icy wind only freezes him more surely into the polluted ice. In a grotesque parody of the Trinity, he has three faces, each a different color, and in each mouth he clamps a sinner whom he rips eternally with his teeth. Judas Iscariot is in the central mouth; Brutus and Cassius in the mouths of either side. Having seen all, the Poets now climb through the center, grappling hand over hand down the hairy flank of Satan himself—a last supremely symbolic action—and at last, when they have passed the center of all gravity, they emerge from Hell. A long climb from the earth's center to the Mount of Purgatory awaits them, and they push on without rest, ascending along the sides of the river Lethe, till they emerge once more to see the stars of Heaven, just before dawn on Easter Sunday.

The Divine Comedy

"On march the banners of the King of Hell,"
    my Master said. "Toward us. Look straight ahead;
    can you make him out at the core of the frozen shell?"
Like a whirling windmill seen afar at twilight,
    or when a mist has risen from the ground—
    just such an engine rose upon my sight
stirring up such a wild and bitter wind
    I cowered for shelter at my Master's back,
    there being no other windbreak I could find.
I stood now where the souls of the last class
    (with fear my verses tell it) were covered wholly;
    they shone below the ice like straws in glass.
Some lie stretched out; others are fixed in place
    upright, some on their heads, some on their soles;
    another, like a bow, bends foot to face. 15
When we had gone so far across the ice
    that it pleased my Guide to show me the foul creature
    which once had worn the grace of Paradise,
he made me stop, and, stepping aside, he said:
    "Now see the face of Dis! This is the place
    where you must arm your soul against all dread."
Do not ask, reader, how my blood ran cold
    and my voice choked up with fear. I cannot write it;
    this is a terror that cannot be told.
I did not die, and yet I lost life's breath;
    imagine for yourself what I became,
    deprived at once of both my life and death.
The Emperor of the Universe of Pain
    jutted his upper chest above the ice;
    and I am closer in size to the great mountain 30
the Titans make around the central pit,
    than they to his arms. Now, starting from this part,
    imagine the whole that corresponds to it!
If he was once as beautiful as now
    he is hideous, and still turned on his Maker,
    well may he be the source of every woe!
With what a sense of awe I saw his head
    towering above me! for it had three faces:
    one was in front, and it was fiery red;

the other two, as weirdly wonderful,
    merged with it from the middle of each shoulder
    to the point where all converged at the top of the skull;
the right was something between white and bile;
    the left was about the color that one finds
    on those who live along the banks of the Nile.   45
Under each head two wings rose terribly,
    their span proportioned to so gross a bird,
    I never saw such sails upon the sea.
They were not feathers—their texture and their form
    were like a bat's wings—and he beat them so
    that three winds blew from him in one great storm:
it is these winds that freeze all Cocytus.
    He wept from his six eyes, and down three chins
    the tears ran mixed with bloody froth and pus.
In every mouth he worked a broken sinner
    between his rakelike teeth. Thus he kept three
    in eternal pain at his eternal dinner.
For the one in front the biting seemed to play
    no part at all compared to the ripping; at times
    the whole skin of his back was flayed away.   60
"That soul that suffers most," explained my Guide,
    "is Judas Iscariot, he who kicks his legs
    on the fiery chin and has his head inside.
Of the other two, who have their heads thrust forward,
    the one who dangles down from the black face
    is Brutus; note how he writhes without a word.
And there, with the huge and sinewy arms, is the soul
    of Cassius—but the night is coming on
    and we must go, for we have seen the whole."
Then, as he bade, I clasped his neck, and he,
    watching for a moment when the wings
    were opened wide, reached over dexterously
and seized the shaggy coat of the king demon;
    then grappling matted hair and frozen crusts
    from one tuft to another, clambered down.   75
When we had reached the joint where the great thigh
    merges into the swelling of the haunch,
    my Guide and Master, straining terribly,

turned his head to where his feet had been
    and began to grip the hair as if he were climbing;
    so that I thought we moved toward Hell again.
"Hold fast!" my Guide said, and his breath came shrill
    with labor and exhaustion. "There is no way
    but by such stairs to rise above such evil."
At last he climbed out through an opening
    in the central rock, and he seated me on the rim;
    then joined me with a nimble backward spring.
I looked up, thinking to see Lucifer
    as I had left him, and I saw instead
    his legs projecting high into the air.   90
Now let all those whose dull minds are still vexed
    by failure to understand what point it was
    I had passed through, judge if I was perplexed.
"Get up. Up on your feet," my Master said.
    "The sun already mounts to middle tierce,
    and a long road and hard climbing lie ahead."
It was no hall of state we had found there,
    but a natural animal pit hollowed from rock
    with a broken floor and a close and sunless air.
"Before I tear myself from the abyss,"
    I said when I had risen, "O my Master,
    explain to me my error in all this.
Where is the ice? and Lucifer—how has he
    been turned from top to bottom? and how can the sun
    have gone from night to day so suddenly?"   105
And he to me: "You imagine you are still
    on the other side of the center where I grasped
    the shaggy flank of the Great Worm of Evil
which bores through the world—you *were* while I climbed down,
    but when I turned myself about, you passed
    the point to which all gravities are drawn.
You are under the other hemisphere where you stand;
    the sky above us is the half opposed
    to that which canopies the great dry land.
Under the midpoint of that other sky
    the Man who was born sinless and who lived
    beyond all blemish came to suffer and die.

My Guide and I crossed over and began
　to mount that little known and lightless road
　to ascend into the shining world again.

You have your feet upon a little sphere
   which forms the other face of the Judecca.
   There it is evening when it is morning here.   120
And this gross fiend and image of all evil
   who made a stairway for us with his hide
   is pinched and prisoned in the ice pack still.
On this side he plunged down from Heaven's height,
   and the land that spread here once hid in the sea
   and fled north to our hemisphere for fright;
and it may be that moved by that same fear,
   the one peak that still rises on this side
   fled upward leaving this great cavern here."
Down there, beginning at the further bound
   of Beelzebub's dim tomb, there is a space
   not known by sight, but only by the sound
of a little stream descending through the hollow
   it has eroded from the massive stone
   in its endlessly entwining lazy flow.   135
My Guide and I crossed over and began
   to mount that little known and lightless road
   to ascend into the shining world again.
He first, I second, without thought of rest,
   we climbed the dark until we reached the point
   where a round opening brought in sight the blest
and beauteous shining of the heavenly cars.
And we walked out once more beneath the stars.

Purgatorio

Canto 1

The Poets emerge from Hell just before dawn of Easter Sunday (April 10, 1300), and Dante revels in the sight of the rediscovered heavens. As he looks eagerly about at the stars, he sees nearby an old man of impressive bearing. The ancient is Cato of Utica, guardian of the shores of Purgatory. Cato challenges the Poets as fugitives from Hell, but Virgil, after first instructing Dante to kneel in reverence, explains Dante's mission and Beatrice's command. Cato then gives them instructions for proceeding. The Poets have emerged at a point a short way up the slope of Purgatory. It is essential, therefore, that they descend to the lowest point and begin from there, an allegory of Humility. Cato, accordingly, orders Virgil to lead Dante to the shore, to wet his hands in the dew of the new morning, and to wash the stains of Hell from Dante's face and the film of Hell's vapors from Dante's eyes. Virgil is then to bind about Dante's waist one of the pliant reeds, symbolizing Humility, that grow in the soft mud of the shore. Having so commanded, Cato disappears. Dante arises in silence and stands waiting, eager to begin. His look is all the communication that is necessary. Virgil leads him to the shore and performs all that Cato has commanded. Dante's first purification is marked by a miracle: when Virgil takes a reed, the stalk immediately regenerates a new reed, restoring itself exactly as it had been.

f OR BETTER waters now the little bark
of my indwelling powers raises her sails
and leaves behind that sea so cruel and dark.

Now shall I sing that second kingdom given
  the soul of man wherein to purge its guilt
  and so grow worthy to ascend to Heaven.
Yours am I, sacred Muses! To you I pray.
  Here let dead poetry rise once more to life,
  and here let sweet Calliope rise and play
some far accompaniment in that high strain
  whose power the wretched Pierides once felt
  so terribly they dared not hope again.
Sweet azure of the sapphire of the east
  was gathering on the serene horizon
  its pure and perfect radiance—a feast   15
to my glad eyes, reborn to their delight,
  as soon as I had passed from the dead air
  which had oppressed my soul and dimmed my sight.
The planet whose sweet influence strengthens love
  was making all the east laugh with her rays,
  veiling the Fishes, which she swam above.
I turned then to my right and set my mind
  on the other pole, and there I saw four stars
  unseen by mortals since the first mankind.
The heavens seemed to revel in their light.
  O widowed northern hemisphere, bereft
  forever of the glory of that sight!
As I broke off my gazing, my eyes veered
  a little to the left, to the other pole
  from which, by then, the Wain had disappeared.   30
I saw, nearby, an ancient man, alone.
  His bearing filled me with such reverence,
  no father could ask more from his best son.
His beard was long and touched with strands of white,
  as was his hair, of which two tresses fell
  over his breast. Rays of the holy light
that fell from the four stars made his face glow
  with such a radiance that he looked to me
  as if he faced the sun. And standing so,
he moved his venerable plumes and said:
  "Who are you two who climb by the dark stream
  to escape the eternal prison of the dead?

The planet whose sweet influence strengthens love
was making all the east laugh with her rays,
veiling the Fishes, which she swam above.

Who led you? or what served you as a light
  in your dark flight from the eternal valley,
  which lies forever blind in darkest night?   45
Are the laws of the pit so broken? Or is new counsel
  published in Heaven that the damned may wander
  onto my rocks from the abyss of Hell? "
At that my Master laid his hands upon me,
  instructing me by word and touch and gesture
  to show my reverence in brow and knee,
then answered him: "I do not come this way
  of my own will or powers. A Heavenly Lady
  sent me to this man's aid in his dark day.
But since your will is to know more, my will
  cannot deny you; I will tell you truly
  why we have come and how. This man has still
to see his final hour, though in the burning
  of his own madness he had drawn so near it
  his time was perilously short for turning.   60
As I have told you, I was sent to show
  the way his soul must take for its salvation;
  and there is none but this by which I go.
I have shown him the guilty people. Now I mean
  to lead him through the spirits in your keeping,
  to show him those whose suffering makes them clean.
By what means I have led him to this strand
  to see and hear you, takes too long to tell;
  from Heaven is the power and the command.
Now may his coming please you, for he goes
  to win his freedom; and how dear that is
  the man who gives his life for it best knows.
You know it, who in that cause found death sweet
  in Utica where you put off that flesh
  which shall rise radiant at the Judgment Seat.   75
We do not break the laws; this man lives yet,
  and I am of that round not ruled by Minos,
  with your own Marcia, whose chaste eyes seem set
in endless prayers to you. O blessed breast
  to hold her yet your own! for love of her
  grant us permission to pursue our quest

across your seven kingdoms. When I go
   back to her side I shall bear thanks of you,
   if you will let me speak your name below."
"Marcia was so pleasing in my eyes
   there on the other side," he answered then,
   "that all she asked, I did. Now that she lies
beyond the evil river, no word or prayer
   of hers may move me. Such was the decree
   pronounced upon us when I rose from there.   90
But if, as you have said, a Heavenly Dame
   orders your way, there is no need to flatter;
   you need but ask it of me in her name.
Go then, and lead this man, but first see to it
   you bind a smooth green reed about his waist
   and clean his face of all trace of the pit.
For it would not be right that one with eyes
   still filmed by mist should go before the angel
   who guards the Gate; he is from Paradise.
All round the wave-wracked shoreline, there below,
   reeds grow in the soft mud. Along that edge
   no foliate nor woody plant could grow,
for what lives in that buffeting must bend.
   Do not come back this way; the rising sun
   will light an easier way you may ascend."   105
With that he disappeared; and silently
   I rose and moved back till I faced my Guide,
   my eyes upon him, waiting. He said to me:
"Follow my steps and let us turn again;
   along this side there is a gentle slope
   that leads to the low boundaries of the plain."
The dawn, in triumph, made the day-breeze flee
   before its coming, so that from afar
   I recognized the trembling of the sea.
We strode across that lonely plain like men
   who seek the road they strayed from and who count
   the time lost till they find it once again.
When we had reached a place along the way
   where the cool morning breeze shielded the dew
   against the first heat of the gathering day,   120

with gentle graces my sweet Master bent
   and laid both outspread palms upon the grass.
   Then I, being well aware of his intent,
lifted my tear-stained cheeks to him, and there
   he made me clean, revealing my true color
   under the residues of Hell's black air.
We moved on then to the deserted strand
   which never yet has seen upon its waters
   a man who found his way back to dry land.
There, as it pleased another, he girded me.
   Wonder of wonders! when he plucked a reed
   another took its place there instantly,
arising from the humble stalk he tore
so that it grew exactly as before.

Canto 2

It is dawn. Dante, washed, and girded by
the reed, is standing by the shore when he sees a
light approaching at enormous speed across the
sea. The light grows and becomes visible as the
Angel Boatman who ferries the souls of the elect
from their gathering place at the mouth of the
Tiber to the shore of Purgatory. The newly arrived
souls debark and, taking the Poets as familiars of
the place, ask directions. Virgil explains that he
and Dante are new arrivals but that they have
come by the dark road through Hell. The newly
arrived souls see by his breathing that Dante is
alive and crowd about him. One of the new souls
is Casella, a musician who seems to have been a
dear friend of Dante's. Dante tries three times to
clasp him to his bosom, but each time his arms
pass through empty air. Casella explains the func-
tion of the Angel Boatman and then, at Dante's
request, strikes up a song, one of Dante's own
canzone that Casella had set to music. Instantly,
Cato descends upon the group, berating them,
and they break like startled pigeons up
the slope toward the mountain.

The sun already burned at the horizon,
   while the high point of its meridian circle
   covered Jerusalem, and in opposition
equal Night revolved above the Ganges
   bearing the Scales that fall out of her hand
   as she grows longer with the season's changes;
thus, where I was, Aurora in her passage
   was losing the pale blushes from her cheeks
   which turned to orange with increasing age.

We were still standing by the sea's new day
  like travelers pondering the road ahead
  who send their souls on while their bones delay;
when low above the ocean's western rim,
  as Mars, at times, observed through the thick vapors
  that form before the dawn, burns red and slim,   15
just so—so may I hope to see it again!—
  a light appeared, moving above the sea
  faster than any flight. A moment then
I turned my eyes to question my sweet Guide,
  and when I looked back to that unknown body
  I found its mass and brightness magnified.
Then from each side of it came into view
  an unknown something white; and from beneath it,
  bit by bit, another whiteness grew.
We watched till the white objects at each side
  took shape as wings, and Virgil spoke no word.
  But when he saw what wings they were, he cried:
"Down on your knees! It is God's angel comes!
  Down! Fold your hands! From now on you shall see
  many such ministers in the high kingdoms.   30
See how he scorns man's tools; he needs no oars
  nor any other sail than his own wings
  to carry him between such distant shores.
See how his pinions tower upon the air,
  pointing to Heaven; they are eternal plumes
  and do not moult like feathers or human hair."
Then as that bird of Heaven closed the distance
  between us, he grew brighter and yet brighter
  until I could no longer bear the radiance
and bowed my head. He steered straight for the shore,
  his ship so light and swift it drew no water;
  it did not seem to sail so much as soar.
Astern stood the great pilot of the Lord,
  so fair his blessedness seemed written on him;
  and more than a hundred souls were seated forward,   45
singing as if they raised a single voice
  in exitu Israel de Aegypto.
  Verse after verse they made the air rejoice.

"Down on your knees! It is God's angel comes!
Down! Fold your hands!"

The angel made the sign of the cross, and they
   cast themselves, at his signal, to the shore.
   Then, swiftly as he had come, he went away.
The throng he left seemed not to understand
   what place it was, but stood and stared about
   like men who see the first of a new land.
The sun, who with an arrow in each ray
   had chased the Goat out of the height of heaven,
   on every hand was shooting forth the day,
when those new souls looked up to where my Guide
   and I stood, saying to us: "If you know it,
   show us the road that climbs the mountainside."   60
Virgil replied: "You think perhaps we two
   have had some long experience of this place,
   but we are also pilgrims, come before you
only by very little, though by a way
   so steep, so broken, and so tortuous
   the climb ahead of us will seem like play."
The throng of souls, observing by my breath
   I was still in the body I was born to,
   stared in amazement and grew pale as death.
As a crowd, eager for news, will all but smother
   a messenger who bears the olive branch,
   and not care how they trample one another—
so these, each one of them a soul elect,
   pushed close to stare at me, well-nigh forgetting
   the way to go to make their beauty perfect.   75
One came forward to embrace me, and his face
   shone with such joyous love that, seeing it,
   I moved to greet him with a like embrace.
O solid seeming shadows! Three times there
   I clasped my hands behind him, and three times
   I drew them to my breast through empty air.
Amazed, I must have lost all color then,
   for he smiled tenderly and drew away,
   and I lunged forward as if to try again.
In a voice as gentle as a melody
   he bade me pause; and by his voice I knew him,
   and begged him stay awhile and speak to me.

He answered: "As I loved you in the clay
    of my mortal body, so do I love you freed;
    therefore I pause. But what brings you this way?"   90
"Casella mine, I go the way I do
    in the hope I may return here," I replied.
    "But why has so much time been taken from you?"
And he: "I am not wronged if he whose usage
    accepts the soul at his own time and pleasure
    has many times refused to give me passage;
his will moves in the image and perfection
    of a Just Will; indeed, for three months now
    he has taken all who asked, without exception.
And so it was that in my turn I stood
    upon that shore where Tiber's stream grows salt,
    and there was gathered to my present good.
It is back to the Tiber's mouth he has just flown,
    for there forever is the gathering place
    of all who do not sink to Acheron."   105
"If no new law has stripped you of your skill
    or of the memory of those songs of love
    that once could calm all passion from my will,"
I said to him, "oh, sound a verse once more
    to soothe my soul which, with its weight of flesh
    and the long journey, sinks distressed and sore."
"Love that speaks its reasons in my heart,"
    he sang then, and such grace flowed on the air
    that even now I hear that music start.
My Guide and I and all those souls of bliss
    stood tranced in song, when suddenly we heard
    the noble Elder cry: "What's this! What's this!
Negligence! Loitering! O laggard crew,
    run to the mountain and strip off the scurf
    that lets not God be manifest in you!"   120
Exactly as a flock of pigeons gleaning
    a field of stubble, pecking busily,
    forgetting all their primping and their preening,
will rise as one and scatter through the air,
    leaving their feast without another thought
    when they are taken by a sudden scare—

so that new band, all thought of pleasure gone,
  broke from the feast of music with a start
  and scattered for the mountainside like one
who leaps and does not look where he will land.
Nor were my Guide and I inclined to stand.

Canto 3

*The souls scatter for the mountain, and
Dante draws close to Virgil as they both race
ahead. The newly risen sun is at Dante's back. He
runs, therefore, with his shadow stretched long
and directly before him. Suddenly he becomes
aware that there is only one shadow on the
ground and he turns in panic, thinking Virgil is no
longer at his side. Virgil reassures him, explaining
that souls are so made as to cast no shadows. His
remarks on the nature of souls give him occasion
to define the limits of reason in the scheme of creation. The Poets reach the base of the cliff and are
dismayed to find that it rises sheer, offering no
way by which they may climb. While Virgil is
pondering this new difficulty, Dante looks about
and sees a band of souls approaching so slowly
that they seem scarcely to move. These are the
first of the Late Repentant souls the Poets will
encounter. In life they put off the desire for grace;
now, as they were laggard in life, so must they
wait before they may begin their purification. The
souls in this band are all souls of the Contumacious; they died excommunicated, but surrendered their souls to God when they were at the
point of death. Their punishment is that they
must wait here at the base of the cliff for thirty
times the period of their contumacy. One soul
among them identifies himself as Manfred and
begs Dante to bear a message to his daughter
Constance in order that she may offer prayer for
Manfred's soul and thereby shorten his period of
waiting. Manfred explains that prayer can greatly
assist the souls in Purgatory. He also explains that
though contumacy is punished, no act of priest
or Pope may keep from salvation a soul
that has truly given itself to God.*

Those routed souls scattered across the scene,
  their faces once again turned toward the mountain
  where Reason spurs and Justice picks us clean;
but I drew ever closer to my Guide;
  and how could I have run my course without him?
  who would have led me up the mountainside?
He seemed gnawed by remorse for his offense.
  O noble conscience without stain! how sharp
  the sting of a small fault is to your sense!
When he had checked that haste that urges men
  to mar the dignity of every act,
  my mind, forced in upon itself till then,
broke free; and eager to see all before me,
  I raised my eyes in wonder to that mountain
  that soars highest to Heaven from the sea.   15
Low at my back, the sun was a red blaze;
  its light fell on the ground before me broken
  in the form in which my body blocked its rays.
I gave a start of fear and whirled around
  seized by the thought that I had been abandoned,
  for I saw one shadow only on the ground.
And my Comfort turned full to me then to say:
  "Why are you still uncertain? Why do you doubt
  that I am here and guide you on your way?
Vespers have rung already on the tomb
  of the body in which I used to cast a shadow.
  It was taken to Naples from Brindisium.
If now I cast no shadow, should that fact
  amaze you more than the heavens which pass the light
  undimmed from one to another? We react   30
within these bodies to pain and heat and cold
  according to the workings of that Will
  which does not will that all Its ways be told.
He is insane who dreams that he may learn
  by mortal reasoning the boundless orbit
  Three Persons in One Substance fill and turn.
Be satisfied with the *quia* of cause unknown,
  O humankind! for could you have seen All,
  Mary need not have suffered to bear a son.

Purgatorio

You saw how some yearn endlessly in vain;
  such as would, else, have surely had their wish,
  but have, instead, its hunger as their pain.
I speak of Aristotle and Plato," he said.
  "Of them and many more." And here he paused,
  and, sorrowing and silent, bowed his head.   45
Meanwhile we reached the mountain's foot; and there
  we found so sheer a cliff, the nimblest legs
  would not have served, unless they walked on air.
The most forsaken and most broken goat-trace
  in the mountains between Lerici and Turbia
  compared to this would seem a gracious staircase.
My Guide exclaimed: "Now who is there to say
  in which direction we may find some slope
  up which one without wings may pick his way!"
While he was standing, head bowed to his shoulders,
  and pondering which direction we might take,
  I stood there looking up among the boulders
and saw upon my left beside that cliff-face
  a throng that moved its feet in our direction,
  and yet seemed not to, so slow was its pace.   60
"Master," I said, "look up and you will find
  some people coming who may solve the problem,
  if you have not yet solved it in your mind."
He looked up then and, openly relieved,
  said: "Let us go to them, since they lag so.
  And you, dear son, believe as you have believed."
We were as far off yet from that slow flock
  (I mean when we had gone a thousand paces)
  as a strong slingsman could have thrown a rock,
when they drew in against the cliff and stood there
  like men who fear what they see coming toward them
  and, waiting for it, huddle close and stare.
"O well-concluded lives! O souls thus met
  already among the chosen!" Virgil said.
  "By that sweet crown of peace that shall be set   75
on each of you in time, tell us which way
  leads to some slope by which we two may climb.
  Who best knows time is most grieved by delay."

As sheep come through a gate—by ones, by twos,
  by threes, and all the others trail behind,
  timidly, nose to ground, and what the first does
the others do, and if the first one pauses,
  the others huddle up against his back,
  silly and mute, not knowing their own causes—
just so, I stood there watching with my Guide,
  the first row of that happy flock come on,
  their look meek and their movements dignified.
And when the souls that came first in that flock
  saw the light broken on the ground to my right
  so that my shadow fell upon the rock,   90
they halted and inched back as if to shy,
  and all the others who came after them
  did as the first did without knowing why.
"Let me confirm the thought you leave unspoken;
  it is a living body you see before you
  by which the sunlight on the ground is broken.
Do not be astonished; you may rest assured
  he does not seek the way to climb this wall
  without a power from Heaven." Thus my Lord
addressed them, and those worthy spirits said,
  waving the backs of their hands in our direction:
  "First turn around, and then go straight ahead."
And one soul said to me: "Whoever you are,
  as you move on, look back and ask yourself
  if you have ever seen me over there."   105
I studied him with care, my head turned round;
  gold-blond he was, and handsomely patrician,
  although one brow was split by a sword wound.
When I, in all humility, confessed
  I never before had seen him, he said: "Look!"
  and showed me a great slash above his breast.
Then, smiling, added: "I am Manfred, grandson
  of the blessed Empress Constance, and I beg you,
  when you return there over the horizon,
go to my sweet daughter, noble mother
  of the honor of Sicily and of Aragon,
  and speak the truth, if men speak any other.

My flesh had been twice hacked, and each wound mortal,
    when, tearfully, I yielded up my soul
    to Him whose pardon gladly waits for all.   120
Horrible were my sins, but infinite
    is the abiding Goodness which holds out
    Its open arms to all who turn to It.
If the pastor of Cosenza, by the rage
    of Clement sent to hunt me down, had first
    studied the Book of God at this bright page,
my body's bones would still be in the ground
    there by the bridgehead outside Benevento,
    under the heavy guard of the stone mound.
Now, rattled by the wind, by the rain drenched,
    they lie outside the kingdom, by the Verde,
    where he transported them with tapers quenched.
No man may be so cursed by priest or Pope
    but what the Eternal Love may still return
    while any thread of green lives on in hope.   135
Those who die contumacious, it is true,
    though they repent their feud with Holy Church,
    must wait outside here on the bank, as we do,
for thirty times as long as they refused
    to be obedient, though by good prayers
    in their behalf, that time may be reduced.
See, then, how great a service you may do me
    when you return, by telling my good Constance
    of my condition and of this decree
that still forbids our entrance to the Kingdom.
For here, from those beyond, great good may come."

Canto 4

*Listening to Manfred's discourse, Dante
has lost track of time. Now, at midmorning, the
Poets reach the opening in the cliff-face and begin
the laborious climb. Dante soon tires and cries
that he can go no farther, but Virgil urges him to
pull himself a little higher yet—significantly—to
the ledge of the Indolent, those souls whose sin
was their delay in pulling themselves up the same
hard path. Seated on the ledge, Virgil explains
that in the nature of the mountain the beginning
of the ascent, or the first turning from sin to true
repentance, is always hardest. The higher one
climbs from sin to repentance, the easier it becomes to climb still higher until, in the perfection
of grace, the climb becomes effortless. But to that
ultimate height, as Virgil knows, human reason
cannot reach. It is Beatrice, divine love, who must
guide him there. As Virgil finishes speaking, an
ironic reply comes from behind a boulder. The
speaker is Belacqua, an old friend of Dante's and
the laziest man in Florence. Because of his indo-
lence, he put off good works and the active desire
for grace until he lay dying. In life he made God
wait. Now God makes him wait an equal period
before he may pass through the Gate into Purgatory and begin his purification. Unless, as Belacqua adds, the prayers of the devout intercede for
him. But now Virgil points out that the sun is
already at its noon height and that Dante,
unlike the Indolent, must not delay.*

When any sense of ours records intense
    pleasure or pain, then the whole soul is drawn
    by such impressions into that one sense

and seems to lose all other powers. And thus
  do I refute the error that asserts
  that one soul on another burns in us.
And, for this reason, when we see or hear
  whatever seizes strongly on the soul,
  time passes, and we lose it unaware.
For that which senses is one faculty;
  and that which keeps the soul intact, another:
  the first, as it were, bound; the second, free.
To this, my own experience bears witness;
  for while I listened to that soul and marveled,
  the sun had climbed—without my least awareness—   15
to fifty full degrees of its noon peak
  when, at one point along the way, that band
  cried out in chorus: "Here is what you seek."
Often when grapes hang full on slope and ledge
  the peasant, with one forkful of his thorns,
  seals up a wider opening in his hedge
than the gap we found there in that wall of stone;
  up which—leaving that band of souls behind—
  my Guide led and I followed, we two alone.
Go up to San Leo or go down to Noli;
  go climb Bismantova—two legs suffice;
  here nothing but swift wings will answer wholly.
The swift wings and the feathers, I mean to say,
  of great desire led onward by that Guide
  who was my hope and light along the way.   30
Squeezed in between two walls that almost meet
  we labor upward through the riven rock,
  a climb that calls for both our hands and feet.
Above the cliff's last rise we reached in time
  an open slope. "Do we go right or left?"
  I asked my Master, "or do we still climb?"
And he: "Take not one step to either side,
  but follow yet, and make way up the mountain
  till we meet someone who may serve as guide."
Higher than sight the peak soared to the sky;
  much steeper than a line drawn from midquadrant
  to the center was the slope that met my eye.

The climb had sapped my last strength when I cried:
    "Sweet Father, turn to me; unless you pause
    I shall be left here on the mountainside!"   45
He pointed to a ledge a little ahead
    that wound around the whole face of the slope.
    "Pull yourself that much higher, my son," he said.
His words so spurred me that I forced myself
    to push on after him on hands and knees
    until at last my feet were on that shelf.
There we sat, facing eastward, to survey
    the trail we had just climbed; for oftentimes
    a backward look comforts one on the way.
I looked down first to the low-lying shore,
    then upward to the sun—and stopped amazed,
    for it was from the left its arrows bore.
Virgil was quick to note the start I gave
    when I beheld the Chariot of the Sun
    driven between me and the North Wind's cave.   60
"Were Castor and Pollux," he said, "in company
    of that bright mirror which sends forth its rays
    equally up and down, then you would see
the twelve-toothed cogwheel of the Zodiac
    turned till it blazed still closer to the Bears
    —unless it were to stray from its fixed track.
If you wish to understand why this is so,
    imagine Zion and this mount so placed
    on earth, the one above, the other below,
that the two have one horizon though they lie
    in different hemispheres. Therefore, the path
    that Phaëthon could not follow in the sky
must necessarily, in passing here
    on the one side, pass there upon the other,
    as your own reasoning will have made clear."   75
And I then: "Master, I may truly vow
    I never grasped so well the very point
    on which my wits were most astray just now;
that the midcircle of the highest heaven,
    called the Equator, always lies between
    the sun and winter, and, for the reason given,

"Sweet Father, turn to me; unless you pause
I shall be left here on the mountainside!"

lies as far north of this place at all times
    as the Hebrews, when they held Jerusalem,
    were wont to see it toward the warmer climes.
But—if you please—I should be glad to know
    how far we have yet to climb, for the peak soars
    higher to Heaven than my eye can go."
And he: "Such is this mount that when a soul
    begins the lower slopes it most must labor;
    then less and less the more it nears its goal.   90
Thus when we reach the point where the slopes seem
    so smooth and gentle that the climb becomes
    as easy as to float a skiff downstream,
then will this road be run, and not before
    that journey's end will your repose be found.
    I know this much for truth and say no more."
His words were hardly out when, from nearby,
    we heard a voice say: "Maybe by that time
    you'll find you need to sit before you fly!"
We turned together at the sound, and there,
    close on our left, we saw a massive boulder
    of which, till then, we had not been aware.
To it we dragged ourselves, and there we found
    stretched in the shade, the way a slovenly man
    lies down to rest, some people on the ground.   105
The weariest of them, judging by his pose,
    sat hugging both knees while his head, abandoned,
    dropped down between them halfway to his toes.
"Master," I said, "look at that sorry one
    who seems so all-let-down. Were Sloth herself
    his sister, he could not be so far gone!"
That heap took heed, and even turned his head
    upon his thigh—enough to look at us.
    "You climb it if you're such a flash," he said.
I knew him then, and all the agony
    that still burned in my lungs and raced my pulse
    did not prevent my going to him. He,
raising his head—just barely—when I stood by,
    drawled: "So you really know now why the sun
    steers to the left of you across the sky?"   120

Purgatorio

His short words and his shorter acts, combined,
   made me half smile as I replied: "Belacqua,
   your fate need never again trouble my mind.
Praise be for that. But why do you remain
   crouched here? Are you waiting for a guide, perhaps?
   Or are you up to your old tricks again?"
"Old friend," he said, "what good is it to climb?—
   God's bird above the Gate would never let me
   pass through to start my trials before my time.
I must wait here until the heavens wheel past
   as many times as they passed me in my life,
   for I delayed the good sighs till the last.
Prayer could help me, if a heart God's love
   has filled with grace should offer it. All other
   is worthless, for it is not heard above."   135
But now the Poet already led the way
   to the slope above, saying to me: "Come now;
   the sun has touched the very peak of day
above the sea, and night already stands
with one black foot upon Morocco's sands."

Canto 5

The Poets continue up the mountain, and Dante's shadow once more creates excitement among the waiting souls. These are the souls of Those Who Died by Violence Without Last Rites. Since their lives were cut off, they did not have full opportunity to repent, and therefore they are placed a step higher than the simply Indolent. These souls crowd about Dante, eager to have him bear news of them back to the world and so to win prayers that will shorten their delay. Virgil instructs Dante to listen to these souls, but warns him not to interrupt his own climb to Grace. The Poets, therefore, continue to press on while the souls cluster about them, each eager to tell his story and to beg that Dante speak of them when he returns to the world.

I was following the footsteps of my Guide,
   having already parted from those shades,
   when someone at my back pointed and cried:
"Look there! see how the sun's shafts do not drive
   through to the left of that one lower down,
   and how he walks as if he were alive!"
I looked behind me to see who had spoken,
   and I saw them gazing up at me alone,
   at me, and at the light, that it was broken.
At which my Master said: "Why do you lag?
   what has so turned your mind that you look back?
   what is it to you that idle tongues will wag?
Follow my steps, though all such whisper of you;
   be as a tower of stone, its lofty crown
   unswayed by anything the winds may do.

For when a man lets his attention range
    toward every wisp, he loses true direction,
    sapping his mind's force with continual change."
What could I say except "I come"? I said it
    flushed with that hue that sometimes asks forgiveness
    for which it shows the asker to be fit.
Meanwhile across the slope a little before us
    people approached chanting the *Miserere,*
    verse by verse in alternating chorus.
But when they noticed that I blocked the course
    of the sun's arrows when they struck my body,
    their song changed to an "Oh! . . . ." prolonged and hoarse.
Out of that silenced choir two spirits ran
    like messengers and, reaching us, they said:
    "We beg to know—are you a living man?"   30
My Guide replied: "You may be on your way.
    And bear back word to those who sent you here
    he does indeed still walk in mortal clay.
If, as I think, it was his shadow drew them
    to stand and stare, they know already. Tell them
    to honor him; that may be precious to them."
I never saw hot vapors flashing through
    the first sweet air of night, or through the clouds
    of August sunsets, faster than those two
ran up to join their band, wheeled round again,
    and, with the whole band following, came toward us,
    like cavalry sent forward with a loose rein.
"There are hundreds in that troop that charges so,"
    my Guide said, "and all come to beg a favor.
    Hear them, but press on, listening as you go."   45
"Pure spirit," they came crying, "you who thus
    while still inside the body you were born to
    climb to your bliss—oh, pause and speak to us.
Is there no one here you recognize? Not one
    of whom you may bear tidings to the world?
    Wait! Won't you pause? Oh, please! Why do you run?
We all are souls who died by violence,
    all sinners to our final hour, in which
    the lamp of Heaven shed its radiance

into our hearts. Thus from the brink of death,
   repenting all our sins, forgiving those
   who sinned against us, with our final breath
we offered up our souls at peace with Him
   who saddens us with longing to behold
   His glory on the throne of Seraphim."   60
"O well-born souls," I said, "I can discover
   no one among you that I recognize
   however much I search your faces over;
but if you wish some service of me, speak,
   and if the office is within my power
   I will perform it, by that peace I seek
in following the footsteps of this Guide,
   that peace that draws me on from world to world
   to my own good." I paused, and one replied:
"No soul among us doubts you will fulfill
   all you declare, without your need to swear it,
   if lack of power does not defeat your will.
I, then, who am no more than first to plead,
   beg that if ever you see that land that lies
   between Romagna and Naples, you speak my need   75
most graciously in Fano, that they to Heaven
   send holy prayers to intercede for me;
   so may my great offenses be forgiven.
I was of Fano, but the wounds that spilled
   my life's blood and my soul at once were dealt me
   among the Antenori. I was killed
where I believed I had the least to fear.
   Azzo of Este, being incensed against me
   beyond all reason, had me waylaid there.
Had I turned toward La Mira when they set
   upon me first outside of Oriaco,
   I should be drawing breath among men yet.
I ran into the swamp, and reeds and mud
   tangled and trapped me. There I fell. And there
   I watched my veins let out a pool of blood."   90
Another spoke: "So may the Love Divine
   fulfill the wish that draws you up the mountain,
   for sweet compassion, lend your aid to mine.

I am Bonconte, once of Montefeltro.
  Because Giovanna and the rest forget me,
  I go among these souls with head bowed low."
And I: "What force or chance led you to stray
  so far from Campaldino that your grave
  remains to be discovered to this day?"
And he: "There flows below the Casentino
  a stream, the Archiana, which arises
  above the hermitage in Apennino.
There where its name ends in the Arno's flood
  I came, my throat pierced through, fleeing on foot
  and staining all my course with my life's blood.   105
There my sight failed. There with a final moan
  which was the name of Mary, speech went from me.
  I fell, and there my body lay alone.
I speak the truth. Oh, speak it in my name
  to living men! God's angel took me up,
  and Hell's cried out: 'Why do you steal my game?
If his immortal part is your catch, brother,
  for one squeezed tear that makes me turn it loose,
  I've got another treatment for the other!'
You are familiar with the way immense
  watery vapors gather on the air,
  then burst as rain, as soon as they condense.
To ill will that seeks only ill, his mind
  added intelligence, and by the powers
  his nature gives, he stirred the mist and wind.   120
From Pratomagno to the spine, he spread
  a mist that filled the valley by day's end;
  then turned the skies above it dark as lead.
The saturated air changed into rain
  and down it crashed, flooding the rivulets
  with what the sodden earth could not retain;
the rills merged into torrents, and a flood
  swept irresistibly to the royal river.
  The Archiana, raging froth and mud,
found my remains in their last frozen rest
  just at its mouth, swept them into the Arno,
  and broke the cross I had formed upon my breast

"Along its banks and down its bed it rolled me,
and then it bound and buried me in silt."

in my last agony of pain and guilt.
    Along its banks and down its bed it rolled me,
    and then it bound and buried me in silt."   135
A third spoke when that second soul had done:
   "When you have found your way back to the world,
    and found your rest from this long road you run,
oh, speak my name again with living breath
    to living memory. Pia am I.
    Siena gave me birth; Maremma, death.
As he well knows who took me as his wife
with jeweled ring before he took my life."

Canto 6

The Poets move along with the souls still crowding about them. Dante promises all of them that he will bear word of them back to the world, but he never pauses in his climb. Among the press of souls, Dante specifically mentions seeing Benincasa da Laterina, Guccio de' Tarlati, Federico Novello, Count Orso, and Pierre de la Brosse. Finally free of that crowd, Dante asks Virgil how it is that prayer may sway God's will. Virgil explains in part but once more finishes by declaring that the whole truth is beyond him and that Dante must refer the question to Beatrice when he meets her. The sun passes behind the mountain as they climb (midafternoon of Easter Sunday). The Poets press on, and there on the shady slope they encounter the majestic spirit of Sordello who, like Virgil, is a Mantuan. Dante watches Sordello and Virgil embrace in a transport of love for their common birthplace and is moved to denounce Italy for setting brothers to war on one another; to denounce the Emperor Albert for his failure to bring unity and peace to Italy; and finally to utter an invective against Florence as the type of the war-torn and corrupt state.

The loser, when a game of dice is done,
   remains behind reviewing every roll
   sadly, and sadly wiser, and alone.
The crowd leaves with the winner; one behind
   tugs at him, one ahead, one at his side—
   all calling their long loyalty to his mind.
Not stopping, he hands out a coin or two
   and those he has rewarded let him be.
   So he fights off the crowd and pushes through.

Such was I then, turning my face now here,
   now there, among that rout, and promising
   on every hand, till I at last fought clear.
There was the Aretine who came to woe
   at the murderous hand of Tacco; and the other
   who drowned while he was hunting down his foe.   15
There, hands outstretched to me as I pushed through,
   was Federico Novello; and the Pisan
   who made the good Marzucco shine so true.
I saw Count Orso; and the shade of one
   torn from its flesh, it said, by hate and envy,
   and not for any evil it had done—
Pierre de la Brosse, I mean; and of this word
   may the Lady of Brabant take heed while here,
   lest, there, she find herself in a worse herd.
When I had won my way free of that press
   of shades whose one prayer was that others pray
   and so advance them toward their blessedness,
I said: "O my soul's light, it seems to me
   one of your verses most expressly states
   prayer may not alter Heaven's fixed decree;   30
yet all these souls pray only for a prayer.
   Can all their hope be vain? Or have I missed
   your true intent and read some other there?"
And he: "The sense of what I wrote is plain,
   if you bring all your wits to bear upon it.
   Nor is the hope of all these spirits vain.
The towering crag of Justice is not bent,
   nor is the rigor of its edict softened
   because the supplications of the fervent
and pure in heart cancel the debt of time
   decreed on all these souls who linger here,
   consumed with yearning to begin the climb.
The souls I wrote about were in that place
   where sin is not atoned for, and their prayers—
   they being pagan—were cut off from grace.   45
But save all questions of such consequence
   till you meet her who will become your lamp
   between the truth and mere intelligence.

Do you understand me? I mean Beatrice.
  She will appear above here, at the summit
  of this same mountain, smiling in her bliss."
"My Lord," I said, "let us go faster now;
  I find the climb less tiring than at first,
  and see, the slope already throws a shadow."
"The day leads on," he said, "and we shall press
  as far as we yet may while the light holds,
  but the ascent is harder than you guess;
before it ends, the sun must come around
  from its present hiding place behind the mountain
  and once more cast your shadow on the ground.   60
But see that spirit stationed all alone
  and looking down at us; he will point out
  the best road for us as we travel on."
We climbed on then. O Lombard, soul serene,
  how nobly and deliberately you watched us!
  how distant and majestic was your mien!
He did not speak to us as on we pressed,
  but held us fixed in his unblinking eyes
  as if he were a lion at its rest.
Virgil, nonetheless, climbed to his side
  and begged him to point out the best ascent.
  The shade ignored the question and replied
by asking in what country we were born
  and who we were. My gentle Guide began:
  "Mantua . . ." And that shade, till then withdrawn,   75
leaped to his feet like one in sudden haste
  crying: "O Mantuan, I am Sordello
  of your own country!" And the two embraced.
Ah, servile Italy, grief's hostelry,
  ah, ship unpiloted in the storm's rage,
  no mother of provinces but of harlotry!
That noble spirit leaped up with a start
  at the mere sound of his own city's name
  and took his fellow citizen to his heart;
while still, within you, brother wars on brother,
  and though one wall and moat surrounds them all,
  your living sons still gnaw at one another!

Purgatorio

O wretched land, search all your coasts, your seas,
  the bosom of your hills—where will you find
  a single part that knows the joys of peace?   90
What does it matter that Justinian came
  to trim the bit, if no one sits the saddle?
  Without him you would have less cause for shame!
You priests who, if you heed what God decreed,
  should most seek after holiness and leave
  to Caesar Caesar's saddle and his steed—
see how the beast grows wild now none restrains
  its temper, nor corrects it with the spur,
  since you set meddling hands upon its reins!
O German Albert, you who turn away
  while she grows vicious, being masterless,
  you should have forked her long before today!
May a just judgment from the stars descend
  upon your house, a blow so weirdly clear
  that your line tremble at it to the end.   105
For you, sir, and your father, in your greed
  for the cold conquests of your northern lands,
  have let the Empire's Garden go to seed.
Come see the Montagues and Capulets,
  the Monaldi and Filippeschi, reckless man!
  those ruined already, these whom ruin besets.
Come, cruel Emperor, come and see your lords
  hunted and holed, come tend their wounds and see
  what fine security Santafior affords.
Come see your stricken Rome that weeps alone,
  widowed and miserable, and day and night
  laments: "O Caesar mine, why are you gone?"
Come see your people—everywhere the same—
  united in love; and if no pity for us
  can move you, come and blush for your good name.   120
O Supreme Jove, for mankind crucified,
  if you permit the question, I must ask it:
  are the eyes of Your clear Justice turned aside?
or is this the unfolding of a plan
  shaped in Your fathomless counsels toward some good
  beyond all reckoning of mortal man?

For the land is a tyrant's roost, and any clod
    who comes along playing the partisan
    passes for a Marcellus with the crowd.
Florence, my Florence, may you not resent
    the fact that my digression has not touched you—
    thanks to your people's sober management.
Others have justice at heart but a bow strung
    by careful counsels and not quickly drawn;
    yours shoot the word forever—from the tongue.   135
Others, offered public office, shun
    the cares of service. Yours cry out unasked:
  "I will! I'll take it on! I am the one!"
Rejoice, I say, that your great gifts endure:
    your wealth, your peacefulness, and your good sense.
    What truth I speak, the facts will not obscure.
Athens and Sparta when of old they drew
    the codes of law that civilized the world,
    gave only merest hints, compared to you,
of man's advance. But all time shall remember
    the subtlety with which the thread you spin
    in mid-October breaks before November.
How often within living recollection
    have you changed coinage, custom, law, and office,
    and hacked your own limbs off and sewed them on?   150
But if your wits and memory are not dead
    you yet will see yourself as that sick woman
    who cannot rest, though on a feather bed,
but flails as if she fenced with pain and grief.
Ah, Florence, may your cure or course be brief.

Canto 7

Sordello, discovering Virgil's identity,
pays homage to him and offers to guide the Poets
as far as Peter's Gate. It is nearly sunset, however,
and Sordello explains that by the Law of the As-
cent no one may go upward after sundown. He
suggests that they spend the night in the nearby
Flowering Valley in which the souls of the Negli-
gent Rulers wait to begin their purification. The
three together climb in the failing light to the edge
of the valley. In it, they observe, among others:
Rudolph of Hapsburg, Ottocar of Bohemia, Philip
the Bold of France, Henry of Navarre, Pedro III
of Aragon, Charles I of Anjou, Henry III of Eng-
land, and William VII, Marquis of Monferrato.
All of the rulers, except Henry of England, were
in one way or another connected with the Holy
Roman Empire. Thus they were specially sancti-
fied by the divine right of kings and again sanc-
tified for their place in the temporal hierarchy
of Christ's Empire. Dante signalizes this eleva-
tion by the beauty of the valley in which he
places them, a flower-strewn green hollow of un-
earthly beauty and fragrance. The valley is cer-
tainly a counterpart of the Citadel of the Virtuous
Pagans in Limbo, but it outshines that lower
splendor by as much as divine love
outshines human reason.

Three or four times in brotherhood the two
    embraced and reembraced; and then Sordello
    drew back and said: "Countryman, who are *you?*"
"Before those spirits worthy to be blessed
    had yet been given leave to climb this mountain,
    Octavian had laid my bones to rest.

I am Virgil, and I am lost to Heaven
   for no sin, but because I lacked the Faith."
   In these words was my Master's answer given.
Just as a man who suddenly confronts
   something too marvelous either to believe
   or disbelieve, and so does both at once—
so did Sordello. Then his great head lowered,
   and, turning, he once more embraced my Master,
   but round the knees, as a menial does his lord.   15
"Eternal glory of the Latin race,
   through whom our tongue made all its greatness clear!
   Of my own land the deathless pride and praise!
What grace or merit lets me see you plain?"
   he said. "And oh, if I am worthy, tell me
   if you come here from Hell, and from what pain."
"Through every valley of the painful kingdom
   I passed," my Lord replied. "A power from Heaven
   marked me this road, and in that power I come.
Not what I did but what I left undone,
   who learned too late, denies my right to share
   your hope of seeing the Eternal Sun.
There is a place below where sorrow lies
   in untormented gloom. Its lamentations
   are not the shrieks of pain, but hopeless sighs.   30
There do I dwell with souls of babes whom death
   bit off in their first innocence, before
   Baptism washed them of their taint of earth.
There do I dwell with those who were not dressed
   in the Three Sacred Virtues but, unstained,
   recognized and practiced all the rest.
But if you know and are allowed to say,
   show us how we may reach the true beginning
   of Purgatory by the shortest way."
"We are not fixed in one place," he replied,
   "but roam at will up and around this slope
   far as the Gate, and I will be your guide.
But the day is fading fast, and in no case
   may one ascend at night; we will do well
   to give some thought to a good resting place.   45

Some souls are camped apart here on the right.
    If you permit, I will conduct you to them;
    I think you will find pleasure in the sight."
"What is it you say?" my Guide asked. "If one sought
    to climb at night, would others block his way?
    or would he simply find that he could not?"
"Once the sun sets," that noble soul replied,
    "you would not cross this line"—and ran his finger
    across the ground between him and my Guide.
"Nor is there anything to block the ascent
    except the shades of night; they of themselves
    suffice to sap the will of the most fervent.
One might, indeed, go down during the night
    and wander the whole slope, were he inclined to,
    while the horizon locks the day from sight."   60
I heard my Lord's voice, touched with wonder, say:
    "Lead us to the place of which you spoke
    where we may win some pleasure from delay."
We had not traveled very far from there
    before I saw a hollow in the slope
    such as one often finds in mountains here.
"There," said that spirit, "where the mountain makes
    a lap among its folds; that is the place
    where we may wait until the new day breaks."
The dell's rim sank away from left to right.
    A winding path, half-level and half-steep,
    led us to where the rim stood at midheight.
Indigo, phosphorescent wood self-lit,
    gold, fine silver, white lead, cochineal,
    fresh emerald the moment it is split—   75
all colors would seem lusterless as shade
    if placed beside the flowers and grassy banks
    that made a shining of that little glade.
Nor has glad Nature only colored there,
    but of a thousand sweet scents made a single
    earthless, nameless fragrance of the air.
Salve Regina!—from that green the hymn
    was raised to Heaven by a choir of souls
    hidden from outer view by the glade's rim.

Salve Regina!—from the green the hymn
was raised to Heaven by a choir of souls
hidden from outer view by the glade's rim.

"Sirs," said that Mantuan, "do not request
    that I conduct you there while any light
    remains before the sun sinks to its nest.
You can observe them from this rise and follow
    their actions better, singly and en masse,
    than if you moved among them in the hollow.   90
He who sits highest with the look of one
    ashamed to move his lips when others praise,
    in life left undone what he should have done.
He was the Emperor Rudolph whose high state
    could once have stayed the death of Italy.
    Now, though another try, 't will be too late.
That one who comforts him ruled formerly
    the land where rise the waters that flow down
    the Moldau to the Elbe to the sea.
He was Ottocar, and more respected and feared
    while still in diapers than his dissipated
    son Wenceslaus is now with a full beard.
That snubnose there who talks with head close-pressed
    to the kindly looking one, died while in flight,
    dishonoring the lily on his crest.   105
Observe the way he beats his breast and cries,
    and how the other one has made his palm
    a bed to rest his cheek on while he sighs.
They are father and father-in-law of The Plague of France.
    They know his dissolute and vicious ways,
    and hence their grief among these holy chants.
The heavy-sinewed one beside that spirit
    with the manly nose, singing in harmony,
    bore in his life the seal of every merit.
And if that younger one who sits in place
    behind him had remained king after him,
    true merit would have passed from vase to vase,
as it has not, alas, in their successors.
    Frederick and James possess the kingdoms now.
    Their father's better heritage none possesses.   120
Rare is the tree that lifts to every limb
    the sap of merit—He who gives, so wills
    that men may learn to beg their best from Him.

And what I say goes for that bignosed one
   no less than for the other who sings with him.
   On his account Provence and Puglia mourn.
By as much as Margaret and Beatrice
   must yield when Constance speaks her husband's worth,
   that much less than the tree the seedling is.
See Henry of England seated there alone,
   the monarch of the simple life; his branches
   came to good issue in a noble son.
The other lone one seated on the ground
   below the rest and looking up to them
   was the Marquis William Longsword, he who found   135
such grief in Allesandria, for whose pride
both Monferrato and Canavese cried."

Canto 8

As the light fades, Dante, Virgil, and Sordello stand on the bank and watch the souls below gather and sing the Compline hymn, asking for protection in the night. In response to the hymn two green angels descend from Heaven and take their posts, one on each side of the valley. Full darkness now settles, and the Poets may make their descent into the valley. Dante immediately finds a soul he knows, Judge Nino de' Visconti, and has a long conversation with him in which both bemoan the infidelity of widows who remarry. When Judge Nino has finished speaking, Dante looks at the South Pole and sees that three stars (the Three Theological Virtues) have replaced the four stars (the Four Cardinal Virtues) he had seen at dawn. As he is discussing them with Virgil, the serpent appears and is immediately routed by the angels, who return to their posts. Dante then has a conversation with Conrad Malaspina, whom Judge Nino had summoned when he found out Dante was a living man. Dante owes a debt of gratitude to the Malaspina House for its hospitality to him in his exile, and he takes this opportunity to praise it and to have Conrad prophesy that Dante shall live to know more about it.

It was the hour that turns the memories
   of sailing men their first day out to home
   and friends they sailed from on that morning's breeze;
that thrills the traveler newly on his way
   with love and yearning when he hears afar
   the bell that seems to mourn the dying day—

when I began, for lack of any sound,
    to count my hearing vain and watched a spirit
    who signaled for attention all around.
Raising his hands, he joined his palms in prayer
    and turned his rapt eyes east, as if to say:
    "I have no thought except that Thou art there."
"Te lucis ante" swelled from him so sweetly,
    with such devotion and so pure a tone,
    my senses lost the sense of self completely.   15
Then all the others with a golden peal
    joined in the hymn and sang it to the end,
    their eyes devoutly raised to Heaven's wheel.
Reader, if you seek truth, sharpen your eyes,
    for here the veil of allegory thins
    and may be pierced by any man who tries.
I saw that host of kings, its supplication
    sung to a close, stand still and pale and humble,
    eyes raised to Heaven as if in expectation.
I saw two angels issue and descend
    from Heaven's height, bearing two flaming swords
    without a point, snapped off to a stub end.
Green as a leaf is at its first unfurling,
    their robes; and green the wings that beat and blew
    the flowing folds back, fluttering and whirling.   30
One landed just above me, and one flew
    to the other bank. Thus, in the silent valley,
    the people were contained between the two.
I could see clearly that their hair was gold,
    but my eyes drew back bedazzled from their faces,
    defeated by more light than they could hold.
"They are from Mary's bosom," Sordello said,
    "and come to guard the valley from the serpent
    that in a moment now will show its head."
And I, not knowing where it would appear,
    turned so I stood behind those trusted shoulders
    and pressed against them icy-cold with fear.
Once more Sordello spoke: "Now let us go
    to where the great souls are and speak to them.
    The sight of you will please them much, I know."   45

It was, I think, but three steps to the base
   of the little bank; and there I saw a shade
   who stared at me as if he knew my face.
The air was closing on its darkling hour,
   yet not so fast but what it let me see,
   at that close range, what it had veiled before.
I took a step toward him; he, one toward me—
   Noble Judge Nin! how it rejoiced my soul
   to see you safe for all eternity!
No welcome was left unsaid on either side.
   Then he inquired: "How long since did you come
   to the mountain's foot over that widest tide?"
"Oh," I replied, "I came by the pits of woe—
   this morning. I am still in my first life,
   though I gain the other on the road I go."   60
He and Sordello, when they heard me thus
   answer the question, suddenly drew back
   as if surprised by something marvelous.
One turned to Virgil, and one turned aside
   to a shade who sat nearby. "Conrad! Get up!
   See what the grace of God has willed!" he cried.
And then to me: "By all the thankful praise
   you owe to Him who hides His primal cause
   so deep that none may ever know His ways—
when you have once more crossed the enormous tide,
   tell my Giovanna to cry out my name
   there where the innocent are gratified.
I do not think her mother cares for me
   since she put off the weeds and the white veil
   that she will once more long for presently.   75
She shows all men how long love's fire will burn
   within a woman's heart when sight and touch
   do not rekindle it at every turn.
Nor will the Milanese viper she must bear
   upon her tomb do her such honor in it
   as would Gallura's cock emblazoned there."
So spoke he; and his features bore the seal
   of that considered anger a good man
   reaches in reason and may rightly feel.

I looked up at the heavens next, and eyed
    that center point at which the stars are slowest,
    as a wheel is next the axle. And my Guide:
"My son, what is it that you stare at so?"
    And I: "At those three stars there in whose light
    the polar regions here are all aglow."   90
And he to me: "Below the rim of space
    now ride the four bright stars you saw this morning,
    and these three have arisen in their place."
Sordello started as my Guide said this;
    and clutching him, he pointed arm and finger,
    crying: "Our adversary! There he is!"
Straight through the valley's unprotected side
    a serpent came, perhaps the very one
    that gave the bitter food for which Eve cried.
Through the sweet grass and flowers the long sneak drew,
    turning its head around from time to time
    to lick itself as preening beasts will do.
I did not see and cannot tell you here
    how the celestial falcons took to flight;
    but I did see that both were in the air.   105
Hearing their green wings beating through the night,
    the serpent fled. The angels wheeled and climbed
    back to their posts again in equal flight.
The shade the judge had summoned with his cry
    had not moved from his side; through all that fray
    he stared at me without blinking an eye.
"So may the lamp that leads to what you seek
    find oil enough," he said, "in your own will
    to light your way to the enameled peak;
if you can say for certain how things stand
    in Val di Magra or those parts, please do,
    for I was once a great lord in that land.
Conrad Malaspina I was—the grandson
    and not the Elder. Here I purify
    the love I bore for those who were my own."   120
"Oh," I replied, "I never have been near
    the lands you held; but is there in all Europe
    a hamlet ignorant of the name you bear?

The glories of your noble house proclaim
    its lords abroad, proclaim the lands that bear them;
    and he who does not know them knows their fame.
I swear to you—so may my present course
    lead me on high—your honored house has never
    put by its strict sword and its easy purse.
Usage and nature have so formed your race
    that, though the Guilty Head pervert all else,
    it still shuns ill to walk the path of grace."
And he: "Go now, for the sun shall not complete
    its seventh rest in that great bed the Ram
    bestrides and covers with its four spread feet,   135
before this testimony you have given
    shall be nailed to the center of your head
    with stouter nails, and more securely driven,
than ever hearsay was. And this shall be
certain as Fate is in its fixed decree."

Canto 9

Dawn is approaching. Dante has a dream
of a golden eagle that descends from the height
of Heaven and carries him up to the Sphere of
Fire. He wakes to find that he has been trans-
ported in his sleep and that it was Lucia who
bore him, laying him down beside an enormous
wall, through an opening in which he and Virgil
may approach the Gate of Purgatory. Having
explained these matters, Virgil leads Dante to
the Gate and its angel guardian. The angel is
seated on the topmost of three steps that symbol-
ize the three parts of a perfect act of confession.
Dante prostrates himself at the feet of the an-
gel, who cuts seven P's in Dante's forehead with
the point of a blazing sword. He then allows the
Poets to enter. As the Gate opens with a sound of
thunder, the mountain resounds
with a great hymn of praise.

Now pale upon the balcony of the east
   ancient Tithonus' concubine appeared,
   but lately from her lover's arms released.
Across her brow, their radiance like a veil,
   a scroll of gems was set, worked in the shape
   of the cold beast whose sting is in his tail.
And now already, where we were, the night
   had taken two steps upward, while the third
   thrust down its wings in the first stroke of flight;
when I, by Adam's weight of flesh defeated,
   was overcome by sleep and sank to rest
   across the grass on which we five were seated.
At that new hour when the first dawn light grows
   and the little swallow starts her mournful cry,
   perhaps in memory of her former woes;

15

and when the mind, escaped from its submission
    to flesh and to the chains of waking thought,
    becomes almost prophetic in its vision;
in a dream I saw a soaring eagle hold
    the shining height of Heaven, poised to strike,
    yet motionless on widespread wings of gold.
He seemed to hover where old history
    records that Ganymede rose from his friends,
    borne off to the supreme consistory.
I thought to myself: "Perhaps his habit is
    to strike at this one spot; perhaps he scorns
    to take his prey from any place but this."
Then from his easy wheel in Heaven's spire,
    terrible as a lightning bolt, he struck
    and snatched me up high as the Sphere of Fire.   30
It seemed that we were swept in a great blaze,
    and the imaginary fire so scorched me
    my sleep broke and I wakened in a daze.
Achilles must have roused exactly thus—
    glancing about with unadjusted eyes,
    now here, now there, not knowing where he was—
when Thetis stole him sleeping, still a boy,
    and fled with him from Chiron's care to Scyros,
    whence the Greeks later lured him off to Troy.
I sat up with a start; and as sleep fled
    out of my face, I turned the deathly white
    of one whose blood is turned to ice by dread.
There at my side my Comfort sat—alone.
    The sun stood two hours high and more. I sat
    facing the sea. The flowering glen was gone.   45
"Don't be afraid," he said. "From here our course
    leads us to joy, you may be sure. Now, therefore,
    hold nothing back, but strive with all your force.
You are now at Purgatory. See the great
    encircling rampart there ahead. And see
    that opening—it contains the Golden Gate.
A while back, in the dawn before the day,
    while still your soul was locked in sleep inside you,
    across the flowers that made the valley gay,

It seemed that we were swept up in a great blaze,
and the imaginary fire so scorched me
my sleep broke and I wakened in a daze.

a Lady came. 'I am Lucia,' she said.
  'Let me take up this sleeping man and bear him
  that he may wake to see his hope ahead.'
Sordello and the others stayed. She bent
  and took you up. And as the light grew full,
  she led, I followed, up the sweet ascent. 60
Here she put you down. Then with a sweep
  of her sweet eyes she marked that open entrance.
  Then she was gone; and with her went your sleep."
As one who finds his doubt dispelled, sheds fear,
  and feels it change into new confidence
  as bit by bit he sees the truth shine clear—
so did I change; and seeing my face brim
  with happiness, my Guide set off at once
  to climb the slope, and I moved after him.
Reader, you know to what exalted height
  I raised my theme. Small wonder if I now
  summon still greater art to what I write.
As we drew near the height, we reached a place
  from which—inside what I had first believed
  to be an open breach in the rock-face— 75
I saw a great gate fixed in place above
  three steps, each its own color; and a guard
  who did not say a word and did not move.
Slow bit by bit, raising my lids with care,
  I made him out seated on the top step,
  his face more radiant than my eyes could bear.
He held a drawn sword, and the eye of day
  beat such a fire back from it, that each time
  I tried to look, I had to look away.
I heard him call: "What is your business here?
  Answer from where you stand. Where is your guide?
  Take care you do not find your coming dear."
"A little while ago," my Teacher said,
  "a Heavenly Lady, well versed in these matters,
  told us, 'Go there. That is the Gate ahead.'" 90
"And may she still assist you, once inside,
  to your soul's good! Come forward to our three steps,"
  the courteous keeper of the Gate replied.

We came to the first step: white marble gleaming
    so polished and so smooth that in its mirror
    I saw my true reflection past all seeming.
The second was stained darker than blue-black
    and of a rough-grained and a fire-flaked stone,
    its length and breadth crisscrossed by many a crack.
The third and topmost was of porphyry,
    or so it seemed, but of a red as flaming
    as blood that spurts out of an artery.
The angel of the Lord had both feet on
    this final step and sat upon the sill
    which seemed made of some adamantine stone.   105
With great goodwill my Master guided me
    up the three steps and whispered in my ear:
    "Now beg him humbly that he turn the key."
Devoutly prostrate at his holy feet,
    I begged in Mercy's name to be let in,
    but first three times upon my breast I beat.
Seven *P*'s, the seven scars of sin,
    his sword point cut into my brow. He said:
    "Scrub off these wounds when you have passed within."
Color of ashes, of parched earth one sees
    deep in an excavation, were his vestments,
    and from beneath them he drew out two keys.
One was of gold, one silver. He applied
    the white one to the gate first, then the yellow,
    and did with them what left me satisfied.   120
"Whenever either of these keys is put
    improperly in the lock and fails to turn it,"
    the angel said to us, "the door stays shut.
One is more precious. The other is so wrought
    as to require the greater skill and genius,
    for it is that one which unties the knot.
They are from Peter, and he bade me be
    more eager to let in than to keep out
    whoever cast himself prostrate before me."
Then opening the sacred portals wide:
    "Enter. But first be warned; do not look back
    or you will find yourself once more outside."

Purgatorio

The Tarpeian rock-face, in that fatal hour
    that robbed it of Metellus, and then the treasure,
    did not give off so loud and harsh a roar   135
as did the pivots of the Holy Gate—
    which were of resonant and hard-forged metal—
    when they turned under their enormous weight.
At the first thunderous roll I turned half-round,
    for it seemed to me I heard a chorus singing
    Te Deum laudamus mixed with that sweet sound.
I stood there and the strains that reached my ears
    left on my soul exactly that impression
    a man receives who goes to church and hears
the choir and organ ringing out their chords
and now does, now does not, make out the words.

Canto 10

*The Gate closes behind them, and the
Poets begin the ascent to the first cornice through
a tortuous passage that Dante describes as a needle's eye. They reach the cornice about 9:00 or
10:00 of Monday morning. At first the cornice
seems deserted. Dante's eye is caught by a series
of three marvelously wrought bas-reliefs in the
marble of the inner cliff-face. Three panels depict
three scenes that serve as the Whip of Pride, exemplifying to each sinner as he enters how far
greater souls have put by far greater reasons for
pride in order to pursue the grace of humility. As
Dante stands in admiration before the carvings,
Virgil calls his attention to a band of souls approaching from the left, and Dante turns for his
first sight of the souls of the Proud, who crawl
agonizingly round and round the cornice under
the crushing weight of enormous slabs of rock.
Their punishment is so simple and so terrible that
Dante can scarcely bear to describe it, and he
cries out in anguish to the proud of this world to
take heed of the nature of their sin and of
its unbearable punishment.*

When we had crossed the threshold of that Gate
    so seldom used because man's perverse love
    so often makes the crooked path seem straight,
I knew by the sound that it had closed again;
    and had I looked back, to what water ever
    could I have gone to wash away that stain?
We climbed the rock along a narrow crack
    through which a zigzag pathway pitched and slid
    just as a wave swells full and then falls back.

"This calls for careful judgment," said my Guide.
  "Avoid the places where the rock swells up
    and weave among the troughs from side to side."
Our steps became so difficult and few,
  the waning moon had reached its western bed
    and sunk to rest before we could work through   15
that needle's eye. But when we had won clear
  to an open space above, at which the mountain
    steps back to form a ledge, we halted there;
I tired, and both of us confused for lack
  of any sign or guide. The ledge was level,
    and lonelier even than a desert track.
From brink to cliff-face measured three men's height,
  and the cornice did not vary in its width
    as far as I could see to left or right.
Our feet had not yet moved a step up there,
  when I made out that all the inner cliff
    which rose without a foothold anywhere
was white and flawless marble and adorned
  with sculptured scenes beside which Polyclitus',
    and even Nature's, best works would be scorned.   30
The angel who came down from God to man
  with the decree of peace the centuries wept for,
    which opened Heaven, ending the long ban,
stood carved before us with such force and love,
  with such a living grace in his whole pose,
    the image seemed about to speak and move.
One could have sworn an *Ave!* sounded clear,
  for she who turned the key that opened to us
    the Perfect Love, was also figured there;
and all her flowing gesture seemed to say—
  impressed there as distinctly as a seal
    impresses wax—*Ecce ancilla Dei.*
"Do not give all your thoughts to this one part,"
  my gentle Master said. (I was then standing
    on that side of him where man has his heart.)   45
I turned my eyes a little to the right
  (the side on which he stood who had thus urged me)
    and there, at Mary's back, carved in that white

and flawless wall, I saw another scene,
    and I crossed in front of Virgil and drew near it
    the better to make out what it might mean.
Emerging from the marble were portrayed
    the cart, the oxen, and the Ark from which
    the sacrilegious learned to be afraid.
Seven choirs moved there before it, bringing
    confusion to my senses; with my hearing
    I thought, "No," with my sight, "Yes, they are singing."
In the same way, the smokes the censers poured
    were shown so faithfully that eyes and nose
    disputed yes and no in happy discord.   60
And there before the Holy Vessel, dancing
    with girt-up robes, the humble Psalmist moved,
    less than a king, and more, in his wild prancing.
Facing him, portrayed with a vexed frown
    of mingled sadness and contempt, Michal
    stood at a palace window looking down.
I moved a little further to the right,
    the better to observe another panel
    that shown at Michal's back, dazzling and white.
Here was portrayed from glorious history
    that Roman prince whose passion to do justice
    moved Gregory to his great victory.
I speak of Trajan, blessed Emperor.
    And at his bridle was portrayed a widow
    in tears wept from the long grief of the poor.   75
Filling the space on both sides and behind
    were mounted knights on whose great golden banners
    the eagles seemed to flutter in the wind.
The widow knelt and by consummate art
    appeared to say: "My lord, avenge my son
    for he is slain and I am sick at heart."
And he to answer: "Justice shall be done;
    wait only my return." And she: "My lord"—
    speaking from the great grief that urged her on—
"if you do not?" And he: "Who wears my crown
    will right your wrong." And she: "Can the good deed
    another does grace him who shuns his own?"

And he, then: "Be assured. For it is clear
  this duty is to do before I go.
  Justice halts me, pity binds me here."   90
The Maker who can never see or know
  anything new, produced that "visible speaking";
  new to us, because not found below.
As I stood relishing the art and thought
  of those high images—dear in themselves,
  and dearer yet as works His hand had wrought—
the Poet said: "Look there; they seem to crawl
  but those are people coming on our left;
  they can tell us where to climb the wall."
My eyes, always intent to look ahead
  to some new thing, finding delight in learning,
  lost little time in doing as he said.
Reader, I would not have you be afraid,
  nor turn from your intention to repent
  through hearing how God wills the debt he paid.   105
Do not think of the torments; think, I say,
  of what comes after them; think that at worst
  they cannot last beyond the Judgment Day.
"Master," I said, "those do not seem to me
  people approaching us; nor do I know—
  they so confuse my sight—what they may be."
And he to me: "Their painful circumstance
  doubles them to the very earth; my own eyes
  debated what they saw there at first glance.
Look hard and you will see the people pressed
  under the moving boulders there. Already
  you can make out how each one beats his breast."
O you proud Christians, wretched souls and small,
  who by the dim lights of your twisted minds
  believe you prosper even as you fall—   120
can you not see that we are worms, each one
  born to become the angelic butterfly
  that flies defenseless to the Judgment Throne?
What have your souls to boast of and be proud?
  You are no more than insects, incomplete
  as any grub until it burst the shroud.

Sometimes at roof or ceiling beam one sees
   a human figure set there as a corbel,
   carved with its chest crushed in by its own knees,
so cramped that what one sees imagined there
   makes his bones ache in fact—just such a sense
   grew on me as I watched those souls with care.
True, those who crawled along that painful track
   were more or less distorted, each one bent
   according to the burden on his back;   135
yet even the most patient, wracked and sore,
seemed to be groaning: "I can bear no more!"

Canto 11

*As the souls of the Proud creep near, the
Poets hear them recite a long and humble prayer
based on the Paternoster. When the prayer is
ended, Virgil asks one of the souls, hidden from
view under its enormous burden, the way to the
ascent. The sinner, who identifies himself as
Omberto Aldobrandesco, instructs the Poets to
follow along in the direction the souls are crawling. He recites his history in brief, and it becomes
clear that Dante means him to exemplify Pride
of Birth. The conversation between Dante and
Omberto is overheard by Oderisi d'Agobbio, who
turns in pain and speaks to Dante, explaining his
sin of Pride of Talent, the avidity of the artist for
preeminence. Oderisi also points out the soul that
struggles along just ahead of him as Provenzano
Salvani, once warlord of Siena, who is being punished for Pride of Temporal Power, though he
has been advanced toward his purification in recognition of a single act of great humility performed in order to save the life of a friend. Oderisi
concludes with a dark prophecy of
Dante's exile from Florence.*

*O*ur *Father in Heaven, not by Heaven bounded*
   but there indwelling for the greater love
   Thou bear'st Thy first works in the realm first-founded,
hallowed be Thy name, hallowed Thy power
   by every creature as its nature grants it
   to praise Thy quickening breath in its brief hour.
Let come to us the sweet peace of Thy reign,
   for if it come not we cannot ourselves
   attain to it however much we strain.

And as Thine angels kneeling at the Throne
offer their wills to Thee, singing Hosannah,
so teach all men to offer up their own.
Give us this day Thy manna, Lord we pray,
for if he have it not, though man most strive
through these harsh wastes, his speed is his delay.   15
As we forgive our trespassers the ill
we have endured, do Thou forgive, not weighing
our merits, but the mercy of Thy will.
Our strength is as a reed bent to the ground;
do not Thou test us with the Adversary,
but deliver us from him who sets us round.
This last petition, Lord, with grateful mind,
we pray not for ourselves who have no need,
but for the souls of those we left behind.
—So praying godspeed for themselves and us,
those souls were crawling by under such burdens
as we at times may dream of. Laden thus,
unequally tormented, weary, bent,
they circled the first cornice round and round,
purging away the world's foul sediment.   30
If they forever speak our good above,
what can be done for their good here below
by those whose will is rooted in God's love?
Surely, we should help those souls grow clear
of time's deep stain, that each at last may issue
spotless and weightless to his starry sphere.
"Ah, so may justice and pity soon remove
the load you bear, that you may spread your wings
and rise rejoicing to the Perfect Love—
help us to reach the stairs the shortest way,
and should there be more than one passage, show us
the one least difficult to climb, I pray;
for my companion, who is burdened still
with Adam's flesh, grows weak in the ascent,
though to climb ever higher is all his will."   45
I heard some words in answer to my Lord's,
but could not tell which of those souls had spoken,
nor from beneath which stone. These were the words:

246

"Your way is to the right, along with ours.
   If you will come with us, you will discover
   a pass within a living person's powers.
And were I not prevented by the stone
   that masters my stiff neck and makes me keep
   my head bowed to the dust as I move on,
I would look up, hoping to recognize
   this living and still nameless man with you,
   and pray to find compassion in his eyes.
I was Italian. A Tuscan of great fame—
   Guglielmo Aldobrandesco—was my father.
   I do not know if you have heard the name.   60
My ancient lineage and the hardihood
   my forebears showed in war, went to my head.
   With no thought that we all share the one blood
of Mother Eve, I scorned all others so
   I died for it; as all Siena knows,
   and every child in Campagnatico.
I am Omberto, and my haughty ways
   were not my ruin alone, but brought my house
   and all my followers to evil days.
Here until God be pleased to raise my head
   I bear this weight. Because I did not do so
   among the living, I must among the dead."
I had bowed low, better to know his state,
   when one among them—not he who was speaking—
   twisted around beneath his crushing weight,   75
saw me, knew me, and cried out. And so
   he kept his eyes upon me with great effort
   as I moved with those souls, my head bowed low.
"Aren't you Od'risi? " I said. "He who was known
   as the honor of Agobbio, and of that art
   Parisians call illumination? "
"Brother," he said, "what pages truly shine
   are Franco Bolognese's. The real honor
   is all his now and only partly mine.
While I was living, I know very well,
   I never would have granted him first place,
   so great was my heart's yearning to excel.

Here pride is paid for. Nor would I have been
    among these souls, had I not turned to God
    while I still had in me the power to sin.   90
O gifted men, vainglorious for first place,
    how short a time the laurel crown stays green
    unless the age that follows lacks all grace!
Once Cimabue thought to hold the field
    in painting, and now Giotto has the cry
    so that the other's fame, grown dim, must yield.
So from one Guido has another shorn
    poetic glory, and perhaps the man
    who will un-nest both is already born.
A breath of wind is all there is to fame
    here upon earth; it blows this way and that,
    and when it changes quarter it changes name.
Though loosed from flesh in old age, will you have
    in, say, a thousand years, more reputation
    than if you went from child's play to the grave?   105
What, to eternity, is a thousand years?
    Not so much as the blinking of an eye
    to the turning of the slowest of the spheres.
All Tuscany once sounded with the fame
    of this one who goes hobbling on before me;
    now, one hears scarce a whisper of his name,
even in Siena, where he was in power
    when he destroyed the rage of Florence (then,
    as much a shrew as she is, now, a whore).
The fame of man is like the green of grass;
    it comes, it goes, and He by whom it springs
    bright from earth's plenty makes it fade and pass."
And I to him: "These truths bend my soul low
    from swollen pride to sweet humility.
    But who is he of whom you spoke just now?"   120
"That's Provenzan Salvani, and the stone
    is on him," he replied, "for his presumption
    in making all Siena his alone.
So he goes on and has gone since his death,
    without a pause. Such coin must one pay here
    for being too presumptuous on earth."

Purgatorio

And I: "But if the souls that do not mend
   their sinful ways until the brink of life,
   must wait below before they can ascend
(unless the prayers of those whom God holds dear
   come to their aid) the period of their lives—
   how was he given license to be here?"
"At the peak of his life's glory," said the ghost,
  "in the Campo of Siena, willingly,
   and putting by all pride, he took his post;   135
and there, to free his dear friend from the pains
   he suffered in the dungeons of King Charles,
   stood firm, although he trembled in his veins.
I say no more; and though you well may feel
   I speak in riddles, it will not be long
   before your neighbors' actions will reveal
all you need know to fathom what I say.
It was this good work spared him his delay."

Canto 12

Virgil instructs Dante to arise from where he has been walking bent beside Oderisi and to move on. Dante follows obediently, and soon Virgil points out to him the Rein of Pride carved in thirteen scenes into the stone beneath their feet. The scenes portray dreadful examples of the destruction that follows upon great pride. The Poets pass on and find the Angel of Humility approaching to welcome them. The angel strikes Dante's forehead with his wings and, though Dante does not discover it till later, the first P instantly disappears without a trace, symboliz-ing the purification from the sin of Pride. The Poets pass on, up a narrow ascent to the second cornice, but though the way is narrow, Dante finds it much easier than the first, since steps have been cut into it and since he is lighter by the weight of the first P. As they climb they hear the first beatitude ring out behind them, sung by the Angel of Humility.

As oxen go in yoke—step matched, head bowed—
  I moved along beside that laden soul
  as long as the sweet Pedagogue allowed.
But when he said: "Leave him his weary trail;
  here each must speed his boat as best he can
  urging it onward with both oars and sail"—
I drew myself again to the position
  required for walking; thus my body rose,
  but my thoughts were still bent double in contrition.
I was following my Guide, and we had put
  those laden souls behind us far enough
  to make it clear that we were light of foot,

As oxen go in yoke—step matched, head bowed—
I moved along beside that laden soul
as long as the sweet pedagogue allowed.

when he said, without turning back his head:
  "Look down. You will find solace on the way
    in studying what pavement your feet tread."   15
In order that some memory survive
  of those who die, their slabs are often carved
    to show us how they looked while yet alive.
And often at the sight a thought will stir
  the passerby to weep for what has been—
    though only the compassionate feel that spur.
Just so, but with a far more lifelike grace—
  they being divinely wrought—stone figures covered
    the track that jutted from the mountain's face.
Mark there, on one side, him who had been given
  a nobler form than any other creature.
    He plunged like lightning from the peak of Heaven.
Mark, on the other, lying on the earth,
  stricken by the celestial thunderbolt,
    Briareus, heavy with the chill of death.   30
Mark there, still armed, ranged at their father's side,
  Thymbraeus, Mars, and Pallas looking down
    at the Giants' severed limbs strewn far and wide.
Mark Nimrod at the foot of his great tower,
  bemused, confounded, staring at his people
    who shared at Shinar his mad dream of power.
Ah, Niobe! with what eyes wrung with pain
  I saw your likeness sculptured on that road
    between your seven and seven children slain!
Ah, Saul! how still you seemed to me, run through
  with your own sword, dead upon Mount Gilboa,
    which never after that felt rain nor dew.
Ah, mad Arachne! so I saw you there—
  already half turned spider—on the shreds
    of what you wove to be your own despair.   45
Ah, Rehoboam! your image in that place
  no longer menaces; a chariot bears it
    in panic flight, though no one gives it chase.
Now see Alcmaeon, there on the hard pavement,
  standing above his mother when she learned
    the full cost of the fatal ornament.

Purgatorio

Now see there how his own sons fell upon
    Sennacherib at prayer within the temple,
    and how they left him dead when they were done.
Now see Tomyris bloody with her kill
    after the ruin she wrought, saying to Cyrus:
    "Your thirst was all for blood. Now drink your fill."
Now see how the Assyrians broke and ran
    from Israel after Holofernes' murder;
    and showed the slaughtered remnants of the man.   60
Mark Troy there in its ashes overthrown.
    Ah, Ilion! how lowly and how lost!
    Now see your hollow shell upon that stone!
What brush could paint or etching-stylus draw
    such lineaments and shadings? At such skill
    the subtlest genius would have stared in awe.
The dead seemed dead, the living alive. A witness
    to the event itself saw it no better
    than I did, looking down there at its likeness.
Now swell with pride and cut your reckless swath
    with head held high, you sons of Eve, and never
    bow down to see the evil in your path!
We had, I found, gone round more of the mount,
    and the sun had run more of its daily course,
    than my bound soul had taken into account,   75
when Virgil, ever watchful, ever leading,
    commanded: "Lift your head. This is no time
    to be shut up in your own thoughts, unheeding.
Look there and see an angel on his way
    to welcome us; and see—the sixth handmaiden
    returns now from her service to the day.
That he may gladly send us up the mountain,
    let reverence grace your gestures and your look.
    Remember, this day will not dawn again."
I was well used to his warnings to abjure
    all that delayed me from my good; on that point
    nothing he said to me could be obscure.
Toward us, dressed in white, and with a face
    serenely tremulous as the Morning Star,
    the glorious being came, radiant with grace.   90

First his arms and then his wings spread wide.
  "Come," he said, "the stars are near, and now
    the way is easy up the mountainside.
Few, all too few, come answering to this call.
  O sons of man, born to ascend on high,
    how can so slight a wind-puff make you fall?"
Straight to where the rock was cut he led.
  There he struck my forehead with his wings,
    then promised us safe journeying ahead.
When a man has climbed the first slope toward the crown
  on which is built the church that overhangs
    at the Rubaconte, the well-managed town,
the abrupt ascent is softened on his right
  by steps cut in the rock in other days,
    before the stave and ledger had grown light—   105
just so the bank here, plunging like a slide
  from the round above, has been made easier,
    though towering cliffs squeeze us from either side.
We set out on the climb, and on the way
  "Beati pauperes spiritu" rang out,
    more sweetly sung than any words could say.
Ah, what a difference between these trails
  and those of Hell; here every entrance fills
    with joyous song, and there with savage wails!
We were going up the holy steps, and though
  the climb was steep, I seemed to feel much lighter
    than I had felt on level ground below.
"Master," I said, tell me what heaviness
  has been removed from me that I can climb
    yet seem to feel almost no weariness."   120
He answered: "When the *P*'s that still remain,
  though fading, on your brow, are wiped away
    as the first was, without a trace of stain—
then will your feet be filled with good desire;
  not only will they feel no more fatigue,
    but all their joy will be in mounting higher."
A man with some strange thing lodged on his hat
  will stroll, not knowing, till the stares of others
    set him to wonder what they're staring at;

whereat his hand seeks out and verifies
   what he suspected, thus performing for him
   the office he could not serve with his eyes—
just so, I put my right hand to my brow,
   fingers outspread, and found six letters only
   of those that had been carved there down below   135
by the angel with the keys to every grace;
at which a smile shone on my Master's face.

Canto 13

The Poets reach the second cornice and
find the blue-black rock unadorned by carvings.
There are no souls in sight to guide them and Vir-
gil, therefore, turns toward the sun as his guide,
bearing right around the cornice. As they walk on,
Dante hears voices crying out examples of great
love of others (Caritas), the virtue opposed to
Envy. These voices are the Whip of Envy. A short
way beyond, Dante comes upon the souls of the
Envious and describes their punishment. The cor-
nice on which they sit is the color of a bruise, for
every other man's good fortune bruised the souls
of the Envious. They offended with their eyes,
envying all the good they saw of others, and there-
fore their eyes are wired shut. So blinded, they sit
supporting one another, as they never did in life,
and all of them lean for support against the blue-
black cliff. They are dressed in haircloth, the
further to subdue their souls, and they intone
endlessly the Litany of the Saints. Among them
Dante encounters Sapìa of Siena, who relates her
story. When she questions him, Dante confesses
his fear of his own besetting sin, Pride.

We climbed the stairs and stood, now, on the track
   where, for a second time, the mount that heals
   all who ascend it had been terraced back.
The terrace circles the entire ascent
   in much the same way as the one below,
   save that the arc it cuts is sooner bent.
There were no spirits and no carvings there.
   Bare was the cliff-face, bare the level path.
   The rock of both was livid, dark and bare.

Purgatorio

"Were we to wait till someone came this way
    who might direct us," Virgil said to me,
    "I fear that would involve a long delay."
Then he looked up and stared straight at the sun;
    and then, using his right side as a pivot,
    he swung his left around; then he moved on.   15
"O blessed lamp, we face the road ahead
    placing our faith in you; lead us the way
    that we should go in this new place," he said.
"You are the warmth of the world, you are its light;
    if other cause do not urge otherwise,
    your rays alone should serve to lead us right."
We moved on with a will, and in a while
    we had already gone so far up there
    as would be reckoned, here on earth, a mile,
when we began to hear in the air above
    invisible spirits who flew toward us speaking
    sweet invitations to the feast of love.
The first voice that flew past rang to the sky,
    "Vinum non habent!" And from far behind us
    we heard it fade repeating the same cry.   30
Even before we heard it cry its last
    far round the slope, another voice rang out:
    "I am Orestes!"—and it, too, sped past.
"Sweet Father," I began, "what are these cries?"—
    and even as I asked, I heard a third
    bodiless voice say: "Love your enemies."
And my good Master then: "This circle purges
    the guilt of envious spirits, and for these
    who failed in love, love is the lash that scourges.
The rein must cry the opposite of love;
    you will hear it, I expect, before you reach
    the pass of absolution that leads above.
But now look carefully across the air
    ahead of us, and you will see some people
    seated against the inner cliff up there."   45
I opened my eyes wider; further on
    I saw a group of spirits dressed in cloaks
    exactly the same color as the stone.

As we drew nearer I heard prayers and plaints.
 "O Mary, pray for us!" I heard them cry;
 and to Michael, and to Peter, and all saints.
I cannot think there walks the earth today
 a man so hard that he would not be moved
 by what I saw next on that ashen way.
For when I drew near and could see the whole
 penance imposed upon those praying people,
 my eyes milked a great anguish from my soul.
Their cloaks were made of haircloth, coarse and stiff.
 Each soul supported another with his shoulder,
 and all leaned for support against the cliff.   60
The impoverished blind who sit all in a row
 during Indulgences to beg their bread
 lean with their heads together exactly so,
the better to win the pity they beseech,
 not only with their cries, but with their look
 of fainting grief, which pleads as loud as speech.
Just as the sun does not reach to their sight,
 so to those shades of which I spoke just now
 God's rays refuse to offer their delight;
for each soul has its eyelids pierced and sewn
 with iron wires, as men sew new-caught falcons,
 sealing their eyes to make them settle down.
Somehow it seemed to me a shameful act
 to stare at others and remain unseen.
 I turned to Virgil. He, with perfect tact,   75
knew what the mute was laboring to say
 and did not wait my question. "Speak," he said,
 "but count your words and see they do not stray."
Virgil was walking by me down the ledge
 on the side from which—because no parapet
 circled the cliff—one might plunge off the edge.
On the other side those spirits kept their places
 absorbed in prayer, while through the ghastly stitches
 tears forced their way and flowed down from their faces.
I turned to them and said: "O souls afire
 with hope of seeing Heaven's Light, and thus
 already certain of your heart's desire—

so may High Grace soon wash away the scum
    that clogs your consciousness, that memory's stream
    may flow without a stain in joys to come—   90
tell me if there is any Latin soul
    among you here. I dearly wish to know,
    and telling me may help him to his goal."
"We are all citizens of one sublime
    and final city, brother; you mean to ask
    who lived in Italy in his pilgrim-time."
These are the words I heard a spirit say
    from somewhere further on. I moved up, therefore,
    in order to direct my voice that way.
I saw one shade who seemed to have in mind
    what I had said.—How could I tell? She sat
    chin raised, the waiting gesture of the blind.
"O soul self-humbled for the climb to Grace,"
    I said, "if it was you who spoke, I beg you,
    make yourself known either by name or place."   105
"I was Sienese," she answered. "On this shelf
    I weep away my world-guilt with these others
    in prayers to Him that He vouchsafe Himself.
Sapìa was I, though sapient I was not;
    I found more joy in the bad luck of others
    than in the good that fell to my own lot.
If this confession rings false to your ears,
    hear my tale out; then see if I was mad.
    In the descending arc of my own years,
the blood of my own land was being spilled
    in battle outside Colle's walls, and I
    prayed God to do what He already willed.
So were they turned—their forces overthrown—
    to the bitter paths of flight; and as I watched
    I felt such joy as I had never known;   120
such that I raised my face, flushed with false power,
    and screamed to God: 'Now I no longer fear You'—
    like a blackbird when the sun comes out an hour.
Not till my final hour had all but set
    did I turn back to God, longing for peace.
    Penance would not yet have reduced my debt

had not Pier Pettinaio in saintly love
   grieved for my soul and offered holy prayers
   that interceded for me there above.
But who are you that you come here to seek
   such news of us; and have your eyes unsewn,
   as I believe; and breathe yet when you speak?"
"My eyes," I said, "will yet be taken from me
   upon this ledge, but not for very long;
   little they sinned through being turned in envy.   135
My soul is gripped by a far greater fear
   of the torment here below, for even now
   I seem to feel the burden those souls bear."
And she: "Then who has led you to this round,
   if you think to go below again?" And I:
  "He who is with me and who makes no sound.
And I still live; if you would have me move
   my mortal feet down there in your behalf,
   ask what you will, O soul blessed by God's love."
"Oh," she replied, "this is a thing so rare
   it surely means that God has loved you greatly;
   from time to time, then, help me with a prayer.
I beg by all you most desire to win
   that if you walk again on Tuscan soil
   you will restore my name among my kin.   150
You will find them in that foolish mob whose dream
   is Talamone now and who will lose there
   more than they did once in their silly scheme
to find the lost Diana. Though on that coast
it is the admirals who will lose the most."

Canto 14

Dante's conversation with Sapìa of Siena
is overheard by two spirits who sit side by side
against the inner cliff-face. They are Guido del
Duca and Rinieri da Calboli. Dante enters into
conversation with them, and Guido denounces
the inhabitants of the cities of the Valley of the
Arno. He then prophesies the slaughter that
Rinieri's grandson, Fulcieri, shall visit upon Flor-
ence, and also that Fulcieri's actions will have a
bearing on Dante's approaching exile from Flor-
ence. Guido concludes with a lament for the past
glories of Romagna as compared to its present
degeneracy. Leaving the two spirits in tears,
Dante and Virgil move on. Suddenly Dante is
struck with terror by two bodiless voices that
break upon them like thunder. The voices are
the Rein of Envy. The first is the voice of Cain la-
menting that he is forever cut off from man-
kind. The second is the voice of Aglauros, who
was changed to stone as a consequence of her
envy of her sister. The canto ends with Virgil's
denunciation of mankind's stubborn refusal to
heed the glory of the heavens and
to prepare for eternal grace.

"Who do you think that is? He roams our hill
    before death gives him wings, and he's left free
    to shut his eyes or open them at will."
"I don't know, but I know he's not alone.
    Ask him—you're nearer—but put in a way
    that won't offend him. Take a careful tone."
Thus, on my right, and leaning head to head,
    two of those spirits were discussing me.
    Then they turned up their faces, and one said:

"O soul that though locked fast within the flesh
   still makes its way toward Heaven's blessedness,
   in charity, give comfort to our wish;
tell us your name and city, for your climb
   fills us with awe at such a gift of grace
   as never has been seen up to this time."   15
And I: "In Falterona lies the source
   of a brook that grows and winds through Tuscany
   till a hundred miles will not contain its course.
From its banks I bring this flesh. As for my name—
   to tell you who I am would serve no purpose;
   I have as yet won very little fame."
And the first spirit: "If I rightly weigh
   your words upon the balance of my mind,
   it is the Arno you intend to say."
And the other to him: "Why is he so careful
   to avoid the river's name? He speaks as men do
   when they refer to things too foul or fearful."
To which the shade he had addressed replied:
   "That I don't know; but it would be a mercy
   if even the name of such a valley died.   30
From its source high in the great range that outsoars
   almost all others (from whose chain Pelorus
   was cut away) to the point where it restores
in endless soft surrender what the sun
   draws from the deep to fall again as rain,
   that every rill and river may flow on,
men run from virtue as if from a foe
   or poisonous snake. Either the land is cursed,
   or long corrupted custom drives them so.
And curse or custom so transform all men
   who live there in that miserable valley,
   one would believe they fed in Circe's pen.
It sets its first weak course among sour swine,
   indecent beasts more fit to grub and grunt
   for acorns than to sit to bread and wine.   45
It finds next, as it flows down and fills out,
   a pack of curs, their snarl worse than their bite;
   and in contempt it turns aside its snout.

Down, down it flows, and as the dogs grow fewer
   the wolves grow thicker on the widening banks
   of that accursed and Godforsaken sewer.
It drops through darkened gorges, then, to find
   the foxes in their lairs, so full of fraud
   they fear no trap set by a mortal mind.
Nor will I, though this man hear what I say,
   hold back the prophecy revealed to me;
   for well may he recall it on his way.
I see your grandson riding to the chase.
   He hunts the wolves that prowl by the fierce river.
   He has become the terror of that place.   60
He sells their living flesh, then—shame on shame—
   the old beast slaughters them himself, for sport.
   Many will die, and with them, his good name.
He comes from that sad wood covered with gore
   and leaves it in such ruin, a thousand years
   will not serve to restock its groves once more."
Just as a man to whom bad chance announces
   a dreadful ill, distorts his face in grief,
   no matter from what quarter the hurt pounces—
just so that shade, who had half turned his head
   better to listen, showed his shock and pain
   when he had registered what the other said.
So moved by one's words and the other's face,
   I longed to know their names. I asked them, therefore,
   phrasing my plea with prayers to win their grace;   75
at which the spokesman of the two replied:
   "You beg me of my good grace that I grant you
   what I have asked of you and been denied;
but God has willed His favor to shine forth
   so greatly in you, I cannot be meager.
   Guido del Duca was my name on earth.
The fires of envy raged so in my blood
   that I turned livid if I chanced to see
   another man rejoice in his own good.
This seed I sowed; this sad straw I reap here.
   O humankind, why do you set your hearts
   on what it is forbidden you to share?

This is Rinier, the honor and the pride
  of the house of the Calboli, of which no one
  inherited his merit when he died.   90
Nor in that war-torn land whose boundary-lines
  the sea and the Reno draw to the east and west;
  and, north and south, the Po and the Apennines,
is his the only house that seems to be
  bred bare of those accomplishments and merits
  which are the good and truth of chivalry.
For the land has lost the good of hoe and plow,
  and poisonous thorns so choke it that long years
  of cultivation would scarce clear it now.
Where is Mainardi? Have you lost the seed
  of Lizio? Traversaro? di Carpigna?
  O Romagnoles changed to a bastard breed!
When will a Fabbro evermore take root
  in all Bologna? or in Faenza, a Fosco?—
  who was his little plant's most noble shoot.   105
O Tuscan, can I speak without a tear
  of Ugolino d'Azzo and Guido da Prata,
  who shared our time on earth? and with them there
Federico di Tignoso and his train?
  the house of the Traversari and the Anastagi,
  both heirless now? or, dry-eyed, think again
of knights and ladies, of the court and field
  that bonded us in love and courtesy
  where now all hearts are savagely self-sealed?
O Brettinoro, why do you delay?
  Your lords and many more have fled your guilt;
  and why, like them, will you not melt away?
Bagnacaval does well to have no heirs;
  and Castrocaro badly, and Conio worse
  in bothering to breed such counts as theirs.   120
The Pagani will do well enough, all told,
  when once their fiend is gone, but not so well
  their name will ever again shine as pure gold.
O Ugolin de' Fantolini, your name
  remains secure, since you have none to bear it
  and, in degeneracy, bring it to shame.

But leave me Tuscan, I am more inclined
   to spell my grief in tears now than in words;
   for speaking thus has wrung my heart and mind."
We knew those dear souls heard us go away.
   Their silence, therefore, served as our assurance
   that, leaving them, we had not gone astray.
We had scarce left those spirits to their prayer,
   when suddenly a voice that ripped like lightning
   struck at us with a cry that split the air: 135
"All men are my destroyers!" It rolled past
   as thunder rolls away into the sky
   if the cloud bursts to rain in the first blast.
Our ears were scarcely settled from that burst
   when lo, the second broke, with such a crash
   it seemed the following thunder of the first:
"I am Aglauros who was turned to stone!"
   Whereat, to cower in Virgil's arms, I took
   a step to my right instead of going on.
The air had fallen still on every hand
   when Virgil said: "That was the iron bit
   that ought to hold men hard to God's command.
But still you gulp the Hellbait hook and all
   and the Old Adversary reels you in.
   Small good to you is either curb or call.   150
The heavens cry to you, and all around
   your stubborn souls wheel their eternal glory,
   and yet you keep your eyes fixed on the ground.
And for each turning from the joys of love
the All-Discerning flails you from above."

Canto 15

It is 3:00 P.M. and the Poets are walking straight into the sun when an even greater radiance blinds Dante and he finds himself in the presence of the Angel of Caritas who passes the Poets on to the ledge above. As they ascend, they hear the angel sing the fifth beatitude. As soon as the Poets enter the third cornice, Dante is entranced by three visions which constitute the Whip of Wrath, extolling the virtue of meekness toward kin, toward friends, and toward enemies. Since these events consume three hours, it is 6:00 P.M. of the second day in Purgatory when the Poets, moving forward, observe an enormous cloud of smoke ahead of them.

Of that bright sphere that, like a child at play,
   skips endlessly, as much as lies between
   the third hour's end and the first light of day
remained yet of the sun's course toward the night.
   Thus, it was Vespers there upon the mountain
   and midnight here in Italy, where I write.
The sun's late rays struck us full in the face,
   for in our circling course around the mountain
   we now were heading toward his resting place.
Suddenly, then, I felt my brow weighed down
   by a much greater splendor than the first.
   I was left dazzled by some cause unknown
and raised my hands and joined them in the air
   above my brows, making a sunshade of them
   which, so to speak, blunted the piercing glare.
When a ray strikes glass or water, its reflection
   leaps upward from the surface once again
   at the same angle but opposite direction

15

from which it strikes, and in an equal space
  spreads equally from a plumb line to midpoint,
  as trial and theory show to be the case.
Just so, it seemed to me, reflected light
  struck me from up ahead, so dazzlingly
  I had to shut my eyes to spare my sight.
"Dear Father, what is that great blaze ahead
  from which I cannot shade my eyes enough,
  and which is still approaching us?" I said.
"Do not be astonished," answered my sweet Friend,
  "if those of the heavenly family still blind you.
  He has been sent to bid us to ascend.   30
Soon now, such sights will not aggrieve your sense
  but fill you with a joy as great as any
  Nature has fitted you to experience."
We stand before the blessed angel now.
  With joyous voice he cries: "Enter. The stair
  is far less steep than were the two below."
We had gone past him and were climbing on
  when *"Blessed are the merciful"* hymned out
  behind us, and *"Rejoice you who have won."*
My Guide and I were going up the stair—
  we two alone—and I, thinking to profit
  from his wise words as we were climbing there,
questioned him thus: "What deep intent lay hidden
  in what the spirit from Romagna said?
  He spoke of 'sharing' and said it was 'forbidden.'"   45
And he: "He knows the sad cost of his own
  besetting sin; small wonder he reviles it
  in hope that you may have less to atone.
It is because you focus on the prize
  of worldly goods, which every sharing lessens
  that Envy pumps the bellows for your sighs.
But if, in true love for the highest sphere,
  your longing were turned upward, then your hearts
  would never be consumed by such a fear;
for the more there are there who say 'ours'—not 'mine'—
  by that much is each richer, and the brighter
  within that cloister burns the love divine."

"I am left hungrier being thus fed,
 and my mind is more in doubt being thus answered,
 than if I had not asked at all," I said.   60
"How can each one of many who divide
 a single good have more of it, so shared,
 than if a few had kept it?" He replied:
"Because within the habit of mankind
 you set your whole intent on earthly things,
 the true light falls as darkness on your mind.
The infinite and inexpressible Grace
 which is in Heaven, gives itself to Love
 as a sunbeam gives itself to a bright surface.
As much light as it finds there, it bestows;
 thus, as the blaze of Love is spread more widely,
 the greater the Eternal Glory grows.
As mirror reflects mirror, so, above,
 the more there are who join their souls, the more
 Love learns perfection, and the more they love.   75
And if this answer does not yet appease
 your hunger, you will soon see Beatrice,
 and this, and every wish, shall find surcease.
Only strive hard that soon no trace may show
 of the five scars which true contrition heals—
 as the first two have faded from your brow."
I was about to say, "I am satisfied,"
 when suddenly we came to the next round,
 and my eyes' avidity left me tongue-tied.
Here suddenly, in an ecstatic trance,
 I find myself caught up into a vision.
 I see a crowded temple, and in the entrance
a Lady by herself, her eyes aglow
 with the sweet grace of a mother, saying gently:
 "My son, my son, why do you treat us so?   90
Your father and I were seeking you in tears."
 So saying, she falls silent, and as quickly
 as it first came, the vision disappears.
Another Lady now appears, her cheeks
 bathed in those waters that are born of grief
 when grief is born of anger. Now she speaks:

"O Pisistratus, if you are true lord
   of the city for whose name the gods debated,
   and whence all learning shone forth afterward,
avenge yourself on the presumptuous one
   who dared embrace our daughter." And her master,
   . sweetly forbearing, in a placid tone,
and smiling gently at her, answers thus:
   "What shall we do to those that wish us harm
   if we take vengeance upon those that love us?"   105
Then there appears a wild and murderous spill
   of people hate-incensed, stoning a boy,
   and roaring to each other's wrath: "Kill! Kill!"
I see the boy sink to the ground, his death
   already heavy on him, but his eyes,
   like gates of Heaven, open through such wrath;
and even in his last extremity
   he prays God to forgive his murderers,
   turning to Him the look that unlocks pity.
When finally my soul could see and feel
   things which were true outside it, I understood
   my not-false errors had been dreams, though real.
My Guide, who watched me as I moved along
   like one just wakened and still sleep-stunned, said:
   "You barely seem to keep your feet—what's wrong?   120
You've stumbled on now for a good half-league
   with eyes half-shut and legs too wide, like one
   groggy with wine or dropping with fatigue."
"O my sweet Father, if you wish to know,
   listen, and I shall tell you what I saw,"
I answered, "when my legs were stricken so."
"Were you to wear a hundred masks," he said,
   "to hide your face, it would lie open to me
   so that your slightest thought might yet be read.
These visions warn your soul on no account
   still to refuse the water of that peace
   which flows to man from the Eternal Fount.
I did not ask 'what's wrong' as a man might
   who sees with eyes alone, and when the body
   is lying senseless has no other sight;   135

Then there appears a wild and murderous spill
of people hate-incensed, stoning a boy
and roaring to each other's wrath: "Kill! Kill!"

Purgatorio

but rather to put strength into your stride;
  for so must laggards be spurred on to use
  their reawakening senses as a guide."
Through the last vesper-hour we traveled on,
  looking ahead as far as eye could see
  against the level rays of the late sun.
And there ahead of us against the light
  we saw come billowing in our direction
  by slow degrees, a smoke as black as night.
Nor was there refuge from it anywhere.
It took our sight from us, and the pure air.

Canto 16

The Poets enter the acrid and blinding smoke in which the Wrathful suffer their purification. As Wrath is a corrosive state of the spirit, so the smoke stings and smarts. As Wrath obscures the true light of God, so the smoke plunges all into darkness. Within it, Dante hears souls singing the Litany of the Lamb of God. The Lamb, of course, is the symbol of the meekness of divine love. As such, it is the opposite of Wrath. A further purification is implicit in the fact that the souls all sing as if with one voice, for Wrath is the sin that soonest breeds division among men, and only spiritual concord can reunite them. Marco Lombardo hears Dante speak and calls to him. Invited by Dante, Marco accompanies the Poets to the edge of the smoke, discoursing on the causes of the modern world's corruption, which he locates in the usurpation of temporal power and wealth by the Church. As Marco concludes, a light begins to appear through the smoke. Marco explains that it is the radiance of the angel who waits ahead. He then turns back, for he is not yet fit to show himself to the angel of the Lord.

No gloom of Hell, nor of a night allowed
   no planet under its impoverished sky,
   the deepest dark that may be drawn by cloud,
ever drew such a veil across my face,
   nor one whose texture rasped my senses so,
   as did the smoke that wrapped us in that place.
The sting was more than open eyes could stand.
   My wise and faithful Guide drew near me, therefore,
   and let me grasp his shoulder with my hand.

Just as a blind man, lest he lose his road
    or tumble headlong and be hurt or killed,
    walks at his guide's back when he goes abroad—
so moved I through that foul and acrid air,
    led by my sweet Friend's voice, which kept repeating:
    "Take care. Do not let go of me. Take care."   15
And I heard other voices. They seemed to pray
    for peace and pardon to the Lamb of God
    which, of Its mercy, takes our sins away.
They offered up three prayers, and every one
    began with *Agnus Dei,* and each word
    and measure rose in perfect unison.
"Master, do I hear spirits on this path?"
    I said. And he to me: "You do indeed,
    and they are loosening the knot of wrath."
"And who are you, then, that you cleave our smoke,
    yet speak of us as if you still kept time
    by kalends?"—without warning, someone spoke
these words to me; at which my Lord and Guide
    said: "Answer. And inquire respectfully
    if one may find a way up on this side."   30
And I: "O spirit growing pure and free
    to go once more in beauty to your Maker—
    you will hear wonders if you follow me."
"As far as is permitted me," he said,
    "I will. And if the smoke divide our eyes,
    our ears shall serve to join us in their stead."
So I began: "I make my way above
    still in these swathings death dissolves. I came here
    through the infernal grief. Now, since God's love
incloses me in grace so bounteous
    that He permits me to behold His court
    by means wholly unknown to modern use—
pray tell me who you were before you died,
    and if I go the right way to the pass
    that leads above. Your words shall be our guide."   45
"I was a Lombard. Marco was my name.
    I knew the ways of the world and loved that good
    at which the bows of men no longer aim.

"And who are you, then, that you cleave our smoke,
　　yet speak of us as if you still kept time
　　by kalends?"

You are headed the right way to reach the stair
   that leads above," he added. And: "I pray you
   to pray for me when you have mounted there."
And I: "On my faith I vow it. But a doubt
   has formed within me and has swelled so large
   I shall explode unless I speak it out.
It was a simple doubt at first, but now
   it doubles and grows sure as I compare
   your words with what was said to me below.
The world, as you have said, is truly bare
   of every trace of good; swollen with evil;
   by evil overshadowed everywhere.   60
But wherein lies the fault? I beg to know
   that I may see the truth and so teach others.
   Some see it in the stars; some, here below."
A deep sigh wrung by grief, almost a moan
   escaped as a long "Ah!" Then he said: "Brother,
   the world is blind and you are its true son.
Mankind sees in the heavens alone the source
   of all things, good and evil; as if by law
   they shaped all mortal actions in their course.
If that were truly so, then all free will
   would be destroyed, and there would be no justice
   in giving bliss for virtue, pain for evil.
The spheres *do* start your impulses along.
   I do not say *all*, but suppose I did—
   the light of reason still tells right from wrong;   75
and free will also, which, though it be strained
   in the first battles with the heavens, still
   can conquer all if it is well sustained.
You are free subjects of a more immense
   nature and power which grants you intellect
   to free you from the heavens' influence.
If, therefore, men today turn from God's laws,
   the fault is in yourselves to seek and find;
   and I shall truly explicate the cause.
From the hand of God, whose love shines like a ray
   upon it, even before birth, comes forth
   the simple soul which, like a child at play,

cries, laughs, and ignorant of every measure
    but the glad impulse of its joyous Maker,
    turns eagerly to all that gives it pleasure.   90
It tastes small pleasures first. To these it clings,
    deceived, and seeks no others, unless someone
    curb it or guide its love to higher things.
Men, therefore, need restraint by law, and need
    a monarch over them who sees at least
    the towers of the True City. Laws, indeed,
there are, but who puts nations to their proof?
    No one. The Shepherd who now leads mankind
    can chew the cud, but lacks the cloven hoof.
The people, then, seeing their guide devour
    those worldly things to which their hunger turns
    graze where he grazes and ask nothing more.
The bad state of the modern world is due—
    as you may see, then—to bad leadership;
    and not to natural corruption in you.   105
Rome used to shine in two suns when her rod
    made the world good, and each showed her its way:
    one to the ordered world, and one to God.
Now one declining sun puts out the other.
    The sword and crook are one, and only evil
    can follow from them when they are together;
for neither fears the other, being one.
    Look closely at the ear, if still you doubt me,
    for by the seed it bears is the plant known.
Honor and courtesy once made their home
    in the land the Po and the Adige water—
    till Frederick came to loggerheads with Rome.
Now any man who has good cause to fear
    the sound of truth or honest company
    may cross it safely—he will find none there.   120
True, three old men are left in whom the past
    reproves the present. How time drags for them
    till God remove them to their joy at last—
Conrad da Palazzo, the good Gherard',
    and Guido da Castel, who is better named,
    in the fashion of the French, 'The Honest Lombard.'

Say, then, that since the Church has sought to be
    two governments at once, she sinks in muck,
    befouling both her power and ministry."
"O Marco mine," I said, "you reason well!
    And now I know why Levi's sons alone
    could not inherit wealth in Israel.
But who is this Gherard' in whom you say
    the past survives untarnished to reprove
    the savage breed of this degenerate day?"   135
"Your question seeks to test me," said Lombardo,
    "or else to trick me. How can you speak Tuscan
    and still seem to know nothing of Gherardo?
Just what his surname is, I do not know—
    unless he might be known as Gaia's father.
    Godspeed; this is as far as I may go.
See there across the smoke, like dawn's first rays,
    the light swell like a glory and a guide.
    The angel of this place gives forth that blaze,
and it is not fit he see me." Thus he spoke,
and said no more, but turned back through the smoke.

Canto 17

*The Poets emerge from the smoke, and
Dante is immediately enrapt by the visions that
make up the Rein of Wrath. In succession he
beholds the destruction caused by Wrath to
Procne, to Haman, and to Queen Amata. Dante
emerges from his trance to hear the Angel of
Meekness calling to him to show him the ascent,
and the Poets mount at once as the beatitude,
"Blessed are the peacemakers," is sounded behind them. They reach the top of the ascent just as
night falls, and though they might normally continue along the level way Dante feels his body so
weighted down that he has to pause and rest. As
the Poets rest, Virgil gives Dante a discourse on
love, demonstrating to him that all actions spring
from either natural or spiritual love and that it is
the various perversions of love that lead to
the sins that are punished in Purgatory.*

Reader, if you have ever been closed in
   by mountain mist that left you with no eyes
   to see with, save as moles do, through the skin,
think how those dense damp vapors thinned away
   slow bit by bit till through them the sun's ball
   was once more dimly visible—thus you may,
and without strain, imagine from your own
   recalled experience how I came again
   to see the sun, which now was almost down.
Thus, matching steps with my true Guide once more,
   I passed beyond the cloud into those rays
   which lay already dead on the low shore.
O Fantasy, which can entrance us so
   that we at times stand and are not aware
   though in our ears a thousand trumpets blow!—

15

Purgatorio

what moves you since our senses lie dead then?
 A light that forms in Heaven of itself,
 or of His will who sends its rays to men.
A vision grew within me of the wrong
 she did who for her cruelty was changed
 into that bird which most delights in song;
and my imagination was so shut
 into itself that what I saw revealed
 could never have come to me from without.
Next, down like rain, a figure crucified
 fell into my high fantasy, his face
 fierce and contemptuous even as he died.
Nearby him great Ahasuerus stood,
 Esther his wife, and the just Mordecai,
 whose word and deed were always one in good. 30
And as soap bubbles rise in air and seem
 full-bodied things, then rupture of themselves
 when the film about them breaks—just so, that dream
vanished, and through my vision rose an image
 in which a maid cried: "O Queen! Queen no more!
 Your very being canceled by your rage!
All not to lose Lavinia? Ah, mother,
 now have you truly lost her. I am she,
 and mourn your death before I mourn another."
When strong light beats against a man's closed eyes
 his sleep is broken in him; yet, though broken,
 gives a last twitch before it wholly dies;
my vision fell from me exactly so
 the instant a new light beat on my face,
 a light outshining any that men know. 45
I was looking all about, as if to find
 where I might be, when a new voice that cried,
 "Here is the ascent!" drove all else from my mind
and kindled in my spirit such a fire
 to see who spoke, as cannot ever rest
 till it stand face to face with its desire.
But, as in looking at the sun, whose rays
 keep his form hidden from our stricken eyes—
 so I lacked power to look into that blaze.

279

"A spirit of Heaven guides us toward the height;
    he shows us the ascent before we ask
    and hides himself in his own holy light.
He does for us what men in the world's uses
    do only for themselves; for who sees need
    and waits a plea, already half refuses.   60
To such sweet bidding let our feet reply
    by striving as they may before night fall;
    for then they may not, till day light the sky."
So spoke my Guide, and he and I as one
    moved toward the ascent; and soon as I had mounted
    the first step cut into that ramp of stone,
I felt what seemed to be a great wing fan
    my face and heard: "Blessèd are the peacemakers,
    who feel no evil wrath toward any man."
The last rays, after which night rules the air,
    were now so far above us that already
    the stars began to shine through, here and there.
"O strength, why do you melt away?" I said
    several times over to myself, for now
    it seemed my legs were turning into lead.   75
We had come to where the stair ascends no more
    and we were stuck fast on the topmost step
    like a vessel half drawn up upon the shore.
I waited with my head cocked to one side
    for any sound that might reveal the nature
    of the new ledge. Then, turning to my Guide,
I said: "Dear Father, what impurity
    is washed in pain here? Though our feet must stay,
    I beg you not to stay your speech." And he:
"That love of good which in the life before
    lay idle in the soul is paid for now.
    Here Sloth strains at the once-neglected oar.
But that you may more clearly know the Way,
    give your entire attention to my words;
    thus shall you gather good fruit from delay.   90
Neither Creator nor His creatures move,
    as you well know," he said, "but in the action
    of animal or of mind-directed love.

Natural love may never fall to error.
  The other may, by striving to bad ends,
  or by too little, or by too much fervor.
While it desires the Eternal Good and measures
  its wish for secondary goods in reason,
  this love cannot give rise to sinful pleasures.
But when it turns to evil, or shows more
  or less zeal than it ought for what is good,
  then the creature turns on its Creator.
Thus you may understand that love alone
  is the true seed of every merit in you
  and of all acts for which you must atone.   105
Now inasmuch as love cannot abate
  its good wish for the self that loves, all things
  are guarded by their nature from self-hate.
And since no being may exist alone
  and apart from the First Being, by their nature,
  all beings lack the power to hate that One.
Therefore, if I have parsed the truth of things,
  the evil that man loves must be his neighbor's.
  In mortal clay such bad love has three springs:
some think they see their own hope to advance
  tied to their neighbor's fall, and thus they long
  to see him cast down from his eminence;
some fear their power, preferment, honor, fame
  will suffer by another's rise, and thus,
  irked by his good, desire his ruin and shame;   120
and some at the least injury catch fire
  and are consumed by thoughts of vengeance; thus,
  their neighbor's harm becomes their chief desire.
Such threefold love those just below us here
  purge from their souls. The other, which seeks good,
  but without measure, I shall now make clear.
All men, though in a vague way, apprehend
  a good their souls may rest in, and desire it;
  each, therefore, strives to reach his chosen end.
If you are moved to see good or pursue it,
  but with a lax love, it is on this ledge—
  after a proper penance—you will rue it.

There is another good which bears bad fruit;
   it is not happiness, nor the true essence
   of the Eternal Good, its flower and root.   135
The love that yields too much to this false good
   is mourned on the three cornices above us;
   but in what way it may be understood
as a tripartite thing, I shall not say.
That, you may learn yourself upon our way."

Canto 18

Virgil continues his discourse on love, explaining the relation of love and free will, but warns Dante that reason is limited. Dante must seek the final answer from Beatrice, for the question involves one of the mysteries of faith. It is near midnight when Virgil concludes, and Dante is starting to drowse when he is suddenly brought awake by a long train of souls who come running and shouting from around the mountain. They are the Slothful, the souls of those who recognized the good but were not diligent in pursuit of it. As once they delayed, so now they are all hurry and zeal and will not even pause to speak to the Poets. Two souls run before the rest shouting aloud the Whip of Sloth, one citing Mary as an example of holy zeal, the other citing Caesar as an example of temporal zeal. Virgil hails the racing souls to ask the nearer way to the ascent, but not even the news that Dante is still alive slows them. One soul, a former abbot of San Zeno, shouts back an answer while still running. Behind the train come two more souls shouting the Rein of Sloth, citing as examples of the downfall of the laggard, the Israelites in the desert, and those followers of Aeneas who remained in Sicily. The souls pass from sight and hearing. Dante sinks into sleep, his head full of confused thoughts, which are transformed into a dream.

His explanation at an end, my Guide,
   that lofty scholar, scrutinized my face
   as if to see if I seemed satisfied.
And I, my thirst already sprung anew,
   said nothing, thinking, "He may well be tired
   of all this questioning I put him through."

But that true Father, sensing both my thirst
   and that I was too timid to reveal it,
   encouraged me to speak by speaking first.
I, therefore: "Master, in the light you shed
   my sight grows so acute that I see clearly
   all that your argument implied or said.
But, dear and gentle Father, please discourse
   more fully on that love in which you say
   all good and evil actions have their source."   15
And he: "Focus the keen eyes of your mind
   on what I say, and you will see made clear
   the error of the blind who lead the blind.
The soul, being created prone to love,
   is drawn at once to all that pleases it,
   as soon as pleasure summons it to move.
From that which really is, your apprehension
   extracts a form which it unfolds within you;
   that form thereby attracts the mind's attention,
then if the mind, so drawn, is drawn to it,
   that summoning force is love; and thus within you,
   through pleasure, a new natural bond is knit.
Then, just as fire yearns upward through the air,
   being so formed that it aspires by nature
   to be in its own element up there—   30
so love, which is a spiritual motion,
   fills the trapped soul, and it can never rest
   short of the thing that fills it with devotion.
By now you will, of course, have understood
   how little of the truth they see who claim
   that every love is, in itself, a good;
for though love's substance always will appear
   to be a good, not every impress made,
   even in finest wax, is good and clear."
"Your words and my own eager mind reveal
   exactly what love is," I said, "but now
   there is an even greater doubt I feel.
If love springs from outside the soul's own will,
   it being made to love, what merit is there
   in loving good, or blame in loving ill?"   45

And he to me: "As far as reason sees,
   I can reply. The rest you must ask Beatrice.
   The answer lies within faith's mysteries.
Every substantial form distinct from matter,
   and yet united with it in some way,
   has a specific power in it. This latter
is not perceivable save as it gives
   evidence of its workings and effects—
   as the green foliage tells us a plant lives.
Therefore, no man can know whence springs the light
   of his first cognizance, nor of the bent
   of such innate primordial appetite
as springs within you, as within the bee
   the instinct to make honey; and such instincts
   are, in themselves, not blamable nor worthy.   60
Now, that all later wills and this first bent
   may thrive, the innate counsel of your reason
   must surely guard the threshold of consent.
This is the principle from which accrue
   your just deserts, according as it reaps
   and winnows good or evil love in you.
Those masters who best reasoned Nature's plan
   discerned this innate liberty, and therefore
   they left their moral science to guide man.
Or put it this way: all love, let us say,
   that burns in you, springs from necessity;
   but you still have the power to check its sway.
These noble powers Beatrice will comprehend
   as 'The Free Will.' Keep that term well in mind
   if she should speak of it when you ascend."   75
It was near midnight. The late-risen moon,
   like a brass bucket polished bright as fire,
   thinned out the lesser stars, which seemed to drown.
It traveled retrograde across that sign
   the sun burns when the Romans look between
   the Sards and Corsicans to its decline.
And he who made Piètola shine above
   all other Mantuan towns had discharged fully
   the burden I had laid on him for love;

because of which I, being pleased to find
    such clear and open answers to my questions,
    was rambling drowsily within my mind.
I wakened in an instant to a pack
    of people running toward us, a great mob
    that broke around the mountain at my back;   90
as once, of old, wild hordes ran through the night
    along Ismenus' and Asopus' banks
    when Thebes invoked no more than Bacchus' might—
in such a frenzy, far as I could see,
    those who were spurred by goodwill and high love
    ran bent like scythes along that cornice toward me.
They were upon us soon, for all that rout
    was running furiously, and out in front
    two spirits streaming tears were calling out:
"Mary *ran* to the hills"—so one refrain;
    and the other: "Caesar, to subdue Ilerda,
    struck at Marseilles, and then *swooped* down on Spain."
"Faster! Faster! To be slow in love
    is to lose time," cried those who came behind.
    "Strive on that grace may bloom again above."   105
"O souls in whom the great zeal you now show
    no doubt redeems the negligence and delay
    that marred your will to do good, there below,
this man lives—truly—and the instant day
    appears again, he means to climb. Please show him
    how he may reach the pass the nearer way."
So spoke my Master, and one running soul
    without so much as breaking step replied:
    "Come after us, and you will find the hole.
The will to move on with all speed so fills us
    we cannot stop; we humbly beg your pardon
    if duty makes us seem discourteous.
I was Abbot of San Zeno in the reign
    of the good emperor Frederick Barbarossa,
    of whom the Milanese still speak with pain.   120
And another with one foot now in the grave
    will shed tears for that monastery soon
    and rue the evil orders he once gave.

Purgatorio

For he has set his son up as the head—
   a man deformed in body, worse in mind,
   and bastard born—in its true pastor's stead."
He had by then left us so far behind
   that if he said more, it was lost to me;
   but I was pleased to keep this much in mind.
My aid on all occasion, the prompt Master,
   said: "Look, for here come two who cry aloud
   the Scourge of Sloth, that souls may flee it faster."
At the tail end one runner cried: "They died
   before the Jordan saw its heirs, those people
   for whom the Red Sea's waters stood aside."   135
The other: "Those who found it too laborious
   to go the whole way with Anchises' son
   cut from their own lives all that was most glorious."
Then when those shades had drawn so far ahead
   that I could not make out a trace of them,
   a new thought seized upon me, and it bred
so many more, so various, and so scrambled,
   that turning round and round inside itself
   so many ways at once, my reason rambled;
I closed my eyes and all that tangled theme
was instantly transformed into a dream.

Canto 19

Just before morning (when the truth is dreamed) Dante dreams of the Siren that lures the souls of men to incontinent worldliness. Hideous in her true form, the Siren grows irresistible in men's eyes as they look upon her. A Heavenly Lady races in upon the dream and calls to Virgil who, thus summoned, strips the Siren, exposing her filthy body. Such a stench rises from her, so exposed, that Dante wakens shuddering to find Virgil calling him to resume the journey. The Angel of Zeal shows them the passage, and when his wings have fanned the Poets, Dante casts off his depression and lethargy, and rushes up the remaining length of the passage. Arrived at the fifth cornice, Virgil inquires the way of one of the souls of the Hoarders and Wasters, who lie motionless and outstretched, bound hand and foot, with their faces in the dust. The soul of Pope Adrian V replies that if they have incurred no guilt by hoarding or wasting, they may pass on the right. Dante kneels in reverence to Adrian and is scolded for doing so. After dismissing Dante in order to resume his purification, Adrian requests that his niece, Alagia, be asked to pray for his soul.

At the hour when the heat of the day is overcome
   by earth, or at times by Saturn, and can no longer
   temper the cold of the moon; when on the dome
of the eastern sky the geomancers sight
   Fortuna Major rising on a course
   on which, and soon, it will be drowned in light;
there came to me in a dream a stuttering crone,
   squint-eyed, clubfooted, both her hands deformed,
   and her complexion like a whitewashed stone.

I stared at her; and just as the new sun
    breathes life to night-chilled limbs, just so my look
    began to free her tongue, and one by one
drew straight all her deformities, and warmed
    her dead face till it bloomed as love would wish it
    for its delight. When she was thus transformed,   15
her tongue thus loosened, she began to sing
    in such a voice that only with great pain
    could I have turned from her soliciting.
"I am," she sang, "Sirena. I am she
    whose voice is honeyed with such sweet enticements
    it trances sailing men far out to sea.
I turned Ulysses from his wanderer's way
    with my charmed song, and few indeed who taste
    how well I satisfy would think to stray."
Her mouth had not yet shut when at my side
    appeared a saintly Lady, poised and eager
    to heap confusion on the Siren's pride.
"O Virgil, Virgil! Who," she cried, "is this?"
    Roused by her indignation, Virgil came;
    his eyes did not once leave that soul of bliss.   30
He seized the witch and with one rip laid bare
    all of her front, her loins and her foul belly:
    I woke sick with the stench that rose from there.
I turned then, and my Virgil said to me:
    "I have called at least three times now. Rise and come
    and let us find your entrance." Willingly
I rose to my feet. Already the high day
    lit all the circles of the holy mountain.
    The sun was at our backs as we took our way.
I followed in his steps, my brow as drawn
    as is a man's so bowed with thought he bends
    like half an arch of a bridge. And moving on,
I heard the words: "Come. This is where you climb"
    pronounced in such a soft and loving voice
    as is not heard here in our mortal time.   45
With swanlike wings outspread, he who had spoken
    summoned us up between the walls of rock.
    He fanned us with his shining pinions then,

affirming over us as we went by,
  "Blessed are they that mourn"—for they shall have
  their consolation given them on high.
"What ails you?" said my Guide. "What heavy mood
  makes you stare at the ground?" (We were by then
  above the point at which the angel stood.)
And I: "An apparition clouds my spirit,
  a vision from a dream so strange and dreadful
  I cannot seem to leave off thinking of it."
"Did you see that ageless witch," he said, "for whom
  —and for no other—those above us weep?
  And did you see how men escape her doom? 60
Let it teach your heels to scorn the earth, your eyes
  to turn to the high lure the Eternal King
  spins with His mighty spheres across the skies."
As falcons stare at their feet until they hear
  the wished-for call, then leap with wings outspread
  in eagerness for the meat that waits them there,
so did I move; filled with desire, I ran
  up the remaining length of the rock passage
  to the point at which the next great round began.
When I stood on the fifth ledge and looked around,
  I saw a weeping people everywhere
  lying outstretched and face-down on the ground.
"My soul cleaves to the dust," I heard them cry
  over and over as we stood among them;
  and every word was swallowed by a sigh. 75
"O chosen of God, spirits whose mournful rites
  both hope and justice make less hard to bear,
  show us the passage to the further heights."
"If you have not been sentenced to lie prone
  in the bitter dust and seek the nearest way,
  keep the rim to your right as you go on."
So spoke the Poet, and so a voice replied
  from the ground in front of us. I took good note
  of what its way of speaking did not hide.
I turned my eyes to Virgil then, and he
  gave me a happy sign of his permission
  to do what my eyes asked. Being thus free

to act according to my own intention,
   I moved ahead and stood above that soul
   whose speaking had attracted my attention,   90
saying: "O soul in whom these tears prepare
   that without which no soul can turn to God,
   put off awhile, I beg, your greater care,
to tell me who you were, why you lie prone,
   and if there is some way that I may serve you
   in the world I left while still in flesh and bone."
"Why Heaven makes us turn our backs shall be
   made known to you," the spirit said, "but first,
   scias quod ego fui successor Petri.
Between Sestri and Chiaveri, flowing on
   through a fair land, there is a pleasant river
   from which the title of my line is drawn.
A single month, a month and some few days,
   I came to know on my own weary body
   how heavily the Papal Mantle weighs   105
upon the wearer who would take good care
   to keep it from the mire; compared to that
   all other burdens are as light as air.
My conversion, alas, came late; for only when
   I had been chosen Pastor of Holy Rome
   did I see the falseness in the lives of men.
I saw no heart's rest there, nor ease from strife,
   nor any height the flesh-bound soul might climb,
   and so I came to love this other life.
My soul was lost to God until that moment,
   and wholly given over to avarice;
   such was my sin, such is my punishment.
The nature of avarice is here made plain
   in the nature of its penalty; there is not
   a harsher forfeit paid on the whole mountain.   120
We would not raise our eyes to the shining spheres
   but kept them turned to mundane things; so Justice
   bends them to earth here in this place of tears.
As avarice, there, quenched all our souls' delight
   in the good without which all our works are lost,
   so, here, the hand of Justice clamps us tight.

"Why do you lower
your knees into the dust?" he said to me.
        And I: "My conscience troubled me for standing
in the presence of your rank and dignity."

Taken and bound here hand and foot, we lie
  outstretched and motionless; and here we stay
  at the just pleasure of the Father on High."
I had knelt to him. Now I spoke once more.
  That spirit sensed at once my voice was nearer
  and guessed my reverence. "Why do you lower
your knees into the dust?" he said to me.
  And I: "My conscience troubled me for standing
  in the presence of your rank and dignity."   135
"Straighten your legs, my brother! Rise from error!"
  he said. "I am, like you and all the others,
  a fellow servant of one Emperor.
It is written in Holy Scripture, *Neque nubent;*
  if ever you understood that sacred text,
  my reason for speaking will be evident.
Now go your way. I wish to be alone.
  Your presence here distracts me from the tears
  that make me ready. And to your last question—
I have a niece, Alagia, still on earth.
  If she can but avoid the bad example
  those of our line have set, her native worth
will lead her yet the way the blessed go.
And she alone remains to me below."

Canto 20

*Dante walks on after Adrian has dis-
missed him, wishing he might have continued the
conversation, but bowing to Adrian's wish to resume his purification. The Poets find the ledge so
crowded with the souls of the Avaricious that
only one narrow passage is left open to them.
Dante hears a soul cry out the Whip of Avarice, a
litany in praise of Mary, Fabricius, and St. Nicholas. The sinner identifies himself as Hugh Capet
and proceeds to a denunciation of the Capetian kings, the dynasty he himself founded, but
which has degenerated into a succession of kings
distinguished only for their bloodthirsty avarice. Hugh Capet then explains the Rein of Avarice, citing several examples of the downfall
of the Avaricious. Dante has hardly left Capet
when he feels the mountain shake as if stricken
by an earthquake, and he hears a shout of triumph. Dante is frightened but Virgil reassures
him. The Poets move on at top speed, but Dante
remains deep in thought, his mind pondering
these new phenomena.*

What's willed must bow to what is stronger willed;
    against my pleasure, to please him, I drew
    my sponge back from the water still unfilled.
I turned; my Guide set off along the space
    left clear next to the rock; for they who drain,
    slow tear by tear, the sin that eats the race
left little room along the outer edge.
    Thus, as one hugs the battlements in walking
    atop a wall, we moved along the ledge.

Purgatorio

Hell take you, She-Wolf, who in the sick feast
   of your ungluttable appetite have taken
   more prey on earth than any other beast!
You heavens, in whose turnings, as some say,
   things here below are changed—when will he come
   whose power shall drive her from the light of day? 15
We moved along with measured step and slow,
   and all my thoughts were centered on those shades,
   their tears and lamentations moved me so.
And walking thus, I heard rise from the earth
   before us: "Blessed Mary!"—with a wail
   such as is wrung from women giving birth.
"How poor you were," the stricken voice went on,
   "is testified to all men by the stable
   in which you laid your sacred burden down."
And then: "O good Fabricius, you twice
   refused great wealth that would have stained your honor
   and chose to live in poverty, free of vice."
These words had pleased me so that I drew near
   the place from which they seemed to have been spoken,
   eager to know what soul was lying there. 30
The voice was speaking now of the largesse
   St. Nicholas bestowed on the three virgins
   to guide their youth to virtuous steadiness.
"O soul," I said, "whose words recite such good,
   let me know who you were and why no other
   joins in your praises of such rectitude.
If I return to finish the short race
   remaining of that life that ends so soon,
   your words will not lack some reward of grace."
"Not for such comfort as the world may give
   do I reply," he said, "but that such light
   of grace should shine on you while yet you live.
I was the root of that malignant tree
   which casts its shadow on all Christendom
   so that the soil bears good fruit only rarely. 45
But if Douay and Lille and Bruges and Ghent
   were strong again, their vengeance would be swift;
   and that it may, I pray the King of Judgment.

I was Hugh Capet in my mortal state.
  From me stem all the Philips and the Louis'
  who have occupied the throne of France of late.
I was born in Paris as a butcher's son.
  When the old line of kings had petered out
  to one last heir, who wore a monk's gray gown,
I found that I held tight in my own hand
  the reins of state and that my new wealth gave me
  such power, and such allies at my command,
that my son's head, with pomp and sacrament,
  rose to the widowed crown of France. From him
  those consecrated bones took their descent.   60
Till the great dowry of Provence increased
  my race so that it lost its sense of shame,
  it came to little, but did no harm at least.
That was the birth of its rapacity,
  its power, its lies. Later—to make amends—
  it took Normandy, Ponthieu, and Gascony.
Charles came to Italy, and—to make amends—
  he victimized Conradin. Then he sent
  St. Thomas back to Heaven—to make amends.
I see a time, not far off, that brings forth
  another Charles from France. It shall make clear
  to many what both he and his are worth.
He comes alone, unarmed but for the lance
  of Judas, which he drives so hard he bursts
  the guts of Florence with the blow he plants.   75
He wins no land there—only sin and shame.
  And what is worse for him is that he holds
  such crimes too lightly to repent his blame.
The third, once hauled from his own ship, I see
  selling his daughter, haggling like a pirate
  over a girl sold into slavery.
O Avarice, what more harm can you do?
  You have taken such a hold on my descendants
  they sell off their own flesh and blood for you!
But dwarfing all crimes, past or yet to be,
  I see Alagna entered, and, in His Vicar,
  Christ himself dragged in captivity.

Purgatorio

I see Him mocked again and crucified,
   the gall and vinegar once more sent up.
   He dies again—with *live* thieves at His side.   90
I see another Pilate, so full of spite
   not even that suffices; his swollen sails
   enter the very Temple without right.
O God, my Lord, when shall my soul rejoice
   to see Thy retribution, which, lying hidden,
   sweetens Thine anger in Thy secret choice?
What you first heard me cry in adoration
   of that one only Bride of the Holy Ghost,
   which made you turn and ask an explanation,
is the litany we add to every prayer
   as long as it is day. When the sun sets
   we raise the countercry on the night air.
We cry then how Pygmalion of old
   was made a traitor, thief, and parricide
   by his insatiable sick lust for gold;   105
how Midas suffered when his miser's prayer
   was answered, and became forever after
   the legend of a ludicrous despair;
and then we tell how Achan, covetous,
   stole from the booty, for which Joshua's rage
   still falls upon him—so it seems to us.
We cry Sapphira's and her husband's blame;
   we praise the hooves that battered Heliodorus;
   then round the ledge runs Polymnestor's name,
foul to all time with Polydorus' blood.
   Then we conclude the litany crying: 'Crassus,
   you supped on gold—tell us, did it taste good?'
We wail or mutter in our long remorse
   according to the inner spur that drives us,
   at times with more, at others with less force;   120
thus I was not the only one who praised
   the good we tell by day; but, as it happened,
   the only one nearby whose voice was raised."
We had already left him to his prayers
   and were expending every ounce of strength
   on the remaining distance to the stairs,

when suddenly I felt the mountain shake
   as if it tottered. Such a numb dread seized me
   as a man feels when marching to the stake.
Not even Delos, in that long ago
   before Latona went there to give birth
   to Heaven's eyes, was ever shaken so.
Then there went up a cry on every side,
   so loud that the sweet Master, bending close
   said: "Do not fear, for I am still your guide."   135
"Glory to God in the Highest!" rang a shout
   from every throat—as I could understand
   from those nearby, whose words I could make out.
We stood there motionless, our souls suspended—
   as had the shepherds who first heard that hymn—
   until the ground grew still and the hymn ended.
Then we pushed on our holy way once more,
   studying those prostrate souls who had already
   resumed their lamentation, as before.
I never felt my soul assaulted so—
   unless my memory err—as in that war
   between my ignorance and desire to know
the explanation of that shock and shout;
   nor dared I ask, considering our haste;
   nor could I of myself, looking about,   150
find anywhere the key to what I sought.
So I moved on, timid and sunk in thought.

Canto 21

*Burning with desire to know the cause of
the shock and shout, Dante hurries after Virgil
along the narrow way. Suddenly they are over-
taken by a figure that salutes them. Virgil answers, and the new soul, taking the Poets to be
souls who may not enter Heaven, expresses as-
tonishment at finding them in this place. Virgil
explains his and Dante's state and asks the
explanation of the earthquake and of the great
cry. The new soul explains that these phenomena
occur only when a soul arises from its final purification and begins its final ascent to Heaven. The
newcomer then reveals that he is Statius and
recites his earthly history, ending with a glowing
statement of his love for the works of Virgil. To
have lived in Virgil's time, says Statius, he would
have endured another year of the pains he has just
ended. Virgil warns Dante, with a glance, to be
silent, but Dante cannot suppress a half smile,
which Statius notices and asks Dante to explain.
He thus learns that he is, in fact, standing in
the presence of Virgil. He kneels to embrace Virgil's knees, but Virgil tells him to arise at once,
for such earthly vanities are out
of place between shades.*

The natural thirst that nothing satisfies
    except that water the Samaritan woman
    begged of Our Lord, as St. John testifies,
burned me; haste drove me on the encumbered way
    behind my Guide, and I was full of grief
    at the just price of pain those spirits pay;
when suddenly—just as Luke lets us know
    that Christ, new risen from the tomb, appeared
    to the two travelers on the road—just so,

as we moved there with bowed heads lest we tread
   upon some soul, a shade appeared behind us;
   nor did we guess its presence till it said:
"Brothers, God give you peace." My Guide and I
   turned quickly toward his voice, and with a sign
   my Master gave the words their due reply.   15
Then he began: "May the True Court's behest,
   which relegates me to eternal exile,
   establish you in peace among the blest."
"But how, if you are souls denied God's bliss,"
   he said—and we forged onward as he spoke—
   "have you climbed up the stairs as far as this?"
My Teacher then: "You cannot fail to see,
   if you observe the angel's mark upon him,
   that he will reign among the just. But she
whose wheel turns day and night has not yet spun
   the full length of the thread that Clotho winds
   into a hank for him and everyone.
Therefore, his soul, sister to yours and mine,
   since it cannot see as we do, could not
   climb by itself. And, therefore, Will Divine   30
has drawn me out of the great Throat of Woe
   to guide him on his way, and I shall lead him
   far as my knowledge gives me power to go.
But tell me, if you can, what was the shock
   we felt just now? And why did all the mountain
   cry with one voice down to its last moist rock?"
He struck the needle's eye of my desire
   so surely with his question, that my thirst,
   by hope alone, lost something of its fire.
The shade began: "The holy rules that ring
   the mountain round do not permit upon it
   any disordered or unusual thing,
nor any change. Only what Heaven draws
   out of itself into itself again—
   that and nothing else—can be a cause.   45
Therefore, there never can be rain nor snow,
   nor hail, nor dew, nor hoarfrost higher up
   than the little three-step stairway there below.

Purgatorio

Neither dense clouds nor films of mist appear,
 nor lightning's flash, nor Thaumas' glowing daughter,
 who shifts about from place to place back there;
nor can dry vapors raise their shattering heat
 above the top of these three steps I mentioned
 upon which Peter's Vicar plants his feet.
Shocks may occur below, severe or slight,
 but tremors caused by winds locked in the earth
 —I know not how—do not reach to this height.
It trembles here whenever a soul feels
 so healed and purified that it gets up
 or moves to climb; and then the great hymn peals.   60
The soul, surprised, becomes entirely free
 to change its cloister, moved by its own will,
 which is its only proof of purity.
Before purgation it does wish to climb,
 but the will High Justice sets against that wish
 moves it to will pain as it once willed crime.
And I, who in my torments have lain here
 five hundred years and more, have only now
 felt my will free to seek a better sphere.
It was for that you felt the mountain move
 and heard the pious spirits praise the Lord—
 ah, may He call them soon to go above."
These were the spirit's words to us, and mine
 cannot express how they refreshed my soul,
 but as the thirst is greater, the sweeter the wine.   75
And my wise Leader: "Now I see what snare
 holds you, how you slip free, why the mount trembles,
 and why your joint rejoicing fills the air.
Now it would please me greatly, if you please,
 to know your name and hear in your own words
 why you have lain so many centuries."
"In the days when the good Titus, with the aid
 of the Almighty King, avenged the wounds
 that poured the blood Iscariot betrayed,
I lived renowned back there," replied that soul,
 "in the most honored and enduring name,
 but still without the faith that makes us whole.

The Divine Comedy

My verses swelled with such melodious breath
　　that, from Toulouse, Rome called me to herself,
　　and there I merited a laurel wreath.   90
Statius my name, and it still lives back there.
　　I sang of Thebes, then of the great Achilles,
　　but found the second weight too great to bear.
The sparks that were my seeds of passion came
　　from that celestial fire which has enkindled
　　more than a thousand poets; I mean the flame
of the *Aeneid,* the mother that brought forth,
　　the nurse that gave suck to my song. Without it
　　I could not have weighed half a penny's worth.
And to have lived back there in Virgil's time
　　I would agree to pass another year
　　in the same banishment from which I climb."
Virgil, at these last words, shot me a glance
　　that said in silence, "Silence!" But man's will
　　is not supreme in every circumstance;   105
for tears and laughter come so close behind
　　the passions they arise from that they least
　　obey the will of the most honest mind.
I did no more than half smile, but that shade
　　fell still and looked me in the eye—for there
　　the secrets of the soul are most betrayed.
"So may the road you travel lead to grace,"
　　he said, "what was the meaning of the smile
　　that I saw flash, just now, across your face?"
Now am I really trapped on either side;
　　one tells me to be still, one begs me speak.
　　So torn I heave a sigh, and my sweet Guide
understands all its meaning. "Never fear,"
　　he says to me, "speak up, and let him know
　　what he has asked so movingly to hear."   120
At which I said: "Perhaps my smiling thus
　　has made you marvel, ancient soul; but now
　　listen to something truly marvelous;
this one who guides my eyes aloft is he,
　　Virgil, from whom you drew the strength to sing
　　the deeds of men and gods in poetry.

302

The only motive for my smiling lay
  in your own words. If you conceived another,
  as you love truth, pray put the thought away."
He was bending to embrace my Teacher's knee,
  but Virgil said: "No, brother. Shade you are,
  and shade am I. You must not kneel to me."
And Statius, rising, said: "So may you find
  the measure of the love that warms me to you
  when for it I lose all else from my mind,   135
forgetting we are empty semblances
and taking shadows to be substances."

Canto 22

The Poets have passed the angel who guards the ascent, and Dante has had one more P removed from his forehead. So lightened, he walks easily behind Virgil and Statius despite their rapid ascent, listening eagerly to their conversation. Virgil declares his great regard for Statius, and Statius explains that he was on the fifth cornice for Wasting rather than for Hoarding. He adds that he would certainly have been damned had Virgil's poetry not led him to see his error. For Virgil, he acknowledges, not only inspired his song, but also showed him the road to faith, whereby he was baptized, though secretly, for fear of the persecutions—a lukewarmness for which he spent five hundred years on the fourth cornice. Statius then names his favorite poets of antiquity and asks where they are. Virgil replies that they are with him in Limbo. He then cites many who have not been mentioned before as being among his eternal companions. At this point the Poets arrive at the sixth cornice and, moving to the right, come upon an enormous tree laden with fruits. From its foliage a voice cries out the examples of abstinence that constitute the Whip of Gluttony.

We had, by now, already left behind
    the angel who directs to the sixth round.
    He had erased a stigma from my brow
and said that they who thirst for rectitude
    are blessèd, but he did not say "who hunger"
    when he recited that beatitude.
I, lighter than on any earlier stairs,
    followed those rapid spirits, and I found it
    no strain at all to match my pace to theirs.

Virgil began: "When virtue lights in us
  a fire of love, that love ignites another
  within the soul that sees its burning. Thus,
ever since Juvenal came down to be
  one of our court in the infernal Limbo,
  and told me of your great regard for me,   15
my goodwill toward you has been of a sort
  I had not felt for any unseen person,
  such as will make the climb ahead seem short.
But tell me—and if I presume too much
  in slackening the rein this way, forgive me
  as a friend would and answer me as such,
how, amid all the wisdom you possessed—
  and which you won to by such diligence—
  could avarice find a place within your breast?"
At these words Statius let a brief smile play
  across his lips, and fade. Then he replied:
  "I hear love's voice in every word you say.
Often, indeed, appearances give rise
  to groundless doubts in us, and false conclusions,
  the true cause being hidden from our eyes.   30
Seeing me on the ledge from which I rose,
  you have inferred my sin was avarice,
  an inference your question clearly shows.
Know then that my particular offense
  was all too far from avarice; I wept
  thousands of months for riotous expense.
Had I not turned from prodigality
  in pondering those lines in which you cry,
  as if you raged against humanity:
'To what do you not drive man's appetite
  O cursèd gold-lust!'—I should now be straining
  in the grim jousts of the infernal night.
I understood then that our hands could spread
  their wings too wide in spending and repented
  of that, and all my sins, in grief and dread.   45
How many shall rise bald to Judgment Day
  because they did not know this sin to grieve it
  in life or as their last breaths slipped away!

For when the opposite of a sin, as here,
  is as blameworthy as the sin itself,
   both lose their growth together and turn sere.
If, then, I lay so long in my distress
  among the Avaricious where they weep,
   it was to purge the opposite excess."
"But when you sang of the fierce warfare bred
  between the twin afflictions of Jocasta,"
   the singer of the sweet *Bucolics* said,
"from what you said when Clio tuned your strain,
  it would not seem that you had found the faith
   without the grace of which good works are vain.   60
If that be so, what sun or beacon shone
  into your mist that you set sail to follow
   the Fisherman?" And that long-waiting one:
"You were the lamp that led me from that night.
  You led me forth to drink Parnassian waters;
   then on the road to God you shed your light.
When you declared, 'A new birth has been given.
  Justice returns, and the first age of man.
   And a new progeny descends from Heaven'—
you were as one who leads through a dark track
  holding the light behind—useless to you,
   precious to those who followed at your back.
Through you I flowered to song and to belief.
  That you may know all, let me stretch my hand
   to paint in full what I have sketched in brief.   75
The world, by then, was swollen with the birth
  of True Belief sown by those messengers
   the Everlasting Kingdom had sent forth.
Those words of yours I quoted, so agreed
  with the new preachers', that I took to going
   to where they gathered to expound the Creed.
In time, they grew so holy in my eyes
  that in the persecutions of Domitian
   the tears burst from me when I heard their cries.
And long as I remained upon the vexed
  shores of that life, I helped them, and they taught me,
   by their strict ways, to scorn all other sects.

Before my poem sang how the Greeks drew near
   the Theban rivers, I had been baptized,
   but kept my faith a secret, out of fear,   90
pretending to be pagan as before;
   for which lukewarmness I was made to circle
   the Ledge of Sloth four hundred years and more.
Now may you please to tell me—you who rent
   the veil that hid me from this good I praise—
   while we have time to spare in the ascent,
where is our ancient Terence now? and where
   Caecilius, Varro, Plautus?—are they damned?
   and if they are, what torments must they bear?"
"All these are there with Persius and the rest,
   myself among them, who surround that Greek
   who outsucked all men at the Muses' breast.
All walk the first ledge of the dark of Hell;
   and we speak often of the glorious mountain
   on which the Nine who suckled us still dwell.   105
Euripides is with us, Antiphon,
   Athenian Agathon, Simonides,
   and many more who wore the laurel crown.
And there, of your own people, one may see
   Ismene, mournful as she was before,
   Deiphyle, Argia, Antigone,
Hypsipyle, who led to Langia's water,
   Thetis, Deidamia with her sisters,
   and there, too, one may see Tiresias' daughter."
We stepped from the walled stairs to level ground,
   and both the Poets now had fallen still,
   attentive once again to look around.
Of the day's handmaids, four had fallen back,
   and now the fifth stood at the chariot's pole,
   pointing the bright tip on its upward track,   120
when Virgil said: "I think we ought to go
   with our right shoulders to the outer edge,
   circling the slope as we have done below."
So custom served to guide us, and we went
   as Virgil said, with all the more assurance
   since Statius' silence gave us his consent.

They walked ahead and I came on behind
  treasuring their talk, which was of poetry,
  and every word of which enriched my mind.
But soon, in midroad, there appeared a tree
  laden with fragrant and delicious fruit,
  and at that sight the talk stopped instantly.
As fir trees taper up from limb to limb,
  so this tree tapered down; so shaped, I think,
  that it should be impossible to climb.   135
From that side where the cliff closed off our way,
  a clear cascade fell from the towering rock
  and broke upon the upper leaves as spray.
The Poets drew nearer, reverent and mute,
  and from the center of the towering tree
  a voice cried: "You shall not eat of the fruit!"
Then said: "Mary thought more of what was due
  the joy and honor of the wedding feast
  than of her mouth, which still speaks prayers for you.
Of old, the mothers of Rome's noble blood
  found joy in water. And great wisdom came
  to holy Daniel in despising food.
Bright as pure gold was mankind's state at first;
  then, hunger seasoned acorns with delight,
  and every rill ran sweet to honest thirst.   150
No wine nor meat were in the wilderness.
  Honey and locusts—that and nothing more
  nourished the Baptist in his holiness;
and to that fact is his great glory due,
as the Gospel clearly testifies to you."

Canto 23

*Dante stares up into the tree to see who
has spoken, but he is called away by Virgil who
leads on, talking to Statius, while Dante walks
behind, drinking in their conversation. Suddenly,
from behind him, Dante hears a psalm, and turning, he sees a band of Gluttons overtaking them,
souls so emaciated that one can read in their
sunken eyes and in the lines of the cheeks and
nose the word OMO. After some difficulty Dante
recognizes one of the hideously wasted souls
as his old friend Forese, who had died only five
years before, but who had been advanced into
Purgatory and directly to this cornice by the
prayers of his widow, Nella. In praising Nella for
her devotion, Forese takes occasion to deliver
a rather salty invective against the women of
Florence for their immodest dress and behavior.
In answer to Forese's plea, Dante explains how
he has mounted into Purgatory and
with whom he is traveling.*

In hope of seeing who had cried those words
   I drew near and peered up at the green boughs
   like one who wastes his lifetime stalking birds.
At that, my more-than-father said: "My son,
   come now, for we must portion out more wisely
   the time allotted us." And he moved on.
I looked down and turned round to join those Sages
   in the same instant. And their talk was such
   that every step I took paid double wages.
Then suddenly at my back I heard the strain
   of *Labia mea, Domine,* so sung
   that it was both a hymn and cry of pain.

"Father," I said, "what is this sound?" And he:
  "Spirits who, circling so, loosen perhaps
    the knot of debt they owe eternity."   15
As pilgrims wrapped in holy meditation,
  when they encounter strangers on the way,
    look, but do not pause for conversation—
so from behind us, turning half about
  to stare as they went by, a band of souls
    came up and passed us, silent and devout.
The sockets of their eyes were caves agape;
  their faces death-pale, and their skin so wasted
    that nothing but the gnarled bones gave it shape.
I doubt that even Erysichthon's skin,
  even when he most feared that he would starve,
    had drawn so tight to bone or worn so thin.
"Behold," I thought, although I did not speak,
  "the face of those who lost Jerusalem
    when Miriam ripped her son with her own beak."   30
Their eye pits looked like gem rims minus gem.
  Those who read OMO in the face of man
    would easily have recognized the M.
Who could imagine, without knowing how,
  craving could waste souls so at the mere smell
    of water and of fruit upon the bough?
I was still wondering how they could have grown
  so thin and scabby (since what famished them
    had not yet been made clear to me), when one
turning his eyes from deep inside his skull,
  stared at me fixedly, then cried aloud:
    "How have I earned a grace so bountiful?"
I never would have recognized his face,
  but in his voice I found that which his features
    had eaten from themselves without a trace.   45
That spark relit my memory and, in awe,
  I understood beneath those altered features
    it was Forese's very self I saw.
"Ah, do not stare," he pleaded, "at my hide,
  bleached like a leper's by these flaming scabs,
    nor at the fleshless bones I bear inside;

but tell me all about yourself, and who
   these two souls are that bear you company;
   and tell me with all haste, I beg of you."
"I wept to see your face once when it lay
   in death," I said, "and I weep no less now
   to see what pain has wasted it away;
in God's name tell me how. Do not demand
   I speak while still bemused, for he speaks badly
   whose mind is too full to be at command."   60
And he: "From the Eternal Counsel flow
   the powers whereby the water and the tree
   we have just passed emaciate us so.
All those who sing while weeping in their pain
   once loved their stomach-sacs beyond all measure.
   Here, thirst and hunger wring them clean again.
Hunger and thirst that nothing can assuage
   grow in us from the fragrance of the fruit
   and of the spray upon the foliage.
And not once only as we round this place
   do we endure renewal of our pain.
   —Did I say 'pain'? I should say 'gift of grace.'
For the same will that drives us to the tree
   drove Christ on gladly to cry, '*Eli! Eli!*'
   when He paid with His blood to set us free."   75
And I to him: "Forese, from the day
   in which you changed worlds for the better life,
   less than five years, as yet, have passed away.
If your ability to sin had fled
   before the hour of that sublime sweet sorrow
   that weds us back to God, among his blessèd,
how have you reached so high in the great climb?
   I thought to find you still below, with those
   who sit and wait, repaying time for time."
"My Nella's flood of tears," he answered me,
   "have borne me up so soon to let me drink
   the blessed wormwood of my agony.
Her sighs and prayers were heard where love abounds;
   they raised me from the slope where I lay waiting
   and set me free of all the other rounds.   90

"But tell me all about yourself, and who
    these two souls are that bear you company;
    and tell me with all haste, I beg of you."

The dearer and more pleasing in God's sight
  is the poor widow of my love, as she
  is most alone in doing what is right.
For the Barbagia of Sardinia breeds
  chaste women as compared to that Barbagia
  in which I left her to her widow's weeds.
O my dear brother, what is there to say?
  In vision I already see a time—
  and it is not far distant from this day—
in which the pulpit shall denounce by writ
  the shameless jades that Florentines call ladies,
  who go about with breasts bare to the tit.
What Moslem woman ever has required
  a priestly discipline, or any other,
  before she would go decently attired?   105
But if the chippies only could foresee
  swift Heaven's punishment, they'd have their mouths
  already open to howl misery.
For if what we foresee here does not lie,
  they shall be sad before those sons grow beards
  who can be soothed now with a lullaby.
Now, brother, answer in your turn. You see
  your shadow there and how these other souls
  are staring at the spot along with me."
I then: "If you call back to mind from here
  my past life in your company, yours in mine,
  memory will seem too great a load to bear.
I was recalled from such ways by that one
  who leads me here, and just the other day
  when that one's sister" (pointing to the sun)   120
"was at the full. Through the profoundest night
  of final death he led me in this flesh
  which follows him to find the final right.
From there with many a sweet encouragement
  he led me upward and around the mountain
  which straightens in you what the world has bent.
And he has pledged himself to go with me
  until I stand by Beatrice, above.
  Then I must do without his company.

The one who pledges this" (and as I spoke
 I pointed to him standing there) "is Virgil.
 The other is the shade of him who woke
to blessedness just now when every rim,
the mountain round, shook in releasing him."

Canto 24

*The Poets move on as Dante continues
his talk with Forese, who identifies many of the
souls of the Gluttons, among them Bonagiunta of
Lucca. Bonagiunta mutters a prophecy concerning Dante's future meeting with Gentucca. He
then questions Dante about the sweet new style
and ends by concluding that had he and the
others of his school of poetry grasped the principle of natural expression, they would have written as well as do the poets of Dante's school.
All the other souls speed ahead, but Forese
remains to prophesy the death of his brother,
Corso Donati, leader of the Black Guelphs. Then
he speeds away and soon disappears. The Poets
move on and come to the Tree of Knowledge
from which a voice cries the Rein of Gluttony,
citing Eve, the Centaurs, and Gideon's army.
Having skirted the tree carefully, warned away
by the voice, the Poets move ahead and meet
the Angel of Abstinence, who shows
them to the ascent.*

Talk did not slow our steps, nor they in turn
   our talk, but still conversing we moved on
   like ships at sea with a brisk wind astern.
And all those shades, looking like things twice dead,
   were drinking in through their sepulchral eyes
   the awe of seeing me as I had been bred.
And I, continuing as I had begun,
   said: "His ascent, I think, is somewhat slower
   than it would be but for that other one.
But where now is Piccarda? Do you know?
   And is there anyone of special note
   among these people who stare at me so?"

And all those shades, looking like things twice dead,
were drinking in through their sepulchral eyes
the awe of seeing me as I had been bred.

Purgatorio

"My sister, who was good as she was fair,
  and fair as good, sits crowned on High Olympus,
  rejoicing in eternal triumph there."   15
Thus he began. Then: "To identify
  anyone here is certainly permitted,
  for abstinence has milked our features dry.
This" (and he pointed to him) "dearest brother,
  was Bonagiunta of Lucca. That behind him,
  his face more sunken in than any other,
once fathered Holy Church. Of Tours his line;
  and here in the long fast he expiates
  Bolsena's eels and the Vernaccia wine."
Then he named many others, one by one,
  at which I saw not one black look among them,
  but all seemed pleased at being thus made known.
Ubaldino della Pila hungered there,
  and Boniface, shepherd to all those bellies—
  they were so starved they used their teeth on air.   30
I saw my Lord Marchese. Before he died
  he drank with somewhat less thirst at Forlì,
  yet no man ever saw him satisfied.
As one who notes one face especially
  among a crowd, I noted him of Lucca
  who seemed most to desire a word with me.
He muttered something, and I seemed to hear
  the word "Gentucca" issue from the wound
  where most he felt High Justice pluck him bare.
"Spirit," I said, "since you seem so intent
  on talking to me, do so audibly,
  and speaking so, make both of us content."
"Though men may mock my city," he replied,
  "she who will teach you how to treasure it
  is born there, though she is not yet a bride.   45
This presage you shall take with you from here,
  and if you misconstrued what I first muttered
  the facts themselves, in time, will make it clear.
But is this really the creator of
  those new *canzoni*, one of which begins
  'Ladies who have the intellect of Love'?"

317

And I: "When Love inspires me with delight,
  or pain, or longing, I take careful note,
  and as he dictates in my soul, I write."
And he: "Ah, brother, now I see the thong
  that held Guittone, and the Judge, and me
  short of that sweet new style of purest song.
I see well how your pens attained such powers
  by following exactly Love's dictation,
  which certainly could not be said of ours.   60
And if one scan the two styles side by side,
  that is the only difference he will find."
With that he fell still, as if satisfied.
Just as the cranes that winter by the Nile
  form close-bunched flights at times, then, gathering speed,
  streak off across the air in single file;
so all the people there faced straight ahead
  and, being lightened by both will and wasting,
  quickened their paces, and away they sped.
And as a runner who must take a rest
  lets his companions pull ahead and walks
  till he has eased the panting in his chest—
just so Forese let that blessed train
  outdistance him and held his pace to mine
  and said to me: "When shall we meet again?"   75
"I do not know how long my life will be,"
  I said, "but I cannot return so soon
  but what my wish will reach the shore before me;
for from that city where I came to life
  goodness is disappearing day by day;
  a place foredoomed to ruin by bloody strife."
"Take heart," he said, "for I see him whose crime
  exceeds all others' dragged at a beast's tail
  to where sin lasts beyond the end of time.
At every stride the beast goes faster, faster,
  until its flashing hooves lash out, and leave
  the foul ruin of what was once its master.
Those spheres" (and he looked toward the heavens here)
  "will not turn far before what I have said,
  and may not add to now, shall be made clear.   90

Purgatorio

Now I must leave you far behind; your pace
    has cost me a considerable delay;
    and time is precious to us in this place."
At times during a horse charge, one brave knight
    will spur ahead, burning to claim the honor
    of having struck the first blow in the fight—
just so his lengthened stride left us behind,
    and I trailed on, accompanied by those two
    who were such mighty marshals of mankind.
And when, in such haste, he had pulled ahead
    so far that I could only make him out
    as I could understand what he had said;
we turned a corner and there came in sight,
    not far ahead, a second tree, its boughs
    laden with fruit, its foliage bursting bright.   105
Sometimes when greedy children beg and screech
    for what they may not have, the one they cry to
    holds it in plain sight but beyond their reach
to whet their appetites—so, round that tree,
    with arms raised to the boughs, a pack of souls
    begged and was given nothing. Finally
they gave up and moved on unsatisfied,
    and we drew close in our turn to that plant
    at which such tears and pleadings were denied.
"Pass on. Do not draw near. The tree whose fruit
    Eve took and ate grows further up the slope,
    and this plant sprouted from that evil root."
Thus, from the boughs, an unknown voice called down.
    And thus warned, Virgil, Statius, and myself
    drew close, and hugged the cliff, and hurried on.   120
"Recall," the voice went on, "those cursed beasts
    born of a cloud. When they had swilled the wine,
    Theseus had to slash their double breasts.
Recall those Jews who once showed Gideon
    how to abandon all to thirst, whereat
    he would not lead them down the hills to Midian."
So we strode on along the inner way
    while the voice cried the sins of gluttony
    which earn, as we had seen, such fearful pay.

Then the road cleared, and with more room for walking
    we spread out and had gone a thousand paces
    in meditation, with no thought of talking,
when suddenly a voice cried, startling me
    as if I were a panic-stricken colt:
    "What are you thinking of alone, you three?"   135
I looked up to see who had spoken so;
    no man has ever seen in any furnace,
    metal or glass raised to so red a glow.
"If your wish is to ascend," I heard one say,
    "this is the place where you must turn aside.
    All you who search for peace—this is the way."
His glory blinded me. I groped and found
    my Teacher's back and followed in his steps
    as blind men do who guide themselves by sound.
Soft on my brow I felt a zephyr pass,
    soft as those airs of May that herald dawn
    with breathing fragrances of flowers and grass;
and unmistakably I felt the brush
    of the soft wing releasing to my senses
    ambrosial fragrances in a soft rush.   150
And soft I heard the angel voice recite:
    "Blessed are they whom grace so lights within
    that love of food in them does not excite
excessive appetite, but who take pleasure
in keeping every hunger within measure."

Canto 25

*It is 2:00 P.M. as the three poets leave the
cornice of the Gluttonous and begin their hurried
ascent to the seventh cornice. Dante, burning
with eagerness to ask how the Gluttons could
give the appearance of advanced starvation despite the fact that they are airy bodies and do not
need food, fears to speak but is finally encouraged
to do so by Virgil. Dante immediately offers his
question, and Virgil, as an act of courtesy, invites
Statius to answer it. The rest of the rapid ascent is
then occupied by the discourse of Statius on the
nature of the generative principle, the birth of the
human soul, and the nature of aerial bodies. By
the time Statius is finished, the Poets have
reached the seventh cornice. There, enwrapped
in sheets of flame, the souls of the Lustful sing
over and over the hymn,* Summae Deus Clementiae. *At each conclusion of the hymn, they cry
out in praise of an example of high chastity.
These examples form the Whip of Lust. It is
in this way, singing and praising as they move
through the flames, that the Lustful
perform their purification.*

It was an hour to climb without delay.
   Taurus succeeded to the Sun's meridian,
   and Scorpio to Night's—a world away;
thus, as a man spurred on by urgent cause
   will push ahead, no matter what appears
   along the way inviting him to pause—
just so we filed, one of us at a time,
   into the gap, and started up those stairs
   whose narrowness divides all those who climb.

And as a little stork, eager to fly
   but afraid to leave the nest, will raise a wing
   then let it fall again—just such was I,
the will within me now strong and now weak,
   eager to ask, but going only so far
   as to make me clear my throat, and then not speak.   15
The pace was swift; nor did my sweet Lord slow
   his stride, but said: "I see the bow of speech
   drawn back to the very iron. Let it go."
My doubts resolved, I did not hesitate
   to use my mouth. "How can they grow so thin,"
   I said, "who need no food in their new state?"
"Recall Meleager wasting as the brand
   wasted in fire," he said, "and you will find
   the matter not so hard to understand.
Or think how your least move before a glass
   is answered by your image and what seemed hard
   is bound to grow much clearer than it was.
But this wish burns you, I know, and to put out
   all of its flames, I shall beg Statius now
   to be the one to heal the wounds of doubt."   30
"If, in your presence," Statius first replied,
   "I explain eternal things, let my excuse
   be only that your wish be not denied."
And then to me: "Son, let it be your task
   to hear and heed my words, and they will be
   a light upon the how of what you ask.
Perfect blood—that pure blood that remains
   as one might say, like food upon the table,
   and never goes to slake the thirsty veins—
acquires, within the heart, formative power
   over all human organs, as that which flows
   into the veins forms *them*. It is once more
changed in the heart, then flows down to that place
   the better left unmentioned. Thence, it drips
   over another blood in its natural vase.   45
There, the two commingle; and one blood shows
   a passive bent, while the other blood is active,
   due to the perfect place from which it flows.

So joined, the active force within the latter
  first clots, then quickens what it has made firm
  of the former blood to serve as working matter.
The active force has now become a soul
  like that of a plant, but with the difference
  that this begins where that achieves its goal.
Soon, like some sea thing, half beast and half weed,
  it moves and feels. It then begins to form
  those powers of sense of which it is the seed.
Now, my son, the formative power expands
  and elongates within, till every member
  takes form and place as nature's plan commands.   60
But how this animal thing grows human powers
  you do not yet see; and this very point
  has led astray a wiser head than yours.
By him, the *possible intellect* was thought
  (since it occupied no organ) to be disjoined
  from the *vegetative soul*—and so he taught.
Open your heart to the truth I shall explain,
  and know that at the instant articulation
  has been perfected in the foetal brain,
that instant the First Mover turns to it.
  And there, rejoicing at such art in nature,
  breathes into it a new and powerful spirit.
All that is active there, this spirit draws
  into itself, forming a single soul
  that lives, and feels, and measures its own cause.   75
(Consider, if you find these words of mine
  too strange to understand, how the sun's heat
  joined to the sap of the vine turns into wine.)
Then when Lachesis' flax is drawn, it frees
  itself from flesh, but takes with it the essence
  of its divine and human faculties—
its lower powers grown passive now and mute;
  but memory, intelligence, and will
  more active than they were and more acute.
Miraculously then, by its own will,
  it falls at once to one or the other shore.
  There it first learns its way, for good or ill.

And once inclosed in that new atmosphere,
  the *formative power* rays out, as it did first
  in shaping the bodily parts it left back there. 90
Then, as the air after a rain will glow
  inside itself, reflecting an outer ray,
  and clothe itself in many colors—so
wherever the soul may stop in its new hour,
  the air about it takes on that soul's image.
  Such is the virtue of the *formative power.*
Thereafter, in the same way one may see
  flame follow fire wherever it may shift,
  the new form follows the soul eternally.
From air it draws its visibility. Hence,
  it is called a *shade.* And out of air it forms
  the organs of sight, speech, and every sense.
Thus are we able to speak and laugh. And thus
  are we able to weep such tears and breathe such sighs
  as you have seen and heard, passing among us. 105
As desire, or other feelings move us—so
  our shades change their appearances. And that
  is that cause of what amazed you just below."
We had come, by then, to the last turn of the stairs
  from which we bore to the right along the cornice,
  and our minds were drawn already to other cares.
Here, from the inner wall, flames blast the ledge,
  while from the floor an air blast bends them back,
  leaving one narrow path along the edge.
This path we were forced to take as best we might,
  in single file. And there I was—the flames
  to the left of me, and the abyss to the right.
My Leader said: "In this place, it is clear,
  we all must keep a tight rein on our eyes.
  To take a false step would be easy here." 120
"*Summae Deus clementiae,*" sang a choir
  inside that furnace, and despite my road
  I could not help but look into the fire.
Then I saw spirits moving through the flames,
  and my eyes turned now to them, now to my feet,
  as if divided between equal claims.

"Summae Deus clementiae," sang a choir
inside that furnace, and despite my road
I could not help but look into the fire.

When they had sung the hymn, those souls in pain
  cried out in full voice: *"Virum non cognosco!"*
  Then, softly, they began the hymn again.
That done, they cried: "Diana kept to the wood,
  and drove Helicé from her when that nymph
  had felt Venus' poison in her blood."
Then, once again, the hymn swelled from their choir;
  and after it they praised husbands and wives
  who were chaste as virtue and marriage vows require.   135
And in this way, I think, they sing their prayer
  and cry their praise for as long as they must stay
  within the holy fire that burns them there.
Such physic and such diet has been thought fit
before the last wound of them all may knit.

Canto 26

Dante's shadow falls on the wall of flame and it is noticed by the souls of the Lustful who approach (without leaving the flames) to question him. Dante's answer, however, is interrupted by the approach of a second band of souls from the opposite direction. These are the Sodomites. The two bands of souls exchange brief embraces and then cry out the Rein of Lust as they move on, drawing rapidly apart. The first group again approaches Dante and the soul of Guido Guinizelli speaks to him. Dante pays high homage to Guinizelli and discusses with him the growth of the sweet new style. With a final request for a prayer for his soul, Guido withdraws, and Dante then addresses Arnaut Daniel, who answers in the langue d'oc. He begs that Dante say a prayer for him and then disappears into the purifying flame.

So, one before the other, we moved there
   along the edge, and my sweet Guide kept saying:
"Walk only where you see me walk. Take care."
The sun, already changing from blue to white
   the face of the western sky, struck at my shoulder,
   its rays now almost level on my right;
and my shadow made the flames a darker red.
   Even so slight an evidence, I noticed,
   made many shades that walked there turn their heads.
And when they saw my shadow, these began
   to speak of me, saying to one another:
"He seems to be no shade, but a living man!"
And some of them drew near me then—as near
   as they could come, for they were ever careful
   to stay within the fire that burned them there.

15

"O you who trail the others—with no desire
    to lag, I think, but out of deference—
    speak to me who am burned by thirst and fire.
Not I alone need what your lips can tell;
    all these thirst for it more than Ethiopes
    or Indians for a drink from a cold well.
How is it that you cast a shadow yet,
    making yourself a barrier to the sun,
    as if death had not caught you in its net?"
So one addressed me. And I should have been
    explaining myself already, but for a new
    surprising sight that caught my eye just then;
for down the center of that fiery way
    came new souls from the opposite direction,
    and I forgot what I had meant to say.   30
I saw them hurrying from either side,
    and each shade kissed another, without pausing,
    each by the briefest greeting satisfied.
(Ants, in their dark ranks, meet exactly so,
    rubbing each other's noses, to ask perhaps
    what luck they've had or which way they should go.)
As soon as they break off their friendly greeting,
    before they take the first step to pass on,
    each shade outshouts the other at that meeting.
"Sodom and Gomorrah!" the new souls cry.
    And the others: "Pasiphaë enters the cow
    to call the young bull to her lechery."
As if cranes split into two flocks, and one
    flew to the Rhipheans, one to the sands,
    these to escape the ice, and those the sun—   45
so, then, those shades went their opposing ways;
    and all returned in tears to their first song,
    and each to crying an appropriate praise.
Then those who came my way drew close once more—
    the same shades that had first entreated me.
    They seemed as eager to hear me as before.
I, having had their wish presented twice,
    replied without delay: "O souls assured—
    whenever it may be—of Paradise,

I did not leave my limbs beyond the flood,
    not green nor ripe, but bear them with me here
    in their own jointure and in their own blood.
I go to be no longer blind. Above
    there is a Lady wins us grace, and I,
    still mortal, cross your world led by her love.   60
But now I pray—so may it soon befall
    you have your greater wish to be called home
    into that heaven of love that circles all—
tell me, that I may write down what you say
    for all to read, who are you? and those others
    who move away behind you—who are they?"
Just as our mountaineers, their first time down,
    half-wild and shaggy, gape about the streets
    and stare in dumb amazement at the town—
just such a look I saw upon those shades;
    but when they had recovered from their stupor
    (which from a lofty heart the sooner fades),
the first shade spoke again: "Blessèd are you
    who for a better life, store in your soul
    experience of these realms you travel through!   75
Those souls you saw going the other way
    grew stained in that for which triumphant Caesar
    heard his own legions call him 'Queen' one day.
Therefore their band, at parting from us, cries
    'Sodom!'—as you have heard—that by their shame
    they aid the fire that makes them fit to rise.
We were hermaphroditic in our offenses,
    but since we did not honor human laws,
    yielding like animals to our lusting senses,
we, when we leave the other band, repent
    by crying to our shame the name of her
    who crouched in the mock-beast with beast's intent.
And now you know our actions and our crime.
    But if you wish our names, we are so many
    I do not know them all, nor is there time.   90
Your wish to know mine shall be satisfied.
    I am Guido Guinizelli, here so soon
    because I repented fully before I died."

In King Lycurgus' darkest hour, two sons
    discovered their lost mother; I was moved
    as they had been (but could not match their actions)
when I heard his name, for he had fathered me
    and all the rest, my betters, who have sung
    sweet lilting rhymes of love and courtesy.
Enraptured, I can neither speak nor hear,
    but only stare at him as we move on,
    although the flames prevent my drawing near.
When at last my eyes had fed, I spoke anew;
    and in such terms as win belief, I offered
    to serve him in whatever I could do.   105
And he to me then: "What you say has made
    such a profound impression on my mind
    as Lethe cannot wash away nor fade.
But if the words you swore just now are true,
    let me know why you show by word and look
    such love as I believe I see in you?"
And I to him: "Your songs so sweet and clear
    which, for as long as modern usage lives,
    shall make the very ink that writes them dear."
"Brother," he said, "that one who moves along
    ahead there" (and he pointed) "was in life
    a greater craftsman of the mother tongue.
He, in his love songs and his tales in prose,
    was without peer—and if fools claim Limoges
    produced a better, there are always those   120
who measure worth by popular acclaim,
    ignoring principles of art and reason
    to base their judgments on the author's name.
So, once, our fathers sent Guittone's praise,
    and his alone, bounding from cry to cry,
    though truth prevails with most men nowadays.
And now, if you enjoy such privilege
    that you are free to go up to that cloister
    within which Christ is abbot of the college,
say an Our Father for me in that host,
    as far as it may serve us in this world
    in which the very power to sin is lost."

With that, perhaps to yield his place with me
  to someone else he vanished through the fire
  as a fish does to the dark depths of the sea.   135
I drew ahead till I was by that shade
  he had pointed to and said that in my heart
  a grateful place to feast his name was laid.
And he replied at once and willingly:
  "Such pleasaunce have I of thy gentilesse,
  that I ne can, ne will I hide from thee.
Arnaut am I, and weepe and sing my faring.
  In grievousnesse I see my follies past;
  in joie, the blistful daie of my preparing.
And by that eke virtue, I thee implour,
  that redeth thee, that thou amount the staire,
  be mindful in thy time of my dolour."
Then he, too, hid himself within the fire
that makes those spirits ready to go higher.

Canto 27

*A little before sunset of the third day on
the mountain, the Poets come to the further limit
of the seventh cornice and are greeted by the
Angel of Chastity, who tells them they must pass
through the wall of fire. Dante recoils in terror,
but Virgil persuades him to enter in Beatrice's
name. They are guided through the fire by a chant
they hear coming from the other side. Emerging,
they find it is sung by the Angel Guardian of the
Earthly Paradise, who stands in a light so brilliant that Dante cannot see him. (It is probably
here that the last P is stricken from Dante's brow;
or perhaps it was consumed by the fire.) The angel
hurries them toward the ascent, but night over-
takes them, and the Poets lie down to sleep, each
on the step on which he finds himself. (For Statius
it will be the last sleep, since there is no night in
Heaven.) There, just before dawn, Dante has a
prophetic dream of Leah and Rachel, which fore-
shadows the appearance, above, of Matilda and
Beatrice. Day arrives; the Poets rise and race up
the rest of the ascent until they come in sight
of the Earthly Paradise. Here Virgil speaks his
last words, for the Poets have come to the limit
of reason, and Dante is free to follow his every
impulse, since all motion of sin in
him has been purged away.*

As the day stands when the Sun begins to glow
   over the land where his Maker's blood was shed,
   and the scales of Libra ride above the Ebro,

while Ganges' waters steam in the noonday glare—
   so it stood, the light being nearly faded,
   when we met God's glad angel standing there

on the rocky ledge beyond the reach of the fire,
   and caroling *"Beati mundo corde"*
   in a voice to which no mortal could aspire.
Then: "Blessèd ones, till by flame purified
   no soul may pass this point. Enter the fire
   and heed the singing from the other side."
These were his words to us when we had come
   near as we could and, hearing them, I froze
   as motionless as one laid in his tomb.   15
I lean forward over my clasped hands and stare
   into the fire, thinking of human bodies
   I once saw burned, and once more see them there.
My kindly escorts heard me catch my breath
   and turned, and Virgil said: "Within that flame
   there may be torment, but there is no death.
Think well, my son, what dark ways we have trod . . .
   I guided you unharmed on Geryon;
   shall I do less now we are nearer God?
Believe this past all doubt; were you to stay
   within that womb of flame a thousand years,
   it would not burn a single hair away.
And if you still doubt my sincerity,
   but reach the hem of your robe into the flame;
   your hands and eyes will be your guarantee.   30
My son, my son, turn here with whole assurance.
   Put by your fears and enter to your peace."
   And I stood fixed, at war with my own conscience.
And seeing me still stubborn, rooted fast,
   he said, a little troubled: "Think, my son,
   you shall see Beatrice when this wall is past."
As Pyramus, but one breath from the dead,
   opened his eyes when he heard Thisbe's name
   and looked at her, when the mulberry turned red—
just so my hard paralysis melted from me,
   and I turned to my Leader at that name
   which wells forever in my memory,
at which he wagged his head, as at a child
   won over by an apple. Then he said:
   "Well, then, what are we waiting for?" and smiled.   45

He turned then and went first into the fire,
   requesting Statius, who for some time now
   had walked between us, to bring up the rear.
Once in the flame, I gladly would have cast
   my body into boiling glass to cool it
   against the measureless fury of the blast.
My gentle Father, ever kind and wise,
   strengthened me in my dread with talk of Beatrice,
   saying: "I seem already to see her eyes."
From the other side, to guide us, rose a paean,
   and moving toward it, mindless of all else,
   we emerged at last where the ascent began.
There I beheld a light that burned so brightly
   I had to look away; and from it rang:
   "Venite, benedicti Patris mei." 60
"Night falls," it added, "the sun sinks to rest;
   do not delay but hurry toward the height
   while the last brightness lingers in the west."
Straight up through the great rock-wall lay the way
   on such a line that, as I followed it,
   my body blocked the sun's last level ray.
We had only climbed the first few stairs as yet
   when I and my two Sages saw my shadow
   fade from me; and we knew the sun had set.
Before the vast sweep of the limned horizon
   could fade into one hue and night win all
   the immeasurable air to its dominion,
each made the step on which he stood his bed,
   for the nature of the mount not only stopped us
   but killed our wish to climb, once day had fled. 75
As goats on a rocky hill will dance and leap,
   nimble and gay, till they find grass, and then,
   while they are grazing, grow as tame as sheep
at ease in the green shade when the sun is high
   and the shepherd stands by, leaning on his staff,
   and at his ease covers them with his eye;
and as the herdsman beds down on the ground,
   keeping his quiet night watch by his flock
   lest it be scattered by a wolf or hound—

Purgatorio

just so we lay there, each on his stone block,
   I as the goat, they as my guardians,
   shut in on either side by walls of rock.
I could see little ahead—rock blocked the way—
   but through that little I saw the stars grow larger,
   brighter than mankind sees them. And as I lay,   90
staring and lost in thought, a sleep came on me—
   the sleep that oftentimes presents the fact
   before the event, a sleep of prophecy.
At the hour, I think, when Venus, first returning
   out of the east, shone down upon the mountain—
   she who with fires of love comes ever-burning—
I dreamed I saw a maiden innocent
   and beautiful, who walked a sunny field
   gathering flowers, and caroling as she went:
"Say I am Leah if any ask my name,
   and my white hands weave garlands wreath on wreath
   to please me when I stand before the frame
of my bright glass. For this my fingers play
   among these blooms. But my sweet sister Rachel
   sits at her mirror motionless all day.   105
To stare into her own eyes endlessly
   is all her joy, as mine is in my weaving.
   She looks, I do. Thus live we joyously."
Now eastward the new day rayed Heaven's dome
   (the sweeter to the returning wanderer
   who wakes from each night's lodging nearer home),
and the shadows fled on every side as I
   stirred from my sleep and leaped upon my feet,
   seeing my Lords already standing by.
"This is the day your hungry soul shall be
   fed on the golden apples men have sought
   on many different boughs so ardently."
These were the very words which, at the start,
   my Virgil spoke to me, and there have never
   been gifts as dear as these were to my heart.   120
Such waves of yearning to achieve the height
   swept through my soul, that at each step I took
   I felt my feathers growing for the flight.

335

When we had climbed the stairway to the rise
    of the topmost step, there with a father's love
    Virgil turned and fixed me with his eyes.
"My son," he said, "you now have seen the torment
    of the temporal and the eternal fires;
    here, now, is the limit of my discernment.
I have led you here by grace of mind and art;
    now let your own good pleasure be your guide;
    you are past the steep ways, past the narrow part.
See there the sun that shines upon your brow,
    the sweet new grass, the flowers, the fruited vines
    which spring up without need of seed or plow.   135
Until those eyes come gladdened which in pain
    moved me to come to you and lead your way,
    sit there at ease or wander through the plain.
Expect no more of me in word or deed;
    here your will is upright, free, and whole,
    and you would be in error not to heed
whatever your own impulse prompts you to;
lord of yourself I crown and miter you."

Canto 28

It is the morning of the Wednesday after Easter, Dante's fourth day on the mountain, and, having been crowned lord of himself by Virgil, Dante now takes the lead for the first time, wandering at his leisure into the sacred wood of the Earthly Paradise until his way is blocked by the waters of Lethe. His feet stopped, Dante sends his eyes on to wander that wood and there suddenly appears to him a solitary Lady, singing and gathering flowers. She is Matilda, who symbolizes the active life of the soul. In reply to Dante's entreaty, Matilda approaches to the other bank of the river. So standing, three paces across from him, she offers to answer all that Dante wishes to ask. Dante replies that he is in some confusion about the sources of the wind and the water of the Earthly Paradise. Matilda promises to dispel the mists from his understanding and proceeds to explain in great detail the natural phenomena of the Earthly Paradise, which is to say, the source of the wind, the vegetation, and the water. She further explains the special powers of the waters of Lethe and of Eunoë and concludes with some remarks on the errors of the ancient poets in the location of the Earthly Paradise. At her last words, Dante turns to his two ancient Poets to see how they are taking her remarks. Finding them smiling, he turns back once more to Matilda.

Eager now to explore in and about
   the luxuriant holy forest evergreen
   that softened the new light, I started out,
without delaying longer, from the stair
   and took my lingering way into the plain
   on ground that breathed a fragrance to the air.

With no least variation in itself,
   and with no greater force than a mild wind,
   the sweet air stroked my face on that sweet shelf,
and at its touch the trembling branches swayed,
   all bending toward that quarter into which
   the holy mountain cast its morning shade;
yet not so far back that in any part
   of that sweet wood the small birds in the tops
   had reason to stop practicing their art;   15
but bursting with delight those singing throngs
   within their green tents welcomed the new breeze
   that murmured a sweet burden to their songs
like that one hears gathering from bough to bough
   of the pine wood there on Chiassi's shore
   when Aeolus lets the Sirocco blow.
I had already come, slow bit by bit,
   so far into that ancient holy wood
   I could not see where I had entered it,
when I came upon a stream that blocked my way.
   To my left it flowed, its wavelets bending back
   the grasses on its banks as if in play.
The purest waters known to man would seem
   to have some taint of sediment within them
   compared to those, for though that holy stream   30
flows darkly there, its surface never lit
   in its perpetual shade by any shaft
   of sun or moon, nothing could hide in it.
My feet stopped, but my eyes pursued their way
   across that stream, to wander in delight
   the variousness of everblooming May.
And suddenly—as rare sights sometimes do,
   the wonder of them driving from the mind
   all other thoughts—I saw come into view
a Lady, all alone, who wandered there
   singing, and picking flowers from the profusion
   with which her path was painted everywhere.
"Fair Lady who—if outward looks and ways
   bear, as they ought, true witness to the heart—
   have surely sunned yourself in Love's own rays,   45

be pleased," I said to her, "to draw as near
  the bank of this sweet river as need be
  for me to understand the song I hear.
You make me see in my imagining
  Persephone as she appeared that day
  her mother lost a daughter; she, the spring."
As a dancer, keeping both feet on the ground
  and close together, hardly putting one
  before the other, spins herself around—
so did she turn to me upon the red
  and yellow flowerlets, virgin modesty
  making her lower her eyes and bow her head.
And she did all I asked, for she came forward
  till I not only heard the melody
  of what she sang, but made out every word.   60
And when she stood where the bright grasses are
  bathed and bent by the waves of the clear river,
  she raised her eyes—and gave my soul a star.
I cannot think so glorious a ray
  shot out of Venus' eyes that time her son
  wounded her inadvertently in play.
There, on the other bank, smiling she stood
  and gathered to her arms more of the flowers
  that sprang up without seeds in that high wood.
The stream between us was three paces wide,
  but the Hellespont where Persian Xerxes crossed
  to leave a dire example to all pride,
in its raging between Sestos and Abydos,
  caused less hate in Leander than this in me,
  for not dividing so that I might cross.   75
"You are newcomers, and perhaps you find
  because I smile," she said, "here in this place
  chosen to be the nest of humankind,
some doubt that makes you wonder at the sight.
  To pierce such mists as gather on your thoughts
  the psalm, *Delectasti me,* will give you light.
And you in front who first entreated me,
  speak if you would know more. I came prepared
  to answer you as fully as need be."

"The way the wood hums and the waters flow,"
  I said then, "are at odds with the conclusions
  I drew from what I heard a while ago."
"I shall explain from what cause," she replied,
  "these things that have confused your mind proceed,
  and thus brush its obscuring mist aside.   90
That Highest Good which only Itself can please
  made man good, and for goodness, and It gave him
  this place as earnest of eternal peace.
But man defaulted. All too brief his stay.
  Defaulted, and exchanged for tears and toil
  his innocent first laughter and sweet play.
When vapors of the earth and water meet
  a storm is born, below there. Now these vapors
  reach up, as far as possible, toward heat.
To guard man from such warring elements
  this mountain soared so high that no earth vapor
  could rise above the Gate of Penitence.
Now since the air revolves in one conjoint
  and perfect circuit with the Primal Motion,
  unless its wheel is broken at some point,   105
here at this altitude, where it goes round
  in its pure state, it strikes the foliage
  which, being dense, is made to give off sound.
The stricken plant impregnates the pure air
  with its particular powers, which are then borne
  on the Great Wheel and scattered everywhere;
and the other earth, according to the powers
  of soil and climate in its various zones,
  conceives and bears its various fruits and flowers.
When this is understood there, no man need
  believe it strange when plants take root and spring
  out of the earth without apparent seed.
Know, too, the sacred soil on which you stand
  is bursting-full of species of all sorts
  and bears fruits never picked by human hand.   120
The water you see here is from no source
  that needs replenishment from cloudy vapors,
  like streams that rise and fall; with constant force

it leaves a fountain that receives again,
    from God's will, every drop that it pours forth
    to the two streams it sends across this plain.
On this side, it removes as it flows down
    all memory of sin; on that, it strengthens
    the memory of every good deed done.
It is called Lethe here, Eunoë there.
    And one must drink first this and then the other
    to feel its powers. No sweetness can compare
with the savor of these waters. And although
    you may at once, and with no more instruction,
    drink your soul's fill from the eternal flow,   135
let me bestow one thing more for good measure.
    Though I exceed my promise, I cannot think
    what I add now will meet with your displeasure.
Those ancients who made songs to celebrate
    man's Age of Gold, placed probably on Parnassus
    this perfect garden of his first pure state.
Here mankind lived its innocent first days.
    Here is the eternal spring and every fruit.
    This is the nectar that the poets praise."
She paused. I turned around to face my Lords,
    the Poets whose strains had honored ancient song,
    and saw they had received her final words
with smiles that lingered yet upon their faces;
then turned back to that Lady of glad graces.

Canto 29

Chanting a blessing on those whose sins are forgiven, Matilda moves upstream along one bank of Lethe, and Dante keeps pace with her on the other side. A glorious light and a sweet melody grow on the air, filling Dante with such rapture that he cries out against Eve's daring, through which such joys were lost to mankind. Soon thereafter he sees the approach of the Heavenly Pageant. It is led by seven golden Candelabra that paint a seven-striped rainbow on the sky. Behind them come twenty-four Elders (the Books of the Old Testament), and behind them four Beasts (the Four Gospels), who guard a Triumphal Chariot (the Church), drawn by a Griffon (Christ). At the right wheel of the chariot dance the Three Theological Virtues; at its left wheel, the Four Cardinal Virtues. This group is followed, in order, by two Elders representing Luke as the author of Acts and Paul as the author of the fourteen Epistles; by four Elders representing James, Peter, John, and Jude as authors of the four Catholic Epistles; and finally by a single Elder representing John as the author of Revelation. When the chariot reaches a point directly across from Dante, a thunderclap resounds, and the entire pageant halts.

Her words done, she began her song again—
　"Beati quorum tecta sunt peccata"—
　as if in love when love is free of pain.
As nymphs of old went wandering alone
　through the deep-shaded woodlands, some pursuing,
　and others seeking to evade, the sun—

so, then, she started up the riverside
   and, on my own bank, I kept pace with her,
   matching her little steps with shortened stride.
Some fifty paces each we moved this way,
   when both banks curved as one; and now I found
   my face turned to the cradle of the day.
Nor had we gone as far again, all told,
   beyond the curve, when she turned to me, saying:
   "Dear brother, look and listen." And behold!—   15
through all that everlasting forest burst
   an instantaneous flood of radiance.
   I took it for a lightning-flash at first.
But lightning comes and goes. The light I saw
   not only stayed on but grew more resplendent.
   "What can this be?" I asked myself in awe.
And a sweet melody filled the bright air—
   so sweet that I reproached in righteous zeal
   Eve's fatal recklessness. How could she dare?—
one woman alone, made but a moment since—
   all Heaven and earth obedient—to refuse
   the one veil willed by High Omnipotence,
beneath which, had she stayed God's acolyte,
   I should have known before then, and for longer,
   those raptures of ineffable delight.   30
My soul hung tranced in joy beyond all measure
   and yearning for yet more, as I moved on
   through those first fruits of the eternal pleasure;
when, under the green boughs that spread before us
   the air became a blaze, and the sweet sound
   we had been hearing grew into a chorus.
O holy, holy Virgins, if for you
   I ever suffered vigils, cold, or fasts,
   occasion spurs me now to claim my due.
Empty all Helicon! Now is the time!
   Urania, help me here with your full choir
   to bring things scarce conceivable to rhyme!
I saw next, far ahead, what I believed
   were seven golden trees (at such a distance
   and in such light the eye can be deceived);   45

but in a while, when I had drawn so near
   that chance resemblances confused by distance
   no longer made false images appear,
that power that reaps for reason's mill could see
   that they were candelabra; and in the chant
   it heard the word *Hosanna!* ringing free.
Above the gold array flamed seven times seven
   candles more lucent than the midmonth moon
   at midnight in the calm of clearest heaven.
I turned about, amazed at what I saw,
   to my good Virgil, and he answered me
   in silence, with a look of equal awe.
I turned back then to those sublimities
   that were approaching at so slow a pace
   that new brides might outdistance them with ease.   60
The Lady cried: "Why have you set your mind
   so fixedly upon those living lights
   that you do not observe what comes behind?"
Then I saw people walking like attendants
   behind their lords and clothed in robes so white
   earth has no snow of such a pure resplendence.
Upon my left the polished river shone
   bright as a mirror, and when I looked in
   I saw my left side there, perfectly drawn.
And when I had moved close enough to be
   kept at a distance by no more than water,
   I halted my slow steps, better to see.
I saw the flames advance, leaving the air
   painted behind, as if by massive strokes
   or by bright pennons they were trailing there;   75
thus, all the trailing heavens were aglow
   with seven bands of light of the same color
   as Delia's girdle or Apollo's bow.
Those bands stretched back further than I could see,
   and the distance separating side from side
   came to ten paces, as it seemed to me.
And there, advancing two by two beneath
   that seven-striped sky came four-and-twenty Elders,
   each crowned in glory with a lily wreath.

And there, advancing two by two beneath
that seven-striped sky came four-and-twenty Elders,
each crowned in glory with a lily wreath.

And all sang with one voice, triumphantly:
  "Blessèd art thou among the daughters of Adam!
  Blessèd thy beauty to eternity!"
And when those souls elect, as in a dream,
  had left behind the flowers and the new grass
  that shone before me, there across the stream,   90
as star follows on star in the serene
  of heaven's height, there came on at their backs
  four beasts, and these wore wreaths of living green.
Each had three pairs of wings, and every pair
  was full of eyes. Were Argus living yet,
  his eyes would be most like what I saw there.
I cannot spend my rhymes as liberally
  as I should like to in describing them,
  for, reader, other needs are pressing me;
but read Ezekiel where he sets forth
  how they appeared to him in a great storm
  of wind and cloud and fire out of the north;
and such as he recounts, such did I see;
  except that in the number of their wings
  John differs with him and agrees with me.   105
Within the space they guarded there came on
  a burnished two-wheeled chariot in triumph,
  and harnessed to the neck of a great Griffon
whose wings, upraised into the bands of light,
  inclosed the middle one so perfectly
  they cut no part of those to left or right.
Higher than sight its wing tips soared away.
  Its birdlike parts were gold; and white the rest
  with blood-red markings. Will it serve to say
Rome never saw such a caparison,
  no, not for Africanus, nor yet Augustus?
  The Sun's own would seem shabby by comparison;
yes, even the Sun's own chariot, which strayed
  and was destroyed in fire by Jove's dark justice
  that day the frightened Earth devoutly prayed.   120
Beside the right wheel, dancing in a gyre,
  three maidens came. The first one was so red
  she would be barely visible in fire.

The second looked as if both flesh and bone
    were made of flawless emerald. The third
    seemed a new snow no slightest wind has blown.
And now the white one led the dance, and now
    the red; and from the song the red one sang
    the others took their measure, fast or slow.
Beside the left wheel, dancing in a flame
    of purple robes, and led by one who had
    three eyes within her head, four glad nymphs came.
Behind these seven came on, side by side,
    two Elders, different in dress, but both
    by the same massive bearing dignified.   135
One showed he was a follower of the art
    of great Hippocrates, whom Nature made
    to heal the creatures dearest to her heart.
The other, his counterpart, carried a blade
    so sharp and bright that at the sight of it,
    even across the stream, I was afraid.
Next I saw four who walked with humble mien.
    And last of all, one who moved in a trance,
    as if asleep, but his face was firm and keen.
These seven were robed like the first twenty-four
    in flowing robes of white, but, for their crowns,
    it was not wreaths of lilies that they wore,
but roses and whatever blooms most red.
    One would have sworn, seeing them at a distance,
    that they were wearing flames about the head.   150
And when the chariot had reached the place
    across from me, I heard a thunderclap
    that seemed a signal to those souls in grace,
for there, in unison with the exalted
first flaming standards, all that pageant halted.

Canto 30

The procession halts and the Prophets turn to the chariot and sing, "Come, my bride, from Lebanon." They are summoning Beatrice, who appears on the left side of the chariot, half-hidden from view by showers of blossoms poured from above by a hundred angels. Dante, stirred by the sight, turns to Virgil to express his overflowing emotions, and discovers that Virgil has vanished. Because he bursts into tears at losing Virgil, Dante is reprimanded by Beatrice. The angel choir overhead immediately breaks into a psalm of compassion, but Beatrice, still severe, answers by detailing Dante's offenses in not making proper use of his great gifts. It would violate the ordering of the divine decree to let Dante drink the waters of Lethe and wash all memory of sin from his soul, before he had shed the tears of a real repentance.

When the Septentrion of the First Heaven,
    which does not rise nor set, and which has never
    been veiled from sight by any mist but sin,
and which made every soul in that high court
    know its true course (just as the lower Seven
    direct the helmsman to his earthly port),
had stopped; the holy prophets, who till then
    had walked between the Griffon and those lights,
    turned to the car like souls who cry, "Amen."
And one among them who seemed sent from Heaven
    clarioned: *"Veni, sponsa, de Libano,"*
    three times, with all the others joining in.
As, at the last trump every saint shall rise
    out of the grave, ready with voice new-fleshed
    to carol *Alleluliah!* to the skies—

Purgatorio

just so, above the chariot, at the voice
  of such an Elder, rose a hundred Powers
  and Principals of the Eternal Joys,
all saying together: *"Benedictus qui venis"*;
  then, scattering flowers about on every side:
"Manibus o date lilia plenis."
Time and again at daybreak I have seen
  the eastern sky glow with a wash of rose
  while all the rest hung limpid and serene,
and the sun's face rise tempered from its rest
  so veiled by vapors that the naked eye
  could look at it for minutes undistressed.
Exactly so, within a cloud of flowers
  that rose like fountains from the angels' hands
  and fell about the chariot in showers,   30
a Lady came in view; an olive crown
  wreathed her immaculate veil, her cloak was green,
  the colors of live flame played on her gown.
My soul—such years had passed since last it saw
  that Lady and stood trembling in her presence,
  stupefied by the power of holy awe—
now, by some power that shone from her above
  the reach and witness of my mortal eyes,
  felt the full mastery of enduring love.
The instant I was smitten by the force,
  which had already once transfixed my soul
  before my boyhood years had run their course,
I turned left with the same assured belief
  that makes a child run to its mother's arms
  when it is frightened or has come to grief,   45
to say to Virgil: "There is not within me
  one drop of blood unstirred. I recognize
  the tokens of the ancient flame." But he,
he had taken his light from us. He had gone.
  Virgil had gone. Virgil, the gentle Father
  to whom I gave my soul for its salvation!
Not all that sight of Eden lost to view
  by our First Mother could hold back the tears
  that stained my cheeks so lately washed with dew.

349

A Lady came in view; an olive crown
   wreathed her immaculate veil, her cloak was green,
   the colors of live flame played on her gown.

Purgatorio

"Dante, do not weep yet, though Virgil goes.
  Do not weep yet, for soon another wound
  shall make you weep far hotter tears than those!"
As an admiral takes his place at stern or bow
  to observe the handling of his other ships
  and spur all hands to do their best—so now,   60
on the chariot's left side, I saw appear
  when I turned at the sound of my own name
  (which, necessarily, is recorded here)
that Lady who had been half-veiled from view
  by the flowers of the angel-revels. Now her eyes
  fixed me across the stream, piercing me through.
And though the veil she still wore, held in place
  by the wreathed flowers of wise Minerva's leaves,
  let me see only glimpses of her face,
her stern and regal bearing made me dread
  her next words, for she spoke as one who saves
  the heaviest charge till all the rest are read.
"Look at me well. I am she. I am Beatrice.
  How dared you make your way to this high mountain?
  Did you not know that here man lives in bliss?"   75
I lowered my head and looked down at the stream.
  But when I saw myself reflected there,
  I fixed my eyes upon the grass for shame.
I shrank as a wayward child in his distress
  shrinks from his mother's sternness, for the taste
  of love grown wrathful is a bitterness.
She paused. At once the angel chorus sang
  the blessed psalm: *"In te, Domine, speravi."*
  As far as *"pedes meos"* their voices rang.
As on the spine of Italy the snow
  lies frozen hard among the living rafters
  in winter when the northeast tempests blow;
then, melting if so much as a breath stir
  from the land of shadowless noon, flows through itself
  like hot wax trickling down a lighted taper—   90
just so I froze, too cold for sighs or tears
  until I heard that choir whose notes are tuned
  to the eternal music of the spheres.

But when I heard the voice of their compassion
   plead for me more than if they had cried out:
   "Lady, why do you treat him in this fashion?"
the ice, which hard about my heart had pressed,
   turned into breath and water, and flowed out
   through eyes and throat in anguish from my breast.
Still standing at the chariot's left side,
   she turned to those compassionate essences,
   whose song had sought to move her, and replied:
"You keep your vigil in the Eternal Day
   where neither night nor sleep obscures from you
   a single step the world takes on its way;   105
but I must speak with greater care that he
   who weeps on that far bank may understand
   and feel a grief to match his guilt. Not only
by the workings of the spheres that bring each seed
   to its fit end according to the stars
   that ride above it, but by gifts decreed
in the largesse of overflowing Grace,
   whose rain has such high vapors for its source
   our eyes cannot mount to their dwelling place;
this man, potentially, was so endowed
   from early youth that marvelous increase
   should have come forth from every good he sowed.
But richest soil the soonest will grow wild
   with bad seed and neglect. For a while I stayed him
   with glimpses of my face. Turning my mild   120
and youthful eyes into his very soul,
   I let him see their shining, and I led him
   by the straight way, his face to the right goal.
The instant I had come upon the sill
   of my second age, and crossed and changed my life,
   he left me and let others shape his will.
When I rose from the flesh into the spirit,
   to greater beauty and to greater virtue,
   he found less pleasure in me and less merit.
He turned his steps aside from the True Way,
   pursuing the false images of good
   that promise what they never wholly pay.

Not all the inspiration I won by prayer
   and brought to him in dreams and meditations
   could call him back, so little did he care.   135
He fell so far from every hope of bliss
   that every means of saving him had failed
   except to let him see the damned. For this
I visited the portals of the dead
   and poured my tears and prayers before that spirit
   by whom his steps have, up to now, been led.
The seal Almighty God's decree has placed
   on the rounds of His creation would be broken
   were he to come past Lethe and to taste
the water that wipes out the guilty years
without some scot of penitential tears!"

Canto 31

*Beatrice continues her reprimand, forc-
ing Dante to confess his faults until he swoons
with grief and pain at the thought of his sin. He
wakes to find himself in Lethe, held in the arms
of Matilda, who leads him to the other side of
the stream and there immerses him that he may
drink the waters that wipe out all memory of
sin. Matilda then leads him to the Four Cardinal
Virtues, who dance about him and lead him
before the Griffon where he may look into the
eyes of Beatrice. In them Dante sees, in a first
beatific vision, the radiant reflection of the Griffon, who appears now in his human and now in
his godly nature. The Three Theological Virtues
now approach and beg that Dante may behold
the smile of Beatrice. Beatrice removes her
veil, and in a second beatific vision, Dante beholds the splendor of the unveiled
shining of Divine Love.*

"You, there, who stand upon the other side—"
    (turning to me now, who had thought the edge
    of her discourse was sharp, the point) she cried
without pause in her flow of eloquence,
    "Speak up! Speak up! Is it true? To such a charge
    your own confession must give evidence."
I stood as if my spirit had turned numb;
    the organ of my speech moved, but my voice
    died in my throat before a word could come.
Briefly she paused, then cried impatiently:
    "What are you thinking? Speak up, for the waters
    have yet to purge sin from your memory."

Confusion joined to terror forced a broken
  "Yes" from my throat, so weak that only one
    who read my lips would know that I had spoken.   15
As an arbalest will snap when string and bow
  are drawn too tight by the bowman, and the bolt
    will strike the target a diminished blow—
so did I shatter, strengthless and unstrung,
  under her charge, pouring out floods of tears,
    while my voice died in me on the way to my tongue.
And she: "Filled as you were with the desire
  I taught you for that Good beyond which nothing
    exists on earth to which man may aspire,
what yawning moats or what stretched chain-lengths lay
  across your path to force you to abandon
    all hope of pressing further on your way?
What increase or allurement seemed to show
  in the brows of others that you walked before them
    as a lover walks below his lady's window?"   30
My breath dragged from me in a bitter sigh;
  I barely found a voice to answer with;
    my lips had trouble forming a reply.
In tears I said: "The things of the world's day,
  false pleasures and enticements, turned my steps
    as soon as you had ceased to light my way."
And she: "Had you been silent, or denied
  what you confess, your guilt would still be known
    to Him from Whom no guilt may hope to hide.
But here, before our court, when souls upbraid
  themselves for their own guilt in true remorse,
    the grindstone is turned back against the blade.
In any case that you may know your crime
  truly and with true shame and so be stronger
    against the Siren's song another time,   45
control your tears and listen with your soul
  to learn how my departure from the flesh
    ought to have spurred you to the higher goal.
Nothing in art or nature could call forth
  such joy from you, as sight of that fair body
    which clothed me once and now sifts back to earth.

The Divine Comedy

And if my dying turned that highest pleasure
    to very dust, what joy could still remain
    in mortal things for you to seek and treasure?
At the first blow you took from such vain things
    your every thought should have been raised to follow
    my flight above decay. Nor should your wings
have been weighed down by any joy below—
    love of a maid, or any other fleeting
    and useless thing—to wait a second blow.
The fledgling waits a second shaft, a third;
    but nets are spread and the arrow sped in vain
    in sight or hearing of the full-grown bird."
As a scolded child, tongue-tied for shame, will stand
    and recognize his fault, and weep for it,
    bowing his head to a just reprimand,
so did I stand. And she said: "If to hear me
    grieves you, now raise your beard and let your eyes
    show you a greater cause for misery."
The blast that blows from Libya's hot sand,
    or the Alpine gale, overcomes less resistance
    uprooting oaks than I, at her command,
overcame then in lifting up my face;
    for when she had referred to it as my beard,
    I sensed too well the venom of her phrase.
When I had raised my eyes with so much pain,
    I saw those primal beings, now at rest,
    who had strewn blossoms round her thick as rain;
and with my tear-blurred and uncertain vision
    I saw her turned to face that beast which is
    one person in two natures without division.
Even veiled and across the river from me
    her face outshone its first-self by as much
    as she outshone all mortals formerly.
And the thorns of my repentance pricked me so
    that all the use and substance of the world
    I most had loved, now most appeared my foe.
Such guilty recognition gnawed my heart
    I swooned for pain; and what I then became
    she best knows who most gave me cause to smart.

356

Purgatorio

When I returned to consciousness at last
   I found the Lady who had walked alone
   bent over me. "Hold fast!" she said. "Hold fast!"
She had drawn me into the stream up to my throat
   and, pulling me behind her, she sped on
   over the water, light as any boat.
Nearing the sacred bank, I heard her say
   in tones so sweet I cannot call them back,
   much less describe them here: *"Asperges me."*
Then the sweet Lady took my head between
   her open arms and, embracing me, she dipped me
   and made me drink the waters that make clean.
Then raising me in my new purity
   she led me to the dance of the Four Maidens;
   each raised an arm and so joined hands above me.   105
"Here we are nymphs; stars are we in the skies.
   Ere Beatrice went to earth we were ordained
   her handmaids. We will lead you to her eyes;
but that your own may see what joyous light
   shines in them, yonder Three, who see more deeply,
   will sharpen and instruct your mortal sight."
Thus they sang, then led me to the Griffon.
   Behind him, Beatrice waited. And when I stood
   at the Griffon's breast, they said in unison:
"Look deep, look well, however your eyes may smart.
   We have led you now before those emeralds
   from which Love shot his arrows through your heart."
A thousand burning passions, every one
   hotter than any flame, held my eyes fixed
   to the lucent eyes she held fixed on the Griffon.   120
Like sunlight in a glass the twofold creature
   shone from the deep reflection of her eyes,
   now in the one, now in the other nature.
Judge, reader, if I found it passing strange
   to see the thing unaltered in itself
   yet in its image working change on change.
And while my soul in wonder and delight
   was savoring that food which in itself
   both satisfies and quickens appetite,

357

Then the sweet Lady took my head between
her open arms and embracing me, she dipped me
and made me drink the waters that make clean.

Purgatorio

the other Three, whose bearing made it clear
    they were of higher rank, came toward me dancing
    to the measure of their own angelic air.
"Turn, Beatrice, oh, turn the eyes of grace,"
    was their refrain, "upon your faithful one
    who comes so far to look upon your face.   135
Grant us this favor of your grace; reveal
    your mouth to him, and let his eyes behold
    the second beauty, which your veils conceal."
O splendor of the eternal living light!
    who that has drunk deep of Parnassus' waters,
    or grown pale in the shadow of its height,
would not, still, feel his burdened genius fail
    attempting to describe in any tongue
    how you appeared when you put by your veil
in that free air open to heaven and earth
whose harmony is your shining shadowed forth!

Canto 32

*Beatrice unveils and for the first time in
ten years Dante looks upon her face. When he recovers from that blinding sight, Dante finds the
Heavenly Pageant has wheeled about and is
heading east. Dante and Statius follow the chariot to the Tree of Good and Evil, which rises to
vast heights but bears neither leaves nor flowers.
The Griffon ties the pole of the chariot to the tree,
and the tree immediately breaks into leaf and
flower. The Heavenly Pageant greets this wonder
with a hymn unknown to mortals. Overpowered
by the singing Dante sleeps. He awakens to find
himself, as he believes at first, alone with Matilda. The Heavenly Pageant has, in fact, departed, but as Dante soon learns, Beatrice has
remained behind to guard the chariot, and the
Seven Nymphs have remained to attend her. She
is seated upon the ground, on the roots of the tree
and under its shade. Dante then witnesses an allegorical masque of the Corruption of the Church
Through Wealth. First an eagle (the Roman
Empire) and then a fox (heresy) attack the tree
and the chariot. Then the eagle returns and covers
the chariot with feathers. Immediately a dragon
(Satan) rips at the chariot's foundation. The chariot then covers itself with the eagle's feathers
(riches) and is converted into a monstrous beast
on which rides a harlot (the corrupt Papacy) attended by a giant (the French Monarchy) that
beats the harlot and drags the monster
into the woods and out of sight.*

Purgatorio

My eyes were fixed with such intensity
   on quenching, at long last, their ten years' thirst
   that every sense but sight abandoned me.
Tranced by the holy smile that drew me there
   into the old nets, I forgot all else—
   my eyes wore blinders, and I could not care.
When suddenly my gaze was wrenched away
   and forced to turn left to those goddesses.
   "He stares too fixedly," I heard them say.
And as a man is blinded by the light
   when he has looked directly at the sun—
   just so I found that I had lost my sight.
When I could make out lesser (I mean, of course,
   less sensible objects) as compared to the greater
   from which I had been called away by force,   15
I saw the legion of those souls in grace
   had turned right-wheel-about and marched back now
   with the sun and the seven torches in its face.
As forward troops when they are giving ground
   turn under their shields, and their standards face about
   before the rest of the column has turned round—
just so the vanguard of that heavenly force
   had all gone by before the chariot
   had swung its pole around to the new course.
Then to their wheels the Ladies turned together,
   and the Griffon once more pulled the sacred car,
   not ruffling so much as a single feather.
Statius and I followed across that park
   with the Lady who had led me through the ford,
   behind the wheel that turned the lesser arc.   30
We marched across the sacred wood which she
   who heeded a forked tongue had left deserted,
   our steps timed by angelic melody.
We had moved on, I think, about as far
   as three good bowshots, end to end, might reach,
   when Beatrice descended from the car.
"Adam!" I heard all murmur, censuring him.
   Then they all formed a circle round a tree
   that bore no leaf nor flower on any limb.

It soared so high that even in woods like those
   the Indians know it would have seemed a wonder;
   and the crown spread out the more the more it rose.
"Blessed art thou, Griffon, whose beak hath rent
   no morsel of the sweet wood of this tree,
   for it grips the belly with a raging torment!"   45
So shouted all the others as they stood
   about the tree. And the two-natured being:
   "Thus is preserved the seed of every good!"
Then he drew up before the widowed mast
   the chariot's pole, and what came from the tree
   he gave it back, and tied the two stems fast.
As in the spring on earth, when the great light
   falls mingled with the rays of those sweet stars
   that follow Pisces into Heaven's height,
the trees begin to swell, then burgeon full,
   each one in its own hue, before the Sun
   harnesses his team beneath the Bull—
just so the boughs that had been bare before
   took color, turning something less than rose
   and more than violet as they bloomed once more.   60
The hymn I heard those blessed souls sing then
   is not sung here, nor did I understand it;
   nor did I hear it through to the "Amen."
Could I portray the eyes of Argus here,
   lulled one by one by drowsy tales of Syrinx,
   that time their pitiless watch cost him so dear,
as a painter paints his model, I would try
   to show exactly how I fell asleep.
   But who can image drowsiness? Not I.
Therefore, I pass to my waking, and declare
   a radiance tore the veil of sleep; a voice
   cried out: "Arise! What are you doing there?"
When they were shown the flowering of that Tree
   that makes the angels hungry for Its fruit
   and sets a feast in Heaven eternally,   75
Peter, John, and James, awe-stricken, fell
   into a sleep from which they were recalled
   by the same word that broke a greater spell;

and saw their company reduced, as both
   Moses and Elijah vanished from them;
   and saw the Master's robe change back to cloth—
just so did I awaken from my dream
   to find, bent over me, the compassionate Lady
   who had conducted me along the stream.
Fearful I cried out, "Beatrice! Where is she?"
   And the Lady: "She is seated on the roots
   of the new foliage, as you can see,
encircled by the seven shining Graces.
   The others mount to Heaven behind the Griffon,
   intoning sweeter and profounder praises." 90
If she said more, her words were lost on me,
   for now my eyes were fixed once more on Beatrice,
   my senses closed to all that was not she.
She sat on the bare earth alone, left there
   to guard the chariot that the Biformed Beast
   had fastened to the tree with such great care.
A living cloister ringing her about,
   the Seven Nymphs stood, holding in their hands
   those candles no wind ever shall blow out.
"Here briefly in this forest shall you dwell;
   and evermore, with me, be of that Rome
   in which Christ is a Roman. Hence, look well
there at the great car, and that you may be
   a light to the dark world, when you return
   set down exactly all that you shall see." 105
Thus Beatrice; and I, devoutly bent
   at the feet of her commands, turned mind and eye
   as she had willed, in all obedient.
No flash from densest clouds when the rains fall
   from the remotest reaches of the sky
   ever shot down as fast out of the squall
as did the bird of Jove that I saw break
   down through the tree, ripping the flowers, the leaves,
   even the bark, with its fierce claws and beak.
He struck the chariot a tremendous blow,
   at which it lurched like a storm-battered ship,
   now rolled to port, now starboard, to and fro.

Next came a fox, so gaunt and angular
  it seemed to know no fit food; and it pounced
  upon the cab of the triumphal car.   120
But threatening all its filthy sins with woe
  my Lady sent it reeling back from there
  as fast as such a bag of bones could go.
Then, through the tree, I saw the bird descend
  once more into the car and shed its plumes
  to feather it in gold from end to end.
And from the sky, as if a heart let slip
  all of its grief in one sound, a voice cried:
  "Oh, what a load you bear, my little ship!"
Then, as I watched, I saw a fissure split
  the earth between the two wheels, and a dragon
  rise to the car and sink its tail in it.
Much as an angry wasp draws back its stinger,
  it drew its tail back, ripping the car's floor,
  and wandered off as if it meant to linger.   135
Like rich soil left to weeds, what then remained
  covered itself with feathers, which no doubt
  had been intended to burnish what they stained.
And both the wheels and the pole were overgrown,
  and all the car to the last part, and all
  in less time than the lips part for a moan.
So changed, the holy ark began to sprout
  heads from its various parts: three from the pole,
  one from each corner. Seven in all grew out.
The three were horned like oxen, but the four
  were each armed with a single evil horn.
  No one had seen the monster's like before.
Secure as a great fortress on a crag,
  an ungirt harlot rode the beast, her eyes
  darting with avarice. Beside that hag,   150
and ready to risk all to keep her his,
  a giant strode erect, and as they passed,
  from time to time the two exchanged a kiss.
But when she turned her hungry eyes on me,
  her savage lover in a bestial rage
  whipped her from head to foot unmercifully.

And ready to risk all to keep her his,
a giant strode erect, and as they passed,
from time to time the two exchanged a kiss.

Then in a jealous fit the brute untied
  the monster from the tree, and dragged it off
  into the woods, far toward the other side,
until between me and that doxie queen
on her weird beast, he made the trees a screen.

Canto 33

*The Seven Nymphs sing a hymn of sor-
row for the grief of the Church, and Beatrice
answers with Christ's words announcing his
resurrection. All then move onward, Beatrice
summoning Dante to her side as they walk on.
Beatrice begins her discourse with an obscure-
ly worded prophecy of the deliverance of the
Church. In much simpler language, she then utters her final reproach to Dante for having so lost
sight of the truth. As she finishes, the train halts
before the great spring from which flow the waters of Lethe and Eunoë. At Beatrice's command,
the Seven Nymphs lead Dante forward, and he
drinks the waters of Eunoë. When he drank the
waters of Lethe, Dante forgot all sin and error;
now every good is strengthened in him. Thus,
his final purification completed, Dante rises
"perfect, pure, and ready for the stars."*

"*Deus, venerunt gentes*"—the Holy Seven,
    in alternating chorus through their tears,
    first three, then four, raised a sweet chant to Heaven;
and Beatrice, when she heard them mourn such loss
    sighed with a grief so deep that even Mary
    could not have changed more at the foot of the cross.
But when the other virgins in their choir
    fell still for her reply, she rose erect
    in holy zeal, and said, as if afire:
"*Modicum, et non videbitis me;*
    et iterum, dearly beloved sisters,
    modicum, et vos videbitis me."
Then placing the Seven before her, she moved ahead
    with a nod to me, to the Lady, and to the Sage
    that had remained, to follow where she led.

15

So she strolled on, and she had not yet laid
   her tenth step on the sward, when she turned round
   and struck my eyes with her eyes as she said
with a serene tranquillity: "Draw near,
   that you may, if I wish to speak to you
   as we move on, be better placed to hear."
When I was, as I should be, at her side,
   she said: "Dear brother, why are you not moved
   to question me as we move on? "—Tongue-tied,
like one who knows his station is beneath
   that of the presences in which he stands,
   and cannot drag his voice across his teeth,
so did I, with a voice almost choked through,
   manage to say: "My Lady, all my need
   and all that is my good is known to you."   30
And she to me: "My wish is that you break
   the grip of fear and shame, and from now on
   no longer speak like one but half awake.
The cart the dragon broke was, and is not;
   let him whose fault that is believe God's wrath
   will not be calmed by soup, however hot.
The eagle you saw shed its plumes back there
   to make the cart a monster and a prey,
   will not remain forever without heir;
for certain as my words, my eyes foresee,
   already nearing, the unstayable stars
   that bring the time in which, by God's decree,
five hundred, ten, and five shall be the sign
   of one who comes to hunt down and destroy
   the giant and his thievish concubine.   45
My prophecy, being obscure as those
   of Themis and the Sphinx, may fail to move you,
   since all such words hide what they should disclose;
but soon now, like an Oedipus reborn,
   events themselves shall solve the dark enigma,
   and without loss of either sheep or corn.
Note my words well, and when you give them breath,
   repeat them as I said them, to the living
   whose life is no more than a race toward death.

And when you come to write them down, make clear
   what you have seen of the tree, now twice-despoiled
   since all-creating God first raised it here.
All those who rob or break those boughs commit
   a blasphemy-in-deed, offending God
   who sacred to Himself created it.   60
For just one bite, the first soul's tears were spilt
   five thousand years and more, yearning for Him
   who suffered in His own flesh for that guilt.
Your wits must be asleep not to have known
   that a particular reason must account
   for its great height and its inverted crown.
Had not your idle thoughts been to your brain
   an Elsan water, and your pleasure in them
   a Pyramus to the mulberry's new stain,
those two facts surely should have made you see
   the justice of God's interdict shine forth
   as the moral meaning of the form of the tree.
It is my wish—because I see your mind
   turned into stone, and like a stone, so darkened
   that the light of what I tell you strikes it blind—   75
that you bear back, if not in writing, then
   in outline, what I say, as pilgrims wreathe
   their staffs with palm to show where they have been."
And I to her: "As pressed wax will retain
   a faithful imprint of the signet ring,
   so is your seal imprinted on my brain.
But why do your desired words fly so high
   above my power to follow their intent
   that I see less and less the more I try?"
"They fly so high," she said, "that you may know
   what school you followed and how far behind
   the truth I speak its feeble doctrines go;
and see that man's ways, even at his best,
   are far from God's as earth is from the heaven
   whose swiftest wheel turns above all the rest."   90
"But," I replied, "I have no recollection
   of ever having been estranged from you.
   Conscience does not accuse me of defection."

And she then with a smile: "If, as you say
   you lack that memory, then call to mind
   how you drank Lethe's waters here today.
As certainly as smoke betrays the fire,
   this new forgetfulness of your wish to stray
   betrays the sinfulness of that desire.
But I assure you that I shall select
   the simplest words that need be from now on
   to make things clear to your dull intellect."
Now with a brighter flame and slower pace
   the sun was holding its meridian height,
   which varies round the world from place to place,   105
when suddenly—as one who leads a line
   of travelers as their escort will stop short
   at a strange sight or an unusual sign—
so stopped the Seven at an edge of shade
   pale as a shadow cast by a cold peak
   on a cold stream deep in an Alpine glade.
And there ahead of them, in a single flow,
   Tigris and Euphrates seemed to rise
   and part as friends who linger as they go.
"O light and glory of mankind," I cried,
   "what is this flood that pours forth from one source
   and then parts from itself to either side?"
In answer to that prayer I heard the name
   "Matilda" and "Ask her." Who spoke up then
   as one does who absolves himself of blame: 120
"This, and much more, I have this very day
   explained to him, and Lethe certainly
   could not have washed that memory away."
And Beatrice: "Perhaps a greater care,
   as often happens, dims his memory
   and his mind's eye. But see Eunoë there—
lead him, as is your custom, to the brim
   of that sweet stream, and with its holy waters
   revive the powers that faint and die in him."
Then as a sweet soul gladly shapes its own
   good will to the will of others, without protest,
   as soon as any sign has made it known,

Reader, had I the space to write at will,
I should, if only briefly, sing a praise
of that sweet draught.

so the sweet maid, taking me by the hand
  and saying in a modest voice to Statius,
  "Come you with him," obeyed the good command.   135
Reader, had I the space to write at will,
  I should, if only briefly, sing a praise
  of that sweet draught. Would I were drinking still!
But I have filled all the pages planned
  for this, my second, canticle, and Art
  pulls at its iron bit with iron hand.
I came back from those holiest waters new,
  remade, reborn, like a sun-wakened tree
  that spreads new foliage to the spring dew
in sweetest freshness, healed of winter's scars;
perfect, pure, and ready for the stars.

Paradiso

Canto 1

Dante states his supreme theme as Paradise itself and invokes the aid not only of the Muses but of Apollo. He and Beatrice are in the Earthly Paradise, the sun is at the vernal equinox, it is noon at Purgatory and midnight at Jerusalem when Dante sees Beatrice turn her eyes to stare straight into the sun and reflexively imitates her gesture. At once it is as if a second sun had been created, its light dazzling his senses, and Dante feels the ineffable change of his mortal soul into Godliness. These phenomena are more than his senses can grasp, and Beatrice must explain to him what he himself has not realized: that he and Beatrice are soaring toward the height of Heaven at an incalculable speed. Thus Dante climaxes the master metaphor in which purification is equated to weightlessness. Having purged all dross from his soul he mounts effortlessly, without even being aware of it at first, to his natural goal in the Godhead. So they pass through the Sphere of Fire, and so Dante first hears the music of the spheres.

THE glory of Him who moves all things rays forth
    through all the universe and is reflected
    from each thing in proportion to its worth.
I have been in that Heaven of His most light,
    and what I saw those who descend from there
    lack both the knowledge and the power to write.
For as our intellect draws near its goal
    it opens to such depths of understanding
    as memory cannot plumb within the soul.
Nevertheless, whatever portion time
    still leaves me of the treasure of that Kingdom
    shall now become the subject of my rhyme.

O good Apollo, for this last task, I pray
   you make me such a vessel of your powers
   as you deem worthy to be crowned with bay.   15
One peak of cleft Parnassus heretofore
   has served my need, now must I summon both
   on entering the arena one time more.
Enter my breast, I pray you, and there breathe
   as high a strain as conquered Marsyas
   that time you drew his body from its sheath.
O power divine, but lend to my high strain
   so much as will make clear even the shadow
   of that High Kingdom stamped upon my brain,
and you shall see me come to your dear grove
   to crown myself with those green leaves which you
   and my high theme shall make me worthy of.
So seldom are they gathered, Holy Sire,
   to crown an emperor's or a poet's triumph
   (oh, fault and shame of mortal man's desire!)   30
that the glad Delphic god must surely find
   increase of joy in the Peneian frond
   when any man thirsts for it in his mind.
Great flames are kindled where the small sparks fly.
   So after me, perhaps, a better voice
   shall raise such prayers that Cyrrha will reply.
The lamp of the world rises to mortal view
   from various stations, but that point which joins
   four circles with three crosses, it soars through
to a happier course in happier conjunction,
   wherein it warms and seals the wax of the world
   closer to its own nature and high function.
That glad conjunction had made it evening here
   and morning there; the south was all alight,
   while darkness rode the northern hemisphere;   45
when I saw Beatrice had turned left to raise
   her eyes up to the sun; no eagle ever
   stared at its shining with so fixed a gaze.
And as a ray descending from the sky
   gives rise to another, which climbs back again,
   as a pilgrim yearns for home—so through my eye

her action, like a ray into my mind,
   gave rise to mine. I stared into the sun
   so hard that here it would have left me blind;
but much is granted to our senses there,
   in that garden made to be man's proper place,
   that is not granted us when we are here.
I had to look away soon, and yet not
   so soon but what I saw him spark and blaze
   like new-tapped iron when it pours white-hot.   60
And suddenly, as it appeared to me,
   day was added to day, as if He who can
   had added a new sun to Heaven's glory.
Beatrice stared at the eternal spheres
   entranced, unmoving; and I looked away
   from the sun's height to fix my eyes on hers.
And as I looked, I felt begin within me
   what Glaucus felt eating the herb that made him
   a god among the others in the sea.
How speak trans-human change to human sense?
   Let the example speak until God's grace
   grants the pure spirit the experience.
Whether I rose in only the last created
   part of my being, O Love that rulest Heaven
   Thou knowest, by whose lamp I was translated.   75
When the Great Wheel that spins eternally
   in longing for Thee captured my attention
   by that harmony attuned and heard by Thee,
I saw ablaze with sun from side to side
   a reach of Heaven; not all the rains and rivers
   of all of time could make a sea so wide.
That radiance and that new-heard melody
   fired me with such a yearning for their Cause
   as I had never felt before. And she
who saw my every thought as well as I,
   saw my perplexity; before I asked
   my question she had started her reply.
Thus she began: "You dull your own perceptions
   with false imaginings and do not grasp
   what would be clear but for your preconceptions.   90

You think you are still on earth; the lightning's spear
   never fled downward from its natural place
   as rapidly as you are rising there."
I grasped her brief and smiling words and shed
   my first perplexity, but found myself
   entangled in another, and I said:
"My mind, already recovered from the surprise
   of the great marvel you have just explained,
   is now amazed anew; how can I rise
in my gross body through such aery substance?"
   She sighed in pity and turned as might a mother
   to a delirious child. "The elements
of all things," she began, "whatever their mode,
   observe an inner order. It is this form
   that makes the universe resemble God.   105
In this the higher creatures see the hand
   of the Eternal Worth, which is the goal
   to which these norms conduce, being so planned.
All being within this order, by the laws
   of its own nature, is impelled to find
   its proper station round its Primal Cause.
Thus every nature moves across the tide
   of the great sea of being to its own port,
   each with its given instinct as its guide.
This instinct draws the fire about the moon.
   It is the mover in the mortal heart.
   It draws the earth together and makes it one.
Not only the brute creatures, but all those
   possessed of intellect and love, this instinct
   drives to their mark as a bow shoots forth its arrows.   120
The Providence that makes all things hunger here
   satisfies forever with Its light
   the heaven within which whirls the fastest sphere.
And to it now, as to a place foretold,
   are we two soaring, driven by that bow
   whose every arrow finds a mark of gold.
It is true that oftentimes the form of a thing
   does not respond to the intent of the art,
   the matter being deaf to summoning—

just so, the creature sometimes travels wide
    of this true course, for even when so driven
    it still retains the power to turn aside
(exactly as we may see the heavens' fire
    plunge from a cloud), and its first impulse may
    be twisted earthward by a false desire.   135
You should not, as I see it, marvel more
    at your ascent than at a river's fall
    from a high mountain to the valley floor.
If you, free as you are of every dross,
    had settled and had come to rest below,
    that would indeed have been as marvelous
as a still flame there in the mortal plain."
So saying, she turned her eyes to Heaven again.

Canto 2

Dante and Beatrice are soaring to the Sphere of the Moon at a speed approaching that of light. Dante warns back the shallow reader: only those who have eaten of the knowledge of God may hope to follow him into the last reaches of his infinite voyage, for it will reveal such wonders as only faith can grasp. His warning concluded, he and Beatrice enter the Sphere of the Moon and pass into the substances of the moon as light into water, as God incarnated Himself into man, or as the saved soul reenters God, without disruption of the substance thus entered. Still unenlightened by the ultimate revelation, Dante does not understand how those markings we know as the Man in the Moon, and which the Italians knew as Cain With His Bush of Thorns, can appear on the surface of the moon—a surface which he conceives as diamond-smooth. Beatrice asks for his explanation, refutes it, and proceeds to explain the truth of the moon's markings.

O you who in your wish to hear these things
   have followed thus far in your little skiffs
   the wake of my great ship that sails and sings,
turn back and make your way to your own coast.
   Do not commit yourself to the main deep,
   for, losing me, all may perhaps be lost.
My course is set for an uncharted sea.
   Minerva fills my sail. Apollo steers.
   And nine new Muses point the Pole for me.
You other few who have set yourselves to eat
   the bread of angels, by which we live on earth,
   but of which no man ever grew replete;

you may well trust your keel to the salt track
   and follow in the furrow of my wake
   ahead of the parted waters that close back   15
Those heroes who sailed to Colchis, there to see
   their glorious Jason turned into a plowman,
   were not as filled with wonder as you will be.
The connate and perpetual thirst we feel
   for the God-like realm bore us almost as swiftly
   as the sight soars to see the heavens wheel.
Beatrice was looking upward and I at her
   when—in the time it takes a bolt to strike,
   fly, and be resting in the bowstring's blur—
I found myself in a place where a wondrous thing
   drew my entire attention; whereat she
   from whom I could not hide my mind's least yearning
turned and said, as much in joy as beauty:
   "To God, who has raised us now to the first star,
   direct your thoughts in glad and grateful duty."   30
It seemed to me a cloud, as luminous
   and dense and smoothly polished as a diamond
   struck by a ray of sun, enveloped us.
We were received into the elements
   of the eternal pearl as water takes
   light to itself, with no change in its substance.
If I was a body (nor need we in this case
   conceive how one dimension can bear another,
   which must be if two bodies fill one space)
the more should my desire burn like the sun
   to see that Essence in which one may see
   how human nature and God blend into one.
There we shall witness what we hold in faith,
   not told by reason but self-evident,
   as men perceive an axiom here on earth.   45
"My Lady," I replied, "in every way
   my being can, I offer up my thanks
   to Him who raised me from the world of clay.
But tell me what dark traces in the grain
   of this bright body show themselves below
   and cause men to tell fables about Cain?"

She smiled a moment and then answered me:
  "If the reckoning of mortals fails to turn
    the lock to which your senses hold no key,
the arrows of wonder should not run you through;
  even when led by the evidence of the senses
    the wings of reason often do not fly true.
But what do *you* believe the cause to be?"
  And I: "That these variations we observe
    are caused by bodies of varying density."   60
And she: "You will certainly come to know your view
  is steeped in falsehood. If you listen well
    to the counter-arguments I shall offer you.
The eighth sphere shines with many lamps, and these
  may be observed to shine with various aspects,
    both in their qualities and quantities.
If rare or dense alone could have produced
  all this, one power would have to be in all,
    whether equally or variously diffused.
Diversity of powers can only spring
  from formal principles, and all but one
    would be excluded by your reasoning.
Now if rarity produced the marks you mention,
  then the matter of this planet must be transparent
    at certain points, due to its rarefaction;   75
or it must be arranged like fat and lean
  within a body, as, so to speak, a book
    alternates pages. But it may be seen
in an eclipse that the first cannot be true,
  for then the sun's light, as it does in striking
    rare matter of any sort, would pass right through.
Since it does not, we may then pass along
  to the second case, and if I prove it false,
    I shall have shown that your whole thought is wrong.
If this rare matter is not spread throughout
  the planet's mass, then there must be a limit
    at which the denser matter will turn about
the sun's rays, which, not being allowed to pass,
  will be reflected as light and color are
    from the leaded back of a clear looking glass.   90

Paradiso

Now you may argue, in Avicenna's track,
    that the ray seems darker in one place than in others
    since it is being reflected from further back.
From such an *instance* (if you will do your part)
    you may escape by experiment (that being
    the spring that feeds the rivers of man's art).
Take three clear mirrors. Let two be set out
    at an equal distance from you, and a third
    between them, but further back. Now turn about
to face them, and let someone set a light
    behind your back so that it strikes all three
    and is reflected from them to your sight.
Although the image from the greater distance
    is smaller than the others, you must note
    that all three shine back with an equal brilliance.   105
Now, as the power of the sun's rays will strip
    the wintry ground on which the snow has lain
    of the cold and color that held it in their grip,
so you, with mind stripped clean, shall I delight
    with such a radiance of the living truth
    that it will leap and tremble in your sight.
Within the Heaven of Peace beyond the sky
    there whirls a body from whose power arises
    the being of all things that within it lie.
The next sphere, that which is so richly lit,
    distributes this power to many essences
    distinct from itself, yet all contained within it.
The other spheres, in various degrees,
    dispose the special powers they have within
    to their own causes and effects. All these   120
great universal organs, as you now know,
    proceed from grade to grade. Each in its order
    takes power from above and does its work below.
Now then, note carefully how I move on
    through this pass to the truth you seek, for thus
    you shall learn how to hold the ford alone.
The motion and the power of the sacred gyres—
    as the hammer's art is from the smith—must flow
    from the Blessed Movers. It is their power inspires.

And thus that heaven made loveliest in its wheel
   by many lamps, from the deep Mind that turns it,
   takes the image and makes itself the seal.
And as the soul within your mortal clay
   is spread through different organs, each of which
   is shaped to its own end; in the same way   135
the high angelic Intelligence spreads its goodness
   diversified through all the many stars
   while yet revolving ever in its Oneness.
This varying power is variously infused
   throughout the precious body that it quickens,
   in which, like life in you, it is diffused.
Because of the glad Nature from which it flows,
   this many-faceted power shines through that body
   as through the living eye the glad soul glows.
From this source only, not from rare and dense,
   comes that by which one light and another differs—
   the formal principle whose excellence,
conforming to its own purposes, makes appear
those markings you observe as dark and clear."

Canto 3

*As Dante is about to speak to Beatrice he
sees the dim traceries of human faces, and taking
them to be reflections he turns to see what souls
are being so reflected. Beatrice, as ever, explains
that these pallid images are the souls themselves.
They are the Inconstant, the souls of those who
registered holy vows in Heaven, but who broke or
scanted them. Among them, Piccarda Donati
identifies herself and then the Empress Constance. Both had taken vows as nuns but were
forced to break them in order to contract a political marriage. Not all the souls about them need
have failed in the same vows, however. Any failure to fulfill a holy vow —of Holy Orders, to go on
a pilgrimage, to offer special services to God—
might place the soul in this lowest class of the
blessed. Piccarda explains that every soul in
Heaven rejoices in the entire will of God and cannot wish for a higher place, for to do so would be
to come into conflict with the will of God. In the
perfect harmony of bliss, everywhere
in Heaven is Paradise.*

That sun that breathed love's fire into my youth
    had thus resolved for me, feature by feature—
    proving, disproving—the sweet face of truth.
I, raising my eyes to her eyes to announce
    myself resolved of error, and well assured,
    was about to speak; but before I could pronounce
my first word, there appeared to me a vision.
    It seized and held me so that I forgot
    to offer her my thanks and my confession.

The Divine Comedy

As in clear glass when it is polished bright,
   or in a still and limpid pool whose waters
   are not so deep that the bottom is lost from sight,
a footnote of our lineaments will show,
   so pallid that our pupils could as soon
   make out a pearl upon a milk-white brow—   15
so I saw many faces eager to speak,
   and fell to the error opposite the one
   that kindled love for a pool in the smitten Greek.
And thinking the pale traces I saw there
   were reflected images, I turned around
   to face the source—but my eyes met empty air.
I turned around again like one beguiled
   and took my line of sight from my sweet Guide,
   whose sacred eyes grew radiant as she smiled.
"Are you surprised that I smile at this childish act
   of reasoning?" she said, "since even now
   you dare not trust your sense of the true fact,
but turn, as usual, back to vacancy?
   These are true substances you see before you.
   They are assigned here for inconstancy   30
to holy vows. Greet them. Heed what they say,
   and so believe; for the True Light that fills them
   permits no soul to wander from Its ray."
So urged, I spoke to those pale spirits, turning
   to one who seemed most eager, and began
   like one whose mind goes almost blank with yearning.
"O well created soul, who in the sun
   of the eternal life drinks in the sweetness
   which, until tasted, is beyond conception;
great would be my joy would you confide
   to my eager mind your earthly name and fate."
   That soul with smiling eyes at once replied:
"The love that fills us will no more permit
   hindrance to a just wish than does that Love
   that wills all of Its court to be like It.   45
I was a virgin sister there below,
   and if you search your memory with care,
   despite my greater beauty, you will know

386

So I saw many faces eager to speak,
   and fell to the error opposite the one
   that kindled love for a pool in the smitten Greek.

I am Piccarda, and I am placed here
    among these other souls of blessedness
    to find my blessedness in the slowest sphere.
Our wishes, which can have no wish to be
    but in the pleasure of the Holy Ghost,
    rejoice in being formed to His decree.
And this low-seeming post which we are given
    is ours because we broke, or, in some part,
    slighted the vows we offered up to Heaven."
And I then: "Something inexpressibly
    divine shines in your face, subliming you
    beyond your image in my memory;   60
therefore I found you difficult to place;
    but now, with the assistance of your words,
    I find the memory easier to retrace.
But tell me, please, do you who are happy here
    have any wish to rise to higher station,
    to see more, or to make yourselves more dear?"
She smiled, as did the spirits at her side;
    then, turning to me with such joy she seemed
    to burn with the first fire of love, replied:
"Brother, the power of love, which is our bliss,
    calms all our will. What we desire, we have.
    There is in us no other thirst than this.
Were we to wish for any higher sphere,
    then our desires would not be in accord
    with the high will of Him who wills us here;   75
and if love is our whole being, and if you weigh
    love's nature well, then you will see that discord
    can have no place among these circles. Nay,
the essence of this blessèd state of being
    is to hold all our will within His will,
    whereby our wills are one and all-agreeing.
And so the posts we stand from sill to sill
    throughout this realm, please all the realm as much
    as they please Him who wills us to His will.
In His will is our peace. It is that sea
    to which all moves, all that Itself creates
    and Nature bears through all Eternity."

Then was it clear to me that everywhere
   in Heaven is Paradise, though the Perfect Grace
   does not rain down alike on all souls there.   90
But as at times when we have had our fill
   of one food and still hunger for another,
   we put this by with gratitude, while still
asking for that—just so I begged to know,
   by word and sign, through what warp she had not
   entirely passed the shuttle of her vow.
"The perfection of her life and her great worth
   enshrine a Lady here above," she said,
   "in whose rule some go cloaked and veiled on earth,
that till their death they may live day and night
   with that sweet Bridegroom who accepts of love
   all vows it makes that add to His delight.
As a girl, I fled the world to walk the way
   she walked, and closed myself into her habit,
   pledged to her sisterhood till my last day.   105
Then men came, men more used to hate than love.
   They tore me away by force from the sweet cloister.
   What my life then became is known above.
This other splendor who lets herself appear
   here to my right to please you, shining full
   of every blessedness that lights this sphere,
understands in herself all that I say.
   She, too, was a nun. From her head as from mine
   the shadow of the veil was ripped away.
Against her will and all propriety
   she was forced back to the world. Yet even there
   her heart was ever veiled in sanctity.
She is the radiance of the Empress Constance,
   who by the second blast of Swabia
   conceived and bore its third and final puissance."   120
She finished, and at once began to sing
   Ave Maria, and singing, sank from view
   like a weight into deep water, plummeting
out of my sight, which followed while it could,
   and then, having lost her, turned about once more
   to the target of its greater wish and good

and wholly gave itself to the delight
    of the sweet vision of Beatrice. But she
    flashed so radiantly upon my sight
that I, at first, was blinded, and thus was slow
to ask of her what I most wished to know.

Canto 4

*Piccarda has told Dante that she inhab-
its the sphere of the inconstant moon because
she broke her vows against her will. Dante is
torn by doubts that could lead to heresy. Was
Plato right in saying souls come from their various
stars preformed and then return to them? If so,
what of free will? And if Heaven is Justice, how
have these souls sinned in being forced against
their wills? And if Heaven is Truth, what of the
contradiction between Piccarda's statements and
Beatrice's? After Beatrice has resolved Dante's
doubts, he asks if men may offer other
recompense for broken vows.*

A man given free choice would starve to death
   between two equal equidistant foods,
   unable to get either to his teeth.
So would a lamb, in counterbalanced fear,
   tremble between two she-wolves and stand frozen.
   So would a hound stand still between two deer.
If I stood mute, then, tugged to either side,
   I neither blame myself nor take my doubt—
   it being necessary—as cause for pride.
I did not speak, but on my face, at once,
   were written all my questions and my yearnings,
   far more distinctly than I could pronounce.
And Beatrice did as Daniel once had done
   when he raised Nebuchadnezzar from the wrath
   that made him act unjustly in Babylon.
"I see full well how equal wish and doubt
   tear you two ways," she said, "so that your zeal
   tangles upon itself and cannot breathe out.

15

You reason: 'If the will that vowed stays true,
  how can another's violence take away
  from the full measure of bliss that is my due?'
And I see a second doubt perplex that thought
  because the souls you see seem to return
  to the stars from which they came, as Plato taught.
These are the questions that bear down your will
  with equal force. Therefore, I shall treat first
  the one whose venom has more power to kill.
Choose the most God-like of the Seraphim—
  take Moses, or Samuel, or take either John,
  or even Mary—not one is nearer Him   30
nor holds his seat atop the blessed spheres
  in any heaven apart from those you saw;
  nor has his being more or fewer years.
All add their beauty to the highest Wheel,
  share the sweet life, and vary in it only
  by how much of the Eternal Breath they feel.
They showed themselves here not because this post
  has been assigned them, but to symbolize
  that they stand lowest in the Heavenly Host.
So must one speak to mortal imperfection,
  which only from the *sensible* apprehends
  whatever it then makes fit for intellection.
Scripture in like manner condescends,
  describing God as having hands and feet
  as signs to men of what more it portends.   45
So Holy Church shows you in mortal guise
  the images of Gabriel and of Michael
  and of the other who gave back Tobit's eyes.
For if Timaeus—as seems rather clear—
  spoke literally, what he says about souls
  is nothing like the truth shown to us here.
He says the soul finds its own star again,
  from which, as he imagines, Nature chose it
  to give form to the flesh and live with men.
But it may be the words he uses hide
  a second meaning, which, if understood,
  reveals a principle no man may deride.

If he means that the blame or honor due
   the influence of each sphere returns to it,
   his arrow does hit something partly true.   60
This principle, misunderstood, once drove
   almost the whole world to attach to planets
   such names as Mars and Mercury and Jove.
The other doubt that agitates your mind
   is not as venomous, for not all its malice
   could drive you from my side to wander blind.
For mortal men to argue that they see
   injustice in our justice is in itself
   a proof of faith, not poisonous heresy.
But since the truth of this lies well within
   the reach of your own powers, I shall explain it,
   just as you wish. If violence, to begin,
occurs when those who suffer its abuse
   contribute nothing to what forces them,
   then these souls have no claim to that excuse.   75
For the will, if it will not, cannot be spent,
   but does as nature does within a flame
   a thousand or ten thousand winds have bent.
If it yields of itself, even in the least,
   then it assists the violence—as did these
   who could have gone back to their holy feast.
If their whole will had joined in their desire—
   as whole will upheld Lawrence on the grill,
   and Mucius with his hand thrust in the fire—
just so, it would have forced them to return
   to their true way the instant they were free.
   But such pure will is too rare, we must learn!
If you have gleaned them diligently, then
   these words forever destroy the argument
   that would have plagued your mind time and again.   90
But now another pass opens before you,
   so strait and tortuous that without my help
   you would tire along the way and not win through.
I made you understand beyond all doubt
   that these souls cannot lie, for they exist
   in the First Truth and cannot wander out.

Later you heard Piccarda say that she
  who stood beside her kept her love of the veil;
  and it seems that what she said contradicts me.
Time and again, my brother, men have run
  from danger by a path they would not choose,
  and on it done what ought not to be done.
So, bending to his father's prayer, did he
  who took his mother's life. Alcmaeon I mean,
  who sought his piety in impiety.   105
Now weigh within your own intelligence
  how will and violence interact, so joining
  that no excuse can wipe out the offense.
Absolute will does not will its own harm,
  but fearing worse may come if it resists,
  consents the more, the greater its alarm.
Thus when Piccarda spoke as she did to you,
  she meant the absolute will; and I, the other.
  So both of us spoke only what was true."
Such was the flowing of that stream so blest
  it flows down from the Fountain of All Truth.
  Such was the power that laid my doubts to rest.
"Beloved of the First Love! O holy soul!"
  I said then, "You whose words flow over me
  and with their warmth quicken and make me whole,   120
there is not depth enough within my love
  to offer you due thanks, but may the One,
  who sees and can, answer for me above.
Man's mind, I know, cannot win through the mist
  unless it is illumined by that Truth
  beyond which truth has nowhere to exist.
In That, once it has reached it, it can rest
  like a beast within its den. And reach it can;
  else were all longing vain, and vain the test.
Like a new tendril yearning from man's will
  doubt sprouts to the foot of truth. It is that in us
  that drives us to the summit from hill to hill.
By this am I encouraged, by this bidden,
  my Lady, in all reverence, to ask
  your guidance to a truth that still lies hidden.   135

Paradiso

Can such as these who put away their veils
   so compensate by other good works done
   that they be not found wanting on your scales? "
Beatrice looked at me, and her glad eyes,
   afire with their divinity, shot forth
   such sparks of love that my poor faculties
gave up the reins. And with my eyes cast down
I stood entranced, my senses all but flown.

Canto 5

Beatrice explains the sanctity of the vow,
its relation to free will, the limited range within
which vows may be altered, and the dangers of
evil vows. When she has finished, she and Dante
soar to the second sphere. There a host of radiant
souls gathers to dance homage around Beatrice
and Dante. These are the Seekers of Honor, souls
who were active in their pursuit of the good, but
who were motivated in their pursuit by a desire
for personal honor, a good enough motive, but the
least of all good motives. One soul among them
addresses Dante with particular joy. In the next
canto this soul identifies itself as the radiance
that in mortal life was the
Emperor Justinian.

"If, in the warmth of love, I manifest
   more of my radiance than the world can see,
   rendering your eyes unequal to the test,
do not be amazed. These are the radiancies
   of the perfected vision that sees the Good
   and step by step moves nearer what it sees.
Well do I see how the Eternal Ray,
   which, once seen, kindles love forevermore,
   already shines on you. If on your way
some other thing seduce your love, my brother,
   it can only be a trace, misunderstood,
   of this, which you see shining through the other.
You ask if there is any compensation
   the soul may offer for its unkept vows
   that will secure it against litigation."
So Beatrice, alight from Heaven's Source,
   began this canto; and without a pause,
   continued thus her heavenly discourse:

15

"Of all creation's bounty realized,
  God's greatest gift, the gift in which mankind
  is most like Him, the gift by Him most prized,
is the freedom he bestowed upon the will.
  All his intelligent creatures, and they alone,
  were so endowed, and so endowed are still.
From this your reasoning should make evident
  the value of the vow, if it is so joined
  that God gives His consent when you consent.
When, therefore, God and man have sealed the pact,
  the man divests himself of that great treasure
  of which I speak—and by his own free act.   30
What can you offer, then, to make amends?
  How can you make good use of what is His?
  Would you employ extortion to good ends?
This much will make the main point clear to you.
  But since the Church grants dispensations in this,
  whereby what I have said may seem untrue,
you must yet sit at table, for the food
  you have just taken is crusty; without help
  you will not soon digest it to your good.
Open your mind to what I shall explain,
  then close around it, for it is no learning
  to understand what one does not retain.
The essence of this sacrificial act
  lies, first, in *what* one does, and, second, in *how*—
  the *matter* and the *manner* of the pact.   45
This second part cannot be set aside
  except by full performance; on this point
  what I said earlier stands unqualified.
Thus it was mandatory to sacrifice
  among the Jews, though the offering itself
  might vary, or a substitute might suffice.
The other—what I have called the *matter*—may
  be of the sort for which a substitution
  will serve without offending in any way.
But let no man by his own judgment or whim
  take on himself that burden unless the keys
  of gold and silver have been turned for him.

And let him think no change a worthy one
   unless what he takes up contains in it,
   at least as six does four, what he puts down.   60
There are, however, things whose weight and worth
   tip every scale, and for these there can be
   no recompense by anything on earth.
Let no man make his vow a sporting thing.
   Be true and do not make a squint-eyed choice
   as Jephthah did in his first offering.
He had better have cried, 'I had no right to speak!'
   than, keeping his vow, do worse. And in like case
   will you find that chief war leader, the great Greek
whose Iphigenia wept her loveliness
   and made both fools and wise men share her tears,
   hearing of such dark rites and her distress.
Be slower to move, Christians, be grave, serene.
   Do not be like a feather in the wind,
   nor think that every water washes clean.   75
You have the Testaments, both old and new,
   and the Shepherd of the Church to be your guide;
   and this is all you need to lead you true.
If cunning greed comes promising remission,
   be men, not mad sheep, lest the Jew among you
   find cause to point his finger in derision.
Do not be like the lamb that strays away
   from its mother's milk and, simple and capricious,
   fights battles with itself in silly play!"
Thus Beatrice to me, just as I write.
   Then she turned, full of yearning, to that part
   where the world is quickened most by the True Light.
Her silence, her transfigured face ablaze
   made me fall still although my eager mind
   was teeming with new questions I wished to raise.   90
And like an arrow driven with such might
   it strikes its mark before the string is still,
   we soared to the second kingdom of the light.
My Lady glowed with such a joyous essence,
   giving herself to the light of that new sky,
   that the planet shone more brightly with her presence.

And if the star changed then and laughed with bliss,
    what did I do, who in my very nature
    was made to be transformed through all that is?
As in a fish pond that is calm and clear
    fish swim to what falls in from the outside,
    believing it to be their food, so, here,
I saw at least a thousand splendors move
    toward us, and from each one I heard the cry:
    "Here is what will give increase to our love!"   105
And as those glories came to where we were,
    each shade made visible, in the radiance
    that each gave off, the joy that filled it there.
Imagine, reader, that I had started so
    and not gone on—think what an anguished famine
    would then oppress your hungry will to know.
So may you, of yourself, be able to see
    how much I longed to know their names and nature
    the instant they had shown themselves to me.
"O well born soul, permitted by God's grace
    to see the thrones of the Eternal Triumph
    while still embattled in the mortal trace,
the lamp that shines through all the vaults of Heaven
    is lit in us; if, therefore, you seek light
    on any point, ask and it shall be given."   120
So spoke one of those pious entities.
    And my Lady said: "Speak. Speak with full assurance.
    And credit them as you would deities!"
"I do indeed see that you make your nest
    in your own light, and beam it through your eyes
    that dazzle when you smile, O spirit blest.
But I know not who you are, nor why you are
    assigned here, to this sphere that hides itself
    from men's eyes in the rays of another star."
These were my words, my face turned to the light
    that had just spoken; at which it made itself
    far more resplendent yet upon my sight.
Just as the sun, when its rays have broken through
    a screen of heavy vapors, will itself
    conceal itself in too much light—just so,   135

I saw at least a thousand splendors move
  toward us, and from each one I heard the cry:
  "Here is what will give increase to our love!"

Paradiso

in its excess of joy that sacred soul
   hid itself from my sight in its own ray,
   and so concealed within its aureole
it answered me, unfolding many things,
the manner of which the following canto sings.

Canto 6

The spirit identifies itself as the soul of the Emperor Justinian and proceeds to recount its life on earth, its conversion by Agapetus, and its subsequent dedication to the codification of the law. It then proceeds to a discourse on the history of the Roman Eagle, and concludes by identifying the spirit of Romeo da Villanova among the souls of the second heaven.

"Once Constantine had turned the eagle's wing
    against the course of Heaven, which it had followed
    behind the new son of the Latian king,
two hundred years and more, as mankind knows,
    God's bird stayed on at Europe's furthest edge,
    close to the mountains out of which it rose.
And there, his wings spread over land and sea,
    he ruled the world, passing from hand to hand;
    and so, through many changes, came to me.
Caesar I was, Justinian I am.
    By the will of the First Love, which I now feel,
    I pruned the law of waste, excess, and sham.
Before my work absorbed my whole intent,
    I knew Christ in one nature only, not two;
    and so believing, I was well content.
But Agapetus, blessed of the Lord,
    he, the Supreme Shepherd, pure in faith,
    showed me the true way by his holy word.
Him I believed, and in my present view
    I see the truth as clearly as you see
    how a contradiction is both false and true.

15

Paradiso

As soon as I came to walk in the True Faith's way,
   God's grace moved all my heart to my great work;
   and to it I gave myself without delay.
To my Belisarius I left my spear,
   and God's right hand so moved his that the omen
   for me to rest from war was more than clear.
Of the two things you asked about before
   this puts a period to my first reply.
   But this much said impels me to say more   30
that you may see with how much right men go
   against the sacred standard when they plot
   its subornation or its overthrow.
You know what heroes bled to consecrate
   its holy destiny from that first hour
   when Pallas died to give it its first state.
You know that for two centuries then its home
   was Alba, till the time came when the three
   fought with the three and carried it to Rome.
What it did then from the Sabines' day of woe
   to good Lucretia's, under the seven kings
   who plundered the neighboring lands, you also know,
and how it led the Chosen Romans forward
   against the powers of Brennus and of Pyrrhus
   and of many a rival state and warring lord.   45
Thence the fame of Torquatus, curly Quintius,
   and the Decii and Fabii. How gladly
   I bring it myrrh to keep it glorious.
It dashed to earth the hot Arabian pride
   that followed Hannibal through the rocky Alps,
   from which, you, Po, sweet river, rise and glide.
Under it triumphed at an early age
   Scipio and Pompey. Against the mountain
   that looked down on your birth it screamed its rage.
Then as that age dawned in which Heaven planned
   the whole world to its harmony, Caesar came
   and, by the will of Rome, took it in hand.
What it did then from the Var to the Rhine is known
   to Isère, Arar, Seine, and every valley
   from which the waters of the Rhone flow down.   60

And what it did when it had taken flight
  from Ravenna and across the Rubicon
  no tongue may hope to speak nor pen to write.
It turned and led the cohorts into Spain;
  then to Dyrrachium; and then struck Pharsalus
  so hard that even the hot Nile felt the pain.
Antandros and the Simoïs, where it first saw light,
  it saw again, and Hector's grave, and then—
  woe to Ptolemy—sprang again to flight.
Like a thunderbolt it struck at Juba next;
  then turned once more and swooped down on your west
  and heard again the Pompeian trumpet vexed.
For what it did above its next great chief
  Brutus and Cassius wail in Cocytus;
  and Modena and Perugia came to grief.   75
For that the tears still choke the wretched wraith
  of Cleopatra, who running to escape it
  took from the asp her black and sudden death.
With him it traveled far as the Red Sea;
  and with him brought the world such peace that Janus
  was sealed up in his temple with lock and key.
But what this sign that moves my present theme
  had done before, all it was meant to do
  through the mortal realm it conquered—all must seem
dim shadows of poor things, if it be scanned
  with a clear eye and pure and honest heart,
  as it appears in the third Caesar's hand;
for the Living Justice whose breath I here breathe in
  gave it the glory, while in that same hand,
  of avenging His just wrath at Adam's sin.   90
Now ponder the double marvel I unfold;
  later, under Titus, it *avenged*
  the vengeance taken for the crime of old!
And when the sharp tooth of the Lombard bit
  the Holy Church, victorious Charlemagne,
  under those same wings, came and rescued it.
Now are you truly able to judge those
  whom I accused above and their wrongdoing,
  which is the cause of all your present woes.

Paradiso

One speeds the golden lilies on to force
  the public standard; and one seizes it
  for private gain—and who knows which is worse?
Let them scheme, the Ghibellines, let them plot and weave
  under some other standard, for all who use
  this bird iniquitously find cause to grieve! 105
Nor let the new Charles think his Guelphs will be
  its overthrow, but let him fear the talons
  that have ripped the mane from fiercer lions than he.
Many a father's sinfulness has sealed
  his children's doom; let him not think his lilies
  will take the place of God's bird on His shield.
This little star embellishes its crown
  with the light of those good spirits who were zealous
  in order to win honor and renown;
and when desire leans to such things, being bent
  from the true good, the rays of the True Love
  thrust upward with less force for the ascent;
but in the balance of our reward and due
  is part of our delight, because we see
  no shade of difference between the two. 120
By this means the True Judge sweetens our will,
  so moving us that in all eternity
  nothing can twist our beings to any ill.
Unequal voices make sweet tones down there.
  Just so, in our life, these unequal stations
  make a sweet harmony from sphere to sphere.
Within this pearl shines, too, the radiance
  of Romeo, whose good and beautiful works
  were answered by ingratitude and bad chance.
But the Provençals who worked his overthrow
  have no last laugh; he walks an evil road
  who finds his loss in the good that others do.
Four daughters had Count Raymond, each the wife
  of a Christian king, thanks to this Romeo,
  a humble man, a pilgrim in his life. 135
Envy and calumny so moved Raymond then
  that he demanded accounting of this just soul
  whose management had returned him twelve for ten.

For this he wandered, aged, poor, and bent,
  into the world again; and could the world
  know what was in his heart, that road he went,
begging his life by crusts from door to door,
much as it praises him now, it would praise him more."

Canto 7

*Justinian and his companions break into
a hymn to the God of Battles and, dancing, disappear into the distance. Dante, torn by doubt,
longs to ask how a just vengeance may justly be
avenged, but dares not speak. Beatrice, sensing
his confusion, answers his unspoken question
and explains the double nature of the Crucifixion,
and why the Jews, though blameless in the crucifixion of the man, were still guilty of sacrilege
against the God. She then explains why God
chose this means of redemption and why that
choice was the greatest act of all eternity. She
then explains the difference between direct and
indirect creation and concludes by proving why
the resurrection of the flesh is certain.*

"*Osanna sanctus Deus Sabaoth
    superillustrans claritate tua
    felices ignes horum malachoth!*"
So, giving itself to its own harmony,
    the substance of that being, over which
    two lights were joined as one, appeared to me.
And all those souls joined in a holy dance,
    and then, like shooting sparks, gone instantly,
    they disappeared behind the veil of distance.
I stood, torn by my doubts. "Speak up. Speak up,"
    I said inside myself. "Ask the sweet Lady
    who slakes your every thirst from the sweet cup."
But the awe that holds my being in its sway,
    even at the sound of BEA or of TRICE
    kept my head bent as if I dozed away.
But she soon soothed my warring doubt and dread,
    for with a smile whose ray could have rejoiced
    the soul of a man tied to the stake, she said:

15

"I know by my infallible insight
   you do not understand how a just vengeance
   can justly be avenged. To set you right
I shall resolve your mind's ambivalence.
   Listen and learn, for what I shall now say
   will be a gift of lofty consequence.
Because he would not, for his own good, take
   God's bit and rein, the man who was not born,
   damning himself, damned mankind for his sake.
Therefore, for many centuries, men lay
   in their sick error, till the Word of God
   chose to descend into the mortal clay.   30
There, moved by His Eternal Love alone,
   He joined in His own Person that other nature
   that had wandered from its Maker and been cast down.
Now heed my reasoning; so joined again
   to its First Cause, this nature (as it had been
   at its creation) was good and without stain.
But by its own action, when it turned its face
   from the road of truth that was its road of life,
   it was driven from the garden of God's grace.
If the agony on the cross, considering this,
   was a punishment of the nature thus assumed,
   no verdict ever bit with greater justice—
just so, no crime to match this can be cited
   when we consider the Person who endured it,
   in whom that other nature was united.   45
Thus, various sequels flow from one event;
   God and the Jews concurred in the same death;
   for it the earth shook and the heavens were rent.
You should no longer find it hard to see
   what is meant in saying that just vengeance taken
   was afterwards avenged by just decree.
I see now that your mind, thought upon thought,
   is all entangled and that it awaits
   most eagerly the untying of the knot.
You think: 'I grasp the truth of what I hear.
   But why God chose this means for our redemption—
   this and no other—I cannot make clear.'

No one may grasp the hidden meaning of
 this edict, brother, till his inborn senses
 have been made whole in the sweet fire of Love.   60
Truly, therefore, since so many sight,
 and so few hit, this target, I shall now
 explain exactly why this means was right.
That Good, which from Itself spurns every trace
 of envy, in Itself sends out such sparks
 as manifest the everlasting grace.
Whatever is uttered by Its direct expression
 thereafter is eternal; His seal once stamped,
 nothing can ever wipe out the impression.
Whatever is poured directly from Its spring
 is wholly free; so made, it is not subject
 to the power of any secondary thing.
The Sacred Fire that rays through all creation
 burns with most joy in what is most like It;
 the more alike, the greater Its elation.   75
All of these attributes endow the nature
 of humankind; and if it fail in one,
 it cannot help but lose its noble stature.
Sin is the one power that can take away
 its freedom and its likeness to True Good,
 whereby it shines less brightly in Its ray.
Its innate worth, so lost, it can regain
 only by pouring back what guilt has spilled,
 repaying evil pleasure with just pain.
Your nature, when it took sin to its seed,
 sinned totally. It lost this innate worth,
 and it lost Paradise by the same deed.
Nor could they be regained (if you heed my words
 with scrupulous attention) by any road
 that does not lead to one of these two fords: 90
either that God, by courtesy alone,
 forgive his sin; or that the man himself,
 by his own penitence and pain, atone.
Now fix your eye, unmoving, on the abyss
 of the Eternal Wisdom, and your mind
 on every word I say concerning this!

Limited man, by subsequent obedience,
could never make amends; he could not go
as low in his humility as once,
rebellious, he had sought to rise in pride.
Thus was he shut from every means himself
to meet God's claim that He be satisfied.
Thus it was up to God, to Him alone
in His own ways—by one or both, I say—
to give man back his whole life and perfection.   105
But since a deed done is more prized the more
it manifests within itself the mark
of the loving heart and goodness of the doer,
the Everlasting Love, whose seal is plain
on all the wax of the world was pleased to move
in all His ways to raise you up again.
There was not, nor will be, from the first day
to the last night, an act so glorious
and so magnificent, on either way.
For God, in giving Himself that man might be
able to raise himself, gave even more
than if He had forgiven him in mercy.
All other means would have been short, I say,
of perfect justice, but that God's own Son
humbled Himself to take on mortal clay.   120
And now, that every wish be granted you,
I turn back to explain a certain passage,
that you may understand it as I do.
You say: 'I see the water, I see the fire,
the air, the earth; and all their combinations
last but a little while and then expire.
Yet all these were creations! Ought not they—
if what you said of them before is true—
to be forever proof against decay?'
Of angels and this pure kingdom of the soul
in which you are, it may be said they sprang
full-formed from their creation, their beings whole.
But the elements, and all things generated
by their various compoundings, take their form
from powers that had themselves to be created.   135

Paradiso

Created was the matter they contain.
   Created, too, was the informing power
   of the stars that circle them in Heaven's main.
From the given potencies of these elements
   the rays and motions of the sacred lamps
   draw forth the souls of all brutes and all plants.
But the Supreme Beneficence inspires
   your life directly, filling it with love
   of what has made it, so that it desires
that love forever.—And from this you may
   infer the sure proof of your resurrection,
   if you once more consider in what way
man's flesh was given being like no other
when He made our first father and first mother."

Canto 8

Dante and Beatrice reach the Sphere of Venus, the third heaven. Instantly, a band of souls that had been dancing in the Empyrean descends to the travelers. These are the souls of the Amorous. As we learn in Canto 9, many of them, perhaps all, were so full of the influence of Venus that they were in danger of being lost to carnality. Through the love of God, however, their passion was converted from physical love to true caritas, and thus do they rejoice in Heaven. Their spokesman is Charles Martel of Anjou. He identifies himself and prophesies dark days for the Kingdom of Naples because of the meanness of King Robert, his brother. Dante asks how it is that mean sons can be born of great fathers, and Charles answers with a discourse on the diversity of natural talents, a diversity he assigns to the influence of the stars, as God provided them for man's own good as a social being, for only by diversity of gifts can society function. God had planned these variations to a harmonious end. Mankind, by forcing men into situations not in harmony with their talents, strays from God's plan.

The world, to its own jeopardy, once thought
    that Venus, rolling in the third epicycle,
    rayed down love-madness, leaving men distraught.
Therefore the ancients, in their ignorance,
    did honor not to her alone, but offered
    the smokes of sacrifice and votive chants
to Dione and to Cupid, her mother and son,
    and claimed that he had sat on Dido's lap
    when she was smitten by love's blinding passion.

Paradiso

From her with whom my song began just now
   they took the name of the star that woos the sun,
   now shining at its nape, now at its brow.
I reached it unaware of my ascent,
   but my Lady made me certain I was there
   because I saw her grow more radiant.   15
And as a spark is visible in the fire,
   and as two voices may be told apart
   if one stays firm and one goes lower and higher,
so I saw lights circling within that light
   at various speeds, each, I suppose, proportioned
   to its eternal vision of delight.
No blast from cold clouds ever shot below,
   whether visible or not, so rapidly
   but what it would have seemed delayed and slow
to one who had seen those holy lights draw nigh
   to where we were, leaving the dance begun
   among the Seraphim in Heaven on high.
And from the first who came, in purest strain
   Hosanna rang, so pure that, ever since,
   my soul has yearned to hear that sound again.   30
Then one of them came forward and spoke thus:
   "We are ready, all of us, and await your pleasure
   that you may take from us what makes you joyous.
In one thirst and one spiraling and one sphere
   we turn with those High Principalities
   to whom you once cried from the world down there:
'O you whose intellects turn the third great wheel!'
   So full of love are we that, for your pleasure,
   it will be no less bliss to pause awhile."
I raised my eyes to the holy radiance
   that was my Lady and, only after she
   had given them her comfort and assurance,
did I turn to the radiance that had made
   such promises. "Who are you?" were my words,
   my voice filled with the love it left unsaid.   45
Ah, how it swelled and grew even more bright,
   taking increase of bliss from my few words
   and adding new delight to its delight.

So changed, it said: "My life there among men
    was soon concluded; had it lasted longer
    great evils yet to be would not have been.
The ecstasy that is my heavenly boon
    conceals me; I am wrapped within its aura
    as a silkworm is inclosed in a cocoon.
You loved me much, and you had reason to,
    for had I stayed below you would have seen
    more than the green leaves of my love for you.
The left bank of the land washed by the Rhone
    after its waters mingle with the Sorgue's
    waited, in due course, to become my own;   60
as did that horn of Italy that lies
    south of the Tronto and Verde, within which
    Bari, Gaeta, and Catona rise.
Already on my brow there shone the crown
    of the land the Danube bathes when it has left
    its German banks. And though not yet my own,
beautiful Sicily, the darkened coast
    between the capes of Faro and Passero,
    there on the gulf that Eurus lashes most
(not dimmed by Typhoeus, as mythology
    would have men think, but by its rising sulfur)
    would yet have looked to have its kings, through me,
from Charles and Rudolph, but that the bitter breath
    of a populace subjected to misrule
    cried out through all Palermo's streets, 'Death! Death!'   75
And could Robert have foreseen how tyranny
    will drive men mad, he would have fled in fear
    from Catalonia's greedy poverty.
For some provision surely must be made,
    by him or by another, lest on his ship,
    already heavy laden, more be laid.
His nature, born to avarice from the loins
    of a liberal sire, would have required lieutenants
    who cared for more than filling chests with coins."
"Sire, I hold dearer this felicity
    that fills me when you speak, believing it
    as visible to you as it is to me,

"The left bank of the land washed by the Rhone
after its waters mingle with the Sorgue's
waited, in due course, to become my own."

there where every good begins and ends.
  And this, too, I hold dear—that you discern it
  in looking on Him from whom all love descends.   90
You have given me joy. Now it is in your power
  to give me light. For your words leave me in doubt.
  How, if the seed is sweet, may the fruit be sour?"
Thus I. And he: "Could I make you recognize
  one truth of what you ask, then what is now
  behind your back would be before your eyes.
The Good by which this Kingdom you now climb
  is turned and gladdened makes Its foresight shine
  as powers of these great bodies to all time.
Not only does that Perfect Mind provide
  for the diversities of every nature,
  but for their good and harmony beside.
And, thus, whatever arrow takes its arc
  from this bow flies to a determined end,
  it being aimed unerringly to its mark.   105
Else would these heavens you now move across
  give rise to their effect in such a way
  that there would be not harmony, but chaos.
This cannot be unless the intellects
  that move these stars are flawed, and flawed the first,
  which, having made them, gave them such defects.
Should I expound this further?" he said to me.
  And I: "There is no need, for now I know
  nature cannot fall short of what must be."
And he: "Would man be worse off than he is,
  there on earth, without a social order?"
"Yes!" I replied, "nor need I proof of this."
"And can that be, unless men there below
  lived variously to serve their various functions?
  Your master, if he knows, answers you no."   120
So point by point that radiant soul disputes.
  Now he concludes: "Your various aptitudes,
  it follows, therefore, must have various roots.
So one man is born Xerxes, another Solon;
  one Melchizedek, and another he
  who, flying through the air, lost his own son.

Paradiso

That ever-revolving nature whose seal is pressed
   into our mortal wax does its work well,
   but takes no heed of where it comes to rest.
So Esau parted from Jacob in the seed;
   and Romulus was born of such humble stock
   that Mars became his father, as men agreed.
Begotten and begetter, but for the force
   of overruling Providence, the son's nature
   would always follow in the father's course.   135
And now what was behind shines out before.
   But to make you understand how much you please me,
   I would wrap you in one corollary more.
What Nature gives a man Fortune must nourish
   concordantly, or nature, like any seed
   out of its proper climate, cannot flourish.
If the world below would learn to heed the plan
   of nature's firm foundation and build on that,
   it then would have the best from every man.
But into Holy Orders you deflect
   the man born to strap on a sword and shield,
   and make a king of one whose intellect
is given to writing sermons. And in this way
your footprints leave the road and go astray."

Canto 9

Cunizza da Romano next appears, lamenting the woes that have befallen her native Venetia and prophesying great grief to her countrymen for pursuing false fame on earth. Cunizza had begun her remarks by pointing out a soul who rejoices beside her in Heaven as one who pursued good ends. When she finishes speaking that soul identifies itself as Folquet, once Bishop of Marseilles. Folquet narrates his life and indicates that, like Cunizza, his amorous nature first led him to carnality but later filled him with passion for the true love of God. Folquet then answers Dante's questions about the nature of the third heaven, identifies Rahab, the Whore of Jericho, as the first soul to ascend to that sphere, and concludes with a denunciation of Boniface VIII, for neglecting the Holy Land and all things spiritual, and of Florence, as a corrupt state and as the source of Papal corruption. A just vengeance, he prophesies, will not be long delayed.

Fair Clemence, when your Charles, in speaking thus
   had shone his light into my mind, he told me
   of the schemes and frauds that would attack his house.
But he said to me: "Say nothing. Let the years
   turn as they must." And so I can say only
   that they who wrong you shall find cause for tears.
Now to the Sun, the all-sufficing good,
   the eternal being of that sacred lamp
   had turned itself again to be renewed.
O souls deceived! ill-born impieties
   who turn your hearts away from the True Love
   and fix your eyes on empty vanities!

Paradiso

And lo! another of those splendors now
    draws near me, and his wish to give me pleasure
    shows in the brightening of his outward glow.   15
The eyes of Beatrice, which as before
    were fixed on me, saw all my wish and gave it
    the assurance of their dear consent once more.
"O blessed spirit, be pleased to let me find
    my joy at once," I said. "Make clear to me
    that you are a true mirror of my mind!"
Thereat the unknown spirit of that light,
    who had been singing in its depths, now spoke,
    like one whose whole delight is to delight.
"In that part of the sinful land men know
    as the Italy which lies between Rialto
    and the springs from which the Brenta and Piave flow,
there stands a hill of no imposing height;
    down from it years ago there came a firebrand,
    who laid waste all that region like a blight.   30
One root gave birth to both of us. My name
    was Cunizza, of Romano, and I shine here
    because this star conquered me with its flame.
Yet gladly I embrace the fate that so
    arranged my lot, and I rejoice in it,
    although it may seem hard to the crowd below.
This bright and precious jewel of our sky,
    whose ray shines here beside me, left great fame
    behind him on the earth; nor will it die
before this centenary is five times told.
    Now ask yourself if man should seek that good
    that lives in name after the flesh is cold.
The rabble that today spills through the land
    bound by the Tagliamento and the Adige
    think little of that, nor, though war's bloody hand   45
rips them, do they repent. But Paduan blood,
    having shunned its duty, shall soon stain the water
    that bathes Vicenza and drains into mud.
And there rules one who yet holds high his head,
    there where the Sile and the Cagnano join,
    for whom the net already has been spread.

And Feltro shall yet weep the treachery
    of its foul priest; no man yet entered Malta
    for a crime as infamous as his shall be.
Great would that ewer be that could hold at once
    the blood Ferrara will spill, and tired the man
    who set himself to weigh it ounce by ounce.
All this the generous priest will freely give
    to prove his party loyalty; but then
    such gifts conform to how those people live.   60
On high are mirrors (you say Thrones) and these
    reflect God's judgment to us; so enlightened,
    we have thought it well to speak these prophecies."
Here she fell still and, turning, made it clear
    she was drawn to other things, joining once more
    the wheel of souls that dance through that third sphere.
That other bliss, he I had heard her say
    was precious to her, now showed himself to me
    like a fine ruby struck by the sun's ray.
Up there, joy makes those souls add light to light,
    as here it makes us laugh; while down below,
    souls darken as they grieve through Hell's long night.
"God sees all, and your insight, blessed being,
    makes itself one with His," I said, "and thus
    no thought or wish may hide beyond your seeing.   75
Why does your voice, then, which forever sings
    Heaven's delight as one with those Blest Flames
    who wrap themselves about with their six wings,
not grant my wish? Had I the intuition
    with which to read your wish as you read mine,
    I should not be still waiting for *your* question!"
"The greatest basin to which earth's waters flow
    —aside from the sea that girdles all the land—"
    his voice began when I had spoken so,
"extends so far against the course of the sun,
    between opposing shores, that at its zenith
    the sun must cross what first was its horizon.
I first saw light on that basin's shore between
    the Ebro and that river whose short course
    parts Tuscan from Genoese—the Magra, I mean.   90

Paradiso

Sunrise and sunset are about the same
  for Bougiah and my city, whose blood flowed
  to warm its harbor's waters when Caesar came.
My name—to such as knew it on the earth—
  was Folquet; here eternally my ray
  marks all this sphere, as its ray marked my birth.
Dido did not burn hotter with love's rage,
  when she offended both Sichaeus and Creusa,
  than I, before my locks grew thin with age.
Nor she of Rhodopè who felt the smart
  of Demophoön's deception, nor Hercules
  when he had sealed Iole in his heart.
But none repents here; joy is all our being;
  not at the sin—that never comes to mind—
  but in the All-Ordering and All-Foreseeing.   105
Here all our thoughts are fixed upon the Love
  that beautifies creation, and here we learn
  how world below is moved by world above.
But that you may take with you from this sphere
  full knowledge of all it makes you wish to know,
  I must speak on a little further here.
You wish to know who is within this blaze
  you see in all its splendor here beside me,
  like purest water lit by the sun's rays.
Know, then, that in it Rahab finds her good;
  and that, one with our choir, she seals upon it
  the highest order of beatitude.
Of all Christ's harvest, her soul was the one
  first summoned by this heaven, on which the shadow
  the earth casts rests the points of its long cone.   120
It was fitting in every way that she should thus
  adorn one of these heavens as a palm
  of the high victory two palms won for us,
for she it was who helped win the first glory
  of Joshua's victory in the Holy Land
  (which seems to have slipped from the Pope's memory).
Your Florence—which was planted by the One
  who first turned on his Maker, and whose envy
  has given men such cause for lamentation—

brings forth and spreads the accursed flower of gold
  that changes the Shepherd into a ravening wolf
  by whom the sheep are scattered from the fold.
And so the Gospels and Great Doctors lie
  neglected, and the Decretals alone
  are studied, as their margins testify.   135
So Pope and Cardinal heed no other things.
  Their thoughts do not go out to Nazareth
  where the blessed Gabriel opened wide his wings.
But the Vatican, and the other chosen parts
  of Holy Rome that have been, from the first,
  the cemetery of those faithful hearts
that followed Peter and were his soldiery,
shall soon be free of this adultery."

Canto 10

*Dante revels in the joy of God's creation
and especially in the art shown by the placement
of the equinoctial point. So rejoicing, he enters the
Sphere of the Sun, unaware of his approach until
he has arrived. A garland of twelve souls immediately surrounds him and Beatrice, the glory of each
soul shining so brilliantly that it is visible even
against the background of the Sun itself. These
are twelve Doctors of the Church, philosophers
and theologians whose writings have guided the
Church in creed and canon law. Their spokesman
is Thomas Aquinas, who identifies the souls in
order around the ring. When Aquinas has finished, the souls dance around Dante and Beatrice, raising their voices in harmonies
unknown except to Heaven itself.*

Contemplating His Son with that Third Essence
   of Love breathed forth forever by Them both,
   the omnipotent and ineffable First Presence
created all that moves in mind and space
   with such perfection that to look upon it
   is to be seized by love of the Maker's grace.
Therefore, reader, raise your eyes across
   the starry sphere. Turn with me to that point
   at which one motion and another cross,
and there begin to savor your delight
   in the Creator's art, which He so loves
   that it is fixed forever in His sight.
Note how the wheel on which the planets ride
   branches from there obliquely; only thus
   may the earth that calls to them be satisfied.

15

For if these two great motions never crossed,
    the influence of the heavens would be weakened
    and most of its power upon the earth be lost.
For if its deviation were to be
    increased or lessened, much would then be wanting,
    both north and south, from the earth's harmony.
Stay on at table, reader, and meditate
    upon this foretaste if you wish to dine
    on joy itself before it is too late.
I set out food, but you yourself must feed!
    For the great matters I record demand
    all my attention, and I must proceed.
Nature's majestic minister, the Sun,
    who writes the will of Heaven on the earth
    and with his light measures the hours that run,   30
now in conjunction (as I have implied)
    with Aries, rode those spirals whose course brings him
    ever earlier from the eastern side.
And I was with the Sun; but no more aware
    of my ascent than a man is of a thought
    that comes to mind, until he finds it there.
It is Beatrice, she it is who leads our climb
    from good to better, so instantaneously
    that her action does not spread itself through time.
How radiant in its essence that must be
    which in the Sun (where I now was) shows forth
    not by its color but its radiancy.
Though genius, art, and usage stored my mind,
    I still could not make visible what I saw;
    but yet may you believe and seek to find!   45
And if our powers fall short of such a height,
    why should that be surprising, since the sun
    is as much as any eye has known of light?
Such, there, was the fourth family of splendors
    of the High Father who fills their souls with bliss,
    showing them how He breathes forth and engenders.
"Give thanks!" my Lady said. "With all devotion
    give thanks to the Sun of Angels, by whose grace
    you have been lifted to this physical one!"

Paradiso

The heart of mortal never could so move
   to its devotion, nor so willingly
   offer itself to God in thankful love,
as mine did when these words had passed her lips.
   So wholly did I give my love to Him
   that she sank to oblivion in eclipse.   60
Nothing displeased, she laughed so that the blaze
   of her glad eyes pierced my mind's singleness
   and once again divided it several ways.
Splendors of living and transcendent light
   circle us now and make a glowing crown,
   sweeter in voice than radiant in sight.
Latona's daughter sometimes seems to us
   so banded when the vaporous air weaves round her
   the thread that makes her girdle luminous.
In Heaven's courts, from which height I have come,
   are many gems so precious and so lovely
   that they cannot be taken from the Kingdom.
Of such those splendors sang. Who does not grow
   wings that will fly him there must learn these things
   from the tidings of the tongueless here below.   75
When, so singing, those Sun-surpassing souls
   had three times turned their blazing circuit round us,
   like stars that circle close to the fixed poles,
they stood like dancers still caught in the pleasure
   of the last round, who pause in place and listen
   till they have caught the beat of the new measure.
And from within its blaze I heard one start:
   "Since the ray of grace from which true love is kindled—
   and then by loving, in the loving heart
grows and multiplies—among all men
   so shines on you to lead you up these stairs
   that none descend except to climb again;
whoever refused your soul, it being thirsty,
   wine from his flask, would be no freer to act
   than water blocked from flowing to the sea.   90
You wish to know what flowering plants are woven
   into this garland that looks lovingly
   on the lovely Lady who strengthens you for Heaven.

The Divine Comedy

I was a lamb among the holy flock
   Dominic leads to where all plenty is,
   unless the lamb itself stray to bare rock.
This spirit on my right, once of Cologne,
   was my teacher and brother. Albert was his name,
   and Thomas, of Aquinas, was my own.
If you wish, similarly, to know the rest
   let your eyes follow where my words shall lead
   circling through all this garland of the blest.
The next flame springs from the glad smile of Gratian,
   who so assisted one court and the other
   that in him Heaven found good cause for elation.   105
The next to adorn our chorus of the glad
   was the good Peter who, like the poor widow,
   offered to Holy Church all that he had.
The fifth light, and the loveliest here, shines forth
   from so magnificent a love that men
   hunger for any news of it on earth;
within it is that mind to which were shone
   such depths of wisdom that, if truth be true,
   no mortal ever rose to equal this one.
See next the taper whose flame, when formerly
   it burned in mortal flesh, saw most profoundly
   the nature of angels and their ministry.
Within the lesser lamp next on my right
   shines the defender of the Christian Age
   whose treatise led Augustine toward the light.   120
Now if your mind has followed on my praise
   from light to light, you are already eager
   to know what spirit shines in the eighth blaze.
In it, for having seen the sum of good,
   there sings a soul that showed the world's deceit
   to any who would heed. The bones and blood
from which it was cruelly driven have their tomb
   down there in Cieldauro; to this peace
   it came from exile and from martyrdom.
See next the flames breathed forth by Isidore,
   by Bede, and by that Richard whose Contemplations
   saw all that a mere man can see and more.

The next, from whom your eyes return to me,
   is the glory of a soul in whose grave thoughts
   death seemed to be arriving all too slowly;
it is the flame, eternally elated,
   of Siger, who along the Street of Straws
   syllogized truths for which he would be hated."
Then as a clock tower calls us from above
   when the Bride of God rises to sing her matins
   to the Sweet Spouse, that she may earn his love,
with one part pulling and another thrusting,
   tin-tin, so glad a chime the faithful soul
   swells with the joy of love almost to bursting—
just so, I saw that wheel of glories start
   and chime from voice to voice in harmonies
   so sweetly joined, so true from part to part,
that none can know the like till he go free
where joy begets itself eternally.

135

Canto 11

The spirits complete their song and their joyous dance and once more gather around Dante and Beatrice. Aquinas reads Dante's mind and speaks to make clear several points about which Dante was in doubt. He explains that Providence sent two equal princes to guide the Church: St. Dominic, the wise law-giver, and St. Francis, the ardent soul. Aquinas was himself a Dominican. To demonstrate the harmony of Heaven's gift and the unity of the Dominicans and Franciscans, Aquinas pronounces a praise of the life of St. Francis. His account finished, he returns to the theme of the unity of the Dominicans and Franciscans, and proceeds to illustrate it further by himself lamenting the degeneracy of the Dominican Order.

O senseless strivings of the mortal round!
   how worthless is that exercise of reason
   that makes you beat your wings into the ground!
One man was giving himself to law, and one
   to aphorisms; one sought sinecures,
   and one to rule by force or sly persuasion;
one planned his business, one his robberies;
   one, tangled in the pleasure of the flesh,
   wore himself out, and one lounged at his ease;
while I, of all such vanities relieved
   and high in Heaven with my Beatrice,
   arose to glory, gloriously received.
When each had danced his circuit and come back
   to the same point of the circle, all stood still,
   like votive candles glowing in a rack.

15

Paradiso

And I saw the splendor of the blazing ray
    that had already spoken to me, smile,
    and smiling, quicken; and I heard it say:
"Just as I take my shining from on high,
    so, as I look into the Primal Source,
    I see which way your thoughts have turned, and why.
You are uncertain and would have me find
    open and level words in which to speak
    what I expressed too steeply for your mind
when I said 'leads to where all plenty is,'
    and 'no mortal ever rose to equal this one.'
    And it is well to be exact in this.
The Providence that governs all mankind
    with wisdom so profound that any creature
    who seeks to plumb it might as well be blind,   30
in order that the Bride seek her glad good
    in the Sweet Groom who, crying from on high,
    took her in marriage with His blessèd blood,
sent her two Princes, one on either side
    that she might be secure within herself,
    and thereby be more faithfully His Bride.
One, in his love, shone like the Seraphim.
    The other, in his wisdom, walked the earth
    bathed in the splendor of the Cherubim.
I shall speak of only one, though to extol
    one or the other is to speak of both
    in that their works led to a single goal.
Between the Tupino and the little race
    sprung from the hill blessèd Ubaldo chose,
    a fertile slope spreads up the mountain's face.   45
Perugia breathes its heat and cold from there
    through Porta Sole, and Nocera and Gualdo
    behind it mourn the heavy yoke they bear.
From it, at that point where the mountainside
    grows least abrupt, a sun rose to the world
    as this one does at times from Ganges' tide.
Therefore, let no man speaking of that place
    call it *Ascesi*—'I have risen'—but rather,
    Oriente—so to speak with proper grace.

Nor was he yet far distant from his birth
  when the first comfort of his glorious powers
  began to make its warmth felt on the earth;
a boy yet, for that Lady who, like death
  knocks on no door that opens to her gladly,
  he had to battle his own father's wrath.   60
With all his soul he married her before
  the diocesan court *et coram patre;*
  and day by day he grew to love her more.
Bereft of her First Groom, she had had to stand
  more than eleven centuries, scorned, obscure;
  and, till he came, no man had asked her hand;
none, at the news that she had stood beside
  the bed of Amyclas and heard, unruffled,
  the voice by which the world was terrified;
and none, at word of her fierce constancy,
  so great, that even when Mary stayed below,
  she climbed the Cross to share Christ's agony.
But lest I seem obscure, speaking this way,
  take Francis and Poverty to be those lovers.
  That, in plain words, is what I meant to say.   75
Their harmony and tender exultation
  gave rise in love, and awe, and tender glances
  to holy thoughts in blissful meditation.
The venerable Bernard, seeing them so,
  kicked off his shoes and toward so great a peace
  ran, and running, seemed to go too slow.
O wealth unknown! O plenitude untried!
  Egidius went unshod. Unshod, Sylvester
  followed the Groom. For so it pleased the Bride!
Thenceforth this father and this happy lord
  moved with his wife and with his family,
  already bound round by the humble cord.
He did not grieve because he had been born
  the son of Bernardone; he did not care
  that he went in rags, a figure of passing scorn.   90
He went with regal dignity to reveal
  his stern intentions to Pope Innocent,
  from whom his order first received the seal.

Then as more souls began to follow him
   in poverty—whose wonder-working life
   were better sung among the Seraphim—
Honorius, moved by the Eternal Breath,
   placed on the holy will of his chief shepherd
   a second crown and everflowering wreath.
Then, with a martyr's passion, he went forth
   and in the presence of the haughty Sultan
   he preached Christ and his brotherhood on earth;
but when he found none there would take Christ's pardon,
   rather than waste his labors, he turned back
   to pick the fruit of the Italian garden.   105
On the crag between Tiber and Arno then, in tears
   of love and joy, he took Christ's final seal,
   the holy wounds of which he wore two years.
When God, whose loving will had sent him forward
   to work such good, was pleased to call him back
   to where the humble soul has its reward,
he, to his brothers, as to rightful heirs
   commended his dearest Lady, and he bade them
   to love her faithfully for all their years.
Then from her bosom, that dear soul of grace
   willed its return to its own blessed kingdom;
   and wished its flesh no other resting place.
Think now what manner of man was fit to be
   his fellow helmsman, holding Peter's ship
   straight to its course across the dangerous sea.   120
Such was our patriarch. Hence, all who rise
   and follow his command will fill the hold,
   as you can see, with fruits of Paradise.
But his flock has grown so greedy for the taste
   of new food that it cannot help but be
   far scattered as it wanders through the waste.
The more his vagabond and distant sheep
   wander from him, the less milk they bring back
   when they return to the fold. A few do keep
close to the shepherd, knowing what wolf howls
   in the dark around them, but they are so few
   it would take little cloth to make their cowls.

Now, if my words have not seemed choked and blind,
   if you have listened to me and taken heed,
   and if you will recall them to your mind,   135
your wish will have been satisfied in part,
   for you will see how the good plant is broken
   and what rebuke my words meant to impart
when I referred, a while back in our talk,
to 'where all plenty is' and to 'bare rock.'"

Canto 12

As soon as Aquinas has finished speaking the wheel of souls begins to turn, and before it has completed its first revolution it is surrounded by a second garland of twelve souls. The spokesman of this second company is St. Bonaventure. In the harmonious balances of Heaven, the Dominican Aquinas had spoken the praise of the life of St. Francis. In the same outgoing motion of love, the Franciscan Bonaventure now speaks the praise of the life of St. Dominic. And as Aquinas had concluded by lamenting the degeneracy of the Dominican Order, so Bonaventure concludes his account with a lament for the degeneracy of the Franciscan Order. He then identifies the other souls in his garland.

So spoke the blessèd flame and said no more;
    and at its final word the holy millstone
    began revolving round us as before
and had not finished its first revolution
    before a second wheel had formed around it,
    matching it tone for tone, motion for motion.
As a reflection is to the source of light,
    such is the best our Sirens and Muses sing
    to the chanting of those sheaths of pure delight.
As through thin clouds or mists twin rainbows bend
    parallel arcs and equal coloring
    when Juno calls her handmaid to attend—
the outer band born of the inner one,
    like the voice of that wandering nymph of love consumed,
    as vapors are consumed by the summer sun—
whereby all men may know what God made plain
    in the pledge he gave to Noah that the waters
    of the great deluge would not come again—

15

Just so, those sempiternal roses wove
   their turning garland round us, and the outer
   answered the inner with the voice of love.

just so, those sempiternal roses wove
   their turning garland round us, and the outer
   answered the inner with the voice of love.
And when the exalted festival and dance
   of love and rapture, sweet song to sweet song,
   and radiance to flashing radiance,
had in a single instant fallen still
   with one accord—as our two eyes make one,
   being moved to open and close by a single will—
from one of those new splendors a voice came;
   and as the North Star draws a needle's point,
   so was my soul drawn to that glorious flame.   30
Thus he began: "The love that makes me shine
   moves me to speak now of that other leader
   through whom so much good has been said of mine.
When one is mentioned the other ought to be;
   for they were militant in the same cause
   and so should shine in one light and one glory.
The troops of Christ, rearmed at such great cost,
   were struggling on behind the holy standard,
   fearful, and few, and laggard, and half lost,
when the Emperor who reigns eternally—
   of His own grace and not for their own merit—
   took thought of His imperiled soldiery;
and, as you have heard say, He sent His Bride
   two champions by whose teachings and example
   the scattered companies were reunified.   45
In the land to which the West Wind, soft and glad,
   returns each spring to open the new leaves
   with which, soon, all of Europe will be clad,
at no great distance from the beat and bite
   of those same waves behind which, in its course,
   the sun, at times, hides from all mortal sight,
a fortunate village lies in the protection
   of the great shield on which two lions are,
   one subjugating and one in subjection.
Within its walls was born the ardent one,
   true lover and true knight of the Christian Faith;
   bread to his followers, to his foes a stone.

His mind, from the instant it began to be,
swelled with such powers that in his mother's womb
he made her capable of prophecy.   60
And when he and his Lady Faith before
the holy font had married and endowed
each other with new gifts of holy power,
the Lady who had spoken for him there
saw, in a dream, the wonder-working fruit
that he and his inheritors would bear.
To speak him as he was, a power from Heaven
was moved to give him the possessive form
of His name unto Whom he was wholly given.
Dominicus he was called. Let him be known
as the good husbandman chosen by Christ
to help Him in the garden He had sown.
A fitting squire and messenger of Christ
he was, for his first love was poverty,
and such was the first counsel given by Christ.   75
Often his nurse found him in meditation
at night on the bare floor, awake and silent,
as if he were saying, 'This is my vocation.'
O Felix, his father in true 'felicity!'
O mother, truly Joan, 'whom God has graced!'
—if the names can be translated literally!
Not as men toil today for wealth and fame,
in the manner of the Ostian and Taddeo,
but for love of the true manna, he soon became
a mighty doctor, and began to go
his rounds of that great vineyard where the vine,
if left untended, pales and cannot grow.
Before that Seat where once the poor were fed
and tended (now, through no fault of its own,
but by its degenerate occupant, corrupted)   90
he did not ask the right to keep as pay
three out of every six, nor a benifice,
nor *decimas quae sunt pauperum Dei;*
but license in the sick world there below
to battle for that seed from which are sprung
the four and twenty plants that ring you now.

Then, will and doctrine joined, and in the light
   of Apostolic Office, he burst forth,
   like a torrent from a mountain vein, to smite
the stumps and undergrowths of heresy.
   And where the thickets were least passable,
   there his assault bore down most heavily.
And from him many rivulets sprang to birth
   by which the Catholic orchard is so watered
   that its little trees spring greener from the earth.   105
If such was the one wheel of the great car
   in which the Church rode to defend herself
   and win in open field her civil war,
you cannot fail to see with a clear mind
   the excellence of that other, about whom,
   before I joined you, Thomas was so kind.
But the track its great circumference cut of old
   is so abandoned that the casks are empty,
   and where there once was crust, now there is mold.
His family, that formerly used to go
   in his very footsteps, is so turned around
   that it prints toe on heel and heel on toe.
Soon shall we see the harvest of these years
   of lazy cultivation and hear the darnel,
   the storehouse shut against it, shed its tears.   120
Search our book leaf by leaf and you will see,
   I have no doubt, written upon some page:
   'I am today all that I used to be.'
But not at Casal' nor Acquasparta—there
   they come to keep our rule, and in the keeping
   one loosens it, one tightens it like a snare.
I am the life of Bonaventure, on earth
   of Bagnoregio, who in great offices
   always put back the things of lesser worth.
Illuminato and Augustine are here,
   two of the first-come of the barefoot poor.
   For the cord they wore God holds them ever dear.
The prior Hugo is here, and the deathless glow
   of Peter Mangiadore, and Peter of Spain
   whose light still shines in twelve small books below.   135

And the prophet Nathan, and the eternal part
   of Chrysostom, and Anselm, and that Donatus
   who gladly turned his hand to the first art.
Rabanus is also here; and here beside me
   shines the Calabrian abbot Joachim
   whose soul was given the power of prophecy.
The ardent courtesy of my holy brother
   and his apt praise of one great paladin
   moved me to say this much about the other
in emulous and loving eulogy;
and so moved all these of my company."

Canto 13

*The twenty-four blessed spirits, moved
by the concluding words of Bonaventure, manifest themselves as a mystical constellation and
ring forth a hymn of praise that fills all Heaven.
When the hymn has been sung, Aquinas speaks
again. He has read Dante's mind and addresses
its perplexity, explaining why none ever equaled
Solomon's wisdom. He concludes with a
warning against hasty judgment.*

If you would understand what I now write
   of what I saw next in that heaven, imagine
   (and hold the image rock-fast in your sight)
the fifteen brightest stars the heavens wear
   in their living crown, stars of so clear a ray
   it pierces even the mist-thickened air;
imagine that Wain that on our heaven's breast
   lies night and day, because the tiller's turning
   causes no part of it to sink to rest;
imagine the bright mouth of the horn one sees
   flower from the axle star, around which spins
   the first wheel—and imagine all of these
forming two constellations, each a wreath
   (like that the daughter of King Minos made
   when through her limbs she felt the chill of death)
and imagine, last, that one wreath has its rays
   inside the other, and that both are turning
   around one center but in opposite ways.
So might you dimly guess (if mankind could)
   what actual stars, joined in their double dance,
   circled around the point on which I stood;

15

though such experiences outrun our knowing
    as the motion of the first and fastest heaven
    outruns the low Chiana's sluggish flowing.
There they sang no Bacchic chant nor paean,
    but Three Persons in One Divine Nature
    and It and human nature in One Person.
The song and circling dance ran through their measure,
    and now those holy lights waited on us,
    turning rejoiced from pleasure to new pleasure.   30
The silence of these numina was broken
    by the same lamp from which the glorious life
    of God's beloved pauper had been spoken.
It said: "Since one sheaf has been thrashed, my brother,
    and the good grain of it has been put by,
    sweet love invites me now to thrash the other.
Into that breast, you think, from which was carved
    the rib that went to form the lovely cheek
    for whose bad palate all mankind was starved,
and into that the lance pierced when it made
    such restitution for the past and future
    that every guilt of mankind was outweighed,
as much of wisdom's light, to the last ray,
    as human nature can contain, He breathed
    by whose power they were clad in mortal clay.   45
And, therefore, you were puzzled when I came
    to the fifth light and said no mortal ever
    had matched the wisdom sheathed within its flame.
Now open your eyes to what I shall say here
    and see your thought and my words form one truth,
    like the center and circumference of a sphere.
All things that die and all that cannot die
    are the reflected splendor of the Form
    our Father's love brings forth beyond the sky.
For the Living Light that streams forth from the Source
    in such a way that it is never parted
    from Him, nor from the Love whose mystic force
joins Them in Trinity, lets its grace ray down,
    as if reflected, through nine subsistent natures
    that sempiternally remain as one.   60

From thing to thing to the last least potencies
    the ray comes down, until it is so scattered
    it brings forth only brief contingencies;
and these contingencies, I would have you see,
    are those *generated things* the moving heavens
    bring forth from seeds or not, as the case may be.
The wax of these things, and the powers that press
    and shape it, vary; thus the Ideal Seal
    shines through them sometimes more and sometimes less.
So trees of the same species may bring forth
    fruit that is better or worse; so men are born
    different in native talent and native worth.
Were the wax most ready and free of every dross,
    and were the heavens in their supreme conjunction,
    the light of the seal would shine through without loss;   75
but nature scants that light in all it makes,
    working in much the manner of a painter
    who knows the true art, but whose brush hand shakes.
But if the Fervent Love move the Pure Ray
    of the First Power to wield the seal directly,
    the thing so stamped is perfect in every way.
So once a quickening of the dust of earth
    issued the form of the animal perfection;
    so once the Virgin Womb quickened toward birth.
Therefore I say that I am one with you
    in the opinion that mankind was never,
    nor will be, what it once was in those two.
Having said this much, I must yet go on
    or you would ask: 'How then can it be said,
    no mortal ever rose to equal this one?'   90
But to make clear what yet seems not to be,
    think who he was, and what it was that moved him
    to answer when God said, 'What shall I give thee?'
I speak these words that you may understand
    he was a king, and asked the Lord for wisdom
    in governing his people and his land,
and not to know the number and degree
    of our motor-angels, nor if a premised 'may'
    can ever conclude, in logic, 'this must be,'

nor if there is prime motion, nor if in the space
  of a semicircle a non-right triangle
  may be drawn with the diameter as its base.
Hence you may see that when I spoke before
  of unmatched wisdom, it was on royal prudence
  that the drawn arrow of my intention bore.   105
Note well that I said 'rose' when I spoke of it.
  Thus you will see I spoke only of kings,
  of whom there are many, though so few are fit.
Such were my words, and taken in this light
  they are consistent with all that you believe
  of our first father and of our Best Delight.
And lead weights to your feet may my words be,
  that you move slowly, like a weary man,
  to the yes and no of what you do not see.
For he is a fool, and low among his kind,
  who answers yea or nay without reflection,
  nor does it matter on which road he runs blind.
Opinions too soon formed often deflect
  man's thinking from the truth into gross error,
  in which his pride then binds his intellect.   120
It is worse than vain for men to leave the shore
  and fish for truth unless they know the art;
  for they return worse off than they were before.
Of this, Parmenides and Melissus bear
  their witness to all men, along with Bryson,
  and others who set out without knowing where;
so Arius, Sabellius, and their schools
  who were to Scripture like a mirroring sword,
  distorting the straight faces to mislead fools.
Men should not be too smug in their own reason;
  only a foolish man will walk his field
  and count his ears too early in the season;
for I have seen a briar through winter's snows
  rattle its tough and menacing bare stems,
  and then, in season, open its pale rose;   135
and I have seen a ship cross all the main,
  true to its course and swift, and then go down
  just as it entered its home port again.

Let Tom and Jane not think, because they see
   one man is picking pockets and another
   is offering all his goods to charity,
that they can judge their neighbors with God's eyes;
for the pious man may fall, and the thief may rise."

Canto 14

*Thomas Aquinas has finished speaking.
Beatrice, anticipating the wish Dante has not yet
realized is his own, begs the double circle of Philosophers and Theologians to explain to Dante the
state in which the blessed will find themselves
after the resurrection of the flesh. The radiant
spirit of Solomon answers. As Solomon finishes
his discourse and as the souls about him cry,
"Amen!" Dante becomes aware of a third circle
of souls, higher and more radiant than the first
two. Its radiance dawns slowly and indistinctly
at first, and then suddenly bursts upon him. Only
then does he realize that he and Beatrice have
been ascending and that he has entered the fifth
sphere, Mars. The souls he had seen in the third
great circle are those of the Warriors of God. There
Dante beholds, shining through the Sphere of
Mars (in about the way the rays of a star sapphire
shine within the stone), the vision of
Christ on the Cross.*

"The water in a round vessel moves about
    from center to rim if it is struck from within,
    from rim to center if it is struck from without."
Such was the thought that suddenly occurred
    to my rapt mind when the immortal ray
    of Thomas had pronounced its final word,
occasioned by the likeness to the flow
    of his speech and my Lady's, she being moved
    to speak when he had done, beginning so:
"There is another need this man must find
    the holy root of, though he does not speak it,
    nor know, as yet, he has the thought in mind.

Explain to him if the radiance he sees flower
   about your beings will remain forever
   exactly as it shines forth in this hour;   15
and if it will remain so, then explain
   how your restored eyes can endure such brilliance
   when your beings have grown visible again."
As dancers in a country reel flush brighter
   as they spin faster, moved by joy of joy,
   their voices higher, and all their gestures lighter—
so at my Lady's prompt and humble plea
   the sacred circles showed yet greater joy
   in their dance and in their heavenly harmony.
Those who mourn, here, that we must die to gain
   the life up there, have never visualized
   that soul-refreshing and eternal rain.
That One and Two and Three that is eternal,
   eternally reigning in Three and Two and One,
   uncircumscribed, and circumscribing all,   30
was praised in three great paeans by each spirit
   of those two rings, and in such melody
   as would do fitting honor to any merit.
And I heard, then, from the most glorious ray
   of the inner circle, a voice as sweetly low
   as the angel's must have sounded to Mary, say:
"Long as the feast of Paradise shall be,
   so long shall our love's bliss shine forth from us
   and clothe us in these radiant robes you see.
Each robe reflects love's ardor shining forth;
   the ardor, the vision; the vision shines down to us
   as each is granted grace beyond his worth.
When our flesh, made glorious at the Judgment Seat,
   dresses us once again, then shall our persons
   become more pleasing in being more complete.   45
Thereby shall we have increase of the light
   Supreme Love grants, unearned, to make us fit
   to hold His glory ever in our sight.
Thereby, it follows, the vision shall increase;
   increase the ardor that the vision kindles;
   increase the ray its inner fires release.

But as a coal, in giving off its fire,
   outshines it by its living incandescence,
   its form remaining visible and entire—
so shall this radiance that wraps us round
   be outshone in appearance by the flesh
   that lies this long day through beneath the ground;
nor will it be overborne by so much light;
   for the organs of the body shall be strengthened
   in all that shall give increase of delight."   60
And "Amen!" cried the souls of either chain
   with such prompt zeal as to make evident
   how much they yearned to wear their flesh again;
perhaps less for themselves than for the love
   of mothers, fathers, and those each soul held dear
   before it became an eternal flame above.
And lo! all round me, equal in all its parts,
   a splendor dawned above the splendor there
   like a horizon when the new day starts.
And as, at the first coming on of night,
   new presences appear across the sky,
   seeming to be, and not to be, in sight—
so did I start to see existences
   I had not seen before, forming a ring
   around the other two circumferences.   75
O sparkling essence of the Holy Ghost!
   How instantly it blazed before my eyes,
   defeating them with glory, their function lost!
But Beatrice let herself appear to me
   so glad in beauty, that the vision must lie
   with those whose glory outdoes memory.
From her I drew again the power of sight
   and looked up, and I saw myself translated,
   with her alone, to the next estate of light.
I was made aware that I had risen higher
   by the enkindled ardor of the red star
   that glowed, I thought, with more than usual fire.
With all my heart, and in the tongue which is
   one in all men, I offered God my soul
   as a burnt offering for this new bliss.   90

Paradiso

Nor had the flame of sacrifice in my breast
  burned out, when a good omen let me know
  my prayer had been received by the Most Blest;
for with such splendor, in such a ruby glow,
  within two rays, there shone so great a glory
  I cried, "O Helios that arrays them so!"
As, pole to pole, the arch of the Milky Way
  so glows, pricked out by greater and lesser stars,
  that sages stare, not knowing what to say—
so constellated, deep within that sphere,
  the two rays formed into the holy sign
  a circle's quadrant lines describe. And here
memory outruns my powers. How shall I write
  that from that cross there glowed a vision of Christ?
  What metaphor is worthy of that sight?   105
But whoso takes his cross and follows Christ
  will pardon me what I leave here unsaid
  when *he* sees that great dawn that rays forth Christ.
From arm to arm, from root to crown of that tree,
  bright lamps were moving, crossing and rejoining.
  And when they met they glowed more brilliantly.
So, here on earth, across a slant of light
  that parts the air within the sheltering shade
  man's arts and crafts contrive, our mortal sight
observes bright particles of matter ranging
  up, down, aslant; darting or eddying;
  longer and shorter; but forever changing.
And as a viol and a harp in a harmony
  of many strings, make only a sweet tinkle
  to one who has not studied melody—   120
so from that choir of glories I heard swell
  so sweet a melody that I stood tranced,
  though what hymn they were singing, I could not tell.
That it was raised in lofty praise was clear,
  for I heard "Arise" and "Conquer"—but as one
  may hear, not understanding, and still hear.
My soul was so enraptured by those strains
  of purest song, that nothing until then
  had bound my being to it in such sweet chains.

447

How shall I write
that from that cross there glowed a vision of Christ?

Paradiso

My saying so may seem too bold at best,
  since I had not yet turned to those dear eyes
  in which my every yearning found its rest.
But think how the living seals of every beauty
  grow stronger toward their heights, and though I had not
  turned to those others yet in love and duty,   135
reason may yet dismiss the charge I bring
  against myself in order to dismiss it;
  and see the holy truth of what I sing;
for my sacred pleasure in those sacred eyes
can only become purer as we rise.

Canto 15

The souls of the Great Cross stop their singing in order to encourage Dante to speak, and one among them descends to the foot of the cross like a shooting star, glowing with joy at the sight of Dante. It is, as Dante will discover, Cacciaguida, Dante's own great-great-grandfather. He addresses Dante as "O blood of mine!" and although he knows Dante's thoughts, he begs his descendant to speak them for the joy of hearing his voice. Dante does as he is bid, and Cacciaguida, in answer to Dante's request, identifies himself, gives an account of ancient Florence, and explains how he followed Conrad in the Crusades, became a knight, and died in battle, passing from martyrdom to bliss.

Goodwill, in which there cannot fail to be
   the outgoing love of right (just as we find
   self-seeking love in all iniquity),
stopped the sweet trembling harp and let fall still
   the blessed viol, upon whose many strings
   the Hand of Heaven plays Its sacred will.
How shall those beings not heed a righteous prayer
   when, to encourage me to speak my wish,
   they stopped with one accord and waited there?
Justly they mourn in their eternal wasting
   who, in their love for what does not endure,
   stripped off the hope of this love everlasting.
As through the pure sky of a peaceful night
   there streaks from time to time a sudden fire,
   and eyes that had been still move at the sight
as if they saw a star changing its post
   (except that none is gone from where it started,
   and blazed its little while, and soon was lost)—

so, in a trail of fire across the air,
    from the right arm to the foot of the great cross,
    a star streaked from the constellation there.
Nor did that gemstone leave its diadem.
    Like fire behind an alabaster screen,
    it crossed those radiant ranks, still one with them.
Just so did the shade of ancient Ilium
    (if we may trust our greatest muse) go forth
    to greet Aeneas in Elysium.
"*O sanguis meus, o superinfusa*
    gratia Dei, sicut tibi, cui
    bis unquam coeli ianua reclusa?"   30
So spoke that radiance as I stared wide-eyed.
    Then I turned my eyes back to my blessed Lady,
    and between those two souls I stood stupefied;
for such a fire of love burned in her eyes
    that mine, I thought, had touched the final depth
    both of my Grace and of my Paradise.
Then, radiating bliss in sight and sound,
    the spirit added to his opening words
    others I could not grasp; they were too profound.
Nor did the spirit's words elude my mind
    by his own choice. Rather, his thoughts took place
    above the highest target of mankind.
And when the bow recovered from the effect
    of its own ardor, and its words arced down
    nearer the target of our intellect,   45
the first on which my straining powers could feed
    were: "Praised be Thou, O Triune Unity
    which showeth me such favor in my seed!"
Continuing: "The sight of you assuages
    a long dear hunger that grew within this lamp
    from which I speak, as I perused the pages
of the Great Book where neither black nor white
    can ever change. I give thanks to this spirit
    whose love gave you the wings for this high flight.
You believe that what you think rays forth to me
    from the Primal Intellect, as five and six,
    if understood, ray forth from unity.

And for that reason you do not inquire
  who I may be, nor why I am more joyous
  than the other spirits of this joyous choir.   60
And you are right; for here in Paradise
  greatest and least alike gaze in that Mirror
  where thoughts outsoar themselves before they rise.
But, that the Sacred Love in which I wake
  to the eternal vision, and which fills me
  with a sweet thirst, you may the sooner slake,
let your own voice, assured, frank, and elated,
  sound forth your will, sound forth your soul's desire,
  to which my answer is already fated!"
I turned to Beatrice and while I still
  sought words, she heard, and smiled such glad assent
  the joy of it gave wings to my glad will.
Thus I began: "When the First Equipoise
  shone forth to you, love and the power to speak love
  became in each of you an equal voice;   75
because the Sun that warmed and lighted you
  contains its heat and light so equally
  that though we seek analogies, none will do.
But mortal utterance and mortal feelings
  for reasons that are evident to you—
  have no such equal feathers to their wings.
I, then, being mortal, in the perturbation
  of my unequal powers, with heart alone
  give thanks for your paternal salutation.
I do indeed beseech you, holy flame,
  and living topaz of this diadem,
  that you assuage my hunger to know your name."
"O leaf of mine, which even to foresee
  has filled me with delight, I was your root."
  So he began in answer to my plea.   90
And then: "The first to take your present surname
  (whose soul has crawled the first round of the mountain
  a century and more), he who became
father of your grandfather, was my son.
  You would do well, by offering up good works,
  to shorten his long striving at his stone.

Florence, within her ancient walls secure—
  from them she still hears Tierce and Nones ring down—
  lived in sweet peace, her sons sober and pure.
No golden chains nor crowns weighed down her spirit,
  nor women in tooled sandals and studded belts
  more to be admired than the wearer's merit.
A father, in those days, was not terrified
  by the birth of a daughter, for marriage and marriage portion
  had not escaped all bounds on either side.   105
No mansions then stood uninhabited.
  No Sardanapalus had yet arrived
  to show what may be done in hall and bed.
Montemario had not yet been outshone
  by your Uccellatoio, which having passed it
  in the race up, shall pass it going down.
Bellincion Berti, with whom I was acquainted,
  went belted in leather and bone; and his good wife
  came from the mirror with her face unpainted.
I have seen the lords of Vecchio and of Nerli
  content to wear plain leather, and their wives
  working the spindle and distaff late and early.
Fortunate they! and blest their circumstance!
  Each sure of her own burial place; none yet
  deserted in her bed because of France.   120
One watched the cradle, babbling soft and low
  to soothe her child in the sweet idiom
  that is the first delight new parents know.
Another, spinning in her simple home,
  would tell old tales to children gathered round her,
  of Troy, and of Fiesole, and of Rome.
A Cornelia or Cincinnatus would amaze
  a modern Florentine as a Cianghella
  or a Lapo would have startled men in those days.
To so serene, so fair a townsman's life,
  to a citizenry so wedded in good faith,
  to such sweet dwelling, free of vice and strife,
Mary gave me—called in the pain of birth—
  and in your ancient Baptistry I became
  a Christian—and Cacciaguida, there on earth.   135

Moronto and Eliseo my brothers were.
   My wife came from the valley of the Po.
   The surname you now bear derives from her.
I served with Conrad in the Holy Land,
   and my valor so advanced me in his favor
   that I was knighted in his noble band.
With him I raised my sword against the might
   of the evil creed whose followers take from you—
   because your Shepherds sin—what is yours by right.
There, by that shameless and iniquitous horde,
   I was divested of the flesh and weight
   of the deceitful world, too much adored
by many souls whose best hope it destroys;
and came from martyrdom to my present joys."

Canto 16

*Dante thrills with pleasure on learning
that his ancestor had been elevated to knighthood, and, feeling the power of pride of ancestry
even in Heaven, in which there is no temptation
to evil, he has a new insight into the family pride
in which mortals glory. Spurred by pride, Dante
addresses Cacciaguida with the formal* voi, *an
affectation at which Beatrice, half amused, ad-
monishes him with a smile. Dante then asks
Cacciaguida for details of his birth and ancestry
and of the history of early Florence. As if to warn
Dante away from pride of ancestry, Cacciaguida
dismisses the question of his birth and of his forebears as a matter best passed over in silence,
and proceeds to a detailed account of the lords
and people of Florence in the days when her
bloodlines and traditions had not been diluted
by the arrival of new families. It is to this mon-
grelization of the Florentines that Cacciaguida
attributes the subsequent degen-
eracy of Florence.*

O trivial pride of ours in noble blood!
   that in possessing you men are possessed,
     down here, where souls grow sick and lose their good,
will never again amaze me; for there, too,
   where appetite is never drawn to evil—
     in Heaven, I say—my own soul gloried in you!
You are a mantle that soon shrinks and tears.
   Unless new cloth is added day by day,
     time will go round you, snipping with its shears!
I spoke again, addressing him with that *voi*
   whose usage first began among the Romans—
     and which their own descendants least employ—

at which my Lady, who stood apart, though near,
   and smiling, seemed to me like her who coughed
   at the first recorded fault of Guinevere.   15
"You are my father," I started in reply.
   "You give me confidence to speak out boldly;
   you so uplift me, I am more than I.
So many streams of happiness flow down
   into my mind that it grows self-delighting
   at being able to bear it and not drown.
Tell me, then, dear source of my own blood,
   who were your own forefathers? when were you born?
   and what transpired in Florence in your boyhood?
Tell me of St. John's sheepfold in those days.
   How many souls were then within the flock,
   and which of them was worthy of high place?"
As glowing coals fanned by a breath of air
   burst into flames, so did I see that light
   increase its radiance when it heard my prayer.   30
And as its light gave off a livelier ray,
   so, in a sweeter and a softer voice—
   though not in the idiom we use today—
it said: "From the day when *Ave* sounded forth
   to that in which my mother, now a saint,
   being heavy laden with me, gave me birth,
this flame had come back to its Leo again
   to kindle itself anew beneath his paws
   five hundred times plus fifty plus twenty plus ten.
My ancestors and I were born in the place
   where the last quarter of the course begins
   for those who take part in your annual race.
Of my fathers, be content with what you have heard.
   Of who they were and whence they came to Florence
   silence is far more fitting than any word.   45
Of men who could bear arms there were counted then,
   between Mars and the Baptist, the fifth part
   of what may be mustered there from living men.
But the citizenry, now mongrelized by the blood
   of Campi, of Certaldo, and of Figghine,
   was pure then, down to the humblest planer of wood.

Oh, how much better to have been neighbors of these
   of whom I speak, and to have Trespiano
   and Galuzzo still fixed as your boundaries,
than to have swallowed them and to bear the stink
   of the yokel of Aguglione, and of Signa's boor
   who still has eyes to swindle and hoodwink.
Had the world's most despicable crew not shown
   a hard stepmother's face and greed to Caesar
   but been a loving mother, one who is known   60
as a Florentine, and who trades in goods and debt,
   would be back in Simifonti, where his grandsire
   once gypsied in the streets for what he could get.
Montemurlo would still be owned by its own counts,
   the Cerchi would be in the parish of Acone,
   and in Valdigreve, still, the Bondelmounts.
It has always been a fact that confusion of blood
   has been a source of evil to city-states,
   just as our bodies are harmed by too much food;
and that a bull gone blind will fall before
   a blind lamb does. And that one sword may cut
   better than five has been proved in many a war.
If you will think of Luni and Urbisaglia,
   how they have passed away, and how, behind them,
   are dying now Chiusi and Sinigaglia,   75
it should not be too hard to comprehend,
   or strange to hear, that families dwindle out,
   when even cities come at last to an end.
All mankind's institutions, of every sort,
   have their own death, though in what long endures
   it is hidden from you, your own lives being short.
And as the circling of the lunar sphere
   covers and bares the shore with never a pause,
   so Fortune alters Florence year by year.
It should not, therefore, seem too wondrous strange
   to hear me speak of the good Florentines,
   whose fame is veiled behind time's endless change.
I knew the Ughi, the Catellini, the line
   of the Greci, Filippi, Ormanni, and Alberichi—
   illustrious citizens, even in decline.   90

I knew those of Sannella, and those of the Bow,
  and the Soldanieri, Ardinghi, and Bostichi;
  as grand as they were ancient, there below.
Not far from the portal that now bears the weight
  of such a cargo of new iniquity
  as soon, now, will destroy the ship of state,
once lived the Ravignani, from whom came
  Count Guido Guerra, and whoever else
  has since borne Bellincione's noble name.
The della Pressa were already furnished
  with knowledge of how to rule, and Galigaio
  had his gold hilt and pommel already burnished.
Great already were the lands of the vair,
  Sacchetti, Giuochi, Fifanti, Barucci, and Galli,
  and of those who blush now for the stave affair.   105
The trunk that bore the many-branched Calfucci
  had grown already great; already called
  to the curule were Sizii and Arrigucci.
How great I have seen them who are now undone
  by their own pride! And even the balls of gold—
  in all great deeds of Florence, how they shone!
So shone the fathers of that gang we see
  in the bishop's palace when your See falls vacant,
  fattening themselves as a consistory.
That overweening and presumptuous tribe—
  a dragon to all who run from it, a lamb
  to any who stand and show a tooth or bribe—
were coming up, though still so parvenu
  Donato was hardly pleased when his father-in-law
  made him a relative of such a crew.   120
The Caponsacchi had come down by then
  from Fiesole to market; the Infangati
  and Giudi were established as good townsmen.
And here's an astonishing fact, though little known:
  in ancient times a gate of the inner wall
  was named for those of the Pera, now all gone.
All those whose various quarterings display
  the staves of the great baron whose name and worth
  are kept alive every St. Thomas' Day

"But it was fitting that to the broken stone
    that guards the bridge, Florence should offer a victim
    to mark the last day's peace she has ever known."

owe him the rank and privilege they enjoy,
   though one who binds those arms with a gold fringe
   makes common cause today with the hoi polloi.
Gualterotti and Importuni were then well known.
   And Borgo would still be a peaceful place
   had it not acquired new neighbors from Montebuon'.   135
The line from which was born your grief and strife,
   because of the righteous anger that ruined you
   and put an end to all your happier life,
was honored in itself and its allies.
   O Buondelmonti, what ill you did in fleeing
   its nuptials to find comfort in other ties!
Many would still be happy whom we now pity,
   had God seen fit to let the Ema drown you
   on the first day you started for the city.
But it was fitting that to the broken stone
   that guards the bridge, Florence should offer a victim
   to mark the last day's peace she has ever known.
With such as these, and others, my first life's years
   saw Florence live and prosper in such peace
   that she had, then, no reason to shed tears.   150
With such as these I saw there in my past
   so valiant and so just a populace
   that none had ever seized the ensign's mast
and hung the lily on it upside down.
Nor was the red dye of division known."

Canto 17

Beatrice and Cacciaguida already know what question is burning in Dante's mind, but Beatrice nevertheless urges him to speak it, that by practicing heavenly discourse he be better able to speak to men when he returns to earth. So urged, Dante asks Cacciaguida to make clear the recurring dark prophecies of Dante's future. Cacciaguida details Dante's coming banishment from Florence, identifies the patrons Dante will find, and assures Dante of his future fame. He warns Dante not to become bitter in adversity, assuring him that the Divine Comedy, once it becomes known, will outlive the proudest of the Florentines and bring shame to their evil memories for ages to come.

Like him who went to Clymene to learn
    if what he had heard was true, and who makes fathers
    unwilling to yield to their sons at every turn—
such was I, and such was I taken to be
    by Beatrice and by the holy lamp
    that, earlier, had changed its place for me.
Therefore my Lady: "Speak. And let the fire
    of your consuming wish come forth," she said,
    "well marked by the inner stamp of your desire;
not that we learn more by what you say,
    but that you better learn to speak your thirst,
    that men may sooner quench it on your way."
"Dear root of my existence, you who soar
    so high that, as men grasp how a triangle
    may contain one obtuse angle and no more,
you grasp contingent things before they find
    essential being, for you can see that focus
    where all time is time-present in God's mind.

15

While I was yet with Virgil, there below,
    climbing the mountain where the soul is healed
    and sinking through the dead world of its woe,
dark words of some dark future circumstance
    were said to me, whereby my soul is set
    four-square against the hammering of chance;
and, therefore, my desire will be content
    with knowing what misfortune is approaching;
    for the arrow we see coming is half spent."
Such were the words of my reply, addressed
    to the light that had spoken earlier; and with them
    as Beatrice wished, my own wish was confessed.   30
Not in dark oracles like those that glued
    the foolish like limed birds, before the Lamb
    that takes our sins away suffered the rood;
but in clear words and the punctilious style
    of ordered thought that father-love replied,
    concealed in and revealed by his own smile:
"*Contingency*, whose action is confined
    to the few pages of the world of matter,
    is fully drawn in the Eternal Mind;
but it no more derives *necessity*
    from being so drawn, than a ship dropping down river
    derives its motion from a watcher's eye.
As a sweet organ-harmony strikes the ear,
    so, from the Primal Mind, my eyes receive
    a vision of your future drawing near.   45
As Hippolytus left Athens, forced to roam
    by his two-faced and merciless stepmother,
    just so shall you leave Florence, friends, and home.
So is it willed, so does it already unfold,
    so will it soon be done by him who plots it,
    there where Christ is daily bought and sold.
The public cry, as usual, will blame you
    of the offended party, but the vengeance
    truth will demand will yet show what is true.
All that you held most dear you will put by
    and leave behind you; and this is the arrow
    the longbow of your exile first lets fly.

You will come to learn how bitter as salt and stone
   is the bread of others, how hard the way that goes
   up and down stairs that never are your own.   60
And what will press down on your shoulders most
   will be the foul and foolish company
   you will fall into on that barren coast.
Ingrate and godless, mad in heart and head
   will they become against you, but soon thereafter
   it will be they, not you, whose cheeks turn red.
Their bestiality will be made known
   by what they do; while your fame shines the brighter
   for having become a party of your own.
Your first inn and first refuge you shall owe
   to the great Lombard whose escutcheon bears
   the sacred bird above, the ladder below.
In such regard and honor shall he hold you,
   that in the act of granting and requesting,
   what others do late, shall be first between you two.   75
With him you will see another, born of this star
   and so stamped by the iron of its virtues
   that he shall be renowned for deeds of war.
The world has not yet noticed him; these spheres
   in their eternal course above his youth
   have turned about him now only nine years.
Before the Gascon sets his low intrigue
   to snare high Henry, men will start to speak
   of his disregard of money and fatigue.
The knowledge of his magnanimities
   will spread so far that men will hear of it
   out of the mouths of his very enemies.
Look you to him and his great works. The fate
   of many shall be altered by his deeds,
   the rich and poor exchanging their estate.   90
And write this in your mind but remain silent
   concerning it . . ." and he said things about him
   to astonish even those who shall be present.
Then added: "Son, these are the annotations
   to what was told you. These are the snares that hide
   behind a few turns of the constellations.

But do not hate your neighbors; your future stretches
  far beyond the reach of what they do
  and far beyond the punishment of wretches."
When, by his silence, that blessed soul made clear
  that he had finished passing his dark shuttle
  across the threads I had combed for him there,
I then, as one who has not understood
  longs for the guidance of a soul that sees,
  and straightway wills, and wholly loves the good: 105
"Father, I do indeed see time's attacks
  hard spurred against me to strike such a blow
  as shall fall most on him who is most lax.
And it is well I arm myself with foresight.
  Thus, if the dearest place is taken from me,
  I shall not lose all place by what I write.
Down through that world of endless bitter sighs,
  and on the mountain from whose flowering crown
  I was uplifted by my Lady's eyes,
and then through Heaven from ray to living ray,
  I have learned much that would, were it retold,
  offend the taste of many alive today.
Yet if, half friend to truth, I mute my rhymes,
  I am afraid I shall not live for those
  who will think of these days as 'the ancient times.'"   120
The light in which my Heaven-found treasure shone
  smiled brighter in its rapture, coruscating
  like a gold mirror in a ray of sun;
then answered me: "A conscience overcast
  by its own shame, or another's, may indeed
  be moved to think your words a bitter blast.
Nevertheless, abjure all lies, but match
  your verses to the vision in fullest truth;
  and if their hides are scabby, let them scratch!
For if your voice is bitter when first tested
  upon the palate, it shall yet become
  a living nutriment when it is digested.
This cry you raise shall strike as does the wind
  hardest at highest peaks—and this shall argue
  no little for your honor, as you will find.   135

Paradiso

Therefore you have been shown—here in these spheres,
    there on the mount, and in the valley of woe—
    those souls whose names most ring in mortal ears;
for the feelings of a listener do not mark
    examples of things unknown, nor place their trust
    in instances whose roots hide in the dark;
nor will men be persuaded to give ear
to arguments whose force is not made clear."

Canto 18

*Beatrice comforts Dante, who is ponder-
ing the bitter and the sweet of Cacciaguida's
prophecy, then instructs him to turn back to
Cacciaguida, who proceeds to name among the
souls who form the Cross of Mars the great Warriors of God. They flash like shooting stars along
the arms of the cross. Finished, Cacciaguida re-
ascends to his original place in the right arm and
the whole choir resumes its hymn. Dante turns
back to Beatrice, sees her grow yet more beautiful, and knows they have made the ascent to the
sixth sphere. He sees the pale glow of Jupiter re-
place the red glow of Mars and in that silvery
sheen he sees the vision of Earthly Justice, a spec-
tacular arrangement of lights that spell out a
message, letter by letter, and then form as an
Eagle (the Empire) ornamented by glowing lilies
(France). Moved by this vision, Dante prays that
these souls of Heavenly Justice will visit their
wrath upon the corrupt Pope, who, like a money-
changer in the temple, denies the Sacraments to
God's people by excommunication and interdic-
tion, in order to sell back what is rightfully theirs.
So, for the love of money does the successor
of Peter and Paul betray Holy Office.*

Now that holy mirror rejoiced alone,
    rapt in its own reflections; and I tasted
    the bitterness and sweetness of my own.
My Guide to God said: "Turn your thoughts along
    a happier course. Remember I dwell near
    the One who lifts the weight of every wrong."

Paradiso

I turned to the loving sound of my soul's aid,
    and the love my eyes beheld in her sacred eyes
    I leave unsaid—not only am I afraid
my powers of speech fail, but my memory
    cannot return so far above itself
    unless Another's grace be moved to guide me.
This much of what I felt I can report—
    that as I looked at her my will was freed
    of every other wish of any sort,   15
for the Eternal Bliss that rayed down whole
    into my Beatrice shone back from her face,
    and its reflection there gladdened my soul.
And with a smile so radiant that my eyes
    were overcome, she said then: "Turn and listen;
    not in my eyes alone is Paradise."
As, here on earth, the face sometimes reveals
    the wish within, if it is wished so strongly
    that all the soul is gripped by what it feels—
so, in the flaming of the holy ray
    to which I turned, I read the inner will,
    and knew that it had something more to say.
It spoke thus: "In this fifth limb of the tree
    whose life is from its crown, and bears forever,
    and never sheds a leaf, I would have you see   30
elected spirits who, in the world's use,
    before they came to Heaven, were so renowned
    their great worth would make greater every Muse.
Look at the arms of the cross. As the swift flame
    within a flame does, so, within that choir,
    shall flash the splendor of each soul I name."
I saw along the cross a streak of light
    as he pronounced the name of Joshua;
    nor did the saying reach me before the sight.
And at the name of the great Maccabee
    I saw another, spinning; and the string
    that whirled that top was its own ecstasy.
And just as hunters follow their falcons' flights,
    so, at the names of Charlemagne and Roland,
    my rapt attention followed two more lights.   45

Then William of Orange and then Rinoard
  drew my eyes after them along that cross.
  And then the good duke Godfrey and Robert Guiscard.
Then, moving once more through those lights, the light
  that had come down to greet me, let me hear
  its art among the choir of Heaven's height.
I turned to my right to learn from Beatrice,
  whether by word or sign, what I should do,
  and I beheld her eyes shine with such bliss,
with such serenity, that she surpassed
  the vision of every other accustomed beauty
  in which she had shone, including even the last.
And as a man, perceiving day by day
  an increase of delight in doing good,
  begins to sense his soul is gaining way—   60
so, seeing that Miracle surpass the mark
  of former beauty, I sensed that I was turning,
  together with Heaven, through a greater arc.
And such a change as fair-skinned ladies show
  in a short space of time, when from their faces
  they lift the weight of shame that made them glow—
such change grew on my eyes when I perceived
  the pure white radiance of the temperate star—
  the sixth sphere—into which I was received.
Within that jovial face of Paradise
  I saw the sparkling of the love that dwelt there,
  forming our means of speech before my eyes.
As birds arisen from a marshy plain
  almost as if rejoicing in their forage
  form, now a cluster, now a long-drawn skein—   75
so, there, within their sheaths of living light,
  blest beings soared and sang and joined their rays,
  and D, then I, then L formed on my sight.
First they sang and moved to their own song;
  then having formed themselves into a letter,
  they stopped their song and flight, though not for long.
O holy Pegasean who consecrates
  the power of genius, giving it long life,
  as it, through you, gives life to cities and states—

As birds arisen from a marshy plain
   almost as if rejoicing in their forage
   form, now a cluster, now a long-drawn skein.

so fill me with your light, that as it shines
  I may show forth their image as I conceive it;
  let your own power appear in these few lines!
In five times seven vowels and consonants
  they showed themselves, and I grasped every part
  as if those lights had given it utterance.   90
The first words of that message as it passed
  before me were *DILIGITE IUSTITIAM.*
  QUI IUDICATIS TERRAM were the last.
Then, in the fifth word, at the final *M*
  they stayed aligned, and silvery Jupiter
  seemed to be washed in a gold glow around them.
More lights descended then and took their place
  on top of the *M*, and sang, as I believe,
  a hymn to the Good that draws them to Its grace.
Then—just as burning logs, when poked, let fly
  a fountain of innumerable sparks
  (from which fools used to think to prophesy)—
more than a thousand of those lights arose,
  some to a greater height, some to a lesser,
  each to the place the Sun that lit it chose.   105
And as each took its place in that still choir
  I saw the head and shoulders of an eagle
  appear in the fixed pattern of that fire.
The One who paints there needs no guide's behest.
  He is Himself the guide. From Him derives
  the skill and essential form that builds a nest.
The other sparks, at first content to twine
  in the form of golden lilies round the *M*
  now moved a bit, completing the design.
O lovely star, how rich a diadem
  shown forth to let me understand our justice
  flows to us from the heaven you begem.
Therefore I pray the mind that initiated
  your power and motion, to observe the source
  of the smoke by which your ray is vitiated   120
that it be moved to anger once again
  against the buyers and sellers in the temple
  whose walls were built of blood and martyr's pain.

Paradiso

O soldiery of Heaven to whose array
    my mind returns, pray for all those on earth
    who follow bad example and go astray.
In earlier eras wars were carried on
    by swords; now, by denying this man or that
    the bread the Heavenly Father denies to none.
But you who scribble only to scratch out,
    remember that Peter and Paul, who died for the vineyard
    you trample, still defend the good you flout.
Well may you say: "My heart's wish is so set
    on the image of the saint who lived alone
    and who was forced to give his head in forfeit,   135
as if it were a favor at a ball—
what do I care for the Fisherman or old Paul!"

Canto 19

The Eagle, made up of the many souls of the Just and Temperate Rulers, moves its beak and speaks as if it were a single entity, announcing that it is the chosen symbol of Divine Justice. Dante is afire to understand the nature of the Divine Justice and begs the Eagle to explain it, but he is told that the infinity of God's excellence must forever exceed His creation, and that none may fathom His will, whereby it is presumptuous of any creature to question the Divine Justice. Man must be content with the guidance of Scripture and with the sure knowledge that God is perfect, good, and just. Dante had once pondered the justice of denying salvation to virtuous pagans. The Eagle tells him it is not for him to sit in judgment on God's intent. It affirms that except as he believes in Christ no soul may ascend to Heaven, yet it adds that the virtuous pagan shall sit nearer Christ than many another who takes Christ's name in vain. The Eagle concludes with a denunciation of the bestialized kings of Christendom in 1300.

Before me, its great wings outspread, now shone
   the image of the eagle those bright souls
   had given form to in glad unison.
Each seemed a little ruby in the sky,
   and the sun's ray struck each in such a way
   the light reflected straight into my eye.
What I must now call back from memory
   no voice has ever spoken, nor ink written,
   nor has its like been known to fantasy.

For I saw and heard the beak move and declare
   in its own voice the pronouns *I* and *mine*
   when *we* and *ours* were what conceived it there.
"For being just and pious in my time,"
   it said, "I am exalted here in glory
   to which, by wish alone, no one may climb;   15
and leave behind me, there upon the earth,
   a memory honored even by evildoers,
   though they shun the good example it sets forth."
Just as the glow of many living coals
   issues a single heat, so from that image
   one sound declared the love of many souls.
At which I cried: "O everlasting blooms
   of the Eternal Bliss, who make one seeming
   upon my sense of all your many perfumes—
my soul has hungered long; breathe forth at last
   the words that will appease it. There on earth
   there is no food with which to break its fast.
I know that if God's justice has constructed
   its holy mirror in some other realm,
   your kingdom's view of it is not obstructed.   30
You know how eagerly I wait to hear;
   you know the what and wherefore of the doubt
   I have hungered to resolve for many a year."
Much as a falcon freed of hood and jess
   stretches its head and neck and beats its wings,
   preening itself to show its readiness—
so moved the emblem that was all compounded
   of praises of God's grace; and from it, then,
   a hymn they know who dwell in bliss resounded.
Then it began to speak: "The One who wheeled
   the compass round the limits of the world,
   and spread there what is hidden and what revealed,
could not so stamp His power and quality
   into His work but what the creating Word
   would still exceed creation infinitely.   45
And this explains why the first Prideful Power,
   highest of creatures, because he would not wait
   the power of the ripening Sun, fell green and sour.

And thus we see that every lesser creature
  is much too small a vessel to hold the Good
  that has no end; Itself is Its one measure.
Therefore, you understand, our way of seeing,
  which must be only one ray of the Mind
  that permeates all matter and all being,
cannot, by its very nature, be so clear
  but what its Author's eye sees far beyond
  the furthest limits that to us appear.
In the Eternal Justice, consequently,
  the understanding granted to mankind
  is lost as the eye is within the sea;   60
it can make out the bottom near the shore
  but not on the main deep; and still it is there,
  though at a depth your eye cannot explore.
There is no light but from that ever fresh
  and cloudless Halcyon; all else is darkness,
  the shadow and the poison of the flesh.
By now, much that was hidden from your view
  by the living Justice of which you used to ask
  so many questions, has been shown to you.
For you used to say, 'A man is born in sight
  of Indus' water, and there is none there
  to speak of Christ, and none to read or write.
And all he wills and does, we must concede,
  as far as human reason sees, is good;
  and he does not sin either in word or deed.   75
He dies unbaptized and cannot receive
  the saving Faith. What justice is it damns him?
  Is it his fault that he does not believe?'
But who are you to take the judgment seat
  and pass on things a thousand miles away,
  who cannot see the ground before your feet?
The man who would split hairs with me could find
  no end of grounds for questioning had he not
  the Scriptures over him to guide his mind.
O earthbound animals! minds gross as wood!
  Itself good in Itself, the Primal Will
  does not move from Itself, the Supreme Good!

Only what sorts with It is just. It sways
    toward no created good, but of Itself
    creates all Good by sending forth Its rays."   90
As a stork that has fed its young flies round and round
    above the nest, and as the chick it fed
    raises its head to stare at it, still nest-bound—
so did that blessed image circle there,
    its great wings moved in flight by many wills,
    and so did I lift up my head and stare.
Circling, it sang, then said: "As what I sing
    surpasses your understanding, so God's justice
    surpasses the power of mortal reasoning."
Those blazing glories of the Holy Ghost
    stopped, still formed in the sign that spread the honor
    of Rome across the world, to its last coast,
grew still, then said: "To this high empery
    none ever rose but through belief in Christ,
    either before or after His agony.   105
But see how many now cry out 'Christ! Christ!'
    who shall be farther from him at the Judgment
    than many who, on earth, did not know Christ.
Such Christians shall the Ethiopian scorn
    when the two bands are formed to right and left,
    one blest to all eternity, one forlorn.
What shall the Persians say to your kings there
    when the Great Book is opened and they see
    the sum of their depravities laid bare?
There shall be seen among the works of Albert
    that deed the moving pen will soon record
    by which Bohemia shall become a desert.
There shall be seen the Seine's grief for the sin
    of that debaser of the currency
    whose death is waiting for him in a pig's skin.   120
There shall be seen the pride whose greed confounds
    the mad Scot and the foolish Englishman
    who cannot stay within their proper bounds.
There, the debaucheries and the vain show
    of the Spaniard and the Bohemian who knew
    nothing of valor and chose not to know.

And there, the cripple of Jerusalem:
   a *1* put down to mark the good he did,
    and then, to mark his villainies, an *M*.
There, the baseness and the greedy rage
   of the watchdog who patrols the burning island
   on which Anchises closed his long old age;
and to make clear how paltry is his case,
   his entry will be signs and abbreviations
   that the record may say much in little space.   135
And there the filthy deeds shall be set down
   of his uncle and his brother, each of whom
   cuckolded a great family and a crown.
There shall be marked for all men to behold
   Norway's king and Portugal's; and Rascia's,
   who lost most when he saw Venetian gold.
O happy Hungary, had she suffered all
   without more griefs ahead! Happy Navarre
   were she to make her peaks a fortress wall!
And every Navarrese may well believe
   the omen of Nicosìa and Famagosta
   whose citizens have present cause to grieve
the way their beast, too small for the main pack,
keeps to one side but hunts on the same track."

Canto 20

*The Eagle pauses briefly and the spirits of
the blest sing a hymn, not as one symbolic entity,
but each in its own voice. The hymn ended, the
Eagle resumes speaking in its single voice, and
identifies as the chief souls of this sphere those
lusters that compose its eye: David, Trajan,
Hezekiah, Constantine, William of Sicily, and
Ripheus. Dante is astonished to find Trajan and
Ripheus in Heaven, both of whom he had thought
to be pagans, but the Eagle explains how by the
special grace of God Ripheus was converted by a
vision of Christ a millennium before His descent
into the flesh, and Trajan was returned from
Limbo to his mortal body long enough to undergo
conversion to Christ and to allow his soul to
mount to Heaven. As for Dante's doubts about
the virtuous Hindu and God's justice, who can
say how many more God has so chosen to His
grace? The Eagle concludes with a praise of God's
predestined justice, rejoicing even in the limita-
tion of its own knowledge, resting in the assurance that the unknown consequences of
God's will cannot fail to be good.*

When the sun, from which the whole world takes its light,
    sinks from our hemisphere and the day fades
    from every reach of land, and it is night;
the sky, which earlier it alone had lit,
    suddenly changes mode and reappears
    in many lights that take their light from it.
I thought of just that change across night's sill
    when that emblem of the world and of its leaders
    had finished speaking through its sacred bill;

For all those living lights now shone on me
more brightly than before, and began singing
a praise too sweet to hold in memory.

for all those living lights now shone on me
   more brightly than before, and began singing
   a praise too sweet to hold in memory.
O heavenly love in smiling glory wreathed,
   how ardently you sounded from those flutes
   through which none but the holiest impulse breathed.   15
When then those precious gems of purest ray
   with which the lamp of the sixth heaven shone
   let their last angel-harmony fade away,
I seemed to hear a great flume take its course
   from stone to stone, and murmur down its mountain
   as if to show the abundance of its source.
And as the sound emerging from a lute
   is tempered at its neck; and as the breath
   takes form around the openings of a flute—
just so, allowing no delay to follow,
   the murmur of the eagle seemed to climb
   inside its neck, as if the neck were hollow.
There it was given voice, and through the bill
   the voice emerged as words my heart awaited.
   And on my heart those words are written still.   30
"Look closely now into that part of me
   that in earth's eagles can endure the sun,"
   the emblem said, "—the part with which I see.
Of all the fires with which I draw my form
   those rays that make the eye shine in my head
   are the chief souls of all this blessèd swarm.
The soul that makes the pupil luminous
   was the sweet psalmist of the Holy Ghost,
   who bore the Ark of God from house to house:
now, insofar as he himself gave birth
   to his own psalms, he is repayed in bliss,
   and by that bliss he knows what they are worth.
Of the five that form my eyebrow's arc, the one
   whose glory shines the closest to my beak
   consoled the widow who had lost her son;   45
now he understands what price men pay
   who do not follow Christ, for though he learns
   the sweet life, he has known the bitter way.

The next in line on the circumference
    of the same upper arc of which I speak,
    delayed his own death by true penitence;
now he knows that when a worthy prayer
    delays today's event until tomorrow,
    the eternal judgment is not altered there.
The third, to give the Shepherd sovereignty,
    (with good intentions though they bore bad fruit)
    removed to Greece, bearing the laws and me;
now he knows the evil that began
    in his good action does not harm his soul
    although it has destroyed the world of man.   60
And him you see upon the arc beneath
    was William of that land that mourns the life
    of Charles and Frederick, as it mourns his death;
now he knows how Heaven's Heart inclines
    to love a just king, as he makes apparent
    by the radiance with which his being shines.
Who would believe in the erring world down there
    that Ripheus the Trojan would be sixth
    among the sacred lusters of this sphere?
Now he knows grace divine to depths of bliss
    the world's poor understanding cannot grasp.
    Even *his* eye cannot plumb that abyss."
Like a lark that soars in rapture to the sky,
    first singing, and then silent, satisfied
    by the last sweetness of its soul's own cry—   75
such seemed that seal of the Eternal Bliss
    that stamped it there, the First Will at whose will
    whatever is becomes just what it is.
And though my eagerness to know shone clear
    as colors shining through a clearest glass,
    I could not bear to wait in silence there,
but from my tongue burst out, "How can this be?"
    forced by the weight of my own inner doubt
    —at which those lights flashed in new revelry.
And soon then, not to keep me in suspense,
    the blessèd emblem answered me, its eye
    flashing a yet more glorious radiance.

"I see that you believe these things are true
    because I say them. Yet, you do not see how.
    Thus, though believed, their truth is hidden from you.   90
You are like one who knows the name of a thing
    whose quiddity, until it is explained
    by someone else, defies his understanding.
By every living hope and ardent love
    that bends the Eternal Will—by these alone
    the Kingdom of Heaven suffers itself to move.
Not as men bend beneath a conqueror's will;
    it bends because it wishes to be bent;
    conquered, its own beneficence conquers still.
You marvel at the first and the fifth gem
    here on my brow, finding this realm of angels
    and gift of Christ made beautiful by them.
They did not leave their bodies, as you believe,
    as pagans but as Christians, in firm faith
    in the pierced feet one grieved and one would grieve.   105
One rose again from Hell—from whose dead slope
    none may return to Love—into the flesh;
    and that was the reward of living hope;
of living hope, whose power of love made good
    the prayers he raised to God to bring him back
    to life again, that his will might be renewed.
And so the glorious soul for whom he prayed,
    back in the flesh from which it soon departed,
    believed in Him who has the power to aid.
Believing, he burst forth with such a fire
    of the true love, that at his second death
    he was worthy of a seat in this glad choir.
The other, by that grace whose blessings rise
    out of so deep a spring that no one ever
    has plumbed its sources with created eyes,   120
gave all his love to justice, there on earth,
    and God, by grace on grace, let him foresee
    a vision of our redemption shining forth.
So he believed in Christ, and all his days
    shunning the poisonous stink of pagan creeds,
    he warned the obstinate to change their ways.

More than a thousand years before the grace
   of baptism was known, those maids you saw
   at the right wheel, stood for him in its place.
Predestination! Oh, how deep your source
   is rooted past the reach of every vision
   that cannot plumb the whole of the First Cause!
Mortals, be slow to judge! Not even we
   who look on God in Heaven know, as yet,
   how many He will choose for ecstasy.   135
And sweet it is to lack this knowledge still,
   for in this good is our own good refined,
   willing whatever God Himself may will."
In these words the blest emblem of that sphere
   gave me these gentle curatives of love
   with which my clouded vision was made clear.
And as the skillful harpist, string by string,
   makes every cord attend on a good singer,
   adding a greater pleasure to the singing;
so, I recall, that as it spoke to me
   these paradisal words, the holy lights
   of Trajan and Ripheus in sweet harmony,
as if they blinked their eyes with one accord,
made their flames pulse in time with every word.

Canto 21

Beatrice and Dante enter the Sphere of Saturn. Beatrice does not smile in her new bliss to announce their arrival, for her radiance would then be such that Dante's mortal senses would be consumed, as Semele was consumed by the god-head of Jupiter. Rather, Beatrice announces that they are there and commands Dante to look into the crystalline substance of that heaven for the vision he will see of the souls of the Contempla-tive. Dante turns and beholds a vision of a Golden Ladder on which countless splendors arise and descend wheeling like birds in flight. That host of the blessèd descends only as far as a given rung, but one radiance among them draws closer to Dante and indicates by its radiance that it is eager to bring him joy. It is the soul of Peter Damiano, a Doctor of the Church, renowned for a severely ascetic life even in high Church Office. Peter Damiano explains to Dante that the mys-tery of predestination is beyond the reach of all but God and that men should not presume to grasp it. He concludes with a denunciation of Papal corruption, and at his words all the souls of Saturn fly down to form a ring around him and thunder forth Heaven's righteous indignation at evildoers. So loud is their cry that Dante cannot make out their words, his senses reeling at that thunderclap of sound.

My eyes were fixed once more on my Lady's face;
    and with my eyes, my soul, from which all thought,
    except of her, had fled without a trace.
She did not smile. "Were I to smile," she said,
  "you would be turned to ash, as Semele was
    when she saw Jupiter in his full godhead;

because my beauty, which, as it goes higher
    from step to step of the eternal palace,
    burns, as you know, with ever brighter fire;
and if it is not tempered in its brightening,
    its radiance would consume your mortal powers
    as a bough is shattered by a bolt of lightning.
We have soared to the seventh splendor, which is now
    beneath the Lion's blazing breast, and rays
    its influence, joined with his, to the world below.   15
Now make your eyes the mirror of the vision
    this mirror will reveal to you, and fix
    your mind behind your eyes in strict attention."
Could any man conceive what blessed pasture
    my eyes found in her face when I turned away,
    at her command, to find another nurture—
then would he know with what a rush of bliss
    I obeyed my heavenly escort, balancing
    one side and the other, that joy against this.
Within the crystal that bears round the world
    the name of its great king in that golden age
    when evil's flag had not yet been unfurled,
like polished gold ablaze in full sunlight,
    I saw a ladder rise so far above me
    it soared beyond the reaches of my sight.   30
And I saw so many splendors make their way
    down its bright rungs, I thought that every lamp
    in all of Heaven was pouring forth its ray.
As grackles flock together at first light,
    obeying a natural impulse to move as one
    to warm their night-chilled feathers in glad flight;
after which, some go off and do not come back,
    others return to the points from which they came,
    and others stay with the flock in its wheeling track—
just such an impulse seemed to work among
    those sparkling essences, for they flocked together
    the instant they had reached a certain rung.
One that came nearest where we stood below
    then made itself so bright I said to myself:
    "I well know with what love for me you glow!"   45

Just such an impulse seemed to work among
   those sparkling essences, for they flocked together
   the instant they had reached a certain rung.

But she from whom I await the how and when
  of my speech and silence, was still; and despite my yearning
  I knew it was well to ask no questions then.
She saw in the vision of Him who sees all things
  what silence held my eager tongue in check,
  and said to me: "Give your soul's impulse wings!"
"O blessèd being hidden in the ray
  of your own bliss," I said in reverence,
  "I am not worthy, but for her sake, I pray,
who gives me leave to question, let me know
  why you, of all this sacred company,
  have placed yourself so near me, here below;
and tell me why, when every lower sphere
  sounds the sweet symphony of Paradise
  in adoration, there is no music here."   60
"Your sight is mortal. Is not your hearing, too?"
  he said. "Our song is still for the same reason
  Beatrice holds back her smile—for love of you.
Only that I might make your spirit gladder
  by what I say and by the light that robes me
  have I come so far down the sacred ladder.
Nor was it greater love that spurred me; here
  as much—and more—love burns in every soul,
  as the flaming of these radiances makes clear.
But the high love that makes us prompt to serve
  the Judge who rules the world, decrees the fate
  of every soul among us, as you observe."
"O sacred lamp," I said, "I understand
  that in this court glad love follows the will
  of Eternal Providence, needing no command;   75
but the further point I cannot grasp is this:
  why, among all these blisses with whom you dwell,
  were you alone predestined to this office?"
Before I finished speaking, that lamp of grace
  like a millstone at full speed, making an axle
  of its own center, began to spin in place.
And then the Love within the lamp replied:
  "I feel the ray of God's light focused on me.
  It strikes down through the ray in which I hide.

Its power, joined to my own, so elevates
  my soul above itself, that I behold
  the Primal Source from which it emanates.
My bliss flames only as that ray shines down.
  As much of glory as I am given to see
  my flame gives back in glory of its own.   90
But in all Heaven, the soul granted most light,
  the Seraph that has God in closest view,
  could not explain what you have asked to know.
The truth of this is hidden so far down
  in the abyss of the Eternal Law,
  it is cut off from all created vision.
Report what I have said when you are back
  in the mortal world, that no man may presume
  to move his feet down so profound a track.
On earth the mind is smoke; here, it is fire.
  How can it do there what it cannot do
  even when taken into Heaven's choir?"
I left that question, his own words having thus
  prescribed me from it, and, so limited,
  was content to ask him humbly who he was.   105
"Not far from your own birthplace, row on row
  between Italy's two shores, peaks rise so high
  that on them thunder sounds from far below.
A humpback ridge called Catria rises there.
  Beneath it stands a holy hermitage
  once given entirely to meditation and prayer."
So, for the third time now, that soul of grace
  began to speak, continuing: "I became
  so rooted in God's service in that place,
I lived on Lenten olive-food alone
  and bore both heat and cold indifferently,
  rejoicing ever more in contemplation.
Once that cloister sent here, sphere on sphere,
  harvests of souls. Now all its works are vain
  as, soon now, righteous punishment shall make clear.   120
I was Peter Damiano there, and became
  Pcter the Sinner by the Adriatic
  in the abbey sacred to Our Lady's name.

The Divine Comedy

Little was left me of my mortal course
    when I was chosen and summoned to wear the hat
    that seems forever to pass from bad to worse.
Cephas, and the great Ark of the Holy Ghost
    once came among mankind barefoot and gaunt,
    eating by chance, with charity as their host.
But now your pastors are so bloated and vain
    they go propped on either side, with a man before
    and another coming behind to bear the train.
They cover even their mounts with the cloaks they wear
    so that two beasts move under a single hide.
    O Heavenly Patience, how long will you forebear!"   135
As he spoke these words, I saw more ardors yearning
    downward in circling flight, from rung to rung;
    and grow more radiant with every turning.
Round him they came to rest, and all burst forth
    in unison of love—a cry so loud
    the like of it has not been heard on earth.
Nor could I understand it, for the peal
of that ominous thunder made my senses reel.

Canto 22

*Dante's senses still reeling, he turns to
Beatrice, who reassures him and prophesies that
he will live to see God's vengeance descend on the
corruptors of the Church. She then calls his attention to the other souls of this sphere. Looking
up, Dante sees a hundred radiant globes, one of
which draws near and identifies itself as the
heavenly splendor that had been St. Benedict.
Benedict explains that the Golden Ladder, like
the contemplative life, soars to the summit of
God's glory, and he laments that so few of his
Benedictine monks remain eager to put the world
behind them and begin the ascent, for they are
lost in the degeneracy of bad days. Yet God has
worked greater wonders than would be required
to restore the purity of the Church. So saying,
Benedict is gathered into his heavenly choir of
radiances, and the whole company ascends to
the top of the sky and out of sight. Beatrice then
makes a sign and Dante feels himself making
the ascent to the eighth sphere, the Sphere of the
Fixed Stars. But before the souls of that sphere are
revealed to him, Beatrice bids him look back
to see how far she has raised him. Dante looks
down, seeing all the heavens at a glance and the
earth as an insignificant speck far below. Then
turning from it as from a puny thing, he turns
his eyes back to the eyes of Beatrice.*

My sense reeled and, as a child in doubt
  runs always to the one it trusts the most,
  I turned to my Guide, still shaken by that shout;
and she, like a mother, ever prompt to calm
  her pale and breathless son with kindly words,
  the sound of which is his accustomed balm,

said: "Do you not know you are in the skies
   of Heaven itself? that all is holy here?
   that all things spring from love in Paradise?
Their one cry shakes your senses; you can now see
   what would have happened to you had they sung
   or had I smiled in my new ecstasy.
Had you understood the prayer within their cry
   you would know now what vengeance they called down,
   though you shall witness it before you die.   15
The sword of Heaven is not too soon dyed red,
   nor yet too late—except as its vengeance seems
   to those who wait for it in hope or dread.
But look now to the others. Turn as I say
   and you shall see among this company
   many great souls of the Eternal Ray."
I did as she commanded. Before my eyes
   a hundred shining globes entwined their beams,
   soul adding grace to soul in Paradise.
I stood there between longing and diffidence
   and fought my longing back, afraid to speak
   for fear my questioning might give offense.
And the largest and most glowing globe among
   the wreath of pearls came forward of its own prompting
   to grant the wish I had not given tongue.   30
These words came from within it: "Could you see,
   as I do, with what love our spirits burn
   to give you joy, your tongue would have been free.
To cause you no delay on the high track
   to the great goal, I shall address myself
   to none but the single question you hold back.
The summit of that mountain on whose side
   Cassino lies, once served an ill-inclined
   and misted people in their pagan pride.
And I am he who first bore to that slope
   the holy name of Him who came on earth
   to bring mankind the truth that is our hope.
Such grace shone down on me that men gave heed
   through all that countryside and were won over
   from the seductions of that impious creed.   45

These other souls were all contemplatives,
    fired by that warmth of soul that summons up
    the holy flowers and fruits of blessèd lives.
Here is Romualdus, and Maccarius, too.
    Here are my brothers who kept within the cloister
    and, never straying, kept hearts sound and true."
And I to him: "The love you have made clear
    in speaking as you have, and the good intent
    I see in all the glories of this sphere,
have opened all my confidence; it grows
    and spreads wide on your warmth, rejoicing in it
    as does, in the sun's heat, a full-blown rose.
I therefore beg you, Father: can I rise
    to such a height of grace that I may see
    your unveiled image with my mortal eyes?"   60
And he then: "Brother, this shall be made known
    in the last sphere. Your wish will be answered there
    where every other is, including my own.
There, every wish is perfect, ripe, and whole.
    For there, and there alone, is every part
    where it has always been; for it has no pole,
not being in space. It is to that very height
    the golden ladder mounts; and thus you see
    why it outsoars the last reach of your sight.
The patriarch Jacob saw it, saw it mount
    to lean on that very sill, that time he dreamed it
    covered with angels beyond all mortal count.
To climb it now, however, none makes haste
    to lift his feet from earth. My rule lives on
    only to fill the parchments it lays waste.   75
The walls that were retreats in their good hour
    are dens for beasts now; what were holy cowls
    are gunnysacks stuffed full of evil flour.
But even compound usury strikes less
    against God's will and pleasure, than does that fruit
    whose poison fills the hearts of monks with madness.
For all the goods of the Church, tithes and donations,
    are for the poor of God, not to make fat
    the families of monks—and worse relations.

The flesh of mortals is so weak down there
  that a good beginning is not reason enough
  to think the seedling tree will live to bear.
Peter began with neither silver nor gold;
  I, with prayer and fasting. And Brother Francis
  in humble poverty gathered souls to his fold.   90
And if you look at the origins of each one,
  then look again at what it has become,
  you will see that what was white has changed to dun.
Yet Jordan flowing backward, and the sea
  parting as God willed, were more wondrous sights
  than God's help to His stricken Church would be."
So did he speak; then faded from my eye
  into his company, which closed about him,
  and then, like a whirlwind, spun away on high.
And my sweet Lady with a simple sign
  raised me along that ladder after them,
  conquering my nature with her power divine.
There never was known down here, where everything
  rises or falls as natural law determines,
  a speed to equal the motion of my wing.   105
Reader, so may I hope once more to stand
  in that holy Triumph, for which I weep my sins
  and beat my breast—you could not draw your hand
out of a tongue of flame and thrust it back
  sooner than I sighted and had entered
  the sign that follows Taurus on Heaven's track.
O glorious constellation! O lamp imbued
  with great powers, to whose influence I ascribe
  all my genius, however it may be viewed!
When I drew my first breath of Tuscan air
  the sun, the father of all mortal life,
  was rising in your rays and setting there.
And then when I was granted Heaven's grace
  to enter the Great Wheel that gives you motion,
  I was led upward through your zone of space.   120
To you devoutly now my prayer is sped:
  make my soul worthy of the call it hears
  to the great passage that still lies ahead!

Paradiso

"You are so near the final health of man
    you will do well to go clear-eyed and keen
    into that good," my Beatrice began.
"Therefore, before you enter further here,
    look down and see how vast a universe
    I have put beneath your feet, bright sphere on sphere.
Thus may you come in the fullness of delight
    to the Triumphant Court that comes in joy
    through the round ether to your mortal sight."
My eyes went back through the seven spheres below,
    and I saw this globe, so small, so lost in space,
    I had to smile at such a sorry show.   135
Who thinks it the least pebble in the skies
    I most approve. Only the mind that turns
    to other things may truly be called wise.
I saw Latona's daughter glowing there
    without that shadow that had once misled me
    to think her matter was part dense, part rare.
My eyes looked on your son, Hyperion,
    nor did they falter. And wheeling close around him,
    I saw the motion of Maia and Dione.
Next I saw how Jupiter mediates
    between his father and son, and I understood
    why the motion of one and the other vacillates.
And all the seven, in a single view,
    showed me their masses, their velocities,
    and the distances between each in its purlieu.   150
And turning there with the eternal Twins,
    I saw the dusty little threshing ground
    that makes us ravenous for our mad sins,
saw it from mountain crest to lowest shore.
Then I turned my eyes to Beauty's eyes once more.

Canto 23

*Beatrice stares expectantly toward that
part of the sky where the sun is at its highest
point, and Dante, moved by the joy of her expectation, follows her look. Almost at once there
descends from the highest Heaven the radiant
substance of the vision of Christ Triumphant as it
rays forth on the garden of all those souls who
have been redeemed through Christ. The splendor
too much for his senses, Dante swoons. He is recalled to himself by Beatrice and discovers that,
newly strengthened as he has been by the vision
of Christ, he is able to look upon her smile of bliss.
Beatrice urges him to look at the Garden of
Christ's Triumph, upon the Rose of the Virgin
Mary and the Lilies of the Apostles. Christ, taking
mercy on Dante's feeble powers, has withdrawn
from direct view and now rays down from above.
Dante fixes his eyes on the brightest splendor (the
Virgin Mary) and sees a crown of flame descend to
summon her back to the Empyrean. It is the Angel
Gabriel. So summoned, Mary ascends to where
her Son is, and the flames of the souls yearn
higher toward her. Among the souls that remain below, Dante identifies St. Peter.*

As a bird in its sweet canopy of green
   covers the nest of its beloved young
   through all the night when nothing can be seen;
but eager for the loved, lit face of things,
   and to go hunting for its fledglings' food
   in toil so glad that, laboring, she sings;
anticipates the day on an open bough
   and in a fire of love awaits the sun,
   her eyes fixed eagerly on the predawn glow—

just so my Lady waited—erect, intense—
   all her attention toward that part of Heaven
   beneath which the sun's daily pace relents;
and I, observing her blissful expectation,
   became like one who yearns for more than he has,
   feeding his hope with sweet anticipation.   15
But the interval between *when* and *when* was slight—
   the *when* of my waiting, I say, and the *when* of seeing
   the sky begin to swell with a new light.
And Beatrice said: "Before you now appears
   the militia of Christ's triumph, and all the fruit
   harvested from the turning of the spheres."
I saw her face before me, so imbued
   with holy fire, her eyes so bright with bliss
   that I pass on, leaving them unconstrued.
As Trivia in the full moon's sweet serene
   smiles on high among the eternal nymphs
   whose light paints every part of Heaven's scene;
I saw, above a thousand thousand lights,
   one Sun that lit them all, as our own sun
   lights all the bodies we see in Heaven's heights;   30
and through that living light I saw revealed
   the Radiant Substance, blazing forth so bright
   my vision dazzled and my senses reeled.
O my Beatrice, sweet and loving Guide!
   "What blinds you," she said to me, "is the very Power
   nothing withstands and from which none may hide.
This is the Intellect and the sceptered Might
   that opened the golden road from earth to Heaven,
   for which mankind had yearned in its long night."
Fire sometimes spreads so wide that it shoots forth
   from a cloud that can no longer hold it in,
   and against its nature, hurtles down to earth.
That feast of bliss had swollen my mind so
   that it broke its bounds and leapt out of itself.
   And what it then became, it does not know.   45
"Open your eyes and turn them full on me!
   You have seen things whose power has made you able
   to bear the bright smile of my ecstasy!"

As one whose senses have been stricken blind
  by a forgotten vision comes to himself
  and racks his wits to call it back to mind—
such was I at that summons, my spirit moved
  to a thankfulness that shall live on forever
  within the book where what is past is proved.
If there should sound now all the tongues of song
  Polyhymnia with her eight sisters nourished,
  giving their sweetest milk to make them strong,
they could not help me, singing thus, to show
  a thousandth part of my Lady's sacred smile,
  nor with what glory it made her features glow.   60
Just so, that Heaven may be figured forth,
  my consecrated poem must make a leap,
  as a traveler leaps a crevice there on earth.
My theme is massive, mortal shoulders frail
  for such a weight. What thoughtful man will blame me
  for trembling under it for fear I fail?
The seas my ardent prow is plowing here
  are no place for small craft, nor for a helmsman
  who will draw back from toil or cringe in fear.
"Why are you so enamored of my face
  you do not turn your eyes to see the garden
  that flowers there in the radiance of Christ's grace?
The Rose in which the Word became incarnate
  is there. There are the lilies by whose odor
  men found the road that evermore runs straight."   75
Thus Beatrice. And I, prompt to her guidance
  in fullest eagerness, raised my feeble lids
  once more to battle with that radiance.
At times when the sun, through broken clouds, has rayed
  one perfect beam, I have seen a field of flowers
  blazing in glory, my own eyes still in shade—
just so, I saw a host of hosts made bright
  by rays of splendor striking from above,
  but could not see the source of that pure light.
O Majesty that seals them in such glory!
  You raised Yourself on high, withdrawing there
  in order that my feeble eyes might see!

The name of that Sweet Flower to which I pray
  morning and night, seized all my soul and moved it
  to fix my eyes upon the brightest ray;   90
and when both my eyes had been allowed to know
  the luster and magnitude of that chosen star
  that triumphs there as it triumphed here below,
from Heaven's height a torch of glory came,
  shaped like a ring or wreath, and spinning round her,
  it wound and crowned her in its living flame.
The sweetest strain that ever swelled aloud
  to draw the soul into itself down here
  would be as thunder from a shattered cloud,
compared to the melody that then aspired
  from the bright lyre that crowned the purest gem
  by which the brightest heaven is ensapphired.
"I am the Angelic Love that wheels around
  the lofty ecstasy breathed from the womb
  in which the hostel of Our Wish was found;   105
so shall I wheel, Lady of Heaven, till
  you follow your great Son to the highest sphere
  and, by your presence, make it holier still."
Thus the encircling melody of that flame
  revealed itself; and all the other lamps
  within that garden rang out Mary's name.
The royal mantle whose folds are spread abroad
  round all the spheres and that most burns and quickens,
  being nearest to the breath and ways of God,
turned its inner shore at such a height
  above the point at which I then was standing
  that I could not yet bring it into sight.
I could not, therefore, with my mortal eyes
  follow the flight of that crowned flame that soared
  to join her Son in the highest Paradise.   120
And as a newly suckled infant yearns
  after its mother with its upraised arms,
  expressing so the love with which it burns;
each of the splendors of that company
  extended its flame on high in such a way
  as made its love of Mary plain to me.

Then they remained there, still within my sight,
  singing *"Regina coeli"* in tones so sweet
  the memory still fills me with delight.
Oh, what treasures cram and overflow
  those richest coffers of the Eternal Grace
  who sowed such good seed in the world below!
Here is true life and relish of the treasure
  their tears laid up in the Babylonian exile,
  in which Christ left man gold beyond all measure.   135
Here sits in triumph under the lofty Son
  of God and the Virgin Mary in His triumph,
  and in the company of everyone
crowned from the New or the Old Consistory,
the soul that holds the great keys to such glory.

Canto 24

Christ and Mary having ascended to the Empyrean, St. Peter remains as the chief soul of the Garden of Christ's Triumph. Beatrice addresses the souls in Dante's behalf, and they, in their joy, form into a dazzling vertical wheel of spinning radiances. Beatrice then begs St. Peter to conduct an examination of Dante's faith. St. Peter questions Dante on the nature of faith, the possession of faith, the sources of faith, the proof of the truth of faith, man's means of knowing that the miracles of faith actually took place, and finally on the content of Christian faith. Dante answers eagerly, as would a willing candidate being examined by his learned master. The examination concluded, St. Peter shows his pleasure by dancing three times around Dante.

"O spirits of that chosen company
 that feeds on the Lamb of God, the flesh of which
 satisfies hunger to all eternity—
if by God's grace this man is given a foretaste
 of what falls from your table, before death
 takes him from time and lays his body waste,
consider the boundless thirst with which he burns;
 bedew him from your plenty. You drink forever
 the waters of that spring for which he yearns!"
So spoke Beatrice, and those blissful souls,
 flaming as bright as comets, formed themselves
 into a sphere revolving on fixed poles.
As the wheels within a clockwork synchronize
 so that the innermost, when looked at closely
 seems to be standing, while the outermost flies—

just so those rings of dancers whirled to show
    and let me understand their state of bliss,
    all joining in the round, some fast, some slow.
From one I saw, the loveliest of them all,
    there grew a radiance of such blessedness
    that it outshone the hosts of the celestial.
Three times it danced round Beatrice to a strain
    so heavenly that I have not the power
    so much as to imagine it again.
Therefore my pen leaps and I do not write;
    not words nor fantasy can paint the truth;
    the folds of Heaven's draperies are too bright.
"O sacred sister whose prayer is so devout,
    the ardor of your love enters my bliss
    within that lovely sphere and calls me out."   30
When it had come to rest, that fire of love
    directed its breath to my Lady and spoke these words
    exactly as I have set them down above.
And she: "Eternal Light of the great priest
    to whom Our Lord brought down and gave the keys
    to the sublimities of this joyous feast;
at your own pleasure, whatever it may be,
    test this man on the greater and lesser points
    of the faith in which you once walked on the sea.
If love and hope and faith are truly his
    you will discover it, for your eyes are turned
    where you can see the image of all that is.
But since this realm is peopled from the seed
    of the True Faith, he will the better praise it,
    could he discuss with you the perfect creed."   45
As a bachelor arms himself for disquisition
    in silence till the master sets the terms
    for defending, not deciding, the proposition;
so did I arm myself for the expression
    of every proof, preparing while she spoke
    for such an examiner, and such profession.
"Speak, good Christian, manifest your worth:
    what is faith?" —At which I raised my eyes
    to the light from which these words had been breathed forth;

then turned to look at Beatrice, and she
   urged me with her eyes to let the waters
   of the spring that welled within my soul pour free.
"May the Grace that grants the grace of this confession
   to the captain of the first rank," I began,
   "grant that my thoughts may find worthy expression!"   60
Continuing: "Father, as it was set down
   by the pen of your dear brother, who, with you,
   set Rome on the road that leads to glory's crown,
faith is the *substance* of what we hope to see
   and the *argument* for what we have not seen.
   This is its *quiddity*, as it seems to me."
Next I heard: "This is, in fact, the essence.
   But do you understand why he classifies it
   first with *substances*, then with argument?"
And I in answer: "The profundities
   that here reveal themselves so liberally
   are so concealed, down there, from mortal eyes
they exist in belief alone. On belief the structure
   of high hope rises. It is *substant*, therefore,
   or 'standing under' by its very nature.   75
Starting with this belief, it is evident,
   we must reason without further visible proofs.
   And so it partakes, by nature, of *argument*."
I heard: "If all that mortal man may know
   through mortal teaching were as firmly grasped,
   sophists would find no listeners there below."
Such was the breath from that love's ecstasy,
   continuing then: "You have assayed this coinage,
   its weight and metal content, accurately;
now tell me if you have it in your possession."
   And I then: "Yes, I have. So bright, so round,
   usage has worn down none of its impression."
After these words the breath once more resounded
   from the light that shone before me: "This dear gem
   on which all good and power of good are founded—   90
whence comes it to you?" And I, "The shower of gold
   of the Holy Ghost, which pours down endlessly
   over the sacred Scrolls, both New and Old,

reasons it to such logical certainty
    that, by comparison, all other reasoning
    can only seem confused and dull to me."
And I heard: "These propositions, the Old and New
    that move you to this conclusion, for what reason
    do you accept them as divinely true?"
And I: "The proof that shows the truth to me
    is in the works that followed. Never has nature
    heated and forged such iron in its smithy."
And I was answered: "Tell me how you know
    there were such works. What seeks to prove itself—
    it only and nothing more—swears it was so."   105
"If the whole world became Christian without the aid
    of the miraculous, that is a miracle
    a hundred times greater than the rest," I said,
"for poor and hungry, by faith alone upborne,
    you entered the field and sowed there the good plant
    that was a vine once and is now a thorn."
 This said, that high and holy choir let ring
    "Te Deum laudamus!" sounding through the spheres
    such melody as the souls of Heaven sing.
And that Baron, who, examining my belief
    from branch to branch, had drawn me out already
    to where we were approaching the last leaf,
began again: "The grace whose loving good
    had pledged itself to your mind, has moved your mouth,
    up to this point, to open as it should.   120
I approve what has emerged thus far, but now
    it is time you should explain *what* you believe,
    and from what source it comes to you, and how."
"O holy Father, spirit that now can see
    what faith once held so firmly that you were prompter
    than younger feet to the tomb in Galilee,"
my answer ran, "you wish me to expound
    the *form* of my own promptness to believe,
    and you ask what reasons for it I have found.
And I reply: I believe in one God, loved,
    desired by all creation, sole, eternal,
    who moves the turning heavens, Himself unmoved.

Paradiso

And for this faith I have the evidences
  not only of physics and of metaphysics,
  but of the truth that rains down on my senses   135
through Moses, the prophets, the psalms, through the Evangel,
  and through you and what you wrote when the Ardent Spirit
  made you the foster father of God's people.
And I believe in three Persons; this Trinity,
  an essence Triune and Single, in whose being
  is and *are* conjoin to eternity.
That this profound and sacred nature is real
  the teachings of the evangels, in many places,
  have stamped on the wax of my mind like a living seal.
This is the beginning, the spark shot free
  that gnaws and widens into living flame,
  and, like a star in Heaven, shines in me."
As a master who is pleased by what he hears
  embraces his servant as soon as he has spoken,
  rejoicing in the happy news he bears—   150
so, that glorious apostolic blaze
  at whose command I had spoken heard me out
  and, blessing me in a glad chant of praise,
danced three times round me there in the eighth great rim,
such pleasure had my speaking given him.

503

Canto 25

Dante, blessed by St. Peter himself as a reward for his labors and his hope, declares that if his poem may serve to soften his sentence of exile from Florence, he will return to his baptismal font at San Giovanni and there place on his own head the poet's laurel wreath. Such is one of the great hopes of his poem, and on that note St. James, the Apostle of Hope, shows himself. Beatrice begs James to conduct the examination of hope and she herself, in answer to the first question, testifies to Dante's possession of hope. Dante then replies on the nature of hope, on the content of his hope, and on the sources of hope. The examination triumphantly concluded, a cry in praise of the grace of hope rings through Paradise, and thereupon St. John the Apostle appears. Dante stares into John's radiance hoping to see the lineaments of his mortal body, and the voice of John, the Apostle of Love (caritas) *calls to him that what he seeks is not there. Dante looks away, blinded by the radiance of love.*

If ever it comes to pass that the sacred song,
    to which both Heaven and earth so set their hand
    that I grew lean with laboring years long,
wins over the cruelty that exiles me
    from the sweet sheepfold where I slept, a lamb,
    and to the raiding wolves an enemy;
with a changed voice and with my fleece full grown
    I shall return to my baptismal font,
    a poet, and there assume the laurel crown;
for there I entered the Faith that lets us grow
    into God's recognition; and for that Faith
    Peter, as I have said, circled my brow.

Paradiso

Thereafter another radiance came forth
   from the same sphere out of whose joy had come
   the first flower of Christ's vicarage on earth.   15
And my Lady, filled with ecstasy and aglow,
   cried to me: "Look! Look there! It is the baron
   for whom men throng to Galicia there below!"
At times, on earth, I have seen a mating dove
   alight by another, and each turn to each,
   circling and murmuring to express their love—
exactly so, within the eighth great sphere,
   one glorious great lord greeted the other,
   praising the diet that regales them there.
Those glories, having greeted and been greeted,
   turned and stood before me, still and silent,
   so bright I turned my eyes away defeated.
And Beatrice said, smiling her blessedness:
   "Illustrious being in whose chronicle
   is written our celestial court's largesse,   30
let hope, I pray, be sounded at this height.
   How often you personified that grace
   when Jesus gave His chosen three more light!"
"Lift up your head, look up and do not fear,
   for all that rises from the mortal world
   must ripen in our rays from sphere to sphere."
So spoke the second flame to comfort me;
   and I raised my eyes to the mountains that before
   had borne them down by their weight of majesty.
"Since of His grace Our Lord and Emperor calls
   and bids you come while still in mortal flesh
   among His counts in His most secret hails,
that you, the truth of this great court made clear,
   may make the stronger, in yourself and others,
   the hope that makes men love the good down there,   45
say what it is, what power helped you to climb,
   and how you bear its flowering in your mind."
   So spoke the second flame a second time.
And that devout sweet spirit that had led
   the feathers of my wings in that high flight
   anticipated my reply and said:

505

"Church Militant, as is written in the Sun
  whose ray lights all our hosts, does not possess
  a single child richer in hope—not one.
It was for that he was allowed to come
  from Egypt to behold Jerusalem
  before his warring years had reached their sum.
The other two points—raised not that you may know
  but that he may report how great a pleasure
  hope is to you, when he returns below—   60
I leave to him. They will not be difficult,
  nor will the truth seem boastful. Let him answer
  and may God's grace appear in the result."
As a pupil who is eager to reply
  to his professor, knowing his subject well,
  and quick to show his excellence—such was I.
"Hope," I said, "is the certain expectation
  of future glory. It is the blessèd fruit
  of grace divine and the good a man has done.
From many stars this light descends to me,
  but it was first distilled into my heart
  by the ultimate singer of Ultimate Majesty.
'Let them hope in Thee,' sang the God-praising poet,
  'whoso doth know Thy name!' And who can feel
  a faith as firm as mine is and not know it?   75
And your epistle sent down once again
  a fresh dew on his dew, till I was full
  and overflowed to others your sweet rain."
While I was speaking thus a luminescence
  trembled within the bosom of that flame,
  sudden and bright as lightning's incandescence.
"Love that still burns in me," I heard it breathe,
  "for that grace that followed even to the palm,
  and till I left the field for happy death,
moves me to speak further. You know the true
  and lasting joy she brings; gladden me, therefore,
  by telling me what hope holds forth to you."
And I: "From Scripture, new and old, descends
  the symbol, and the symbol points me to it.
  All those whom God has chosen as His friends—   90

as Isaiah testifies—they shall be dressed
  in double raiment in their native land;
  and that land is this sweet life with the blest.
And your brother, where he writes so ardently
  of the white robes, sets forth this revelation
  in great detail for all of us to see."
As soon as I had spoken there rang clear
  from overhead, "Let them hope in Thee, O Lord!"
  and the response rang back from all that sphere.
At once within that choir there blazed a ray
  so bright that if the Crab had such a star
  one month of winter would be a single day.
And as a joyous maid will rise and go
  to join the dance, in honor of the bride
  and not for any reasons of vain show, 105
so did that radiant splendor, there above,
  go to the two who danced a joyous reel
  in fit expression of their burning love.
It joined them in the words and melody;
  and like a bride, immovable and silent,
  my Lady kept her eyes fixed on their glory.
"This is he who lies upon the breast
  of Our Pelican; and this is he elected
  from off the cross to make the great behest."
So spoke my Lady, nor, her pose unbroken,
  did she once let her rapt attention stray,
  either before or after she had spoken.
As one who stares, squinting against the light,
  to see the sun enter a partial eclipse,
  and in the act of looking loses his sight— 120
so did I stare at the last flame from that sphere
  until a voice said, "Why do you blind yourself
  trying to see what has no true place here?
My body is earth in earth where it shall be
  one with the rest until our numbers grow
  to fill the quota of eternity.
Only the Two Lamps that are most aglow
  rose to their blessèd cloister doubly clad.
  Explain this to your world when you go below."

And when these words were said the flaming wreath
   broke off the dancing and the sweet accord
   in which it had combined its three-part breath,
as oars that have been striking through the sea
   pause all together when a whistle sounds
   to signal rest or some emergency.   135
Ah, what a surge of feeling swept my mind
   when I turned away an instant from such splendor
   to look at Beatrice, only to find
I could not see her with my dazzled eyes,
though I stood near her and in Paradise!

Canto 26

John assures Dante that Beatrice will
restore his sight. Dante expresses his willingness
to await her will since he knows her to be Love.
John, thereupon, begins the examination of love,
asking Dante to explain how he came into the
possession of love, and what drove him to seek
it. He then asks Dante to describe the intensity
of love and to discuss the sources of love. Dante
concludes with a praise of God as the source
of love. At his words all Heaven responds with
a paean, and immediately Dante's vision is re-
stored. There appears before him a fourth great
splendor which Beatrice identifies as the soul
of Adam. Dante begs Adam to speak and learns
from him the date of Adam's creation, how long
Adam remained in Eden, the cause of God's
wrath, and what language Adam spoke
in his time on earth.

While I stood thus confounded, my light shed,
    out of the dazzling flame that had consumed it
    I heard a breath that called to me, and said:
"Until your eyes once more regain their sense
    of the light you lost in me, it will be well
    for discourse to provide a recompense.
Speak, therefore, starting with the thing that most
    summons your soul to it, and be assured
    your sight is only dazzled and not lost;
for she who guides you through this holy land
    has, in a single turning of her eyes,
    the power that lay in Ananias' hand."
"As she wills, late or soon, let remedy
    come to my eyes," I said, "the gates through which
    she brought the fire that ever burns in me.

"Speak, therefore, starting with the thing that most
summons your soul to it, and be assured
your sight is only dazzled and not lost."

The Good that is this cloister's happiness
    is the Alpha and Omega of the scripture
    love reads to me with light and heavy stress."
The same voice that had soothed my fear away
    when I found suddenly that I could not see
    called me back to the question. I heard it say:
"Surely a finer sieve must sift this through.
    You must explain what made you draw your bow
    at this exalted target—what and who."
And I: "By the arguments of philosophy
    and by authority that descends from here
    such love has clearly stamped its seal upon me.
For the Good, to the extent imperfect sense
    grasps its goodness, kindles love; the brighter
    the more we understand its excellence.   30
To the Essence then in which lies such perfection
    that every good thing not immediate to It
    is nothing more than Its own ray's reflection—
to It, above all else, the mind must move
    once it has seen the truth that is the proof
    and argument that so compels man's love.
That truth he first made evident to me
    whose proofs set forth the First Cause and First Love
    of every sempiternal entity.
It was proved by the True Maker's voice sent forth
    to Moses when It said, meaning Itself,
    'I shall cause you to see a vision of all worth.'
And proved by you in the high proclamation
    that cries to earth the secrets of this heaven
    more clearly than any other revelation."   45
And I heard: "As human reason and Holy Writ
    in harmony have urged you, keep for God
    the first, most sovereign passion of your spirit.
But tell me if you feel yet other ties
    bind you to Him. Say with how many teeth
    this love consumes you." So in Paradise
Christ's Eagle spoke his sacred purpose whole,
    concealing nothing; rather, urging me
    to make a full profession of my soul.

I therefore: "All those teeth with power enough
    to turn the heart of any man to God
    have joined in my heart, turning it to Love.
The existence of the world, and my own, too;
    the death He took on Himself that I might live;
    and what all believers hope for as I do—   60
these and the living knowledge mentioned before
    have saved me from the ocean of false love
    and placed me by the true, safe on the shore.
The leaves that green the Eternal Garden's grove
    I love to the degree that each receives
    the dew and ray of His all flowering love."
The instant I fell still, my love professed,
    all Heaven rang with "Holy! Holy! Holy!"
    my Lady joining with the other blest.
As bright light shatters sleep, the man being bid
    to waken by the visual spirit running
    to meet the radiance piercing lid by lid,
and the man so roused does not know what he sees,
    his wits confounded by the sudden waking,
    till he once more regains his faculties—   75
so from my eyes, my Lady's eyes, whose ray
    was visible from a thousand miles and more,
    drove every last impediment away;
in consequence of which I found my sight
    was clearer than before, and half astonished
    I questioned her about a fourth great light
near us; and she: "In that ray's Paradise
    the first soul from the hand of the First Power
    turns ever to its Maker its glad eyes."
As a bough that bends its crown to the wind's course,
    and then, after the blow, rises again
    uplifted by its own internal force—
so did I as she spoke, all tremulous;
    then calmed again, assured by a desire
    to speak that burned in me, beginning thus: 90
"O first and only fruit earth ever saw
    spring forth full ripe; O primal sire, to whom
    all brides are equally daughters and daughters-in-law;

speak, I beg, devoutly as I may.
    You know my wish. To hear you speak the sooner
    I leave unsaid what there is no need to say."
An animal, were it covered with a shawl
    and moved beneath it, would reveal its motion
    by the way in which the cloth would rise and fall;
in the same way, that first soul let me see
    through the motion of its covering, with what joy
    it moved in Heaven to bring joy to me.
Then breathed forth: "Without any need to hear
    what you would say, I know your wish more surely
    than you know what you take to be most clear.   105
I see it in the True Mirror, Itself the perfect
    reflector of all things in Its creation,
    which nothing in creation can reflect.
You wish to know how many years it is
    since God created me in the high garden
    where she prepared you for these stairs to bliss;
and how long my eyes enjoyed the good they prized;
    and the true reason for the great rejection;
    and the tongue I spoke, which I myself devised.
Know, my son, that eating from the tree
    was not itself the cause of such long exile,
    but only the violation of God's decree.
Longing to join this company, my shade
    counted four thousand three hundred and two suns
    where your Lady summoned Virgil to your aid.   120
And circling all its signs, I saw it go
    nine hundred and thirty times around its track
    during the time I was a man below.
The tongue I spoke had vanished utterly
    long before Nimrod's people turned their hands
    to the work beyond their capability,
for nothing of the mind is beyond change;
    man's inclination answers to the stars
    and ranges as the starry courses range.
That man should speak is nature's own behest;
    but that you speak in this way or in that
    nature lets you decide as you think best.

Till I went down to the agony of Hell
    the Supreme Good whose rays send down the joy
    that wraps me here was known on earth as *EL*;   135
and then was known as *JAH*; and it must be so,
    for the usage of mankind is like a leaf
    that falls from the branch to let another grow.
On the peak that rises highest, my total stay,
    in innocence and later in disgrace,
    was from the first bright hour of my first day,
to the hour after the sixth, at which the sun
changed quadrant, being then at meridian."

Canto 27

*St. Peter grows red with righteous indig-
nation and utters a denunciation of papal corruption. All Heaven darkens at the thought of such
evil. Peter's charge, of course, is that the Papacy
has become acquisitive, political, and therefore
bloody. Having so catalogued the crimes of the
bad Popes, Peter specifically charges Dante to repeat among mankind the wrath that was spoken
in Heaven. The triumphant court soars away, and
Dante is left with Beatrice who tells him to look
down. Dante finds he is standing above a point
midway between Jerusalem and Spain, and, having seen earth (and all its vaunted pomps) as
an insignificant mote in space, Dante once more
turns his thoughts upward as Beatrice leads him
in the ascent to the Primum Mobile, discoursing en route on the nature of time, which has
its source in the Primum Mobile. The time of
earth's corruption, Beatrice tells Dante,
is drawing to a close.*

"Glory to the Father, the Son, and the Holy Ghost"—
  a strain so sweet that I grew drunk with it
  rang from the full choir of the Heavenly Host.
I seemed to see the universe alight
  with a single smile; and thus my drunkenness
  came on me through my hearing and my sight.
O joy! O blessedness no tongue can speak!
  O life conjoint of perfect love and peace!
  O sure wealth that has nothing more to seek!
The four great torches were still burning there,
  and the one that had descended to me first
  began to outshine all else in that sphere.

"Glory to the Father, the Son, and the Holy Ghost"—
a strain so sweet that I grew drunk with it
rang from the full choir of the Heavenly Host.

Paradiso

As Jupiter might appear if it and Mars
    were birds and could exchange their glowing plumes—
    such it became among the other stars.   15
The Providence that assigns to Heaven's band
    the offices and services of each
    had imposed silence there on every hand
when I heard: "You need not wonder that I change hue,
    for as I utter what I have to say
    you shall see all these beings change theirs, too.
The usurper of the throne given to me,
    to me, to me, there on the earth that now
    before the Son of God stands vacant, he
has made a sewer of my sepulcher, a flow
    of blood and stink at which the treacherous one
    who fell from here may chuckle there below."
With the same color I have seen clouds turn
    when opposite the rising or setting sun,
    I saw the sweet face of all Heaven burn.   30
And as a modest lady whose pure bearing
    is self-secure, may blush at another's failings,
    though they be only mentioned in her hearing—
so Beatrice changed complexion at a breath,
    and such eclipse came over Heaven then
    as when Supreme Might suffered mankind's death.
Then he continued speaking as before,
    his voice so changed, so charged with indignation
    that his appearance could not darken more:
"The Bride of Christ was not suckled of old
    on blood of mine, of Linus, and of Cletus
    to be reared as an instrument for grabbing gold.
It was to win this life of blessedness
    Sixtus, and Pius, and Calixtus, and Urban
    let flow the blood and tears of their distress.   45
We never meant that men of Christian life
    should sit part on the right, part on the left
    of our successors, steeled for bloody strife.
Nor that the keys consigned into my hand
    should fly as emblems from a flag unfurled
    against the baptized in a Christian land.

517

Nor that my head should, in a later age,
    seal privilege sold to liars. The very thought
    has often made me burn with holy rage!
From here in every pasture, fold, and hill
    we see wolves dressed as shepherds. O hand of God,
    mankind's defender, why do you yet lie still?
Gascons and Cahorsines are crouched to drink
    our very blood. O excellent beginning,
    to what foulest conclusion will you sink?   60
Yet the high Providence that stood with Rome
    and Scipio for the glory of the world
    will once again, and soon, be seen to come.
You, son, who must yet bear around earth's track
    your mortal weight, open your mouth down there;
    do not hold back what I have not held back!"
Just as the frozen vaporings sift down
    out of our earthly atmosphere when the horn
    of heaven's Goat is burnished by the sun—
just so, up there, I saw the ether glow
    with a rising snow of the triumphant vapors
    who had remained awhile with us below.
My eyes followed their traces toward the height,
    followed until the airy medium
    closed its vast distance on my upward sight;   75
at which my Lady, seeing me absolved
    from service to the height, said: "Now look down
    and see how far the heavens have revolved."
I looked down once again. Since the last time,
    I had been borne, I saw, a length of arc
    equal to half the span of the first clime;
so that I saw past Cadiz the mad route
    Ulysses took; and almost to the shore
    from which Europa rode the godly brute.
And yet more of this little threshing floor
    would have been visible but, below my foot,
    the sun was ahead of me by a sign and more.
My mind, which ever found its Paradise
    in thinking of my Lady, now more than ever
    burned with desire to look into her eyes.   90

Paradiso

If nature or art ever contrived a lure
  to catch the eye and thus possess the mind,
  whether in living flesh or portraiture,
all charms united could not move a pace
  toward the divine delight with which I glowed
  when I looked once more on her smiling face.
In one look then I felt my spirit given
  a power that plucked it out of Leda's nest
  and sent it soaring to the swiftest heaven.
From its upper and lower limits to its center
  it is so uniform, I cannot say
  what point my Lady chose for me to enter.
But she, knowing what yearning burned in me,
  began thus—with so rapturous a smile
  God seemed to shine forth from her ecstasy: 105
"The order of the universe, whose nature
  holds firm the center and spins all else around it,
  takes from this heaven its first point of departure.
This heaven does not exist in any place
  but in God's mind, where burns the love that turns it
  and the power that rains to it from all of space.
Light and Love contain it in one band
  as it does all the rest; and such containment
  only the Cunctitenant can understand.
Its own motion unfactored, all things derive
  their motions from this heaven as precisely
  as ten is factored into two and five.
So may you understand how time's taproot
  is hidden in this sphere's urn, while in the others
  we see its spreading foliage and its fruit.   120
O greed that has drawn down all Adam's blood
  so deep into its dark that none has strength
  to raise his eyes above its evil flood!
The will of man comes well to its first flower,
  but then the rain that sets in endlessly
  blights the good fruit and leaves it green and sour.
Faith and innocence are found nowhere
  except in little children; and both have fled
  before their cheeks have sprouted a first hair.

519

Still young enough to lisp, one fasts and prays;
   then, his tongue freed, devours all sorts of food
   even in Lent, even on fasting days.
Another will love his mother and behave
   while yet a lisper, who, with his freed speech
   will be impatient to see her in her grave.   135
So the fair daughter of Him who leaves us night
   and brings us morning, changes her complexion,
   and her white skin turns black in Heaven's sight.
Consider, if you marvel at what I say,
   how there is none to govern on the earth,
   whereby the human family goes astray.
But before January falls in spring
   because of that odd day in each hundred years
   that all neglect down there, these spheres shall ring
so loud with portents of a season's turn
   that the long awaited storm will sweep the fleet,
   blowing the bows around to dead astern
and set the true course straight. Then all shall see
first blossom turn to good fruit on the tree."

Canto 28

*Dante turns from Beatrice and beholds a
vision of God as a nondimensional Point of Light
ringed by nine glowing spheres representing the
Angel Hierarchy. Dante is puzzled because the
vision seems to reverse the order of the universe,
the highest rank of the angels being at the center
and represented by the smallest sphere. Beatrice
explains the mystery and then catalogues
the Orders of the Angels.*

When she whose powers imparadise my mind
    had so denounced and laid bare the whole truth
    of the present state of miserable mankind;
just as a man before a glass can see
    a torch that burns behind him and know it is there
    before he has seen or thought of it directly;
and turns to see if what the glass has shown
    is really there; and finds, as closely matched
    as words to music, the fact to its reflection;
just so, as I recall, did I first stare
    into the heaven of those precious eyes
    in which, to trap me, Love had set his snare;
then turned, and turning felt my senses reel
    as my own were struck by what shines in that heaven
    when we look closely at its turning wheel.   15
I saw a Point that radiated light
    of such intensity that the eye it strikes
    must close or ever after lose its sight.

The star that seems the smallest, seen from here,
   would seem a moon, were it placed next to this,
   as often we see star by star appear.
And at about the distance that a halo
   surrounds a heavenly radiance that paints it
   on the densest mist that will yet let it show—
so close around the Point, a ring of fire
   spun faster than the fastest of the spheres
   circles creation in its endless gyre.
Another surrounded this, and was surrounded
   by a third, the third by a fourth, the fourth
   by a fifth, and by a sixth the fifth, in turn, was bounded.   30
The seventh followed, already spread so wide
   that were Juno's messenger to be made complete
   she could not stretch her arc from side to side.
And so the eighth and the ninth, and each ring spun
   with an ever slower motion as its number
   placed it the further out from the first one,
which gave forth the most brilliant incandescence
   because, I think, being nearest the Scintilla,
   it drew the fullest share of the True Essence.
I was on tenterhooks, as my Lady saw.
   To ease my mind she said: "From that one Point
   are hung the heavens and all nature's law.
Look at the closest ring. I would have you know
   it spins so fast by virtue of Love's fire,
   the ray of which pierces it through and through."   45
And I to her: "Were the ordering we find
   in the universe like that of these bright wheels,
   what I have seen would satisfy my mind.
But in the sensible universe one can see
   the motions of the spheres become more God-like
   the nearer they are to the periphery.
If there is food for my soul's appetite
   in this most glorious and angelic temple
   whose only boundaries are love and light,
you must explain why it has been so planned
   that the form and the exemplum are at odds;
   for by myself I cannot understand."

"It is small wonder such a knot defies
    your fingers, for since none has ever tried it,
    the coils have set together like a vise."   60
So spoke my Lady, going on to say:
    "If you would understand, grasp what I tell you,
    and around it give your mind's best powers full play.
The physical spheres are graduated in size
    according to the power that infuses each
    and fixes it to its station in the skies.
The greater good intends a greater grace.
    A greater body can hold more of good
    if all its parts are perfect, as in this case.
This sphere, then, that spins with it as it goes
    all of the universe, must correspond
    to the angel sphere that most loves and most knows.
If you will measure not by what appears
    but by the power inherent in these beings
    that manifest themselves to you as spheres,   75
you will observe a marvelous correspondence
    of greater power to larger, and lesser to smaller,
    between each heaven and its Intelligence."
As the airy hemisphere serenes and glows,
    cloudless and blue into its furthest reach,
    when from his gentler cheek Boreas blows,
purging and dissolving with that breeze
    the turbulent vapors, so that Heaven smiles
    with the beauty of its every diocese—
so was it in my mind, once I was given
    my Lady's clear reply; and I saw the truth
    shining before me like a star in Heaven.
And at her last word every angel sphere
    began to sparkle as iron, when it is melted
    in a crucible, is seen to do down here.   90
And every spark spun with its spinning ring;
    and they were numberless as the sum of grain
    on the last square of the chessboard of the king.
From choir to choir their hymn of praise rang free
    to the Fixed Point that holds them in fixed place,
    as ever was, as evermore shall be.

And at her last word every angel sphere
  began to sparkle as iron, when it is melted
  in a crucible, is seen to do down here.

And she who felt uncertainty bedim
  my dazzled mind explained: "The first two circles
  have shown you the Seraphim and Cherubim.
Being led, they chase the reins in their eagerness
  to resemble the Point the more, and they can the more
  the more they look upon Its blessedness.
The beings in the next bright wheel you see
  are titled Thrones of the Eternal Aspect;
  and they complete the first great trinity.   105
And know that all these raptures are fulfilled
  to the degree that each can penetrate
  the Truth in which all questioning is stilled.
Hence one may see that the most blest condition
  is based on the act of seeing, not of love,
  love being the act that follows recognition.
They see as they are worthy; they arc made
  to their degrees by grace and their own goodwill;
  and so their ranks proceed from grade to grade.
The second trinity that blossoms here
  in this eternal springtime of delight
  whose leaves nocturnal Aries does not sear,
warble 'Hosanna!' everlastingly,
  and their three melodies sound the three degrees
  of blessedness that form this trinity.   120
These are the divinities therein found:
  Dominations first, then Virtues, then, in order,
  the ranks of Powers within the widest round.
In the next two dances of this exaltation
  whirl Principalities first, then the Archangels.
  The last contains the Angelic jubilation.
All fix their eyes on high and as their sight
  ascends their power descends to all below.
  So are all drawn, as all draw, to God's height.
Dionysius gave himself to contemplation
  of these same orders with such holy zeal
  that he named and ranked them just as I have done.
Gregory, later, differed with his conclusions;
  but hardly had he wakened in this heaven
  then he was moved to laugh at his own delusions.   135

525

And if a truth so hidden was made clear
  by one still in the weight of mortal dust,
   you need not wonder; one who saw it here
returned and told him this—this and much more
of the bright truth these circles hold in store."

Canto 29

Beatrice, gazing on God, sees Dante's unspoken questions and explains to him God's intent in willing the creation, the eternity of God, and the simultaneity of creation. She then explains the time from the creation to the revolt of the angels, how the loving angels began their blissful art, and that grace is received according to the ardor of love. She denounces foolish teachings and concludes by pointing out the infinity and the distinction of the angels.

When Latona's twins, one setting in the sign
   of Aries and the other rising in Libra,
   are belted by the same horizon's line;
as long then as the zenith's fulcrum bears
   their perfect balance, till one and other leave
   their common belt and change their hemispheres—
so long did Beatrice, smiling her delight,
   stay silent, her eyes fixed on the Fixed Point
   whose power had overcome me at first sight.
Then she began: "I do not ask, I say
   what you most wish to hear, for I have seen it
   where time and space are focused in one ray.
Not to increase Its good—no mil nor dram
   can add to true perfection, but that reflections
   of His reflection might declare 'I am'—
in His eternity, beyond time, above
   all other comprehension, as it pleased Him,
   new loves were born of the Eternal Love.
Nor did He lie asleep before the Word
   sounded above these waters; 'before' and 'after'
   did not exist until His voice was heard.

15

Pure essence, and pure matter, and the two
  joined into one were shot forth without flaw,
  like three bright arrows from a three-string bow.
And as in glass, in amber, or in crystal
  a ray shines so that nothing intervenes
  between its coming and being, which is total—
so the threefold effect rayed from its Sire
  into created being, without beginning
  and without interval, instantly entire.   30
Order was the co-created fact
  of every essence; and at the peak of all,
  these angel loves created as pure act.
Pure potential held the lowest ground;
  between, potential-and-act were tied together
  so tight they nevermore shall be unbound.
Hieronymus wrote to you of the long span
  of centuries in which such beings existed
  before the other world was made for man;
but the Scribes of the Holy Ghost clearly declare
  the true account in many passages,
  as you will see if you will read with care.
It can, in part, be grasped by intellection,
  which cannot grant such powers could long exist
  apart from the functioning of their perfection.   45
This much will answer where, and when, and how
  the angels were created; and so are quenched
  the first three flames of your desire to know.
Nor could you count to ten and ten before
  some of those angels fell from Heaven to roil
  the bedrock of the elemental core.
The rest remained here and around their Cause
  began the art you see, moved by such bliss
  that their glad revolutions never pause.
It was accursèd pride for which they fell,
  the pride of that dark principal you saw
  crushed by the world's whole weight in deepest Hell.
These you see here were humble, undemanding,
  and prompt in their acknowledgment of the Good
  that made them capable of such understanding;   60

whereby their vision was exalted higher
  by illuminating grace and their own merit,
  in which their wills are changeless and entire.
Now hear this and, beyond all doubt, believe it;
  the good of grace is in exact proportion
  to the ardor of love that opens to receive it.
And now, if you have heeded what I said,
  you should be able to observe this college
  and gather much more without further aid.
But since your earthly schoolmen argue still
  that the angelic nature is composed
  of understanding, memory, and will,
I will say this much more to help you see
  the truth that is confounded there below
  by the equivocations of sophistry;   75
these beings, since their first bliss in the sight
  of God's face, in which all things are revealed,
  have never turned their eyes from their delight.
No angel's eye, it follows, can be caught
  by a new object; hence, they have no need
  of memory, as does divided thought.
So men, awake but dreaming, dare to claim,
  believing it or not, they speak the truth—
  though the hypocrite's is the greater sin and shame.
You mortals do not walk a single way
  in your philosophies, but let the thought
  of being acclaimed as wise lead you astray.
Yet, Heaven bears even this with less offense
  than it must feel when it sees Holy Writ
  neglected or perverted of all sense.   90
They do not count what blood and agony
  planted it in the world, nor Heaven's pleasure
  in those who search it in humility.
Each man, to show off, strains at some absurd
  invented truth; and it is these the preachers
  make sermons of; and the Gospel is not heard.
One says the moon reversed its course to throw
  a shadow on the sun during Christ's passion
  so that its light might not shine down below;

others say that the sun itself withdrew
  and, therefore, that the Indian and the Spaniard
  shared the eclipse in common with the Jew.
These fables pour from pulpits in such torrents,
  spewing to right and left, that in a year
  they outnumber the Lapi and Bindi in all Florence. 105
Therefore the ignorant sheep turn home at night
  from having fed on wind. Nor does the fact
  that the pastor sees no harm done set things right.
Christ did not say to His first congregation:
  'Go and preach twaddle to the waiting world.'
  He gave them, rather, Holy Truth's foundation.
That, and that only, was the truth revealed
  by those who fought and died to plant the Faith.
  They made the Gospel both their sword and shield.
Now preachers make the congregation roar
  with quips and quirks, and so it laugh enough,
  their hoods swell, and they ask for nothing more.
But in their tippets there nests such a bird
  that the people, could they see it, would soon know
  what faith to place in pardons thus conferred. 120
Because of these such folly fills the earth
  that, asking neither proof nor testimonials,
  men chase whatever promise is held forth.
On such St. Anthony's pig feeds on, unstinted,
  and others yet more swinish feast and guzzle
  and pay their way with money never minted.
But we have strayed. Therefore before we climb
  turn your attention back to the straight path
  that we may fit our journey to our time.
So many beings are ranked within this nature
  that the number of their hosts cannot be said
  nor even imagined by a mortal creature.
Read well what Daniel saw at Heaven's height.
  You will soon see that when he speaks of 'thousands'
  every finite number is lost from sight. 135
To all, the Primal Light sends down Its ray.
  And every splendor into which It enters
  receives that radiance in its own way.

Paradiso

Therefore, since the act of loving grows
    from the act of recognition, the bliss of love
    blazes in some of these, and in some it glows.
Consider then how lofty and how wide
    is the excellence of the Eternal Worth
    which in so many mirrors can divide
Its power and majesty forevermore,
Itself remaining One, as It was before."

Canto 30

The great theme is drawing to a close.
Here is the Empyrean; Beatrice is at last at home,
her beauty made perfect; and Dante utters a lofty
praise of Beatrice. Beatrice promises Dante a vi-
sion of both Hosts of Paradise. He is blinded by a
new radiance, hears a voice announce that he
shall be given new powers, and immediately sees
a vision of a River of Light. As in the Earthly Para-
dise, he is commanded to drink. With his face sub-
merged in the water, his vision grows circular
and re-forms as a vision of the Mystic Rose.

When, as may be, the sun's noon heat is shed
 six thousand miles away, while, where we are,
 earth's shadow makes an almost level bed;
when, at our zenith, the sky begins to show
 such changes that a star or two begins
 to fade from the eyes of watchers here below;
and as the sun's most radiant serving maid
 comes nearer yet, and heaven puts out its lamps
 one by one, till the loveliest, too, must fade—
just so that Triumph that forever races
 around the blinding ray of the Fixed Point
 that seems embraced by what Itself embraces,
faded from sight, degree by slow degree;
 at which I turned my eyes from the lost vision
 to Beatrice, as love commanded me.
If all that I have said of her below
 were gathered now into a single paean,
 that would be scant praise of her beauty now.
The beauty I saw there transcends all measure
 of mortal minds. I think only her Maker
 can wholly comprehend so great a treasure.

15

Paradiso

Here I concede defeat. No poet known,
  comic or tragic, challenged by his theme
  to show his power, was ever more outdone.
As feeblest eyes, struck by the sun, go blind,
  so the remembrance of my Lady's smile
  strikes every recognition from my mind.
From the first day I looked upon her face
  in this life, to this present sight of her,
  my song has followed her to sing her praise.   30
But here I must no longer even try
  to walk behind her beauty. Every artist,
  his utmost done, must put his brushes by.
So do I leave her to a clarion
  of greater note than mine, which starts to draw
  its long and arduous theme to a conclusion.
She, like a guide who has his goal in sight,
  began to speak again: "We have ascended
  from the greatest sphere to the heaven of pure light.
Light of the intellect, which is love unending;
  love of the true good, which is wholly bliss—
  bliss beyond bliss, all other joys transcending.
Here shall you see both hosts of Paradise,
  one of them in the aspect you shall see
  when you return the day all bodies rise."   45
As a flash of lightning striking on our sight
  destroys our visual spirits, so that the eye
  cannot make out even a brighter light—
just so, an aureole burst all about me,
  swathing me so completely in its veil
  that I was closed in light and could not see.
"The Love that keeps this Heaven ever the same
  greets all who enter with such salutation,
  and thus prepares the candle for His flame."
No sooner had these few words penetrated
  my hearing than I felt my powers increase
  beyond themselves; transcendent and elated,
my eyes were lit with such new-given sight
  that they were fit to look without distress
  on any radiance, however bright.   60

I saw a light that was a river flowing
   light within light between enameled banks
   painted with blossoms of miraculous spring;
and from the river as it glowed and rolled
   live sparks shot forth to settle on the flowers.
   They seemed like rubies set in bands of gold;
and then, as if the fragrance overthrew
   their senses, they dove back into the river;
   and as one dove in there, out another flew.
"The flame of high desire that makes you yearn
   for greater knowledge of these things you see
   pleases me more the more I see it burn.
But only this same water satisfies
   such thirst as yours. You must bend down and drink."
   So spoke the sun and pole-star of my eyes,   75
and added: "The river and the jewels you see
   dart in and out of it, and the smiling flowers
   are dim foretastes of their reality.
Not that these fruits are in their natures tart
   and unformed, but that you still lack the vision
   of such high things. The defect is on your part."
No babe in arms that ever wakened hungry
   from having slept too long could turn its face
   to its dear mother's milk more eagerly
than I bent down to drink in Paradise
   of the sweet stream that flows its grace to us,
   so to make better mirrors of our eyes.
No sooner were my eyes' eaves sweetly drowned
   in that bright stream to drink, than it appeared
   to widen and change form till it was round.   90
I have seen masqueraders here below
   shed the disguises that had hidden them
   and show their true appearances. Just so,
the sparks and spring flowers changed before my eyes
   into a greater festival, and I saw
   the vision of both courts of Paradise.
O splendor of God eternal through which I saw
   the supreme triumph of the one True Kingdom,
   grant me the power to speak forth what I saw!

Paradiso

There in Heaven, a lamp shines in whose light
   the Creator is made visible to His creature,
   whose one peace lies in having Him in sight.
That lamp forms an enormous circle, such
   that its circumference, fitted to the sun
   as a bright belt, would be too large by much.   105
It is made up entirely of the reflection.
   of rays that strike the top of the first-moved sphere,
   imparting to it all its power and motion.
And as a slope shines in the looking glass
   of a lake below it, as if to see itself
   in its time of brightest flower and greenest grass—
so, tier on tier, mounting within that light,
   there glowed, reflected in more than a thousand circles,
   all those who had won return to Heaven's height.
And if so vast a nimbus can be bound
   within its lowest tier, what then must be
   the measure of this rose at its topmost round?
Nor were my eyes confounded by that sea
   and altitude of space, but took in all,
   both number and quality, of that ecstasy.   120
There, far and near cause neither loss nor gain,
   for where God rules directly, without agents,
   the laws that govern nature do not pertain.
Into the gold of the rose that blooms eternal,
   rank on rank, in incenses of praise
   it sends up to the Sun forever vernal—
I, yearning to speak and silent—Beatrice drew me
   and said: "Now see how many are in the convent
   of the white robes. Behold our far-flung city.
And see the benches—every one a throne—
   how every rank of them is filled so full
   but few are wanted before all is done.
That great throne with the crown already set
   above it draws your eyes. To it shall come—
   before your own call to this nuptial banquet—   135
the soul, already anointed, of Henry the Great,
   who will come to Italy to bring law and order
   before the time is ripe to set things straight.

Tranced in blind greed, your ever deepening curse,
  you have become as mindless as an infant
  who screams with hunger, yet pushes away his nurse.
The prefect of the holy court will be
  a man who will profess his cause in public
  while working to defeat it secretly.
But after that God will not long permit
  his simony; he shall be stuffed away
  where Simon Magus, headfirst in the pit,
pays for his guilt. There, paying for his own,
he shall force the guilt of Alagna further down."

Canto 31

*The Second Soldiery of the Church Tri-
umphant is the Angel Host. Dante now receives a
vision of them as a swarm of bees in eternal transit between God and the Rose. Dante turns from
that rapturous vision to speak to Beatrice and
finds in her place a reverend Elder. It is St. Bernard, who will serve as Dante's guide to the ultimate vision of God. Bernard shows Dante his last
vision of Beatrice, who has resumed her throne
among the blessed. Across the vastness of Paradise, Dante sends his soul's prayer of thanks to
her. Beatrice smiles down at Dante a last time,
then turns her eyes forever to the Eternal Fountain
of God. Bernard, the most faithful of the worship-
ers of the Virgin, promises Dante the final vision
of God through her intercession. Accordingly, he
instructs Dante to raise his eyes to her throne.
Dante obeys and burns with bliss at
the vision of her splendor.*

Then, in the form of a white rose, the host
   of the sacred soldiery appeared to me,
   all those whom Christ in His own blood espoused.
But the other host (who soar, singing and seeing
   His glory, who to will them to His love
   made them so many in such blissful being,
like a swarm of bees, who in one motion dive
   into the flowers and in the next return
   the sweetness of their labors to the hive)
flew ceaselessly to the many-petaled rose
   and ceaselessly returned into that light
   in which their ceaseless love has its repose.

Then, in the form of a white rose, the host
of the sacred soldiery appeared to me,
all those whom Christ in his own blood espoused.

Like living flame their faces seemed to glow.
    Their wings were gold. And all their bodies shone
    more dazzling white than any earthly snow.   15
On entering the great flower they spread about them,
    from tier to tier, the ardor and the peace
    they had acquired in flying close to Him.
Nor did so great a multitude in flight
    between the white rose and what lies above it
    block in the least the glory of that light;
for throughout all the universe God's ray
    enters all things according to their merit,
    and nothing has the power to block its way.
This realm of ancient bliss shone, soul on soul,
    with new and ancient beings, and every eye
    and every love was fixed upon one goal.
O Threefold Light which, blazoned in one star,
    can so content their vision with your shining,
    look down upon us in the storm we are!   30
If the barbarians (coming from that zone
    above which Helice travels every day
    wheeling in heaven with her beloved son)
looking at Rome were stupefied to see
    her works in those days when the Lateran
    outshone all else built by humanity;
what did I feel on reaching such a goal
    from human to blest, from time to eternity,
    from Florence to a people just and whole—
by what amazement was I overcome?
    Between my stupor and my new-found joy
    my bliss was to hear nothing and be dumb.
And as a pilgrim at the shrine of his vow
    stares, feels himself reborn, and thinks already
    how he may later describe it—just so, now   45
I stood and let my eyes go wandering out
    into that radiance from rank to rank,
    now up, now down, now sweeping round about.
I saw faces that compelled love's charity
    lit by Another's lamp and their own smiles,
    and gestures graced by every dignity.

Without having fixed on any part, my eyes
   already had taken in and understood
   the form and general plan of Paradise;
and—my desire rekindled—I wheeled about
   to question my sweet Lady on certain matters
   concerning which my mind was still in doubt.
One thing I expected; another greeted me.
   I thought to find Beatrice there; I found instead
   an Elder in the robes of those in glory.   60
His eyes and cheeks were bathed in the holy glow
   of loving bliss; his gestures, pious grace.
   He seemed a tender father standing so.
"She—where is she?" I cried in sudden dread.
   "To lead you to the goal of all your wish
   Beatrice called me from my place," he said,
"and if you raise your eyes you still may find her
   in the third circle down from the highest rank
   upon the throne her merit has assigned her."
Without reply I looked up to that height
   and saw her draw an aureole round herself
   as she reflected the Eternal Light.
No mortal eye, though plunged to the last bounds
   of the deepest sea, has ever been so far
   from the topmost heaven to which the thunder sounds   75
as I was then from Beatrice; but there
   the distance did not matter, for her image
   reached me unblurred by any atmosphere.
"O Lady in whom my hope shall ever soar
   and who for my salvation suffered even
   to set your feet upon Hell's broken floor;
through your power and your excellence alone
   have I recognized the goodness and the grace
   inherent in the things I have been shown.
You have led me from my bondage and set me free
   by all those roads, by all those loving means
   that lay within your power and charity.
Grant me your magnificence that my soul,
   which you have healed, may please you when it slips
   the bonds of flesh and rises to its goal."   90

Such was my prayer, and she—far up a mountain,
  as it appeared to me—looked down and smiled.
  Then she turned back to the Eternal Fountain.
And the holy Elder said: "I have been sent
  by prayer and sacred love to help you reach
  the perfect consummation of your ascent.
Look round this garden, therefore, that you may
  be gazing at its radiance, be prepared
  to lift your eyes up to the Trinal Ray.
The Queen of Heaven, for whom in whole devotion
  I burn with love, will grant us every grace
  because I am Bernard, her faithful one."
As a stranger from afar—a Croat, if you will—
  comes to see our Veronica and, awed
  by its ancient fame, can never look his fill,   105
but says to himself as long as it is displayed:
  "My Lord, Jesus Christ, true God, and is this then
  the likeness of Thy living flesh portrayed?"—
just so did I gaze on the living love
  of him who in this world, through contemplation,
  tasted the peace which ever dwells above.
"Dear son of Grace," he said, "you cannot know
  this state of bliss while you yet keep your eyes
  fixed only on those things that lie below;
rather, let your eyes mount to the last round
  where you shall see the Queen to whom this realm
  is subject and devoted, throned and crowned."
I looked up. By as much as the horizon
  to eastward in the glory of full dawn
  outshines the point at which the sun went down,   120
by so much did one region on the height
  to which I raised my eyes out of the valley
  outshine the rays of every other light.
And as the sky is brightest in that region
  where we on earth expect to see the shaft
  of the chariot so badly steered by Phaeton,
while to one side and the other it grows dim—
  just so, that peaceful oriflamme lit the center
  and faded equally along either rim.

541

And in the center, great wings spread apart,
   more than a thousand festive angels shone,
   each one distinct in radiance and in art.
I saw there, smiling at this song and sport,
   she whose beauty entered like a bliss
   into the eyes of all that sainted court.   135
And even could my speech match my conception,
   yet I would not dare make the least attempt
   to draw her delectation and perfection.
Bernard, seeing my eyes so fixed and burning
   with passion on his passion, turned his own
   up to that height with so much love and yearning
that the example of his ardor sent
new fire through me, making my gaze more ardent.

Canto 32

His eyes fixed blissfully on the vision of
the Virgin Mary, Bernard recites the orders of the
Mystic Rose, identifying the thrones of the most
blessed. Mary's throne is on the topmost tier of
the Heavenly Stadium. Directly across from it
rises the throne of John the Baptist. From her
throne to the central arena (the yellow of the
Rose) descends a line of Christian saints. These
two radii form a diameter that divides the sta-
dium. On one side are throned those who believe
in Christ to Come; on the other, those who be-
lieved in Christ Descended. The lower half of the
Rose contains, on one side, the pre-Christian chil-
dren saved by Love, and on the other, the Chris-
tian children saved by Baptism. Through all these
explanations, Bernard has kept his eyes fixed
in adoration upon the Virgin. Having finished
his preliminary instruction of Dante, Bernard
now calls on him to join in a
prayer to the Virgin.

Still rapt in contemplation, the sainted seer
    assumed the vacant office of instruction,
    beginning with these words I still can hear:
"The wound that Mary healed with balm so sweet
    was first dealt and then deepened by that being
    who sits in such great beauty at her feet.
Below her, in the circle sanctified
    by the third rank of loves, Rachel is throned
    with Beatrice, as you see, there at her side.
Sarah and Rebecca and Judith and she
    who was the great-grandmother of the singer
    who for his sins cried, 'Lord, have mercy on me!'—

as I go down the great ranks tier by tier,
    naming them for you in descending order,
    petal by petal, you shall see them clear.   15
And down from the seventh, continuing from those
    in the first six tiers, a line of Hebrew women
    forms a part in the tresses of the rose.
Arranged to form a wall thus, they divide
    all ranks according to the view of Christ
    that marked the faith of those on either side.
On this side, where the flower is in full bloom
    to its last petal, are arranged all those
    whose faith was founded upon Christ to Come;
on that, where the half circles show the unblended
    gaps of empty seats, are seated those
    whose living faith was fixed on Christ Descended.
And as, on this side, the resplendent throne
    of Heaven's Lady, with the thrones below it,
    establishes the line of that division;   30
so, facing hers, does the throned blessedness
    of the great John who, ever holy, bore
    the desert, martyrdom, and Hell's distress;
and under him, forming that line are found
    Francis, Benedict, Augustine, and others
    descending to this center round by round.
Now marvel at all-foreseeing profundity:
    this garden shall be complete when the two aspects
    of the one faith have filled it equally.
And know that below that tier that cuts the two
    dividing walls at their centerpoint, no being
    has won his seat of glory by his own virtue,
but by another's, under strict condition;
    for all of these were spirits loosed from flesh
    before they had matured to true volition.   45
You can yourself make out their infant graces;
    you need no more than listen to their treble
    and look attentively into their faces.
You do not speak now; many doubts confound you.
    Therefore, to set you free I shall untie
    the cords in which your subtle thoughts have bound you.

Infinite order rules in this domain.
   Mere accidence can no more enter in
   than hunger can, or thirst, or grief, or pain.
All you see here is fixed by the decree
   of the eternal law, and is so made
   that the ring goes on the finger perfectly.
These, it follows, who had so short a pause
   in the lower life are not ranked higher or lower
   among themselves without sufficient cause.   60
The King in whom this realm abides unchanging
   in so much love and bliss that none dares will
   increase of joy, creating and arranging
the minds of all in the glad Paradise
   of His own sight, grants them degrees of grace
   as He sees fit. Here let the effect suffice.
Holy Scripture clearly and expressly
   notes this effect upon those twins who fought
   while still within their mother. So we see
how the Supreme Light fittingly makes fair
   Its aureole by granting them their graces
   according to the color of their hair.
Thus through no merit of their works and days
   they are assigned their varying degrees
   by variance only in original grace.   75
In the first centuries of man's creation
   their innocence and the true faith of their parents
   was all they needed to achieve salvation.
When the first age of man had run its course,
   then circumcision was required of males,
   to give their innocent wings sufficient force.
But when the Age of Grace came to mankind
   then, unless perfectly baptized in Christ,
   such innocents went down among the blind.
Look now on her who most resembles Christ,
   for only the great glory of her shining
   can purify your eyes to look on Christ."
I saw such joy rain down upon that face—
   borne to it by those blest Intelligences
   created thus to span those heights of space—   90

that through all else on the long road I trod
nothing had held my soul so fixed in awe,
nor shown me such resemblances to God.
The self-same Love that to her first descended
singing *"Ave Maria, gratia plena"*
stood before her with its wings extended.
Thus rang the holy chant to Heaven's Queen
and all the blessed court joined in the song,
and singing, every face grew more serene.
"O holy Father, who endures for me
the loss of being far from the sweet place
where fate has raised your throne eternally,
who is that angel who with such desire
gazes into the eyes of our sweet Queen,
so rapt in love he seems to be afire?" 105
Thus did I seek instruction from that Great One
who drew the beauty of his light from Mary
as the morning star draws beauty from the sun.
And he: "As much as angel or soul can know
of exultation, gallantry, and poise
there is in him; and we would have it so,
for it was he who brought the victory
to Mary when the Son of God had willed
to bear the weight of human misery.
But let your eyes go where my words point out
among this court, and note the mighty peers
of the empire of the just and the devout.
Those two whose bliss it is to sit so close
to the radiance of the Empress of All Joy
are the two eternal roots of this our rose. 120
The one just to the left of her blessedness
is the father whose unruly appetite
left man the taste for so much bitterness;
and on her right, that ancient one you see
is the father of Holy Church to whom Christ gave
the twin keys to this flower of timeless beauty.
And that one who in his prophetic sight
foretold the evil days of the Sweet Bride
won by the spear and nails, sits on his right.

Paradiso

While by the other father and first man
   sits the great leader to whom manna fell
   to feed an ingrate and rebellious clan.
Across the circle from Peter, behold Anna.
   She feels such bliss in looking at her daughter
   she does not move her eyes to sing '*Hosanna!*'   135
And opposite the father of us all
   sits Lucy, who first urged your Lady to you
   when you were blindly bent toward your own fall.
But the time allowed for this dream vision flies.
   As a tailor must cut the gown from what cloth is given—
   just so must we move on, turning our eyes
to the Primal Love, that as your powers advance
   with looking toward Him, you may penetrate
   as deep as may be through His radiance.
But lest you should fall backward when you flare
   your mortal wings, intending to mount higher,
   remember grace must be acquired through prayer.
Therefore I will pray that blessèd one
   who has the power to aid you in your need.
   See that you follow me with such devotion   150
your heart adheres to every word I say."
And with those words the saint began to pray.

Canto 33

*St. Bernard offers a lofty prayer to the
Virgin, asking her to intercede in Dante's behalf,
and in answer Dante feels his soul swell with
new power and grow calm in rapture as his eyes
are permitted the direct vision of God. There can
be no measure of how long the vision endures. It
passes, and Dante is once more mortal and falli-
ble. Raised by God's Presence, he had looked into
the Mystery and had begun to understand its
Power and Majesty. Returned to himself, there is
no power in him capable of speaking the truth of
what he saw. Yet the impress of Truth is stamped
upon his soul, which he now knows will
return to be one with God's Love.*

"Virgin Mother, daughter of thy Son,
    humble beyond all creatures and more exalted,
    predestined turning point of God's intention,
thy merit so ennobled human nature
    that its divine Creator did not scorn
    to make Himself the creature of His creature.
The Love that was rekindled in thy womb
    sends forth the warmth of the eternal peace
    within whose ray this flower has come to bloom.
Here, to us, thou art the noon and scope
    of Love revealed; and among mortal men,
    the living fountain of eternal hope.
Lady, thou art so near God's reckonings
    that who seeks grace and does not first seek thee
    would have his wish fly upward without wings.
Not only does thy sweet benignity
    flow out to all who beg, but oftentimes
    thy charity arrives before the plea.

15

Paradiso

In thee is pity, in thee munificence,
  in thee the tenderest heart, in thee unites
  all that creation knows of excellence!
Now comes this man who from the final pit
  of the universe up to this height has seen,
  one by one, the three lives of the spirit.
He prays to thee in fervent supplication
  for grace and strength, that he may raise his eyes
  to the all-healing final revelation.
And I, who never more desired to see
  the vision myself than I do that he may see It,
  add my own prayer, and pray that it may be   30
enough to move you to dispel the trace
  of every mortal shadow by thy prayers
  and let him see revealed the Sum of Grace.
I pray thee further, all-persuading Queen,
  keep whole the natural bent of his affections
  and of his powers after his eyes have seen.
Protect him from the stirrings of man's clay;
  see how Beatrice and the blessèd host
  clasp reverent hands to join me as I pray."
The eyes that God reveres and loves the best
  glowed on the speaker, making clear the joy
  with which true prayer is heard by the most blest.
Those eyes turned then to the Eternal Ray,
  through which, we must indeed believe, the eyes
  of others do not find such ready way.   45
And I, who neared the goal of all my nature,
  felt my soul, at the climax of its yearning,
  suddenly, as it ought, grow calm with rapture.
Bernard then, smiling sweetly, gestured to me
  to look up, but I had already become
  within myself all he would have me be.
Little by little as my vision grew
  it penetrated further through the aura
  of the High Lamp which in Itself is true.
What then I saw is more than tongue can say.
  Our human speech is dark before the vision.
  The ravished memory swoons and falls away.

As one who sees in dreams and wakes to find
  the emotional impression of his vision
  still powerful while its parts fade from his mind—   60
just such am I, having lost nearly all
  the vision itself, while in my heart I feel
  the sweetness of it yet distill and fall.
So, in the sun, the footprints fade from snow.
  On the wild wind that bore the tumbling leaves
  the Sybil's oracles were scattered so.
O Light Supreme who doth Thyself withdraw
  so far above man's mortal understanding,
  lend me again some glimpse of what I saw;
make Thou my tongue so eloquent it may
  of all Thy glory speak a single clue
  to those who follow me in the world's day;
for by returning to my memory
  somewhat, and somewhat sounding in these verses,
  Thou shalt show man more of Thy victory.   75
So dazzling was the splendor of that Ray,
  that I must certainly have lost my senses
  had I, but for an instant, turned away.
And so it was, as I recall, I could
  the better bear to look, until at last
  my vision made one with the Eternal Good.
O grace abounding that had made me fit
  to fix my eyes on the Eternal Light
  until my vision was consumed in It!
I saw within Its depth how It conceives
  all things in a single volume bound by Love,
  of which the universe is the scattered leaves;
substance, accident, and their relation
  so fused that all I say could do no more
  than yield a glimpse of that bright revelation.   90
I think I saw the universal form
  that binds these things, for as I speak these words
  I feel my joy swell and my spirits warm.
Twenty-five centuries since Neptune saw
  the Argo's keel have not moved all mankind,
  recalling that adventure, to such awe

as I felt in an instant. My tranced being
   stared fixed and motionless upon that vision,
   ever more fervent to see in the act of seeing.
Experiencing that Radiance, the spirit
   is so indrawn it is impossible
   even to think of ever turning from It.
For the good which is the will's ultimate object
   is all subsumed in It; and, being removed,
   all is defective which in It is perfect.   105
Now in my recollection of the rest
   I have less power to speak than any infant
   wetting its tongue yet at its mother's breast;
and not because that Living Radiance bore
   more than one semblance, for It is unchanging
   and is forever as It was before;
rather, as I grew worthier to see,
   the more I looked, the more unchanging semblance
   appeared to change with every change in me.
Within the depthless deep and clear existence
   of that abyss of light three circles shown—
   three in color, one in circumference:
the second from the first, rainbow from rainbow;
   the third, an exhalation of pure fire
   equally breathed forth by the other two.   120
But oh, how much my words miss my conception,
   which is itself so far from what I saw
   that to call it feeble would be rank deception!
O Light Eternal fixed in Itself alone,
   by Itself alone understood, which from Itself
   loves and glows, self-knowing and self-known;
that second aureole which shone forth in Thee,
   conceived as a reflection of the first—
   or which appeared so to my scrutiny—
seemed in Itself of Its own coloration
   to be painted with man's image. I fixed my eyes
   on that alone in rapturous contemplation.
Like a geometer wholly dedicated
   to squaring the circle, but who cannot find,
   think as he may, the principle indicated—   135

The Divine Comedy

so did I study the supernal face.
  I yearned to know just how our image merges
  into that circle, and how it there finds place;
but mine were not the wings for such a flight.
  Yet, as I wished, the truth I wished for came
  cleaving my mind in a great flash of light.
Here my powers rest from their high fantasy,
  but already I could feel my being turned—
  instinct and intellect balanced equally
as in a wheel whose motion nothing jars—
by the Love that moves the Sun and the other stars.

Notes

Cosmography

In the fifteenth century, Copernicus laid the foundation of modern astronomy by establishing that the earth was not the stationary center of the universe, but merely a planet that revolves around the sun. His theory refuted the Ptolemaic system, which had been devised by the ancients and which, interpreted in the light of Christian doctrine, was the accepted explanation of the workings of the universe in Dante's time.

According to the Ptolemaic system (Diagram A), the earth is a solid, motionless sphere in the center of the universe. Around it revolve nine transparent, hollow spheres, each within its outside neighbor. The ninth sphere, the Primum Mobile, imparts its motion to the others and constitutes the frontier of the material world. Each of the other spheres governs the movement of one of the heavenly bodies: the eighth, the fixed stars; the seventh, Saturn; the sixth, Jupiter; the fifth, Mars; the fourth, the sun; the third, Venus; the second, Mercury; the first, the moon.

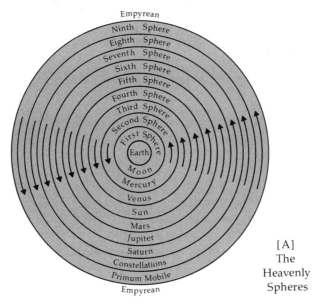

[A] The Heavenly Spheres

All the spheres move around the earth together, from east to west, once in twenty-four hours. In addition, each of the heavenly bodies has an independent movement within its sphere: the moon, for example, accomplishes its special revolution in one month; the sun, in a year; and so on. The earth alone of the material universe is without motion. It is surrounded by air and separated from the moon by a sphere of fire.

In the Christian interpretation of the Ptolemaic universe, the Primum Mobile encompasses the finite universe as created by God. Beyond it lies the Empyrean. Outside time and space, it is the abode of God and His chosen elect. In *The Divine Comedy*, Dante's journey begins on the earth, which is explored from its darkest abyss (Hell) to its most glorious height (Purgatory), and culminates with an ascension through the spheres to the Empyrean and the final vision of God.

The earth, where the vision begins, is conceived as a perfect sphere, about 20,000 miles in circumference and divided into two hemispheres: the Hemisphere of Land and the Hemisphere of Water. (These do not correspond to the northern and southern hemispheres as we know them.) The Hemisphere of Land contains all the continents, as well as the Mediterranean and part of the great ocean (Diagram B). Jerusalem lies at the exact center of this hemisphere, with the river Ganges at its eastern extremity and the Straits of Gibraltar on the west, each 90° from Jerusalem.

Hell is a vast cavity in the form of an inverted cone beneath the Hemisphere of Land. Its apex is at the center of the earth, directly under Jerusalem, and it extends at its widest point from Italy to mid-Asia (Diagram C). The round sides of the cone are broken into nine steps, or circles, each of which runs all the way around it. These circles are of unequal width and are separated by cliffs of varying height and steepness. A huge wall, circling around the sixth circle, separates the outermost section from the other two, making an Upper and a Lower Hell. The latter is called the City of Dis, and all the fires of Hell are within

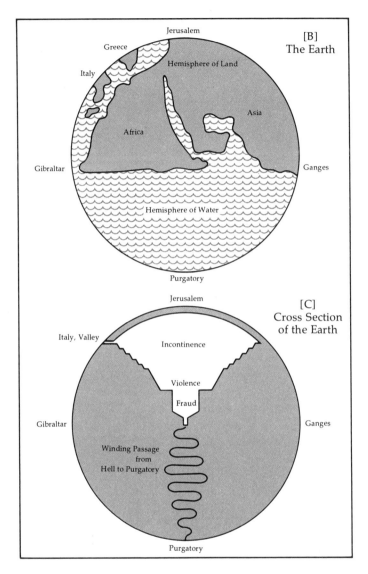

its boundaries. Within each of the nine circles is punished a particular type of sin: in Upper Hell, the sins of Incontinence; in Lower Hell, the sins of Violence and Fraud. A detailed diagram showing each of the circles and the spe-

557

cific sinners punished therein is presented on page 559, at the opening of the notes to the Inferno.

With Virgil as his guide, Dante descends through all the circles of Hell to the bottom of the abyss, where he sees Satan, frozen in the ice of the lake of Cocytus. He and Virgil then climb down Satan's belly to the exact center of the earth where the force of gravity is reversed. Here they climb up a winding passage and emerge in the center of the Hemisphere of Water, where Dante places the Mount of Purgatory.

Directly opposite Jerusalem, the towering mountain is the only land mass in this hemisphere, and on it Dante finds the souls of those who must do penance for their sins before they can assume their seats among the blessed. The mountain is formed by a series of plateaus or ledges, corresponding to the Seven Deadly Sins. At the top of the mountain lies the Earthly Paradise (the Garden of Eden), in which the souls about to enter Heaven are purged by the river Lethe of all remembrance of their sins. Its waters then flow down to Hell, delivering all memory of sin to its source—Satan. A detailed diagram showing the ledges of purgation and the sinners punished there is presented on page 595, at the opening of the notes to the Purgatorio.

Dante is guided through the spheres of Heaven by Beatrice. Just as he saw sin punished below, here he sees virtue rewarded and has the mysteries of God's creation revealed to him. As he rises towards the Empyrean, the blessed manifest themselves to Dante in the sphere corresponding to the particular virtue through which they found their redemption. The Warriors of God, for example, are found in the Sphere of Mars, named for the mythological god of war; those whose faithfulness was marred by inconstancy, on the other hand, are found in the sphere of the ever-changing moon. A diagram showing the divine spheres and the blessed within them is presented on page 643, at the opening of the notes to the Paradiso.

Cross-Section of the Inferno

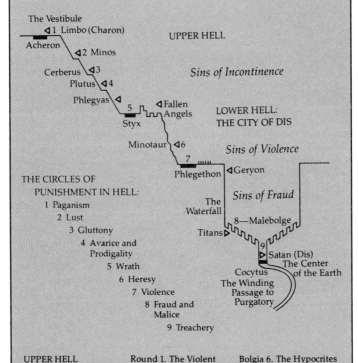

The Vestibule
◁1 Limbo (Charon)
Acheron
◁2 Minos
Cerberus ◁3
Plutus ◁4
Phlegyas ◁
5 ◁ Fallen Angels
Styx
Minotaur ◁6
7
Phlegethon ◁Geryon
The Waterfall
8—Malebolge
Titans ▷
9 ▷ Satan (Dis)
Cocytus
The Winding Passage to Purgatory

UPPER HELL

Sins of Incontinence

LOWER HELL:
THE CITY OF DIS

Sins of Violence

Sins of Fraud

The Center of the Earth

THE CIRCLES OF
PUNISHMENT IN HELL:
1 Paganism
2 Lust
3 Gluttony
4 Avarice and Prodigality
5 Wrath
6 Heresy
7 Violence
8 Fraud and Malice
9 Treachery

UPPER HELL
The Vestibule. The Opportunists
Circle 1. Limbo. The Virtuous Pagans

The Sins of Incontinence
Circle 2. The Carnal
Circle 3. The Gluttons
Circle 4. The Hoarders and the Wasters
Circle 5. The Wrathful and the Sullen

LOWER HELL:
THE CITY OF DIS
Circle 6. The Heretics

The Sins of Violence
Circle 7. The Violent

Round 1. The Violent Against Their Neighbors
Round 2. The Violent Against Themselves
Round 3. The Violent Against God, Nature and Art

The Sins of Fraud
Circle 8. Malebolge. The Fraudulent and Malicious
Bolgia 1. The Seducers and Panderers
Bolgia 2. The Flatterers
Bolgia 3. The Simoniacs
Bolgia 4. The Fortune Tellers and Diviners
Bolgia 5. The Grafters

Bolgia 6. The Hypocrites
Bolgia 7. The Thieves
Bolgia 8. The Evil Counselors
Bolgia 9. The Sowers of Discord
Bolgia 10. The Falsifiers
Circle 9. Cocytus. The Treacherous
Caïna. The Treacherous to Kin
Antenora. The Treacherous to Country
Ptolemea. The Treacherous to Guests and Hosts
Judaïca. The Treacherous to Their Masters

Notes to Inferno

1. *Midway in our life's journey:* The Biblical life span is three-score years and ten. The action opens in Dante's thirty-fifth year, A.D.1300.

17. *that planet:* The sun.

33–48. *Leopard . . . Lion . . . She-Wolf:* These three beasts undoubtedly are taken from Jer. 5:6. They foreshadow the three divisions of Hell (Incontinence, Violence, and Fraud) which Virgil explains at length in Canto 11.

38–39. *Aries . . . that rode with him to light the new creation:* In medieval tradition, the sun was in Aries at the time of the creation. In Dante's allegory, he awakens just before dawn of Good Friday, 1300, and thus begins his new life under Aries (creation), at dawn (rebirth), in the Easter season (resurrection).

69. *sub Julio:* In the reign of Julius Caesar. Virgil was born in 70 B.C.

95–98. *the Greyhound . . . Feltro and Feltro:* Probably Can Grande della Scala (1290–1329), the great Italian leader born in Verona, which lies between the towns of Feltre and Montefeltro.

100–101. *Nisus . . . Turnus . . . Euryalus . . . Camilla:* In the *Aeneid,* these four were killed in the war between the Trojans and the Latians, which established Trojan dominance of the peninsula.

110. *the second death:* Damnation.

118. *forbids me to come there:* Salvation is only through Christ in Dante's theology. Virgil lived and died before the establishment of Christ's teachings in Rome, and therefore he cannot enter Heaven.

125. *Peter's Gate:* The Gate of Purgatory, only open to the elect.

CANTO 2

13. *father of Sylvius:* Aeneas.

78. *the heaven of the smallest circle:* The moon.

97. *Lucia:* The patron saint of eyesight.

Notes

CANTO 3

7. *Only those elements time cannot wear:* The Angels, the Empyrean, and the First Matter.

57. *who, in his cowardice, made the Great Denial:* Celestine V, who became Pope in 1294. He was a man of saintly life, but allowed himself to be convinced by a priest named Benedetto that his soul was in danger, since no man could live in the world without being damned. In fear for his soul he withdrew from all worldly affairs and renounced the papacy. Benedetto promptly assumed the mantle himself and became Boniface VIII, a Pope who symbolized for Dante the worst corruptions of the Church. Celestine's great guilt is that his selfish terror for his own welfare served as the door through which so much evil entered the Church.

88. *By other windings:* Charon recognizes Dante not only as a living man but as a soul in grace and knows, therefore, that the infernal ferry is not intended for him. He is probably referring to the fact that souls destined for Purgatory and Heaven assemble on the banks of the Tiber, from which they are transported by an angel.

100. *they blasphemed God:* The souls of the damned cannot repent, for repentance is a divine grace.

123. *they yearn for what they fear:* Hell (allegorically Sin) is the deliberate choice of the damned, who consciously hardened their hearts to God in life; divine grace is denied to none who wish for it.

CANTO 4

53. *a Mighty One:* Christ; His name is never spoken in Hell. *descended here:* The legend of the Harrowing of Hell is that Christ in the glory of His resurrection descended into Limbo and took with Him to Heaven the souls of the Hebrews who believed in the coming of the Messiah.

106. *a great Citadel:* The Citadel represents philosophy, which is human reason without the light of God.

119. *the master souls of time were shown to me:* The inhabitants of the Citadel fall into three groups:

1. The heroes and heroines, all of whom are associated with the Trojans and their Roman descendants. The exception is the Saladin who was defeated by Richard the Lion-Heart, but whose great qualities as a ruler were legend in medieval Europe. The Electra mentioned is not the sister of Orestes, but the mother of Dardanus, the founder of Troy.

561

2. The philosophers, whose teachings represent the highest achievements of human reason unaided by divine love.

3. The naturalists, or historians of science. Avicenna and Averroës were Arab philosophers and physicians known for their commentaries on Aristotle.

CANTO 5

4. *Minos:* A great king and legislator of ancient Crete. In the *Odyssey* and *Aeneid*, he is given the office of judge of the dead. Dante transforms him into a hideous demon, apparently the symbol of a guilty conscience.

58. *Semiramis:* Legendary Queen of Assyria who assumed the throne at the death of her husband, Ninus.

61. *Dido:* Queen of Carthage who fell in love with Aeneas after the death of her husband, Sichaeus, to whose memory she had sworn eternal fidelity. When Aeneas abandoned her, she stabbed herself on a funeral pyre.

65. *Achilles:* According to medieval legend, for love of Polyxena, the daughter of Priam, Achilles agreed to desert the Greeks and join the Trojans; when he went to the temple for the wedding, he was killed by Paris.

74. *those two swept together:* Francesca of Rimini and her lover, Paolo Malatesta. Francesca was the daughter of Guido da Polenta, a powerful citizen of Ravenna. In 1275 she was married, for political reasons, to Giovanni Malatesta of Rimini, called Giovanni the Lame, a deformed but powerful warrior. About ten years later, Giovanni surprised his wife and his younger brother Paolo in her bedroom and stabbed them.

104. *Caïna waits for him:* Giovanni Malatesta was still alive at the writing, but his fate has nevertheless been decided; at death, his soul is doomed to Caïna, the first ring of the last circle of Hell, reserved for those who were treacherous against their kin.

124–125. *the rhyme of Launcelot:* The story exists in many forms; Dante uses details from an Old French version.

134. *That book, and he who wrote it, was a pander: Galeotto,* the Italian word for pander, is also the Italian rendering of the name Gallehault, who, in the French romance Dante refers to here, was the intermediary between Launcelot and Guinevere.

562

Notes

13. *Cerberus:* In classical mythology, the three-headed dog placed at the Gate of the Underworld; he allowed all to enter, but none to escape. Dante presents him as a part-human monster; his three heads and ravenous disposition make him an apt symbol of gluttony.

49. *Ciacco, the Hog:* A Florentine renowned both for his gluttony and his ready wit; he is said to have died in 1286.

62. *it shall come to blood:* Ciacco prophesies the political history of Florence from 1300 to 1302. In May of 1300 the White Guelphs (Dante's party) drove the Black Guelphs from Florence in bloody fighting. Two years later ("within three suns"), the Blacks, aided by the corrupt Pope, Boniface VIII, returned and expelled most of the prominent Whites, among them Dante. This was the beginning of his long exile from Florence.

67. *Black shall ride on White for many years:* Dante did not live to see his party triumph.

76–77. *Farinata* appears in Canto 10 among the Heretics; *Tegghiaio* and *Jacopo Rusticucci* in Canto 16 with the Sodomites; *Mosca* in Canto 28 with the Sowers of Discord; *Arrigo* does not appear again, but is probably Arrigo (or Oderigo) dei Fifanti, a fellow-conspirator of Mosca.

103. *your science:* The writings of Aristotle and the commentaries on them, particularly those of Thomas Aquinas.

CANTO 7

1. *Papa Satán, Papa Satán, aleppy:* Apparently a threat against the travelers and a warning to Satan below.

2. *Plutus:* In Greek mythology, the god of wealth, a role which makes him the ideal overseer of the miserly and prodigal.

22. *Charybdis:* A whirlpool in the Straits of Sicily.

68. *Dame Fortune:* A central figure in medieval mythology, usually shown holding an ever-revolving wheel, symbolizing chance. Dante incorporates her into his scheme of the universe, ranking her among the angels.

87. *the other gods:* The angelic orders that control the spheres.

97. *the stars that marked our starting fall away:* It is now after midnight of Good Friday.

107. *Styx:* In classical mythology, a river of the Underworld; Dante makes it a filthy marsh, which marks the first great division of Hell. Between Acheron and Styx are punished the sins of Incontinence (the sins of the She-Wolf); beyond Styx rise the flaming walls of Dis, within which are punished the sins of Violence (the Lion) and Fraud (the Leopard).

CANTO 8

19. *Phlegyas:* Mythological king of Boeotia. Angry at Apollo, who had seduced his daughter, he set fire to Apollo's temple at Delphi. For this offense, the god killed him and threw his soul into Hades.

58. *Filippo Argenti:* One of the Adimari of Florence, who were bitter political enemies of Dante; his savagery toward Filippo is intended as an insult to the entire family.

64. *Dis:* In classical mythology, another name for Pluto, King of the Underworld; used by Dante as an alternate name for Satan and here applied to Lower Hell, his fortified city.

80. *spirits purged from Heaven for its glory:* The Rebellious Angels.

122. *a less secret gate:* The Gate of Hell. In the legend of the Harrowing of Hell, these demons opposed Christ's entry, but He broke open the gate and it has remained so ever since.

125. *a Great One:* The Heavenly Messenger whose coming is described in the next canto.

CANTO 9

20. *Erichtho:* A sorceress drawn from Lucan's *Pharsalia.*

24. *a spirit from Judaïca:* Judaïca (or Judecca) is the final pit of Hell. Erichtho called up the spirit in order to foretell the outcome of the campaign between Pompey and Caesar. There is no trace of the legend in which Virgil is chosen for the descent; Virgil, in fact, was still alive at the time of the battle of Pharsalia.

35. *Furies:* In classical mythology, especially malign spirits who pursued and tormented those who had violated fundamental taboos (desecration of temples, murder of kin, etc.). The symbols of the guilty conscience of the damned, they are also called Erinyes.

41. *the Queen of Woe:* Proserpine (or Hecate), wife of Pluto, and Queen of the Underworld.

50. *Medusa:* The Gorgon; she turned to stone whoever looked at her. Allegorically she represents despair of ever winning the mercy of God.

Notes

51. *Too lightly we let Theseus go free:* Theseus and Pirithous tried to kidnap Hecate. Pirithous was killed in the attempt and Theseus was punished by being chained to a great rock. He was later set free by Hercules, who descended to his rescue in defiance of all the powers of Hell. The meaning of the Furies' cry is that Dante must be made an example of their power. Had they punished Theseus properly, men would have acquired more respect for their powers and would not still be attempting to invade the Underworld.

95. *Cerberus:* When Cerberus opposed the fated entrance of Hercules into Hell, Hercules threw a chain about his neck and dragged him to the upperworld. Cerberus' throat, according to Dante, is still peeled raw from this experience.

109–110. *Arles . . . Pola:* Situated as indicated on the Rhone and the Quarnaro Gulf, respectively, these cities were the sites of great cemeteries dating back to the time of Rome.

CANTO 10

11. *Jehoshaphat:* A valley outside Jerusalem. The popular belief that it would serve as the scene of the Last Judgment was based on Joel 3:2, 12.

14. *Epicurus:* The Greek philosopher. The central aim of his philosophy was to achieve happiness, which he defined as the absence of pain. For Dante this doctrine meant the denial of the eternal life, since the whole aim of the Epicurean was temporal happiness.

32. *Farinata:* Farinata degli Uberti, who became leader of the Ghibellines of Florence in 1239 and played a large part in expelling the Guelphs in 1248. The Guelphs returned in 1251, but Farinata remained. His arrogant desire to rule singlehanded led to difficulties, however, and he was expelled in 1258. With the aid of the Manfredi of Siena, he gathered a large force and defeated the Guelphs of Montaperti on the river Arbia in 1260. Reentering Florence in triumph, he again expelled the Guelphs, but at the Diet of Empoli, held by the victors after the battle of Montaperti, he alone rose in open counsel to resist the general sentiment that Florence should be razed. He died in Florence in 1264. In 1266 the Guelphs returned and crushed forever the power of the Uberti, destroying their palaces and issuing special decrees against persons of the Uberti line. In 1283 a decree of heresy was published against Farinata.

52. *another shade:* Cavalcante dei Cavalcanti, a famous Epicurean and the father of Guido Cavalcanti, a poet and friend of Dante. Guido was married to Farinata's daughter.

79. *her who reigns in Hell:* Hecate, also the moon goddess. Dante was

banished from Florence in 1302, well within the fifty months of the prophecy.

119–120. *The second Frederick:* Emperor Frederick II, commonly reputed to be an Epicurean. *the Cardinal of the Ubaldini:* In the original Dante refers to him simply as *il Cardinale.* Ottaviano degli Ubaldini (c. 1209–1273) became Cardinal in 1245, but his energies seem to have been directed exclusively to money and political intrigue. When he was refused an important loan by the Ghibellines, he is reported to have remarked: "I may say that if I have a soul, I have lost it in the cause of the Ghibellines, and no one of them will help me now." The words "if I have a soul" would be enough to make him guilty in Dante's eyes of the charge of heresy.

CANTO 11

8–9. *Anastasius . . . Photinus:* Medieval tradition confused Pope Anastasius II (496–498) with his contemporary, Anastasius I, who was Emperor from 491–518; it is the latter who was induced by Photinus, a deacon of Thessalonica, to adopt the Acacian heresy, which denied the divine paternity of Christ.

50. *Sodom and Cahors:* Cities used as symbols for the sins that flourished within them: Sodom is identified with unnatural sex practices; Cahors, in southern France, was notorious in the Middle Ages for its usurers.

64. *the center point of all creation:* In the Ptolemaic system, the earth was the center of the universe; in Dante's geography, the bottom of Hell is the center of the earth.

73. *the rust-red city:* Dis.

113. *the Wain lies over Caurus:* Virgil indicates the hour (in Jerusalem) by a description of the sky, which is not visible from Hell, but which he reads by a special power Dante does not explain. The Fish (the constellation Pisces, which precedes Aries) is just rising; the Wain, or Great Bear, lies in the quarter of Caurus, the Northwest Wind. The time is thus three or more hours after midnight.

CANTO 12

4. *the Slides of Mark:* The landslide known as *Li Slavoni di Marco,* about two miles from Rovereto, on the left bank of the river Adige.

12–18. *the Infamy of Crete:* The Minotaur of classical mythology. Pasiphaë, wife of Minos, King of Crete, became enamored of a bull and, in order to mate with it, she crept into a wooden cow. From this union the Minotaur was born, half-man, half-beast. It devoured an annual tribute of youths and maidens from Athens and was killed by Theseus with the help of Ariadne, Minos' daughter. More beast than human in Dante's conception, the Minotaur was conceived in a sodomitic union and was a devourer of human flesh; thus he is a fitting symbol of the souls he guards.

40–42. *the universe felt love . . . as some believe:* The Greek philosopher Empedocles taught that the universe existed by the counterbalance (discord or mutual repulsion) of its elements. Should the elemental matter feel harmony (love or mutual attraction) all would fly together into chaos.

47. *the river of boiling blood:* Phlegethon.

55. *Centaurs:* In classical mythology, creatures who were half-horse, half-men: They were skilled and savage hunters and, as creatures of passion and violence, are a fitting choice for the tormentors of these sinners.

64. *Chiron:* The wisest and most just of the Centaurs; reputedly the teacher of Achilles and of other Greek heroes to whom he imparted great skill in bearing arms, medicine, astronomy, music, and augury.

67. *Nessus:* A Centaur who tried to abduct Dejanira, the wife of Hercules, but was killed by the outraged husband with a poisoned arrow. While dying, he whispered to Dejanira that a shirt stained with his poisoned blood would act as a love charm should Hercules' affections stray. When Hercules fell in love with Iole, Dejanira sent him a shirt stained with Nessus' blood. It poisoned Hercules, and he died in agony.

72. *Pholus:* A number of classical poets mention Pholus, but nothing is known about him.

107. *Alexander:* Alexander the Great. *Dionysius:* Either Dionysius I (died 367 B.C.) or his son, Dionysius II (died 343). Both were tyrants of Sicily and infamous as prototypes of the bloodthirsty and exorbitant ruler.

110. *Azzolino:* Ezzelino da Romano, Count of Onora (1194–1259), the cruelest of the Ghibelline tyrants, especially infamous for his slaughter of the Paduans.

111. *Opizzo da Esti:* Marquis of Ferrara (1264–1293). The account of his life is confused, and one must accept Dante's facts as given.

119–120. *That one . . . a heart still honored on the Thames:* The sinner indicated is Guy de Montfort. His father, Simon de Montfort, was a leader of the barons who rebelled against Henry III and was killed at the battle of Evesham (1265) by Prince Edward (later Edward I). In 1271, Guy (then Vicar General of Tuscany) avenged his father's death by murdering Henry's nephew (who was also named Henry) in a church at Viterbo. The murdered Henry's heart was sealed in a casket and sent to London, where it was accorded various honors.

134. *Sextus:* Probably the younger son of Pompey the Great; his piracy is mentioned by Lucan. *Pyrrhus:* Either Pyrrhus, the son of Achilles, who was especially bloodthirsty at the sack of Troy, or Pyrrhus, King of Epirus (319–272 B.C.), who waged relentless and bloody war against the Greeks and Romans.

135. *Attila:* King of the Huns from 433 to 453; he was called the Scourge of God.

137. *Rinier da Corneto . . . Rinier Pazzo:* Two especially bloodthirsty robber-barons of Dante's time.

CANTO 13

6–9. The reference here is to the Maremma district of Tuscany, which lies between the mountains and the sea. The river Cecina is the northern boundary of this district; Corneto is on the river Marta, which forms the southern boundary. The Maremma is a wild district of marsh and forest.

10. *Harpies:* These hideous birds with the faces of malign women were often associated with the Erinyes (Furies). Their original function in mythology was to snatch away the souls of men at the commands of the gods. Later, they were portrayed as defilers of food, and, by extension, of everything they touched. The islands of the Strophades were their legendary abode. Aeneas and his men landed there and fought with the Harpies, who drove them back and pronounced a prophecy of unbearable famine upon them.

48. *in my verses only:* The *Aeneid* describes a similar bleeding plant. There, Aeneas pulls at a myrtle growing on a Thracian hillside. It bleeds where he breaks it and the voice of Polydorus cries out of the ground. He had been treacherously murdered by the Thracian king.

58. *I am he:* Pier delle Vigne (1190–1249), a famous and once-powerful minister of Emperor Frederick II. He enjoyed Frederick's whole confidence until 1247, when he was accused of treachery, imprisoned, and blinded. He committed suicide to escape further torture. Pier delle Vigne was famous for his eloquence and for his mastery of the ornate Provençal-inspired Sicilian School of Italian Poetry, and Dante styles his speech accordingly. *who held both keys:* The phrasing suggests the papal keys; delle Vigne may be suggesting that he was to Frederick as the Pope is to God.

120. *Lano:* Lano da Siena, a famous squanderer. He died at the ford of the river Toppo near Arezzo in 1287 in a battle against the Aretines. Boc-

caccio writes that he deliberately courted death, having squandered all his great wealth and being unwilling to live on in poverty. Thus his companion's jeer probably means: "You were not so ready to run then, Lano; why are you running now?"

133. *Jacomo da Sant' Andrea:* A Paduan with an infamous lust for laying waste his own goods and those of his neighbors. Arson was his favorite prank. He was murdered in 1239, probably by assassins hired by Ezzolino da Romano (Canto 12).

143. *the city that tore down Mars and raised the Baptist:* Florence. Mars was the first patron of the city, and when the Florentines were converted to Christianity they pulled down his equestrian statue and built a church on the site of his temple. The statue of Mars was placed on a tower beside the Arno. When Totila destroyed Florence the tower fell into the Arno and the statue with it. Legend has it that Florence could never have been rebuilt had not the mutilated statue been rescued. It was placed on the Ponte Vecchio, but was carried away in the flood of 1333.

150. *Attila:* Dante confuses Attila with Totila, King of the Ostrogoths (died 552). He destroyed Florence in 542. Attila (died 453), King of the Huns, destroyed many cities of northern Italy, but not Florence.

CANTO 14

12. *just such a waste as Cato marched across:* In 47 B.C., Cato of Utica led an army across the Libyan desert.

28–33. *Like those Alexander met, etc.:* This incident of Alexander the Great's campaign in India is described by Albertus Magnus and was taken by him, with considerable alteration, from a letter reputedly sent to Aristotle by Alexander.

43. *that wraith who lies along the rim:* Capaneus, one of the Seven who warred on Thebes. As he scaled the walls, he defied Jove to protect them, and Jove replied with a thunderbolt that killed him with this blasphemy still on his lips.

53. *Mongibello:* Mt. Etna; Vulcan was believed to have his smithy inside the volcano.

55. *as he did at Phlegra:* At the battle of Phlegra in Thessaly, the Titans tried to storm Olympus; Jove drove them back with the help of the thunderbolts Vulcan forged for him.

76. *the Bulicame:* A hot sulphur spring near Viterbo, whose waters boil and steam and have a distinctly reddish tint as a consequence of their mineral content. A part of the Bulicame flows through what was once a quarter reserved to prostitutes, who were not permitted to use the public baths.

94. *Rhea:* Wife of Saturn and mother of Jove (Zeus). It had been prophesied to Saturn that one of his children would dethrone him and, to nullify the prophecy, he devoured each of them at birth. On the birth of Jove, Rhea duped Saturn by letting him bolt down a stone wrapped in baby clothes. As a further precaution, she hid the infant on Mt. Ida in Crete. There she posted her Corybantes (or Bacchantes) as guards, instructing them to set up a great din whenever the baby cried so that Saturn would not hear him.

97. *An ancient giant:* The Old Man of Crete, who first occurs in Dan. 2:32–34, in Nebuchadnezzar's dream. Dante follows most of the details of the original, but adds a totally different interpretation. In Dante each metal represents one of the ages of man, each deteriorating from the Golden Age of Innocence. The left foot, terminating the Age of Iron, is the Holy Roman Empire. The right foot, of terra cotta, is the Roman Catholic Church, a more fragile base than the left, but the one upon which the greater weight descends. The tears of the woes of man flow down the great fissure that defaces all but the Golden Age. Thus, starting in woe, they flow through man's decline, into the hollow of the mountain and become the waters of all Hell. Dante's other major addition is the site and position of the figure: equidistant from the three continents, the Old Man stands at the center of Time, his back turned to Damietta in Egypt (symbolizing the East, the past, the birth of religion), his gaze fixed upon Rome (the West, the future, the Catholic Church).

CANTO 15

4–9. Dante compares the banks of the rill of Phlegethon to the dikes built by the Flemings to hold back the sea, and to those built by the Paduans to hold back the spring floods of the river Brent. Chiarentana was a duchy of the Middle Ages, whose territory included the headwaters of the Brent.

30. *Ser Brunetto:* Brunetto Latino or Latini (born between 1210 and 1230, died 1294), a prominent Florentine Guelph who held, among many other posts, that of notary, whence the title *Ser.* He was not Dante's schoolmaster as many have supposed; Dante's use of the word *màster* is to indicate spiritual indebtedness to Brunetto and his works. It is worth noting that Dante addresses him in Italian as *voi* instead of using the less respectful *tu* form. Farinata (Canto 10) is the only other sinner so addressed in the Inferno. Brunetto's two principal books, both of which Dante admires, were the prose *Livre dou Tresor* (*The Book of the Treasure*) and the poetic *Tesoretto* (*The Little Treasure*). Dante learned a number of his devices from the allegorical journey which forms the *Tesoretto.*

40. *I will walk at your hem:* Dante is standing on the dike at approximately the level of Brunetto's head and he cannot descend because of the rain of fire and the burning sands.

61. *that ungrateful and malignant stock:* The ancient Etruscan city of Fiesole was situated on a hill about three miles north of the present site of Florence. According to legend, Fiesole sided with Catiline in his war with Julius Caesar. Caesar destroyed the town and set up a new city called Florence on the Arno, peopling it with Romans and Fiesolans. The Romans were the aristocracy of the new city, but the Fiesolans were a majority. Dante ascribes the endless bloody conflicts of Florence largely to the internal strife between these two strains, and, at the same time, proudly proclaims his descent from the Roman strain.

67. *the old adage calls them blind:* The source of this proverbial expression, "Blind as a Florentine," is not known.

71. *shall make both sides hunger for you:* Both sides will hunger to destroy Dante.

94–99. *Twice already . . . is well heard:* Ciacco (Canto 6) and Farinata (Canto 10) have prophesied Dante's exile and suffering. Dante's reply (come what may he will remain true to his purpose) earns Virgil's praise.

109. *Priscian:* Latin grammarian and poet of the first half of the sixth century.

110. *Francesco d'Accorso:* A Florentine scholar, who died in Bologna in 1294.

112–113. *that one the Servant of Servants . . . Arno to the Bacchiglione:* Servus servorum, a correct papal title, is here ironically applied to Dante's old enemy, Boniface VIII. In 1295 Boniface transferred Bishop Andrea de' Mozzi from the Bishopric of Florence (on the Arno) to that of Vicenza (on the Bacchiglione). The transfer was reputedly brought about at the request of the Bishop's brother, Tommaso de' Mozzi of Florence, who wished to remove from his sight the spectacle of his brother's stupidity and unnatural vices.

114. *unnatural organ:* The original, *mal protesi nervi,* contains an untranslatable word-play. *Nervi* may be taken as "the male organ" and *protesi* for "erected"; thus the organ aroused to passion for unnatural purposes (*mal*).

121. *the green cloth:* On the first Sunday of Lent all the young men of Verona ran a race for the prize of green cloth. The last runner in was given a live rooster and was required to carry it through the town.

CANTO 16

37. *Guido Guerra:* "Guido of War" (c. 1220–1272), a valiant leader of the Guelphs despite his Ghibelline origin as one of the Counts of Guidi.

38. *the good Gualdrada:* Guido Guerra's grandmother, renowned in her youth both for her beauty and for her industry.

41. *Tegghiaio Aldobrandi:* Guelph noble (died 1265) of the degli Adimari family. With Guido Guerra he advised the Florentines not to move against the Sienese at the disastrous battle of Montaperti (see Farinata, Canto 10), knowing that the Sienese had been heavily reinforced by mercenaries. It is probably these good counsels that "the world would have done well to understand."

44. *Jacopo Rusticucci:* A Florentine knight of Dante's time; no details of his life are known. Dante had inquired of Ciacco (Canto 6) about Tegghiaio and Rusticucci.

70. *Borsiere:* Guglielmo Borsiere. *Borsiere* in Italian means pursemaker, and the legend has grown without verification that this was his origin. He was a courtier, peacemaker, and arranger of marriages, of whom Boccaccio speaks highly in the *Decameron.*

93–101. *that river:* The water course described by Dante and made up of the Acquacheta and the Montone flows directly into the sea without draining into the Po. The placement of it as "first one on the left of the Apennines" results from the peculiar orientation of the maps of Dante's time. The "river" has its source and course along a line running almost exactly northwest from Florence. *San Benedetto dell' Alpe:* A small monastery situated on that line about twenty-five miles from Florence.

CANTO 17

1. *the sharp-tailed beast:* Geryon, a mythical king of Spain represented as a giant with three heads and three bodies; he was killed by Hercules. A later tradition represents him as killing and robbing strangers whom he lured into his realm. It is probably on this account that Dante chose him as the prototype of Fraud, though in a radically altered bodily form. Some of the details of Dante's Geryon may be drawn from Rev. 9:9–20, but most of them seem his own invention: a monster with a general shape of a dragon but with the tail of a scorpion, hairy arms, a gaudily-marked reptilian body, and the face of a just and honest man.

17. *Tartar . . . Turk:* The most skilled weavers of Dante's time.

18. *Arachne:* In classical mythology, a spinner and weaver so famous

Notes

that she challenged Minerva to a contest; there are various accounts of the outcome, but all end with the goddess so angry that she changed Arachne into a spider.

33. *some people:* The Usurers.

56. *azure on or, a kind of lion:* The arms of the Gianfigliazzi of Florence were a lion azure on a field of gold. The sinner bearing this purse must be Catello di Rosso Gianfigliazzi, who set up as a usurer in France and was made a knight on his return to Florence.

57. *on a blood-red field, a goose whiter than whey:* A white goose on a red field was the arms of the noble Ghibelline family of the Ubriachi, or Ebriachi, of Florence. The wearer is probably Ciappo Ubriachi, a notorious usurer.

58-59. *sow azure on field argent:* These are the arms of the Scrovegni of Padua. The bearer is probably Reginaldo Scrovegni.

62. *Vitaliano:* Vitaliano di Iacopo Vitaliani, another Paduan.

66. *the sovereign cavalier:* Giovanni di Buiamonte was esteemed in Florence as "the sovereign cavalier" and was chosen for many high offices. He was a usurer and a gambler who lost great sums at play. Dante's intent is clearly to bewail the decay of standards which permits Florence to honor so highly a man for whom Hell is waiting so dismally. Buiamonte was of the Becchi family whose arms were three black goats on a gold field. *Becchi* in Italian is the plural form of the word for goat.

79. *quartanary chill:* Quartan fever is an ague that runs a four-day cycle with symptoms roughly like those of malaria. At the approach of the chill, Dante intends his figure to say, any thought of coolness strikes terror into the shivering victim.

101. *Phaeton:* Son of Apollo, who drove the chariot of the sun. Phaeton begged his father for a chance to drive the chariot himself, but he lost control of the horses and Zeus killed him with a thunderbolt for fear the whole earth would catch fire. The scar left in the sky by the runaway horses is marked by the Milky Way.

103. *Icarus:* Daedalus, the father of Icarus, made wings for himself and his son, and they flew into the sky. Icarus, ignoring his father's commands, flew too close to the sun. The heat melted the wax with which the wings were fastened, and Icarus fell into the Aegean and was drowned.

121. *flight-worn falcon:* Falcons, when sent aloft, were trained to circle until sighting a bird, or until signaled back by the lure (a stuffed bird). Flight-weary, Dante's metaphoric falcon sinks bit by bit, rebelling against his training and sulking away from his master in wide slow circles.

CANTO 18

2. *Malebolge: Bolgia* in Italian means ditch or pouch. That combination of meanings is not possible in a single English word, but clearly Dante intends both meanings: not only a ditch of evil, but a pouch full of it, a filthy treasure of ill-gotten souls.

5. *a well:* This is the final pit of Hell, in which the Treacherous are punished.

29. *the year of the Jubilee:* Boniface VIII had proclaimed 1300 a Jubilee Year, and consequently throngs of pilgrims had come to Rome. Since the date of the vision is also 1300, the Roman throngs are moving across the Tiber via Ponte Castello Sant' Angelo at the very time Dante is watching the sinners in Hell.

47. *thought to hide his face:* The general rule of the sinners above the great barrier cliff has been an eagerness to make themselves known and to be remembered in the world. From this point to the bottom of Hell that rule is reversed, and the sinners, with a few exceptions, try to conceal their identity, asking only to be forgotten.

50. *Venedico Caccianemico:* A nobleman of Bologna. To win the favor of the Marquis Obbizo da Este of Ferrara, Caccianemico acted as the procurer of his own sister Ghisola, called *la bella* or *Ghisolabella.*

86. *Jason:* Leader of the Argonauts, who carried off the Colchian Ram (the Golden Fleece). The good advice that helped him win the Fleece was given by Medea, daughter of the King of Colchis, whom Jason took with him and later abandoned for Creusa. Jason had previously seduced Hypsipyle and deserted her to continue his voyage after the Fleece. She was one of the women of Lemnos whom Aphrodite cursed with a foul smell which made them unbearable to their husbands and lovers. The women took their revenge by banding together to kill all their males, but Hypsipyle managed to save her father, King Thoas, by pretending to the women that she had already killed him.

122. *Alessio Interminelli da Lucca:* One of the noble family of the Interminelli or Interminei, a prominent White family of Lucca. All that is known of Alessio is the fact that he was still alive in 1295.

CANTO 19

1. *Simon Magus:* Simon the Samarian magician (Acts 8:9–24) from whom the term simony derives. Upon his conversion to Christianity, he offered to buy the power to administer the Holy Ghost and was severely rebuked by Peter.

17. *the font of my beautiful San Giovanni:* It was the custom in Dante's

time to baptize only on Holy Saturday and on Pentecost. These occasions were naturally thronged, and to protect the priests a special font was built in the Baptistry of San Giovanni with marble stands for the priests, who were thus protected both from the crowds and from the water in which they immersed those to be baptized. The Baptistry is still standing, but the font is no longer in it. A similar font still exists, however, in the Baptistry at Pisa.

19-21. In these lines Dante is replying to a charge of sacrilege that had been rumored against him. One day a boy playing in the baptismal font became jammed in the marble tube and could not be extricated. To save the boy from drowning, Dante smashed the tube. This is his answer to all men on the charge of sacrilege.

29. *more than all the others:* The fire is proportioned to the guilt of the sinner; these are the feet of the chief sinner of this *bolgia.*

42. *one whose legs did penance for him:* Giovanni Gaetano degli Orsini, or Pope Nicholas III, who held the office from 1277 to 1280. He is awaiting the arrival of his successor, Boniface VIII, who will take his place in the stone tube and who will in turn be replaced by Clement V, a Pope even more corrupt than Boniface. With the foresight of the damned he had read the date of Boniface's death (1303) in the Book of Fate. Mistaking Dante for Boniface, he thinks his foresight has erred by three years, since it is now 1300.

46. *like a friar:* Persons convicted of murdering for hire were sometimes executed by being buried alive upside down. If the friar was called back at the last moment, he had to bend over the hole in which the man was fixed upside down awaiting the first shovelful of earth.

66. *the Great Mantle:* Of the Papacy.

67. *son of the She-Bear:* Nicholas's family name, degli Orsini, means "of the bear cubs."

69. *pursed:* A play on the second meaning of *bolgia* (purse): "Just as I put wealth in my purse when alive, so am I put in this foul purse now that I am dead."

77–81. *a lawless Shepherd . . . Jason of the Maccabees . . . the French king:* The reference is to Clement V, Pope from 1305 to 1314. He came from Gascony (the West) and was involved in many intrigues with the King of France. It was Clement V who moved the Papal See to Avignon, where it remained until 1377. He is compared to Jason, who bought an appointment as High Priest of the Jews from King Antiochus and thereupon introduced pagan and venal practices into the office in much the same way as Clement used his influence with Philip of France to secure and corrupt his high office. Clement will succeed Boniface in Hell because Boniface's successor, Benedictus XI (1303–1304), was a good and holy man.

88–89. *Nor did Peter . . . of Matthias:* Upon the expulsion of Judas from the bands of Apostles, Matthias was chosen in his place.

93. *Charles of Anjou:* The seventh son of Louis VIII of France, who became King of Naples and of Sicily largely through the help of Pope Urban IV and later of Clement IV; Nicholas III withdrew the high favor his predecessors had shown Charles. In Dante's time it was believed that Nicholas instigated the massacre called the Sicilian Vespers, in which the Sicilians overthrew the rule of Charles and held a general slaughter of the French who had been their masters. The Sicilian Vespers, however, was a popular and spontaneous uprising, and it did not occur until Nicholas had been dead for two years.

95. *the Great Keys:* Of the Papacy.

100–102. *the Evangelist . . . She Who Sits Upon the Waters:* St. John the Evangelist. His vision of She Who Sits Upon the Waters is set forth in Revelation, Chapter 17. The Evangelist intended it as a vision of pagan Rome, but Dante interprets it as a vision of the Roman Church in its simoniacal corruption. The seven heads are the Seven Sacraments; the ten horns, the Ten Commandments.

109. *Ah, Constantine:* The first rich Father was Silvester, who was Pope from 314 to 355. Before him the Popes possessed nothing, but when Constantine was converted and Catholicism became the official religion of the Empire, the Church began to acquire the wealth that to Dante was the root of its corruption. Dante makes Constantine directly responsible for this misfortune because the scholars of his time argued (based on a document called "The Donation of Constantine") that Constantine moved his Empire to the East in order to leave the sovereignty of the West to the Church.

CANTO 20

8. *at about the pace of a litany procession:* The litanies are chanted not only in church (before the Mass), but sometimes in procession, the priest chanting the prayers and the marchers the response. These processions move very slowly.

34. *Amphiareus:* Another of the Seven captains who fought against Thebes. Statius tells how Amphiareus foresaw his own death in this war and attempted to run away from it, but was swallowed in his flight by an earthquake.

40. *Tiresias:* A Theban diviner and magician. Ovid tells how he came on two twined serpents, struck them apart with his stick, and was thereupon transformed into a woman. Seven years later he came on two

serpents similarly entwined, struck them apart, and was changed back into a man.

46–48. *Aruns:* An Etruscan soothsayer who foretold the war between Pompey and Julius Caesar, Caesar's victory, and Pompey's death. *Luni:* An ancient Etruscan city. *Carrara's valley:* The Carrarese valley is famous for its white (Carrara) marble.

63. *Benacus:* The ancient name for the Lago di Garda, which lies a short distance north of Mantua. The other places named in this passage lie around Lago di Garda. On an island in the lake the three dioceses mentioned conjoined, giving all three bishops jurisdiction on the island.

95–96. *Casalodi . . . Pinamonte:* Albert, Count of Casalodi and Lord of Mantua, let himself be persuaded by Pinamonte de Buonaccorsi to banish the nobles from Mantua as a source of danger to his rule. Once the nobles had departed, Pinamonte headed a rebellion against the weakened lord and took over the city himself.

106. *That one whose beard:* Eurypylus, a Greek augur. According to Greek custom an augur was summoned before each voyage to choose the exact propitious moment for departure. Dante has Virgil imply that Eurypylus and Calchas were selected to choose the moment for Agamemnon's departure from Aulis to Troy. According to the *Aeneid*, Eurypylus was not at Aulis; rather, he and Calchas were both consulted in choosing the moment for the departure from Troy.

116. *Michael Scott:* An Irish scholar of the first half of the thirteenth century, whose studies were largely in the occult.

118. *Guido Bonatti:* A thirteenth-century astrologer of Forlì. He was court astrologer to Guido da Montefeltro (Canto 27) advising him in his wars. *Asdente:* A shoemaker of Parma who turned diviner and won wide fame for his forecastings in the last half of the thirteenth century.

124. *Cain with his bush of thorns:* The medieval equivalent of our Man in the Moon. Dante seems to mean by Seville the whole area of Spain and the Straits of Gibraltar (Pillars of Hercules) which were believed to be the western limit of the Hemisphere of Land. The moon is setting on the western waves on the morning of Holy Saturday, 1300.

CANTO 21

7. *the Venetian arsenal:* An arms manufactory and a great center of shipbuilding and repairing.

37. *Blacktalons:* The original is Malebranche, or Evil Claws.

38. *Santa Zita:* The patron saint of the city of Lucca. One of Santa Zita's Elders would therefore equal one of Lucca's Senators, or Aldermen. Dante apparently has no specific man in mind. Rather, he means to underscore the fact that Lucca was a city of grafters, just as Bologna was represented as a city of panderers and seducers.

41. *Bonturo:* Bonturo Dati, a politician of Lucca.

51. *the Sacred Face: Il volto santo* was an ancient wooden image of Christ venerated by the Luccanese.

52. *Serchio:* A river near Lucca.

61. *You had best not be seen:* This is the only place in the total journey that Dante presents himself as being in physical danger. Since his dismissal from office and exile from Florence (on pain of death if he return) was based on a false charge of grafting, the reference is pointedly autobiographical.

79. *Malacoda:* The name means Bad Tail, or Evil Tail.

97–99. *Pisan infantry . . . of the enemy:* A Tuscan army attacked the fortress of Caprona near Pisa in 1289, and after fierce fighting the Pisan defenders were promised a safe-conduct if they would surrender. In some accounts it is reported that the Tuscans massacred the Pisans despite their promised safe-conduct, but in any case, the emerging Pisans would feel profoundly uneasy at being surrounded by their enemies under such conditions.

112–114. *In just five hours . . . a thousand two hundred and sixty-six years and a day:* Christ died on Good Friday of the year 33, and it is now Holy Saturday of the year 1300, five hours before the hour of his death. Many commentators (and Dante himself in the *Convivio*) place the hour of Christ's death at exactly noon. Accordingly, it would now be 7:00 A.M. of Holy Saturday—exactly eight minutes since the Poets left the bridge over the fourth *bolgia* (at moonset). According to the Synoptic Gospels, however, with which Dante was certainly familiar, Christ's death is precisely stated as 3:00 P.M., and it would now be 10:00 A.M. As far as the action of the poem is concerned, the only question of consequence is the time lapse from the bridge over the fourth *bolgia* to the talk with Malacoda, a matter of eight minutes or of three hours and eight minutes. One certainly seems too short, the other needlessly long; either answer can be supported.

CANTO 22

4. *Aretines:* The people of Arezzo. Dante was present in 1289 when the Guelphs of Florence and Lucca defeated the Ghibellines of Arrezo at Campaldino.

578

Notes

5–6. *tourney . . . tilts:* A tourney was contested by groups of knights in a field; a tilt by individuals who tried to unhorse one another across a barrier.

7. *bells:* The army of each town used a highly decorated chariot as a rallying point; bells, mounted on the chariot, were used for battle signals.

8. *signals from a castle:* Troops in sight of their castle were directed from the castle towers by banners in daytime and by fires at night.

19–21. *dolphins . . . secure ship:* It was a common belief that when dolphins began to leap around a ship they were warning the sailors of an approaching storm.

31–32. *I saw . . . one linger:* The Navarrese Grafter; his speech tells all that is known about him.

53. *King Thibault:* Thibault II, King of Navarre.

66. *Italians:* Dante uses the term *Latino* for a person from the area of ancient Latium, now Lazio, the province in which Rome is located.

82. *Friar Gomita of Gallura:* In 1300 Sardinia was a Pisan possession and was divided into four districts, of which Gallura was the northeast. Friar Gomita administered Gallura for his own profit and was hanged by the Pisan governor when he was found guilty of taking bribes to let prisoners escape.

89. *Michel Zanche of Logodoro:* Made Vicar of Logodoro when the King of Sardinia went off to war. When the king was captured and did not return, Michel maneuvered a divorce for the queen and married her. About 1290 he was murdered by his son-in-law, Branca d'Oria (Canto 33).

CANTO 23

4. *the fable of the Mouse and the Frog:* The fable was not by Aesop, but was attributed to him in Dante's time. A mouse comes to a body of water and wonders how to cross. A frog, thinking to drown the mouse, offers to ferry him, but the mouse is afraid he will fall off. The frog thereupon suggests that the mouse tie himself to one of the frog's feet. In this way they start across, but in the middle the frog dives from under the mouse, who struggles desperately to stay afloat while the frog tries to pull him under. A hawk sees the mouse struggling and swoops down and seizes him; but since the frog is tied to the mouse, he too is carried away, and so both of them are devoured.

6. *point by point:* The mouse would be the Navarrese Grafter; the frog would be the two fiends, Grizzly and Hellken. By seeking to harm the Navarrese they came to grief themselves.

579

22. *a pane of leaded glass:* A mirror.

43. *land mill:* As distinguished from the floating mills, built on rafts and anchored in rivers, that were common in Dante's time.

44–45. *ran faster . . . at the point nearest the paddles:* The sharp drop of the sluice makes the water run fastest at the point at which it hits the wheel.

59. *the Benedictines of Cluny:* The habit of these monks was especially ample and elegant.

62. *Frederick's capes:* Frederick II executed persons found guilty of treason by fastening them into a leaden shell. The doomed man was then placed in a cauldron over a fire and the lead was melted around him.

100. *Jovial Friars:* A nickname given to the military monks of the Order of the Glorious Virgin Mary founded at Bologna in 1261. Their original aim was to serve as peacemakers, enforcers of order, and protectors of the weak, but their observance of their rules became so scandalously lax, and their management of worldly affairs so self-seeking, that the order was disbanded by papal decree.

101–102. *We were chosen jointly . . . to keep the peace:* Catalano dei Malavolti (c. 1210–1285), a Guelph, and Loderingo degli Andolo (c. 1210–1293), a Ghibelline, were both Bolognese and, as brothers of the Jovial Friars, both had served as *podestà* (the chief officer charged with keeping the peace) of many cities for varying terms. In 1266 they were jointly appointed to the office of *podestà* of Florence on the theory that a bipartisan administration by men of God would bring peace to the city. Their tenure of office was marked by great violence, however, and they were forced to leave in a matter of months. Modern scholarship has established the fact that they served as instruments of Clement IV's policy in Florence, working at his orders to overthrow the Ghibellines under the guise of an impartial administration.

103. *Gardingo:* The site of the palace of the Ghibelline family degli Uberti. In the riots resulting from the maladministration of the two Jovial Friars, the Ghibellines were forced out of the city and the Uberti palace was razed.

107. *a figure crucified upon the ground:* Caiaphas; his words were: "It is expedient that one man shall die for the people and that the whole nation perish not" (John 11:50).

118. *His father-in-law:* Annas, father-in-law of Caiaphas, was the first before whom Jesus was led upon His arrest. He had Jesus bound and delivered to Caiaphas.

Notes

121. *I saw Virgil marvel:* Caiaphas had not been there on Virgil's first descent into Hell.

CANTO 24

2. *Aquarius:* The zodiacal sign for the period from January 21 to February 21. The Italian spring comes early, and the first warm days would normally occur under Aquarius.

85–90. *Libya . . . Ethiopia . . . lands that lie by the Red Sea:* The desert areas of the Mediterranean shores. Lucan's *Pharsalia* describes the assortment of monsters listed here by Dante. Their names have been rendered from Latin to English jabberwocky to avoid problems of pronunciation. In Lucan *chelydri* make their trails smoke and burn, they are amphibious; *jaculi* fly through the air like darts piercing what they hit; *pharese* plow the ground with their tails; *cenchri* waver from side to side when they move; and *amphisboenae* have a head at each end.

93. *heliotrope:* The bloodstone. A spotted chalcedony, it was believed to make the wearer invisible.

107. *the Phoenix:* The Phoenix of Arabia was the only one of its kind in the world. Every five hundred years it built a nest of spices and incense which took fire from the heat of the sun and the beating of the Phoenix's wings. The Phoenix was thereupon cremated and was then reborn from its ashes.

124. *Vanni Fucci:* The bastard son of Fuccio de Lazzeri, a nobleman (Black) of Pistoia. In 1293 with two accomplices he stole the treasure of San Jacopo in the Duomo of San Zeno. Others were accused, and one man spent a year in jail on this charge before the guilty persons were discovered. Vanni Fucci had escaped from Pistoia by then, but his accomplices were convicted.

129. *a man of blood and anger:* The traveler within the narrative (rather than Dante the author) claims that he did not know Fucci was a thief, but only that he was a man of blood and violence, who should therefore be punished in the seventh circle.

141. *listen to what I say:* Vanni Fucci's prophesy is as follows. In May of 1301 the Whites of Florence joined with the Whites of Pistoia to expel the Pistoian Blacks and destroy their houses. The Blacks fled to Florence and joined forces with the Florentine Blacks. On November 1st of the same year, Charles of Valois took Florence and helped the Blacks drive out the Whites. Piceno was the scene of a battle in which the Blacks of Florence and Lucca combined in 1302 to capture Serravalle, a White strong point near Pistoia.

145. *a fiery vapor:* Dante's meteorological figure is based on the contemporary belief that electric storms were caused by a conflict between fiery vapors and the preponderant watery vapors. By their contraries the watery vapors (mist) surround the fiery vapors, seeking to extinguish them, and the fiery vapors combat to shatter the mist. Here the fiery vapor is the Blacks and the shattered mist is the Whites.

CANTO 25

2. *figs:* An obscene gesture made by closing the hands into a fist with the thumb protruding between the first and second fingers. The fig is an ancient symbol for the vulva.

25. *Cacus:* The son of Vulcan. He lived in a cave at the foot of Mt. Aventine, from which he raided the herds of Hercules, which pastured on the plain below. Hercules clubbed him to death for his thievery, beating him in rage long after he was dead. Cacus is condemned to the lower pit for his greater crime, instead of guarding Phlegethon with his brother Centaurs.

35. *three wraiths came:* Agnello Brunelleschi, Buoso degli Abati, and Puccio Sciancato. These are the first of the five Florentine noblemen whom Dante encounters in this *bolgia.* They have been walking with Cianfa de' Donati, but they suddenly miss him and ask about him with some concern. Cianfa reappears in the form of a six-legged lizard and immediately fixes himself on Agnello and merges his lizard body with Agnello's human form. Cianfa and Agnello go off together, and a tiny reptile (Francesco dei Cavalcanti) bites Buoso degli Abati and exchanges forms with him. Only Pucci Sciancato is left unchanged for the time being. Little is known of the lives of these sinners beyond the fact that they were thieves.

82. *that part:* The navel.

91–94. *let Lucan be still . . . be Ovid silent:* Lucan relates how Sabellus and Nassidius, two soldiers of the army Cato led across the Libyan desert, were bitten by monsters. Sabellus melted into a puddle, and Nassidius swelled until he popped his coat of mail. In *Metamorphoses,* Ovid wrote how Cadmus was changed into a serpent and how Arethusa was changed into a fountain.

146. *he for whom you weep, Gaville:* Francesco dei Cavalcanti. He was killed by the people of Gaville, a village in the Arno Valley. His kinsmen rallied immediately to avenge his death, and many of the townsmen of Gaville were killed in the resulting feud.

Notes

8. *Prato:* Cardinal Niccolò da Prato, papal legate from Benedict XI to Florence. In 1304 he tried to reconcile the warring factions, but found that neither side would accept mediation. Since none would be blessed, he cursed all impartially and laid the city under an interdict (i.e., forbade the offering of the Sacraments). Shortly after this rejection by the Church, a bridge collapsed in Florence, and later a great fire broke out. Both disasters cost many lives, and both were promptly attributed to the papal curse.

34. *he the bears avenged:* Elisha saw Elijah translated to Heaven in a fiery chariot. Later he was mocked by some children, who called out tauntingly that he should "Go up" as Elijah had. Elisha cursed the children in the name of the Lord, and bears came suddenly upon the children and devoured them.

53–54. *the pyre where Eteocles and Polynices lay:* Eteocles and Polynices, sons of Oedipus, succeeded jointly to the throne of Thebes and came to an agreement whereby each would rule separately for a year at a time. Eteocles ruled the first year and, when he refused to surrender the throne at the appointed time, Polynices led the Seven against Thebes in a bloody war. In single combat the two brothers killed one another. Statius wrote that their mutual hatred was so great that when they were placed on the same funeral pyre the very flame of their burning drew apart in two great raging horns.

56. *Ulysses and Diomede:* They suffer here for their guilt in counseling and carrying out many stratagems which Dante considered evil. They are in one flame for their joint guilt, but the flame is divided, perhaps to symbolize the moral that men of evil must sooner or later come to a falling out, for there can be no lasting union except by virtue. Their first sin was the stratagem of the Wooden Horse, as a result of which Troy fell and Aeneas went forth to found the Roman line. Another sin was Ulysses' theft of the sacred statue of Pallas from the Palladium. Upon the statue, it was believed, depended the fate of Troy. Its theft, therefore, would result in Troy's downfall.

72. *since they were Greek:* Dante knew no Greek, and these sinners might scorn him, first, because he spoke what to them would seem a barbarous tongue, and second, because as an Italian he would seem a descendant of Aeneas and the defeated Trojans. Virgil, on the other hand, appeals to them as a man of virtuous life (who therefore has a power over sin) and as a poet who celebrated their earthly fame.

80. *one of you:* Ulysses. He is the figure in the larger horn of the flame (which symbolizes that his guilt, as leader, is greater than that of Diomede). His account of his last voyage and death is Dante's invention.

583

86. *Circe:* A sorceress, who changed Ulysses' men to swine and kept him a prisoner.

87. *Gaëta:* Southeastern Italian coastal town. According to the *Aeneid* it was earlier named Caieta by Aeneas in honor of his aged nurse.

90. *Penelope:* Ulysses' wife.

98. *both shores:* Of the Mediterranean.

101. *narrow pass:* The Straits of Gibraltar, formerly called the Pillars of Hercules. They were presumed to be the western limit beyond which no man could navigate.

104. *Ceuta:* In Africa, opposite Gibraltar.

105. *Seville:* In Dante's time this was the name given to the general region of Spain. Having passed through the Straits, the men are now in the Atlantic.

115. *morning . . . night:* East and west.

118. *we raised the other pole ahead:* They drove south across the equator, observed the southern stars, and found that the North Star had sunk below the horizon.

124. *a peak:* Purgatory. They sight it after five months of passage.

CANTO 27

3. *another came:* Guido da Montefeltro (1223–1298). As head of the Ghibellines of Romagna, he was reputed the wisest and most cunning man in Italy.

7. *the Sicilian bull:* In the sixth century B.C. Perillus of Athens constructed for Phalaris, Tyrant of Sicily, a metal bull to be used as an instrument of torture. When victims were placed inside it and roasted to death, their screams passed through tuned pipes and emerged as a burlesque bellowing of the bull. Phalaris accepted delivery and showed his gratitude by appointing the inventor the bull's first victim. Later Phalaris was overthrown, and he, too, took his turn inside the bull.

29–30. *Urbino . . . the Tiber springs to birth:* The Romagna district runs south from the Po along the east side of the Apennines. Urbino is due east of Florence and roughly south of Rimini. Between Urbino and Florence rise the Coronaro Mountains which contain the headwaters of the Tiber.

39–41. *Ravenna . . . Polenta's eagles . . . Cervia:* In 1300 Ravenna was ruled by Guido Vecchio da Polenta, father of Francesca da Rimini.

Notes

His arms bore an eagle, and his domain included the small city of Cervia about twelve miles south of Ravenna.

42–44. *The city . . . the* Green Claws: The city is Forlì. In 1282 Guido da Montefeltro defended Forlì from the French, but in 1300 it was under the despotic rule of Sinibaldo degli Ordelaffi, whose arms were a green lion.

44–46. Verrucchio *the Aged Mastiff and his Pup . . .* Montagna: Verrucchio was the castle of Malatesta and his son Malatestino, Lords of Rimini, whom Dante calls dogs for their cruelty. Montagna de' Parcitati, the leader of Rimini's Ghibellines, was captured by Malatesta in 1295 and murdered in captivity by Malatestino.

47–48. Lamone *and* Santerno . . . *the white den's Lion:* Maginardo de' Pagani (died 1302) ruled Faenza, on the river Lamone, and Imola, close by the river Santerno. His arms were a blue lion on a white field. He supported the Ghibellines in the north, but in the south (Florence) he supported the Guelphs, thus changing his politics according to the direction in which he was facing.

49–50. *the city the Savio washes:* Cesena. It ruled itself for a number of years, but was taken over by Malatestino in 1314. It lies between Forlì and Rimini.

67. *the Great Priest:* Boniface VIII, so called as Pope.

82. *the Prince of the New Pharisees:* Also Boniface.

83. *marched upon the Lateran:* Boniface had had a long-standing feud with the Colonna family. In 1297 the Colonna walled themselves in a castle twenty-five miles east of Rome at Penestrino (now called Palestrina) in the Lateran. On Guido's advice the Pope offered a fair-sounding amnesty which he had no intention of observing. When the Colonna accepted the terms and left the castle, the Pope destroyed it, leaving the Colonna without a refuge.

86–87. Acre . . . *trader in the Sultan's land:* It was the Saracens who opposed the crusaders at Acre, the Jews who traded in the Sultan's land.

90–92. Constantine . . . Silvestro . . . Soracte: In the persecutions of the Christians by the Emperor Constantine, Pope Sylvester I took refuge in the caves of Mt. Soracte (now called Santo Oreste) near Rome. Later, according to legend, Constantine was striken by leprosy and sent for Sylvester, who cured him and converted him to Christianity, in return for which the Emperor was believed to have made the famous "Donation of Constantine" (see Canto 19).

102. *so easily let go by Celestine:* Celestine V under the persuasion of Boniface abdicated the Papacy.

107. *long promise and short observance:* This is the advice upon which Boniface acted in trapping the Colonna with his hypocritical amnesty.

109. *St. Francis came:* To gather in the soul of one of his monks.

110. *one of the Black Angels:* A devil.

CANTO 28

8. *Puglia:* The modern name, but some of the events Dante narrates took place in the ancient province of Apulia. The southeastern area of Italy is the scene of all the fighting Dante mentions in the following passage.

10. *the war of the Trojans:* The Romans (descended from the Trojans) fought the native Samnites in a long series of raids and skirmishes from 343–290 B.C.

10–12. *and in that long war . . . Livy:* The Punic Wars (264–146 B.C.). Livy writes that in the battle of Cannae (216 B.C.) so many Romans fell that Hannibal gathered three bushels of gold rings from the fingers of the dead and produced them before the Senate at Carthage.

14. *Robert Guiscard:* Dante places Guiscard (1015–1085) in Paradise among the Warriors of God (Paradiso, 18). He fought the Greeks and Saracens in their attempted invasion of Italy.

16. *Ceperano:* In 1266 the Pugliese under Manfred, King of Sicily, were charged with holding the pass at Ceperano against Charles of Anjou. The Pugliese, probably under papal pressure, allowed the French free passage, and Charles went on to defeat Manfred at Benevento. Manfred himself was killed in that battle.

17–18. *Tagliacozzo . . . Alardo:* At Tagliacozzo (1268) in a continuation of the same strife, Charles of Anjou used a stratagem suggested to him by Alard de Valéry and defeated Conradin, nephew of Manfred. "Won without weapons" is an overstatement: what Alardo suggested was a simple but effective concealment of reserve troops. When Conradin seemed to have carried the day and was driving his foes before him, the reserve troops broke on his flank and rear and defeated Conradin's outpositioned forces.

32. *Ali:* Ali succeeded Mahomet to the Caliphate, but not until three of the disciples had preceded him. Mahomet died in 632, and Ali did not assume the Caliphate until 656.

56. *Fra Dolcino:* In 1300 Fra Dolcino took over the reformist order called the Apostolic Brothers, who preached, among other things, the community of property and of women. Clement V declared them hereti-

cal and ordered a crusade against them. The brotherhood retired with
its women to an impregnable position in the hills between Novara
and Vercelli, but their supplies gave out in the course of a year-long
siege, and they were finally starved out in March of 1307. Dolcino
and Margaret of Trent, his "Sister in Christ," were burned at the
stake at Vercelli the following June.

74. *Vercelli . . . Marcabò:* Vercelli is the most western town in Lombardy. Marcabò stands near the mouth of the Po.

76–90. *this warning, etc.:* Malatestino da Rimini (Canto 27), in a move
to annex the city of Fano, invited Guido del Cassero and Angioletto
da Carignano, leading citizens of Fano, to a conference at La Cattolica, a point on the Adriatic midway between Fano and Rimini. At
Malatestino's orders the two were thrown overboard off Focara, a
headland swept by such dangerous currents that approaching sailors
used to offer prayers for a safe crossing.

83. *Cyprus to Majorca:* These islands are at opposite ends of the Mediterranean.

84. *nor the Argive time:* The Greeks were raiders and pirates.

85. *The one-eyed traitor:* Malatestino.

86. *one who walks here beside me:* This is the Roman Tribune Curio,
who was banished from Rome by Pompey and joined Caesar's forces,
advising him to cross the Rubicon, which was then the boundary
between Gaul and the Roman Republic. The crossing constituted
invasion, and thus began the Roman Civil War. The Rubicon flows
near Rimini.

106. *Mosca dei Lamberti:* Dante had asked Ciacco (Canto 6) for news of
Mosca as a man of good works. Now he finds him, his merit canceled
by his greater sin. Buondelmonte dei Buondelmonti had insulted the
honor of the Amidei by breaking off his engagement to a daughter of
that line in favor of a girl of the Donati. When the Amidei met to
discuss what should be done, Mosca spoke for the death of Buondelmonte. The Amidei acted upon his advice, and from that murder
sprang the bloody feud between the Guelphs and Ghibellines of
Florence.

119. *a body without a head:* Bertrand de Born (1140–1215), a great
knight and master of the troubadours of Provence. He is said to have
instigated a quarrel between Henry II of England and his son Prince
Henry, called "The Young King" because he was crowned within his
father's lifetime.

137. *Achitophel:* One of David's counselors, who deserted him to assist
the rebellious Absalom.

The Divine Comedy

CANTO 29

10–11. *the moon . . . is under our feet:* If the moon, nearly full, is under their feet, the sun must be overhead. It is therefore approximately noon of Holy Saturday.

27. *Geri del Bello:* A cousin of Dante's father. He became embroiled in a quarrel with the Sacchetti of Florence and was murdered. At the time of the writing he had not been avenged by his kinsmen in accord with the clan code of a life for a life.

29. *master of Altaforte:* Bertrand de Born was Lord of Hautefort.

47. *Maremma, Valdichiano, and Sardinia:* Malarial plague areas. Valdichiano and Maremma were swamp areas of eastern and western Tuscany.

59. *the Aeginian people dying:* Juno, incensed that the nymph Aegina let Jove possess her, set a plague upon the island that bore her name. Every animal and every human died until only Aeacus, the son born to Aegina of Jove, was left. He prayed to his father for aid, and Jove repopulated the island by transforming the ants at his son's feet into men. The Aeginians have since been called Myrmidons, from the Greek word for ant.

85. *my Guide called out to one:* The sinner spoken to is Griffolino d'Arezzo, an alchemist who extracted large sums of money from Alberto da Siena on the promise of teaching him to fly like Daedalus. When the Sienese finally discovered he had been tricked, he had his "uncle," the Bishop of Siena, burn Griffolino as a sorcerer. Griffolino, however, is not punished for sorcery but for falsification of silver and gold through alchemy.

125–132. *Stricca . . . Niccolò . . . Caccia . . . Abbagliato:* These Sienese noblemen were members of the Spendthrift Brigade and wasted their substance in competitions of riotous living. Lano (Canto 13) was also of this company. Niccolò dei Salimbeni discovered some recipe (details unknown) prepared with fabulously expensive spices.

137. *Capocchio:* Reputedly a Florentine friend of Dante's student days. For practicing alchemy he was burned at the stake at Siena in 1293.

CANTO 30

1–2. *Juno took her furious revenge:* When Juno's husband (Jove) begot a son (Bacchus) upon a mortal (Semele, daughter of King Cadmus of Thebes), Juno turned her fury upon the mortals in a number of godlike ways, among them inducing the madness of King Athamas (Semele's brother-in-law).

Notes

16. *Hecuba:* Wife of King Priam. When Troy fell she was taken to Greece as a slave. En route she was forced to witness the sacrifice of her daughter and to look upon her son lying murdered and unburied. She went mad in her affliction and fell to howling like a dog. Ovid describes her anguish, but does not say she was changed into a dog.

31. *the Aretine:* Capocchio's companion, Griffolino.

32. *Gianni Schicchi:* Of the Cavalcanti of Florence. When Buoso di Donati died, his son, Simone, persuaded Schicchi to impersonate the dead man and to dictate a will in Simone's favor. Buoso was removed from the deathbed, Schicchi took his place in disguise, and the will was dictated to a notary as if Buoso were still alive. Schicchi took advantage of the occasion to make several bequests to himself, including a famous and highly-prized mare.

38. *Myrrha:* Daughter of Cinyras, King of Cyprus. Moved by an incestuous passion for her father, she disguised herself and slipped into his bed. After he had mated with her, the king discovered who she was and threatened to kill her, but she ran away and was changed into a myrtle. Adonis was born from her trunk.

61. *Master Adam:* Of Brescia. Under the orders of the Counts Guidi of Romena, he counterfeited Florentine florins of twenty-one rather than twenty-four carat gold, and on such a scale that a currency crisis arose in northern Italy. He was burned at the stake by the Florentines in 1281.

65. *Casentino:* A mountainous district in which the Arno rises.

74. *the Baptist's image:* John the Baptist's. As patron of Florence, his image was stamped on the florins.

76–77. *Guido . . . Alessandro . . . their filthy brother:* The Counts Guidi.

79. *Branda:* A spring near Romena. The famous fountain of Branda is in Siena, but Adam is speaking of his home country and must mean the spring.

79–81. *One of the three . . . is here already:* Guido died before 1300.

97. *the liar who charged young Joseph:* Potiphar's wife bore false witness against Joseph.

98. *Sinon:* The Greek who glibly talked the Trojans into taking the Horse inside the city walls.

116. *a single crime:* Dante must reckon each false florin as a separate sin.

128. *Narcissus' mirror:* A pool of water. Ovid tells how the young Narcissus fell in love with his own reflection in a pool. He remained bent over the reflection till he wasted away and was changed into a flower.

CANTO 31

5. *the lance that was Achilles':* Peleus, father of Achilles, left his magic lance to his son. Sonneteers of Dante's time made frequent metaphoric use of this lance; just as the lance could cure and then heal, so could the lady's look destroy with love and her kiss make whole.

17. *Roland:* Nephew of Charlemagne, hero of the French epic poem, *Chanson de Roland.* He protected the rear of Charlemagne's column on the return march through the Pyrenees from a war against the Saracens. When he was attacked he was too proud to blow his horn as a signal for help, but as he was dying he blew so prodigious a blast that it was heard by Charlemagne eight miles away.

40. *Montereggione:* A castle in Val d'Elsa near Siena built in 1213. Its walls had a circumference of more than half a kilometer and were crowned by fourteen great towers, most of which are now destroyed.

59. *the bronze pine cone in St. Peter's:* Originally part of a fountain, in Dante's time it stood in front of the Basilica of St. Peter. It is now inside the Vatican. It stands about thirteen feet high but shows signs of mutilation that indicate it was once higher.

63. *Frieslanders:* The men of Friesland were reputed to be the tallest in Europe.

77. *Nimrod:* The first king of Babylon, supposed to have built the Tower of Babel, for which he is punished by the confusion of his own tongue and understanding. Nothing in the Biblical references portrays him as one of the earth-giants.

94. *Ephialtes:* Son of Neptune (the sea) and Iphimedia. With his brother, Otus, he warred against the gods, striving to pile Mt. Ossa on Mt. Olympus, and Mt. Pelion on Mt. Ossa. Apollo restored order by killing the two brothers.

99. *Briareus:* Another of the giants who rose against the Olympian gods. Virgil speaks of him as having a hundred arms and fifty hands, but Dante has need only of his size and of his sin, which he seems to view as a kind of revolt of the angels, just as the action of Ephialtes and Otus may be read as a pagan distortion of the Tower of Babel legend. He was the son of Uranus and Tellus.

100. *Antaeus:* The son of Neptune and Tellus (the Earth). In battle, his strength grew every time he touched the earth, his mother. He was accordingly invincible until Hercules killed him by lifting him over his head and strangling him in midair. Lucan describes Antaeus' great lion-hunting feat in the valley of Zama where, in a later era, Scipio defeated Hannibal. Antaeus did not join in the rebellion against the gods, and therefore he is not chained.

124. *Tityos or Typhon:* Also sons of Tellus. They offended Jupiter, who had them hurled into the crater of Etna, below which the lake Tartarus was supposed to lie.

136. *the Carisenda:* A leaning tower of Bologna.

CANTO 32

10. *those Ladies of the Heavenly Spring:* The Muses. They so inspired Amphion's hand upon the lyre that the music charmed blocks of stone out of Mt. Cithaeron, and the blocks formed themselves into the walls of Thebes.

28–29. *Tanbernick . . . Pietrapana:* There is no agreement on the location of the mountain Dante called Tanbernick. Pietrapana, today known as *la Pania,* is in Tuscany.

41. *two clamped together:* Alessandro and Napoleone, Counts of Mangona. Among other holdings, they inherited a castle in the Val di Bisenzio. They seemed to have been at odds on all things and finally killed one another in a squabble over their inheritance and their politics (Alessandro was a Guelph and Napoleone a Ghibelline).

61. *him whose breast and shadow:* Mordred, King Arthur's traitorous nephew. He tried to kill Arthur, but the king struck him a single blow of his lance, and when it was withdrawn a shaft of light passed through the gaping wound and split the shadow of the falling traitor.

63. *Focaccia:* Of the Cancellieri of Pistoia. He murdered his cousin (among others) and may have been the principal cause of a great feud that divided the Cancellieri and split the Guelphs into the White and Black parties.

66. *Sassol Mascheroni:* Of the Toschi of Florence. He was appointed guardian of one of his nephews and murdered him to get the inheritance for himself.

68. *Camicion de' Pazzi:* Alberto Camicion de' Pazzi of Valdarno. He murdered a kinsman. *Carlin:* Carlino de' Pazzi, relative of Alberto. He was charged with defending for the Whites the castle of Piantravigne in Valdarno, but surrendered it for a bribe. He belongs therefore in the next lower circle, Antenora, as a traitor to his country, and when he arrives there his greater sin will make Alberto seem almost virtuous by comparison.

78. *the face of one:* Bocca degli Abbati, a traitorous Florentine. At the battle of Montaperti he hacked off the hand of the Florentine standard-bearer. The cavalry, lacking a standard around which it could rally, was soon routed.

116. *Buoso da Duera:* Of Cremona. In 1265 Charles of Anjou marched against Manfred and Naples (see Canto 19). Buoso da Duera was sent out in charge of a Ghibelline army to oppose the passage of one of Charles's armies, but he accepted a bribe and let the French pass unopposed. The event took place near Parma.

119. *Beccheria:* Tesauro dei Beccheria of Pavia, Abbot of Vallombrosa and Papal Legate (of Alexander IV) in Tuscany. The Florentine Guelphs cut off his head in 1258 for plotting with the expelled Ghibellines.

120. *Gianni de' Soldanier:* A Florentine Ghibelline of ancient and noble family. In 1265, however, during the riots that occurred under the Two Jovial Friars, he deserted his party and became a leader of the commoners (Guelphs). In placing him in Antenora, Dante makes no distinction between turning on one's country and turning on one's political party if the end is simply for power.

121. *Ganelon:* Betrayed Roland to the Saracens (see Canto 31).

122. *Tebaldello:* Tebaldello de' Zambrasi of Faenza. At dawn on November 13, 1280, he opened the city gates and delivered Faenza to the Bolognese Guelphs in order to revenge himself on the Ghibelline family of the Lambertazzi who, in 1274, had fled from Bologna to take refuge in Faenza.

130–131. *Tydeus . . . Menalippus:* Statius recounts that Tydeus killed Menalippus in battle but fell himself, mortally wounded. As he lay dying he had Menalippus' head brought to him and fell to gnawing it in his dying rage.

CANTO 33

13–14. *Ugolino . . . Ruggieri:* Ugolino, Count of Donoratico and a member of the Guelph family della Gherardesca. He and his nephew, Nino de' Visconti, led the two Guelph factions of Pisa. In 1288 Ugolino intrigued with Archbishop Ruggieri degli Ubaldini, leader of the Ghibellines, to get rid of Visconti and to take over the command of all the Pisan Guelphs. The plan worked, but in the consequent weakening of the Guelphs, Ruggieri saw his chance and betrayed Ugolino, throwing him into prison with his sons and his grandsons. In the following year the prison was sealed up, and they were left to starve to death. It should be noted that two of the boys were grandsons, and all were considerably older than one would gather from Dante's account. Anselm, the younger grandson, was fifteen. The others were really young men and were certainly old enough for guilt despite Dante's charge in line 90.

Notes

22. *coop:* Dante uses the word *muda,* signifying a stone tower in which falcons were kept in the dark to moult. From the time of Ugolino's death it became known as the Tower of Hunger.

29–30. *the mountain that hides Lucca from Pisa:* These two cities would be in view of one another were it not for Monte San Giuliano.

32. *Gualandi and Sismondi and Lanfranchi:* Three Pisan nobles, Ghibellines and friends of the Archbishop.

79–80. *the land where "si" sounds sweet and clear:* Italy.

82. *Caprara and Gorgona:* These two islands near the mouth of the Arno were Pisan possessions in 1300.

86. *betrayed your castles:* In 1284, Ugolino gave up certain castles to Lucca and Florence. He was at war with Genoa at the time, and it is quite likely that he ceded the castles to buy the neutrality of these two cities, for they were technically allied with Genoa. Dante, however, must certainly consider the action as treasonable, for otherwise Ugolino would be in Caïna for his treachery to Visconti.

88. *you modern Thebes:* Thebes was the site of some of the most hideous crimes of antiquity.

105. *Is not all heat extinguished:* Dante believed that all winds resulted from "exhalations of heat." Cocytus, however, is conceived as wholly devoid of heat, a metaphysical absolute zero. The source of the wind is Satan (Canto 34).

118. *Friar Alberigo:* Of the Manfredi of Faenza. He was another Jovial Friar. In 1284 his brother Manfred struck him in the course of an argument. Alberigo pretended to let it pass, but in 1285 he invited Manfred and his son to a banquet and had them murdered. The signal to the assassins was the words: "Bring in the fruit." "Friar Alberigo's bad fruit," became a proverbial saying.

125. *Atropos:* The Fate who cuts the thread of life.

137. *Branca d'Oria:* A Genoese Ghibelline. His sin is identical in kind to that of Friar Alberigo. In 1275 he invited his father-in-law, Michel Zanche (Canto 22), to a banquet and had him and his companions cut to pieces. He was assisted in the butchery by his nephew.

CANTO 34

1. *On march the banners of the King:* The hymn *(Vexilla regis prodeunt)* was written in the sixth century by Venantius Fortunatus, Bishop of Poitiers. The original celebrates the Holy Cross and is part of the service for Good Friday to be sung at the moment of uncovering the cross.

67. *huge and sinewy arms:* The Cassius who betrayed Caesar was more generally described in terms of Shakespeare's "lean and hungry look." Another Cassius is described by Cicero as huge and sinewy. Dante probably confused the two.

95. *middle tierce:* In the canonical day tierce is the period from about 6:00 to 9:00 A.M. Middle tierce, therefore, is seven-thirty. In going through the center point, they have gone from night to day and have moved ahead twelve hours.

128. *the one peak:* The Mount of Purgatory.

129. *this great cavern:* The natural animal pit of line 98. It is also Beelzebub's dim tomb, line 131.

133. *a little stream:* Lethe. In classical mythology, the river of forgetfulness, from which souls drank before being born. In Dante's symbolism it flows down from Purgatory, where it has washed away the memory of sin from the souls who are undergoing purification. That memory it delivers to Hell, which draws all sin to itself.

143. *stars:* As part of his total symbolism Dante ends each of the three divisions of the *Commedia* with this word. Every conclusion of the upward soul is toward the stars, God's shining symbols of hope and virtue.

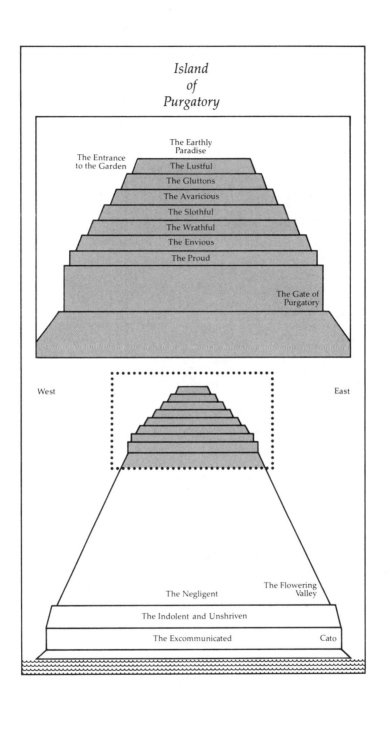

Island
of
Purgatory

The Earthly
Paradise

The Entrance
to the Garden

The Lustful

The Gluttons

The Avaricious

The Slothful

The Wrathful

The Envious

The Proud

The Gate of
Purgatory

West   East

The Flowering
Valley

The Negligent

The Indolent and Unshriven

The Excommunicated   Cato

Notes to Purgatorio

7–12. *Yours am I, sacred Muses, etc.:* Dante invokes all the Muses as he did in the Inferno, but there the exhortation was to his own powers, to high genius, and to memory. Here he exhorts Calliope, the Muse of Epic Poetry, to fill him with the strains of the music she played in the defeat of the Pierides, the nine daughters of Pierius, King of Thessaly. They presumed to challenge the Muses to a contest of song. After their defeat they were changed into magpies for their presumption.

19. *The planet whose sweet influence strengthens love:* Venus. Here, as the morning star, Venus is described as rising in Pisces, the sign preceding Aries, in which the sun will rise.

23. *four stars:* The Four Cardinal Virtues. Modern readers are always tempted to identify these four stars as the Southern Cross, but it is almost certain that Dante did not know about that formation.

24. *the first mankind:* Adam and Eve. After their sin, they were driven from the Earthly Paradise into the Hemisphere of Land.

29. *the other pole:* The North Pole. The Wain (Ursa Major) is below the horizon.

31. *an ancient man:* Cato of Utica, or Marcus Porcius Cato, the Younger (95–46 B.C.). In the name of freedom, he opposed the policies both of Caesar and of Pompey, but because he saw Caesar as the greater evil he joined forces with Pompey. After the defeat of his cause at the battle of Thapsus, Cato killed himself rather than lose his freedom. Virgil lauds him in the *Aeneid* as a symbol of perfect devotion to liberty, and all writers of Roman antiquity gave him a similar high place. Why Cato should be so signally chosen by God as the special guardian of Purgatory has been much disputed. Despite his suicide he was sent to Limbo as a Virtuous Pagan. From Limbo he was especially summoned to his present office, and it is clear that he will find a special triumph on Judgment Day. The key to Dante's intent seems to lie in the four stars, the Four Cardinal Virtues, that shine so brightly on Cato's face when Dante first sees him. Once Cato is forgiven his suicide (in this case viewed as a positive act, a death for freedom), he may be taken as a figure of Prudence, Justice, Fortitude and Temperance and a symbol of the natural love of freedom. Purgatory, it should be remembered, is the road to Ultimate Freedom.

78. *Marcia:* Daughter of the Consul Philippus, she became Cato's second wife, bearing his three children. In 56 B.C., in an unusual transac-

Notes

tion approved by her father, Cato released her in order that she might marry his friend Hortensius. After the death of Hortensius, Cato took her back. In *Il Convivio,* Dante presents the newly widowed Marcia praying to be taken back in order that she may die the wife of Cato and that it may be said of her that she was not cast forth from his love. Dante treats that return as an allegory of the return of the strayed soul to God.

89. *the decree:* The law that makes an absolute separation between the damned and the saved.

CANTO 2

1–9. *The sun, etc.:* It is dawn.

47. *in exitu Israel de Aegypto:* "When Israel out of Egypt came" (Psalm 114).

71. *who bears the olive branch:* In Dante's time couriers bore the olive branch to indicate not only peace but good news in general.

91. *Casella:* Practically all that is known about Casella has been drawn from the text itself. He seems to have died several months before Dante began his journey, hence early in 1300 or late in 1299. There is no explanation of his delay in reaching Purgatory, but clearly it is Dante's conception that the souls bound for Purgatory do not always proceed instantly to their destination, but may be required to expiate by a delay at their gathering point by the mouth of the Tiber.

99. *he has taken all who asked:* Boniface VIII decreed a Jubilee Year from Christmas, 1299, to Christmas, 1300. His decree extended special indulgences even to the dead, hence the angel's permissiveness.

CANTO 3

27. *It was taken to Naples from Brindisium:* Virgil died in 19 B.C. in Brindisium. His bones were later exhumed and reinterred in Naples by order of the Emperor Augustus.

29. *the heavens which pass the light:* The spheres of the Ptolemaic system, conceived as crystalline and as so clear that light passes from one to the other undiminished.

40–45. *You saw how some yearn, etc.:* Dante saw them in Limbo. Virgil's implication is that if such monuments of human intellect could never penetrate the mystery of the All, it is folly for mankind to seek to explain the reasons for God's ways. *Of them and many more:* Part of Virgil's sorrow is due to the fact that he is one of the "many more."

50. *Lerici and Turbia:* Lerici lies on the shores of the Mediterranean near the river Magra, and Turbia stands a bit inland from the Mediterranean on the other side of Liguria. The tract of mountains between them is one of the most rugged in Europe.

52. *Now who is there to say:* Virgil had traveled through Hell once before and knew that way, but the road of Purgatory is unknown to him.

59. *a throng:* The Contumacious. The section of the Mount of Purgatory that lies below the Gate (the Ante-Purgatory) is occupied by the Late Repentant who put off their surrender to God until the end of their lives. As they made God wait, so must they now wait before they may begin their purification. These souls suffer no pain but the burning of their own frustrated desire to mount to God.

74. *already among the chosen:* The souls in Purgatory must suffer their purification, but they are already, in effect, saved and will eventually enter Heaven.

101. *waving the backs of their hands in our direction:* To indicate the way. The gesture is Italian; we should be inclined to point.

105. *over there:* In Purgatory "over there" always means "back in the world."

112. *I am Manfred:* Manfred, King of Sicily, the legitimized natural son of Frederick II. He was born in Sicily in 1231 and was killed at the battle of Benevento after a defeat by Charles of Anjou in 1266. He was famous as an Epicurean and for his taste for physical pleasures rather than for godliness. In the everlasting internal wars of Italy, Manfred often opposed the Papal States, but was too powerful to be excommunicated while alive. He was nevertheless disobedient to Mother Church and therefore must pass thirty times the period of his disobedience outside the cliff.

112–113. *grandson of the blessed Empress Constance:* Constance was the mother of Frederick II. Since Manfred was not a legitimate son, he identifies himself by his grandmother as a delicate way of avoiding any reference to his illegitimacy.

115. *my sweet daughter:* Also named Constance. She married Peter of Aragon and bore him three sons. One died before full manhood. Of the remaining two, Frederick became King of Sicily and Iacapo succeeded his father to the throne of Aragon.

118. *My flesh had been twice hacked:* At the battle of Benevento. After Manfred's defeat and death, Charles of Anjou ordered that every soldier in his army file past the body of the dead Manfred and place a stone upon it. Thus, a great cairn was erected to the memory of a fallen warrior.

Notes

124. *the pastor of Cosenza:* Bartolommeo Pignatelli, Cardinal and Archbishop of Cosenza from 1254 to 1266. On orders from Pope Clement
IV, he disinterred the body of Manfred and had it carried without
honors (with quenched tapers) outside the Kingdom of Naples,
which was then a Papal State.

CANTO 4

5–12. *the error that asserts, etc:* The original doctrine of multiple souls
was set forth by Plato, who claimed that we have three souls within
us, each with its specific function: the Vegetative Soul (roughly corresponding to what we might call the Somatic) which is seated in the
liver; the Sensitive (the Emotional) Soul which is seated in the heart;
and the Intellectual Soul which is seated in the brain.

16. *to fifty full degrees of its noon peak:* Since one degree of arc equals
four minutes of time, it is now three hours and twenty minutes since
sunrise, or about 9:00 A.M.

25–26. *San Leo:* An almost inaccessible town on a mountaintop near
San Marino. *Noli:* A seacoast town accessible (in Dante's time) only
from the sea or by treacherously steep steps cut into the cliffs behind
the town. *Bismantova:* A village on a mountain of the same name
about twenty miles south of Reggio Emilia.

41–42. *a line drawn from midquadrant to the center:* Of an astrolabe;
hence 45 degrees.

55–75. *I looked . . . upward to the sun, etc.:* Dante is astonished to find
that the sun is on his left (i.e., north) when he faces east. Virgil points
out that as the sun moves toward the summer solstice it will move
even further north (toward Ursa Major) into the sign of Gemini. Virgil then asks Dante to visualize the globe with the Mount of Zion and
the Mount of Purgatory so placed that they are in different hemispheres but share the same celestial horizon. Since the sun must pass
between them, Zion must always be north of the sun and Purgatory
must always be south of it. In addition, since the two places are an-
tipodal, the Celestial Equator is always as far south of one as it is
north of the other.

60. *the North Wind's cave:* Aquilon, the North Wind, rules the compass
from NW to NE (for 45° on either side of the North Pole).

62–63. *that bright mirror:* The sun, reflector of God's love. *up and
down:* In two senses: first, to the upper and lower hemispheres; second, up to Heaven and down to earth.

80–84. *the Equator, etc:* The soundest interpretation of these lines is
based on Dante's *Il Convivio:* "And it is to be understood that each

heaven below the Crystalline [the Sphere of the Fixed Stars] has two poles that are constant in relation to that heaven itself; and the ninth [the Crystalline] has two poles that are firm and fixed and immovable in every respect; and each, the ninth like all the others, has a circle which may be called the equator of its proper heaven; the which is equally distant from one pole and the other, as one may clearly understand if he revolves an apple or some other round thing." Hence the following extended paraphrase of lines 79–84: "The mid-circle of the Crystalline Sphere, which is called the Celestial Equator, always lies between the sun and that hemisphere in which it is winter, and, for the reason you have just given [i.e., that Purgatory and Zion are antipodal] the Celestial Equator must always lie as far to the north of this place [Purgatory] as the Hebrews [when, before the dispersion of the Jews, they looked at it from Jerusalem] were accustomed to seeing it toward the south [warmer climes]."

122. *Belacqua:* A Florentine who manufactured parts for musical instruments. Of him the Anonimo Florentino says: "He was the most indolent man who ever lived. . . . Dante was very intimate with him and used often to take him to task for his laziness."

128. *God's bird above the Gate:* God's angel above the Gate of Purgatory, which Dante will come to in Canto 9.

136–140. It is now noon at Purgatory. It must therefore be midnight in Jerusalem. Dante believed Morocco was exactly 90° west of Jerusalem (in the same longitude as Spain). Since 90° west of midnight is six hours earlier, it is six o'clock there, and night would just be beginning.

CANTO 5

23. *Miserere:* The souls are singing Psalm 51: "Have mercy upon us." Each band of souls on the mountain has its particular prayer, except the Contumacious, who have been cut off from the offices of ritual.

37. *hot vapors:* Dante's meteorology was built largely on a theory of the opposition of hot and wet vapors. Here he attributes falling stars and heat lightning to hot or "fiery" vapors.

69. *one replied:* Jacopo del Cassero. Of a leading family of Fano, he served as *podestà* of Bologna from 1296 to 1297 in a manner that offended the powerful Azzo VIII of Este. In 1298, on his way to Milan to serve as *podestà* of that city, he was killed outside the town of Oriaco (or Oriago) by Azzo's hirelings, after a chase in which he foundered among the reeds and mud of a nearby swamp area. Had he turned instead toward La Mira, a Paduan city, he would have found refuge.

600

Notes

81. *among the Antenori:* Among the Paduans. According to legend, Padua was founded by Antenor of Troy.

94–101. *Bonconte:* Son of Guido da Montefeltro, who is in Hell as an Evil Counselor (Inferno, 27). Bonconte was a leader of the Ghibellines at the battle of Campaldino, in which the Florentine Guelphs defeated the Ghibellines and Bonconte was killed (1289). *Giovanna:* Bonconte's wife. Neither she nor anyone else has offered prayers to shorten his time of waiting. *Archiana:* A nearby river that rises in the Apennines and flows into the Arno (the point at which "its name ends").

120. *his nature gives:* The demons are fallen but they still retain many of the powers given them by their angelic origins.

121. *From Pratomagno to the spine:* The Casentino, or upper valley of the Arno, is closed in on the east by the spine of the Apennines, and on the west by the Pratomagno range.

132. *the cross I had formed upon my breast:* His arms crossed in contrition and as a symbol of surrender to God.

140. *Pia:* Traditionally identified as Pia de' Tolomei of Siena, who married a Guelph leader and was murdered by him. The identification is doubtful, however, and the text says all that is certain about her.

CANTO 6

13. *the Aretine:* Benincasa da Laterina, a justice of the city of Arezzo. On the charge of highway robbery and brigandage, he passed the death sentence on the brother of Ghino di Tacco. Soon thereafter Benincasa was called to Rome to a papal judgeship. Ghino, a fierce robber-baron, followed him there, burst in upon him in open court, cut off his head, and escaped safely.

14. *the other:* The other Aretine, Guccio or Ciacco de' Tarlati. He drowned in the Arno after the battle of Montaperti, or perhaps of Campaldino.

17. *Federico Novello:* Little is known about him except that he was the son of Guido Novello and that he was killed in a skirmish with a band of Aretines.

17–18. *the Pisan . . . Marzucco:* Farinata, son of Marzucco degli Scornigiani of Pisa. Farinata was killed in Pisa, and Marzucco, who had become a Minor Friar, went to bury his body. In one account, he preached a funeral sermon of forgiveness and ended by kissing the hand that had murdered his son, thus "shining so true" in Christian charity. In another account, Count Ugolino had ordered that the body be left unburied, and Marzucco went boldly before his enemy and won permission to bury his son, thus "shining so true" in courage.

19. *Count Orso:* Son of Napoleone degli Alberti murdered by his cousin, the son of Alessandro; Alessando is with Napoleone in Hell (Canto 32).

22. *Pierre de la Brosse:* Court physician and favorite of Louis IX and later of Philip III of France. Philip had Pierre hanged in 1278. Dante believed him to have been the innocent victim of the intrigues of Queen Mary of Brabant, "the Lady" he calls upon to repent while still on earth, for fear she may find herself in a worse herd (in Hell) than that in which Pierre finds himself.

29. *one of your verses:* The *Aeneid,* in which Palinurus begs Aeneas to get him out of Hell, but the reply comes from the Sibyl: *Desine fata deum flecti sperare precando* (Do not hope to bend the fixed decree of the gods by prayer).

77. *Sordello:* A troubadour poet of the first three-quarters of the thirteenth century. His life is only sketchily known, but he seems to have been a person of some political consequence. Dante has given him the same relative position in Purgatory and the same majestic dignity he assigns to Farinata in Hell and to Cacciaguida in Paradise. Since all three are political figures, Dante seems to have ennobled Sordello for his politics rather than for his poetry.

91. *Justinian:* The Emperor Justinian. His reorganization and codification of Roman law trimmed the bit and adjusted the bridle of the horse (the Empire), making a unified Italy possible, but his work has gone for nothing.

94–99. *You priests . . . set meddling hands upon its reins:* Dante charges the priests with having helped create the bloody chaos of Italian politics by meddling in temporal affairs. By disregarding the Biblical injunction to render unto Caesar what is Caesar's and unto God what is God's, they have brought corruption upon the Church and destruction upon the state.

100. *German Albert:* Albert of Austria, born 1248, Emperor 1298, assassinated 1308. He was, therefore, Emperor at the purported time of Dante's journey. At that time Italy was a part of the Holy Roman Empire though torn by internal strife between the Ghibellines (nominally the party of the Emperor though the party lines were blurred by local urgencies) and the Guelphs (nominally for independence and more often for anarchy). Many of the warring lords were, moreover, lieges of the Emperor. Dante's lament for Italy is always for her bloody internal wars, which he attributed to the lack of a central authority. The Emperor had that authority and could easily have

brought unification and peace to Italy. But Albert and his father Rudolph concerned themselves with affairs to the north and neither ever so much as visited Italy. Because of their negligence, Italy had all but slipped out of the Empire and the many Italian robber-barons warred on unceasingly at the very time that the northern kingdoms of the Empire were enjoying a long era of peace.

121. *Supreme Jove:* In Dante's view the pagan names Zeus and Jove referred always to the Christian God as (dimly) perceived by the ancients who lacked Christ's clarifying word.

129. *Marcellus:* Marcellus opposed Caesar and was forgiven by him.

CANTO 7

4–6. *Before those spirits . . . to rest:* According to the legend of the Harrowing of Hell, Christ descended into Limbo in A.D. 33 and took with Him to Heaven the first souls to win salvation. From the time of the Fall until then, Purgatory existed but was not in use. Virgil died in 19 B.C. under the Emperor Octavian.

33. *taint of earth:* Original sin. Unbaptized infants have not yet been cleansed of their part in Adam's guilt. They share the fate of the Virtuous Pagans whom they resemble in being sinless but lacking Christ's Sacrament.

35–36. *the Three Sacred Virtues:* Faith, Hope, and Charity; these are the revealed or theological virtues. *the rest:* The Four Cardinal Virtues: Justice, Prudence, Temperance, and Fortitude.

40–60. *We are not fixed, etc.:* The Law of the Ascent described here is allegorical and is centered around the sun as the symbol of divine illumination. The primary meanings of the allegory are first, that one cannot achieve true repentance and purification except in the sight of God (light of the sun); second, that one has no difficulty in backsliding (going down the mountain) once he is out of God's sight (darkness); and third, that once out of sight of God/Sun one simply cannot find within himself the will to climb.

82. *Salve Regina:* The beginning of the Compline hymn in the Roman Catholic Breviary: "Hail Queen, Mother of Mercy . . . to thee we sigh . . . in this valley of tears."

94. *the Emperor Rudolph:* Rudolph of Hapsburg (1218–1291), crowned Emperor in 1273. He is the father of German Albert (Canto 6) and with him shares the blame for failing to unify Italy.

96. *Now, though another try, 't will be too late:* The other is Henry VII of Luxemburg, Emperor from 1308 to 1313. As Emperor, he tried to ac-

complish, under circumstances that had by then made it impossible, what Rudolph and Albert had neglected to do under circumstances that assured success.

97. *That one who comforts him:* Ottocar II, King of Bohemia (the land whose waters drain into the Moldau, to the Elbe, to the sea) from 1253 to 1278. In life he was Rudolph's enemy and a bloodthirsty tyrant, but Dante may have known him only as a valiant warrior. His object in placing him here seems to be to show the reconciliation of enemies after true repentance and forgiveness.

102. *Wenceslaus:* Wenceslaus IV (the Good), born in 1270, succeeded his father as King of Bohemia in 1278. He was elected King of Poland in 1300, and died 1305. Wenceslaus was forced to cede many territories for which his warrior father would have fought to the death. Wenceslaus preferred piety to warfare, habitually hearing several masses daily. With his spirits thus restored, he seems to have found the strength for scouting various bedrooms, for he had begotten numerous illegitimate children by the time he was twenty-five. Hence Dante's charge that he was dissipated.

103. *That snubnose:* Philip III of France (1245–1285), known as the Bold, also the Snubnose, succeeded his father, Louis IX, in 1270. He did not die while actually in flight from the field of battle, but at Perpignan, to which he had retired after the French navy had been annihilated by Pedro III of Aragon.

104. *the kindly looking one:* Henry (the Fat) of Navarre (reigned 1270–1274). He died reportedly "suffocated by the fat of his own body." In life he was quite other than kindly, but Dante obviously credits him with true repentance.

109. *The Plague of France:* Philip IV (the Fair) of France, born 1268, crowned 1285, died 1314. Second son of Philip III, he married Juana, daughter of Henry of Navarre. Philip was for Dante the archetype of the evil ruler, in much the same way that Boniface VIII (whom Philip humiliated and drove to an early death) was the archetype of the evil Pope. Internally, Philip ruined whole provinces by his extortions and currency frauds. He systematically jailed Italian merchants (for ransom) on false charges, cruelly robbed the Jews, and suppressed the Knights Templars in order to confiscate their properties. Externally, he played a disastrous hand in Italian politics. Soon after he had eliminated Boniface VIII, he succeeded in placing one of his puppet cardinals on the Papal Throne as Clement V. Under Clement V the Papal Seat was transferred to Avignon.

112–113. *The heavy-sinewed one . . . that spirit with the manly nose:* Another pair of former enemies reconciled. The first is Pedro III of Aragon (1236–1285), King of Aragon, 1276, and (after the bloody Sicilian Vespers of 1282 in which all the French were massacred) King of Sicily. He married Manfred's "good Constance" (Canto 3). The second spirit is Charles I of Anjou (1220–1285), crowned King of Sicily and Puglia (Apulia) in 1265. It was Charles who destroyed Manfred at Benevento in 1265 and who was overthrown in the Sicilian Vespers.

115. *that younger one:* Alfonso III, the Magnificent (1271–1291), crowned King of Aragon, 1286. He left no heirs and his rule passed to his degenerate younger brothers: the throne of Aragon to James, and that of Sicily to Frederick, both of whom were ruling in 1300. Thus, the younger sons have the material heritage of their father, Pedro, but no one (now that Alfonso is dead) possesses his better heritage (his merit).

130. *Henry of England:* Henry III (1216–1278), a pious but pallid king. His son, Edward I, however (who was ruling in 1300), crowned a glorious reign with an enduring reform of English law. Hence Henry's branches came to a good issue in a noble son. Henry is seated alone because he is unique in this company. He attended so many masses daily that he never got around to governing his kingdom. His sin, therefore, could not have been neglect of God, but rather neglect of his divinely imposed duties to rule his kingdom well.

135. *the Marquis William Longsword:* William VII, Marquis of Monferrato (1245–1292). A lesser prince than the others, hence he sits below and looks up to them. As Imperial Vicar to Italy he headed a coalition of Ghibelline towns. In 1290 the Republic of Asti fomented a rebellion in Alessandria, a town held by William. Attempting to put down the rebellion, William was captured, locked in an iron cage, and exposed to public ridicule. He died in the cage, and even in death his body was shockingly abused by the Alessandrians. William's son moved against Alessandria to avenge his father, but the Alessandrians defeated him and invaded Monferrato and Canavese, the two districts of William's fief.

CANTO 8

53. *Judge Nin:* Nino de' Visconti da Pisa (died 1296), nephew of Count Ugolino (Inferno, 33). He was Justiciary of Gallura in Sardinia, then a Pisan possession, and ordered the hanging of Friar Gomita (Inferno, 22). He was a viceroy for his uncle, not a judge in the modern sense. Dante, who knew him intimately, rejoices that a man so deeply involved in worldly affairs did not lose his soul to worldliness.

70. *enormous tide:* Figuratively, the enormous tide between life and death. Literally, the sea between the mouth of the Tiber and the

shores of Purgatory, the longest sea route on earth as Dante conceived it.

71. *my Giovanna:* Nino's daughter.

73–81. *I do not think her mother, etc.:* Nino's widow was Beatrice, daughter of Opizzo da Este (Inferno, 12). She put off the weeds and white veil (the mourning costume of Dante's time), first, in being betrothed to Alberto Scotti, Lord of Piacenza, and then, in jilting him to marry Galeazzo Visconti of Milan, all under the pressure of her family's political motives. The jilted Scotti took revenge by ruining Visconti, and Beatrice had to share his poverty. In 1328, Beatrice's son (she was then a widow for the second time) was made Lord of Milan and her fortunes thereafter (she died in 1334) rode high—a turn of events Dante did not live to see.

118. *Conrad Malaspina:* Very little is known about Conrad except that he was the son of Frederick I, Marchese di Villafranca, and the grandson of Conrad I. The house of Malaspina, on the other hand, was honorably known, though scarcely as well as Dante declares below. In his praise of the Malaspina family, Dante is paying a debt of gratitude for the honor and hospitality with which it received him after his exile from Florence.

129. *strict sword . . . easy purse:* Valor . . . liberality.

131. *the Guilty Head:* The primary meaning is the Devil; the corrupt Papacy and the negligent Emperor may be secondary meanings.

133–135. *the sun shall not complete its seventh rest:* The sun will not have completed its seventh transit of Aries (the seven years will not pass) before Dante will know from his own experience the truth of what he has here uttered as hearsay (of the virtue and liberality of the Malaspina family). *that great bed the Ram bestrides:* That portion of the zodiac which falls under the sign of Aries. Aries is often depicted with his four feet spread wide.

CANTO 9

1–6. There is no wholly satisfactory explanation of this complex opening description. Dante seems to be saying that the third hour of darkness is beginning (hence, if sunset occurred at 6:00 it is now a bit after 8:00 P.M.) and that the aurora of the rising moon is appearing above the horizon. He describes the moon as the concubine of Tithonus. Tithonus, however, married the daughter of the sun, Aurora (dawn), and it was she who begged Jove to give her husband immortality while forgetting to ask perpetual youth for him. Thus Tithonus lived but grew older and older beside his ageless bride. Despite his advanced years, however, he seems here to be philandering with the

moon as his concubine. Dante describes the moon as rising from
Tithonus' bed and standing on the balcony of the east (the horizon)
with the constellation Scorpio gemmed on her forehead.

15. *former woes:* Tereus, the husband of Procne, raped her sister
Philomela, and cut out her tongue so that she could not accuse him.
Philomela managed to communicate the truth to Procne by means of
her weaving. The two sisters thereupon took revenge by killing Itys,
son of Procne and Tereus, and serving up his flesh to his father.
Tereus, learning the truth, was about to kill the sisters when all were
turned into birds. Ovid has Tereus changed into a hoopoe, and probably Procne into a swallow and Philomela into a nightingale. Dante
clearly takes the swallow to be Philomela.

18. *prophetic in its vision:* It was an ancient belief that the dreams that
came toward dawn were prophetic.

23. *Ganymede:* Son of Tros, the mythical founder of Troy. He was reputedly the most beautiful of mortals, so beautiful that Jove sent an
eagle to snatch up the boy and bring him to Heaven, where he became cupbearer to the gods.

24. *consistory:* The council of the gods on Olympus.

34–39. *Achilles must have roused, etc:* It had been prophesied that
Achilles would be killed at Troy. Upon the outbreak of the Trojan
War, his mother, Thetis, stole him, while he was sleeping, from the
care of the Centaur Chiron who was his tutor and fled with him to
Scyros, where she hid him disguised as a girl. He was found there and
lured away by Ulysses and Diomede, who burn for that sin (among
others) in Malebolge.

77. *three steps:* The entrance into Purgatory involves the ritual of the
Roman Catholic confessional with the angel serving as the confessor. The three steps are the three acts of the perfect confession.

86. *Where is your guide?* It must follow from the angel's question that
souls ready to enter Purgatory are led up the mountain by another
angel. Dante and Virgil are arriving in an irregular way, as they did to
the shore below, where they were asked essentially the same question by Cato.

94. *the first step:* Contrition of the heart. White for purity, shining for
hope, and flawless for perfection.

97. *The second:* Contrition of the mouth, *i.e.,* confession. The color of a
bruise for the shame that envelops the souls as it confesses, rough-
grained and fire-flaked for the pain the confessant must endure, and
cracked for the imperfection (sin) the soul confesses.

100. *The third:* Satisfaction by works. Red for the ardor that leads to good

works. Porphyry is a purple stone, but Dante does not say the stone was porphyry; only that it resembled it.

103–105. The angel represents the confessor and, more exactly, the Church Confessant. Thus the Church is founded on adamant and rests its feet on good works.

112. *Seven P's:* P is for the Latin *peccatum.* Thus there is one P for each of the Seven Deadly Sins for which the sinners suffer on the seven ledges above: Pride, Envy, Wrath, Acedia (Sloth), Avarice (Hoarding and Prodigality), Gluttony, and Lust. Dante has just completed the act of confession and the angel confessor marks him to indicate that even in a shriven soul there remain traces of the seven sins which can be removed only by suffering.

133. *The Tarpeian rock-face:* The public treasury of Rome was kept in the great scarp of Tarpeia on the Campidoglio. The Tribune Metellus was its custodian when Caesar, returned to Rome after crossing the Rubicon, moved to seize the treasury. Metellus opposed him but was driven away and the great gates were opened. Lucan describes the scene and the roar that echoed from the rock-face as the gates were forced open.

CANTO 10

2. *perverse love:* All human actions, in Dante's view, are motivated by love: right love produces good actions and perverse love produces bad.

14. *waning moon:* The moon had been full on the night before Good Friday; it is now four and a half days later.

26. *the inner cliff:* At the entrance to each cornice, Dante presents high examples of the virtue opposite the sin punished on that cornice. Their purpose is clearly to whip the souls on to emulation. At the end of the passage of each cornice, Dante presents examples of the terrible price one must pay for succumbing to each particular sin. The opening exhortations designed to drive the souls on to emulation may be called the Whip of each sin; the closing examples, or admonitions, may be called the Rein, serving to check the impulse toward that sin.

29. *Polyclitus:* Greek sculptor of the late fifth century B.C., contemporary with Phidias. His name seems to have been the word for artistic perfection during the late Middle Ages and early Renaissance, probably because he is often mentioned by Aristotle.

42. *Ecce ancilla Dei:* "Behold the handmaiden of God" (Luke 1:38).

Notes

49. *another scene:* The second panel depicts King David putting aside all the offices of majesty to dance in humility and total abandonment before the Lord on bringing the Ark to Jerusalem from the house of the Gittite, Obed-edom. Dante has confused, or deliberately blended, two scenes into one. The first journey of the Ark began with an ox-drawn cart and it was then that Uzzah (an example of overweening pride) was struck dead for laying unsanctified hands upon the Ark, a sacrilegious act. David laid up the Ark in the house of the Gittite and returned for it three months later, on which occasion it was carried to Jerusalem by the Levites. It was on the second journey that David put by his majesty to dance before the Lord. Michal, daughter of King Saul, and David's first wife, looked on scornfully and was punished for her arrogance by sterility (see II Samuel).

68. *another panel:* The third panel depicts the Emperor Trajan halting his royal cavalry en route to battle and dismounting in order to secure justice for a poor woman. Dante places Trajan in Paradise (Canto 20), his soul according to legend having been summoned back to earth and baptized by St. Gregory.

CANTO 11

59. *Guglielmo Aldobrandesco:* A powerful Ghibelline of the Sienese Maremma and Count of Santafiora, the district Dante has already cited as a lawless robber-barony. The Aldobrandeschi were in constant conflict with Siena. In 1259, according to varying accounts, the Sienese besieged the Aldobrandeschi castle in Campagnatico. Omberto, though with very few men at his disposal, scorned his enemies, refused to surrender, killed many Sienese, and even made a mad charge into the thick of the enemy's forces, where he was killed after giving a bloody account of himself. Omberto's death broke the power of the Aldobrandeschi, their rule passing to the Sienese. Thus (lines 67–69) his pride destroyed not only Omberto but all of his line and its adherents.

79. *Od'risi:* Oderisi d'Agobbio, a famous illuminator of manuscripts and a miniaturist. He is reputed to have illuminated many Vatican manuscripts on papal commission. He probably died in Rome in 1299.

83. *Franco Bolognese:* Oderisi's student. He was alive in 1300, but few mentions of his name or traces of his work still exist.

94. *Cimabue:* Giovanni dei Cimabui (c. 1240–1308), esteemed by his Florentine contemporaries as the master painter. His particular innovation was in liberating painting from strict Byzantine domination in favor of a more natural style.

95. *Giotto:* A shepherd boy who became Cimabue's pupil and who went

609

on to excel his teacher, becoming the true father of the Renaissance tradition of painting from nature.

97–98. *from one Guido has another shorn poetic glory:* The first is Guido Cavalcanti (1250?–1300), a fellow poet whom Dante saluted in the *Vita Nuova* as "he whom I call first among my friends" (see Inferno, 10). The other is generally taken to be Guido Guinizelli of Bologna (died *c.* 1275).

108. *the turning of the slowest of the spheres:* The Ptolemaic cosmography attributed to the Sphere of the Fixed Stars a west-to-east rotation of 1° per 100 years, hence 36,000 years for one revolution.

110. *this one:* Provenzano Salvani, the Ghibelline chief of Siena at the battle of Montaperti, who led the cry for the destruction of Florence. In 1269 the Florentines defeated the Sienese at Colle di Val d'Elsa, and Salvani, taken prisoner, was beheaded on the field of battle.

127–132. *But . . . how was he given license to be here?:* Salvani has been dead thirty-one years. Normally, if (as Dante assumes) he had put off repentance till the end, he would have had to wait in Ante-Purgatory for a period equal to his lifetime. However, an incident of great self-abasement won special grace for Salvani. A friend of his was captured, probably by Charles of Anjou at Tagliacozza, and held for a great ransom to be paid within a month, failing which the friend would be executed. Salvani, despite his great pride, posted himself in the Piazza del Campo in Siena and begged alms to raise the ransom by which his friend was freed.

CANTO 12

23–24. *stone figures covered the track:* The Rein of Pride. The Poets find set before them as a final lesson, examples of great pride and of the downfall to which it brings men.

30. *Briareus:* One of the Titans who now guard the central well of Hell. He stormed Olympus and tried to unseat Jupiter, but was felled by a thunderbolt.

31–33. *their father:* Jupiter. *Thymbraeus:* Apollo, so called after his temple at Thymbra. *Pallas:* Minerva. The scene portrays another repulse of the Titans, this time at Phlegra in Thessaly.

34. *Nimrod:* The first king of Babylon and builder of the Tower of Babel at Shinar.

37. *Niobe:* The mother of seven sons and seven daughters who, in her pride, mocked Latona, concubine of Jupiter, for having only one son (Apollo) and one daughter (Diana). Thereupon, Apollo took his bow and killed all the sons; Diana, hers and killed all the daughters.

Notes

40. *Saul:* The proud first king of Israel. Defeated by the Philistines on Mt. Gilboa, he fell on his own sword to avoid capture. David, mourning his death, cursed Mt. Gilboa: "Ye mountains of Gilboa, let there be no dew, neither let there be rain upon you, nor fields of offerings" (II Samuel 1:21).

46. *Rehoboam:* The arrogant king of Israel who would not lighten the taxes of the ten tribes. He sent Adoram to collect the taxes, and when Adoram was stoned to death, Rehoboam fled in panic from Jerusalem, though no one pursued him.

49. *Alcmaeon:* Son of Amphiareus, a soothsayer. Foreseeing that he would die at Thebes, Amphiareus hid in a place known only to Eriphyle, his wife. Eriphyle accepted a gold necklace as a bribe for revealing his hiding place, whereupon Amphiareus instructed his son, Alcmaeon, to avenge him, and the boy killed his mother. The fatal ornament had been made by Vulcan and bore a charm that brought to grief whoever owned it.

53. *Sennacherib:* King of Assyria. He was defeated by the inferior forces of Hezekiah of Judah. Praying to his gods after his defeat, he was murdered by two of his sons. Thus, Sennacherib, not yet sufficiently humbled, went back to his false gods and met death in the act of prayer, but the true God made Hezekiah rejoice.

55–56. *Tomyris . . . Cyrus:* Cyrus (560–529 B.C.), Emperor of Persia, showed his contempt for Tomyris, the Scythian queen, by killing her son. Tomyris gathered her armies and defeated Cyrus in a battle in which he was killed. She then had Cyrus' head cut off and threw it into an urn full of human blood, commanding the head of the bloodthirsty tyrant to drink its fill.

59. *Holofernes:* He laid siege to Bethulia as general of the army of Nebuchadnezzar. The city, cut off from water, was about to surrender when Judith made her way to Holofernes' tent to spend the night with him. While he slept, she cut off his head and took it back to the city, where it was mounted on the wall. Holofernes' fate threw the Assyrians into a panic and they fled, pursued by the Jews.

80. *the sixth handmaiden:* The figure here conceives of the twelve hours of the light as twelve handmaidens serving the day. The sixth handmaiden is, therefore, the sixth hour of light, hence, noon, sunrise being at six o'clock.

101–102. *the church:* San Miniato, built on a rise across the Arno from Florence. *the Rubaconte:* The bridge that leads most directly to San Miniato (now Ponte alle Grazie).

105. *the stave and ledger:* The stave was formerly an official measure, primarily for salt, which was taxed. One of the Chiaramontesi family, as head of the Salt Tax Department, had given rise to a famous

611

scandal by auditing the salt in with a full stave and auditing it out with a lightened one, thus shaving a certain quantity from each transaction. The "ledger" had grown light when two officials ripped out a page to remove evidence of graft. The exact dates of these events are disputed, but both took place in Dante's time and both were widely known.

110. *Beati pauperes spiritu:* "Blessed are the poor in spirit: for theirs is the kingdom of Heaven" (Matthew 5:3).

CANTO 13

27. *sweet invitations:* The Whip of Envy. Since the Envious have their eyes wired shut, it is appropriate that the Whip of Envy be oral rather than visual. The Whip, accordingly, consists of three disembodied voices that cry out the key lines from scenes that exemplify great charity (*caritas*, the love of others).

29. *Vinum non habent:* "They have no wine." These words were spoken by Mary at the Wedding Feast in Cana of Galilee.

33. *I am Orestes:* The second lesson in love of others clearly reflects John 15:13: "Greater love hath no man than this, that he lay down his life for his friends." Orestes and Pylades were famous for the depth of their friendship. Cicero relates the incident in which, Orestes having been condemned to death, Pylades pretended to be Orestes in order to die in his friend's place. Orestes then came forward asserting his own identity, and thereupon both friends argued, "I am Orestes," each trying to save the other.

36. *Love your enemies:* These words were spoken by Jesus in the Sermon on the Mount: "Love your enemies, bless them that curse you, do good to them that hate you, and pray for them which despitefully use you, and persecute you" (Matt. 5:44).

58. *haircloth:* A coarse, heavy fabric made of goat hair, worn against the skin as a penance, and to discipline the flesh.

71. *sew new-caught falcons:* Since diurnal birds sit still in the dark, the eyelids of newly caught falcons were sewn shut by their trainers to make them sit still, partly to keep them from battering themselves against the cage and partly to break them for their later training. In hunting, the birds were normally carried hooded to the point of release.

86. *Heaven's Light:* God.

97. *a spirit:* Sapìa of Siena, paternal aunt of Provenzano Salvani (Canto 11). As the wife of another nobleman, she resented Salvani's rise to great power. Salvani attacked the Florentines at Colle in 1269, and

Notes

when she saw him defeated and beheaded on the field, she is reported to have cried: "Now God, do what You will with me, and do me any harm You can, for after this I shall live happily and die content." According to another account, she had been exiled from Siena (hence her resentment) and was living at Colle at the time of the battle. The dates of her birth and death are unknown, but she seems to have been about sixty at the time of the battle of Colle, and Dante makes clear that she died before Pier Pettinaio, whose death occurred in 1289.

123. *like a blackbird:* The occasional warm, sunny days that occur in Italy in January and February are called in Tuscany and Lombardy "the days of the blackbird." The European blackbird is reputed by Italians to dread cold. When the winter sun shines brightly, however, it immediately perks up and acts as if it owned the world. But as soon as the cold returns, it huddles shivering and miserable.

127. *Pier Pettinaio:* Literally, Peter Combseller. He came to Siena as a boy from the country, became a Sienese citizen, and grew into a local legend of piety. He was given to public prayer and to elaborate ideas of honesty and was later honored by an annual feast day such as is normally reserved for saints. He operated a small shop in which he sold combs, hence his name.

150. *restore my name:* In her final years Sapìa performed a number of good works for Siena, but there are several reports that she was generally condemned as a traitor.

151–155. A complicated passage of local reference that is certainly put into Sapìa's mouth by Dante as a Florentine jibe at the Sienese. *Talamone:* A point on Italy's west coast about eighty miles almost due south of Siena. The Sienese, lacking a port, and wanting to compete with Genoa, bought the site in 1303 and invested heavily in building and dredging operations. The scheme failed because of malarial conditions and because the hoped-for port silted in almost as fast as it could be dredged. *the lost Diana:* Another project intermittently undertaken by the Sienese over a long period. Siena was water-poor, but the magnificent flow at certain wells suggested to the Sienese the presence of an underground river which they christened the Diana, and which they dug for at great expense. All efforts had failed up to Dante's time, and the failures were used as a standing joke against the Sienese as overambitious crackpots trying to make themselves better than they were. The Sienese, however, continued their expensive digging and did, sometime later, locate a substantial underground flow. There is still a Well of Diana in a convent in Siena. *the admirals:* May be interpreted as contractors or harbor-masters, in which case they would "lose the most" because they would die of malaria, or as ships' captains, in which case they would lose the most if they tried to use the port, or if they waited until the Sienese finished it.

613

The Divine Comedy

CANTO 14

16. *Falterona:* One of the major peaks of the Tuscan Apennines. It is northeast of Florence, and both the Arno and the Tiber spring from its sides.

31–36. The gist of these lines may be stated as: "From the Arno's source to the point at which it enters the sea." *the great range:* The Apennines. *Pelorus:* A mountain in Sicily, part of the Apennine system, but cut off from the rest of the chain by the Straits of Messina.

42. *they fed in Circe's pen:* Circe changed men into beasts of various kinds. Guido goes on to specify four species of beasts into which the Arno transforms the people along its course: the swine of the Casentine, the curs of Arezzo, the wolves of Florence, and the foxes of Pisa.

43. *its first weak course:* In the Upper Casentine the Arno is not yet swollen by any tributaries.

48. *turns aside its snout:* The Arno flows from the Upper Casentine straight toward Arezzo, but at a point a few miles north of the town it swings east without entering the town proper.

58. *your grandson:* Rinieri's grandson was Fulcieri da Calboli, who in 1302 became *podestà* of Florence. In Dante's time many of the city-states of Italy were so torn by internal strife that they could not hope to agree on one of their own citizens as *podestà*. The practice grew, therefore, of electing a (presumably neutral) outsider to administer impartial justice for a given term. Fulcieri (either bribed by the Black Guelphs, or put into office in the first place as part of their plot) arrested and put to painful death many leaders of the White Guelphs as well as some of the few remaining and powerless Ghibellines. The leaders disposed of, he proceeded murderously against the Whites in general. The wolves he hunts are the White Florentines; the sad wood is Florence; the old beast is Fulcieri, who, after selling them alive, piles shame on shame by killing them himself for sport.

81. *Guido del Duca:* A Ghibelline of Brettinoro, a member of the prominent Onesti family of Ravenna. He served in various judicial posts in Romagna from 1195 on, and is known to have been alive in 1229.

85. *This seed:* Envy. *this sad straw:* His present pains.

88. *Rinier:* Rinieri dei Paolucci da Calboli di Forlì, a Guelph leader, *podestà* of Faenza in 1247, and later of other cities. In 1292 he was reelected *podestà* of Faenza, but he and his supporters were expelled by the Ghibellines in 1294. In 1296 Rinieri seized Faenza while the Ghibellines were away paying a social war on Bologna. Those courtesies concluded, they returned in force, and Rinieri was killed in the homecoming festivities.

614

Notes

91–92. *war-torn land:* Romagna. *the sea:* The Adriatic. *Reno:* A river that bounds Romagna on the west.

100–102. All the persons mentioned here were leaders of Romagna during the last decades of the twelfth century and into the first three quarters of the thirteenth. All are cited as examples of knightly grace, bravery, and sound counsel. *Romagnoles:* People of Romagna.

103–104. *Fabbro:* Fabbro de' Lambertazzi, leader of all Romagna's Ghibellines, died in 1259. *Fosco:* Bernardin di Fosco, son of a small landholder, who rose to high estate through great merit and served as *podestà* of Pisa in 1248 and of Siena in 1249. Both men are cited for the same virtues exemplified by Mainardi and the others listed in lines 100–114. These were all prominent leaders of Romagna, and all were alive during some part of Guido's lifetime.

110. *the house of the Traversari:* Guido has cited Pier Traversaro among the best lords of the land. Here he extends his praise to the whole house, along with his lament that it is an expiring line. *the Anastagi:* Of Ravenna. Another great house left without heirs.

115. *Brettinoro:* A small town between Forlì and Cesena. Now called Bertinoro, it was Guido's birthplace.

118–120. The towns here mentioned are small fortified towns of Romagna. In Guido's view, their ruling houses have bred down to degenerate stock. In 1300 the Malvacini di Bagnacavallo had no male heirs and the line was doomed to extinction.

121–123. *The Pagani:* Ruled over various holdings in Romagna, Faenza and Imola among them. The fiend of the Pagani was Count Maginardo (Inferno, 27), who died in 1302. After him his sons ruled well, but never well enough to remove the stain left on the family name by Maginardo's misrule.

124. *Ugolin de' Fantolini:* Of Faenza. A lord of great reputation. He died in 1278 leaving two sons and two daughters, but both sons had died without issue by 1286.

134. *a voice:* The Rein of Envy. Like the Whip, the Rein consists of bodiless voices racing through the air. The first voice is that of Cain crying to God at his punishment: "Everyone that findeth me shall slay me" (Gen. 4:14). Thus the first crash resounds with the cry of the first man punished for envy. The second voice is of Aglauros, daughter of Cecrops, King of Athens. Her sisters were Herse and Pandrace. Mercury fell in love with the beautiful Herse and bribed Aglauros to arrange for him an assignation with her sister. Aglauros took the bribe, but in envy that her sister should lie with a god, she turned Mercury away when he arrived for his appointment. Mercury, enraged, turned her to stone.

The Divine Comedy

CANTO 15

1–2. *that bright sphere that . . . skips endlessly:* The zodiac, which dips above and below the horizon.

54–57. *such a fear:* That someone else will get the material good one cherishes. *that cloister:* Heaven.

86–114. *a vision:* The Whip of Wrath. It consists of three visions that seize upon the soul on their way to enter the cloud of smoke. The first (lines 85–93) is an incident from the life of Christ, in which he stayed behind in the Temple of Jerusalem to instruct the learned men. The second (lines 94–105) is of an incident from the life of Pisistratus, Tyrant of Athens from 560–527 B.C. A suitor of Pisistratus' daughter embraced her in public. The wife of Pisistratus demanded vengeance for this apparent act of dishonor, but Pisistratus turned away wrath with a soft answer. The third (lines 106–114) is of the martyrdom of St. Stephen. Dante is in error in making Stephen a boy at the time of his death.

98. *for whose name the gods debated:* The legend is that Neptune and Athena both wished the new city to bear their names. Ovid describes the resultant contest, which Athena won.

CANTO 16

19. *three prayers:* The Litany of the Mass includes three prayers, each of which begins with *Agnus Dei*—"Lamb of God which taketh away the sins of the world." The first two add "have mercy upon us"; the third adds "give us peace."

27. *kalends:* The kalends were the first day of each Roman month. To reckon time by kalends, therefore, is to use mortal measures which are meaningless in the eternity of the dead. *someone spoke:* Marco Lombardo, or Marco the Lombard. Nothing is definitely known of him, not even his exact name, for his own identification of himself may mean either "I am a man of Lombardy named Marco," or "I am Marco of the Lombardi family."

38. *these swathings death dissolves:* Mortal flesh.

98. *The Shepherd who now leads mankind:* Boniface VIII.

116. *the land the Po and the Adige water:* Lombardy.

117. *till Frederick came to loggerheads with Rome:* Frederick II engaged in a long and disastrous conflict with, successively, Popes Honorius III, Gregory IX, and Innocent IV.

124. *Conrad da Palazzo:* Or Corrado. A nobleman of Brescia, he held various high offices in Florence, Siena, and Piacenza between 1276

Notes

and 1289. *Gherard'*: Gherardo da Cammino, Captain-General of Treviso from 1283 till his death in 1306. Dante cites him as the type of the true noble in *Il Convivio*.

125. *Guido da Castel:* Or Castello. A nobleman of Reggio, famous for his graciousness and liberality.

126. *in the fashion of the French, 'The Honest Lombard':* The French called all Italians "Lombards" and believed all of them to be shrewd and unscrupulous usurers. To be thus called "honest" by them would be to win praise from the least likely source.

131. *why Levi's sons alone:* The Levites, the priests of Israel, were forbidden to inherit wealth, for the Lord was their inheritance, and except for their houses they were commanded to depend on the tithes and offerings of the people. Dante has returned once more to his basic charge against the Church—that in amassing wealth and power it lost spirituality and grew corrupt.

CANTO 17

3. *as moles do, through the skin:* Dante follows a medieval belief that the eyes of moles were completely sealed by a membrane through which they could see a diffused, foggy light only.

19. *a vision:* The Rein of Wrath. The three visions of the ruinous results of wrath may be taken as exemplifying wrath against kin, against neighbor, and against God (and self). The first vision shows Procne killing her own son in wrath. The second vision (lines 25–30) is of the crucifixion of Haman, the powerful minister of Ahasuerus, King of Persia. Enraged against Mordecai, Haman persuaded Ahasuerus to decree the death of all the Jews in Persia. Queen Esther, however, persuaded Ahasuerus of Haman's iniquity and the decree was canceled. Ahasuerus had Haman crucified in Mordecai's place. The third vision (lines 34–39) is of Amata killing herself for wrath. In the *Aeneid*, Amata's daughter, Lavinia, was betrothed to Turnus, against whom Aeneas launched an attack. When a false rumor of Turnus' death reached Amata, she hanged herself in rage. Aeneas later killed Turnus in a duel, and Lavinia married him. Dante's meaning is that Aeneas was God's chosen and was sent to Italy by divine will to found the Roman Empire as the seat of the true Church. It was God's will, therefore, that Aeneas marry Lavinia, daughter of Italy, and thus bring together God's two chosen races. Amata's wrath, therefore, was not only against herself but against God's decree.

47. *a new voice:* The Angel of Meekness.

87. *Sloth:* The fourth of the deadly sins, a torpor of the soul which, loving the good, does not pursue it actively enough.

617

93. *of animal or of mind-directed love:* By either blind instinct or those desires shaped by the God-given light of reason.

106–108. *love cannot abate, etc.:* The doctrine here is Aquinian. Nothing in creation seeks anything but what it takes to be the good of love. Even suicide is an act motivated by self-love, the suicide believing he does himself more good in escaping life than in enduring it.

CANTO 18

18. *the blind who lead the blind:* The teachers of Epicurean philosophy and their students. Both are spiritually blind in Dante's view in that they teach that all desire (all love) is a good thing and should be gratified.

37. *love's substance:* Dante uses the philosophical term *matera* (matter), which may be taken to mean either the thing loved or the natural substance of love, i.e., the soul's naturally created aptitude to love. The Epicureans, according to Dante, err in not seeing that appearances may beguile the soul into loving a bad object.

49. *substantial form:* A Scholastic term for "the essence of a thing." The substantial form of man is his soul, which is distinct from matter, yet united with it.

67. *Those masters:* Aristotle and Plato. Both based their moral philosophy upon free will.

82. *Pietola:* A village near Mantua. One legend has it that Virgil was born in Pietola rather than in Mantua proper. Thus Pietola outshines all other Mantuan towns because it was Virgil's birthplace.

92. *Ismenus and Asopus:* Boetian rivers. The ancient Thebans ran on their banks at night invoking the aid of Bacchus when they needed rain for their vines.

99. *two spirits . . . were calling out:* The Whip of Sloth. The first example of zeal (spiritual) is Mary's haste, after the Annunciation, to go visit Elizabeth in the hill country of Juda. The second (temporal) is Caesar's diligence in the conquest of Ilerda (the modern Spanish town of Lérida). He laid siege to Marseilles, left an army there under Brutus, and pushed by forced marches to take Ilerda.

118. *San Zeno:* The Abbot of San Zeno through most of Barbarossa's reign was Gherardo II, who died in 1187.

119. *Frederick Barbarossa:* Frederick Redbeard or Frederick I, Emperor from 1152–1190. Dante calls him good because he pursued the good of the Empire. Frederick quarreled with Pope Alexander III and was excommunicated by him. Frederick then warred on the Pope's adher-

618

ents in Lombardy. He took Milan in 1163, pulled down its walls, burned the city, plowed the ruins, and sowed the ground with salt that nothing might grow there. After other bloody successes, his fortunes turned, and he had to kneel to Alexander for pardon. He drowned while crusading in the Holy Land.

121. *another with one foot now in the grave:* Alberto della Scala, Lord of Verona, who died in September of 1301. He had three natural sons, among them the famous Can Grande della Scala, who was Dante's host and protector in exile. Another was Giuseppe, and it was this son Alberto forced upon the monks as Abbot of San Zeno, a post he held from 1292 to 1313. The speaker, as former abbot, is especially indignant that an unworthy man should hold so high an office. Giuseppe was triply disqualified, being mentally incapable, physically deformed, and a bastard.

132–138. *the Scourge of Sloth, etc.:* The Rein of Sloth. The first example reminds the sinners that though the Lord delivered Israel from Egyptian bondage, opening the Red Sea for their passage, the people still muttered and would not follow Moses (would not diligently pursue good) and that, therefore, the Lord doomed them to die in the wilderness. The second example, from secular history, reminds the sinners of those followers of Aeneas who chose to live at ease in Sicily rather than follow him to the great end that had been promised. Thus they did not share in the glory of founding Rome.

CANTO 19

5. *Fortuna Major:* A conjunction of the last stars of Aquarius and the first of Pisces, supposed to signify great good fortune.

7. *a stuttering crone:* The Sirens were mythological creatures, usually of great beauty, and with the power of singing so entrancingly that they charmed the souls of men. They were usually presented as luring sailors at sea to their destruction. Dante's Sirena is a Christian adaptation. She symbolizes the three remaining sins, Greed, Gluttony, and Lust, the abandonment to physical appetites.

22. *I turned Ulysses:* In the *Odyssey,* Ulysses escapes the Sirens by stuffing his ears with wax and having himself lashed to the mast of his ship. Dante may, perhaps, be following another version of the myth, but more probably he means to portray the Siren as a liar.

26. *a saintly Lady:* She may be Beatrice, or she may be Provenient Grace, but any identification is speculative.

50. *Blessed are they that mourn:* The fourth beatitude, "Blessed are they that mourn: for they shall be comforted" (Matthew 5:4).

73. *My soul cleaves to the dust:* Psalm 119.

99. *Scias quod ego fui successor Petri:* "Know that I was Peter's successor." The speaker is Pope Adrian V. He died in 1276 after having been Pope for thirty-eight days.

101. *a pleasant river:* The Lavagna, which flows between Sestri and Chiaveri, small coastal towns near Genoa. Adrian, born Ottobuono de' Fieschi, was of the line of the Counts of Lavagna.

139. *Neque nubent:* ". . . they neither marry [nor are given in marriage but are as the angels of God in Heaven]" (Matt. 22:30). These were Christ's words when asked to which husband a remarried widow would belong in Heaven. Adrian obviously extends the meaning to include the cancellation of all earthly contracts, fealties, and honors.

145. *Alagia:* Daughter of Niccolò di Tedisio di Ugone de' Fieschi and wife of Moroello Malaspina, Marquis of Giovagallo. Dante had been well received by Malaspina and knew and admired his wife for her good works.

CANTO 20

19. *I heard rise:* The Whip of Avarice. The first example (lines 20–24) praises the blessed poverty of Mary, so great that she gave birth to Jesus in a manger. The second example (lines 25–27) praises the honorable poverty of Fabricius Caius Luscinus, Roman Consul in 282 B.C. and Censor in 275. He refused to deal in the bribes and gifts which were normally assumed to be perquisites of such high offices, and he died so poor that the state had to bury him and had also to provide dowries for his daughters. The third example (lines 31–33) cites St. Nicholas, Bishop of Myra in Lycia, who was born rich and gave all his riches to the poor. In one example, a local minor nobleman found himself so poor that he could not provide dowries for his daughters. He was about to turn them over to a life of sin in order that they might make a living, when Nicholas heard of their plight and threw three bags of gold through the nobleman's window. Thus the father was able to buy husbands for the girls, and thus Nicholas guided their youth to "virtuous steadiness."

49. *Hugh Capet:* Dante seems to confuse Hugh, Duke of the Franks (died 956), and his son, Hugh Capet (King of France 987–996), into one person. Hugh Capet founded the Capetian dynasty of French kings, succeeding Louis V, the last of the Carlovingian line founded by Charlemagne. The vengeance Hugh Capet prays for as of 1300 had already taken place by the time Dante wrote these lines, the Flemish having inflicted a major defeat upon the French at the battle of Courtrai in 1302.

Notes

50. *all the Philips and the Louis':* From 1060 to 1300 all the kings of France bore one of these names. Louis' is an abbreviation of the plural Louises.

54. *one last heir, who wore a monk's gray gown:* There is no evidence that Charles of Lorraine, the last of the Carlovingians, took Holy Orders. He died in prison, put there by Hugh Capet. Two sons born to him while he was in prison were hustled away to Germany, where they disappeared.

58. *my son's head:* The son of King Hugh Capet was Robert I, but Dante is clearly having King Hugh speak now as if he were Duke Hugh.

60. *those consecrated bones:* The Capetian kings. By the sacramental anointment which was part of the coronation, the king's person became sacred.

61–62. *the great dowry of Provence:* Raymond Berengar was Count of Provence. After his death, Louis IX (St. Louis) married the eldest of the count's four daughters, and Louis' brother, Charles of Anjou, married one of the younger daughters. The brothers then seized all of Provence, claiming it as their wives' dowry. *lost its sense of shame:* In waxing great on so much wealth, they lost all sense of just reckoning.

66. *Normandy, Ponthieu, and Gascony:* Philip II took Normandy from England in 1202. Philip the Fair took Ponthieu and Gascony from England in 1295.

67. *Charles:* Charles of Anjou, brother of Louis IX. When Clement IV excommunicated Manfred (see Canto 3), he summoned Charles to Italy and crowned him King of Sicily. In 1266 Charles defeated Manfred at Benevento. In 1268 he defeated Conradin, Manfred's nephew, at Tagliacozzo and had him beheaded.

68–69. *sent St. Thomas back to Heaven:* Dante is following an unfounded popular legend that Charles had Thomas Aquinas poisoned.

71. *another Charles:* Charles of Valois, brother of Philip the Fair. He was called Charles Sans Terre. Boniface VIII called him to Florence in 1301, presumably as peacemaker, but actually to destroy all who opposed papal policy.

76. *He wins no land there:* A taunt at the fact that Charles had inherited no land. He will not improve his temporal state, says Hugh, and will only blacken his honor and his soul.

79. *The third:* The third Charles is Charles II of Anjou (Charles the Lame), King of Naples and of Apulia (1243–1309). *once hauled from his own ship:* In June of 1284 the admiral of Peter III of Aragon sailed into the Bay of Naples. Charles, against express orders left by his father, allowed himself to be lured out to meet the Aragonese and

was easily taken prisoner. Two hundred of his court were taken with him and were executed by the Aragonese to avenge the death of Conradin. Charles escaped with his life but remained a prisoner in Sicily until 1288.

80. *selling his daughter:* In 1305 Charles concluded a marriage contract between his very young daughter and Azzo (or Ezzo) VIII of Este, then forty-two. For the honor of marrying the king's daughter, Azzo settled for practically no dowry and made very valuable gifts to his father-in-law.

85–93. *But dwarfing all crimes, etc.:* The crime was the capture and humiliation of Pope Boniface VIII at the instigation of Philip the Fair. Philip had charged Boniface with heresy, and Boniface had prepared a bull excommunicating Philip. On September 7, 1303, before the bull could be published, Philip sent a large force to Alagna (now Anagni) under Guillaume de Nogaret and Sciarra Colonna. They ransacked the palace and the cathedral treasury and subjected Boniface to great indignities, threatening to haul him off in chains to execution. Boniface, then eighty-six, was released in a few days but his mind seems to have cracked, and he died of "hysterical seizures" in Rome within a few weeks, on October 12, 1303. Much as Dante loathed Boniface for his corruption of the Papacy, he saw the office itself as sacred, for Boniface was officially Christ's Vicar on earth. Thus to offend his person was to offend the person of Christ Himself. King Philip's all-dwarfing crime, therefore, was against the very body of Christ.

93. *enter the very Temple:* The reference here is to Philip's suppression of the Knights Templars and the seizure of their lands and treasuries in 1314. He tortured those he captured and forced Pope Clement V to legalize the action.

95. *Thy retribution:* God's retribution. It lies hidden from men, but is known to God in His omniscient prevision, and will take place at His pleasure. His anger, therefore, is sweetened by the fact that His vengeance is already calculated and certain.

102. *the countercry:* The Rein of Avarice, consisting of seven examples of the downfall caused by Avarice.

103. *Pygmalion:* Brother of Queen Dido. He killed King Sichaeus in the temple, stole his gold, and drove Dido into exile. Dante calls him a parricide because Sichaeus was not only his brother-in-law but his uncle.

109. *Achan:* After the fall of Jericho, Joshua commanded that all the booty should go into the Temple as the Lord's. Achan pilfered some treasures for himself and Joshua had him and his family stoned to death.

Notes

112. *Sapphira's and her husband's blame:* They were entrusted to sell some property held in common by the Apostles, but they returned only part of the sale price, representing it as the whole sum. When St. Peter reproved them for their fraud, they fell dead at his feet.

113. *Heliodorus:* He was sent to Jerusalem by the King of Syria with orders to steal the Treasury but was driven from the Temple by the apparition of a great horse that battered him with its forefeet.

114. *Polymnestor:* King of Thrace and a friend of King Priam. During the siege of Troy, Priam sent his youngest son, Polydorus, into Thrace for Polymnestor's protection. A considerable treasure accompanied the boy, and Polymnestor killed him for it as soon as Troy fell. Hecuba, mother of Polydorus, later avenged her son by blinding Polymnestor and killing him.

116. *Crassus:* Marcus Licinius Crassus (114–53 B.C.), Triumvir of Rome with Julius Caesar and Pompey, and infamous for his avarice, bribe taking, and plundering. He was taken in battle by the Parthians and his head was brought to King Hyrodes, who had molten gold poured into its mouth, thus mocking the memory of Crassus' bloody avarice by serving his severed head a last feast of gold.

130–132. *Not even Delos ... Latona ... Heaven's eyes:* Latona was pregnant by Jupiter and was chased from place to place by the jealous Juno. According to one legend, Jupiter caused an earthquake to raise the island of Delos from the bottom of the sea as a place of refuge for Latona. According to another, Delos was a floating island left over from the original division of the sea and the land and tossed about by waves until Jupiter fixed it in place for Latona. On Delos, Latona gave birth to Apollo (the sun) and Diana (the moon), hence, the twin eyes of Heaven.

140. *who first heard that hymn:* The shepherds of Bethlehem. It was first sung to announce the birth of Christ.

CANTO 21

2–3. *that water the Samaritan woman begged:* At Jacob's Well, Jesus asked the Samaritan woman for a drink, and she showed surprise that a Jew should make such a request of her; but Jesus replied that had she known who he was, she would have asked him for a drink and he would have given her the living water of the truth. "The woman saith unto him, Sir, give me this water that I thirst not. . . ." (John 4:6–15).

24. *she:* Lachesis. She is the Fate (or Parca) who spins the thread of life. Her sister Clotho winds each man's thread about her distaff, forming it into a hank begun at each man's birth. The third sister, Atropos,

623

cuts the thread at the end of the man's life. Virgil means simply that Dante is not yet dead.

36. *cry with one voice down to its last moist rock:* Down to the shore where the reeds grow.

50. *Thaumas' glowing daughter:* Iris, the rainbow. Daughter of the Centaur Thaumas and of Electra. Her sisters were the Harpies. Like her sisters, she was a messenger of the gods and came and went by way of the rainbow, with which she became identified.

52. *dry vapors:* Dante's theory of wet and dry vapors is from Aristotle. Wet vapors cause rain, hail, dew, and hoarfrost, as specified in lines 46–47. Dry vapors, if they are free, produce lightning and thunder. If, however, they enter the earth as winds and are locked inside, they cause earthquakes. But such terrestrial earthquakes (lines 55–60) cannot be felt above the three steps at the Gate.

82. *the good Titus:* Roman Emperor, A.D. 78–81. In A.D. 70 in the reign of his father, Vespasian, Titus besieged and took Jerusalem. Thus, with God's help, Rome avenged the death (the wounds) of Christ.

86. *in the most honored and enduring name:* Of poet.

91. *Statius:* Publius Papinius Statius (c. A.D. 45–96), a Latin poet much admired by Dante. Statius' main work was the *Thebaid,* an epic of the Seven against Thebes, and he was engaged in an epic of the Trojan War, the *Achilleid,* at his death. He was born in Naples and lived in Rome. Dante confused him in part with Lucius Statius Ursulus, a rhetorician of Toulouse, and has Statius give his birthplace accordingly in line 89.

CANTO 22

13. *Juvenal:* Decius Junius Juvenal, satiric poet (47–130). Since he and Statius were contemporaries, he would be a natural choice as the bearer of tidings of Statius.

56–57. *the twin afflictions of Jocasta:* Eteocles and Polynices, the twin sons of Oedipus by his own mother, Jocasta. When they succeeded to the throne of Thebes they agreed to rule in alternating years, the nonruling brother to pass the year in exile. Eteocles occupied the throne the first year and then refused to surrender it when Polynices came to claim it. Thereupon there broke out the war of the Seven against Thebes which Statius celebrated in his *Thebaid.*

58. *when Clio tuned your strain:* In the *Thebaid,* Statius began with an invocation to Clio, the Muse of History.

59–60. *the faith without the grace of which good works are vain:* The

624

doctrine that there can be no salvation except through the Catholic Church.

63. *the Fisherman:* St. Peter.

67. *A new birth . . . Heaven:* These are the words of the Sybil in Virgil's fourth Eclogue, from his *Bucolics.* Virgil, as a courtier, was celebrating the birth of a son to the well-placed Asinius Pollio. Medieval readers were quick to interpret the lines as a prophecy of the birth of Christ, thus giving rise to the legend of Virgil as a powerful soothsayer and magician.

77. *those messengers:* The Apostles.

88–90. *drew near the Theban rivers:* The ninth book of the *Thebaid* relates the arrival of the Greeks under Adrastus to the Theban rivers, the Ismenus and the Asopus. The *Thebaid* consists of twelve books in all.

97–99. *Terence . . . Caecilius, Varro, Plautus:* All were Latin poets of the third and second centuries B.C. Since all of them died before Christ, none could have won salvation.

100. *Persius:* Latin poet, A.D. 34–62.

101. *that Greek:* Homer.

104. *the glorious mountain:* Parnassus.

106–108. *Euripides . . . Antiphon . . . Agathon, Simonides:* All were Greek poets of the Golden Age.

109–114. *of your own people:* Virgil means "of the people you wrote about in the *Thebaid.*" All those listed may be taken as characters of the poem, only two of whom here require further explanation: *Ismene, mournful as she was:* Daughter of Oedipus and Jocasta, sister of Antigone and of Eteocles and Polynices. Having witnessed the death of all her family and of her betrothed, she was sentenced to death by Creon. *who led to Langia's water:* When the Seven who fought against Thebes were dying of thirst on their march through Boetia, Hypsipyle showed them the way to a spring called Langia.

118–120. It is between 10:00 and 11:00 A.M.

141–155. *a voice:* The Whip of Gluttony. The voice cites examples of abstinence and moderation, first (lines 142–144), the example of Mary at the marriage feast at Cana in Galilee and how she thought only of the good of others, not of her own appetite. Second (lines 145–146), the matrons of ancient Rome. It was the custom during the Republic for noble matrons not to drink wine; thus they "found joy in water." The third example (lines 146–147) is based on Dan. 1:8 and 17. Daniel determined not to defile himself with the king's wine and meat . . . "and Daniel had understanding in all visions and dreams." The fourth example (lines 148–150) cites mankind's earliest and most natural state, when men lived in accord with nature and had not developed the cookery that leads men to gluttonous feasting nor the wine that leads to drunkenness. The final example (lines 151–155) cites John the Baptist, who ate only honey and locusts in the desert and won thereby to the glory the Gospel attests.

CANTO 23

11. *Labia mea, Domine:* "O Lord, open Thou my lips, and my mouth shall pour forth Thy praise." From Psalm 51 of the Vulgate, part of the service of Lauds for Tuesdays. The time is now Easter Tuesday.

25. *Erysichthon:* He mocked the goddess Ceres by felling an oak in her sacred grove, and Ceres visited an insatiable hunger upon him. He ate up all his own substance, sold his daughter in order to buy more food, consumed that, and finally devoured his own limbs.

29–30. *who lost Jerusalem . . . Miriam:* Josephus relates that when Titus was besieging Jerusalem in A.D. 70, the people were so reduced by hunger that a woman named Miriam, the daughter of Eleazar, killed her son, cooked him, and ate half his body.

32. *Those who read OMO in the face of man:* A medieval notion held that the Creator had signed His creation *OMO DEI,* "Man [is] of God"; the eyes forming the two *O*'s, the brows, nose, and cheekbones forming the *M,* the ears the *D,* the nostrils the *E,* and the mouth the *I.* Dante mentions only the OMO, making the point that these souls were so emaciated that one could readily see the *M.*

48. *Forese:* Forese Donati, died in July of 1296. Gemma Donati, Dante's wife, was Forese's kinswoman. Forese was the brother of Corso Donati, head of the Black Guelphs, and Dante was a passionate White, but before politics separated them they had been warm friends. Forese had been something of a poet, and he and Dante had exchanged rhymed lampoons in one of which Dante had accused him of gluttony, and of pride and prodigality as well.

74. *drove Christ on gladly to cry 'Eli! Eli!':* At the ninth hour of his agony Christ cried, *'Eli, Eli, lama sabachthani?'*—"My God, my God, why hast thou forsaken me?" The desire of these sinners to endure their terrible suffering is compared to Christ's eagerness to endure the pain that would redeem the souls of men.

85. *Nella:* Forese's wife, Giovanna, a name whose affectionate diminutive is Giovanella, whence Nella.

90. *set me free of all the other rounds:* Nella's prayers have not only moved Forese out of Ante-Purgatory, but have freed him of all the pains of the rounds below.

Notes

94. *the Barbagia of Sardinia:* Barbagia, a wild region in the Sardinian mountains, was dominated by the Barbacini, a bandit clan reputed to be savages and idolaters. Some medieval sources report their women as going half-naked.

109. *For if what we foresee here does not lie:* As usual, it does not, the calamities here foreseen, as of 1300, having already befallen Florence. In November of 1301 Charles de Valois entered Florence and sowed disaster. In 1302 Rinier da Calboli introduced his reign of terror, and a great famine occurred in the same year. In 1303 Florence was interdicted, and shortly thereafter a bridge collapsed, killing many people. It would take about fifteen years for male children to progress from lullabies to beards, and by 1315 Florence had more than enough to mourn.

120. *that one's sister:* The moon. As Diana, she was said to be the sister of Apollo, the sun. Dante is referring to the moon of the night of Holy Thursday when he was in the Dark Wood of Error.

CANTO 24

10. *Piccarda:* Sister of Forese. She took vows as a nun but was later forced by her other brother, Corso, into a political marriage in violation of her vows. Dante will meet her in the lowest sphere of Paradise.

14. *High Olympus:* Heaven.

20. *Bonagiunta of Lucca:* Bonagiunta degli Overardi. A poet and orator of some repute in Lucca, he was a famous glutton and tippler who died in 1297. *That behind him:* Simon de Brie of Tours, Pope from 1281–1285 as Martin IV.

24. *Bolsena's eels and the Vernaccia wine:* The eels of Lake Bolsena, near Viterbo, are still especially prized. Vernaccia is a rich, sweet, white wine of the mountains near Genoa. Martin IV gorged incessantly on such eels and died of an attack brought on by overindulgence.

28. *Ubaldino della Pila:* A knight of the Ubaldini, brother of the Cardinal of the Ubaldini (Inferno, 10). Another brother was Ugolino d'Azzo, who is mentioned with great honor in Canto 14. Ubaldino was the father of Archbishop Ruggieri (Inferno, 32–33). He was a great feaster and entertainer, once playing host for several months to the Pope and his whole court.

29. *Boniface:* Archbishop of Ravenna, 1274–1294. Dante's charge is that Boniface was shepherd to the bellies rather than to the souls of his archdiocese. There is no evidence outside Dante that Boniface was a glutton.

31. *Marchese:* Marchese of Forlì, *podestà* of Faenza in 1296. He once asked what the people thought of him. When told they spoke of nothing but his incessant drinking, he replied that they should remember he was always thirsty.

35. *him of Lucca:* Bonagiunta (line 20).

38. *Gentucca:* Probably the name of a lady Dante met when he went to live with a friend at Lucca between 1314–1316.

44. *she:* Gentucca. In 1300 she had been born and was living in Lucca, but as a girl not yet married.

56–57. *Guittone . . . the Judge . . . sweet new style:* Guittone d'Arezzo (who first perfected the form of the Italian sonnet), Jacopo da Lentino (a Sicilian poet known as "Il Notaro" or The Judge), and Bonagiunta were all practitioners of a kind of conventionalized verse modeled after the most decadent phase of Provençal poetry. They flourished in the first half of the thirteenth century. Dante was a prime mover in the later "sweet new style" of more natural expression.

82. *him:* Corso Donati, Forese's brother and head of the Black Guelphs. It was Corso who persuaded Boniface VIII to send Charles of Valois to Florence in 1300. Thus the crimes of Charles are indirectly his. In 1309 Corso tried a coalition that would make him the supreme authority in Florence, but the Blacks discovered his plot and condemned him to death. He fled but was pursued and killed. Dante follows an account that has him dragged to death by his horse.

115–126. *Pass on, etc.:* The Rein of Gluttony.

121. *those cursed beasts:* The Centaurs, known for their drunkenness. Invited to a wedding feast by the neighboring Lapithae, the Centaurs became so drunk they tried to make off with the bride, whereupon Theseus and the Lapithae seized arms and killed great numbers of the Centaurs. The Centaurs are spoken of as born of a cloud because they were supposed to have been sired by Ixion upon the cloud Nephele whom Jupiter had formed into the likeness of Juno, beloved of Ixion. They are said to have double breasts because of their two natures, half-horse and half-human.

124. *Recall those Jews:* When Gideon was leading the army of the Jews against Midian, he was instructed by the Lord to lead his men to the river and to watch how they drank. Those who threw aside all caution at the sight of water and plunged their faces into the river were to be set aside. Those who stayed alert despite their thirst, drinking cautiously by scooping the water up in their hands and remaining watchful, were to be chosen. Three hundred were so chosen, and with them alone Gideon moved down to victory.

Notes

17–18. *the bow of speech, etc.:* Dante's speech is conceived to be a bow that he has bent back to the very iron (the head) of the arrow, in his eagerness to let fly, but which he has been afraid to release.

22. *Meleager:* Son of Oeneus, King of Calydon, and of Althaea. When he was born, the Fates threw a branch into the fire and decreed that he should live until fire had consumed it. Althaea pulled it out of the fire and hid it. When he had grown, Meleager fell in love with Atalanta and slew a great bear for her and gave her the skin. His own brothers stole the skin and Meleager, in his rage, killed them. Althaea thereupon brought the fatal branch out of hiding and threw it into the fire. As the flames consumed it, Meleager's life was consumed.

34–108. *And then to me, etc.:* Statius' long discourse may be divided into three parts: I. The Nature of the Generative Principle; II. The Birth of the Human Soul; and III. The Nature of Aerial Bodies. An extended paraphrase is perhaps the best way to deal with the complexities of the discourse.

I. *The Nature of the Generative Principle:*

31–39. Dante's concept of blood includes not only blood as we understand it, but a pre-substance (perfect blood), some of which flows into the veins (the arteries), but some of which remains apart (like food left untouched and in its original state).

40–42. This perfect blood enters the heart (without entering into the general circulation of the bloodstream) and acquires the power (which we now associate with the genes) to determine the development of the bodily organs and members. Similarly, the blood that flows into the "veins" has the power to determine *their* form and function. *formative power:* A technical term from Scholastic philosophy. It may be thought of as the generative principle. It is derived entirely from the male parent.

43–45. Within the heart of the father, this "perfect blood" undergoes a change into sperm. It then flows down to the male organs ("better left unmentioned") and, in the act of conception, drips over the blood of the female in the womb ("another blood in its natural vase").

46–48. These two bloods commingle. One of them (the female blood) is passive, i.e., it is menstrual, tending to flow away rather than to take form. The other (the male blood), because of the perfect place from which it flows (the heart), is active (seeks to generate form).

49–51. The active blood then causes the passive blood to clot. It thus forms it into solid and workable matter, which it then quickens into life. Conception has taken place.

629

II. *The Birth of the Human Soul:*

52–54. With conception the soul is born, not as a coinheritance from the mother and father, but from the active force (the formative power) of the father-blood alone, the maternal blood providing only the matter for the formative power to work on. (Dante's views here are pure Aquinian doctrine.) This newly formed soul is like that of a plant (vegetative only), but with the difference that the plant soul is fully formed at this stage, whereas the human soul is only beginning.

55–57. From this plantlike state the soul grows capable of elementary motion and sensation. It has achieved the state of some "sea-thing." He probably meant some coelenterate, such as the hydra, sea anemone, or jellyfish. In Dante's time such life-forms were believed to be single living masses without differentiated organs of any sort.

58–60. From this "sea-thing" stage, the *formative power* of the soul (from the father) moves within the maternal material shaping each organ and member into its form and place in human anatomy, according to nature's plan.

61–63. One must still ask how this animal foetus acquires the power of human reason (in Scholastic phrasing, "the possible intellect"). And here, before propounding the true doctrine as he sees it, Statius pauses to refute the teaching of Averroës ("a wiser head than yours"), who erred on this point.

64–66. To grasp the importance to Dante's doctrine of the error of Averroës, one must understand that in Scholastic teaching the soul possesses (1) the *vegetative faculty,* which is to say it lives, (2) the *sensitive or perceiving faculty,* which is to say it feels and receives impressions, and (3) the *reflective faculty,* called the *possible intellect,* which is to say it has the power of reasoning from the known to the unknown, and of extracting forms and concepts from nature.

The vegetative and sensitive faculties receive particular impressions only. The organ of those faculties, common in both man and beast, is the brain. Where then was the organ of the higher intellectual faculty, the possible intellect?

Since he could find no such organ, Averroës postulated a generalized universal rationality from which all men could draw rational faculties during their lives, but which was lost to them at death. It must follow, therefore, that no individual and rational soul could be summoned to eternal judgment, since the soul would have lost its possible intellect (rationality) at death. Church scholars would necessarily be required to reject such a doctrine, since it denied the very basis of free will and of just reward and punishment.

67–75. Having refuted error, Statius then explains the truth: the instant the brain is fully formed in the human foetus, God turns to it in his joy at the art of nature in forming so perfect a thing, and breathes into

Notes

it a powerful spirit peculiar to man. This God-infused spirit draws all the life forces (vegetative, sensitive, and rational) into a single soul. Note especially, in reply to Averroës, that the soul so formed is individualized, self-measuring, and, therefore, self-responsible.

76–78. Statius then compares the change wrought by the new spirit with the way the heat of the sun is transformed into the quickened wine when joined to the relatively inert sap of the vine.

III. *The Nature of Aerial Bodies:*

79–81. Then when Lachesis (the Fate who draws out the flaxen thread of life) measures the end of the mortal life, the soul goes free of the flesh but takes with it, by virtue of that essence God breathed into it, all of its faculties both human (vegetative and sensitive) and divine (rational).

82–84. These lower (vegetative and sensitive) faculties grow passive and mute after death, since they have left behind the organs whereby they functioned. The higher faculties, however, since they are God-inspired and now free of their mortal involvement in materiality, become more active and acute.

85–87. At the instant of death the soul miraculously falls, by an act of its own will, either to the shore of Hell for damnation, or to the mouth of the Tiber to await transport to Purgatory.

88–90. As soon as the soul feels itself inclosed in the new atmosphere of the afterlife, the *formative power* from the heart of the father (line 40) sends out its rays, as it first did through the matter of the maternal blood to shape the living organs of the body.

91–93. The process is compared to the way the sun's rays (a force from without) work upon moist air to form a rainbow (within the air).

94–96. On whichever shore the soul lights, the inclosing air takes on the image of that soul by virtue of the soul's indwelling formative power.

97–99. Then, ever after, and just as flame follows fire, the new form follows the soul, wherever it may move.

100–102. This new form is called a *shade* because it is made of insubstantial air and because out of air it forms all the organs of sense.

103–105. Not only is the shade able to receive sensory impressions, but to produce sounds and appearances that can be registered by mortal senses.

106–108. The appearance of the shade, moreover, conforms in detail to the inner feelings of the soul. Thus, if God fills the souls of the gluttonous with a craving for food which is then denied them, their shades appear to wither and starve, their outward appearance conforming to their inner state.

631

121. *Summae Deus clementiae:* God of clemency supreme. These words
are the beginning of the old hymn (now revised) which was sung at
Matins on Saturday. The hymn is a prayer for chastity, begging God,
of His supreme clemency, to burn lust from the soul and to leave the
suppliant chaste.

128. *Virum non cognosco:* "I know not a man." These words were spoken by Mary at the Annunciation. Gabriel had said, "Behold thou
shalt conceive in thy womb, and bring forth a son." Mary replied,
"How shall this be, seeing I know not a man?" (Luke 1:26–38).

130ff. *Diana kept to the wood, etc.:* In order to preserve her virginity,
Diana lived in the woods and became a huntress. One of her attend-
ant nymphs, Helicé, felt the urging of lust and gave herself to Jove.
After she had been driven away by Diana, Helicé was changed into a
bear by Juno, but Jove placed her in the sky as Ursa Major, the Big
Dipper.

CANTO 26

4–8. *changing from blue to white . . . the western sky:* It is now about
4:00 P.M. of the third day on the mountain.

20–21. *Ethiopes or Indians:* Dante thought of Ethiopia and India as
nothing but parched and burning wastes.

32. *and each shade kissed another:* In accordance with the Apostolic
admonition: "Salute one another with a holy kiss" (Rom. 16:16).
These holy kisses not only remind them of the libidinous kisses of
their sin, but help expiate it.

41. *Pasiphaë:* Daughter of Apollo by the nymph Perseis; wife of King
Minos of Crete. Poseidon sent Minos a black bull to be offered as a
sacrifice, but Minos put it in his herd. For revenge, Poseidon made
Pasiphaë fall in love with the bull. She had Daedalus make a cunning
effigy of a cow with wooden ribs, over which a cowhide was spread.
She then crouched inside in order to be possessed by the bull. The
Minotaur was born of the union. Thus, lust gave birth to a monster.
Note that Dante reserves sodomy specifically for homosexuality. In
modern usage sodomy includes sexual relations with animals.
Pasiphaë's example, though it may *seem* unnatural, does not violate
natural law, but only human law.

41. *the Rhipheans:* The Rhiphean Mountains, a mythical range that occurs "somewhere in the north" on some old maps. Dante's phrasing
is best understood to mean north in a generic sense. *the sands:* Of the
African desert.

77–78. *Caesar . . . 'Queen':* Suetonius reports Caesar's homosexual relation with Nicomedes, the conquered King of Bithynia, and that he was called "The Queen of Bithynia" for it.

82–84. *hermaphroditic:* Heterosexual. These sinners were guilty of abandoning themselves to lust, but not of mating with their own sex. *human laws:* Those restraints that govern human but not animal behavior, and which are the functions of intelligence and of a moral sense. To lose those restraints is to be bestial, and therefore the example of Pasiphaë in the Rein of Lust.

92. *Guido Guinizelli:* Guido di Guinizelli de' Principi, vernacular poet of the mid-thirteenth century, esteemed as a forerunner of the sweet new style. Died 1276.

94–96. *Lycurgus' darkest hour:* Hypsipyle, wife of Jason, to whom she had borne twin sons. She was captured by pirates and sold to Lycurgus, King of Nemea, who appointed her as nurse for his infant son. When she met the parched heroes who fought against Thebes, she put the baby down on the grass long enough to point out the spring called Langia. While she was gone, the infant was bitten by a poisonous snake. Lycurgus condemned her to death for negligence, and she was on the point of being executed when her sons (they had been sent to Nemea by Dionysus) discovered her, rushed to embrace her, and won her release. Dante's point is that he felt upon discovering the identity of Guinizelli as the twins had felt on discovering their lost mother.

113. *modern usage:* Of writing about love in the spoken tongue rather than in Latin or in elaborate euphuisms (the sweet new style).

119–120. *Limoges produced a better:* Girault de Bornelh of Limoges, a rival poet.

136–137. *that shade he had pointed to:* Arnaut Daniel, Provençal poet of the second half of the twelfth century. He was especially given to intricate rhyme structures and elaborate phrasing and is generally credited with having invented the sestina.

140–147. *Such pleasaunce, etc.:* Daniel replies, in the original, not in Italian, but in the *language d'oc,* the Provençal tongue in which he wrote.

CANTO 27

1–4. *As the day stands, etc.:* It is shortly before sunset of the third day on the mountain. *the Ebro:* For Spain.

8. *Beati mundo corde:* "Blessed are the pure in heart" (Matthew 5:8).

11. *the fire:* The fire in which the lustful are purified as well as the leg-

endary wall of fire that surrounded the Earthly Paradise. Note that all
souls must pass through that fire.

37–39. _Pyramus . . . Thisbe:_ Famous tragic lovers of Babylon; Ovid tells
their story. At a tryst by a mulberry (which in those days bore white
fruit), Thisbe was frightened by a lion and ran off, dropping her veil.
The lion, his jaws bloody from a recent kill, tore at the veil, staining
it with blood. Pyramus, arriving later, saw the stained veil, concluded that Thisbe was dead, and stabbed himself. Thisbe, returning,
found him and cried to him to open his eyes for his Thisbe. At that
name Pyramus opened his eyes, looked at her, and died; Thisbe, invoking the tree to darken in their memory, thereupon stabbed herself. The mulberry roots drank their blood and the fruit turned red
ever after.

58. _a light:_ The Angel Guardian of the Earthly Paradise. He corresponds
to the angel guarding the Gate.

60. _Venite benedicti Patris mei:_ "Come ye blessed of my Father" (Matthew 25:34).

94. _At the hour . . . when Venus, first returning:_ Venus, the morning star;
it is the hour before dawn, in which the truth is dreamed.

CANTO 28

11. _that quarter:_ The west.

20. _the pine wood there on Chiassi's shore:_ Chiassi (now Classe) was the
seaport of Ravenna in 1300. It is now a desolate place left behind by
the recession of the Adriatic.

21. _Aeolus:_ In ancient mythology the god who kept the winds in his cave
and controlled their blowing. _the Sirocco:_ The south wind, which in
Italy is the wind from Africa.

45. _sunned yourself in Love's own rays:_ In the light of God.

50. _Persephone:_ Daughter of Demeter, the goddess of vegetation. One
day, as Persephone was gathering flowers in a field, she was carried
off to the lower world by Hades (with the consent of Zeus, her father).
At the insistence of Demeter, Zeus sent Hermes to fetch her back.
Persephone, however, had eaten a quarter of a fateful pomegranate
and, in consequence, could only return for three quarters of each
year, being forced to return to the lower world for the fourth quarter.
Thus Persephone represents the vegetative cycle, spending spring,
summer, and fall with Demeter (as Mother Earth) but descending to
the lower world (into the ground) for the winter. When she is in the
lower world she rules beside her husband as the goddess of the dead,
but she forever returns to her mother as the virgin daughter (spring).

634

Matilda not only reminds Dante of Persephone, but of Persephone as she was in that original springtime before she was carried off to the lower world.

65–66. *Venus . . . her son:* Cupid was playing with his mother one day when one of the arrows in his quiver scratched her breast by accident and she was smitten with love of Adonis, the son of Myrrha by her own father.

71. *Hellespont:* Now called the Dardanelles, the strait between Europe and Asia Minor. It is famous for its raging currents. *Xerxes:* Son of Darius, the Persian king. In 485 B.C. Xerxes crossed the Hellespont on a bridge of ships to invade Greece. Decisively defeated in a sea battle off Salamis, Xerxes fled back across the Hellespont undone, thus leaving to all posterity a dire example of the downfall of pride.

73–74. *Sestos and Abydos:* Cities on the Hellespont in, respectively, Greece and Asia Minor. The Hellespont is about a mile wide between them. *Leander:* A young man of Abydos who fell in love with Hero, a priestess of Aphrodite at Sestos. Because of her position and of family opposition, they could not marry but decided to meet clandestinely every night, Leander swimming to her across the Hellespont, guided by a light from Hero's tower. One night the light blew out and Leander lost his direction, was carried off by the current, and drowned. The next morning Hero found his body washed ashore and threw herself into the current.

81. *Delectasti me:* Matilda's phrase is from Psalm 92: "For Thou, Lord, hast made me glad through Thy work."

103–108. *Now since the air revolves in one conjoint, etc.:* The earth is conceived as standing still while the atmosphere moves from east to west at the constant rate imparted to it, as to the heavenly spheres, by the Primum Mobile. On the earth's surface the air is deflected by many obstructions (surface turbulence) that make it flow in all directions, but at the altitude of the Earthly Paradise one experiences only the air's unperturbed original motion. This is the "mild wind" Dante felt (lines 8–9), as it is the wind that makes the whole wood murmur (lines 17–18).

130. *Lethe:* In classical mythology, a river of Hades from which the souls of the dead drank forgetfulness of their first existence. Dante places it in the Earthly Paradise and gives it the power of washing from the souls who drink of it every last memory of sin. Note, too, that Dante's Lethe (Inferno, 34) flows down to the bottom of Hell, bearing down to Satan, to be frozen into the filthy ice around him, the last lost vestiges of the sins of the saved. *Eunoë:* Having adapted Lethe to his purpose, Dante invents as its complement Eunoë (the name meaning, literally, "good memory") and gives it the power to strengthen every memory of good deeds done.

CANTO 29

2. *Beati quorum tecta sunt peccata:* This is Dante's elision of Psalm 32:1, "Blessed are they [whose transgression is forgiven] whose sins are covered."

37–42. *O holy, holy Virgins, etc.:* Dante is about to describe the entrance of the Heavenly Pageant, a spectacle of such splendor that it is difficult to conceive, let alone put into rhyme. For his great effort, therefore, he summons all the Muses from Helicon, calling upon Urania to preside, since she is the Muse of Astronomy, hence of heavenly things.

50. *candelabra:* The seven candelabra may be taken as the light and glory of God from which issue the Seven Gifts of the Holy Spirit: Wisdom, Understanding, Counsel, Might, Knowledge, Piety, and Fear of the Lord.

78. *Delia's girdle:* The rainbow-colored halo around the moon. Delia was another name for Diana, the moon goddess. *Apollo's bow:* The rainbow. Apollo was god of the sun.

95. *Argus:* Jove made love to Io. Juno, in wifely jealousy, turned Io into a cow and set Argus of the hundred eyes to watch her. Mercury, sent by Jove, caused Argus to fall into an enchanted sleep and cut his head off. Juno set Argus' eyes in the tail of the peacock.

108. *Griffon:* A mythical figure with the foreparts of an eagle and the hind parts of a lion, here meant to represent the dual role of Christ as God and man, his birdlike part divine, his lionlike part animal, hence human, and the unity of the two a symbol of his incarnation as the Word.

122. *three maidens:* The Three Theological Virtues: Faith, Hope, and Charity (*Caritas*).

132. *four glad nymphs:* The Four Cardinal Virtues: Prudence, Justice, Fortitude, and Temperance.

136–137. *One showed he was a follower of the art of great Hippocrates:* Luke, as the author of Acts. In Colossians, Paul describes him as "the beloved physician." He is the doctor of souls, as Hippocrates was the doctor of bodies.

139–141. *his counterpart . . . I was afraid:* Paul. The sword he carries may symbolize "the sword of the Spirit, which is the word of God" (Eph. 6:17). Thus he is here the taker rather than the healer of lives, as presented in the Epistles.

Notes

1. *the Septentrion of the First Heaven:* The Septentrion is the seven stars of the Big Dipper. Here Dante means the seven candelabra. They are the Septentrion of the First Heaven (the Empyrean) as distinct from the seven stars of the dipper which occur lower down in the Sphere of the Fixed Stars.

11. *Veni, sponsa, de Libano:* "Come [with me] from Lebanon, my spouse" (Song of Sol. 4:8).

17–18. *a hundred Powers and Principals:* Angels.

19. *Benedictus qui venis:* "Blessed is he who cometh" (Matt. 21:9).

21. *Manibus o date lilia plenis:* "Oh, give lilies with full hands." In the *Aeneid,* these are the words of Anchises in honor of Marcellus.

31. *a Lady:* Beatrice. She is dressed in the colors of Faith (white), Hope (green), and *Caritas* (red).

34. *since last it saw:* Beatrice died in 1290. Thus Dante has passed ten years without sight of her.

36. *stupefied:* Dante describes the stupor of his soul at the sight of the living Beatrice in *La Vita Nouva.* Then, however, it was mortal love, here it is eternal, and the effect accordingly greater.

68. *wise Minerva's leaves:* The olive crown.

83–84. *In te, Domine, speravi . . . pedes meos:* In mercy the angel chorus sings Psalm 31:1–8, beginning "In thee, O Lord, do I put my trust" and continuing as far as "thou hast set my feet in a large room."

85–90. *the spine of Italy:* The Apennines. *the living rafters:* The trees. *the land of shadowless noon:* Africa. In equatorial regions the noonday sun is at the zenith over each point twice a year. Its rays then fall straight down and objects cast no shadows.

101. *compassionate essences:* The angel chorus.

125. *my second age:* Beatrice's womanhood. When she had reached the full bloom of youth Dante turned from her and wrote to his *donna gentile.* Allegorically, he turned from divine "sciences" to an over-reliance upon philosophy (the human "sciences"). For this sin he must suffer.

144. *were he to come past Lethe:* In passing Lethe and drinking its waters, the soul loses all memory of guilt. This, therefore, is Dante's last opportunity to do penance.

637

CANTO 31

16–18. *arbalest . . . snap . . . diminished blow:* The bolt (corresponding to an arrow) of a crossbow strikes the target with less force when the bow snaps.

42. *the grindstone is turned back against the blade:* Turning the grindstone away from the blade sharpens it. Turning it back against the blade dulls it. Thus Beatrice is saying that when a soul openly confesses in true repentance what could not in any case be hidden from God, the sword of Justice is blunted (no longer cuts as deeply).

99. *Asperges me: Asperges me hyssopo, et mundabor; lavabis me, et super nivem dealbabor.* ("Purge me with hyssop, and I shall be clean; wash me, and I shall be whiter than snow.") These are the words the priest utters when he sprinkles holy water over the confessed sinner to absolve him.

116–126. *those emeralds, etc.:* The eyes of Beatrice. Note that Dante does not achieve his revelation by looking at the Griffon, but rather by looking at its reflection in the eyes of Beatrice (as the Church). Thus he achieves here the first fruits of faith, seeing as much of the nature of God as is perceivable in the first life. The final revelation can happen only in Heaven, in the rapturous presence of God.

138. *the second beauty:* The smile of Beatrice (Divine Love). Dante was led to the first beauty by the Four Cardinal Virtues. Now the Three Theological Virtues, as higher beings, lead him to the second, and higher beauty, which is the joy of Divine Love in receiving the purified soul.

140. *Parnassus' waters:* The fountain of Castalia. To drink from it is to receive poetic gifts. To grow pale in the shadow of Parnassus signifies to labor at mastering the art of poetry.

CANTO 32

20. *under their shields:* Troops turning in retreat within range of the enemy held their shields over their heads for protection.

22. *the vanguard of that heavenly force:* The twenty-four Elders.

30. *the wheel that turned the lesser arc:* The right. In making a right turn, it would swing through the lesser arc. The Poets, therefore, are walking behind the Three Theological Virtues.

65. *Syrinx:* When Jupiter sent Mercury to lull Argus to sleep (see Canto 29, line 95), Mercury told a series of tales about Syrinx, who was loved by Pan, and who was changed into a reed by her sisters to save her from Pan's pursuit.

Notes

73. *that Tree:* Christ.

81. *and saw the Master's robe change back to cloth:* Back to its mortal state, as it was before the Transfiguration.

86–87. *She is seated on the roots of the new foliage:* As Christ, after his Transfiguration, resumed his earthly appearance, so Beatrice, having entered as the figure of revelation aboard the triumphal chariot, is now seated upon the ground.

109–111. Dante's meteorological figure here is based on the belief that the highest reaches of the sky are the domain of fire. The highest clouds, therefore, being closest to the sphere of fire would be especially subject to fiery influences and would give forth the most powerful lightning flashes.

142–147. *the holy ark began to sprout, etc.:* The source of this figure is as follows: "And I saw a woman sit upon a scarlet-colored beast full of the names of blasphemy, having seven heads and ten horns" (Rev. 17:3). The seven heads have been interpreted in endless ingenious ways. Let them be taken as representing the Seven Deadly Sins. They thus took root in the Church as soon as it covered itself with wealth. The first three of the seven are Pride, Wrath, and Avarice. Being the worst sins, they sprout from the pole (they come before the others). And since they represent offenses against both God and one's neighbors, they are represented as having two horns. The four lesser sins (Sloth, Envy, Gluttony, and Lust) offend God but not necessarily one's neighbors and they are, therefore, represented as having single horns. Thus the total of ten horns.

149–150. *an ungirt harlot:* She represents the Papacy as it existed under Boniface VIII and Clement V, the two Popes Dante most charges with corruption. "Ungirt" should be understood to imply both lewdness (immodesty of dress) and lack of restraint (knowing no bounds). *her eyes darting with avarice:* Looking everywhere for plunder.

152. *a giant:* The French monarchy, and especially Philip the Fair, who made the Papacy his puppet.

158. *and dragged it off:* In 1304 Philip engineered the election of Clement V and transferred the Papal Seat to Avignon.

CANTO 33

1. *Deus, venerunt gentes:* Psalm 79, the lamentation for the destruction of Jerusalem. "O God, the heathen are come into Thine inheritance; Thy holy temple have they defiled; they have laid Jerusalem on heaps." So have the later unbelievers despoiled and defiled the Church.

639

3. *first three, then four:* The seven nymphs sing the psalm antiphonally, the Three Theological Virtues singing first (they being higher in the scale of things), and then the Four Cardinal Virtues.

5–6. *even Mary could not have changed more:* Beatrice, mourning for the crucifixion of the Church, would endure the same grief Mary suffered at the crucifixion of her son, Christ and the Church being one.

10–12. *Modicum et non . . . videbitis me:* "A little while and ye shall not see me; and again a little while, and ye shall see me" (John 16:16). These are Christ's words to His disciples, announcing His resurrection. Beatrice speaks them afire with her holy zeal in reply to the mournful psalm. She is saying, in effect, that the triumph of the True Faith shall be seen again.

14–15. *the Lady:* Matilda. *the Sage that had remained:* Statius.

35–36. *God's wrath will not be calmed by soup:* In some parts of ancient Greece a murderer could protect himself from all vengeance if for nine successive days he ate soup on the grave of his victim. In Florence it became a custom to stand guard for nine days over the grave of a murdered man to see that no one ate soup upon it. Dante's intent is that no such simple rite will ward off the vengeance of God.

37–39. *The eagle . . . will not remain forever without heir:* The eagle is, of course, the Roman Empire. The true heir of the Caesars, who will restore order and goodness, will come at last. Dante thought of Frederick II as the last real heir of the Caesars.

41. *the unstayable stars:* Nothing can stay the stars in their courses. Beatrice foresees propitious stars already near at hand.

47–51. *Themis:* Daughter of Gaea (Earth) and Uranus (Heaven). She was the second wife of Zeus, and later, no longer as his wife, became his goddess of law and order. She was noted for the obscurity of her oracles. *the Sphinx:* A monster with the head of an innocent maiden and the body of a savage beast. One of the oracles of Themis, she waited for travelers on a rock near Thebes and killed them when they failed to solve her famous riddle: "What walks on four legs in the morning, on two at noon, and on three at night?" *Oedipus:* The ill-fated King of Thebes answered properly that the riddle meant a man in the three stages of his life (for he crawls on all fours as an infant, walks on two legs in the middle of his life, and totters on two legs and a cane thereafter). The Sphinx was so enraged on hearing the right answer that she killed herself. *without loss of either sheep or corn:* Themis, to avenge her oracle, sent a monstrous beast to ravage the flocks and fields of Thebes.

62. *five thousand years and more:* According to Genesis, Adam lived 930 years on earth. According to Paradiso, Canto 26, he then waited

Notes

in Limbo for 4,302 years. Dante follows, in this, the chronology of the ecclesiastical historian Eusebius, who set Christ's birth in the year 5200 since the creation. Christ's death, therefore (and the Harrowing of Hell), would have occurred in the year 5232.

68. *an Elsan water:* The Elsa, a river of Tuscany, is so rich in lime that at some points along its course objects left in its waters will either petrify or become coated. So Dante's idle thoughts (seemingly flowing *around* his brain more than *through* it) have petrified his intellect.

72. *the moral meaning:* The form of the tree symbolizes its essential nature. Interpreted in the moral sense the great height and inverted crown of the tree express how far above and beyond man is the final understanding of good and evil. Hence the justice of God's interdict in forbidding man what lies beyond his grasp.

74. *turned into stone:* As if by Elsan waters. *so darkened:* As was the mulberry.

77–78. *as pilgrims wreathe their staffs with palm:* The palm grows in the Holy Land. Returning pilgrims wreathed their staffs with palm to prove they had been there.

86. *what school you followed:* The school of philosophy, whose error lies in placing its dependence on reason as an end, and which cannot, therefore, comprehend the mysteries of faith.

89–90. *the heaven whose swiftest wheel:* The Primum Mobile, uppermost of the nine spheres. Since all the spheres turn together, the outermost must move most swiftly.

113. *Tigris and Euphrates:* The Tigris flows through Turkey and Iraq (ancient Chaldea) to join the Euphrates, which rises in Armenia and flows into the Persian Gulf. Genesis identifies the Euphrates as one of the four rivers of Eden, all of which rise from the same source. The rivers of Dante's Earthly Paradise are Lethe and Eunoë. They "seem to rise" as if they were Tigris and Euphrates rising from a single spring.

117. *parts from itself to either side:* The two rivers flow off in opposite directions, just as their powers, rising from one source, work in opposite ways to achieve one good.

The Heavenly Spheres

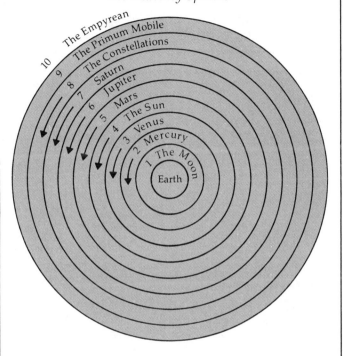

10. The Mystic Rose (God)

 9. The Angelic Orders

 8. The Church Triumphant

 7. Temperance: The Contemplatives

 6. Justice: The Just and Temperate Rulers

 5. Courage: The Warriors of God

 4. Wisdom: The Theologians and Doctors of the Church

 3. Love marred by Wantoness

 2. Service marred by Ambition

 1. Faithfulness marred by Inconstancy

Notes to Paradiso

CANTO 1

15. *crowned with bay:* The laurel wreath awarded to poets and conquerors.

16. *one peak of cleft Parnassus:* Parnassus has two peaks: Nisa, which was sacred to the Muses; and Cyrrha, which was sacred to Apollo. Heretofore Nisa has been enough for Dante's need, but for this last canticle he must summon aid from both the Muses and Apollo.

20. *Marsyas:* The Satyr Marsyas challenged Apollo to a singing contest and was defeated. Apollo punished him by pulling him out of his skin, leaving all the uncovered organs still functioning.

32. *Peneian frond:* The laurel or bay, so called for Daphne, daughter of the river god Peneus. Cupid, to avenge a taunt, fired an arrow of love into Apollo and an arrow of aversion into Daphne. Fleeing from the inflamed Apollo, Daphne prayed to her father and was changed into a laurel tree.

62. *day was added to day:* Dante perceives the increased brilliance of the light as if God had added a second sun to the sky.

68. *Glaucus:* The fisherman Glaucus, noting how his catch revived and leaped into the sea after being laid upon a certain herb, ate some of it and was transformed into a god.

73–75. *the last created part of my being:* The soul, which is created after the body. *O Love that rulest Heaven:* God. *whose lamp:* Beatrice as the reflector of God's love.

79. *ablaze with sun:* Dante believed that the earth's atmosphere extended as high as the Sphere of the Moon. Beyond the moon is another atmosphere of fire. The Sphere of Fire was believed to cause lightning.

93. *there:* To the Sphere of Fire.

104. *an inner order:* In relation to one another, and each in its relation to the total and to its final end, as fire to fire. The end of man is God; therefore, the purified soul ascends naturally and inevitably to Him.

106. *the higher creatures:* The rational beings of creation: angels, heavenly spirits, and men.

123. *the heaven:* The Empyrean. *the fastest sphere:* The Primum Mobile.

Notes

125. *that bow:* The innate impulse of all creatures to seek their place in God.

CANTO 2

11. *the bread of angels:* The knowledge of God.

19. *connate:* Dante says *concreata*. The thirst for God is born in the instant the soul is formed.

29. *the first star:* The moon.

64–66. *The eighth sphere:* The Sphere of the Fixed Stars. *qualities and quantities:* Coloration and intensity.

68. *power:* The influence of the stars upon the earth and upon the lives of men.

71. *formal principles:* Scholastic teaching distinguishes two principles in all bodies: the *material*, or the first matter, which is the same in all; and the *formal*, or the substantial form that produces the various species and innate abilities of living forms. The *formal principle* is active; the *material principle*, passive. Dante's reasoning is false in that it would reduce all to a single principle.

73ff. *the marks you mention, etc.:* Beatrice's explanation of the markings of the moon refutes a position Dante had expressed in his *Il Convivio*. There, Dante had attributed these traces to differences in the density of the lunar matter, whereby the body reflected the light unequally. In this he followed Avicenna. Now, with Beatrice as his revelation, he has her first show that such a belief leads to impossible conclusions and then has her assign the true cause to the special power diffused by the Primum Mobile. That power, though itself indivisible, dispenses itself with varying intensity according to the different bodies it permeates—as the soul, for example, permeates some parts of the body more intensely than it does other.

94. *instance:* A technical term (*instanza*) of Aristotelian and Scholastic logic signifying counter-proposition.

96. *man's art:* Learning.

112. *the Heaven of Peace beyond the sky:* The Empyrean.

113. *a body:* The Primum Mobile. Since the Empyrean (which lies beyond) is beyond space, the sphere of the Primum Mobile contains all of the universe. Taking its power from the all-encompassing Godhead (the Empyrean), it gives rise to all being.

123. *takes power from above:* From God. *and does its work below:* Ultimately upon man (the influence of the heavens upon mortal

645

lives), but intermediately some of the work of each sphere must be to transmit certain powers (undiminished) to the spheres below.

124–126. Beatrice is acting as Dante's teacher. Here, in a military figure, she instructs him to take careful note of how her argument proceeds through the next point, that by her example Dante may learn how to defend the ford (the crossing to the truth) by himself.

131. *from the deep Mind that turns it:* Of God. The Sphere of the Fixed Stars receives its power from God (through the Primum Mobile) and taking His image from above, makes itself the seal that impresses that image on the spheres below (as a seal impresses its given image upon wax).

140. *the precious body:* Of the Sphere of the Fixed Stars, here compared to the human body, because its unity comprises so many varied organs.

147. *formal principle:* The power of the divine and angelic intelligence is the intrinsic and substantial cause which produces the effect of dark and clear according to the various ways in which it enters into conjunction with the stars.

CANTO 3

13. *a footnote of our lineaments:* The image is related to the face as a footnote is related to the text.

18. *the smitten Greek:* Narcissus.

46. *virgin sister:* A nun.

49. *Piccarda:* Piccarda Donati, the daughter of Cianfa Donati (Inferno, 25) and sister of Forese (Purgatorio, 23) and of the war-leader, Corso (Purgatorio, 24). Piccarda was already a nun and living in her convent when her brother Corso, needing to establish a political alliance, forced her to marry Rossellino della Tossa of Florence. Various commentators report that Piccarda sickened and soon died as a consequence of having been so forced against her will and vows.

98. *a Lady:* St. Clara of Assisi (1194–1253). Born Chiara Sciffi, she became a disciple of St. Francis and, under his influence, founded an order of nuns in 1212.

109. *This other splendor:* The Empress Constance (1154–1198). As the last of the line of Norman kings who took southern Italy in the eleventh century, she was Empress of the Two Sicilies (Sicily and Naples). She married Emperor Henry VI in 1185 and became the mother of Frederick II. Dante follows a legend that she had become a nun and was forced to leave her convent to marry Henry.

Notes

119. *blast:* The three blasts of Swabia are the three great princes whose origins were in Swabia (in Germany). Frederick Barbarossa was the first. His son, Henry VI, was the second. To Henry, Constance bore the third, Frederick II.

CANTO 4

13. *as Daniel once had done:* Nebuchadnezzar, King of Babylon, condemned all his diviners to death because they could not interpret a dream he had forgotten. Daniel first divined the dream and then interpreted it, calming the fury of the king.

24. *as Plato taught:* As Dante rendered the *Timaeus,* Plato taught that souls existed in the stars before they entered human bodies and returned, at the body's death, to the same stars from which they had come. Such a doctrine, however, denies free will, the soul being precreated to a fixed place in Heaven's order.

48. *the other:* Raphael, the third Archangel, who cured Tobit of blindness.

62. *almost the whole world:* The exception was the Jews. All others imagined multiple gods whose names they attached to the planets.

81. *their holy feast:* Their convents and their vows.

83. *Lawrence:* In 258, during the reign of Valerius, St. Lawrence, then Deacon of Rome, was ordered by the Roman Prefect to send him the treasure of the Church. Lawrence sent him the poor and the oppressed, declaring that they were the one treasure. He was thereupon martyred. After many other tortures, he was roasted on a grill, but remained steadfast under torture.

84. *Mucius:* Mucius Scaevola, a young man of ancient Rome. He vowed to kill Porsenna and let his right hand be consumed by fire when its thrust missed the mark.

105. *his piety:* To his father. *impiety:* To his mother. For Alcmaeon see Purgatorio, 12.

113. *absolute will . . . the other:* The central idea of this passage is the difference between the absolute and the conditioned will. The absolute will is incapable of willing evil. The conditioned will, when coerced by violence, interacts with it and consents to a lesser harm in order to escape a greater.

127. *In That:* In the truth of God.

647

The Divine Comedy

CANTO 5

49. *Thus it was mandatory:* The law of the Jews absolutely required them to offer sacrifices to the Lord (the *substance* of the covenant) but allowed them some latitude in what might be sacrificed (the *manner*).

61–62. *things whose weight and worth tip every scale:* A vow of chastity would involve such a thing, virginity being irreplaceable. A vow of a lifetime of service would, similarly, involve what is irreplaceable.

66. *Jephthah:* King of Israel. He fought the Ammonites and vowed that if he were victorious he would offer up to God the first thing he saw coming out of the door of his house. The first thing he saw was his daughter and he sacrificed her.

69–70. *the great Greek whose Iphigenia:* Agamemnon. Iphigenia was his daughter. Dante follows the legend in which Agamemnon vowed before the birth of Iphigenia that he would sacrifice to Artemis the loveliest creature the year brought forth. Rather than sacrifice Iphigenia, he did not keep his vow. Years later, when the Greek ships were becalmed at Aulis, the other Greek leaders, especially Menelaus, blamed their distress on the unkept vow, and Agamemnon was finally persuaded to send for Iphigenia and to sacrifice her.

79. *cunning greed:* The greed of those who offer dispensations and other holy offices for money. To Dante such practices were damnable simony.

80. *lest the Jew among you:* The Jew could then point his finger in derision because his law was incorruptible in the matter of sacrifices.

97. *the star:* Mercury.

CANTO 6

1–3. *turned the eagle's wing, etc.:* The Imperial Eagle, standard and symbol of Rome. In 330 Constantine moved the seat of empire to Byzantium. Thus the Roman eagle flew east "against the course of Heaven," which turns from east to west, but also against the will of Heaven, for Dante believed God had decreed Rome to be the seat of His Church and the Roman Empire to be its earthly arm. He also believed that Constantine moved the seat of empire to Byzantium in order to give Rome to the Church. This gift was the "Donation of Constantine" whereby the Church (as Dante believed) grew rich and corrupt. *new son of the Latian king:* Aeneas. He came from Troy (*with* the course of Heaven), married Lavinia, daughter of the Latian king, and founded the line of the Roman Empire.

648

Notes

4. *two hundred years and more:* Byzantium became the imperial seat in 330. Justinian became Emperor in 527. Thus the eagle had stayed in Europe's furthest edge for 197 years before it came to Justinian's hand.

6. *close to the mountains out of which it rose:* The Trojan mountains.

10. *Justinian:* Became Emperor of Rome in 527. A Christian, he subscribed to the Monophysitic heresy, which accepted the divine nature of Christ but rejected His incarnation in mortal flesh. From this heresy he was converted by Agapetus (Pope from 535–536). As soon as he was converted, God's grace moved him to his great task of codifying the Roman Law, and to that work he gave himself wholly, leaving the conduct of his armies (which he had led with great success) to his general, Belisarius. Dante seems not to have known of the tyrannies of Justinian's reign, nor that the Justinian codification was the work of Tribonius, undertaken by him on imperial command.

20. *as clearly as you see:* As a first principle of logic, a statement that contradicts itself contains both truth and falsehood. Of two contradictory terms only one can be true and the other must be false.

25. *Belisarius:* Justinian's general, born 505, died 565. His successful campaigns against the Ostrogoths restored most of the Empire's authority over Italy. Dante seems not to have known that Justinian, in 562, in one of the endless intrigues of the Byzantine court, stripped "his" Belisarius of rank and had him imprisoned.

31–33. *that you may see, etc.:* Justinian denounces both the Guelphs and the Ghibellines for opposing the true purposes of the Holy Roman Empire, whose history (and divine right) he then recounts. *with how much right:* None at all. *the sacred standard:* The Imperial Eagle. *when they plot its subornation:* The Ghibellines sought to suborn imperial authority and leave matters in the hands of local lords.

36. *Pallas:* Son of Evander, a Greek who had founded a kingdom on the present site of Rome. Evander joined Aeneas in fighting Turnus and was killed. Aeneas was victorious, however, and thus acquired a kingdom that included the hereditary rights of Pallas. Thus Pallas died to give the eagle its first kingly state.

37–38. *its home was Alba:* Following his victory over Turnus, Aeneas established his seat at Lavinium. His son, Ascanius, moved it from there to Alba Longa, called the Mother of Rome. There the eagle remained until the seventh century B.C., when the Curiatii (the three heroes of Alba) were vanquished by the three Horatii of Rome.

40–42. *What it did then, etc.:* Expelled from Alba, Romulus established a base in Rome on the Palatine and recruited a band of raiders who carried out the raid on the Sabines in order to get wives. From this robber settlement grew the kingdom of Rome. Through a succession of seven kings it raided and looted its neighbors until Sextus, son of Tarquinius Superbus (the last of the Roman kings), violated Lucretia. When she died as a result of his attack, the people rose in anger, overthrew the king, and founded the Republic of Rome, in 510 B.C.

43–45. *and how it led the Chosen Romans, etc.:* During the Republic, the eagle was carried to many triumphs by Chosen Romans. Condensing almost three full centuries of history into nine lines, Dante cites the defeat of Brennus and his Gauls (*c.* 390 B.C.) and of Pyrrhus and his Greek invaders (280 B.C.).

46–48. *Thence the fame, etc.:* From the Republican victories was born the fame of Torquatus (Titus Manlius Torquatus) who defeated the Gauls. In these battles one of the Fabii also distinguished himself, as did Lucius Quintius, called Cincinnatus because of an unruly lock of hair (from Latin *cincinnus*, a curl). Three generations of the Decii died in battle from 340 to 280 B.C., the last of these engagements being the defeat of the Greeks under Pyrrhus. And in 218 B.C. Quintus Fabius Maximus, the most notable of the Fabii, defeated Hannibal.

49–51. *It dashed to earth, etc.:* The eagle defeated Hannibal in 218 B.C. Dante follows the custom of his times in referring to all inhabitants of north Africa as Arabs.

53. *Scipio and Pompey:* In 218 B.C. Scipio Africanus, then seventeen, saved his father's life in battle against Hannibal at Ticinus. At twenty he defeated Hannibal's forces in Spain. And at thirty-three, by his successful invasion of Africa, he brought about the destruction of Hannibal and of Carthage. Pompey's first great victory (over Marius in 81 B.C.) occurred when he was twenty-five. *the mountain:* Fiesole, where, according to Roman legend, the eagle of the Republic overthrew Catiline.

58–60. *What it did then, etc.:* The territory of the Gallic Wars (58–50 B.C.).

61–63. *when it had taken flight, etc.:* The Rubicon flows between Ravenna and Rimini. In Caesar's time it marked the boundary between Italy and Gaul. In crossing it (49 B.C.), Caesar left his province without permission of the Senate, thus precipitating civil war.

64–66. *into Spain, etc.:* Before the year was out Caesar struck Ilerda in Spain, defeating Pompey's lieutenants. In the next year Caesar laid siege to Pompey in Dyrrachium (modern Durres in Albania), broke off, and then engaged Pompey again at Pharsalus in Thessaly, this time winning a great victory. *even the hot Nile felt the pain:* Because Pompey fled to Egypt and was killed there by Ptolemy.

Notes

67–69. *Antandros, etc.:* Antandros is a coastal town near Troy. The Simoïs is a nearby river. Aeneas sailed from Antandros when he brought the eagle to Italy. After Pompey's death, Caesar visited Troy. Thus the eagle saw its homeland again. From Troy Caesar moved to Egypt, defeated Ptolemy, and gave Egypt to Cleopatra.

70–72. *Like a thunderbolt, etc.:* Led by Caesar, the eagle next overthrew Juba, King of Numidia (46 B.C.) under whom fourteen republican legions had formed. In the next year he struck again at Spain ("on your west") where Pompey's two sons had gathered a new army.

73–78. *its next great chief, etc.:* Augustus, Caesar's nephew. After Caesar's murder Augustus became the standard-bearer. He defeated Marc Antony at Modena in 43 B.C., then formed an alliance with him, and defeated Brutus and Cassius at Philippi in 42 B.C. In 41 B.C. Augustus defeated Marc Antony's brother Lucius at Perugia. And in 31 B.C. Augustus defeated Marc Antony at Actium. Antony committed suicide soon after his defeat, and Cleopatra did the same when she heard the news.

79–81. *him:* Augustus. *far as the Red Sea:* The limit of the Empire. Augustus was now undisputed ruler of all Rome and the Empire was at peace. *Janus:* The gates of his temple were always open in time of war. Now they were closed (as they had been only twice before) to indicate peace throughout the Empire. Thus the serene time was set for the birth of Christ, the Prince of Peace.

87. *the third Caesar:* Tiberius.

89. *gave it the glory:* The great glory given the eagle in his reign was the Crucifixion, for thereby the sin of Adam was wiped clean and the gates of Heaven were opened to redeemed mankind.

91–93. *the double marvel, etc.:* Under Titus, the fourth Caesar, Jerusalem was taken in a bloody conquest which Dante saw as a vengeance taken for a just vengeance.

94. *the Lombard:* Desiderius, an eighth-century king of the Lombards, who rose against the Church but was overthrown by Charlemagne in 774. Charlemagne, as Emperor of the Holy Roman Empire, was still bearing the eagle standard.

100–102. *One speeds the golden lilies on to force the public standard:* The Guelphs urge the lilies of France against the eagle. *one seizes it for private gain:* The Ghibellines seek to pervert the imperial standard to their own ends.

106. *the new Charles:* Charles II (The Lame) of Anjou, King of Naples and leader of the Guelphs.

128. *Romeo:* Romeo da Villanova. He was born *circa* 1170 and became Prime Minister and Chamberlain of Raymond Berenger IV, Count of

Provence from 1209 to 1245. Dante follows the legend that Romeo, passing through Provence on his way back from a pilgrimage, attached himself to Raymond's court and soon achieved high station by his wise management of Raymond's affairs. Among his triumphs, Romeo negotiated the marriages of Raymond's four daughters, each to a king. Later the local nobles, envious of Romeo's position, accused him of mismanaging the treasury. When Raymond demanded an accounting, Romeo pointed to the increase in the treasury, and picking up his pilgrim's staff once more, left the court to wander as he had come.

CANTO 7

1–3. The hymn is addressed to the God of Triumphant Armies (the God, as Dante believed, who led the Roman Eagle) and is compounded of Hebrew and Latin, the two languages of Heaven: "Hosanna, holy God of Sabaoth [of the armies], lighting from above with Your luster the blessed fires [the souls] of these kingdoms!"

26. *the man who was not born:* Adam.

31–33. *Eternal Love:* The Holy Ghost. *His own Person:* Christ, the Son. *that other nature:* Man. *Maker:* God the Father.

104. *His own ways:* Mercy and justice.

124–125. *water . . . fire . . . air . . . earth:* The four elements of which all things were believed to be compounded.

CANTO 8

8. *had sat on Dido's lap:* When she was smitten by love for Aeneas, the passion that led to her death.

11. *the star that woos the sun:* The apparent motion of Venus is from one side of the sun to the other.

22–24. *blast from cold clouds, etc.:* Hot dry vapors colliding with cold wet clouds were believed to discharge visible or invisible blasts of wind at great speeds. Lightning was believed to be a blast of wind moving so fast that the friction of its motion caused it to ignite.

31. *one of them:* Charles Martel (1271–1295), the first son of Charles II (The Lame) of Anjou, crowned King of Hungary (though in title only) 1290. His conversation indicates that he and Dante had met on earth, probably when Charles visited Florence in 1294, and that Charles had intended to be Dante's royal patron. (This Charles Martel should not be confused with the better known Charles Martel, King of the Franks, who lived c. 688–741.)

Notes

58–60. *The left bank, etc.:* The land so marked was Provence. Charles I (King of Naples and brother of the King of France) acquired it by marriage. It thus became attached to the crown of Naples, was passed on to Charles II, and would have passed on to Charles Martel as the firstborn son.

61. *that horn of Italy:* The territory so described was the former Kingdom of Naples, to which Charles was also heir. The Tronto and the Verde (now called the Garigliano) draw a nearly complete line across Italy. Together they were the main boundary between the Papal States to the north and the Kingdom of Naples to the south.

64–66. *the crown of the land the Danube bathes, etc.:* The Danube rises in Germany and flows east through Hungary. Charles Martel had the glow of the Hungarian crown on his brow, but the throne was occupied by Andreas III of Venice. Charles was king in title only. In 1310 Charles Robert, son of Charles Martel, became King of Hungary in fact as well as in title.

66–75. *And though not yet my own, etc.:* The passage is in Dante's denser style and complicated by the strange parenthesis about Typhoeus, a Titan associated with the fires and smokes of the earth's interior. He rose against Zeus, who hurled him deep into the earth and piled Etna upon him. Dante explains that the smoke shrouds of Sicily are caused not by Typhoeus but by the burning sulfur of volcanoes. The gist of the rest of the passage is that Charles Martel, but for the overthrow of the French in the Sicilian Vespers, would have ruled Sicily and so continued in his sons the bloodlines of Anjou (on his side) and of Rudolph of Hapsburg (on his wife's side). *Faro:* Cape Faro, the northeast tip of Sicily. *Passero:* Cape Passero, the southeast tip. *Eurus:* The east wind. *the bitter breath . . . Palermo's streets:* The Sicilian Vespers. *misrule:* Of Charles I of Anjou.

76. *Robert:* Became King of Naples in 1309. He was one of the younger brothers of Charles Martel who remained in Spain from 1288 to 1295 as hostages for Charles II. In Catalonia, Robert made friends among the Spanish, who later became powerful in his government of Naples and who, in the greed of their poverty, oppressed the people. Charles is prophesying that Robert, a weak man, will reap a bad harvest from the seeds of misrule he has sown.

120. *Your master:* Aristotle. In the *Ethics* and elsewhere he expounds the various offices men in society must serve for the good of all.

124–126. *Xerxes:* The Persian King. He is the type of the war-leader. *Solon:* Athenian lawgiver of the seventh century B.C., the type of the legislator. *Melchizedek:* As in Gen. 14:18, "He was the priest of the most high God," hence the type of the spiritual leader. *he who, flying . . . lost his own son:* Daedalus, the type of the artisan and mechanic.

The Divine Comedy

130–132. *Esau . . . Jacob:* Though twins they were markedly different in character. Dante implies that their genetic inheritance was identical. If so, only the diverse influences of the stars could have affected their differences. *Romulus:* His father was so humble that men were able to say he was born of Mars (as they could not have said had his father been sufficiently well known to have been remembered).

145–148. *into Holy Orders:* Charles probably intends an additional reference to his younger brother Lodovico who became Bishop of Toulouse. *and make a king of one:* Charles intends a reference to his brother Robert, who paid little attention to his duties as King of Naples and who composed a number of ornate sermons and other discourses.

CANTO 9

2–6. *he told me, etc.:* The prophecy of Charles Martel is as follows. On the death of Charles Martel (1295) the throne of Naples passed to his son Caroberto, but in 1309 Robert the Wise (younger brother of Charles and, therefore, Caroberto's uncle) usurped the throne. Thus the direct line of Charles Martel lost the crown of Naples. Robert and his followers, however, will yet have cause to weep in the disastrous consequences of their deceptions and of the suffering inflicted upon Robert's subjects by his Spanish lieutenants.

7. *the Sun:* God.

13. *another of those splendors:* Cunizza da Romano (c. 1198–1279), youngest daughter of Ezzolino II, Count of Onora, and the cruelest of the Ghibelline tyrants. He is in Hell with the Violent Against Their Neighbors (Inferno, 12). Cunizza was known as an outgoing woman, her tendencies attested by the fact that she had various lovers as well as three husbands. Sordello was one among her lovers (Purgatorio, 6). Among other bad choices, she willed her estate to Alessandro and Napoleone, Counts of Mangona, two of the worst sinners in Hell (Inferno, 32). There seems to be no way of knowing why Dante put her in Paradise. He must have credited her with a true contrition in her later years, but at best she would have been scheduled for more than twenty-one years in Purgatory. Her case may have been helped by the fact that in 1265 she manumitted a number of slaves who had been in bondage to her father and brothers.

26–27. *Rialto:* The principal island of Venice, here taken for all of Venice. *the Brenta and Piave:* These rivers have their sources in the mountains north and northwest of Florence. The area so defined is Marca Trivigiana whose principal city is Treviso.

29. *a firebrand:* Ezzolino (or Azzolino), Cunizza's brother.

654

Notes

37. *This bright and precious jewel:* Folquet of Marseilles, a troubadour
poet who became a Cistercian monk and who was Bishop of Toulouse from 1205 to 1231. He was a leader in the atrocious crusade
against the Albigensians. Cunizza seems here to honor him as one
who inveighed against the false passions of the people of Marca
Trivigiana, exhorting them to seek the pure and lasting fame of an
honored memory.

40. *this centenary:* The year 1300 was a Jubilee Year.

43–48. *The rabble that today, etc.:* The Tagliamento and the Adige are
rivers. The land they bound is, approximately, the present Venetia.
The Bacchiglione flows through this land a bit south of its center,
passes by Vicenza and then Padua, and empties into the swamps behind Venice. Cunizza prophesies the defeat of the Paduans outside
Vicenza in 1314 by Dante's great patron, Can Grande della Scala. The
duty the Paduans shunned was, in general, the observance of justice
but, specifically, their allegiance to the Empire as represented by Can
Grande.

49. *there rules one:* Rizzardo da Cammino, Lord of Treviso, who was
treacherously murdered in 1312 while playing chess.

52–53. *Feltro . . . its foul priest . . . Malta:* The Malta was a papal prison
near Lake Bolsena. The worst of its criminals had yet to commit a
crime as foul as the one that would be committed by Alessandro
Novella, Bishop of Feltro, who accepted a group of Ghibelline refu-
gees from Ferrara as his guests, and then (in July of 1314) turned them
over to Pino della Tosa, one of the Spanish agents of Robert of Naples,
to be beheaded. Thus the bishop fell to his place in Ptolemea among
those who were treacherous against their guests.

77–78. *those Blest Flames . . . six wings:* The Seraphim.

82–83. *The greatest basin . . . girdles all:* The Mediterranean.

89–92. *the Ebro:* The Spanish river. *the Magra:* Runs south into the
Mediterranean for a bit over 40 miles (its short course) between Tuscany and Liguria (whose capital city is Genoa). Marseilles lies about
halfway between the two rivers and is in almost the same latitude as
Bougiah (line 92) in Algeria. Thus the two cities would see the sun
rise and set at almost the same time.

92–93. *blood flowed . . . when Caesar came:* In 49 B.C., when Caesar left
Brutus to defeat the forces of Pompey at Marseilles while he himself
swooped down on Spain.

100–101. *she of Rhodopè . . . Demophoön:* Phyllis, daughter of King
Sithon of Thrace (wherein rises Mount Rhodopè) was to marry
Demophoön. When he did not arrive on the wedding day, she hanged
herself and was changed into an almond tree. The bridegroom arrived
after a painful delay only to find that Phyllis was dead.

655

115. *Rahab:* When Joshua sent spies before him into Jericho, Rahab, a harlot of that city, hid them from the king's men and helped them to escape. Thus she helped the people of Israel to regain the Promised Land, and immediately following the Crucifixion her soul (which must have been in Limbo) was summoned by the third heaven, the first of its elect.

119–120. *shadow . . . rests the point of its long cone:* Some scholars of Dante's time believed that the cone of the earth's shadow came to a point in the third sphere.

122–123. *as a palm:* As a trophy. *two palms:* Of Christ when He was nailed to the cross. It is fitting that Rahab should be the heavenly trophy of Christ's victory for she had helped Israel win the Promised Land. It is a pity, Dante has Folquet say, that the Pope cares so little for the Holy Land (he had done nothing to reestablish Christianity there after Acre, the last Christian stronghold, fell to the Saracens in 1291).

127. *the One:* Satan was the first to turn on God. It was Mars who founded Florence (Inferno, 13), but Dante's invective has a firm foundation in those Church Fathers who held that Mars and all the pagan gods were fiends.

130. *the accursed flower of gold:* The Florentine florin, a gold coin stamped with a lily. The power of gold transforms the Shepherd (the Church, the Papacy in general, and Boniface VIII in particular) so that he preys on the sheep he should lead and guard.

133–135. *Great Doctors:* The Church Fathers, givers of doctrine. *the Decretals:* The volumes of canon law. Gregory IX ordered the compilation of the first five volumes in 1234 and Boniface VIII had a sixth added. The margins of the Decretals testify (by being worn and covered with annotations) how seriously they were studied, for they covered the temporal rights and privileges of the Church's vast power and wealth, and a knowledge of canon law could make a shyster's fortune.

138. *where . . . Gabriel opened wide his wings:* At the Annunciation.

CANTO 10

7–27. *reader, raise your eyes, etc.:* Dante summons the reader to ponder the perfection of God's creation as exemplified by the point of the vernal equinox. It is at this point that the sun's ecliptic crosses the celestial equator into the northern hemisphere. Were the courses of the equator and the ecliptic to run parallel, or were the angles between them to change, the influences of the spheres would be weakened, and earth that stands ever in need of those influences would lose the full good of their powers.

32. *those spirals:* The path of the sun seems to be a spiral from the Tropic of Capricorn (the southern limit of the sun's motion) to the Tropic of Cancer (the northern limit).

53–54. *the Sun of Angels:* God. *this physical one:* The sun. As the sun lights man, so God lights the angels.

95. *Dominic:* St. Dominic, founder of the Dominican Order.

98. *Albert:* Albertus Magnus (c. 1200–1280), the *Doctor Universalis* who, with Aquinas, reestablished Aristotelian learning in Western thought. He was teaching in Cologne in 1248 when Aquinas went there to be his student. Albertus was not canonized and proclaimed a Doctor of the Church until 1931.

99. *Thomas, of Aquinas:* Aquinas (1227–1274), known as the *Doctor Angelicus,* was author of the *Summa Theologica,* a principal source of Dante's learning; founder of Thomistic philosophy; and perhaps the most learned of Catholic theologians. He was not canonized until 1323, two years after Dante's death. Dante, therefore, was writing of Thomas, not of St. Thomas. As befits the modes of Heaven, Thomas does not mention his own name till he has identified the spirit on his right, a brother Dominican and his teacher.

103. *Gratian:* Or Gratianus, a twelfth-century scholar. It is for his *Decretum Gratiani* that Aquinas credits him with correlating and harmonizing civil and ecclesiastical law.

107. *the good Peter:* Petrus Lombardus. Born early in the twelfth century, Bishop of Paris 1159, died 1160. Called *Magister Sententiarum* because of his *Sententiarum Libri IV,* a compilation of scriptures and texts of the Church Fathers. In a sense, he did for doctrine what Gratianus did for canon law, and Dante typically puts the two side by side. *like the poor widow:* In his preface to *Sententiarum* Peter modestly compares himself to the poor widow who gave her two mites (all she had) to the treasury of the church.

109–111. *The fifth light:* Solomon. *so magnificent a love:* As expressed in the Song of Songs which was thought to be the wedding hymn of the Church and God. *men hunger for any news:* Of Solomon's final fate. I Kings 9:1–9 records the sins of Solomon's age, and theologians of Dante's time debated whether he had been saved or damned.

115. *the taper:* Dionysus the Areopagite, converted by St. Paul and wrongly believed in Dante's time to be the author of "The Celestial Hierarchy."

119. *the defender of the Christian Age:* Either Paulus Orosius, fifth-century Spanish priest whose *Historiarum Adversus Paganos* de-

fended the effect of Christianity upon the Roman Empire, or Marius Victorinus, a fourth-century Roman, who became a Christian theologian and whose example was believed to have contributed to the conversion of St. Augustine.

123. *what spirit shines in the eighth blaze:* Boethius, born in Rome *c.* 470, studied in Greece, became consul of Theodoric the Ostrogoth in 510, later imprisoned by Theodoric in Pavia on charges of treason and magic, and executed in 524. His *De Consolatione Philosophiae,* written in prison, is a work of pagan dignity that defends the joys of the good life without reference to any eternal reward. Despite its essential paganism, its influence upon the Middle Ages was enormous, among other reasons, as a source of late classical learning. In time the death of Boethius came to be thought of as a martyrdom. His remains were formally moved to a tomb in Pavia's Cieldauro (Church of St. Peter) in the eighth century, and though never canonized, he grew to be locally revered as St. Severinus.

130. *Isidore:* Of Seville (*c.* 560–636). Became Archbishop of Seville *c.* 600, canonized St. Isidore, 1598, designated a Doctor of the Church, 1722. His major work, *Etymologiae,* was highly prized as an encyclopedia of medieval learning.

131. *Bede:* The Venerable Bede (*c.* 673–735), English Bible scholar and historian. The title of Venerable (the three orders of holiness are venerable, blessed, and saint, in mounting order) was conferred in the ninth century. Pope Leo declared him a Doctor of the Church in 1899. *Richard:* Richard of St. Victor. Twelfth-century English mystic and theologian. Birth date unknown; died *c.* 1173. He was called the Great Contemplator after one of his treatises, *De Contemplatione.*

137. *Siger:* Siger of Brabant. Born *c.* 1226. An outstanding Averroist philosopher, he taught at the University of Paris (which was then on la rue de Feurre or Street of Straws) and was cited for heresy in 1277 before the Grand Inquisitor of France (hence, the "truths for which he would be hated"). He fled to Orvieto to appeal his case to the Papal Court but was stabbed to death (*c.* 1283) by his secretary.

CANTO 11

34. *two Princes, one on either side:* St. Dominic and St. Francis. Dominic, on one side (line 39), by his wisdom and doctrinal clarity made the Church secure within itself by helping to defend it against error and heresy. Francis, on the other (line 37), set the example that made it more faithfully the Bride of Christ.

43–51. *Between the Tupino, etc.:* The passage is full of local allusions, not all of them relevant to St. Francis, but all describing the situation of Assisi, his birthplace. *the Tupino:* Skirts Mt. Subasio on the south

658

and flows roughly west into the Tiber. *the little race:* The Chiascio flows south along the length of Subasio and empties into the Tupino below Assisi. *blessèd Ubaldo:* St. Ubaldo (1084–1160), Bishop of Gubbio from 1129. He chose a hill near Gubbio as a hermitage in which to end his days, but died before he could retire there. *Porta Sole:* Perugia's west gate. It faces Mt. Subasio. In summer its slopes reflect the sun's ray through Porta Sole; in winter, covered with snow, they send the cold wind. *Nocera . . . Gualdo:* Towns behind Subasio. Their heavy yoke may be their subjugation by Perugia, or Dante may have meant by it the taxes imposed by Robert of Naples and his Spanish brigands.

52–54. *let no man, etc.:* Ascesi, which can mean "I have risen," was a common name for Assisi in Dante's day. *Oriente* is the point at which the sun rises. Let no man, therefore, call Assisi "I have risen" (i.e., a man has risen), but let him call it, rather, the dawning east of the world (a sun has risen).

55ff. *Nor was he yet far distant, etc.:* Francis, born Bernardone, was the son of a relatively prosperous baker and, early in life, assisted his father. In a skirmish between Assisi and Perugia he was taken prisoner and later released. On his return to Assisi (he was then twenty-four) he abandoned all worldly affairs and gave himself entirely to religious works. *that Lady:* Poverty. *his own father's wrath:* In 1207 (Francis was then twenty-five) he sold one of his father's horses along with a load of bread and gave the money to a church. In a rage, his father forced the church to return the money, called Francis before the Bishop of Assisi, and there demanded that he renounce his right to inherit. Francis not only agreed gladly but removed his clothes and gave them back to his father saying, "Until this hour I called you my father on earth; from this hour I can say in truth 'our Father which art in Heaven.'" *he married:* In his "Hymn to Poverty" Francis himself celebrated his union to Poverty as a marriage. He had married her before the diocesan court of Assisi, *et coram patre* (before the court, i.e., in the legal presence of his father). The marriage was solemnized by his renunciation of all possessions.

64–66. *her First Groom:* Christ. *he:* St. Francis.

68. *Amyclas:* Lucan reported how the fisherman Amyclas lay at his ease on a bed of seaweed before Caesar himself, being so poor that he had nothing to fear from any man. Not even this report of the serenity Mistress Poverty could bring to a man, and not even the fact that she outdid even Mary in constancy, climbing the very cross with Christ, had moved any man to seek her in marriage.

79. *Bernard:* Bernard di Quintavalle, a wealthy neighbor, became the first disciple of Francis, kicking off his shoes to go barefoot in imitation of the master.

82–83. *unknown:* To men. Holy Poverty is the wealth none recognize, the plenitude none try. *Egidius . . . Sylvester:* The third and fourth disciples of Francis. Peter, the second disciple, seems not to have been known to Dante.

93. *his order first received the seal:* In 1210. But Innocent III thought the proposed rule of the order so harsh that he granted only provisional approval.

96. *among the Seraphim:* In the Empyrean, rather than in this fourth heaven.

97–99. *Honorius . . . second crown:* In 1223, Pope Honorius III gave his fully solemnized approval of the Franciscan Order.

100–105. *he went forth, etc.:* In 1219, St. Francis and eleven of his followers made a missionary pilgrimage to Greece and Egypt. Dante may have meant that pilgrimage, or he may have meant Francis' projected journey to convert the Moors (1214–1215) when Francis fell ill in southern Spain and had to give up his plans.

106–108. *On the crag, etc.:* In 1224, on a crag of Mt. Alvernia, St. Francis received the stigmata in a rapturous vision of Christ. He wore the wounds two years before his death in 1226, at the age of forty-four.

119. *his fellow helmsman:* St. Dominic. *Peter's ship:* The Church.

122. *his command:* The rule of the Dominicans. *will fill the hold:* With the treasures of Paradise.

CANTO 12

10. *twin rainbows:* Twin rainbows were said to occur when Juno called her handmaiden Iris (the Rainbow) to attend her. Dante believed the outer band of a twin rainbow was a reflection of the inner band.

14. *wandering nymph:* Echo, who wasted away for love of Narcissus (consumed by the fire of love as vapors are consumed by the sun) until the gods changed her to a stone.

28. *one of those new splendors:* St. Bonaventure (1221–1274), born Giovanni di Fidanza at Bagnoregio (now Bagnorea) near Lake Bolsena. He was a scholar saint and a leading theologian. He became Minister General of the Franciscan Order in 1257 and was created Cardinal-Bishop of Albano in 1273. Much of his scholarship was carried out in France, where he died during the sessions of the second Council of Lyons. He was canonized in 1482 by Sixtus IV and pronounced sixth among the Doctors of the Church by Sixtus V in 1587.

37–38. *rearmed:* By the blood of martyrs when persecution had all but scattered it. *the holy standard:* The cross.

Notes

52–54. *a fortunate village:* Calahorra, birthplace of St. Dominic, lies on the Ebro about 60 miles due south of the Bay of Biscay where it washes the westernmost point of the Spanish-French border. *the great shield:* Of the house of Castile. It is quartered and contains on one side a castle above a lion and on the other a lion above a castle, thus one lion is subjugating the castle and the other is being subjugated by it.

55. *the ardent one:* St. Dominic (1170–1221). Not all of the details Dante offers in his account of St. Dominic have a historic base. Dominic may have been born of an ancient family named Guzman, but little is known of his origins. He was an austere but undeviating man of mercy, with faith in pure doctrine. Beginning as an Augustinian, Dominic sought to overcome the heresies of the Albigensians, partly in defense of the pure faith and partly to save them from the terrors of the crusade that eventually destroyed them in a hideous bloodbath. He founded the Dominican Order with the special purpose of saving the Albigensians from destruction in this world and damnation in the next. In 1215 he won provisional papal approval of his order from Innocent III, and, in 1216, full confirmation by Honorius III. He died in Bologna in 1221 and was canonized in 1234. Unlike Francis, who dreaded learning as a corruptive force and praised the holy ignorance of the rude and simple mind, Dominic labored for purity of doctrine and founded his order for missionary scholars who were to go forth and preach the pure faith. The notes that follow comment on Dante's version of the life of St. Dominic, not on the historical record.

59. *such powers:* While still in the womb, Dominic was said to be so gifted that his mother foresaw the Dominican Order in a dream of giving birth to a black and white dog. Black and white are the Dominican colors, and *Domini canes* translates "hounds of the Lord."

64–65. *the Lady . . . saw, in a dream:* Following his baptism, his godmother is supposed to have dreamed that he had a star on his forehead, a sign that he would bring God's light to man.

68–69. *the possessive form of His name:* Dominic is the possessive form of the Latin *Domine* (the Lord).

83–87. *the Ostian:* Enrico di Susa, who became Bishop of Ostia in 1271. *Taddeo:* Probably Taddeo d'Alderotto, a Florentine physician born *c.* 1215. The first was a successful scholar of canon law, the second of medicine. Both acquired money and fame as a result of their secular studies.

91–96. *he did not ask, etc.:* In seeking to find his new order Dominic did not ask permission to dispense Church wealth, nor for a benefice, nor for *decimas quae sunt pauperum Dei* (the tithes that belong to God's poor). He asked only for license to combat heresy, and thus to defend the seed of the true faith from which are sprung, as plants of the everlasting tree, the twenty-four Doctors of the Church who surround Dante as Bonaventure speaks.

98–102. *he burst forth, etc.:* When Dominic was allowed in 1215 to found his Order of Preaching Friars, he had already been laboring for twelve years to wipe out the Albigensian heresy. The Church, under Innocent III, had by that time spent seven years massacring this group, which denied the Resurrection. Dominic attempted to win the heretics back to the faith through his preachments, not by the sword.

118–120. *the harvest of these years, etc.:* The original rule of St. Francis was so harsh that it caused a schism within the order even before his death. One group, the Spiritual Franciscans, insisted on the rule of absolute poverty to the point of being punished for heresy by the Church. The other group sought to modify the rule. St. Bonaventure attempted to resolve the conflict by teaching that all property given to the friars was the property of the Church, but was held for their use (*usus pauperis*) in their life and work. This schism was the lazy cultivation that made a bad harvest inevitable. The bad harvest (the darnel) would be those Franciscans who risked excommunication by insisting, against direct papal orders, on the unmitigated rule, as well as those who observed the modified rule too slackly. Darnel or rye grass or black caraway springs up among the cultivated grains. Its hard seeds, ground up with the edible grains and so eaten as bread, can cause nervous disorders. It must be weeded out carefully and kept out of the good grain, the storehouse shut against it.

121–123. *our book:* The Franciscan Order. *some page:* Some member of the order.

124. *Casal:* The Franciscan monastery at Casale in Monferato. Ubertino di Casale (1259–1338) was General of the Chapter and, favoring the Spirituals, so tightened the rule that he was forced to leave the order. *Acquasparta:* In Todi. From this monastery Matteo d'Acquasparta rose to be General of the Order in 1287 and Cardinal in 1288. Under him the Franciscan rule was substantially relaxed.

130. *Illuminato and Augustino:* Two of the early brothers.

133. *The prior Hugo:* Hugo of St. Victor (1096?–1141). Born in Saxony, he went to the monastery of St. Victor in Paris in 1115, where he taught philosophy and theology. In 1133 he was made prior and given charge of all studies.

134. *Peter Mangiadore:* Of Troyes (1110–1179?), Dean of the Cathedral of Troyes, 1147–1164. His *Historia Scholastica* was long the standard work on Bible history. *Peter of Spain:* Became John XXI in 1276, died in 1277. He was born in Lisbon *c.* 1226. Among the twelve books

here referred to was his well-known summary of logical principles, *Summulae logicales.*

136. *the prophet Nathan:* Nathan spoke out against the sins of King David.

137. *Chrysostom:* The name in Greek means golden mouth, a tribute to his oratorical power. He was John of Antioch (344?–407), Metropolitan of Constantinople. Like Nathan, he denounced the sins of the ruler. He was exiled by the Empress Eudoxia. *Anselm:* Born in Aosta, Lombardy, c. 1033. As Archbishop of Canterbury (from 1093) he fought the king on the question of the recognition of the Pope. Forced into exile in 1103, he returned to Canterbury in 1107, and died there in 1109. *Donatus:* Lived in Rome about the middle of the fourth century. He wrote commentaries on Terence and Virgil and a book on grammar that was widely used in Dante's time.

139. *Rabanus:* Rabanus Maurus (776?–856). Became Archbishop of Mainz in 847. Bible scholar, poet, and author of *De clericorum institutione,* a manual for clerics.

140. *Joachim:* Of Fiore (1132?–1202). A Cistercian mystic whose doctrines were especially popular among the Spiritual Franciscans who opposed Bonaventure.

142–144. *my holy brother:* St. Thomas. *one great paladin:* St. Francis. *the other:* St. Dominic. The paladins were the twelve great champions who surrounded Charlemagne.

CANTO 13

13–15. *two constellations, each a wreath, etc.:* Each like the Corona Borealis, which, according to legend, was made from the bridal wreath of Ariadne (daughter of King Minos) when, abandoned by Theseus, she is found by Dionysus and is taken to heaven to become his wife.

24. *Chiana:* A Tuscan river that, in Dante's time, wound sluggishly through swamplands that have since been drained.

53. *Form:* The Platonic Form, or Idea.

55–57. *the Living Light:* The Son. *the Source:* The Father as Creator. *the Love:* The Holy Ghost.

59. *nine subsistent natures:* The nine orders of angels that attend the spheres.

61–63. *thing:* The Scholastic term for that which actually exists. *potencies:* That which does not exist but that has the power of coming into being. *contingencies:* What could exist but does not.

68. *the Ideal Seal:* A metaphoric equivalent of the Ideal Form of Plato, here, the Divine Concept. It is perfect and unchangeable but, descending through the constant changes of the spheres to the flux of matter, it is transmitted and received in a necessarily diminished way. Thus the Divine Idea shines through all things, and through some more than through others, but never perfectly.

93. *What shall I give thee?:* After Solomon went to Gideon and offered up a thousand burnt offerings, the Lord appeared in a dream and asked what gift he would choose. Solomon asked for the wisdom with which to rule his people.

124–125. *Parmenides . . . Melissus . . . Bryson:* Philosophers refuted by Aristotle. Parmenides taught that all things come from and return to the sun. Melissus, a disciple of Parmenides, taught that there is no motion in the universe but only an appearance of motion. Bryson labored devotedly and at great length to square the circle.

127. *Arius . . . Sabellius:* Heretical philosophers. Arius, an Alexandrian priest (died 336) taught that the Son, having been created by the Father, could not be one with Him. Sabellius advanced the Monarchian heresy that there is no real distinction between Father and Son and that the Trinity is merely a succession of modes in which a single person appears.

CANTO 14

88–89. *the tongue which is one in all men:* The tongue of true prayer.

102. *a circle's quadrant lines:* A quadrant is one fourth of a circle. The lines that describe the four quadrants form a cross within a ring.

133–135. *living seals:* The heavens. Their influences stamp themselves, as a signet does in wax, upon the souls of men. *those others:* The eyes of Beatrice.

CANTO 15

25–27. *ancient Ilium:* Anchises, the ancient king of Ilium. *muse:* For poet, i.e., Virgil.

28–30. *O sanguis meus, etc.:* "O blood of mine! O ever abundant grace of God poured over you! To whom was the Gate of Heaven ever thrown open twice, as it is to you?" *twice:* Now, while Dante is still in the flesh, and again after his death. St. Paul was borne up in a dream to the third heaven, but Dante has come in the flesh. The speaker is Cacciaguida, Dante's great-great-grandfather. The details of Cacciaguida's life are best presented piecemeal, in the notes to the

Notes

conversation that follows. Note, however, that Cacciaguida lived in the twelfth century when the spoken language was still primarily Latin. The reference to Virgil and to the *Aeneid* makes it doubly felicitous that he begin his remarks in Latin.

52. *the Great Book:* Of Fate.

55–57. *You believe, etc.:* Dante is asserting, as a principle of mathematics, that all numbers (five or six, for example) derive from one. So all knowledge derives from the Primal Intellect, which is unity.

73. *the First Equipoise:* God, in whom all attributes coexist equally, as light and heat coexist in the sun.

91. *present surname:* The surname Alighieri (then Aldighiero) is thus identified as having originated with Cacciaguida's son.

98. *from them . . . Tierce and Nones:* The church called La Badia was built on the old Roman walls. This church rang all the canonical hours.

107. *Sardanapalus:* King of Assyria from 667 to 626 B.C. He is cited as the type of the luxurious and libertine debauché of the harem.

109–111. *Montemario:* A hill with a commanding view of Rome. *Uccellatoio:* A hill with a similar view of Florence. The splendor of the view from the Uccellatoio had not yet outdone the view from Montemario, but just as Florence is rising faster than Rome, so will she plunge to ruin faster.

112–113. *Bellincion Berti:* A nobleman of some importance, honorary citizen of Florence, and father of the good Gualdrada (Inferno, 16). *belted in leather and bone:* A leather belt with a bone clasp rather than ornamented with a jeweled clasp.

115. *Vecchio. . . Nerli:* Both were Guelph lords of Cacciaguida's time and leading citizens of Florence.

119. *sure of her own burial place:* As Dante was not, having been exiled. As, by implication, few later Florentines could be, since any of them might find himself banished.

120. *because of France:* In both of two possible senses. Florentine bankers and merchants often traveled to France, hence they were often out of town. But in France, too, they learned vices for which they abandoned their wives even when they were back in Florence.

127–129. *Cornelia:* Daughter of Scipio Africanus and mother of the Roman paragons, the Gracchii. *Cincinnatus:* Roman general. *Cianghella:* A Florentine woman married to a Lord of Imola. She died about 1330, having acquired a reputation for a sharp tongue, a haughty extravagance, and an easy bed. *Lapo:* Lapo Saltorello. A

Florentine poet and lawyer noted for his extravagant living. He and Dante were banished in the same decree of March 10, 1302.

133–134. *Mary . . . called in the pain of birth:* Cacciaguida's mother, in the throes of her birth pains, cried out a plea to the Virgin Mary, who thereupon granted him life and sweet dwelling in ancient Florence. *Baptistry:* Of San Giovanni.

136–138. There is no historic record of any of the persons here mentioned.

139. *Conrad:* Conrad III (reigned 1137–1152). He went crusading in 1147 and was defeated at Damascus. He never visited Florence, however, whereas Conrad II (reigned 1024–1039) knew Florence well. Conrad II crusaded against the Saracens in Calabria. Dante has probably run the two Conrads into one.

143–144. *the evil creed:* Islam. *because your Shepherds sin:* Because of bad Popes the Holy Land, which Dante held to be rightfully Christian, was left to Islam.

149. *from martyrdom to my present joys:* Cacciaguida, having died fighting for the faith—for God—mounted directly to his place in Heaven.

CANTO 16

10. *voi:* The second person plural. It seems to have come into use as the deferential form of address to a single person in about the third century A.D., but Dante is following the popular belief of his time that it was first used in addressing Caesar when he assumed all the high offices of the Republic and so became, in effect, many personages in one.

14–15. *like her who coughed:* The wife of Gallehault (Inferno, 5), who coughed when she first saw Guinevere with Launcelot.

37. *this flame:* Mars. *its Leo:* Astrologers asserted various special connections between Mars and Leo. Both were classified as hot and dry, and Leo is the constellation of the lion, the warlike and heraldic beast perhaps closest to the god of war.

39. *five hundred, etc.:* The date of Cacciaguida's birth is not known. But he is thought to have died when he was about 56.

41. *the last quarter:* Probably Port San Piero.

47. *between Mars and the Baptist:* In Florence.

50. *of Campi, of Certaldo, and of Figghine:* All are nearby places a self-righteous Florentine would think of as the backwoods.

Notes

53–56. *Trespiano:* A crossroads village now at the edge of Florence, but in Cacciaguida's time an hour's walk away on the road to Bologna. *Galuzzo:* A village at about the same distance on the road to Siena. *the yokel of Aguglione:* Baldo d'Aguglione. His family name traces to a "backwoods" castle in Val di Pesa, but he became a power in Florence. On September 3, 1311, he issued a decree recalling a number of Florentine exiles but left Dante's name off the list. *Signa's boor:* Fazio dei Morubaldini of Signa, a hamlet near Florence. Fazio was a lawyer of Dante's time with a considerable reputation as a grafter and swindler.

62. *Simifonti:* A castle and town in Valdessa captured by Florence in 1202.

64. *Montemurlo:* A castle between Pistola and Prata. It formerly belonged to the Counts Guidi (Inferno, 30). In 1254, unable to defend the castle against the Pistoians, the counts sold it to Florence.

65. *Acone:* In Val di Sieve. In Dante's time, the Cerchi had become leaders of the White Party in Dante's ancestral quarter of Porta San Piero.

66. *Valdigreve:* South of Florence where the Buondelmonti had a castle called Montebuoni. In 1135 the castle was taken from them by the Florentines, and they were forced to move into Florence, where they became powerful in Borgo Sant' Apostolo.

73–75. *Luni:* An ancient city on the Magra at the northern boundary of Tuscany, already a ruin in Dante's time. *Urbisaglia:* In the March of Ancona; not quite dead in Dante's time. *Chiusi:* Ancient Clusium, in Val di Chiana. *Sinigaglia:* On the coast north of Ancona. Both were ravaged by malaria in Dante's time, but both have survived their prophesied extinction.

88–90. *Ughi, etc.:* Cacciaguida lists six solid, old families of the first half of the eleventh century and says they were illustrious even in their decline. In 1300 these families had finished declining and were extinct, at least as influential voices in Florentine affairs.

91. *those of the Bow:* The family dell' Arca. They and the other four families here cited were numerous and powerful in Cacciaguida's time. In Dante's time the dell' Arca clan was extinct; the Soldanieri, a Ghibelline clan, still existed but had been banished; and the descendants of the other three clans had lost power and social standing.

94. *the portal:* Of San Piero, where the Cerchi ruled in Dante's time (line 65). The portal shows the destruction of Florence.

97–99. *Ravignani . . . Count Guido Guerra . . . Bellincione:* Berti dei Ravignani was praised in Canto 15. Count Guido Guerra was praised in the Inferno, 16, though he is damned among the Sodomites.

100. *della Pressa:* An emergent family in Cacciaguida's time, who had been elected to govern some of the nearby territories of Florence. Their descendants were charged with betraying the Florentines at Montaperti.

101. *Galigaio:* A noble family of Porta San Piero, here said to have been already of the knighthood in Cacciaguida's time, but reduced to the rank and file by 1300.

103. *vair:* A fur, usually of a small squirrel. Represented in heraldry by rows of little bells. It appeared on the arms of the Pigli, a family of Porta San Pancrazio.

104. A continuation of the early eleventh-century Florentine social register.

105. *those who blush now for the stave affair:* The Chiaramontesi of Porta San Piero.

106. *Calfucci:* Were collateral with the Donati. Dante's wife, Gemma, was a Donati.

108. *the curule:* A chair in which only the highest officers of Rome might sit. Here used to indicate highest rank. *Sizii and Arrigucci:* Neither family was extinct by Dante's time, but the first was nearly so, and the second much reduced.

110. *balls of gold:* From the arms of the Lamberti. Mosca, one of this line, is in the *bolgia* of the Sowers of Discord (Inferno, 28).

112. *So shone the fathers of that gang we see:* As the Lamberti once shone in every great deed of Florence, so shone (in evil deeds) the Visdomini and the Tosinghi, hereditary patrons and defenders of the episcopal see and palace. Whenever the see fell vacant, they were in charge of episcopal affairs until a new bishop was elected. Dante here accuses them of forming themselves into a private consistory in order to fatten themselves on the resources of the see.

115. *That . . . tribe:* The Adimari. When Dante was banished, Boccaccio Adimari took over his forfeited estates and resisted every effort to rescind the decree of banishment.

119. *Donato . . . his father-in-law:* Bellincione married the good Gualdrada to Umbertino Donati of the family of the Counts Guidi. He then married another daughter to the upstart Adimari, thus relating the two families. The Donati refused to acknowledge kinship.

121–123. *Caponsacchi . . . Infangati . . . Giudi:* Three Ghibelline families, once well established, but much diminished by Dante's time.

125. *the inner wall:* The first (Roman) wall of the city. Cacciaguida is saying that Dante would know the long-vanished della Pera family

was an ancient one, but not that it traced back to the very founding of Florence.

128–132. *the great baron, etc.:* Hugh of Brandenburg, known in Italy as Ugo il Grande, Marchese di Toscano, the Imperial Vicar and chief Ghibelline of Tuscany. His arms bore seven staves, which are variously reproduced in the arms of all the families he raised to knighthood and fortune (among them the Giandotti, Pulci, della Bella, and Neri). He died on St. Thomas' Day, 1006, and it is still part of the festival of St. Thomas to offer solemn prayers to Ugo in the abbey he built in Florence. *though one who binds those arms:* Giano della Bella. He was exiled in 1295 and was no longer making common cause with the hoi polloi. But Dante, though he had to become a Guelph once there were no more Ghibellines in Florence, still has his only political hope in the party of the Emperor and will not miss a chance to condemn the great Ghibelline families that identified themselves with the cause of vulgar independence.

133. *Gualterotti and Importuni:* Guelph families of Borgo Santo Apostolo, great in Cacciaguida's time, but common workingmen in Dante's.

135. *new neighbors from Montebuon':* The Buondelmonti.

136–139. *The line:* Of the Amidei. A great family related to the Lamberti and allied to many noble families of Florence. Despite the fact that it was of much higher rank, it betrothed one of its daughters to Buondelmonte dei Buondelmonti, who broke off the nuptials in order to marry a daughter of the Donati. The Amidei, in "righteous anger" at this affront by a man of lower rank, held a council of war. As a result Buondelmonti was murdered at the foot of the statue of Mars in 1215. As a result of that murder Florence, previously united, became divided into Guelph and Ghibelline factions, and was plunged into civil war, thereby ending its "happier life."

143. *the Ema:* A river bounding the lands from which the Buondelmonti were dispossessed before they came to Florence.

153–154. *none had ever seized, etc.:* The Florentines had never been defeated in war.

155. *the red dye of division:* The ancient standard of Florence bore a white lily on a red field. In 1251 the Guelphs changed their standard to a red lily on a white field, the Ghibellines preserving the original. Thus there were two Florentine standards and division had dyed the lily red. The red dye is also the blood spilled in war.

CANTO 17

1. *him who went to Clymene:* Phaeton, son of Clymene and Apollo.

669

Epaphus had told him Apollo was not his father, and the boy had run to his mother to be reassured. Phaeton persuaded Apollo to let him drive the chariot of the sun, but the boy lost control and was killed by Zeus. The reluctance Phaeton teaches fathers is for the good of the sons.

31–32. *that glued the foolish like limed birds:* Bird-lime, a highly viscous substance, is spread on boughs and used to trap birds much as flies are trapped on fly paper. Dante compares the sayings of pagan oracles to that lime, in which the pagan world let itself be trapped before the Lamb of Christ suffered to set men free of such traps.

46. *Hippolytus:* Son of Theseus and the Amazon Antiope. He rejected the advances of his stepmother, Phaedra, and she, accusing him of what she herself wanted, turned Theseus against him. Theseus not only drove him from home, but called on Poseidon for vengeance. Poseidon sent a bull from the sea to kill Hippolytus as he was driving his chariot along the shore.

50. *him who plots it:* Boniface VIII, if not in person then through his corrupt agents.

71–72. *the great Lombard:* Of the Scaligeri (della Scalla) family of Verona. *the sacred bird:* The eagle. The arms of the family displayed a ladder (*scala*) below an eagle.

76. *another:* Can Grande della Scala.

81. *nine years:* Earth years. Cacciaguida does not say nine "times." Nine Martian years would equal about seventeen earth years and Can Grande was nine years old on March 9, 1300.

82–83. *the Gascon . . . high Henry:* The Gascon is Clement V, who succeeded Boniface VIII to the papal throne in 1305 and to the baptismal font of Hell in 1314 (Inferno, 19). Henry VII of Luxemburg, Emperor 1308–1313, was the main prop of Dante's hopes for a general peace and for the end of his exile. Clement invited him to Rome with fair promises, but threatened to excommunicate him in 1312. "Before" therefore means "before 1312." By that time Can Grande was twenty-one, had been joint lord of Verona for four years, and sole lord for one.

CANTO 18

37ff. *I saw, etc.:* Dante sees the great Warriors of God. Joshua, succeeding Moses, led Israel into the promised land. Judas Maccabaeus freed Israel from the Syrian tyranny. Charlemagne, in driving the Moors out of Europe, restored the Empire and freed the Spanish church. Roland was the nephew of Charlemagne and his greatest knight. William of Orange, hero of various medieval French romances, was the ideal of the Christian knight and was said to have died a monk. Rinoardo Rainouart served under William as his chief lieutenant. He was reputed to have been a convert from paganism and to have died in Holy Orders but he, like William, is largely a legendary figure. Godfrey or Gottfried of Bouillon was the leader of the first crusade and became the first Christian king of Jerusalem. He died in 1100. Robert Guiscard, son of Tancred d'Hauteville, a Norman war leader, joined with his brothers in 1046 to war against the Saracens in southern Italy, becoming Duke of Puglia and of Calabria. He died in 1085.

68. *the temperate star:* Ptolemy described Jupiter as a temperate mean between hot Mars and cold Saturn.

72. *our means of speech:* The alphabet.

78–99. *D . . . I . . . L, etc.:* The message formed by the lights, beginning with these letters and running to thirty-five letters, is DILIGITE IUSTITIAM QUI IUDICATIS TERRAM—"Love righteousness, ye that are judges of the earth."

82. *Pegasean:* The Muses drink from the spring called Hippocrene that sprang from the earth where Pegasus struck it with his hoof. The nine Muses together may properly be called Pegaseans. Dante uses the singular form, perhaps to invoke the Muses generally.

95. *silvery Jupiter:* Jupiter was reputed to have a silvery sheen that set it apart from other white stars. The souls, however, are encased in sheaths of golden light.

104–105. *greater . . . lesser . . . to the place the Sun that lit it chose:* It is the Sun (God) who decrees the pattern of the eagle, assigning to each soul its place in the pattern according to the amount of grace It rays forth to each.

115. *O lovely star:* Jupiter.

122. *the temple:* The Church.

126. *bad example:* Of papal corruption.

130. *you:* Dante uses the singular form *tu.* He must, therefore, be referring to a single evil Pope. As of 1300 that Pope would be Boniface VIII. *scribble only to scratch out:* Instead of preparing bulls that will clarify God's intent to all time, the evil Popes merely scribble excommunications, interdictions, and denials of justice in order to cancel them again for a fee.

134. *the image of the saint:* John the Baptist. But in a bitter irony, Dante portrays the corrupt Popes having their hearts set not on the saint but on his image, for it was stamped on the Florentine gold florin. Thus their love of St. John is the love of money.

CANTO 19

46. *the first Prideful Power:* Satan.

65. *Halcyon:* God.

109. *Ethiopian:* Used as a generic term for all pagans.

112. *Persians:* Another generic term for pagans.

115. *Albert:* Albert I, Emperor from 1298 to 1308. He is the German Albert of Purgatorio, 6. He invaded Bohemia in 1304.

118–120. *the Seine:* For France, generally. *debaser of the currency:* Philip the Fair. He debased the coinage to finance his wars and brought misery to France. Dante punished counterfeiters in the Inferno not out of love of money, but because a sound coinage was an essential principle of social order. *death . . . in a pig's skin:* In 1314, in the course of a royal hunt, a wild boar ran under Philip's horse. Philip was thrown and died soon after of his injuries.

121–122. *greed:* For more land. *Scot . . . Englishman:* The Scottish and English kings in their endless border wars.

125. *the Spaniard:* Probably Ferdinand IV. *the Bohemian:* Probably Wenceslaus IV.

127–129. *cripple of Jerusalem:* Charles II of Anjou, known as Charles the Lame. He was King of Jerusalem only by the act of giving himself that title. In the Book of Judgment his virtues will be marked by the number 1 and his villainies by the letter M (a thousand).

131–132. *the watchdog:* Frederick II of Sicily. *burning island:* Sicily. *on which Anchises:* He died at Drepanum, modern Trapani.

137–138. *his uncle and his brother:* King James of Majorca, brother of James I of Aragon; and James II of Aragon, son of James I. Each disgraced the crown he wore; both disgraced the house of Aragon. *cuckolded:* They disgraced their family and their kingdom from within, as a wife does when she cuckolds her husband.

140. *Norway's king:* In 1300, Hacon V. *Portugal's:* Dionysus. *Rascia's:* Orosius II. Rascia was part of Serbia. Orosius seems to have altered the metal content of Venetian money on a substantial scale. *lost most:* His falsifying of the currency would slate him for a meeting with Master Adam in Hell (Inferno, 30).

142. *Hungary:* Andrew III, a good king, ruled in 1300. Hungary had endured many ruinous wars.

143–144. *Navarre . . . fortress wall:* The ancient kingdom of what is now southern France and northern Spain. Joanna of Navarre married Philip the Fair of France in 1284 but remained sole ruler of Navarre.

Notes

After her death in 1304, her son Louis inherited Navarre, and when his father died in 1314, he became Louis X, King of France and Navarre. So Navarre passed under French rule, the bitterness of which they were to learn in full. Hence, they would have been happier had they armed the mountains around them (the Pyrenees) as fortress walls for keeping out the French.

146–148. *Nicosìa and Famagosta:* The two principal cities of Crete. *their beast:* Henry II of the French house of Lusignan was King of Cyprus in 1300, a man given to debaucheries for which the people paid dearly. Every Navarrese would have done well in 1300 to have taken him as an example of French rule and of what Navarre would suffer when it passed under the French crown.

CANTO 20

31. *that part:* The eye. The ancients believed that the eagle could look straight into the sun.

38. *the sweet psalmist:* David.

43. *the one:* Trajan.

48. *he has known the bitter way:* Trajan had been long in Limbo.

49–54. *The next in line:* Hezekiah, who, offering a true repentance on his deathbed, was allowed to live for fifteen more years. *now he knows:* To what extent prayer may vary the preordained divine plan without altering it.

55–60. *The third:* The Emperor Constantine. With the purest of intentions Constantine ceded the Western Empire to the Church (the Shepherd) and moved his seat of Empire to Greece, bearing with him Roman law and "me" (the Roman Eagle). Constantine learns in Heaven that the evil consequences of a good action (or the good consequences of an evil action) do not change the nature of the original action—a point made by Aquinas in his *Summa.*

62. *William:* William II (the Good), King of the Two Sicilies from 1166 to 1189. He was the last of the house of Tancred. In Dante's time, the Kingdom of Naples passed to Charles the Lame and the Kingdom of Sicily to Frederick II. Sicily mourns its present evil as it mourns the passing of its happiness with the death of William.

68. *Ripheus:* Virgil mentioned him once in the *Aeneid* as the one most just man among the Trojans and as the one who most loved the right. No more is known of him, and Dante is thus free (see below) to invent a pre-Christian conversion for him.

92. *quiddity:* In Scholastic terminology: "that which causes a thing to be what it is."

673

103–105. *They did not leave their bodies, etc.:* Ripheus and Trajan did not leave their bodies as pagans but as Christians and firm believers, one (Trajan) in the pierced feet (the Crucifixion) that has already taken place; the other (Ripheus) in the Crucifixion yet to come.

106–117. *One rose, etc.:* In relating the resurrection and conversion of Trajan, Dante follows a legend that Gregory I (Pope from 590 to 604) prayed so ardently for the salvation of Trajan that God's voice replied, "I grant pardon to Trajan." Since none may go from Hell to Heaven (with the exeception of those souls Christ took with Him in the Harrowing of Hell), it was necessary to restore Trajan to the flesh, long enough to permit his conversion to Christ.

124. *So he believed in Christ:* Unhampered by any historical record, Dante creates a legend of Ripheus as a Christian before the fact. Granted a vision of Christ to come, he believed utterly and was saved. In place of baptism the three maids who stood at the right wheel of the Chariot of the Church in the Heavenly Pageant of the Earthly Paradise stood as his godmothers in some equivalent ritual.

CANTO 21

5. *Semele:* Semele loved Jupiter, and Juno tricked the girl into begging Jupiter to show himself to her in the full splendor of his godhead (as the other gods saw him). Semele was consumed to ash by his radiance.

25–27. *the crystal, etc.:* The Sphere of Saturn. It bears around the world the name of Saturn, who was the world's king in the Golden Age of man before sin had appeared.

43. *One:* Peter Damiano (1007–1072). Born in Ravenna, he became a Benedictine and entered the Camaldolese house at Fonte Avellana in 1035, became prior about 1043, and Cardinal-Bishop of Ostia in 1057 or 1058, accepting his elevation, as all reports agree, against his own inclination, and continuing in every high office a life of monastic severity. He was never officially canonized though he was venerated in Ravenna. He was, however, officially pronounced a Doctor of the Church. His many writings enjoin strict monastic rules and mortification of the flesh.

96. *created vision:* The vision of which any created thing is capable. Only God's uncreated vision can plumb the mystery of predestination.

109. *Catria:* Lies between Gubbio and Pergola. Below it stands the monastery of Santa Croce di Fonte Avellana of the Camaldolese rule (established at Camaldoli about 1012 by St. Romualdo). This rule

minimized the community organization of the monastery but established a particularly severe rule for the individual monks.

115–116. *Lenten olive-food:* Olive oil was common in Italy, but butter and lard (like all animal products) were expensive, and therefore luxurious. Lenten food was prepared in nothing but olive oil. Here we should probably understand a diet of simple crusts dipped in olive oil. *both heat and cold:* The rule required the monks to go barefoot.

121–123. *I was, etc.:* Peter went by both names, adopting the second as an act of piety (he had adopted the first in gratitude to his brother, who had made possible his education); he went to Ravenna ("by the Adriatic") as a papal emissary. He lived there for two years in the monastery of Santa Maria Pomposa.

124. *Little was left me of my mortal course:* Peter became Cardinal in 1057 or 1058. He died in 1072.

127. *Cephas:* The name Christ gave to Simon, who became Peter. The word means rock in Hebrew, as *pietra* does in Italian, *Pietro* being the masculine form of the word used as a man's name. *the great Ark of the Holy Ghost:* St. Paul.

130. *pastors:* Popes.

CANTO 22

28. *the largest and most glowing globe:* St. Benedict (480–543). He was born at Nursia in Umbria and went to Rome for his education. There, appalled by the wickedness of the Romans, he left the world about the year 500 and lived in a cave on Mt. Subiaco, his rigid asceticism and holiness drawing disciples to him, though he seems never to have been ordained. About 525 he moved with his followers to Monte Cassino and there, after destroying a temple of Apollo, founded the great central monastery of the Benedictine Order on the rule he had already established for his followers on Subiaco. He died at Monte Cassino on March 21, his feast day.

49. *Romualdus:* St. Romualdo (956–1027), founder of the Camaldolese Order. *Maccarius:* Probably St. Maccarius of Alexandria (died 404), a disciple of St. Anthony. He lived in the desert between the Nile and the Red Sea and was reputed to have been the leader of 5,000 eremites.

144. *Maia and Dione:* Here stand for Mercury and Venus. Maia was one of the seven sisters of the Pleiades and the mother of Mercury. Dione was the mother of Venus.

145–146. *Jupiter . . . his father and son:* Jupiter was the son of Saturn and the father of Mars. The temperate planet Jupiter lies between the excessively hot planet Mars and the excessively cold planet Saturn.

16. *when:* As used in Scholastic terminology, meaning "time of" or "duration."

20–21. *all the fruit harvested from the turning of the spheres:* The first-created angels of Heaven did, of course, share in Christ's triumph, but they were not part of its harvest, which consisted of the redemption of the souls of men. Once the soul had entered into that triumph (mounted to Heaven), it would manifest itself in one of the spheres, though it was in essence in the choir of the Empyrean. Thus the militia of Christ must contain all the souls of glory whose manifestations populate the spheres of Heaven (including now the Sphere of the Fixed Stars).

25–26. *Trivia:* Diana, the moon, in her manifestation as a nymph. *eternal nymphs:* The stars.

30. *lights all the bodies:* Lights all stars (which are supposed, as the moon does, to send forth only the reflection of the sun's light).

40. *Fire:* Lightning.

42. *against its nature:* The nature of fire is to ascend toward the Sphere of Fire. Contrary to its nature (which is to rise to God), Dante's spirit swoons and falls.

56. *Polyhymnia:* The Muse of Sacred Songs. Her name means Many-Hymned.

101–102. *the bright lyre:* The Angel Gabriel. *purest gem:* The Virgin Mary. *the brightest heaven:* The Sphere of the Fixed Stars.

112–113. *The royal mantle:* The Primum Mobile. *most burns:* With ardent joy. *and quickens:* Being the outer sphere whose revolutions control the turning of all those it encloses, it turns faster than any of the others.

128. *Regina coeli:* Queen of Heaven.

139. *New or the Old Consistory:* The New and the Old Testament.

140. *the soul that holds the great keys:* St. Peter.

CANTO 24

53. *what is faith?:* The anonymous Epistle to the Hebrews, Chapter 11, (which Dante attributes to St. Paul) provides the source of the first answer: "Now faith is the substance of things hoped for, the evidence of things not seen."

64. *substance:* In Scholastic terminology "what exists in itself." But

Notes

Aquinas had set forth, "No quality is a substance; but faith is a quality." Faith, therefore, could not be a substance. Dante circumvents this difficulty by rendering the *substantia* of Hebrews as "that which stands under" (*sub* and *stare*).

65. *argument:* The means whereby the intellect reaches toward the inherent truth of things. It is necessary but limited, as reason is limited.

66. *quiddity:* The companion term "quality" signifies the likeness of a thing to something else, "quiddity" signifying the way in which a thing is like itself.

124–125. *now can see what faith once held so firmly:* The Triumph of Christ, a matter of faith during his mortal life, a fact forever before his eyes in Heaven.

125–126. *you were prompter than younger feet:* St. John was the first to approach the tomb of Christ, but Peter was the first to enter it and the first to believe in the Resurrection. The greater promptness indicates the greater zeal, and thus the greater triumph of the heavenly soul.

128. *form:* In Scholastic terminology, the same as the Platonic Form, the idea of the thing, which is independent of particular instances, as, for example, the form of Justice would exist noumenally, if only in God's mind, even if no single instance of justice could be found on earth. Contingency is that which comes into being as an instance of form, the form itself being eternal.

136–138. *Moses, the prophets, the psalms:* The Old Testament. *the Evangel:* The New Testament, commonly divided into the Evangelical and Apostolic books. *you:* The Italian is the plural form *voi*. The reference, therefore, is to all the Apostles.

CANTO 25

14. *the same sphere:* Not from the Sphere of the Fixed Stars, the eighth heaven, in which Dante, Beatrice, and these souls are, but from the sphere of light the souls had formed for joy when Beatrice uttered her prayer in the previous canto.

17–18. *the baron . . . Galicia:* The second of the barons of Christ is St. James. His tomb is in Santiago di Compostela in Galicia, Spain, and was a shrine to which many pilgrimages were made in the Middle Ages.

23. *one glorious great lord:* St. Peter. *the other:* St. James.

24. *the diet that regales them there:* The love of others, *caritas.*

37. *second flame:* St. James.

52. *the Sun:* God. Dante's hope is known to God and, therefore, to all the blessed.

56–57. *Egypt:* The mortal life, earthly bondage. *Jerusalem:* Heaven, deliverance. *warring years:* Dante's mortal years in the Church Militant.

58. *not that you may know:* Since he knows already, informed by the ray of God.

59–60. *how great a pleasure hope is to you:* As the special patron of the grace he himself no longer needs.

83–84. *that grace:* Hope. *the palm:* Martyrdom. *left the field:* Abandoned the warfare of the Church Militant for the bliss of the Church Triumphant, i.e., Heaven.

91–92. *they shall be dressed in double raiment:* The glory in which Dante sees the souls clad, plus the glory of the resurrected flesh after the Day of Judgment.

94–96. *your brother:* St. John. *where he writes ... white robes:* Apocalypse, Chapter 7.

100. *a ray:* St. John.

113. *Our Pelican:* One of the medieval epithets for Christ. The pelican was believed to nourish its young by striking its breast until it bled and then giving them its blood. Another legend ran that the pelican performed in this way when it found its young dead, reviving them with its blood.

113–114. *elected from off the cross:* Chosen by Christ while He was on the cross to remain behind and be a son to Mary.

CANTO 26

12. *the power ... in Ananias' hand:* Ananias cured the blindness of St. Paul by the laying on of hands (Acts 9:10ff).

26. *authority:* Scripture. *from here:* Heaven.

37. *That truth:* That God is the Supreme Good and Supreme Love. *he:* Probably Aristotle who argued a single God of Love as the first principle of creation, the "unmoved mover" of the *Metaphysics,* which is "the object of desire."

43. *the high proclamation:* "I am Alpha and Omega, the beginning and the ending, saith the Lord which is, and which was, and which is to come, the Almighty" (Rev. 1:8).

50. *teeth:* Urgings, promptings. A softer figure would detract from the

Notes

ardor necessary to the love of God, about which there can be nothing bland.

52. *Christ's Eagle:* St. John.

61. *the living knowledge mentioned before:* That God is the Supreme Good.

118–120. *this company:* Of elected souls. *suns:* Annual, not daily. *where your Lady summoned Virgil:* Limbo.

121–122. *all its signs:* Of the zodiac. *nine hundred and thirty:* Adam's age at death is so given in Gen. 5:5.

135–136. *EL . . . JAH:* Dante has Adam speak these syllables as *J* and *EL*, the *J* being a form of *Y*. In that order *Y* or *YEH* or *JAH* followed by *EL* may suggest some primitive form of *JAHVEH* or *JAHVEL*. Such an interpretation is conjectural, however, and I have transposed the two syllables for rhyme purposes.

139–143. *my total stay, etc.:* Adam declares that his whole sojourn in the Earthly Paradise was six hours (and perhaps part of the seventh). His time was from the dawn on the day of his creation, to the hour that follows the sixth. The total circuit of the sun is 360°, which divides into four quadrants of 90° or six hours. Assuming the time of Adam's creation to be at the vernal equinox, when day and night are each twelve hours long, the first hour of light would be from six to seven A.M., the end of the sixth would be at noon, and the hour after the sixth would be from noon to one P.M. Adam says "from the first hour . . . to the hour after the sixth." He does not say how far into that hour he remained, but it would be native to Dante's mind and style to intend Adam's expulsion to fall exactly at high noon. Half an allegorical day is about as long as any man can stay innocent.

CANTO 27

22. *The usurper:* Boniface VIII.

25. *my sepulcher:* Rome as the seat of papal authority. According to tradition, Peter was buried there.

41–44. *Linus . . . Cletus, etc.:* All these here named were early Bishops of Rome, Peter's first successor being traditionally believed to be Linus, and his successor, Cletus (Anacletus). The others followed at various intervals: Sixtus (117–c.127), Pius (141–c.149), Calixtus (217–222), and Urban (222–230). Not all were martyred, as line 45 would seem to suggest, but all suffered in the flesh and in the spirit for the sins of mankind.

49–51. *keys:* The papal keys, emblems of the Pope's authority, were used on the banner of the Vatican States, which had often been carried into battle against Christians—a bloody perversion, in Dante's view, of the papal mission.

52–53. *my head . . . seal:* The papal seal, stamped on many documents whose intent was venial, bore the purported likeness of St. Peter.

58. *Gascons and Cahorsines:* Clement V was from Gascony; John XXII from Cahors. Both filled the Papal Court with greedy favorites from their native lands. And both, of course, were guilty of the further sin of being French in Italy.

62. *Scipio:* God's foreseeing provision, as Dante would have understood it, must have helped Scipio overthrow Hannibal, else Rome would not have remained the glory of the world and could not have become the proper seat of Holy Church.

68–69. *when the horn of heaven's Goat is burnished by the sun:* The sun is in Capricorn at about mid-January, hence at the time when "frozen vaporings" come down as snow.

82–84. *past Cadiz:* The Atlantic. *the mad route Ulysses took:* See Inferno, 26. *the shore from which Europa:* Phoenicia on the eastern coast of the Mediterranean. Zeus appeared to Europa there as a bull and, taking her on his back, bore her to Crete.

85–87. *more . . . would have been visible:* Dante's view is cut off by darkness because the sun is ahead of him in Aries. He is in Gemini. The sign of Taurus lies between. A zodiacal sign covers 30°. The sun, therefore, is something more than two hours ahead of him and perhaps as much as four. Part of the world below Dante must, therefore, lie in shadow.

98. *Leda's nest:* Gemini, the sign of the twins, Castor and Pollux. Zeus appeared to Leda as a swan and, according to the most common legend, she bore him Castor and Pollux.

114. *the Cunctitenant:* God, the All-Containing. He contains the Primum Mobile as it contains all else.

140. *none to govern:* The Church being corrupt and the Emperor having abandoned Italy.

143. *that odd day in each hundred years:* The calendar as reformed under Julius Caesar fixed the year at 365 days and 6 hours, introducing an error of about 13 minutes, approximately one hundredth of a day. In each century, therefore, the calendar would move the months a day forward into the advancing season. In a millennium, January would have moved ten days nearer the spring. In 1582, the Gregorian calendar (developed under Pope Gregory XIII) substantially corrected this error.

Notes

1–21. The figure is based on Psalms 21:1: "The heavens are telling the glory of God and the firmament proclaims His handiwork."

16. *a Point:* The term is used in its strict mathematical sense to symbolize God as an immaterial and non-spatial essence.

25–30. *a ring of fire . . . Another, etc.:* The hierarchy of angels surround God as the heavenly spheres surround the earth, but their motions, contrary to those of the spheres, are greater as they lie closer to the center. In lines 52–57 below, Dante begs Beatrice to explain the mystery of this seeming paradox, and in 58–78 Beatrice resolves Dante's uncertainties, going on then (97–129) to set forth the nine orders of the angelic beings grouped in three trinities. First Trinity: Seraphim, Cherubim, Thrones; Second Trinity: Dominations, Virtues, Powers; Third Trinity: Principalities, Archangels, Angels.

32. *Juno's messenger:* Iris, the rainbow. As Juno's messenger, the rainbow is conceived as descending from Heaven to earth; at most, therefore, as a quarter of a circle. Were the rainbow to be extended to a full 180° across the sky, the distance it could span at its greatest spread could not equal the circumference of the seventh ring.

38. *the Scintilla:* God. The Point.

50. *more God-like:* Possessed of greater powers as indicated by greater speed and greater brilliance.

56. *the form:* Platonic form, the essential, unchanging noumenal concept of which any exemplum is an instance.

58–60. *It is small wonder, etc.:* God is the radiating center of all spiritual energy and He is simultaneously the all-containing bound and limit of physical creation.

65. *the power:* The "virtue" of each, its power to influence the course of what lies below it.

70. *This sphere:* The Primum Mobile, the source of all motion in the physical universe. As the most powerful of the spheres and as the one closest to God, it corresponds to the inner ring of the angel hierarchy, the Seraphim.

78. *Intelligence:* The Angel Intelligence of each sphere.

81. *Boreas:* The North Wind. When he blows straight out of his mouth the wind is from the north, which in Italy is from the Alps. Italians call that wind *il tramontano,* and think of it as the stormy source of bitter winter cold. When Boreas blows from his left cheek, the resultant northeaster (*il grecale*) is thought of as a source of storms and of cloudy skies. But when he blows from the right (the gentler) cheek,

The Divine Comedy

Italians experience *il maestrale,* the sky-clearing wind from the northwest.

88. *every angel sphere:* The rings of the angel hierarchy.

91. *spun with its spinning ring:* On earth, sparks tend to fly away from their sources. Here they stay in place, keeping pace with the rotation of the heavenly ring. The sparks may be taken as the individual Angel Intelligences within each ring; the added brightness of each, as evidence of the increase of its joy.

93. *the chessboard of the king:* The legend is still common and variously told. In one form, the inventor of chess offered the game to the king, who was so pleased with it that he ordered the inventor to name his own reward. The inventor asked that a single grain of wheat be placed on the first square of the board, two on the second, four on the third, and so on until the sixty-fourth increment was reached. The king, no mathematician, agreed gladly. It must have been at about the twelfth square (1,080,576 grains) that the king began to learn the power of mathematics and that the number of grains would mount by the sixty-fourth square to something more than 18,000,000,000,000,000,000.

104. *Thrones:* God's aspect as Supreme Justice.

106. *all these raptures:* All the angelic beings of all the nine ranks, not simply those of the first trinity.

116–117. *springtime . . . nocturnal Aries:* In spring the sun is in Aries and its stars are not visible in the day sky. In autumn the sun has moved to the opposite sign (Libra) and the stars of Aries are visible at night. Thus nocturnal Aries may be said to be the sign under which the plants that blossomed in spring turn to seared leaves.

121–123. *therein:* Within the second trinity. *the widest round:* The third of the second trinity.

124. *dances:* Ranks, orders. Called dances to denote exaltation.

130. *Dionysius:* St. Dionysius the Areopagite. A Greek mystic of the first century A.D. His conversion by St. Paul is recorded in Acts 17:34. To him was attributed the thesis *De coelesti hierarchia,* from which Dante draws the details for his angel hierarchy.

133. *Gregory:* St. Gregory (c. 540–604), called the Great. Pope from 590. Among many other writings he revised Dionysius' treatise on the angel hierarchies.

138. *one who saw it here:* St. Paul (II Cor. 12:2ff.) tells of his ascent to the third heaven "whether in the body or out of the body I do not know." Dante's presumption here is that Paul told Dionysius what he had seen in Heaven, and thus the accuracy of Dionysius' description.

682

Notes

1–9. Latona (or Leto) was, according to early legend, the wife of Zeus before he married Hera. Later legend has her as his mistress. In any case she bore him Apollo (the Sun) and Diana, or Artemis (the Moon). At the vernal equinox the sun sets in Aries as the moon rises in the opposite sign of Libra. For a moment, with the zenith as the fulcrum of these sky-wide scales, they are perfectly balanced and wear the line of the horizon as a common belt. Then, each changing hemisphere—one dropping below the horizon, the other rising above it—the balance is broken. Gist of this passage: "Beatrice looked up a moment in silence."

12. *where time and space focus in one ray:* God, ubiquitous and eternal.

18. *new loves:* The angels.

20. *'before' and 'after':* Conditions of time, and God (line 16) is beyond time.

22–23. *Pure essence:* Immaterial intelligences; the angels. *pure matter:* The physical materials of the universe and the lower animals. *the two joined into one:* Creatures composed of both soul and physical matter; mankind.

37. *Hieronymus:* St. Hieronymus, also known as St. Jerome (c. 342–420), was one of the first great Biblical scholars. *wrote to you:* In one of his epistles he asserted the precreation of the angels, a doctrine opposed to the one Beatrice is expounding.

40. *the Scribes of the Holy Ghost:* The writers of Scripture. All of them were said to have been "entered" (inspired) by the Holy Ghost.

53. *the art:* Of circling around God, their cause. The art of the angels is to receive God's ray from above and to spread its influence below.

62–66. *illuminating grace, etc.:* Dante intends a distinction here between illuminating grace and consuming grace. He is following Aquinas (*Summa Theologica*). *Illuminating grace is God's gift to the soul,* which may then, through zealous love, earn the consuming grace of the direct vision of God. The power of illuminating grace is, in fact, directly measurable by the ardor of love with which the soul receives it.

81. *divided thought:* Human intelligence, lacking absolute content and concentration, must categorize, dividing its attention and putting some things out of mind at times to be summoned back later by memory. The intelligence of angels, on the contrary, is eternally aware of all knowledge and memory and, therefore, irrelevant to it.

105. *the Lapi and Bindi:* Lapo and Bindo were, and are, common Florentine surnames.

111. *Holy Truth's foundation:* "For no other foundation can one lay than that which is laid, which is Jesus Christ" (I Cor. 3:11).

117. *hoods:* Heads.

118. *in their tippets:* The tippet is the long hanging point of a monk's hood or sleeves. Mendicant friars stuffed their tippets with all sorts of dubious religious articles and trade goods to be sold to pious simpletons along with unauthorized indulgences. Thus did they do the Devil's work, and so the bird that nests in their tippets is the Devil himself.

122. *testimonials:* Documents bearing papal or episcopal seals as authority to sell indulgences.

124. *St. Anthony's pig:* St. Anthony the Eremite (251–356) was usually depicted with a pig (representing the Devil) rooting at his feet. In Florence, pigs belonging to the various monastery herds were called St. Anthony's pigs and enjoyed the status of sacred cows, rooting in gardens, and even in houses, with no interference from the superstitious and pious folk. On such credulity, St. Anthony's pigs (these swinish mountebank monks) feed, and with them others yet (concubines, cronies, relatives) who eat and drink their fill, paying with fantastic and worthless promises (money never minted).

CANTO 30

1–15. *When . . . the sun's noon heat is shed, etc.:* When the sun is at its noon height over India (about 6,000 miles away) dawn is just beginning in Italy and the earth's shadow is nearly perpendicular to a line dropped from the zenith. Then the stars directly overhead begin to fade, the dimmest first, then the brighter. Then as dawn (Aurora, the serving maid of Apollo, the sun) draws nearer, all the stars go out, even the loveliest and brightest. Just so nine rings of the three trinities of angelic beings fade as Dante and Beatrice ascend into the first dawning of the direct vision of God.

43. *both hosts of Paradise:* The angels and the blessed.

52. *The Love:* God. *that keeps this Heaven ever the same:* All the other heavens rotate in constant change. The Empyrean, reflecting God's unchanging and unchangeable perfection, is always the same.

88. *my eyes' eaves:* His eyelashes.

108. *power:* Virtue. The ability to influence what lies below it. *motion:* Its own rapid revolution.

112ff. *tier on tier, etc.:* The Mystic Rose. As ever in Paradise, the heavenly beings manifest themselves to Dante at the highest level he is capable of grasping at each point of his development. Now, his vision at last approaching perfection, Dante sees them in their supreme heavenly state, ranked tier on tier in a huge stadium that gives forth the appearance of an enormous white rose basking in the eternal springtime of the direct light of God. The Rose may be thought of as an immense, truncated, inverted, floating cone marked off in many tiers. The tier first reflected to Dante from that sea of light is the bottom one, the upper tiers being only partially visible at this point. The nimbus of the bottom tier (lines 115–116) is far greater than the circumference of the sun (lines 104–105).

124. *Into the gold of the rose:* The central corona of the rose, from which the petals grow, is always golden, or so it was in Dante's time, though some modern hybrids no longer have a golden center.

136. *already anointed:* As Holy Roman Emperor. *Henry:* Henry VII of Luxemburg, Emperor 1308–1313. He was not, strictly speaking, referred to as Henry the Great, but is so called here for purposes of rhyme. For the background of Henry's attempt at order in Italy see Purgatorio, 6. In the Purgatorio Dante says Henry came too late. Here he says he came before the time was ripe. In either case the result was the same and Dante attributes Henry's failure to the evil designs of the bad Popes Beatrice now goes on to denounce before the full court of Heaven. Dante placed his one hope of returning to Florence on the outcome of Henry's efforts to settle the hatreds of Italian politics.

140. *you:* Italians.

142. *The prefect:* The Pope. *The holy court:* Rome, the Vatican. Here Dante intends Clement V, who worked to defeat Henry's policy, though he professed to support it.

145. *God will not long permit:* Clement died eight months after Henry, on April 20, 1314.

147. *where Simon Magus, headfirst in the pit:* With the Simoniacs in the third *bolgia* of the eighth circle (Inferno, 19).

149. *the guilt of Alagna:* Boniface VIII. He was born at Alagna.

CANTO 31

1–4. *the host . . . the other host:* The first host is of the sacred soldiery, those who were once mortal and who were redeemed by Christ. They are seated upon the thrones of the Mystic Rose in which are gathered eternally the essences of all those heavenly souls that manifested themselves to Dante in the various spheres below, moved by *caritas* to reveal themselves to Dante at the various levels of his developing understanding. The second soldiery is of the angels who never left

Heaven. They soar above the Rose like heavenly bees, in constant motion between the Rose and the radiance of God. Unlike earthly bees, however, it is from God, the mystical hive of grace, that they bring the sweetness to the flower, bearing back to God, of course, the bliss of the souls of Heaven. The first host is more emphatically centered on the aspect of God as the Son; the second, on the aspect of God as the Father.

27. *one goal:* God.

32. *Helice:* The nymph Helice attracted Zeus and was turned into a bear by jealous Hera. Zeus translated his nymph to heaven as Ursa Major, the constellation of the Great Bear which contains the Big Dipper. Arcas, her son by Zeus, was translated to Ursa Minor, within which he forms the Little Dipper. The two dippers, being near the Pole, are always above the horizon in the northland, the zone from which the barbarians came.

35. *the Lateran:* The Lateran is today a section of old Rome; here Dante uses it to signify Rome in general.

43. *shrine of his vow:* It was a custom of the pious, as thanks for an answered prayer, to win forgiveness of sins, or as a testimony of faith, to vow a journey to a stated shrine or temple. Such pilgrimages were often dangerous. Travel was rare in the Middle Ages, and the pilgrim returned from far shrines was much sought after for the hopefully miraculous, and in any case rare, news he brought back. Dante, having traveled to the Infinite Summit, cannot fail to think ahead to the way he will speak his vision to mankind.

60. *an Elder:* St. Bernard (1090–1153), the famous Abbot of Clairvaux, a contemplative mystic and author. Under him the Cistercian Order (a branch of the Benedictines with a stricter rule than the original order) flourished and spread. All Cistercian monasteries are especially dedicated to the Virgin, and St. Bernard is particularly identified with her worship.

66. *Beatrice called me from my place:* In succeeding Beatrice, Bernard clearly becomes the allegorical figure of Contemplation, and so a progress of the soul: from human reason the soul mounts to revelation at which time the final bliss becomes contemplation of God as He reveals Himself.

68. *the third circle down:* In the Mystic Rose, Mary sits in the topmost tier, Eve directly below her, Rachel below Eve. Beatrice sits to the right of Rachel.

103. *a Croat:* Probably used here in a generic sense to signify the native of any far off Christian land, but Croatia, aside from lying at one of the outer limits of Christianity, was also known for the ardor of its religious belief.

104. *our Veronica:* From *vera icon,* the true image. Certainly the most famous relic in St. Peter's, the Veronica was the handkerchief of St. Veronica who gave it to Jesus to wipe the blood from his face on the road to Calvary. It was believed that the true likeness of Jesus had appeared on the cloth in His own blood.

110–111. *of him who . . . tasted the peace . . . above:* According to legend, Bernard was rewarded for his holiness by being permitted a vision of Heaven's blessedness while he was yet on earth.

118–123. *By as much as the horizon, etc.:* Bright as Heaven is, Mary outshines it as the east outshines the west at daybreak.

124–129. *as the sky is brightest, etc.:* The shaft of the chariot of the sun would be the first point of light of the new dawn, that moment when light glows on the eastern rim while the horizon to north and south is still dark. Thus Mary not only outshines all Heaven as the east at daybreak outshines the west, but even at the uppermost tier of the blessed, those radiances at either side of her are dim by comparison.

132. *art:* Motion.

CANTO 32

1–2. *Still rapt in contemplation:* Of the Virgin. *the vacant office of instruction:* Formerly held by Beatrice.

4–6. *The wound:* Original sin. *balm so sweet:* Jesus. *dealt:* The first fault, Eve's disobedience. *deepened:* Her seduction of Adam, thus spreading sin to all mankind. *in such great beauty:* Eve, having been created directly by God, was perfect in her beauty.

10–12. *Sarah:* Wife of Abraham. Hebrews 11:11–14, cites her as the mother of the Jews who foresaw Christ's coming and believed in him. *Rebecca:* Wife of Isaac. *Judith:* She killed Holofernes and freed the Jews. *and she:* Ruth, great-grandmother of David. *the singer:* David. *who for his sins:* His lust for Bathsheba, wife of Uriah. In order to marry Bathsheba, David sent Uriah to his death in the first line of battle. David's lament is in Psalm 50.

22. *in full bloom:* That half of the Rose that holds the pre-Christian believers would naturally be completely filled. On the other side there are thrones waiting for those who have yet to win salvation through Christ Descended.

32–33. *the great John:* The Baptist. He denounced Herod Antipos and was beheaded two years before the Crucifixion. He had to wait in Limbo for two years till Christ came for him at the Resurrection.

40–43. *below that tier:* The lower half of the Rose contains the blessed infants, the souls of those who died before they had achieved the true volition of reason and faith. They could not, therefore, win salvation by their own merit. *but by another's, under strict condition:* The necessary qualification for election is belief in Christ. These souls were too young at death to have formed their faith. Salvation is granted them not directly through belief in Christ but through the faith and prayers of their parents, relatives, and others of the faithful who interceded for them.

66. *the effect:* The cause is buried in God's mind. The effect must speak for itself.

68–72. *those twins, etc.:* The reference here is to Jacob and Esau. According to Genesis, they were at odds while still in their mother's womb. Dante follows St. Paul (Rom. 9:11–13) in interpreting the division between Jacob and Esau as a working of God's unfathomable will. "Even as it is written, Jacob I loved, but Esau I hated." Man can note the will of God in such matters ("the effect") but cannot plumb its causes. *according to the color of their hair:* For what may seem to be superficial reasons. Esau was redheaded.

84. *among the blind:* Among the souls of Hell. Such infants were assigned to Limbo.

94. *the self-same Love:* The Archangel Gabriel, the Angel of the Annunciation.

118. *Those two:* Adam and St. Peter. Adam as father of mankind, Peter as father of the Church. Note that Peter has the place of honor on the right.

127. *that one:* St. John the Evangelist. His *Apocalypse* was received as the prophetic book in which the entire history of the Church is foretold. He sits on Peter's right.

131. *the great leader:* Moses. As the second great figure of the Old Testament he sits to the left of Adam.

133–135. *Anna:* St. Anna, mother of the Virgin. Her position directly across the circle from Peter's puts her to the right of John the Baptist. *does not move her eyes to sing 'Hosanna!':* Like all the other heavenly beings, she constantly sings the praise of God. All others, naturally enough, look up as they sing. She, however, is so filled with bliss by the sight of Mary that she does not turn her eyes from her blessed daughter. She praises God while looking at Mary.

137. *Lucy:* It was she who first sent Beatrice to rescue Dante from the Dark Wood of Error. She sits opposite Adam and would, accordingly, be to the left of John the Baptist.

Notes

54. *which in Itself is true:* The light of God is the one light whose source is Itself. All others are a reflection of this.

65–66. *tumbling leaves . . . oracles:* The Cumean Sybil wrote her oracles on leaves, one letter to a leaf, then sent her message scattering on the wind. Presumably, the truth was all contained in that strew, could one only gather all the leaves and put the letters in the right order.

85–87. *how It conceives, etc.:* The idea here is Platonic: the essence of all things (form) exists in the mind of God. All other things exist as exempla.

88. *substance:* Matter, all that exists in itself. *accident:* All that exists as a phase of matter.

130–144. The central metaphor of the entire *Comedy* is the image of God and the final triumphant in-Godding of the elected soul returning to its Maker. On the mystery of that image, the metaphoric symphony of the *Comedy* comes to rest. In the second aspect of Trinal-unity, in the circle reflected from the first, Dante thinks he sees the image of mankind woven into the very substance and coloration of God. He turns the entire attention of his soul to that mystery, as a geometer might seek to shut out every other thought and dedicate himself to squaring the circle. The mystery remains beyond Dante's mortal power. Yet, there in Heaven, in a moment of grace, God revealed the truth to him in a flash of light—revealed it, that is, to the God-enlarged power of Dante's emparadised soul. On Dante's return to the mortal life, the details of that revelation vanished from his mind but the force of the revelation survives in its power on Dante's feelings. So ends the vision of the *Comedy*, and yet the vision endures, for ever since that revelation, Dante tells us, he feels his soul turning ever as one with the perfect motion of God's love.

This Franklin Library edition of
THE DIVINE COMEDY
is set in Trump Mediaeval,
an elegant twentieth-century typeface
named for its designer, Georg Trump;
the display typeface is Rhapsodie.
They were chosen by
designers Colin Joh and Robert Freese
to echo the period in which
Dante wrote his masterpiece
and to harmonize with
Gustave Doré's engravings.
The acid-free book paper is
50-pound Franklin Library Smooth Natural,
made to archival standards by
P. H. Glatfelter Paper Company of
Spring Grove, Pennsylvania, for The Franklin Library.
The book was printed by R. R. Donnelley
& Sons, Co., Chicago, Illinois.

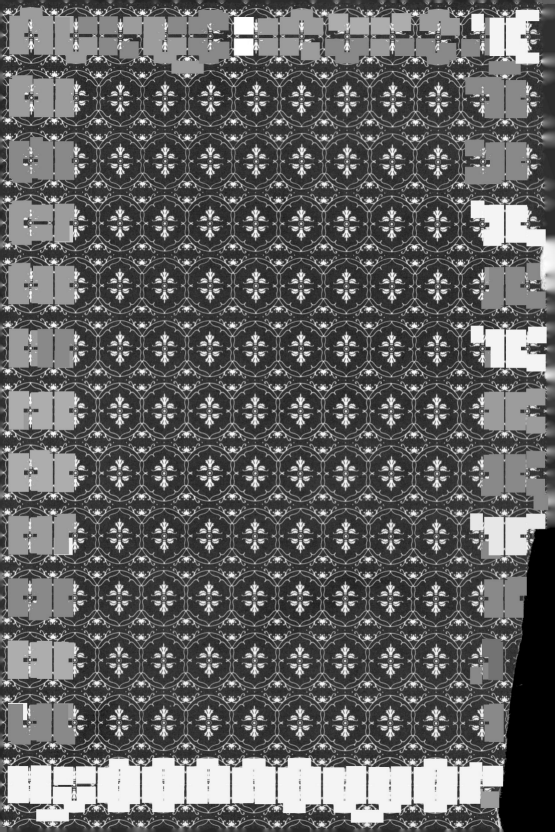